LUTON TOWN FOOTBALL CLUB

THE FULL RECORD

ROGER WASH & SIMON PITTS

Second edition published 2014
First edition published 2010

Roger Wash
5 Downing Close
Newmarket
CB8 8AU

British Library Cataloguing-in-Publication Data
A catalogue record for this book is available from the British Library

ISBN 978-0-9560832-2-7

Printed in Great Britain by Berforts, Stevenage. www.berforts.co.uk

Design and typeset by Alchemy Creations Ltd, Stevenage. www.alchemycreations.co.uk

The publisher acknowledges with thanks Gareth Owen and Bedfordshire Newspapers for the provision of photographs for this book.

CONTENTS

4	AUTHOR'S NOTE
5	THE FULL RECORD 1885-2014
266	THE TABLES
278	THE PLAYERS
290	THE 'OTHER' LEAGUES
294	THE 'OTHER' RECORDS

AUTHOR'S NOTE

The first edition of this book, published in 2010 to coincide with the club's 125th birthday, would not have got off the ground without the computer wizardry of Simon Pitts who converted my old handwritten records which I had compiled following numerous trips to Luton Library in the 1960's.

I always promised that a revised and updated version of the book would be published once we got back into the Football League and after a glorious 2013/14 season, with many club records smashed, I naturally needed to keep my word.

This new version expands on the original, corrects a few errors and provides some new photographs to encompass 5210 first team competitive games played out by 1218 wearers of the sacred jersey.

Sincere thanks are due once again to Dave Cockfield for trawling through the newspaper microfilms at Luton Library, sometimes just to check a single fact. Thanks are also offered to Alan Shury for providing some of the player's first names missing from the original version.

Roger Wash
October 2014

Round	Month	Day	Year	Venue	Opponents	W,L,D Score	Scorers	Attendance	Round
1	Oct 31	1885	(a)	Great Marlow	L 0-3	-		500	1
1	Oct 23	1886	(h)	HOTSPUR	L 1-3	Ellingham		1000	1
1	Oct 15	1887	(a)	Chatham	L 1-5	G. Deacon		800	1
Q1	Oct 6	1888	(a)	READING	W 4-0	Thring, Narburgh, J Lomax (2)		1000	Q1
Q2	Oct 27	1888	(a)	Chesham	D 3-3	Narburgh, J Lomax (2)		750	Q2
Rep	Nov 3	1888	(h)	CHESHAM	W 10-2	Thring (3), G Deacon (3), Narburgh, J Lomax (2)		1500	Rep
Q3	Nov 17	1888	(h)	OLD BRIGHTONIANS	L 1-3	G Deacon		800	Q3
Q2	Oct 26	1889	(a)	Maidenhead	W 2-1	H Whitby, J Lomax		500	Q2
Q3	Nov 16	1889	(a)	Old St. Pauls	L 0-4			750	Q3
Q1	Oct 4	1890	(h)	93rd HIGHLAND REGIMENT	L 0-7			1500	Q1
Q1	Oct 3	1891	(h)	SWINDON TOWN	W 4-3	Chesher (2), H Whitby, G Deacon		1000	Q1
Q2	Oct 24	1891	(a)	WINDSOR PHOENIX ATH	W 3-0	H Whitby, Chesher, G Deacon		2000	Q2
Q3	Nov 14	1891	(a)	Bedminster	W 4-1	F Whitby (2), G Deacon, Oclee		1500	Q3
Q4	Dec 5	1891	(a)	Clifton	W 3-0	H Whitby (3)		1000	Q4
1	Jan 16	1892	(h)	MIDDLESBROUGH	L 0-3			4000	1
Q1	Oct 15	1892	(h)	OLD ST. MARKS	W 4-0	Julian, Brown, F Whitby, H Whitby		1800	Q1
Q2	Oct 29	1892	(h)	OLD ETONIANS	W 4-2	Sanders, Allen, F Whitby, Marten (og)		1500	Q2
Q3	Nov 19	1892	(a)	Polytechnic	L 2-4	F Whitby, Watkins		800	Q3
Q2	Nov 4	1893	(a)	Old Westminsters	W 1-0	Dimmock		3000	Q2
Q3	Nov 25	1893	(h)	NORWICH CEYMS	W 5-1	Finlayson (2), Allen (2), Julian		2500	Q3
Q4	Dec 16	1893	(a)	1st Sherwood Foresters	D 2-2	Dimmock, Brown		1500	Q4
Rep	Dec 23	1893	(h)	1ST SHERWOOD FORESTERS	W 2-1	Galbraith, Allen		2500	Rep
1	Jan 27	1894	(a)	Middlesbrough Ironopolis	L 1-2	Dimmock		1400	1

Player appearance columns (rotated headers): Allen F, Barrett GW, Bee E, Bower PH, Boxford H, Brown WR, Burley J, Chesher W, Deacon A, Deacon G, Dimmock J, Ellingham R, Finlayson John, Galbraith H, Hoy A, Humphrey G, Hunt J, Julian JW, Lawrence T, Lomax D, Lomax E, Lomax J, Long GJ, Martin A, Mileman R, Miller H, Moody J, Munroe E, Narburgh L, Oclee HW, Paul H, Read T, Saddington G, Sanders A, Small GH, Smart A, Taylor AH, Taylor JA, Thring LCR, Vickers RE, Watkins J, Whitby F, Whitby H, Wilson John, Wright J.

Apps: 8, 6, 5, 1, 1, 8, 8, 12, 1, 12, 5, 1, 5, 8, 7, 1, 8, 2, 3, 10, 10, 1, 5, 5, 3, 5, 2, 6, 5, 5, 3, 1, 14, 2, 1, 21, 1, 5, 1, 5, 12, 10, 5, 8

Goals: 4, -, -, -, -, 2, -, 3, -, 8, 3, 1, 2, 1, -, -, 2, -, -, -, 2, -, -, -, -, 2, -, 3, -, -, 1, -, 4, -, 1, 5, 7, -, -

* 1890/91 The 1st Qualifying match versus 93rd Highland Regiment was played at Luton by arrangement

* In 1893/94 Luton were leading 4-2 in a 4th Qualifying tie against 1st Sherwood Foresters at Colchester when the match was abandoned after 24 minutes of extra time. The score of 2-2 at 90mins was recorded.

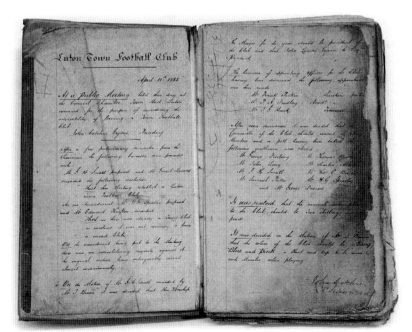

The opening pages from the club's first minute book.

At a public meeting called on April 11th 1885 at the Council Chambers of Luton Town Hall it was moved that a Town Football Club be formed, to be called Luton Town Football Club. The amalgamation of local clubs Luton Excelsior and Luton Wanderers was not without its initial teething problems but the joining together of the two strongest sides in the area made eminent sense especially when the Excelsior ground, an enclosed field in Dallow Lane, was thrown into the equation.

Football was obviously a different game compared to that played today. In 1885 professionalism had only just been legalised but was confined to northern clubs, there were no goal nets and the penalty kick was still six years away from entering the rule books. Players were courteous but on the other hand play was brutal to say the least with little finesse being exhibited as the combatants kicked lumps out of each other. The Luton Town minute book (see left) famously confirms that the 'colors (note the American spelling) of the club should be navy blue and pink with a shirt and cap to be worn by each member when playing.'

Adverts were placed in the popular 'Pastime' and 'Referee' magazines asking for fixtures and a list of likely opponents was also drawn up and letters written. Among the earliest invitees were Old Etonians, Grove House, Old Foresters, Old Wykehamists, Prairie Rangers, Hendon, Hotspur and St Albans. Although most of these names mean little to today's supporter they were, in fact, the Premiership of the day boasting international players galore.

The Town's first competitive game came about on entering the F.A.Cup competition in 1885/86 when on 31st October 1885 Marlow, semi-finalists three years before, ran out easy 3-0 winners.

TIMELINE...

11 April 1885 The Luton Town Football Club is formed.
31 October 1885 The first competitive game is played.
December 1890 Three players are paid 5 shillings a week.
August 1891 The whole team is paid to play.

Arthur Taylor, the Town's first regular captain.

The 1891/92 team – the first professionals. Back row (left to right): Isaac Smith (Director), Sanders, Burley, Hoy, Frank Pitkin (Secretary). Middle row (left to right): Wright, Paul, Taylor. Front row (left to right): F. Whitby, Deacon, Oclee, Chesher, H. Whitby.

◗ **The 1893/94 team with the Luton Charity Cup** – Players only (with badges on their shirts). Back row (left to right): H Whitby, Bee, Chesher. Middle row (left to right): Watkins, Julian, Taylor. Front row (left to right): Brown, Finlayson, Galbraith, Allen, Dimmock.

1894/95 SOUTHERN LEAGUE DIVISION ONE

Match No	Month	Day	Venue	Opponents	W,L,D Score	Scorers	Attendance	Allen F	Bee B	Brown WR	Chesher A	Collins A	Dickerson J	Dimmock J	Finlayson John	Galbraith H	Gallacher W	Groom	Howe A	Jack J	McCartney WJ	McCrindle R	McEwan J	Nicholson MD	Prentice W	Watkins J	Match No
1	Oct	6	(h)	MILLWALL ATHLETIC	L 3-4	Gallacher, Finlayson, Prentice	5000	10	1						8	9	7		6			5	3	2	11	4	1
2	Oct	20	(a)	Reading	W 3-2	Gallacher (2), Allen		10	1		2				8	9	7		6			5	3		11	4	2
3	Oct	27	(h)	SOUTHAMPTON ST MARY'S	W 4-1	Galbraith (2), Allen, Prentice	3000	10	1	7	2				8	9			6			5	3		11	4	3
4	Nov	17	(h)	CHATHAM	W 2-1	Brown (2)	3000	10	1	7				11	8	9			6			5	3	2		4	4
5	Dec	8	(a)	Royal Ordnance Factories	L 0-2	-		9						7	8				6	11		5	3	2	10	4	5
6	Dec	22	(a)	Southampton St Mary's	W 2-1	Galbraith (2)	6000		1		2				8	9	7		6	11		5	3		10	4	6
7	Jan	5	(a)	Ilford	L 1-3	Gallacher	1000		1		4				8	9	7		6	11		5	3	2	10		7
8	Jan	12	(a)	Millwall Athletic	D 2-2	Gallacher, Finlayson	4500				2	4	1		8	9	7		6	11		5	3		10		8
9	Feb	9	(a)	Chatham	D 2-2	Galbraith, Jack	1000	10	1		2	6			8	9	7			11		5	3			4	9
10	Feb	23	(h)	ROYAL ORDNANCE FACTORIES	W 3-0	Finlayson (2), Prentice			1		2	6			8		7		9	11		5	3		10	4	10
11	Mar	2	(h)	READING	W 5-2	Galbraith (3), Prentice (2)	3000		1		2				8	9	7		6	11		5	3		10	4	11
12	Mar	9	(h)	SWINDON TOWN	W 2-0	Gallacher, Prentice	2000		1		2				8	9	7		6	11		5	3		10	4	12
13	Mar	16	(a)	Clapton	D 1-1	Galbraith	3000		1		2				8	9	7		6	11		5	3		10	4	13
14	Mar	18	(h)	ILFORD	D 1-1	Prentice			1		2				8	9	7		6	11		5	3		10	4	14
15	Mar	23	(h)	CLAPTON	W 2-0	Galbraith, Prentice	3000		1			6			8	9	7			11	2	5	3		10	4	15
16	Apr	6	(a)	Swindon Town	W 3-0	Galbraith (2), Ross (og)	2000		1			6			8	9	7			11	2	5	3		10	4	16
				Final League Position: 2nd		1 Own Goal	Apps	6	15	2	7	9	1	2	16	14	13	-	13	12	2	16	16	4	14	14	
							Goals	2	-	2	-	-	-	-	4	12	6	-	-	1	-	-	-	-	8	-	

1894/95 FA CUP

Round	Month	Day	Venue	Opponents	W,L,D Score	Scorers	Attendance	Allen F	Bee B	Brown WR	Chesher A	Collins A	Dickerson J	Dimmock J	Finlayson John	Galbraith H	Gallacher W	Groom	Howe A	Jack J	McCartney WJ	McCrindle R	McEwan J	Nicholson MD	Prentice W	Watkins J	Round
Q1	Oct	13	(h)	CITY RAMBLERS	W 8-2	Prentice (3), Gallacher (2), Galbraith (2), Allen	2000	9	1						11	8	7		6			5	3	2	10	4	Q1
Q2	Nov	3	(a)	St. Albans	W 6-1	Prentice (3), Brown, Galbraith, Dimmock	3000		1	7	2			11	8	9			6			5	3		10	4	Q2
Q3	Nov	24	(a)	Ilford	W 2-0	Allen, Dimmock	1200	10	1	7				11	8	9			6			5	3	2		4	Q3
Q4	Dec	15	(a)	Tottenham Hotspur	D 2-2	Finlayson, Prentice	3000		1					11	8		7	9	6			5	3	2	10	4	Q4
Rep	Dec	19	(h)	TOTTENHAM HOTSPUR	W 4-0	Gallacher (2), Finlayson, Galbraith	2000		1				2	11	8	9	7		6			5	3		10	4	Rep
1	Feb	2	(h)	PRESTON NORTH END	L 0-2	-	4000		1		2	4		11	8	9	7			10		5	3			6	1
							Apps	2	6	2	2	2	-	5	6	5	4	1	5	1	-	6	6	3	4	6	
							Goals	2	-	1	-	-	-	2	2	4	4	-	-	-	-	-	-	-	7	-	

TIMELINE
October 1894 The Town become founder members of the Southern Leag

Hugh Galbraith. Regarded as the top centre forward in the south during the mid 1890's

The 1894/95 team – Back row (left to right): W.Prime (Trainer), Watkins, McCrindle, Nicholson, Squires (Linesman), Bee, Howe, McEwen, Wright (Asst Trainer). Front row (left to right): Gallacher, Finlayson, Galbraith, Prentice, Dimmock.

TIMELINE...

August 1896 The Town resign from the Southern League and apply to join the Football League. The bid fails and a season (1896/97) has to be spent in the United League (see Page 260).

10 January 1897 A record crowd of 6,898 sees the West Bromwich F.A.Cup tie at Dallow Lane.

April 1897 The club moves to a new ground in Dunstable Road.

1895/96 SOUTHERN LEAGUE DIVISION ONE

Match No	Month	Day	Venue	Opponents	W,L,D Score	Scorers	Attendance	Birch E	Brown WR	Coupar J	Dickerson J	Docherty J	Ekins FG	Finlayson John	Galbraith H	Gallacher W	Jack J	McCartney WJ	McCrindle R	McEwen J	Nicholson MD	Parkinson R	Russell AE	Stewart WS	Watkins J	Williams R	Match No
1	Sep	21	(h)	ILFORD	W 5-0	Cosburn (og), Markham (og), Ekins, Galbraith, Coupar	3000	4		10		6	11		9	7	1			3	2	8		5			1
2	Sep	28	(a)	Millwall Athletic	L 0-2	-	10000	4		10		6	11		9	7	1			3	2	8		5			2
3	Oct	5	(h)	READING	W 7-2	Coupar (3), Galbraith (2), Ekins, Parkinson	2000	4		10		6	11		9	7	1			3	2	8		5			3
4	Oct	26	(a)	Southampton St Mary's	L 1-2	Parkinson	6000	4		10	1		11		9	7		2		3		8		5	6		4
5	Nov	9	(h)	ROYAL ORDNANCE FACTORIES	W 4-0	Gallacher, Parkinson, Galbraith (2)	3000	6		10		3	11		9	7		2				8	1	5	4		5
6	Nov	16	(a)	Reading	W 3-0	Parkinson, Coupar (pen), Birch	4000	7		10		6	11		9			2		3		8	1	5	4		6
7	Nov	30	(a)	Swindon Town	W 2-0	Parkinson, Birch	2500	9		10		6	11			7		2		3		8		5	4	1	7
8	Dec	7	(h)	MILLWALL ATHLETIC	L 0-3	-	5500	9		10		6	11			7		2		3		8		5	4	1	8
9	Dec	21	(a)	Royal Ordnance Factories	D 0-0	-	500		7	10		6	11	9				2	5	3		8	1		4		9
10	Jan	4	(a)	Chatham	L 1-2	Galbraith	2000	6		10			11		9	7		2		3		8		5	4	1	10
11	Jan	11	(a)	Ilford	W 5-0	Gallacher, Galbraith, Birch, Stewart (2)	700	8		10			11	6	9	7		2		3				5	4	1	11
12	Feb	8	(a)	New Brompton	W 1-0	Galbraith	3000	8		10		6	11		9	7		2		3				5	4	1	12
13	Feb	22	(h)	SWINDON TOWN	W 7-1	Gallacher (2), Ekins, Birch, Galbraith, Coupar, (og)	3000	8		10		6	11		9	7		2		3				5	4	1	13
14	Feb	29	(h)	CHATHAM	W 9-1	Galbraith (2), Ekins (2), Coupar (2), Gallacher, Stewart, Birch		8		10		6	11		9	7		2		3				5	4	1	14
15	Mar	7	(h)	SOUTHAMPTON ST MARY'S	W 3-0	Stewart, Gallacher, Galbraith		8		10		6	11		9	7		2		3				5	4	1	15
16	Mar	14	(a)	Clapton	W 6-0	Ekins (2), Coupar, Gallacher, Birch, McEwen		8		10		6	11		9	7		2		3				5	4	1	16
17	Apr	4	(h)	NEW BROMPTON	W 8-1	Galbraith (3), Ekins, Gallacher, Stewart, Birch, Coupar	3000	8		10		6	11		9	7		2		3				5	4	1	17
18	Apr	11	(h)	CLAPTON	W 6-0	Coupar (2), Stewart, Birch, Earle (og), Galbraith	1500	6		10		2	11	8	9	7				3				5	4	1	18
				Final League Position: 2nd		4 Own Goals	Apps	17	1	18	1	15	18	3	15	16	3	14	1	17	3	10	3	17	15	11	
							Goals	8	-	12	-	-	8	-	16	8	-	-	-	1	-	5	-	6	-	-	

1895/96 FA CUP

Round	Month	Day	Venue	Opponents	W,L,D Score	Scorers	Attendance	Birch E	Brown WR	Coupar J	Dickerson J	Docherty J	Ekins FG	Finlayson John	Galbraith H	Gallacher W	Jack J	McCartney WJ	McCrindle R	McEwen J	Nicholson MD	Parkinson R	Russell AE	Stewart WS	Watkins J	Williams R	Round
Q1	Oct	12	(h)	TOTTENHAM HOTSPUR	L 1-2	Galbraith	3000	5		8		6	11		9	7	1			3	2	10		4			Q1
							Apps	1		1		1	1		1	1	1			1	1	1		1			
							Goals								1												

1896/97 FA CUP

Round	Month	Day	Venue	Opponents	W,L,D Score	Scorers	Attendance	Birch E	Coupar J	Davies S	Docherty J	Ekins FG	Galbraith H	Gallacher W	McCartney WJ	McEwan T	McInnes T	Stewart WS	Williams R	Round
Q3	Dec	12	(h)	1ST SCOTS GUARDS	W 7-0	McInnes (3), Docherty, Galbraith, Stewart, McCartney	1000		4	6	11	10	9	7	2	3	8	5	1	Q3
Q4	Jan	6	(a)	Marlow	W 5-0	Galbraith, Coupar, Gallacher, Stewart, Docherty	1500		4	6	11	10	9	7	2	3	8	5	1	Q4
Q5	Jan	16	(h)	TOTTENHAM HOTSPUR	W 3-0	McInnes (2), Gallacher	3000		4	6	11	10	9	7	2	3	8	5	1	Q5
1	Jan	30	(h)	WEST BROMWICH ALBION	L 0-1	-	6898	11	10	4	6		9	7	2	3	8	5	1	1
							Apps	1	4	4	4	3	4	4	4	4	4	4	4	
							Goals		1		2		2	2	1		5	2		

SEE PAGE 290 FOR UNITED LEAGUE RESULTS FOR 1896/97

❱ **The 1895/96 team with the Luton Charity Cup** – Players only (with badges
on their shirts). Back row: Williams.
Middle row (left to right): McCartney, Watkins, Stewart, Docherty, McEwen.
Front row (left to right): Gallacher, Coupar, Galbraith, Birch, Ekins.

1897/98 FOOTBALL LEAGUE DIVISION TWO

Match No	Month	Day	Venue	Opponents	W/L/D Score	Scorers	Attendance	Birch E	Catlin W	Clarke J	Coupar J	Davies Samuel	Docherty J	Donaldson R	Durrant AF	Ekins FG	Gallacher W	Little T	McCartney WJ	McEwen J	McInnes T	Perrins G	Stewart WS	Williams R	Match No
1	Sep	4	(a)	Leicester Fosse	D 1-1	Ekins	6000	9			8	4	6			11	7		2	3	10		5	1	1
2	Sep	11	(h)	GAINSBOROUGH TRINITY	W 4-0	Ekins, Little, McInnes, Gallacher	4000				8	4	6			11	7	9	2	3	10		5	1	2
3	Sep	18	(a)	Newton Heath	W 2-1	McInnes, Little	7000				8	4	6			11	7	9	2	3	10		5	1	3
4	Oct	2	(h)	WOOLWICH ARSENAL	L 0-2	-	5000			9	8	4	6				7	11	2	3	10		5	1	4
5	Oct	9	(a)	Woolwich Arsenal	L 0-3	-	14000				8		6			11	7	9	2	3	10	4	5	1	5
6	Oct	16	(a)	Loughborough	L 0-2	-	1500				8		6			11	7	9	2	3	10	4	5	1	6
7	Nov	6	(h)	BURTON SWIFTS	D 1-1	Gallacher	3000				8	4	6			11	7	9	2	3	10		5	1	7
8	Nov	13	(a)	Burnley	L 0-4	-	3000	10				4	6			11	7	9	2	3	8		5	1	8
9	Nov	27	(a)	Gainsborough Trinity	D 3-3	McInnes, Gallacher, Little	1500				8	4	6			11	7	9	2	3	10		5	1	9
10	Nov	29	(h)	BLACKPOOL	W 3-1	Little (2), Coupar					8	4	6			11	7	9	2	3	10		5	1	10
11	Dec	4	(a)	Lincoln City	L 2-4	Stewart, McEwen					8	4	6			11	7	9	2	3	10		5	1	11
12	Dec	18	(h)	LINCOLN CITY	W 9-3	Birch (3), Stewart, Coupar, McInnes (2), Little, Gallacher	3000	9			8	4	6				7	10	2	3	11		5	1	12
13	Dec	25	(a)	Burton Swifts	L 1-2	Donaldson		8				4	6	9		11	7	10	2	3			5	1	13
14	Dec	27	(h)	GRIMSBY TOWN	W 6-0	McInnes, Ekins, Donaldson (2), Coupar, Davies (pen)	5000				8	4	6	9		11	7		2	3	10		5	1	14
15	Jan	1	(h)	MANCHESTER CITY	W 3-0	Donaldson, Coupar, McInnes	4000				8	4	6	9			7	10	2	3	11		5	1	15
16	Jan	8	(a)	Walsall	L 0-5	-	4000				8	4	6	9			7	10	2	3	11		5	1	16
17	Jan	15	(h)	LOUGHBOROUGH	W 7-0	Coupar (2), Stewart (2, 1 pen), Donaldson (2), Little	3000				8		6	9			7	10	2	3	11	4	5	1	17
18	Jan	22	(a)	Grimsby Town	W 3-1	Donaldson, McInnes, Coupar	5000				8	4	6	9			7	10	2	3	11		5	1	18
19	Feb	5	(h)	WALSALL	W 6-0	Stewart (4, 1 pen), Little (2)	2000	6			8		2	9			7	10		3	11	4	5	1	19
20	Feb	12	(a)	Small Heath	L 2-4	Stewart, Donaldson	4000	6			8		2	9			7	10		3	11	4	5	1	20
21	Feb	19	(h)	NEWCASTLE UNITED	W 3-1	Birch, Stewart, Donaldson	3500	11			8	4	6	9			7		2	3	10		5	1	21
22	Feb	26	(a)	Darwen	W 2-0	Gallacher, Birch	3000	11			8	4	6	9			7		2	3	10		5	1	22
23	Mar	12	(a)	Newcastle United	L 1-4	Birch	15000	11			8	4	6	9			7		2	3	10		5	1	23
24	Mar	19	(h)	BURNLEY	W 2-0	Donaldson, Gallacher	3000	11					6	9			7	8	2	3	10	4	5	1	24
25	Mar	21	(h)	NEWTON HEATH	D 2-2	Durrant, McInnes	2000					4	6	9	11		7	8	2	3	10		5	1	25
26	Mar	26	(a)	Manchester City	L 1-2	Coupar	5000	11			8	4	6	9			7		2	3	10		5	1	26
27	Apr	2	(h)	SMALL HEATH	L 1-2	Coupar	3000	11			8	4	6	9			7		2	3	10		5	1	27
28	Apr	8	(h)	LEICESTER FOSSE	L 0-1	-	3000	11			8	4	6	9			7		2	3	10		5	1	28
29	Apr	11	(h)	DARWEN	W 3-0	Gallacher, McInnes, Catlin			11		9	4	6				7	8	2	3	10		5	1	29
30	Apr	30	(a)	Blackpool	L 0-1	-	200				8	4	6	9			7	11	2	3	10		5	1	30
							Apps	13	1	1	26	25	30	17	1	12	30	22	27	30	29	6	30	30	
							Goals	6	1	-	9	1	-	10	1	3	7	9	-	1	10	-	10	-	

Final League Position: 8th

1897/98 FA CUP

Round	Month	Day	Venue	Opponents	W/L/D Score	Scorers	Attendance	Birch E	Catlin W	Clarke J	Coupar J	Davies Samuel	Docherty J	Donaldson R	Durrant AF	Ekins FG	Gallacher W	Little T	McCartney WJ	McEwen J	McInnes T	Perrins G	Stewart WS	Williams R	Round
Q4	Nov	20	(a)	Tottenham Hotspur	W 4-3	Davies, Stewart, McInnes, Ekins	12000				10	4	6			11	7	9	2	3	8		5	1	Q4
Q5	Dec	11	(a)	Clapton	W 2-0	Stewart, Little	2500				10	4	6			11	7	9	2	3	8		5	1	Q5
1	Jan	29	(h)	BOLTON WANDERERS	L 0-1	-	9000				8	4	6	9			7	11	2	3	10		5	1	1
							Apps	-	-	-	3	3	3	1	-	2	3	3	3	3	3	-	3	3	
							Goals	-	-	-	-	1	-	-	-	1	-	1	-	-	1	-	2	-	

▶ John McEwen

▶ John McCartney (*who became manager 30 years later*)

▶ George Ekins

▶ Tom McInnes

▶ Bob Donaldson

▶ Billy Lawson (*Trainer*)

TIMELINE...
September 1897 The Town's bid to join the Football League is successful.

1898/99 FOOTBALL LEAGUE DIVISION TWO

Match No	Month	Day	Venue	Opponents	W,L,D Score	Scorers	Attendance	Birch E	Boutwood J	Brock JS	Clarke W	Crump WH	Dow JM	Draper F	Durrant AF	Ekins FG	Farr H	Ford C	Ford WG	Galbraith H	Gentle P	Hawkes T	Hewitt G	Kemplay J	McInnes T	Moore James	Palmer JF	Perkins WH	Ralley W	Sharpe DA	Smith GH	Williams H	Match No
1	Sep	3	(h)	WOOLWICH ARSENAL	L 0-1		5000			11	5	6			7			4	9			8		10	3			1				2	1
2	Sep	10	(a)	Barnsley	L 1-2	McInnes				11	4				7			6	9			8		10	3			1		5		2	2
3	Sep	17	(a)	Leicester Fosse	D 1-1	Hewitt	3000				2				7			4	11				10	9	8			1	6	5		3	3
4	Sep	24	(h)	DARWEN	W 8-1	Hewitt, McInnes, Kemplay (2), Ekins, Durrant (2), W Ford									7	11		4	10				6	9	8	3		1		5		2	4
5	Oct	1	(a)	Gainsborough Trinity	W 3-2	McInnes, Kemplay, Brock	2000			11			2		7			4	10				6	9	8	3		1		5			5
6	Oct	8	(h)	MANCHESTER CITY	L 0-3		3000						2		7	11		4	10				6	9	8	3		1		5			6
7	Oct	15	(a)	Glossop	L 0-5		2500				4	6	2		7				10					9	8	3		1		5			7
8	Oct	22	(h)	WALSALL	W 3-2	McInnes, Hewitt, Durrant	2000						2		7	11		6	4				10	9	8	3		1		5			8
9	Nov	5	(h)	BURSLEM PORT VALE	L 0-1		2000					6	11		7			4	5	9				10	8			1				3	9
10	Nov	12	(a)	Small Heath	L 0-9		4000					6	2		7	11		4	5	9				10	8			1				3	10
11	Nov	26	(a)	Blackpool	W 3-2	Ekins, Hewitt (2)	1000	7				6				11		4					10	9	8	3		1		5		2	11
12	Dec	3	(h)	GRIMSBY TOWN	W 3-1	Durrant (2), Kemplay	2000					6	2		7	11		4					10	9	8			1		5		3	12
13	Dec	17	(h)	NEW BRIGHTON TOWER	L 2-3	Hewitt, Williams	3000	7				6	2			11		4					10	9	8			1		5		3	13
14	Dec	24	(a)	Lincoln City	L 0-2			7				6	2			11		4	10					9	8	3		1				5	14
15	Dec	26	(a)	Burton Swifts	D 1-1	Brock			10	7		6	2			11		4						9	8	3		1	4	5		5	15
16	Dec	31	(a)	Woolwich Arsenal	L 2-6	Kemplay (2)	4000	10		7		6	2			11		4						9	8			1		5		5	16
17	Jan	7	(h)	BARNSLEY	W 4-1	Kemplay, Birch (3)		7				6	2			11		4						9	8			1	4	5		5	17
18	Jan	14	(h)	LEICESTER FOSSE	L 1-6	W Ford	2000	10				6			7			4	10					9	8			1	4	5		5	18
19	Jan	28	(h)	GAINSBOROUGH TRINITY	W 4-2	Brock, McInnes, Kemplay (2)	1000	10		7		6				11		4						9	8			1		5		2	19
20	Feb	4	(a)	Manchester City	L 0-2		8000	10				6	2		7			6	8					9				1	4	5		3	20
21	Feb	11	(h)	GLOSSOP	L 0-2			10		11		6	2		7			4						9	8			1		5		3	21
22	Feb	18	(a)	Walsall	L 0-6		3000	10		7		6	2			11		4						9	8			1		5		3	22
23	Mar	4	(a)	Burslem Port Vale	L 1-4	Birch	4000	9		7		11	2					6		10					8			1	4	5		3	23
24	Mar	11	(h)	SMALL HEATH	L 2-3	Dow, W Ford	2000	11		7		6	2					4	10					9	8			1		5		4	24
25	Mar	18	(a)	Loughborough	L 1-4	Brock		11		8			2		7			6						9	10	3		1		5		4	25
26	Mar	25	(h)	BLACKPOOL	W 3-2	W Ford (2), Kemplay		10		7		6	2		11			6	8					9				1		5		3	26
27	Mar	31	(h)	LOUGHBOROUGH	D 2-2	McInnes, Durrant	4000	10					2		7	11			9		1				8	3				6		3	27
28	Apr	1	(a)	Grimsby Town	L 0-5		5000	6					2		7	11			10		1			9	8					4		3	28
29	Apr	3	(h)	BURTON SWIFTS	W 3-0	W Ford, Kemplay, Brock				8			2		7	11			10					9					5	4	1	3	29
30	Apr	8	(h)	NEWTON HEATH	L 0-1		2000	4					2		7	11			10		1			9	8				5	4		3	30
31	Apr	11	(a)	Darwen	L 1-4	McInnes							2		7	11		4	5	10	1			9	8						3	31
32	Apr	12	(a)	Newton Heath	L 0-5		3000			8			2		7	11			10		1			9	10	3						3	32
33	Apr	15	(a)	New Brighton Tower	L 0-4				4	7			6			11			10		3			9	8	1	1			5			33
34	Apr	22	(h)	LINCOLN CITY	W 2-0	W Ford, McInnes			4	7			6	3		11	1		10					9	8					5		2	34
				Apps				16	1	21	4	25	26		22	21	1	24	23	3	5	1	12	29	31	19	1	26	11	21	1	30	
				Goals				4		5		1			6	2			7				6	11	8							1	

Final League Position: 15th

1898/99 FA CUP

Round	Month	Day	Venue	Opponents	W,L,D Score	Scorers	Attendance	Birch E	Boutwood J	Brock JS	Clarke W	Crump WH	Dow JM	Draper F	Durrant AF	Ekins FG	Farr H	Ford C	Ford WG	Galbraith H	Gentle P	Hawkes T	Hewitt G	Kemplay J	McInnes T	Moore James	Palmer JF	Perkins WH	Ralley W	Sharpe DA	Smith GH	Williams H	Round
Q3	Oct	29	(h)	WATFORD	D 2-2	Dow, Durrant	2500			11			2		7			6	4	9			10	8				1		5		3	Q3
Rep	Nov	2	(a)	Watford	W 1-0	Galbraith	2000			11		5	2		7			6	4	9			10		8	2		1				3	Rep
Q4	Nov	19	(h)	SHEPHERDS BUSH	W 4-3	Crump, Durrant, Kempley, Hewitt	2000			11	5	2			7			6					10	9	8	4		1				3	Q4
Q5	Dec	10	(a)	Tottenham Hotspur	D 1-1	Hewitt	12000				5	2				11		6	6	4			10	9	8			1		7		3	Q5
Rep	Dec	14	(h)	TOTTENHAM HOTSPUR	D 1-1	McInnes	3500				5	2		4	11			6					10	9	8			1		7		3	Rep
Rep 2	Dec	19	(n)	Tottenham Hotspur	L 0-2		8000				5	2	10		11			6		4				9	8			1		7		3	Rep 2
				Apps						3	5	5	1	4	3			6	3	3			5	5	5	2		6		4		6	
				Goals								1	1		2					1			2	1	1								

5th Qualifying Round 2nd Replay played at Tufnell Park

▶ **The 1898/99 team** – Back row (left to
right): Lawson (Trainer), Williams,
Perkins, Moore, Wiseman (Groundsman),
Galbraith. Middle row (left to right):
Durrant, C.Ford, Sharp, Clarke, Crump,
Ekins. Front row (left to right): Brock,
Kemplay, W.G.Ford, Hewitt, McInnes.

TIMELINE...

April 1899 The cracks begin to show as the Town struggle on and off the pitch.

1899/1900 FOOTBALL LEAGUE DIVISION TWO

Match No	Month	Day	Venue	Opponents	W,L,D Score	Scorers	Attendance	Barnes WT	Brock JS	Brown James	Brown WR	Burbage RW	Daw EC	Dawson	Dimmock E	Dow JM	Draper F	Durrant AF	Eckford J	Fairgrieve RW	Garratt A	Hawkes F	Hawkes T	Holdstock HF	Inglis JA	Marshall FR	McCurdy W	McInnes T	Morrison FR	Ralley W	Stewart WS	Williams H	Match No
1	Sep	2	(a)	Grimsby Town	D 3-3	Fairgrieve, Brock (2)	4000		8				1			2			11	9					7		3	10	4		5	6	1
2	Sep	9	(h)	WOOLWICH ARSENAL	L 1-2	Dow	3000		8				1			2			11	9					7		3	10	4		5	6	2
3	Sep	16	(a)	Barnsley	L 1-2	Williams	2500		8				1			2			11	9					7		3	10	4		5	6	3
4	Sep	23	(h)	LEICESTER FOSSE	D 0-0	-	4000		8		7		1			2	9		11								3	10	4		5	6	4
5	Sep	30	(h)	BURTON SWIFTS	W 5-2	Fairgrieve, Brock (2), Eckford, W Brown	-		8		7		1			2			11	9							3	10	4		5	6	5
6	Oct	7	(a)	Burslem Port Vale	L 0-1	-	2000		8		7		1			2			11	9							3	10	4		5	6	6
7	Oct	14	(h)	WALSALL	W 4-0	Brock, Fairgrieve, Bunch (og), McInnes	3000		8		7		1			2			11	9							3	10	4	6	5		7
8	Oct	21	(a)	Middlesbrough	D 0-0	-	7000		8		7		1			2			11	9							3	10	4	6	5		8
9	Nov	4	(a)	Gainsborough Trinity	D 2-2	Brock, Fairgrieve	-		8		7		1			2			11	9							3	10	4	6	5		9
10	Nov	11	(h)	BOLTON WANDERERS	L 0-2	-	-		8		7		1			2			11	9							3	10	4	6	5		10
11	Nov	25	(h)	NEWTON HEATH	L 0-1	-	3000		8				1			2		7	11	9	3							10	4	6	5		11
12	Dec	2	(a)	Sheffield Wednesday	L 0-6	-	10000	5	4		7		1						8	11				9			3	10		6	2		12
13	Dec	16	(a)	Small Heath	L 0-3	-	2000		4		7		1			2			8	11						9	3	10		6	5		13
14	Dec	23	(h)	NEW BRIGHTON TOWER	L 1-4	Marshall	-		4		7		1			2			8	11						9	3	10		6	5		14
15	Dec	26	(h)	CHESTERFIELD	L 0-3	-	2000		4		7		1			2			8	11						9	3	10		6	5		15
16	Dec	30	(h)	GRIMSBY TOWN	L 0-4	-	500		9		7		1			2			8	11							3	10	4	6	5		16
17	Jan	6	(a)	Woolwich Arsenal	L 1-3	Eckford	3000		4		7		1		11	2	9		10					6			3	8				5	17
18	Jan	13	(h)	BARNSLEY	W 3-0	J Brown, Brock, Draper	-		4	6	7		1		11	2	9		10								3	8				5	18
19	Jan	20	(a)	Leicester Fosse	D 2-2	Draper (2)	6000		4		7		1		11	2	9		10					5			3	8			6		19
20	Feb	3	(a)	Burton Swifts	L 1-3	W Brown	300		4		7		1		11	2	9		10					5			3	8			6		20
21	Feb	10	(h)	BURSLEM PORT VALE	D 1-1	Draper	500		4	5	7		1		11	2	9		10								3	8			6		21
22	Feb	17	(a)	Walsall	L 3-7	Dimmock, Eckford, Draper	1000			5	7		1		11	2	9		10					4			3	8			6		22
23	Feb	24	(h)	MIDDLESBROUGH	D 1-1	W Brown	1000		4	6	7		1		11	2	9		10					5				8			3		23
24	Mar	3	(a)	Lincoln City	L 0-2	-	2500	6	4		7		1		11	2		8	10								3	9				5	24
25	Mar	10	(h)	GAINSBOROUGH TRINITY	W 4-0	Holdstock, Dimmock, Draper, Brock	1000		10	6	7		1		8	2	9		11					5			3				4		25
26	Mar	17	(a)	Bolton Wanderers	L 0-3	-	3658			6	7		1		11	2		8	10					5			3	9			4		26
27	Mar	24	(h)	LOUGHBOROUGH	W 4-0	Dow, Brock (2), F Hawkes	-		9	6	7		1			2			11			4	8	5			3	10					27
28	Mar	26	(a)	Chesterfield	L 0-2	-	-		9		7		1		4	2		11	10					5			3	8				5	28
29	Mar	31	(a)	Newton Heath	L 0-5	-	3000		4	6	7		1		11	2		8	10								3	9			5		29
30	Apr	7	(h)	SHEFFIELD WEDNESDAY	L 0-1	-	1000	8	4			9	1			2		7	11					5			3	10			6		30
31	Apr	16	(h)	LINCOLN CITY	L 0-2	-	1500		4	6	7	9	1					8	11					5			3	10			2		31
32	Apr	17	(a)	Loughborough	D 1-1	Durrant	300		4	6	7		1		11			8	10					5			3	9			2		32
33	Apr	21	(h)	SMALL HEATH	L 1-2	Burbage	1000	8	6		7	9	1			2			11					5			3	10			4		33
34	Apr	28	(a)	New Brighton Tower	L 1-5	McInnes	-		4	6	7		1		11			8	10					5			3	9			2		34
				Final League Position: 17th		1 Own Goal	**Apps**	6	31	13	27	3	34	1	11	30	9	9	34	15	1	2	2	13	3	3	31	33	13	10	16	24	
							Goals	-	10	1	3	1	-	-	2	2	6	1	3	4	-	1	-	1	-	1	-	2	-	-	-	1	

1899/1900 FA CUP

Round	Month	Day	Venue	Opponents	W,L,D Score	Scorers	Attendance	Barnes WT	Brock JS	Brown James	Brown WR	Burbage RW	Daw EC	Dawson	Dimmock E	Dow JM	Draper F	Durrant AF	Eckford J	Fairgrieve RW	Garratt A	Hawkes F	Hawkes T	Holdstock HF	Inglis JA	Marshall FR	McCurdy W	McInnes T	Morrison FR	Ralley W	Stewart WS	Williams H	Round
Q3	Oct	28	(a)	Lowestoft Town	W 2-0	McInnes, Eckford	1000		8		7		1			2			11	9							3	10	4	6	5		Q3
Q4	Nov	18	(h)	WATFORD	W 3-2	Brown, Brock, Fairgrieve	4500		8		7		1			2			11	9							3	10	4	6	5		Q4
Q5	Dec	9	(h)	QUEENS PARK RANGERS	D 1-1	McInnes	4000		8		7		1			2			11	9							3	10	4	6	5		Q5
Rep	Dec	13	(a)	Queens Park Rangers	L 1-4	Fairgrieve	2000				7		1			2		8	11	9							3	10	4	6	5		Rep
							Apps	-	3	-	4	-	4	-	-	4	-	1	4	4	-	-	-	-	-	-	4	4	4	4	4	-	
							Goals	-	1	-	1	-	-	-	-	-	-	-	1	2	-	-	-	-	-	-	-	2	-	-	-	-	

A Match Card for the friendly fixture against Thames Ironworks (now West Ham) on 8th January 1900 which the Town lost 3-5.

The 1899/1900 team – Back row (left to right): Wiseman (Groundsman), Williams, Ralley, Dow, Daw, McCurdy, Lawson (Trainer). Middle row (left to right): Inglis, Morrison, Stewart, Brown, Eckford. Front row (left to right): Brock, Fairgrieve, McInnes.

TIMELINE...

April 1900 Due to financial problems the Town decide not to seek re-election to the Football League. A request to join a now much stronger Southern League is accepted.

1900/1901 SOUTHERN LEAGUE DIVISION ONE

Match No	Month	Day	Venue	Opponents	W,L,D Score	Scorers	Attendance	Barker A	Blessington J	Brown WR	Burbage RW	Clifford T	Cox AG	Dempsey N	Dimmock E	Durrant AF	Farr H	Garratt A	Gray RSM	Hawkes F	Holdstock HF	Lindsay W	McCurdy W	Molyneux F	Monks J	Ord RG	Plummer MM	Saxton AW	Smart T	Street A	Tierney TT	White F	Williams H	Match No
1	Sep	1	(h)	SOUTHAMPTON	L 3-4	Molyneux (2), Brown	3000		8	7		4									5	2	3	9	1			11			10		6	1
2	Sep	15	(h)	BRISTOL CITY	W 2-0	Burbage (2)	3000		8	7	9	4									5	2	3				11	1		10		6	2
3	Sep	22	(a)	Swindon Town	L 1-2	Brown			8	7		4	10			11					5	2	3		1			9				6	3
4	Sep	29	(h)	WATFORD	W 2-0	Saxton, Durrant	3500		8	7	9	4				11					5	2	3		1		10					6	4
5	Oct	6	(a)	Queens Park Rangers	W 3-1	Brown, Blessington, Durrant	4000		8	7	9	4				11					5	2	3		1		10					6	5
6	Oct	20	(h)	WEST HAM UNITED	W 2-0	Blessington (2)	4000		8	7	9	4				11					5	2	3		1		10					6	6
7	Oct	27	(a)	Portsmouth	L 0-2	-	5000	9		7		4		8		11					5	2	3		1		10					6	7
8	Nov	10	(a)	Bristol Rovers	L 0-1	-	5000	9	8	7		4		10							5	2	3		1		11					6	8
9	Dec	1	(h)	GRAVESEND UNITED	W 5-2	Williams, Brown, Blessington, Saxton, Dempsey	1500		8	7		4		10		11					5	2	3		1		9					6	9
10	Dec	15	(a)	Southampton	L 0-5	-			8	7		4		9		11					5	2	3		1		10					6	10
11	Dec	25	(a)	Kettering Town	L 0-2	-		9		7		5				11				8	6	3	2			1		10				4	6	11
12	Dec	29	(a)	Bristol City	L 0-1	-	4000	9		7		4				11	5	6		8		3	2			1		10					6	12
13	Jan	12	(a)	Watford	L 0-2	-	3000		9			4				11	7	6		8		3	2			1					10	5	6	13
14	Jan	19	(h)	QUEENS PARK RANGERS	D 2-2	Williams, Durrant	3000		8	7		4				11					5	3				1					10	2	6	14
15	Jan	26	(h)	SWINDON TOWN	W 2-1	Tierney, Gray	1000		8			4	5			7			9			3				1					10	2	6	15
16	Feb	9	(a)	West Ham United	L 0-2	-	1000		8	7		4	5						9			2				1		11			10	3	6	16
17	Feb	16	(h)	PORTSMOUTH	L 2-4	Tierney, Durrant			8			5				7			9	4		2				1		11			10	3	6	17
18	Feb	23	(a)	New Brompton	L 1-3	Durrant	1500	9	8	11		4				7					5	3				1					10	2	6	18
19	Mar	2	(h)	BRISTOL ROVERS	L 0-1	-	2000	9	8	11		5				7			4			3				1					10	2	6	19
20	Mar	9	(a)	Reading	W 1-0	F Hawkes		9	8	11			5			7			10			3				1				2		4	6	20
21	Mar	23	(a)	Gravesend United	D 2-2	Blessington, Barker		9	8	11						7			4			3				1				2	10	5	6	21
22	Mar	30	(h)	MILLWALL	W 2-0	Brown, Durrant	2500	9	8	11						7			4			3				1				2	10	5	6	22
23	Apr	5	(h)	KETTERING TOWN	W 2-0	Durrant, Barker		9	8	11						7			4	5		3				1				2	10		6	23
24	Apr	6	(a)	Millwall	L 1-3	Durrant	5000	9	8	11			5			7			4							1	10			2		3	6	24
25	Apr	13	(h)	NEW BROMPTON	W 4-2	Tierney (3), Brown	2000	9	8	11		3				7			4							1				2	10	5	6	25
26	Apr	25	(a)	Tottenham Hotspur	L 2-3	Blessington, Durrant	4000		8	7		4		9		11						2				1			1	3	10	5	6	26
27	Apr	27	(h)	READING	W 2-0	Barker, F Hawkes		9	8	11		2				7			4							1				3	10	5	6	27
28	Apr	29	(h)	TOTTENHAM HOTSPUR	L 2-4	Blessington (2)	4500	9	8	11		2				7			4							1				3	10	5	6	28
				Apps				14	25	25	4	23	5	5	1	24	1	2	4	13	14	20	15	1	1	25	2	14	2	11	16	13	28	
				Goals				3	8	6	2	-	-	1	-	9	-	-	1	2	-	-	-	2	-	-	-	2	-	-	5	-	2	

Final League Position: 11th

1900/1901 FA CUP

Round	Month	Day	Venue	Opponents	W,L,D Score	Scorers	Attendance	Barker A	Blessington J	Brown WR	Burbage RW	Clifford T	Cox AG	Dempsey N	Dimmock E	Durrant AF	Farr H	Garratt A	Gray RSM	Hawkes F	Holdstock HF	Lindsay W	McCurdy W	Molyneux F	Monks J	Ord RG	Plummer MM	Saxton AW	Smart T	Street A	Tierney TT	White F	Williams H	Round
Q3	Nov	3	(a)	Kings Lynn	W 4-1	Blessington, Saxton (3)	1000	8	7			4		10		9					5	2	3			1		11					6	Q3
Q4	Nov	17	(h)	CIVIL SERVICE	W 9-1	McCurdy, Lindsay (2), Holdstock, Saxton (2), Blessington (2), Johnson (og)	2500		7	8	9	4		10							5	2	3			1		11					6	Q4
Q5	Dec	8	(h)	QUEENS PARK RANGERS	W 3-0	Durrant (2), Dempsey	3500	7	8			4		10		9					5	2	3			1		11					6	Q5
IR	Jan	5	(h)	BRISTOL ROVERS	L 0-2	-	3000	7	8	11		4				9	2				5		3			1					10		6	IR
				Apps				1	4	3	2	4	-	3	-	3	1	-	-	-	4	3	4	-	-	4	-	3	-	-	1	-	4	
				Goals				-	3	-	-	-	-	1	-	2	-	-	-	-	1	2	1	-	-	-	-	5	-	-	-	-	-	

1 Own Goal

▶ **The 1900/01 team** – Back row (left to right): Smart, Jones. Middle row (left to right): Wiseman (Groundsman), H.Smart (Director), Holdstock, Lindsay, Clifford, McCurdy, Williams, Lawson (Trainer), E.Gibbs (Director). Front row (left to right): Brown, Blessington, Molyneux, Tierney, Saxton.

TIMELINE...

April 1901 Back amongst old friends the Hatters finish a comfortable 11th.

Luton Town Football Club – The Full Record | 19

1901/1902 SOUTHERN LEAGUE DIVISION ONE

Match No	Month	Day	Venue	Opponents	W,L,D Score	Scorers	Attendance	Barker A	Blessington J	Brown John	Colvin R	Dimmock E	Durrant AF	Farr H	Goodge SH	Hall E	Hawkes F	Hawkes R	Holdstock H	Lindsay W	Moody HB	Ord RG	Plummer MM	Sharp A	Street A	Tierney TT	White F	Williams H	Match No
1	Sep	7	(h)	WELLINGBOROUGH	W 1-0	Tierney	1200		8	9	11		7				4			2		1		3		10	5	6	1
2	Sep	14	(a)	Portsmouth	L 0-1	-	9000		8	9	11		7				4			2		1		3		10	5	6	2
3	Sep	21	(h)	SWINDON TOWN	W 3-0	Brown (3)			8	9	11		7				4			2		1		3		10	5	6	3
4	Sep	28	(a)	Brentford	W 1-0	Blessington	2500		8	9	11		7				4			2		1		3		10	5	6	4
5	Oct	12	(a)	West Ham United	L 1-4	White	4000		8	9	11		7			3	4			2		1				10	5	6	5
6	Oct	26	(h)	QUEENS PARK RANGERS	W 1-0	Brown	2000		8	9	11		7				4			2		1		3		10	5	6	6
7	Nov	9	(h)	SOUTHAMPTON	L 0-2	-	3000		8	9	11		7				4			2		1		3		10	5	6	7
8	Nov	23	(h)	NEW BROMPTON	W 3-1	Durrant, Blessington, Tierney	2000		8	9	11		7				4			2		1		3		10	5	6	8
9	Dec	7	(h)	WATFORD	W 1-0	Blessington	4000		8	9	11		7				4	6		2		1		3		10	5		9
10	Dec	21	(a)	Wellingborough	D 2-2	Tierney, (og)	500		8	9	11		7				4			2		1		3		10	5	6	10
11	Dec	25	(a)	Kettering Town	D 2-2	Brown (2)			8	9	11		7				4			2		1			3	10	5	6	11
12	Dec	26	(h)	NORTHAMPTON TOWN	D 0-0	-	4000		10	8	11		7				4	6		2		1			3	9	5		12
13	Jan	4	(a)	Swindon Town	W 2-1	Blessington, Colvin			10	8	11		7				4			2		1			3	9	5	6	13
14	Jan	11	(h)	BRENTFORD	D 1-1	(og)			8	9	11		7					10	4	2		1		3			5	6	14
15	Jan	25	(h)	WEST HAM UNITED	L 0-3	-	2000		8	9	11		7	1			4			2				3		10	5	6	15
16	Feb	1	(h)	MILLWALL	W 1-0	Durrant	1900		8		11		7				4	9		2	10	1		3			5	6	16
17	Feb	8	(a)	Queens Park Rangers	D 2-2	Blessington, Colvin	3000		8	9	11		7				4			2		1		3		10	5	6	17
18	Feb	15	(h)	READING	D 1-1	Tierney	2000		8		11		7		9		4			2		1		3		10	5	6	18
19	Feb	22	(a)	Watford	L 0-2	-	4000	9	8		11		7				4			2		1		3		10	5	6	19
20	Mar	1	(h)	BRISTOL ROVERS	D 1-1	R Hawkes	2000		8	9	11		7				4	6		2		1		3		10	5		20
21	Mar	8	(a)	New Brompton	L 0-3	-	2000	8		9	11		7				4			2		1		3		10	5	6	21
22	Mar	28	(h)	KETTERING TOWN	W 1-0	Tierney			8		11		7				4	6			9	1		3		10	5	6	22
23	Mar	29	(h)	TOTTENHAM HOTSPUR	D 0-0	-	3000		8		11		7				4	6			9	1		3		10	5	2	23
24	Mar	31	(a)	Northampton Town	W 4-2	Durrant (2), Blessington, Brown			8	9	11		7				4					1		3	2	10	5	6	24
25	Apr	1	(a)	Millwall	L 0-1	-	3000		8	9		11	7				4			2		1		3		10	5	6	25
26	Apr	5	(a)	Bristol Rovers	L 0-4	-	3000	9	8		11		7				4			2		1		3	10		5	6	26
27	Apr	9	(a)	Southampton	L 0-1	-		9	8		11		7				4					1		3	2	10	5	6	27
28	Apr	12	(a)	Tottenham Hotspur	D 0-0	-	6000		8	9	11		7				4			2		1		3		10	5	6	28
29	Apr	19	(a)	Reading	D 1-1	Tierney		9	8				7				4			2		1	11	3		10	5	6	29
30	Apr	26	(h)	PORTSMOUTH	W 2-1	Durrant (2)			8		11		7				4	6		2	9	1		3		10	5		30
				Final League Position: 7th		2 Own Goals	**Apps**	5	26	22	28	1	30	1	1	3	29	8	1	23	6	28	1	25	8	27	30	26	
							Goals	-	6	7	2	-	6	-	-	-	-	1	-	-	-	-	-	-	-	6	1	-	

1901/1902 FA CUP

Round	Month	Day	Venue	Opponents	W,L,D Score	Scorers	Attendance	Barker A	Blessington J	Brown John	Colvin R	Dimmock E	Durrant AF	Farr H	Goodge SH	Hall E	Hawkes F	Hawkes R	Holdstock H	Lindsay W	Moody HB	Ord RG	Plummer MM	Sharp A	Street A	Tierney TT	White F	Williams H	Round
Q1	Oct	5	(h)	APSLEY	W 13-1	Lindsay, F Hawkes, White, Blessington (4), Brown (2), Tierney (3), Colvin	3000		7	8	11		9				4			2		1		3		10	5	6	Q1
Q2	Oct	19	(h)	BEDFORD QUEENS WORKS	W 4-2	Lindsay, Blessington, Durrant, Colvin	2000		7	8	11		9			3	4			2		1				10	5	6	Q2
Q3	Nov	2	(a)	Lowestoft Town	W 2-1	Blessington, Brown	1500		7	8	11		9				4			2		1		3		10	5	6	Q3
Q4	Nov	16	(a)	Watford	W 2-1	Blessington, Brown	4000		7	8	11		9				4	6		2		1		3		10	5		Q4
Q5	Nov	30	(h)	QUEENS PARK RANGERS	W 2-0	Durrant, Brown	5000		7	8	11		9				4	6		2		1		3		10	5		Q5
IR	Dec	14	(a)	Woolwich Arsenal	D 1-1	Blessington	10000		7	8	11		9				4	6		2		1				10	5	3	IR
Rep	Dec	18	(h)	WOOLWICH ARSENAL	L 0-2	-	4500		7	8	11		9				4	6		2		1				10	5	3	Rep
							Apps	-	7	7	7	-	7	-	-	1	7	4	-	7	-	7	-	4	-	7	7	5	
							Goals	-	8	5	2	-	2	-	-	-	1	-	-	2	-	-	-	-	-	3	1	-	

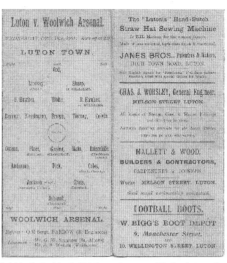

A Match Card for the F.A.Cup replay against Woolwich Arsenal (now Arsenal) which the Town lost 0-2.

H. MOODY (Forward).

A debut season for Luton born Herbert Moody who went on to net over 100 goals for the Town.

The 1901/02 team – Back row (left to right): Lindsay, Ord, Sharp.
Middle row (left to right): Durrant, F.Hawkes, White, Williams,
Colvin. Front row (left to right): Blessington, Brown, Tierney.

TIMELINE...

15 October 1901 A new scoring record as Apsley are seen off 13-1 in an F.A.Cup tie.

1902/1903 SOUTHERN LEAGUE DIVISION ONE

Match No	Month	Day	Venue	Opponents	W.L.D	Score	Scorers	Attendance	Allen F	Allsopp TC	Blessington J	Davidson AB	Draycott W	Durrant AF	Eling A	Everitt	Frail J	Gall L	Hall E	Hawkes F	Hawkes R	Hilsdon J	Hood F	Jeakings RW	Lindsay W	Milam	Moody HB	Sharp A	Stratton L	Street A	White F	Williams H	Woods Herbert	Match No
1	Sep	6	(a)	Portsmouth	L	0-3	-	10000		11	8			7			1	10		4	6				2		9	3			5			1
2	Sep	13	(h)	NEW BROMPTON	D	1-1	Gall	2000		11	8			7			1	10		4	6				2		9	3			5			2
3	Sep	20	(a)	Swindon Town	L	1-2	Durrant				8			7			1	10		4		11		3	2		9				5	6		3
4	Sep	27	(h)	KETTERING TOWN	W	1-0	Gall				8			7			1	10		4		11			2		9	3			5	6		4
5	Oct	4	(h)	MILLWALL	L	0-1	-	3000		11	8			7			1	10		4	6	9						3			5	2		5
6	Oct	11	(a)	Reading	L	3-5	Durrant, Moody, Allsopp	1000		11	8			7			1		2	4		9					10	3			5	6		6
7	Oct	18	(h)	QUEENS PARK RANGERS	W	4-1	Durrant, Blessington, Allsopp, Moody	2000		11	8			7			1		2	4	6	9					10	3			5			7
8	Oct	25	(a)	Southampton	L	0-2	-			11	8			7			1		2	4	6	9					10				5	3		8
9	Nov	8	(a)	Bristol Rovers	L	1-4	White	5000		11	8			7			1			4		9			2		10			3	5	6		9
10	Nov	22	(a)	Watford	W	1-0	Blessington	3500		11	8			7			1			4	6	9			2		10			3	5			10
11	Dec	6	(a)	Tottenham Hotspur	D	1-1	Moody	4000		11	8			7			1	9		4	6				2		10				5	3		11
12	Dec	20	(h)	PORTSMOUTH	L	0-2	-	3000			8			7			1	9		4	6				2		10				5	3	11	12
13	Dec	26	(h)	NORTHAMPTON TOWN	W	4-0	Durrant, Moody, Gall (2)	4000		11	8			7			1	9		4	6				2		10				5	3		13
14	Dec	27	(a)	New Brompton	D	1-1	Durrant	5000			8			7			1	9		4	6				2		10				5	3	11	14
15	Jan	3	(h)	SWINDON TOWN	D	0-0					8			7			1	9		4	6				2		10				5	3	11	15
16	Jan	10	(a)	Kettering Town	D	1-1	Moody	2000	9	11	8			7			1			4					2		10				5	3		16
17	Jan	17	(a)	Millwall	L	0-1	-	2000	9	11	8			7			1			4					2		10				5	6		17
18	Jan	24	(h)	READING	L	0-3				11	8			7			1	9		4	6				2		10				5	6		18
19	Jan	31	(a)	Queens Park Rangers	L	1-3	Gall	5000		11	8			7			1	9		4	6				2		10				5	3		19
20	Feb	14	(a)	Wellingborough	L	1-2	Allsopp	1000		11	8			7			1	9		4	6				2		10				5	3		20
21	Feb	28	(h)	BRISTOL ROVERS	D	1-1	Moody	2000		11	8		10	7			1			4	6				2		9				5	3		21
22	Mar	7	(h)	WATFORD	W	4-1	Durrant, Blessington, Moody, Davidson	2000		11	8	9		7			1			4	6				2		10				5	3		22
23	Mar	14	(a)	Brentford	W	3-1	Blessington, Allsopp, Davidson	3500		11	8	9		7			1			4	6				2		10				5	3		23
24	Mar	21	(h)	TOTTENHAM HOTSPUR	W	3-0	Lindsay, Blessington, Davidson	4000		11	8	9		7			1			4	6				2		10				5	3		24
25	Mar	28	(a)	West Ham United	L	1-4	Davidson	1000		11	8	9		7			1			4	6				2		10				5	3		25
26	Apr	4	(h)	SOUTHAMPTON	L	1-3	Gall	4000		11	8	9			6		1	7		4					2		10				5	3		26
27	Apr	11	(h)	WELLINGBOROUGH	W	3-1	Gall, Davidson (2)	2000		11	8	9		7			1	10		4	6				2						5	3		27
28	Apr	13	(a)	Northampton Town	D	0-0		1800		11	8	9		7			1	10		4	6				2						5	3		28
29	Apr	14	(h)	BRENTFORD	W	2-0	Lindsay, White	1500			8			7			1	9			6				2	1	10		4		5	3	11	29
30	Apr	18	(h)	WEST HAM UNITED	W	4-0	Gall, Allsopp, Davidson (2)	2000		11	8	9					1	7		4	6				2		10				5	3		30
				Final League Position: 11th				Apps	2	24	30	8	1	28	1	1	29	17	3	29	24	8	4	1	26	1	26	6	1	2	30	24	4	
								Goals	-	5	5	8	-	6	-	-	-	8	-	-	-	-	-	-	2	-	7	-	-	-	2	-	-	

1902/1903 FA CUP

Round	Month	Day	Venue	Opponents	W.L.D	Score	Scorers	Attendance	Allen F	Allsopp TC	Blessington J	Davidson AB	Draycott W	Durrant AF	Eling A	Everitt	Frail J	Gall L	Hall E	Hawkes F	Hawkes R	Hilsdon J	Hood F	Jeakings RW	Lindsay W	Milam	Moody HB	Sharp A	Stratton L	Street A	White F	Williams H	Woods Herbert	Round
Q3	Nov	1	(a)	Queens Park Rangers	W	3-0	Blessington, Durrant, Allsopp	8000		11	7			9			1		3	4	6	8			2		10				5			Q3
Q4	Nov	15	(h)	LOWESTOFT TOWN	W	5-1	R Hawkes (2), Blessington, Durrant, Moody	3000		11	7			9			1			4	6				2		10			3	5	8		Q4
Q5	Nov	29	(h)	FULHAM	W	5-1	Blessington, Gall (3), Moody	3500		11	8			7			1	9		4	6				2		10			3	5			Q5
IR	Dec	13	(h)	KIDDERMINSTER HARRIERS	W	3-0	Durrant, Blessington, Gall	2500		11	8			7			1	9		4	6				2		10				5	3		IR
1	Feb	7	(a)	Millwall	L	0-3	-	8826		11	8			7			1	9		4	6				2		10				5	3		1
								Apps	-	5	5	-	-	5	-	-	5	3	1	5	5	1	-	-	5	-	5	-	-	2	5	3	-	
								Goals	-	1	4	-	-	3	-	-	-	4	-	-	2	-	-	-	-	-	2	-	-	-	-	-	-	

R. HAWKES (Half-Back).

▶ Bob Hawkes. The Town's 'superstar' of the Edwardian era. An amateur for most of his time at Luton, Bob won 19 England Amateur International caps, five full caps and starred for his country in the successful 1908 Olympic football side.

▶ **The 1902/03 team** – Back row (left to right): Lindsay, Frail, Sharp, Bygrave (Groundsman). Second row (left to right): Pakes (Trainer), F.Hawkes, White, Williams, R.Hawkes, C.Green (Secretary). Third row (left to right): Durrant, Hilsdon, Allsopp. Front row (left to right): Blessington, Moody, Gall.

1903/1904 SOUTHERN LEAGUE DIVISION ONE

Match No	Month	Day	Venue	Opponents	W/L/D	Score	Scorers	Attendance	Allsopp TC	Bennett JW	Cox AG	Dow JM	Durrant AF	Eaton SL	Hawkes F	Hawkes R	Holdstock H	Madden	McEwen J	McKee J	Moody HB	Storey GC	Thompson F	Turner P	White F	Williams H	Match No
1	Sep	5	(a)	Southampton	D	1-1	Storey		11	2			7	8	4	6			3	9		10	1		5		1
2	Sep	12	(h)	FULHAM	D	0-0	-	3000	11	2			7	8	4	6			3	9		10	1		5		2
3	Sep	19	(a)	Millwall	W	3-2	McKee, Storey, Allsopp	10000	11	2			7	8	4	6			3	9		10	1		5		3
4	Sep	24	(a)	West Ham United	D	0-0	-	3000	11	2			7	8	4	6				9		10	1		5	3	4
5	Sep	26	(h)	QUEENS PARK RANGERS	W	1-0	Storey	6000	11	2			7	8	4				3	9		10	1		5	6	5
6	Oct	3	(a)	Plymouth Argyle	D	0-0	-		11	2			7	8	4		6		3	9		10	1		5	6	6
7	Oct	10	(h)	READING	W	2-1	Eaton, McKee	6000	11	2			7	8	4					9		10	1		5	3	7
8	Oct	24	(h)	BRISTOL ROVERS	W	1-0	Turner	6000	11	2			7	8	4	6			3			9	1	10	5		8
9	Nov	7	(h)	PORTSMOUTH	D	1-1	R Hawkes	5000	11	2			7	8	4	6			3	9		10	1		5		9
10	Nov	21	(h)	BRENTFORD	W	1-0	McKee	4000	11	2			7	8	4	6	5		3	9			1	10			10
11	Dec	5	(h)	TOTTENHAM HOTSPUR	W	3-2	Eaton (2), Storey	6000	11	2			7		4	6			3	9		8	1	10	5		11
12	Dec	12	(h)	SWINDON TOWN	W	3-0	R Hawkes, McKee, Turner		11	2					4	6			3	9		8	1	10	5		12
13	Dec	19	(a)	New Brompton	D	2-2	R Hawkes, Eaton	3000	11	2					4	6			3	9		8	1	10	5		13
14	Dec	26	(h)	NORTHAMPTON TOWN	W	1-0	R Hawkes	6000	11	2			7		4	6			3	9			1	10	5		14
15	Dec	28	(h)	KETTERING TOWN	W	2-1	White (2)	5500	11	2					4	6			3	9			1	10	5		15
16	Jan	2	(h)	SOUTHAMPTON	W	1-0	R Hawkes	7500	11	2			7		4	6			3	9		10	1	11	5		16
17	Jan	9	(a)	Fulham	L	0-1	-	17000	11	2			7		4	6			3	9		8	1	10	5		17
18	Jan	16	(h)	MILLWALL	D	1-1	Turner	7000	11	2			7		4	6			3	9		10	1	8	5		18
19	Jan	30	(h)	PLYMOUTH ARGYLE	D	1-1	Moody		11	2			7	8	4	6			3	9	10		1		5		19
20	Feb	6	(a)	Swindon Town	L	0-1	-			2			7	8	4	6			3	9	10		1	11	5		20
21	Feb	20	(a)	Bristol Rovers	L	1-3	Allsopp	3000	11	2			7	8	4	6	5		3	9			1	10			21
22	Feb	27	(h)	BRIGHTON & HOVE ALBION	W	2-0	Durrant, Eaton	3000	11	2			7	8	4				3	9			1	10	5	6	22
23	Mar	5	(a)	Portsmouth	L	0-3	-	6000	11	2			7	8	4				3	9			1	10	5	6	23
24	Mar	7	(a)	Wellingborough	L	0-2	-		11	2				7	4		8		3	9			1	10	5	6	24
25	Mar	17	(a)	Queens Park Rangers	L	1-2	Eaton	4000	11	2				7	4				3	8	9		1	10	5	6	25
26	Mar	19	(a)	Brentford	L	1-2	R Hawkes	3000	11			2		7	4	8			3		9		1	10	5	6	26
27	Mar	26	(h)	WEST HAM UNITED	W	1-0	McKee	5000	11	2				7	4	8			3	9			1	10	5	6	27
28	Apr	1	(h)	WELLINGBOROUGH	L	1-2	Moody		11	2			7		4				3		9		1	10	5		28
29	Apr	2	(a)	Tottenham Hotspur	D	1-1	R Hawkes	10000	11	2			7		4	6			3	9		10	1	8	5		29
30	Apr	4	(a)	Northampton Town	D	0-0	-	5000	11	2			7		4				3	9	10		1	8	5		30
31	Apr	5	(a)	Brighton & Hove Albion	D	2-2	McKee, Allsopp	3000	11	2			7		4				3	9	10		1	8	5	6	31
32	Apr	13	(a)	Reading	D	1-1	McKee	1500	11	2				7	4		6		3	9			1	8	5		32
33	Apr	16	(h)	NEW BROMPTON	W	1-0	McKee	3000	11	2			7		4	6			3	9	10		1	8	5		33
34	Apr	23	(a)	Kettering Town	W	2-1	White, Moody	1000	11	2			7		4		6		3	9	10		1	8	5		34
								Apps	32	33	-	1	26	27	34	24	5	1	32	31	11	15	34	25	32	11	
								Goals	3	-	-	-	1	6	-	7	-	-	-	8	3	4	-	3	3	-	

Final League Position: 8th

1903/1904 FA CUP

Round	Month	Day	Venue	Opponents	W/L/D	Score	Scorers	Attendance	Allsopp TC	Bennett JW	Cox AG	Dow JM	Durrant AF	Eaton SL	Hawkes F	Hawkes R	Holdstock H	Madden	McEwen J	McKee J	Moody HB	Storey GC	Thompson F	Turner P	White F	Williams H	Round
Q3	Oct	31	(h)	HITCHIN TOWN	W	2-1	Turner, Storey	1000	11	2	9			7	4	6			3			10	1	8	5		Q3
Q4	Nov	14	(h)	WATFORD	W	4-1	Turner (2), McKee, Allsopp	6000	11	2			7	9	4	6	3			10			1	8	5		Q4
Q5	Nov	28	(a)	Fulham	L	1-3	Durrant	10000	11	2			7	9	4	6	3	5		10			1	8			Q5
								Apps	3	3	1	-	2	3	3	3	2	-	2	2	-	1	3	3	2	-	
								Goals	1	-	-	-	1	-	-	-	-	-	-	1	-	1	-	3	-	-	

3rd Qualifying Round played at Luton by arrangement

▶ **The 1903/04 team** – Back row (left to right): Leech (Trainer), Bygrave (Groundsman), Bennett, Thompson, C.Green (Secretary), McEwen, H.Smart (Director). Middle row (left to right): Durrant, F.Hawkes, White, R.Hawkes, Allsopp. Front row (left to right): Eaton, Griffiths, McKee, Storey, Moody.

1904/1905 SOUTHERN LEAGUE DIVISION ONE

Match No	Month	Day	Venue	Opponents	W/L/D Score	Scorers	Attendance	Barnes WE	Brown Joe	Dow JM	Eaton SL	Goodge SH	Hawkes F	Hawkes R	Hunt A	Kellett G	Lamberton GR	Lindsay W	McEwen J	Moody HB	Penman E	Pritchard R	Ross DE	Spencer S	Turner E	Wallace J	White F	Williams H	Match No
1	Sep	1	(a)	Swindon Town	L 0-1	-		11			7		4	6			8	1	3		9		10		2		5		1
2	Sep	3	(h)	SOUTHAMPTON	L 1-2	Lamberton		11			7		4				8	1	3		9				2	10	5	6	2
3	Sep	10	(a)	Fulham	D 0-0		15000	11			7		4	6			8	1	3		9		10		2		5		3
4	Sep	17	(h)	WATFORD	W 2-1	Ross (2)	6000	11			7		4	6			8	1	3		9		10		2		5		4
5	Sep	24	(a)	Plymouth Argyle	L 0-3	-		11			7		4				8	1	3		9	6	10		2		5		5
6	Oct	1	(h)	WEST HAM UNITED	L 0-2	-	4000	11			7		4	6			8	1	3	9			10		2		5		6
7	Oct	8	(a)	Reading	L 0-1	-		11			7		4	6				1	3		9		10		2		5		7
8	Oct	15	(h)	BRISTOL ROVERS	L 1-2	Ross	4000	11			7		4		8			1	3		9	6	10		2		5		8
9	Oct	29	(h)	PORTSMOUTH	W 4-3	White, R Hawkes, Ross (2)	5000	11			8		4	6		9	7	1	3				10		2		5		9
10	Nov	5	(a)	Brentford	L 0-3		6000	11			8		4	6		9	7	1	3				10		2		5		10
11	Nov	12	(h)	QUEENS PARK RANGERS	D 1-1	Ross	6000	11			8		4	6		9	7	1	3				10		2		5		11
12	Nov	19	(a)	Millwall	L 0-2		3000	11			8		4	6			7	1	3				10	9	2		5		12
13	Nov	26	(h)	TOTTENHAM HOTSPUR	W 1-0	Ross	8000	11			8		4	6			7	1	3				10	9	2		5		13
14	Dec	3	(a)	Brighton & Hove Albion	D 1-1	Eaton	3752	11			8		4	6			7	1	3				10	9	2		5		14
15	Dec	17	(h)	NEW BROMPTON	W 1-0	R Hawkes	4000	11			7		4				9	1	3	10		6	8		2		5		15
16	Dec	24	(a)	Wellingborough	L 0-2			11		7			4	6			9	1	3	10			8		2		5		16
17	Dec	26	(h)	NORTHAMPTON TOWN	W 4-2	R Hawkes (3), Lamberton	5000	11		7			4				9	1	3	10		6	8		2		5		17
18	Dec	31	(a)	Southampton	L 1-4	Moody		11			7		4	6			9	1	3	10			8		2		5		18
19	Jan	7	(h)	FULHAM	W 6-0	Eaton (2), Lamberton (2), Ross (2)	5000	11			7		4				9	1	3	10			8		2		5		19
20	Jan	14	(h)	SWINDON TOWN	W 4-1	Barnes (2), Eaton, Moody		11			7		4				9	1	3	10			8		2		5		20
21	Jan	21	(h)	PLYMOUTH ARGYLE	L 0-2			11			7		4				9	1	3	10			8		2		5		21
22	Jan	28	(a)	West Ham United	L 2-6	R Hawkes, Lamberton	5000	11			7		4	6			9	1	3	10			8		2		5		22
23	Feb	11	(a)	Bristol Rovers	L 2-3	Lamberton, Ross	8000	11			7		4	6			9	1	3	10			8		2		5		23
24	Feb	25	(a)	Portsmouth	L 0-1		7000	11			7	1	4				9		3	10		6	8		2		5		24
25	Mar	4	(h)	BRENTFORD	W 1-0	Lamberton		11			7		4				9	1	3	10		6	8		2		5		25
26	Mar	11	(a)	Queens Park Rangers	W 2-1	Moody (2)	4000	11			7		4	6			9	1	3	10			8		2		5		26
27	Mar	18	(h)	MILLWALL	L 1-2	Barnes	5000	11			7		4	6			9	1	3	10			8		2		5		27
28	Mar	25	(a)	Tottenham Hotspur	L 0-1		7000	11			7		4				9	1	3	10		6	8		2		5		28
29	Apr	1	(h)	BRIGHTON & HOVE ALBION	W 2-0	Ross, Moody	4000	11			7		4				9	1	3	10		6	8		2		5		29
30	Apr	15	(a)	New Brompton	L 1-2	White	7000	11			7		4	6			9	1	3	10			8		2		5		30
31	Apr	21	(a)	Watford	L 0-3		7000	11			7		4	6			9	1	3	10			8		2		5		31
32	Apr	22	(h)	WELLINGBOROUGH	W 4-0	Eaton (2), Lamberton, Ross					8		4	6		7	9	1	3	11			10		2		5		32
33	Apr	24	(a)	Northampton Town	L 1-2	Moody			2		8		4	5		7	9	1	3	11		6	10						33
34	Apr	25	(h)	READING	W 2-0	Eaton (2)			2		10		4	11		7		1	3		9	6					5		34
				Apps				31	3	2	29	1	33	28	3	3	33	33	34	20	8	14	30	3	32	1	32	1	
				Goals				3	-	-	8	-	-	6	-	-	8	-	-	6	-	-	12	-	-	-	2	-	

Final League Position: 17th

1904/1905 FA CUP

Round	Month	Day	Venue	Opponents	W/L/D Score	Scorers	Attendance	Barnes WE	Brown Joe	Dow JM	Eaton SL	Goodge SH	Hawkes F	Hawkes R	Hunt A	Kellett G	Lamberton GR	Lindsay W	McEwen J	Moody HB	Penman E	Pritchard R	Ross DE	Spencer S	Turner E	Wallace J	White F	Williams H	Round
Q6	Dec	10	(a)	Fulham	L 0-4	-	16000	11		9			4	6			7	1	5				10	8	2		3		Q6
				Apps				1	-	-	1	-	1	1	-	-	1	1	1	-	-	-	1	1	1	-	1		
				Goals				-	-	-	-	-	-	-	-	-	-	-	-	-	-	-	-	-	-	-	-		

▶ **The 1904/05 team** – Back row (left to right): C.Green (Secretary), Turner, Bygrave (Groundsman), Lindsay, H.Smart (Director), McEwen, W.Soper (Director), Lawson (Trainer). Middle row (left to right): Dow, F.Hawkes, White, R.Hawkes, Williams, Wallace. Front row (left to right): Eaton, Lamberton, Penman, Moody, Ross, Barnes.

TIMELINE...
April 1905 The Town play their last game at Dunstable Road.

1905/1906 SOUTHERN LEAGUE DIVISION ONE

Match No	Month	Day	Venue	Opponents	W/L/D Score	Scorers	Attendance	Barnes WE	Blackett J	Brown Alexander	Dobson E	Gallacher PJ	Hawkes F	Hawkes R	Lane H	Latheron R	Mayes T	McCurdy W	McDonald A	Pickering J	Platt P	Warner A	White F	Match No
1	Sep	4	(h)	PLYMOUTH ARGYLE	D 0-0	-	5000	11	2	9		7	4	6				3		10	1	8	5	1
2	Sep	9	(h)	BRIGHTON & HOVE ALBION	W 4-1	Brown (2), Gallacher, Pickering	5000	11	2	9		7	4	6				3		10	1	8	5	2
3	Sep	16	(a)	West Ham United	W 2-1	Warner, Brown	9500	11	2	9		7	4	6				3		10	1	8	5	3
4	Sep	23	(h)	FULHAM	L 0-1	-	9000	11	2	9		7	4	6				3		10	1	8	5	4
5	Sep	30	(a)	Queens Park Rangers	W 3-2	Barnes (2), Warner	10000	11	2	9			4	6				3	8	10	1	7	5	5
6	Oct	7	(h)	BRISTOL ROVERS	W 7-1	Warner (3), Barnes (2), R Hawkes, McDonald	7000	11	2	9			4	6				3	8	10	1	7	5	6
7	Oct	14	(a)	New Brompton	D 1-1	Brown	4000	11	2	9			4	6				3	8	10	1	7	5	7
8	Oct	21	(h)	PORTSMOUTH	W 3-2	Warner, Brown, McDonald	7000	11	2	9			4	6				3	8	10	1	7	5	8
9	Oct	28	(a)	Swindon Town	D 1-1	R Hawkes	4000	11	2	9			4	6				3	8	10	1	7	5	9
10	Nov	4	(h)	MILLWALL	W 6-1	Warner (2), Brown (2), Barnes, Pickering	7000	11	2	9			4	6				3	8	10	1	7	5	10
11	Nov	18	(a)	Tottenham Hotspur	L 0-1	-	22000	11	2	9			4	6				3	8	10	1	7	5	11
12	Nov	25	(h)	BRENTFORD	L 0-2	-	5000	11	2	9			4	6				3	8	10	1	7	5	12
13	Dec	2	(a)	Norwich City	D 1-1	Blackett	8500	11	2	9			4	6				3	8	10	1	7	5	13
14	Dec	16	(a)	Southampton	L 1-2	McDonald		11	2	9	10	7	4	6				3	8		1		5	14
15	Dec	23	(a)	READING	W 3-0	McDonald (2), R Hawkes	5000	11	2	9	7	6	4	10				3	8		1		5	15
16	Dec	25	(h)	WATFORD	W 2-0	White, R Hawkes	9000		2	9		11	4	6				3	8	10	1	7	5	16
17	Dec	26	(h)	NORTHAMPTON TOWN	W 1-0	Barnes	7500	11	2	9		6	4	10		7		3	8		1		5	17
18	Jan	6	(a)	Brighton & Hove Albion	L 1-2	Pickering	3000	11	2	8		6	4			7		3	10	9	1		5	18
19	Jan	20	(h)	WEST HAM UNITED	D 1-1	Brown	5000	11	2	9			4	6				3	8	10	1	7	5	19
20	Jan	27	(a)	Fulham	L 0-3	-	14000	11	2	9			4	6			7	3	8	10	1		5	20
21	Feb	3	(h)	QUEENS PARK RANGERS	W 3-2	Pickering, McDonald, Blackett	5000	11	2	9			4	6			7	3	8	10	1		5	21
22	Feb	10	(a)	Bristol Rovers	L 2-3	Pickering (2)	5000	11	2		9	6						3	8	10	1	7	5	22
23	Feb	17	(h)	NEW BROMPTON	W 2-1	Brown (2)		11	2	9		6	4					3	8	10	1	7	5	23
24	Feb	24	(a)	Portsmouth	L 0-2	-		11	2	9			4	6				3	8	10	1	7	5	24
25	Mar	3	(h)	SWINDON TOWN	W 4-0	Brown (2), Barnes, McDonald		11	2	9			4	6				3	8	10	1	7	5	25
26	Mar	10	(a)	Millwall	W 2-1	R Hawkes, McDonald	5000	11	2	9		5	4	6				3	8	10	1	7		26
27	Mar	24	(h)	TOTTENHAM HOTSPUR	W 2-0	Brown (2)	6000	11	2	9		5	4	6				3	8	10	1	7		27
28	Mar	31	(a)	Brentford	L 1-2	Pickering	7000	11	2	9		5	4					3	8	10	1	7	6	28
29	Apr	7	(h)	NORWICH CITY	W 2-1	R Hawkes, Dobson	7000	11	2		9		4	6				3	8	10	1	7	5	29
30	Apr	13	(a)	Watford	D 1-1	Brown	7000	11	2	9			4	6				3	8	10	1	7	5	30
31	Apr	14	(a)	Plymouth Argyle	L 0-2	-		11	2	8	9		4	6				3		10	1	7	5	31
32	Apr	16	(a)	Northampton Town	W 2-1	Brown, Pickering	9500	11	2	9		6	4					3	8	10	1	7	5	32
33	Apr	21	(h)	SOUTHAMPTON	W 5-0	R Hawkes, Warner, Brown, Pickering (2)	7000	11	2	8			4	6				3	7	9	1	10	5	33
34	Apr	23	(a)	Reading	D 1-1	Brown		11	2	9		5	4		6	7		3		10	1	8		34
				Apps				33	34	31	6	19	31	27	1	4	2	34	29	30	34	28	31	
				Goals				7	2	18	1	1	-	7	-	-	-	-	8	10	-	9	1	

Final League Position: 4th

1905/1906 FA CUP

Round	Month	Day	Venue	Opponents	W/L/D Score	Scorers	Attendance	Barnes WE	Blackett J	Brown Alexander	Dobson E	Gallacher PJ	Hawkes F	Hawkes R	Lane H	Latheron R	Mayes T	McCurdy W	McDonald A	Pickering J	Platt P	Warner A	White F	Round
Q4	Dec	9	(a)	Crystal Palace	L 0-1	-	8000	11	2	9			4	6				3	8	10	1	7	5	Q4
				Apps				1	1	1	-	-	1	1			-	1	1	1	1	1	1	
				Goals				-	-	-			-	-					-	-		-	-	

▶ **The 1905/06 team** – Back row (left to right): E.Gibbs (Director), Bygrave (Groundsman), Else, F.Hawkes, Blackett, Lewis, McCurdy, Watkins, Wales, C.Green (Secretary), Lawson (Trainer). Middle row (left to right): Gallacher, Warner, Dow, Pickering, McDonald, Barnes. Front row (left to right): White, Brown, R.Hawkes.

TIMELINE...

4 September 1905 The Town play their first competitive game at Kenilworth Road – a 0-0 draw with Plymouth.

1906/1907 SOUTHERN LEAGUE DIVISION ONE

Match No	Month	Day	Venue	Opponents	W,L,D Score	Scorers	Attendance	Barnes WE	Benham GC	Brown Alexander	Fitzpatrick HJ	Gallacher PJ	Gittins AF	Hawkes F	Hawkes R	Hogg J	Hull	Jackson BH	Jones A	Latheron R	McCurdy W	McDonald A	Murphy N	Pickering J	Platt P	Schofield JA	Warner A	White F	Match No
1	Sep	1	(h)	QUEENS PARK RANGERS	D 1-1	Warner	6000	11		9			8	4	6	2			5		3			10	1		7		1
2	Sep	8	(a)	Fulham	D 0-0	-	20000	11		9				4	6				2		3			10	1	7	8	5	2
3	Sep	15	(h)	SOUTHAMPTON	W 2-1	R Hawkes, Brown		11		9				4	6				2		3			10	1	7	8	5	3
4	Sep	22	(a)	West Ham United	L 1-5	White	13000	11		9				4	6				2		3			10	1	7	8	5	4
5	Sep	29	(h)	TOTTENHAM HOTSPUR	L 0-2	-	10000	11				6		4	8	2					3	9		10	1	7	8	5	5
6	Oct	6	(a)	Swindon Town	L 0-4	-		11		9			10	4					2		3				1	7	8	5	6
7	Oct	13	(h)	NORWICH CITY	L 1-3	Schofield	5000	11		9				4	6				2		3			10		8	7	5	7
8	Oct	20	(a)	Bristol Rovers	W 1-0	Brown	5000	11		9	10			4	6	2		5			3	8			1		7	5	8
9	Oct	27	(a)	Crystal Palace	W 1-0	Fitzpatrick	8000	11		9	10			4	6	2		5			3	8	7		1			5	9
10	Nov	3	(h)	BRENTFORD	W 2-0	F Hawkes, Fitzpatrick		11		9	10			4	6	2		5			3	8	7		1				10
11	Nov	10	(a)	Millwall	L 1-5	R Hawkes	5000	11		9	10			4	6	2		5			3	8	7		1				11
12	Nov	17	(h)	LEYTON	W 5-3	Gittins, Brown (2), Fitzpatrick (2)		11		9	10		8	4	6	2		5		7	3				1				12
13	Nov	24	(a)	Portsmouth	L 0-1		5000	11		9	10		8	4	6	2		5		7	3				1				13
14	Dec	1	(h)	NEW BROMPTON	L 0-2	-	3500	11		9	10	6	8	4		2		5		7	3				1				14
15	Dec	8	(a)	Plymouth Argyle	D 0-0	-		11		9			6	4		2					3	8		10	1		7	5	15
16	Dec	15	(h)	BRIGHTON & HOVE ALBION	W 3-1	McDonald (2), Fitzpatrick	5000	11		9			6	4							3	8		10	1		7	5	16
17	Dec	22	(a)	Reading	L 2-7	Barnes, McDonald		11		9	10		6	4							3	8			1		7	5	17
18	Dec	25	(h)	WATFORD	W 2-0	Warner, Pickering	8000	11		9				4	6	2					3	8	9	10	1		7	5	18
19	Dec	29	(a)	Queens Park Rangers	L 0-2		5000	11					10	4	6	2				11	3	8	9		1		7	5	19
20	Jan	5	(h)	FULHAM	W 2-0	Brown (2)	7000	11		9			8	4	6	2					3				1			5	20
21	Jan	19	(a)	Southampton	L 0-1			11		9			8	4		2				7	3				1			5	21
22	Jan	26	(h)	WEST HAM UNITED	D 1-1	Barnes	4000	11		9	10			4		2			6	7	3	8			1			5	22
23	Feb	9	(h)	SWINDON TOWN	W 6-2	Jones, Gittins (2), Brown, Fitzpatrick, Murphy		11		9	10		8	4		2			6		3		7		1			5	23
24	Feb	16	(a)	Norwich City	W 1-0	Brown	5000	11		9	10		8	4		2			6	7	3				1			5	24
25	Mar	2	(h)	CRYSTAL PALACE	W 2-1	Brown, Fitzpatrick	8000	11		9	10		8	4	6	2			7		3				1			5	25
26	Mar	9	(a)	Brentford	W 1-0	Jones	5000	11		9	10		8	4		2			6		3				1		7	5	26
27	Mar	11	(h)	BRISTOL ROVERS	W 1-0	Barnes	5000	11		9	10		8	4	6			2			3				1		7	5	27
28	Mar	16	(h)	MILLWALL	D 1-1	Brown	5000	11		9	10		8	4	6	2					3				1		7	5	28
29	Mar	23	(a)	Leyton	L 0-1	-		11		9			8	4		2			6		3				1		7	5	29
30	Mar	25	(a)	Tottenham Hotspur	W 2-1	Brown, Pickering	8000	11		9			8	4		2			6		3			10	1		7	5	30
31	Mar	29	(a)	Watford	D 2-2	F Hawkes, Brown	9000	11		9			8	4		2	1		6		3			10			7	5	31
32	Mar	30	(h)	PORTSMOUTH	W 3-1	Gittins (2), Brown	6000	11		9			8	4		2			6		3			10	1		7	5	32
33	Apr	1	(a)	Northampton Town	D 0-0	-	9000	11		9			8	4		2			6		3			10	1		7	5	33
34	Apr	2	(h)	NORTHAMPTON TOWN	W 1-0	Benham	5000	11	9				8	4		2			6		3			10	1		7	5	34
35	Apr	6	(a)	New Brompton	D 0-0	-	4000	11		9			8	4		2			6	7	3	9			1			5	35
36	Apr	13	(h)	PLYMOUTH ARGYLE	W 3-2	Jones (2), Brown		11		9			8	4	6	2		5	7		3			10	1			5	36
37	Apr	20	(a)	Brighton & Hove Albion	W 3-1	Jones, Pickering, Murphy	6000	11		9			8	4		2		5	7		3	9		10	1			6	37
38	Apr	27	(h)	READING	D 1-1	Jones		11		9			8	4		2		5	7		3			10	1			6	38
				Apps				37	1	32	20	2	23	38	21	24	1	14	23	12	38	11	8	19	37	7	21	29	
				Goals				3	1	14	7	-	5	2	2	-	-	-	6	-	-	3	2	3	-	1	2	1	

Final League Position: 4th

1906/1907 FA CUP

Round	Month	Day	Venue	Opponents	W,L,D Score	Scorers	Attendance	Barnes WE	Benham GC	Brown Alexander	Fitzpatrick HJ	Gallacher PJ	Gittins AF	Hawkes F	Hawkes R	Hogg J	Hull	Jackson BH	Jones A	Latheron R	McCurdy W	McDonald A	Murphy N	Pickering J	Platt P	Schofield JA	Warner A	White F	Round
1	Jan	12	(a)	Gainsborough Trinity	D 0-0	-	2000	11		9	8		10	4	6			2			3				1		7	5	1
Rep	Jan	16	(h)	GAINSBOROUGH TRINITY	W 2-1	Warner, Brown	4000	11		9	8		10	4	6						3				1		7	5	Rep
2	Feb	2	(h)	SUNDERLAND	D 0-0	-	10500	11		9	8		10	4	6	2				7	3				1	8		5	2
Rep	Feb	6	(a)	Sunderland	L 0-1		18000	11		9	8		10	4	6	2				7	3				1			5	Rep
				Apps				4	-	4	4	-	4	4	4	2	-	1	-	-	4	-	-	2	1	4	-	2	4
				Goals				-	-	1	-	-	-	-	-	-	-	-	-	-	-	-	-	-	-	-	1	-

P. PLATT (Goal)

▶ Peter Platt. Regarded by many commentators as the best goalkeeper in the Southern League, he also scored from the spot in a game at Leyton in 1908!

▶ **The 1906/07 team** – Back row (left to right): Lawson (Trainer), F.Hawkes, Warner, Latheron, Bygrave (Groundsman). Second row (left to right): Dow, White, Jackson, Hogg, Platt, McCurdy, Watkins, Gallacher, C.Green (Secretary). Third row (left to right): McDonald, Schofield, R.Hawkes, Gittins, Barnes. Front row (left to right): Brown, Pickering, Jones.

TIMELINE...

2 February 1907 The five figure barrier is broken when 10,500 turn up at Kenilworth Road to see a 0-0 draw with Sunderland in the F.A.Cup.
16 February 1907 Bob Hawkes becomes Luton's first full England international when winning a cap against Northern Ireland at Goodison Park.

1907/1908 SOUTHERN LEAGUE DIVISION ONE

Match No	Month	Day	Venue	Opponents	W,L,D	Score	Scorers	Attendance	Albone F	Brown Alexander	Dimmock WH	Eling A	Farrant SG	Hall P	Hawkes F	Hawkes R	Hogg J	Jarvis RT	Jones A	Jones AE	Latheron R	McCurdy W	Moody HB	Murphy James	Nicholson B	Parsons F	Pearson F	Pettengell B	Platt P	Porter WM	Rankin B	Rigate WJ	Walders J	Watkins J	White F	Match No
1	Sep	2	(a)	Southampton	L	1-2	A Jones				9			8	4		2		6			3	10						1			11	7		5	1
2	Sep	7	(a)	Northampton Town	D	0-0		5000			9			8	4	6	2						10						1			11	7		5	2
3	Sep	14	(h)	SOUTHAMPTON	L	0-2	-				9		10	8	4	6	2				11	3							1			7			5	3
4	Sep	21	(a)	Plymouth Argyle	L	1-2	Hall							8	4	10	2		6		11	3							1			7			5	4
5	Sep	28	(h)	WEST HAM UNITED	L	0-3	-	7000			9			8	4	6	2				11	3	10						1			7			5	5
6	Oct	5	(a)	Queens Park Rangers	L	1-3	Moody	10000		2				9	10	4			5			3	8								11	7			6	6
7	Oct	12	(h)	TOTTENHAM HOTSPUR	W	3-1	F Hawkes, Moody, Rigate	7000		2				10	9	4		1	6			3	11								8	7			5	7
8	Oct	19	(a)	Swindon Town	L	0-4	-							9	10	4	2	1	6			3	8								11	7			5	8
9	Oct	26	(h)	CRYSTAL PALACE	W	4-0	A Jones, Rankin, Moody (2)			2				8	4				6			3	10						1		9	11	7		5	9
10	Nov	2	(h)	NEW BROMPTON	L	1-2	Rigate	5000		2				8	4				6			3	10						1		9	7	11		5	10
11	Nov	9	(a)	Brighton & Hove Albion	L	0-1	-	6000						8	6	2			4			3	10						1		9	7	11		5	11
12	Nov	16	(h)	PORTSMOUTH	W	2-0	F Hawkes, Moody	3000			3			8	6	2			4				10						1		9	7	11		5	12
13	Nov	23	(a)	Bradford Park Avenue	L	0-1	-	5000			3			8	6	2			4		11		10				9		1			7			5	13
14	Nov	30	(h)	MILLWALL	W	3-1	F Hawkes (2), Moody	5000			3			8	6	2			4				10				9		1			7	11		5	14
15	Dec	7	(a)	Brentford	L	1-3	Pearson	4000						8	2				6			3	10			4	9		1		11	7			5	15
16	Dec	14	(h)	BRISTOL ROVERS	L	0-2	-	3000						8	4	2						3	10				9		1		11	7			5	16
17	Dec	21	(a)	Leyton	L	0-5	-				9	2	8		4	6						3	10						1			7	11		5	17
18	Dec	25	(h)	WATFORD	D	1-1	Walders							8	6				4			3	10	9			5		1			7	11	2		18
19	Dec	26	(h)	NORWICH CITY	D	0-0	-	7000						8	6				4			3	10				9		1			7	11	2	5	19
20	Dec	28	(h)	READING	W	3-1	Walders, Rankin, Moody	4000						8	6	2			4			3	10						1		9	7	11		5	20
21	Jan	18	(h)	PLYMOUTH ARGYLE	D	0-0	-	8000							4	8			6			3	10				5		1		9	7	11			21
22	Jan	25	(a)	West Ham United	L	0-1	-	8000							4	6	2		5			3	10				9	11	1		8	7				22
23	Feb	8	(a)	Tottenham Hotspur	W	2-1	Porter (2)	11000							4	6	2		5		10	3	9						1	8	11	7				23
24	Feb	15	(h)	SWINDON TOWN	W	1-0	Rankin								4	6	2		5		10	3	9						1	8		7	11			24
25	Feb	26	(h)	QUEENS PARK RANGERS	D	0-0	-	4000							4	6	2		5	9		3	10						1	8	11	7				25
26	Feb	29	(a)	New Brompton	W	1-0	Moody	3000							4	6	2	11	5	9		3	10						1		8	7			5	26
27	Mar	4	(a)	Crystal Palace	L	2-4	Moody (2)			11					4	6	2		5		10	3	9						1		8	7				27
28	Mar	7	(h)	BRIGHTON & HOVE ALBION	W	1-0	Moody	4000							4	6			5		10	3	9						1		8	7	11	2		28
29	Mar	14	(a)	Portsmouth	L	0-1	-	5500			2				4	6			5			3	10				9		1		8	7				29
30	Mar	21	(h)	BRADFORD PARK AVENUE	W	1-0	Rankin	5000			2				4	6			5		11	3	10				9		1		8	7				30
31	Mar	28	(a)	Millwall	D	0-0	-	4000			2				4	6			5		11	3	10				9		1		8	7				31
32	Apr	4	(h)	BRENTFORD	W	1-0	Moody	3000			2				4	6			5		11	3	10				9		1		8	7				32
33	Apr	11	(a)	Bristol Rovers	W	1-0	Rankin	5000	6		2				4				5		11	3	10				9		1		8	7				33
34	Apr	17	(a)	Watford	L	1-2	Rankin	9500	6		2				4				5		11	3	10				9		1		8	7				34
35	Apr	18	(h)	LEYTON	L	0-3	-		6		2				4			1	5				10				9		1		8	7			3	35
36	Apr	20	(h)	NORTHAMPTON TOWN	L	0-1	-		6		2				4			1	5	9			11		3						8	7	10			36
37	Apr	21	(a)	Norwich City	L	1-6	Pearson	5000			3		10		4		2	1					6				9				8	7	11		5	37
38	Apr	29	(a)	Reading	L	0-3	-	1500	6		3		8		4		2	1		10							9				7	11		5	38
				Final League Position: 18th				**Apps**	5	6	18	1	3	9	38	28	20	6	33	3	17	31	31	1	1	4	17	1	32	4	30	32	20	4	23	
								Goals	-	-	-	-	1	4	-	-	-	-	2	-	-	-	12	-	-	-	2	-	-	2	6	2	2	-	-	

1907/1908 FA CUP

Round	Month	Day	Venue	Opponents	W,L,D	Score	Scorers	Attendance	Albone F	Brown Alexander	Dimmock WH	Eling A	Farrant SG	Hall P	Hawkes F	Hawkes R	Hogg J	Jarvis RT	Jones A	Jones AE	Latheron R	McCurdy W	Moody HB	Murphy James	Nicholson B	Parsons F	Pearson F	Pettengell B	Platt P	Porter WM	Rankin B	Rigate WJ	Walders J	Watkins J	White F	Round
1	Jan	11	(h)	FULHAM	L	3-8	Rigate, Rankin, Moody	5500							4	6	8					3	10						1		9	7	11	2	5	1
								Apps	-	-	-	-	-	-	1	1	1	-	-	-	-	1	1	-	-	-	-	-	1	-	1	1	1	1	1	
								Goals	-	-	-	-	-	-	-	-	-	-	-	-	-	-	1	-	-	-	-	-	-	-	1	1	-	-	-	

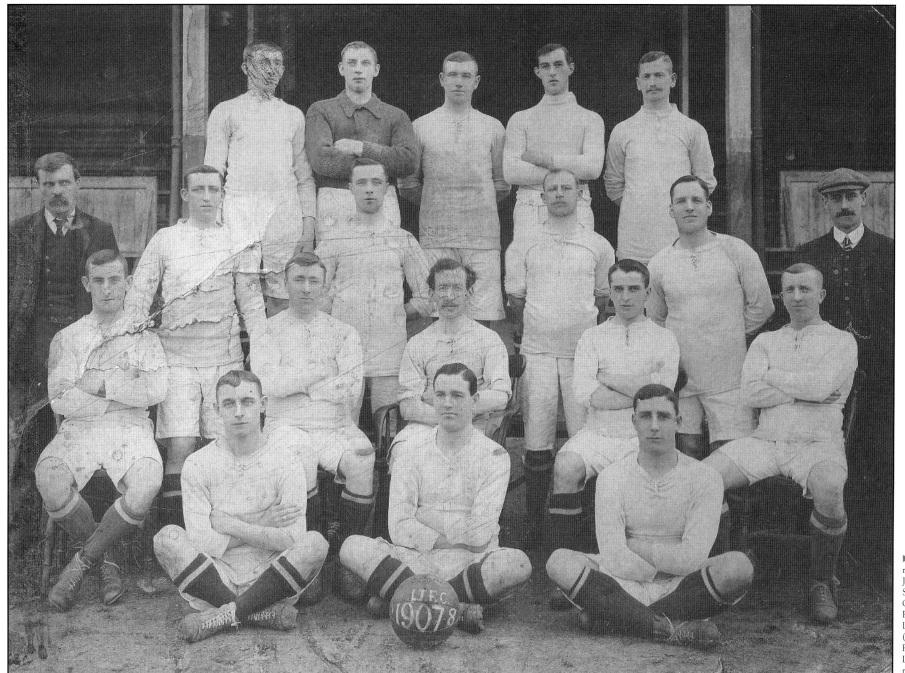

◗ **The 1907/08 team** – Back row (left to right): Nicholson, Jarvis, Hogg, Platt, McCurdy. Second row (left to right): C.Green (Secretary), Rigate, F.Hawkes, White, Jones, Lawson (Trainer). Third row (left to right): Walders, Rankin, R.Hawkes, Farrant, Latheron. Front row (left to right): Hall, Brown, Pearson.

1908/1909 SOUTHERN LEAGUE DIVISION ONE

Match No	Month	Day	Venue	Opponents	W,L,D Score	Scorers	Attendance	Bradley EJ	Brown NL	Chapman R	Dimmock WH	Folley W	Gregory J	Hawkes F	Hawkes R	Haycock FJ	Jarvis RT	Johnson J	Jones A	McCurdy W	Menzies AW	Moody HB	Platt P	Porter WM	Rigate WJ	Stansfield H	Tildesley J	White F	Match No
1	Sep	2	(h)	NORWICH CITY	W 4-0	Bradley (3), Haycock	4000	9	7				2	4	6	8	1	11	5	3		10							1
2	Sep	5	(h)	READING	D 2-2	Moody, Jones	5000	9	7		6		2	4		8	1	11	5	3		10							2
3	Sep	12	(a)	Southampton	L 0-6	-			7		2			4	6			11	5	3	9	10	1			8			3
4	Sep	19	(h)	LEYTON	W 2-1	Bradley (2)	4000	9	7					4	6			11	5	2		10	1			8			4
5	Sep	23	(h)	MILLWALL	L 0-1	-	5000				2			4	6	8		11	5			10	1		7	9			5
6	Sep	26	(a)	West Ham United	L 0-4		3000		7		2			4	6	8			5	3	9	10	1			11			6
7	Oct	3	(h)	BRIGHTON & HOVE ALBION	W 3-1	Jones, Stansfield, Porter	5000				2			4	6	8			5	3	9	10	1	11		7			7
8	Oct	10	(a)	Crystal Palace	L 0-2	-	10000		7		2			4	6	8			5	3	9	10	1			11			8
9	Oct	17	(h)	BRENTFORD	W 3-1	Jones, R Hawkes, Brown	6000	9	7		2		3	4	6				5		8	10	1			11			9
10	Oct	24	(a)	Plymouth Argyle	D 1-1	F Hawkes			7				3	4		8			6	2	9	10	1			11		5	10
11	Oct	31	(a)	Swindon Town	L 1-4	Brown			7				3		6	8			6	2	9	10	1			11		5	11
12	Nov	7	(h)	PORTSMOUTH	W 5-1	Moody (4), Menzies	6000		7		2		3	4	6	8			5		9	10	1			11			12
13	Nov	14	(a)	Exeter City	L 1-2	Menzies	4000		7		2		3	4		8			6		9	10	1			11		5	13
14	Nov	21	(h)	NORTHAMPTON TOWN	W 3-1	Stansfield, Brown, Haycock	8000		7		2		3	4	6	8			5		9	10	1			11			14
15	Nov	28	(a)	New Brompton	L 0-1	-	6000	10	7				3	4	6	8			5	2	9		1			11			15
16	Dec	12	(a)	Southend United	L 0-2	-		9	7				3	4	6	8			5	2		10	1			11			16
17	Dec	19	(h)	COVENTRY CITY	W 6-1	Menzies (2), Stansfield, R Hawkes, Haycock (2)	4000						3	4	6	8		11	5	2	9	10	1			7			17
18	Dec	25	(a)	Bristol Rovers	L 0-1	-	7000						3	4		8		11	5	2	9	10	1			7		5	18
19	Dec	26	(h)	WATFORD	W 1-0	Moody	9000		7				3	4	6	8		11	5	2		10	1						19
20	Dec	28	(a)	Norwich City	L 2-3	Moody (2)	6431		7				3	4	6	8			5	2		10	1			11			20
21	Jan	2	(a)	Reading	D 2-2	Haycock (2)			7				3	4		8			6		9	10	1			11	2	5	21
22	Jan	9	(h)	SOUTHAMPTON	W 1-0	Stansfield	6000		7				3	4	6	8			5	2		10	1			11			22
23	Jan	23	(a)	Leyton	L 0-2				7		2		3	4		8			6		9	10	1			11		5	23
24	Jan	30	(h)	WEST HAM UNITED	W 1-0	Menzies	3000		7	2			3	4	6	8		10	5		9		1			11			24
25	Feb	6	(a)	Brighton & Hove Albion	D 0-0		5000		7				3	4	6	8	1	10	5	2	9					11			25
26	Feb	8	(h)	QUEENS PARK RANGERS	W 1-0	Menzies	5000		7				3	4		8	1	10	5	2	9					11		5	26
27	Feb	13	(h)	CRYSTAL PALACE	W 4-1	Haycock (3), Brown	5000		7				3	4	6	8	1	10	5	2	9					11			27
28	Feb	20	(a)	Brentford	D 2-2	Stansfield, Moody	6000						3	4		8	1	11	6	2		10				7		5	28
29	Feb	27	(h)	PLYMOUTH ARGYLE	L 1-3	Moody							3	4		8	1	11	6	2		10				7		5	29
30	Mar	13	(a)	Portsmouth	L 0-1	-			7				3	4		8			6	2	9	10	1			11		5	30
31	Mar	15	(a)	Queens Park Rangers	L 0-4	-	2000		7		2		3	4		8			6		9	10	1			11		5	31
32	Mar	20	(h)	EXETER CITY	L 0-2	-	4500		7				3	4	6	8			5	2		10	1			11		5	32
33	Mar	27	(a)	Northampton Town	L 0-3	-	1400		7	2				4	6	8			5	3		10	1			11		5	33
34	Apr	3	(h)	NEW BROMPTON	W 3-0	Jones, Moody (2)	3000	9	7	2				4	6	8			5	3		10	1			11			34
35	Apr	9	(a)	Watford	W 3-0	Menzies (2), Moody	9000	9	7	2				4			1		6	3	8	10				11		5	35
36	Apr	10	(a)	Millwall	D 0-0		5000		7	2				4			1	9	6	3	8	10				11		5	36
37	Apr	12	(h)	BRISTOL ROVERS	W 1-0	Stansfield	6000	9	7	2				4			1		6	3	8	10				11		5	37
38	Apr	17	(h)	SOUTHEND UNITED	W 3-0	Stansfield (2), Moody			7	2				4			1	9	6	3		10				11		5	38
39	Apr	19	(h)	SWINDON TOWN	W 1-0	Bradley		9	7	2				4			1		6	3	8	10				11		5	39
40	Apr	24	(a)	Coventry City	L 2-5	Haycock, Stansfield	7069	9	7	2				4		8	1		6	3		10				11		5	40
				Final League Position: 9th			**Apps**	11	34	9	10	2	28	40	22	33	13	15	40	31	33	35	27	1	1	37	1	17	
							Goals	6	4	-	-	-	-	1	2	10	-	-	4	-	8	14	-	1	-	9	-	-	

1908/1909 FA CUP

Round	Month	Day	Venue	Opponents	W,L,D Score	Scorers	Attendance	Bradley EJ	Brown NL	Chapman R	Dimmock WH	Folley W	Gregory J	Hawkes F	Hawkes R	Haycock FJ	Jarvis RT	Johnson J	Jones A	McCurdy W	Menzies AW	Moody HB	Platt P	Porter WM	Rigate WJ	Stansfield H	Tildesley J	White F	Round
Q5	Dec	5	(h)	SOUTHEND UNITED	D 1-1	Johnson	8000	9					2	4	6	8		11	5	3		10	1			7			Q5
Rep	Dec	9	(a)	Southend United	W 4-2	Brown, Haycock, Moody (2)	5500	9	7				2	4	6	8			5	3		10	1			11			Rep
1	Jan	16	(h)	MILLWALL	L 1-2	Menzies	9000		7				2	4	6	8			5	3	9	10	1			11			1
							Apps	2	2	-	-	-	3	3	3	3	-	1	3	3	1	3	3	-	-	3	-	-	
							Goals	-	1	-	-	-	-	-	-	1	-	1	-	-	1	2	-	-	-	-	-	-	

5th Qualifying Round aet, 1-1 after 90 minutes

F. HAWKES
LUTON TOWN

▶ Fred Hawkes, no relation to Bob, was a local lad who became an utterly dependable wing-half in a career spanning over 20 years at Kenilworth Road.

▶ **The 1908/09 team** – Back row (left to right): Dimmock, Gregory, McCurdy. Second row (left to right): Lawson (Trainer), Jarvis, Bradley, Platt, C.Green (Secretary). Third row (left to right): Rigate, Brown, Stansfield, R.Hawkes, Menzies, Moody, Johnson. Front row (left to right): Haycock, F.Hawkes, Jones.

1909/1910 SOUTHERN LEAGUE DIVISION ONE

Match No	Month	Day	Venue	Opponents	W,L,D Score	Scorers	Attendance	Chapman R	Coxhead E	Fry A	Hawkes F	Hawkes R	Hedley GT	Jarvis RT	Johnson J	Jones A	Lashbrooke AE	McCurdy W	Moody HB	Moore T	Porter GC	Potts EJ	Quinn TA	Rayner WJ	Slennett C	Smith J	Stansfield H	Trueman WO	Match No
1	Sep	1	(h)	NORWICH CITY	D 1-1	R Hawkes	4000	2	7		4	6	3	1	11	5			10				9			8			1
2	Sep	4	(a)	Reading	W 1-0	Smith	2900	2	7		4	6	3	1		5			10				9			8	11		2
3	Sep	9	(a)	Norwich City	L 0-6	-	4000	2			4	6	3	1	11				10				8		5	9	7		3
4	Sep	11	(h)	SOUTHEND UNITED	D 3-3	Hedley, Quinn (2)	5000	2	7		4	6	3	1						10			8		5	9	11		4
5	Sep	15	(h)	WATFORD	W 4-2	Smith, Stansfield, Moore (2)	3000	2	7		4		3	1		5				10			8			9	11	6	5
6	Sep	18	(a)	Leyton	L 0-3	-		2	7		4		3	1		5			10				8			9	11	6	6
7	Sep	22	(a)	Watford	D 1-1	Moody	3000	2	7		4		3	1		5			10				8			9	11	6	7
8	Sep	25	(h)	PLYMOUTH ARGYLE	W 3-2	Smith (2), Stansfield	4000	2	7		4		3	1		5			10				8			9	11	6	8
9	Oct	2	(a)	Southampton	L 2-3	Porter, F Hawkes		2			4		3	1		5					10	7	8			9	11	6	9
10	Oct	4	(h)	SWINDON TOWN	D 1-1	Quinn	1000	2	10		4		3	1		5						9	7			8	11	6	10
11	Oct	9	(h)	CROYDON COMMON	D 1-1	Quinn	3500	2	7	1	4		3			5			10				8			9	11	6	11
12	Oct	16	(a)	Millwall	D 2-2	Smith (2)	7000	2	7		4	6		1		5		3	10				8			9	11		12
13	Oct	23	(h)	NEW BROMPTON	W 1-0	Moody	4000	2	7		4	6		1		5		3	10				8			9	11		13
14	Oct	30	(a)	Northampton Town	L 1-6	Moody		2	7		4	6		1		5		3	9	10			8				11		14
15	Nov	6	(h)	QUEENS PARK RANGERS	D 1-1	Quinn	7000		7		4	6	2	1		5		3	10				8			9	11		15
16	Nov	13	(h)	EXETER CITY	W 3-1	Hedley, F Hawkes, Smith	6100		7		4	6	2	1		5			10				8		3	9	11		16
17	Nov	27	(h)	CRYSTAL PALACE	L 2-4	Johnson (2)	4000		7	1	4	6	2		9	5	10	3					8				11		17
18	Dec	11	(h)	WEST HAM UNITED	W 4-2	Quinn (3), Stansfield	3000		7		4		2	1	9	5			10				8				11	6	18
19	Dec	18	(a)	Portsmouth	L 2-3	Moody (2)			7		4	6	2	1		5		3	10				8			9	11		19
20	Dec	24	(a)	Coventry City	L 2-6	Stansfield, (og)	5000				4		2	1	7	5		3	10				9			8	11	6	20
21	Dec	25	(h)	BRISTOL ROVERS	W 2-1	Quinn, Moody	2500	3	7		4	6	2	1		5			10				8			9	11		21
22	Dec	27	(a)	Bristol Rovers	L 1-2	Smith	9000	3	7		4	6		1		5			10				8	2		9	11		22
23	Dec	28	(h)	BRENTFORD	W 4-2	Smith (2), Quinn, Johnson	4000	3	7		4	6		1	10	5		2					8			9	11		23
24	Jan	1	(a)	Brighton & Hove Albion	L 0-3	-	7000	2	7		4	6		1		5		3	10				8			9	11		24
25	Jan	8	(h)	READING	W 2-1	Smith, Quinn	4000	2	7		4	6		1		5		3	10				8			9	11		25
26	Jan	22	(a)	Southend United	L 1-4	Quinn			7		4	6	2	1		5		3	10				8			9	11		26
27	Jan	29	(h)	LEYTON	D 1-1	Jones		2	7		4	6		1		5		3	10				8			9	11		27
28	Feb	5	(a)	Plymouth Argyle	L 2-4	Smith, Moody		2	7		4	6	3	1		5			10				8			9	11		28
29	Feb	12	(h)	SOUTHAMPTON	L 3-4	Coxhead, Quinn, Moody	4000	2	7		4	6	3	1		5			10				8			9	11		29
30	Feb	19	(a)	Croydon Common	W 3-2	Stansfield (2), Moody		2	7		4	6		1		5			10			3	8			9	11		30
31	Feb	26	(h)	MILLWALL	W 4-1	Jones, Quinn, Moody, Stansfield	3000		7		4	6		1		5			10			3	8			9	11		31
32	Mar	5	(a)	New Brompton	L 0-4	-	5000	2	7		4	6		1		5			10			3	8			9	11		32
33	Mar	12	(h)	NORTHAMPTON TOWN	L 0-3	-	4000	2	7		4	6		1		5			10			3	8			9	11		33
34	Mar	19	(a)	Queens Park Rangers	L 0-4	-	6000	2	7		4			1		5			10			3	8			9	11		34
35	Mar	25	(h)	COVENTRY CITY	W 4-1	Quinn (2), Smith (pen), Moody	6000	2	7		4	6		1		5			10			3	8			9	11		35
36	Mar	26	(a)	Exeter City	W 2-1	Quinn (2)	7000	2	7		4	6		1		5			10			3	8			9	11		36
37	Mar	28	(a)	Brentford	D 2-2	Smith, Quinn	8000	2	7		4			1					10			3	8	5		9	11		37
38	Apr	2	(a)	Swindon Town	D 0-0	-		2	7		4	6		1		5			10			3	8			9	11		38
39	Apr	9	(a)	Crystal Palace	W 3-1	F Hawkes, Smith, Quinn		2	7		4			1		5			10			3	8			9	11		39
40	Apr	16	(h)	BRIGHTON & HOVE ALBION	D 1-1	Stansfield	6100	2	7		4			1		5			10			3	8			9	11		40
41	Apr	23	(a)	West Ham United	W 2-1	Smith, Quinn	4000	2	7		4	6		1		5			10			3	8			9	11		41
42	Apr	30	(h)	PORTSMOUTH	L 0-1	-		2	7		4			1		5			10			3	8			9	11		42
				Apps				34	39	2	42	24	21	40	14	40	1	13	36	5	1	14	42	2	3	39	41	9	
				Goals				-	1	-	3	1	2	-	3	2	-	-	11	2	1	-	21	-	-	16	8	-	

Final League Position: 15th *1 Own Goal*

1909/1910 FA CUP

Round	Month	Day	Venue	Opponents	W,L,D Score	Scorers	Attendance	Chapman R	Coxhead E	Fry A	Hawkes F	Hawkes R	Hedley GT	Jarvis RT	Johnson J	Jones A	Lashbrooke AE	McCurdy W	Moody HB	Moore T	Porter GC	Potts EJ	Quinn TA	Rayner WJ	Slennett C	Smith J	Stansfield H	Trueman WO	Round
Q4	Nov	20	(a)	Brentford	L 1-2	Smith	7500		7	1	4	6	2			5		3	10				8			9	11		Q4
				Apps				-	1	1	1	1	1	-	-	1	-	1	1	-	-	-	1	-	-	1	1	-	
				Goals				-	-	-	-	-	-	-	-	-	-	-	-	-	-	-	-	-	-	1	-	-	

A. JONES (Half-Back).

▶ Although standing only 5'7", centre-half Abe Jones was rarely beaten in the air and was a firm favourite at Kenilworth Road for his 'robust' play.

▶ The 1909/10 team – Back row (left to right): Tineman, Hedley, Jarvis, Chapman, Ruffet, Rayner. Middle row (left to right): Stansfield, John Smith, F.Hawkes, R.Hawkes, Quinn, Moody, Johnson. Front row (left to right): Potts, Jones.

1910/1911 SOUTHERN LEAGUE DIVISION ONE

Match No	Month	Day	Venue	Opponents	W,L,D	Score	Scorers	Attendance	Bushell W	Chapman R	Coxhead E	Hawkes F	Hawkes R	Jarvis RT	Johnson J	Lashbrooke AE	McDonald A	Moody HB	Naisby TH	Potts EJ	Quinn TA	Smith J	Stansfield H	Stephenson James	Walker Robbie	Watson C	West G	Wightman S	Match No
1	Sep	3	(h)	SOUTHAMPTON	W	3-2	Moody (2), (og)	8000	5	2	7	4	6					10	1	3	8	9	11						1
2	Sep	10	(a)	Southend United	W	4-1	Moody (3), Quinn	5000		2	7	4	6		5			10	1	3	8	9	11						2
3	Sep	17	(h)	COVENTRY CITY	W	4-2	Smith (2), Stansfield, (og)	8000		2	7	4	6		5			10	1	3	8	9	11						3
4	Sep	21	(h)	BRISTOL ROVERS	W	4-0	Stansfield (3), Moody	3000		2	7	4	6		5			10	1	3	8	9	11						4
5	Sep	24	(a)	New Brompton	L	1-2	Coxhead	7000		2	7	4	6		5		8	10	1	3			11						5
6	Oct	1	(h)	MILLWALL	W	1-0	Moody	8000	5	2	7	4	6		8			10	1	3			11						6
7	Oct	8	(a)	Queens Park Rangers	D	3-3	Bushell, Quinn, Moody	12000	5	2	7	4			6			10	1	3	8	9	11						7
8	Oct	15	(h)	WEST HAM UNITED	D	1-1	Smith	8000	5	2	7	4	6					10	1	3	8	9	11						8
9	Oct	22	(a)	Norwich City	L	2-3	Moody, MacKenzie (og)	8000	5	2	7	4	6					10	1	3	8	9	11						9
10	Oct	29	(a)	Portsmouth	L	1-2	Smith		5	2	7	4	6					10	1	3	8	9	11						10
11	Nov	5	(h)	NORTHAMPTON TOWN	L	1-3	Smith	8000	5	2	7	4	6					10	1	3	8	9	11						11
12	Nov	12	(a)	Brighton & Hove Albion	D	3-3	Quinn, Smith, Moody	7000	5	2	7	4						10	1		8	9	11			3			12
13	Nov	26	(a)	Swindon Town	L	1-4	F Hawkes		5	2	7	4			6			10	1		8	9	11			3			13
14	Dec	10	(a)	Crystal Palace	L	1-3	Smith		5	2	7	4	6					10	1		8	9	11			3			14
15	Dec	17	(h)	BRENTFORD	D	1-1	Moody	5000	5	2	7	4	6					10	1		8	9	11				3		15
16	Dec	24	(a)	Leyton	L	0-3	-	4000	5		7	4	6					10	1		8	9	11				3		16
17	Dec	26	(a)	Watford	L	0-1	-	6000	5		7			1	6	9		10		3	8		11				2		17
18	Dec	27	(h)	WATFORD	W	3-1	Moody (2), F Hawkes	6000	5		7	4		1	9			10		3	8		11				2		18
19	Dec	31	(a)	Southampton	D	0-0	-		5	3	7	4	6	1	9			10			8		11				2		19
20	Jan	7	(h)	SOUTHEND UNITED	W	3-1	Smith (2), Moody	6000	5	2	7	4	6		11			10			8	9					3		20
21	Jan	21	(a)	Coventry City	D	1-1	Smith	7000	5		7	4			6			10	1	3	8	9	11				2		21
22	Jan	28	(h)	NEW BROMPTON	W	3-0	Quinn, Smith, Stansfield	5000	5		7		6					10	1	3	8	9	11				2		22
23	Feb	4	(a)	Millwall	W	3-1	Quinn, Smith, Moody	8000	5		7	4	6					10	1	3	8	9	11				2		23
24	Feb	11	(h)	QUEENS PARK RANGERS	L	0-1	-	6000	5		7	4			6			10	1	3	8	9	11				2		24
25	Feb	18	(a)	West Ham United	L	0-2	-	8000	5		7	4	6					10	1	3	8	9	11				2		25
26	Feb	25	(h)	NORWICH CITY	W	3-1	Smith, Moody, Stansfield	6000	5		7	4	6					10	1	3	8	9	11				2		26
27	Mar	4	(h)	PORTSMOUTH	W	4-1	Coxhead, Smith (2), Moody	4000	5		7	4	6					10	1	3	8	9	11				2		27
28	Mar	11	(a)	Northampton Town	L	1-3	Smith	6000	5		7	4	6					10	1	3	8	9	11				2		28
29	Mar	18	(h)	BRIGHTON & HOVE ALBION	W	1-0	Walker	5000	5		7	4	6		9			10	1	3			11		8		2		29
30	Mar	25	(a)	Exeter City	L	2-4	Bushell, Moody	3500	5		7	4			9	6		10	1	3			11		8		2		30
31	Apr	1	(h)	SWINDON TOWN	W	2-1	Moody, Stephenson		5		7	4						10	1	3			11	9	8		2		31
32	Apr	8	(a)	Bristol Rovers	L	2-4	Bushell, Stephenson	9000	5		7	4			6	10			1	3			11	9	8		2		32
33	Apr	14	(a)	Plymouth Argyle	L	0-4	-		5		7	4				10			1	3			11	9	8		2		33
34	Apr	15	(h)	CRYSTAL PALACE	D	1-1	Stephenson	6000	5		7	4			6				1	3			11	9	8		10	2	34
35	Apr	17	(h)	PLYMOUTH ARGYLE	D	0-0	-				7	4	6		5				1	3			11	9	8		10	2	35
36	Apr	18	(a)	EXETER CITY	W	3-1	Walker, Stephenson (2)	5000		3	7	4			5	10			1				11	9	8			2	36
37	Apr	22	(a)	Brentford	L	0-1	-	3000	5		7	4			6	10			1	3			11	9	8			2	37
38	Apr	29	(h)	LEYTON	W	4-1	Walker (2), Stephenson, Stansfield		5		7	4	6		10				1	3			11	9	8			2	38

Final League Position: 9th   3 Own Goals

	Apps	32	19	38	38	29	3	21	6	1	31	35	30	26	25	37	8	10	3	2	24
	Goals	3	-	2	2	-	-	-	-	-	19	-	-	5	16	7	6	4	-	-	-

1910/1911 FA CUP

Round	Month	Day	Venue	Opponents	W,L,D	Score	Scorers	Attendance	Bushell W	Chapman R	Coxhead E	Hawkes F	Hawkes R	Jarvis RT	Johnson J	Lashbrooke AE	McDonald A	Moody HB	Naisby TH	Potts EJ	Quinn TA	Smith J	Stansfield H	Stephenson James	Walker Robbie	Watson C	West G	Wightman S	Round
Q4	Nov	19	(h)	CAMBRIDGE UNITED	W	9-1	Smith (4), Moody (3), Quinn, Johnson	4000	5	2	7	4			6			10	1	3	8	9	11						Q4
Q5	Dec	3	(a)	Rochdale	D	1-1	Quinn	5500	5	2	7	4	6					10	1	3	8	9	11						Q5
Rep	Dec	7	(h)	ROCHDALE	W	3-2	Quinn (2), Moody	3000	5	2	7	4	6					10	1		8	9	11		3				Rep
1	Jan	14	(a)	Northampton Town	L	1-5	Moody	8000	5	2	7	4	6					10	1		8	9	11					3	1

4th Qualifying Round played at Luton by arrangement

	Apps	4	4	4	4	3	-	1	-	-	4	4	2	4	4	4	-	1	-	-	1
	Goals	-	-	-	-	-	-	1	-	-	5	-	-	4	4	-	-	-	-	-	-

▶ **The 1910/11 team** – Back row (left to right): C.Green (Secretary), F.Hawkes, Bushell, H.Smart (Director), Naisby, H.Woods (Director), Potts, Bygrave (Groundsman), Lawson (Trainer). Front row (left to right): Coxhead, Quinn, John Smith, R.Hawkes, Moody, Stansfield, Johnson.

TIMELINE...

13 March 1911 The Hatters are labelled a 'selling club' for the first time after John Quinn and John Smith are sold to Millwall for a joint fee of £300.

1911/1912 SOUTHERN LEAGUE DIVISION ONE

Match No	Month	Day	Venue	Opponents	W/L/D Score	Scorers	Attendance	Ashton J	Brown Archibald	Bushell W	Clarke H	Coxhead E	Hawkes F	Hawkes R	Johnson J	Lashbrooke AE	Mardle HA	Moody HB	Naisby TH	Potts EJ	Read M	Shepherd James	Smith FG	Stansfield H	Stephenson James	Streeton TA	Walden G	Walker Robbie	Wightman S	Match No
1	Sep	2	(a)	New Brompton	D 0-0	-	5000			6		5	7	4				10	1	3				11	9			8	2	1
2	Sep	9	(h)	STOKE	D 1-1	Walker	8000			6		5	7	4				10	1	3				11	9			8	2	2
3	Sep	16	(a)	Exeter City	L 0-2		6500			6		5	7	4				10	1	3			9	11				8	2	3
4	Sep	23	(h)	COVENTRY CITY	L 2-4	R Hawkes, Moody	7000			6		5	7	4				10	1	3				11	9			8	2	4
5	Sep	30	(a)	Brentford	W 1-0	Shepherd	5700			6		5	7	4				10	1	3		9		11				8	2	5
6	Oct	7	(h)	LEYTON	W 4-1	Coxhead, Walker, Moody, Stansfield				6		5	7	4				10	1	3		9		11				8	2	6
7	Oct	14	(a)	Queens Park Rangers	L 0-2	-	14000			6		5	7	4				10	1	3		9		11				8	2	7
8	Oct	21	(h)	NORWICH CITY	L 0-1		5000			6		5	7	4				10	1	3		9		11				8	2	8
9	Oct	28	(a)	Millwall	D 1-1	F Hawkes	12000			6		5	7	4				10	1	3		9		11					2	9
10	Nov	4	(h)	CRYSTAL PALACE	L 0-1	-	5000	3		6		5	7	4				10	1			9		11				8	2	10
11	Nov	11	(a)	West Ham United	L 0-3	-	9000	3		6		5	7	4	8	11		10	1			9							2	11
12	Nov	18	(h)	SOUTHAMPTON	D 1-1	Johnson	4000			6		5	7	4	8	11		10	1	3		9							2	12
13	Nov	25	(a)	Bristol Rovers	L 1-2	Moody	6000			6		5	7	4	8	11		10	1	3					9				2	13
14	Dec	2	(h)	PLYMOUTH ARGYLE	L 0-3		4000			6		5	7	4	8	11		10	1	3					9				2	14
15	Dec	9	(a)	Swindon Town	L 2-4	Walker (2)				6		5	7	4	9	11		10	1	3								8	2	15
16	Dec	16	(a)	Reading	D 1-1	Johnson				6		5	7	4	9			10	1	3				11				8	2	16
17	Dec	23	(h)	NORTHAMPTON TOWN	D 3-3	Walker (2), Johnson	6000			6		5	7	4	9			10	1	3				11				8	2	17
18	Dec	25	(h)	WATFORD	D 1-1	Moody	8000			6		5	7	4				10	1	3				11	9			8	2	18
19	Dec	26	(a)	Watford	W 1-0	R Hawkes	6000			6		5	7	4				10	1	3				11	9			8	2	19
20	Dec	30	(h)	NEW BROMPTON	W 3-0	Walker (2), Streeton				6		5	7	4				10	1	3				11		9		8	2	20
21	Jan	20	(h)	EXETER CITY	W 4-2	Moody (2), Coxhead, Streeton	4000			6		5	7	4				10	1	3				11		9		8	2	21
22	Jan	27	(a)	Coventry City	L 0-1	-	5000			6		5	7	4				10	1	3				11	9			8	2	22
23	Feb	3	(h)	BRENTFORD	D 0-0					6		5	7	4				10	1	3				11	9			8	2	23
24	Feb	10	(a)	Leyton	D 1-1	Moody				6		5	7	4				10	1	3				11	9			8	2	24
25	Feb	17	(h)	QUEENS PARK RANGERS	L 1-3	Stephenson				6		5	7	4				10	1	3				11	9			8	2	25
26	Feb	24	(a)	Norwich City	D 2-2	Walker, Stephenson	6000			6		5	7	4				10	1	3				11	9			8	2	26
27	Mar	2	(h)	MILLWALL	L 0-1	-	4500			6		5	7	4				10	1	3				11	9			8	2	27
28	Mar	9	(a)	Crystal Palace	L 1-3	Read	7000			6		5	7	4				10	1	3	11				9			8	2	28
29	Mar	16	(h)	WEST HAM UNITED	W 2-1	Moody (2)	6000			6		5	7	4				10	1	3				11	8	9			2	29
30	Mar	18	(a)	Stoke	L 3-4	Moody, Streeton, Walden	6000			6		5	7	4				10	1	3					8	11	9		2	30
31	Mar	23	(a)	Southampton	L 2-3	Stephenson, Walden				6	5		7	4				10	1	3					8	11	9		2	31
32	Mar	30	(a)	BRISTOL ROVERS	W 3-1	Wightman, Stephenson, Moody	4000			6		5	7	4				10	1	3					8	11	9		2	32
33	Apr	5	(h)	BRIGHTON & HOVE ALBION	W 1-0	Stephenson	10000			6		5	7	4				10	1	3					8	11	9		2	33
34	Apr	6	(a)	Plymouth Argyle	L 0-2	-				6		5	7	4				10	1	3					8	11	9		2	34
35	Apr	8	(a)	Brighton & Hove Albion	L 0-1	-	10000			6		5	7	4				10	1	3					8	11	9			2	35
36	Apr	13	(h)	SWINDON TOWN	L 0-3	-			2	6		5	7	4			9	10	1	3				11				8		36
37	Apr	20	(h)	READING	W 7-1	Bushell, Coxhead, Moody (3), Mardle (2)			2	6		5	7	4			9	10	1	3				11	8					37
38	Apr	27	(a)	Northampton Town	L 0-1	-	7000		2	6		5	7	4		9		10	1	3				11	8					38

Final League Position: 19th

| | | | | | | | Apps | 2 | 3 | 37 | 1 | 37 | 38 | 38 | 7 | 6 | 2 | 36 | 38 | 36 | 1 | 8 | 1 | 20 | 22 | 16 | 7 | 28 | 34 | |
| | | | | | | | Goals | - | - | 1 | - | 3 | 1 | 2 | 3 | - | 2 | 14 | - | 1 | 1 | - | - | 1 | 5 | 3 | 2 | 9 | 1 | |

1911/1912 FA CUP

Round	Month	Day	Venue	Opponents	W/L/D Score	Scorers	Attendance	Ashton J	Brown Archibald	Bushell W	Clarke H	Coxhead E	Hawkes F	Hawkes R	Johnson J	Lashbrooke AE	Mardle HA	Moody HB	Naisby TH	Potts EJ	Read M	Shepherd James	Smith FG	Stansfield H	Stephenson James	Streeton TA	Walden G	Walker Robbie	Wightman S	Round
1	Jan	13	(h)	NOTTS COUNTY	L 2-4	Streeton, Moody	6500			6		5	7	4				10	1	2				11		9		8	3	1

| | | | | | | | Apps | - | - | 1 | - | 1 | 1 | 1 | - | - | - | 1 | 1 | 1 | - | - | - | 1 | - | 1 | - | 1 | 1 | |
| | | | | | | | Goals | - | - | - | - | - | - | - | - | - | - | 1 | - | - | - | - | - | - | - | 1 | - | - | - | |

▶ **The 1911/12 team** – Back row (left to right): H.Smart (Director), W.Soper (Director), Wightman, Naisby, J.Smith (Director), Potts, Bygrave (Groundsman), Ashton, C.Green (Secretary), Lawson (Trainer). Middle row (left to right): Coxhead, Walker, R.Hawkes, Stephenson, Moody, Stansfield, Johnson. Front row (left to right): F.Hawkes, Bushell.

TIMELINE...

8 April 1912 Sammy Wightman is accidentally kicked in the stomach at Brighton. He dies four days later from peritonitis.
27 April 1912 The Town are relegated to Division Two of the Southern League.

1912/1913 SOUTHERN LEAGUE DIVISION TWO

Match No	Month	Day	Venue	Opponents	W/L Score	Scorers	Attendance	Abbott RH	Bateman H	Chipperfield JJ	Davidson TK	Day JW	Elvey JR	Hawkes F	Hawkes R	Henderson CG	Holland JJ	Jarvie J	Johnson J	Murphy John	Potts EJ	Price M	Rogers E	Smith W	Stephenson James	Streeton TA	Thompson S	Wileman AH	Wilson TT	Worth A	Match No
1	Sep	14	(a)	Mardy	W 3-2	R Hawkes (2), Murphy						1			6	2				10	3			9	7		5	8	4	11	1
2	Sep	21	(h)	MARDY	W 1-0	Stephenson	5000					1			6	2				10	3			9	7		5	8	4	11	2
3	Sep	28	(a)	Mid-Rhondda	D 2-2	R Hawkes, Stephenson	4000				10	1		4	6	2					3			9	7			8	5	11	3
4	Oct	5	(a)	Aberdare	L 0-3	-		1						4	6	2				10	3			9	7			8	5	11	4
5	Oct	19	(h)	TREHARRIS	W 4-0	Stephenson (2), Streeton (2)		1						4	6	2					3		7	9	10	11		8	5		5
6	Oct	26	(h)	CROYDON COMMON	W 3-1	Stephenson (2), Worth	4000	1						4	6	2					3		7	9	10			8	5	11	6
7	Nov	9	(a)	Treharris	W 3-0	R Hawkes, Stephenson, Streeton		1						4	6	2					3			9	7	10		8	5	11	7
8	Nov	23	(h)	SOUTHEND UNITED	W 4-3	Thompson (2), Stephenson (2)	6500	1						4	6	2					3			9	7		10	8	5	11	8
9	Dec	7	(h)	PONTYPRIDD	D 2-2	F Hawkes (2)		1						4	6	2					3			9	7		10	8	5	11	9
10	Dec	21	(h)	MID-RHONDDA	W 3-1	Thompson (2), Smith	4000	1						4	6	2					3			9	7		10	8	5	11	10
11	Dec	26	(h)	CARDIFF CITY	W 2-0	Smith, Worth	6000	1						4	6	2					3			9	7		10	8	5	11	11
12	Dec	28	(a)	Pontypridd	W 2-1	Wileman, Worth	7000	1						4	6	2					3			9	7		10	8	5	11	12
13	Jan	4	(h)	LLANELLY	W 2-0	Murphy, F Hawkes		1						4	6	2				10	3			9	7			8	5	11	13
14	Jan	18	(a)	Newport County	L 1-5	R Hawkes		1						4	6	2				10	3			9	7			8	5	11	14
15	Feb	8	(h)	SWANSEA TOWN	L 0-4	-	5000	1						4	6	2			10		3			9	7			8	5	11	15
16	Feb	15	(a)	Croydon Common	L 2-4	R Hawkes, Wileman		1						4	6	2					3			9	7	10		8	5	11	16
17	Feb	22	(h)	TON PENTRE	W 7-1	Smith (3), Wileman (2), Stephenson, R Hawkes			1					4	6	2					3			9	7	10		8	5	11	17
18	Mar	1	(a)	Southend United	D 1-1	Smith			1					4	6	2	10	3						9	7			8	5	11	18
19	Mar	15	(a)	Llanelly	D 1-1	Holland			1					4	6	2	10	3						9	7			8	5	11	19
20	Mar	22	(a)	Cardiff City	L 0-3	-	22000		1					4	6	2	10	3						9	7			8	5	11	20
21	Mar	24	(h)	ABERDARE	W 3-1	Wileman (3)			1				10	4	6	2		3						9	7			8	5	11	21
22	Mar	29	(a)	Swansea Town	L 0-2	-			1					4	6	2	10	3						9	7			8	5	11	22
23	Apr	4	(h)	NEWPORT COUNTY	W 5-0	Wilson, Wileman, Chipperfield (3)			1	10			2	6		4					3			9	7			8	5	11	23
24	Apr	12	(a)	Ton Pentre	L 1-2	Smith			1						6	2		4		10	3			9	7			8	5	11	24
				Apps				13	8	1	1	3	2	21	22	19	5	7	1	11	20	1	2	17	20	5	16	23	23	23	
				Goals				-	-	3	-	-	-	3	7	-	1	-	-	2	-	-	-	7	10	3	4	8	1	3	

Final League Position: 5th

1912/1913 FA CUP

Round	Month	Day	Venue	Opponents	W/L Score	Scorers	Attendance	Abbott RH	Bateman H	Chipperfield JJ	Davidson TK	Day JW	Elvey JR	Hawkes F	Hawkes R	Henderson CG	Holland JJ	Jarvie J	Johnson J	Murphy John	Potts EJ	Price M	Rogers E	Smith W	Stephenson James	Streeton TA	Thompson S	Wileman AH	Wilson TT	Worth A	Round
Q4	Nov	30	(h)	TUNBRIDGE WELLS RANGERS	W 3-0	R Hawkes, Wileman, Streeton	4500	1						4	6	3				2					11	9	7	8	5	10	Q4
Q5	Dec	14	(a)	Croydon Common	L 0-2	-	3000	1						4	6	3				2					11	9	7	8	5	10	Q5
				Apps				2						2	2	2				2					2	2	2	2	2	2	
				Goals				-	-	-	-	-	-	-	1	-	-	-	-	-	-	-	-	-	-	1	-	1	-	-	

The 1912/13 team – Back row (left to right): C.Green (Secretary), W.Soper (Director), Wilson, Thompson, Henderson, Streeton, Potts, Bygrave (Groundsman), E.Gibbs (Director), Lawson (Trainer). Front row (left to right): Stephenson, Wileman, W.Smith, R.Hawkes, Murphy, Worth.

1913/1914 SOUTHERN LEAGUE DIVISION TWO

Match No	Month	Day	Venue	Opponents	W,L,D	Score	Scorers	Attendance	Abbott RH	Brewis R	Dodd EJ	Donaghy Michael	Durrant AF	Elvey JR	Frith RW	Hawkes F	Hawkes R	Hoar SW	Jarvie J	Lovell P	Mitchell JT	Robinson J	Rollinson F	Simms E	Stevens E	Wileman AH	Wilkie J	Wilson TT	Match No
1	Sep	13	(h)	MARDY	W	1-0	R Hawkes					7		2	5	4	6		3		1		10	9	8		11		1
2	Sep	17	(a)	Abertillery	W	2-1	Rollinson, Wileman			9				2	5	4	6		3		1		10		7	8	11		2
3	Sep	20	(a)	Mardy	W	2-1	Wileman, Brewis			9				2	5	4	6		3		1		10		7	8	11		3
4	Sep	27	(h)	TREHARRIS	W	6-0	Simms (2), Rollinson (2), Wileman (2)					7		2	5	4	6		3		1		10	9		8	11		4
5	Oct	4	(a)	Barry	W	3-1	Simms, Rollinson, Wileman					7		2	5	4	6		3		1		10	9		8	11		5
6	Oct	18	(a)	Treharris	W	2-1	F Hawkes, Stevens							2	5	4	6		3		1		10	9	7	8	11		6
7	Oct	25	(h)	ABERTILLERY	W	6-0	Wileman (3), Rollinson (2), Simms							2	5	4	6		3		1		10	9	7	8	11		7
8	Nov	1	(a)	Llanelly	L	0-3	-							2	5	4	6		3		1		10	9	7	8	11		8
9	Nov	8	(a)	Pontypridd	L	2-3	Simms, Rollinson					7		2	5	4	6		3		1		10	9		8	11		9
10	Nov	15	(h)	Ton Pentre	W	4-0	Wileman (2), Simms, Rollinson					7		2	5	4			3		1		10	9		8	11	6	10
11	Nov	22	(h)	MID-RHONDDA	W	8-1	R Hawkes, Simms (2), Wileman (3), Rollinson (2)					7		2	5	4	6		3		1		10	9		8	11		11
12	Dec	6	(h)	PONTYPRIDD	W	3-0	R Hawkes, Simms, Durrant			8			7		5	4	6	11	3		1	2	10	9					12
13	Dec	20	(h)	ABERDARE	W	7-0	Brewis (5), Wileman, Rollinson		1	9		7			5	4			3			2	10			8	11	6	13
14	Dec	25	(a)	Newport County	L	0-2	-	10000	1	9		7			5	4			3			2	10			8	11	6	14
15	Dec	26	(h)	NEWPORT COUNTY	W	1-0	R Hawkes	8000	1	8				2	5	4	10		3	9					7		11	6	15
16	Dec	27	(a)	Croydon Common	D	1-1	F Hawkes	10000	1	10				2	5	4	8		3					9	7		11	6	16
17	Jan	17	(h)	CAERPHILLY	W	4-0	F Hawkes, Simms (2), Wileman		1	10			7	2	5	4	6		3					9		8	11		17
18	Jan	24	(a)	Caerphilly	W	9-0	Simms (4), Rollinson, Durrant (2), Wileman (2)						7	2	5	4	6	11			1	3	10	9		8			18
19	Feb	7	(h)	BRENTFORD	W	3-1	Rollinson (2), Wileman						7	2	5	4	6	11			1	3	10	9		8			19
20	Feb	14	(a)	Aberdare	W	5-1	Elvey, Simms, Wileman (3)						7	2	5	4	6	11			1	3	10	9		8			20
21	Feb	21	(h)	BARRY	W	3-1	Simms (2), Wileman						7	2	5	4	6	11			1	3	10	9		8			21
22	Feb	28	(h)	LLANELLY	W	5-1	Elvey, Simms (3), Rollinson						7	2	5	4	6	11			1	3	10	9		8			22
23	Mar	7	(h)	TON PENTRE	W	2=0	Simms (2)						7	2	5	4	6	11			1	3	10	9					23
24	Mar	14	(a)	Swansea Town	W	1-0	Wileman						7	2	5	4	6				1	3	10	9	11	8			24
25	Mar	28	(a)	Mid-Rhondda	D	1-1	Simms						7	2	5	4	6	11			1	3	10	9		8			25
26	Apr	4	(h)	SWANSEA TOWN	W	5-0	Simms (2), Rollinson, Wileman (2)						7	2	5	4	6	11			1	3	10	9		8			26
27	Apr	10	(h)	STOKE	W	2-1	Simms, Rollinson	12000					7	2	5	4	6	11			1	3	10	9		8			27
28	Apr	11	(a)	Brentford	D	0-0	-	8000		10				2	5	4	6				1	3		9	7	8			28
29	Apr	13	(a)	Stoke	W	2-1	Simms, Brewis			10	7			2	5	4	6	11			1	3		9		8			29
30	Apr	18	(h)	CROYDON COMMON	W	2-1	Wileman (2)			10				2	5	4	6	11			1	3		9	7	8			30
				Apps					5	13	1	9	12	27	30	30	26	12	17	1	25	17	24	24	11	24	17	5	
				Goals					-	7	-	-	3	2	-	3	4	-	-	-	-	-	17	28	1	27	-	-	

Final League Position: 2nd

1913/1914 FA CUP

Round	Month	Day	Venue	Opponents	W,L,D	Score	Scorers	Attendance	Abbott RH	Brewis R	Dodd EJ	Donaghy Michael	Durrant AF	Elvey JR	Frith RW	Hawkes F	Hawkes R	Hoar SW	Jarvie J	Lovell P	Mitchell JT	Robinson J	Rollinson F	Simms E	Stevens E	Wileman AH	Wilkie J	Wilson TT	Round
Q4	Nov	29	(h)	CROYDON COMMON	W	3-0	Wileman, Rollinson (2)	8700				7			6	4			3		1	2	11	9		8	10	5	Q4
Q5	Dec	13	(h)	SOUTH SHIELDS	D	0-0	-	9500					7	2	6	4	5		3		1		11	9		8	10		Q5
Rep	Dec	17	(a)	South Shields	L	0-2	-	12000					7	2	6	4	5		3		1		11	9		8	10		Rep
				Apps					-	-	-	1	2	2	3	3	2	-	3	-	3	1	3	3	-	3	3	1	
				Goals					-	-	-	-	-	-	-	-	-	-	-	-	-	-	2	-	-	1	-	-	

The Luton News
FOOTBALL PROMOTION SOUVENIR.

PRICE ONE PENNY.]

LUTON TOWN F.C.

Left to Right—*Back Row*: A. F. DURRANT, M. DONAGHY, R. BREWIS, T. J. MITCHELL, S. HOAR, F. ROLLINSON.
Second Row: J. R. ELVEY, F. HAWKES, R. W. FRITH, R. ABBOTT, E. J. DODD, J. ROBINSON, Mr. H. SMART (Director),
W. LAWSON (Trainer), and Mr. C. GREEN (Secretary).
Third Row: J. JARVIE, Mr. W. SOPER (Director), E. STEVENS, Mr. W. J. ALLEN (Director), R. M. HAWKES,
Mr. F. J. CRICK (Director & Treasurer of the Supporters' Club), J. WILKIE and Mr. E. GIBBS (Director).
Front Row: A. WILKMAN, E. SIMMS and T. T. WILSON.

Photo by W. H. Cox, Gainsborough Studio, Luton.

WEBB BROS., The Luton Tailors,
FOR
* * YOUR Suit to Measure.

▶ Following relegation to Southern League Division Two in 1912, the Town come back two years later in a far healthier state smashing several club records along the way.

▶ The home win over Stoke on Good Friday virtually guaranteed promotion.

▶ Ernie Simms netted 28 goals in only 24 games during the promotion season.

TIMELINE...

10 April 1914 The Kenilworth Road attendance record is broken again with 12,000 going through the turnstiles for the promotion 'four pointer' against Stoke.

1914/1915 SOUTHERN LEAGUE DIVISION ONE

Match No	Month	Day	Venue	Opponents	W,L,D Score	Scorers	Attendance	Abbott RH	Chipperfield JJ	Dunn J	Durrant AF	Elvey JR	Frith RW	Hawkes F	Hawkes R	Heath W	Hoar SW	Johnson J	Lindley F	McFarlane R	Mitchell JT	Needham EG	Roberts HP	Robinson J	Roe A	Rollinson F	Simms E	Wileman AH	Wilson TT	Match No
1	Sep	2	(a)	Southampton	D 3-3	Simms (2), Rollinson						2	5	4			11				1		6	7	3	10	9	8		1
2	Sep	5	(h)	PLYMOUTH ARGYLE	W 2-1	Wileman, Hoar						2	5	4			11				1		6	7	3	10	9	8		2
3	Sep	9	(h)	SOUTHAMPTON	W 3-2	Simms (2), Rollinson						2	5	4			11				1		6	7	3	10	9	8		3
4	Sep	12	(a)	West Ham United	L 0-3	-	5000					2		4	6	5	11				1			7	3	10	9	8		4
5	Sep	16	(h)	QUEENS PARK RANGERS	L 2-4	Hoar, Wilson	4000			4		2					11				1		6	7	3	10	9	8	5	5
6	Sep	19	(h)	NORWICH CITY	D 1-1	Heath	5000					2		4	8	5	11				1		7		3	10	9		6	6
7	Sep	26	(a)	Gillingham	W 4-2	Roberts, Wileman (2), Rollinson	5000					2		4	6			5	11		1		7		3	10	9	8		7
8	Sep	30	(h)	READING	L 1-2	Rollinson						2	5	4				6	11		1		7		3	10	9	8		8
9	Oct	3	(h)	BRIGHTON & HOVE ALBION	L 0-1	-	6000				7	2	5	4	6						1		11	3	8	10	9			9
10	Oct	10	(a)	Cardiff City	L 0-3	-	8000				7	2		4	6						1		11	3	8	10	9		5	10
11	Oct	17	(h)	EXETER CITY	L 0-2	-	5000				7	2	5	4	6						1		11	3	8	10	9			11
12	Oct	21	(h)	BRISTOL ROVERS	W 3-1	Wileman, Rollinson, McFarlane	3000			3		2	5	4	6					7	1		11			10	9	8		12
13	Oct	24	(a)	Crystal Palace	W 3-2	F Hawkes, Simms (2)				3		2	5	4	6					7	1		11			10	9	8		13
14	Oct	31	(a)	Portsmouth	L 1-3	Simms	7000			3		2	5	4	6					7	1		11			10	9	8		14
15	Nov	7	(h)	SWINDON TOWN	D 2-2	Simms (2)				3		2	5	4	6					7	1		11			10	9	8		15
16	Nov	14	(a)	Southend United	L 0-1	-				3		2	5	4	6					7	1		11			10	9	8		16
17	Nov	28	(h)	MILLWALL	L 0-2	-	7000			3		2	5	4	6		11				1		7			10	9	8		17
18	Dec	12	(a)	Croydon Common	D 1-1	Roe				3		2	5	4	6		11				1		7		8	10	9			18
19	Dec	25	(h)	NORTHAMPTON TOWN	D 1-1	Simms	4000			3		2	5	4	6		11				1		7			10	9	8		19
20	Dec	26	(a)	Northampton Town	W 3-0	Rollinson (2), Wileman				3		2	5	4	6		11				1		7			10	9	8		20
21	Jan	2	(a)	Plymouth Argyle	D 3-3	Roberts, Wileman, Simms				3		2	5	4	6		11				1		7		10		9	8		21
22	Jan	23	(a)	Norwich City	L 1-5	Hoar	3000			3		2	5	4	6		11				1		7			10	9	8		22
23	Jan	30	(h)	GILLINGHAM	W 3-1	Roberts (2), Simms				3		2		4	6		11				1		7			10	9	8	5	23
24	Feb	13	(h)	CARDIFF CITY	W 2-1	Robinson, R Hawkes	9000					2	5	4	11	6					1		7	3		10	9	8		24
25	Feb	20	(a)	Exeter City	W 2-1	Wileman, Simms	3000			3		2		4	6				11		1		7			10	9	8	5	25
26	Feb	27	(h)	CRYSTAL PALACE	L 1-2	Hoar		1		3		2	5	4		6	11						7			10	9	8		26
27	Mar	6	(h)	PORTSMOUTH	L 0-2	-		1		3		2	5	4		6	11						7			10	9	8		27
28	Mar	10	(h)	WEST HAM UNITED	L 1-2	Simms	7000			3		2	5	4	6		11				1		7			10	9	8		28
29	Mar	13	(a)	Swindon Town	D 2-2	Rollinson, Hoar						2	5	4	6		11				1		7	3	8	10	9			29
30	Mar	17	(a)	Brighton & Hove Albion	W 1-0	Simms	1000					2	5	4	6		11				1		7	3		10	9	8		30
31	Mar	20	(h)	SOUTHEND UNITED	L 3-4	Simms, Rollinson, Roe						2		4	6	5	11				1		7		3	10	9	8		31
32	Mar	27	(a)	Queens Park Rangers	W 3-0	Simms (3)	3000			3		2	5	4	6		11				1		7		8	10	9			32
33	Apr	2	(a)	Watford	W 4-2	Simms (2), Roberts, Hoar	8000			3		2	5	4	6		11				1		7		8	10	9			33
34	Apr	3	(a)	Millwall	D 3-3	Simms, Rollinson, Hoar	5000			3		2	5	4	6		11				1		7			10	9	8		34
35	Apr	5	(h)	WATFORD	L 0-2	-	7000			3		2	5	4	6		11				1		7			10	9	8		35
36	Apr	10	(a)	Bristol Rovers	L 0-1	-	3000			3		2	5	4			11				1		7			10	9	8	6	36
37	Apr	17	(h)	CROYDON COMMON	W 2-1	Rollinson, Hoar				3		2	5		6		11				1		7			10	9	8	4	37
38	Apr	24	(a)	Reading	L 0-4	-				3		2	5	4	6				11		1		7			10	9	8		38
				Apps				2	1	24	3	37	29	36	27	7	23	6	5	5	36	4	38	16	14	35	38	25	7	
				Goals				-	-	-	-	-	-	1	1	1	8	-	-	1	-	-	5	1	2	11	22	7	1	

Final League Position: 14th

1914/1915 FA CUP

Round	Month	Day	Venue	Opponents	W,L,D Score	Scorers	Attendance	Abbott RH	Chipperfield JJ	Dunn J	Durrant AF	Elvey JR	Frith RW	Hawkes F	Hawkes R	Heath W	Hoar SW	Johnson J	Lindley F	McFarlane R	Mitchell JT	Needham EG	Roberts HP	Robinson J	Roe A	Rollinson F	Simms E	Wileman AH	Wilson TT	Round
Q4	Nov	21	(h)	GT. YARMOUTH	W 15-0	Simms (4), Rollinson (4), Wileman (2), F Hawkes, Frith, Roberts, Hoar, Housego (og)	4000			3		2	5	4	6		11				1		7			10	9	8		Q4
Q5	Dec	5	(a)	Oxford City	W 1-0	Simms	2500			3		2	5	4	6		11				1		7			10	9	8		Q5
Q6	Dec	19	(h)	BROMLEY	W 5-1	Simms (3), F Hawkes, Wileman	2500			3		2	5	4	6		11				1		7			10	9	8		Q6
1	Jan	9	(a)	Southampton	L 0-3	-	11000		10	3		2	5	4	6		11				1		7				9	8		1
				Apps				-	1	4	-	4	4	4	4	-	4	-	-	-	4	-	4	-	-	3	4	4	-	
				Goals				-	-	-	-	-	1	2	-	-	1	-	-	-	-	-	1	-	-	4	8	3	-	

1 Own Goal

▶ **The 1914/15 team** – Back row (left to right): E.Gibbs (Director), Elvey, Dunn, Abbott, Needham, Rollinson, Hoar. Second row (left to right): C.Green (Secretary), Roberts, F.Hawkes, Simms, Frith, Robinson, Lawson (Trainer), Bygrave (Groundsman), Mitchell. Third row (left to right): Chipperfield, Wileman, R.Hawkes, Roe, Heath, Johnson, Lindley. Front row (left to right): McFarlane, Thorpe, Potts, Wilson.

TIMELINE...

21 November 1915 The goalscoring record is smashed, this time for good, as Gt Yarmouth are thrashed 15-0 in an F.A.Cup tie.

1919/1920 SOUTHERN LEAGUE DIVISION ONE

Match No	Month	Day	Venue	Opponents	W,L,D Score	Scorers	Attendance	Abbott RH	Bookman LO	Bowler GH	Bradshaw JH	Brandham J	Bratby JL	Dodd GF	Dunn J	Elvey JR	Furr WS	Fearn J	Ford H	Fryer HC	Grimes WJ	Hawkes F	Hawkes R	Hensman F	Higginbotham H	Hill FWP	Hoar SW	Jones B	Mathieson A	Neale O	Parker TB	Riddle F	Roe A	Rutherford J	Seymour EH	Simms E	Summers P	Tomlinson R	Urwin TA	Whitehead H	Williams D	Match No
1	Aug	30	(h)	SWANSEA TOWN	D 1-1	Elvey (pen)									3	2	7									11					6		8	5		9	1		4		10	1
2	Sep	1	(h)	GILLINGHAM	W 2-0	Simms, Tomlinson	4000								3						2			11							6		7	5		9	1	8	4		10	2
3	Sep	6	(a)	Exeter City	L 2-3	Elvey (pen), Tomlinson	5000								3	2				7				11							6	10		5		9	1	8	4			3
4	Sep	10	(a)	Gillingham	L 0-2	-									3	2				7				11							6	10		5		9	1		4	8		4
5	Sep	13	(h)	CARDIFF CITY	D 2-2	Williams, Rutherford	10000								3	2					7						11				5	10	6				1	8	4		9	5
6	Sep	17	(h)	MERTHYR TOWN	L 0-4	-				5					3				8		2			11							6				7	9	1		4			6
7	Sep	20	(a)	Queens Park Rangers	L 0-4	-	6000			4					3					7	2			11							6	10		5		9	1		4			7
8	Sep	27	(h)	SWINDON TOWN	W 3-1	Rutherford, Simms (2)									3	2											11				6	10	8	5	7	9	1		4			8
9	Oct	4	(a)	Millwall	L 0-2	-	12000								3	2											7				6		8	5	11	9	1		4		10	9
10	Oct	11	(h)	BRIGHTON & HOVE ALBION	W 2-0	Simms, Williams	7000		11						3	2											7				6		8	5		9	1		4		10	10
11	Oct	18	(h)	Newport County	D 0-0	-	6414		11						3	2					7										6		8	5		9	1		4		10	11
12	Oct	25	(h)	PORTSMOUTH	W 2-0	Rutherford (2)			11						3	2											7				6		8	5		9	1		4		10	12
13	Nov	1	(a)	Northampton Town	W 4-1	Simms (2), Williams, Tomlinson			11						3	2															6		7	5		9	1	8	4		10	13
14	Nov	8	(h)	CRYSTAL PALACE	L 1-4	Tomlinson			11						3	2											7				6		7	5		9	1	8	4		10	14
15	Nov	15	(a)	Southend United	L 0-3	-			11			4			3	2											7				6		8	5		9	1		4		10	15
16	Nov	22	(h)	NORWICH CITY	D 1-1	Dodd	6000		11					10	3	2											7				6		5			9	1		4		8	16
17	Nov	29	(a)	Brentford	L 1-3	Dodd	6000		11					10	3	2											7				6		8	5		9	1		4			17
18	Dec	13	(a)	Plymouth Argyle	L 0-1	-			11					10	3	2											7				6		5			9			4	8		18
19	Dec	25	(h)	SOUTHAMPTON	L 0-1	-			11					10	3	2											7		1		6		5			9			4	8		19
20	Dec	26	(a)	Southampton	L 1-2	Bookman		1	11					10	3	2											7				6		5			9			4	8		20
21	Dec	27	(a)	Reading	W 2-1	Williams, Dodd		1	11					10	3	2															6		5			9		7	4		8	21
22	Jan	3	(a)	Swansea Town	L 0-3	-		1	11						3	2															6		8	5		9		7	4		10	22
23	Jan	17	(h)	EXETER CITY	W 3-1	Simms (2), Bookman	5000	1	11					10	3	2											7				6		8	5		9			4			23
24	Jan	24	(a)	Cardiff City	L 1-2	Simms	15000		11					10	3	2					7		3								6			5		9	1		4			24
25	Feb	7	(a)	Swindon Town	L 0-1	-			11						3	2					7			8							6			5		9	1		4			25
26	Feb	14	(h)	MILLWALL	D 2-2	Williams, Bookman	6000		11						3	2						8					7				6			5		9			4		10	26
27	Feb	21	(a)	Brighton & Hove Albion	L 3-4	Rutherford, Williams, Bookman	8000		11		10				3	2						8					7				6			5			1		4		9	27
28	Feb	28	(h)	NEWPORT COUNTY	W 4-0	Simms (2), Tomlinson, Hill	8000		11						3	2						8					7				6			5		9	1	10	4			28
29	Mar	6	(a)	Portsmouth	D 1-1	Hill	13629		11			5			3	2					7	8				10					6					9	1		4			29
30	Mar	13	(h)	NORTHAMPTON TOWN	L 0-2	-	6000		11			5			3	2						8				10	7				6				9		1		4			30
31	Mar	20	(a)	Crystal Palace	L 1-4	Higginbotham			11						3	2									8		7			10	6			5		9	1		4			31
32	Mar	22	(h)	QUEENS PARK RANGERS	W 2-1	Hoar, Hill	4000								3	2					4				8	11	7			10	6			5		9	1		5			32
33	Mar	27	(h)	SOUTHEND UNITED	D 1-1	Simms									3	2		11			7	4			10		7				6			5		9	1					33
34	Apr	2	(a)	Watford	L 2-4	Dodd, Higginbotham	10000							10	3	2						8			9	11	7				6		5				1		4			34
35	Apr	3	(a)	Norwich City	D 1-1	Hill	10000								3	2					7	4			8	10	11				6		9				1		5			35
36	Apr	5	(h)	WATFORD	L 1-2	Elvey (pen)	13000								3	2						4			10	7					6		8			9	1		5		11	36
37	Apr	6	(a)	Bristol Rovers	L 0-5	-	8000		11						3	2					7	8			10						6		9				1		5		4	37
38	Apr	10	(h)	BRENTFORD	D 0-0	-	6000		11						3	2					7	10			8						6		9				1		5		4	38
39	Apr	17	(a)	Merthyr Town	W 3-1	F Hawkes, Higginbotham (2)			11				9		3	2						10			8						6		5				1		4		7	39
40	Apr	24	(h)	PLYMOUTH ARGYLE	L 1-2	Urwin			11				9		3	2						10			8						6		5				1		4		7	40
41	Apr	26	(h)	BRISTOL ROVERS	D 1-1	Higginbotham	3000		11				9		3	2			1		4	10	6		8		7				5								8			41
42	May	1	(h)	READING	L 0-2	-			11						3	2						10					7				6		5			9	1		8			42
				Final League Position: 20th			**Apps**	4	29	2	1	3	3	9	38	41	1	1	1	3	11	14	1	5	11	13	26	1	2	2	40	2	24	29	2	33	32	12	40	3	23	
							Goals	-	4	-	-	-	-	4	-	3	-	-	-	-	-	1	-	-	5	4	1	-	-	-	-	-	-	5	-	12	-	5	1	-	6	

1919/1920 FA CUP

Round	Month	Day	Venue	Opponents	W,L,D Score	Scorers	Attendance	Abbott RH	Bookman LO	Bowler GH	Bradshaw JH	Brandham J	Bratby JL	Dodd GF	Dunn J	Elvey JR	Furr WS	Fearn J	Ford H	Fryer HC	Grimes WJ	Hawkes F	Hawkes R	Hensman F	Higginbotham H	Hill FWP	Hoar SW	Jones B	Mathieson A	Neale O	Parker TB	Riddle F	Roe A	Rutherford J	Seymour EH	Simms E	Summers P	Tomlinson R	Urwin TA	Whitehead H	Williams D	Round
Q6	Dec	20	(a)	Brighton & Hove Albion	W 1-0	Williams	9250	8						7	3	2										11					6			5		9			4	1	10	Q6
1	Jan	10	(h)	COVENTRY CITY	D 2-2	Parker, Dodd	10000		11					10	3	2											7				6	8		5		9	1		4			1
Rep	Jan	16	(a)	Coventry City	W 1-0	Hoar	21893		11					10	3	2											7				6	8		5		9			4	1		Rep
2	Jan	31	(h)	LIVERPOOL	L 0-2	-	12640		11					10	3	2											7				6	8		5		9	1		4			2
						Apps		1	4	-	-	-	-	4	4	4	-	-	-	-	-	-	-	-	-	1	4	-	-	-	4	3	-	4	-	4	2	-	4	2	1	
						Goals		-	-	-	-	-	-	1	-	-	-	-	-	-	-	-	-	-	-	-	1	-	-	-	1	-	-	-	-	-	-	-	-	-	1	

▶ **The 1919/20 team** – Back row (left to right): Lawson (Trainer), C.Green (Secretary). Middle row (left to right): Urwin, Williams, Elvey, Whitehead, Rutherford, Dunn, Hill, Parker. Front row (left to right): Hoar, Roe, Simms, Dodd, Bookman.

TIMELINE...

May 1920 The clubs in the Southern League Division One are to form a new Division Three of the Football League in the following season.

1920/1921 FOOTBALL LEAGUE DIVISION THREE

Match No	Month	Day	Venue	Opponents	W/L/D Score	Scorers	Attendance	Bailey H	Bayliss LR	Bookman LO	Bradley JL	Butcher G	Cockerill HL	Higginbotham H	Hill FWP	Hoar SW	Hull F	Lamb JW	Lennon GF	Mathieson A	McKechnie J	Millar RM	Molyneux W	Parker TB	Pett EF	Roe A	Semple J	Shankland J	Sidney H	Simms E	Tirrell A	Walsh W	Walker Jimmy	Watson J	Match No
1	Aug	28	(a)	Swindon Town	L 1-9	Simms	10000			11	8							5	2	10				6	7	4	3			9				1	1
2	Aug	30	(h)	PORTSMOUTH	D 2-2	Hoar (pen), Simms	8000			11				8		7		5	2	10			4	6						9	3			1	2
3	Sep	4	(h)	SWINDON TOWN	W 2-0	Hoar (pen), Mathieson	11000	1		11			6	8		7			2	10			4	5						9	3				3
4	Sep	8	(a)	Portsmouth	L 0-3		16000	1		11			6	8		7			2	10			4	5						9	3				4
5	Sep	11	(h)	SWANSEA TOWN	W 3-0	Simms, Hill (2)	9000	1		11				8	10	7		6	2				4	5						9	3				5
6	Sep	18	(a)	Swansea Town	D 1-1	Hill	14000	1		11			6	8	10	7			2				4	5						9	3				6
7	Sep	25	(a)	Queens Park Rangers	L 1-4	Hill	20000	1		11			6	8	10	7			2				4	5						9	3				7
8	Oct	2	(h)	QUEENS PARK RANGERS	W 2-1	Simms (2)	10000			11				8	10	7		6	2				4	5						9	3			1	8
9	Oct	9	(h)	GRIMSBY TOWN	W 3-1	Simms (2), Bookman	10000	1		11				8		7		6	2	10			4	5						9	3				9
10	Oct	16	(a)	Grimsby Town	W 1-0	Simms	8000	1		11		8				7		6	2	10			4							9	3	5			10
11	Oct	23	(h)	BRIGHTON & HOVE ALBION	W 3-2	Mathieson, Hayes (og), Simms	11000	1		11		8				7		6	2	10			4							9	3	5			11
12	Oct	30	(a)	Brighton & Hove Albion	D 1-1	Mathieson	11000	1		11						7		6	2	10			4	5			8			9	3				12
13	Nov	6	(h)	CRYSTAL PALACE	D 2-2	Simms, Mathieson	11000	1		11						7		6	2	10			4	5			8			9	3				13
14	Nov	13	(a)	Crystal Palace	L 1-2	Simms	12000	1		11				8		7		6	2	10			4	5						9	3				14
15	Nov	20	(h)	NORWICH CITY	W 4-0	Bookman, Simms (3)	7000	1		11				8		7		6	2	10			4							9	3	5			15
16	Nov	27	(a)	Norwich City	L 0-3		9000	1		11				8		7		6	2	10			4							9	3	5			16
17	Dec	4	(h)	BRENTFORD	W 2-0	Simms, Mathieson	6000	1		11			6	8		7			2	10			4	5						9	3				17
18	Dec	11	(a)	Brentford	L 0-1	-	6000	1		11		8	6			5			2	10			4							9	3				18
19	Dec	25	(h)	SOUTHAMPTON	D 1-1	Simms	14000	1		11				8		7		6	2	10			4	5						9	3				19
20	Dec	27	(a)	Southampton	D 1-1	Mathieson	19793	1		11				8		7		6	2	10			4	5						9	3				20
21	Dec	28	(h)	GILLINGHAM	W 5-0	Mathieson (2), Higginbotham (2), Hoar	11000	1		11				8		7		6	2	10			4	5						9	3				21
22	Jan	1	(h)	BRISTOL ROVERS	L 1-2	Mathieson	9000	1		11			6	8		7			2	10			4	5						9	3				22
23	Jan	15	(a)	Northampton Town	L 0-1	-	7000	1		11	10	8				7		6	2				4	5						9	3				23
24	Jan	22	(h)	NORTHAMPTON TOWN	W 3-1	Bookman, Bradley, Simms	12000	1		11	10	8				7		6	2				4	5						9	3				24
25	Feb	5	(a)	Reading	W 1-0	Butcher	6000	1		11	10	8				7		6	2				4	5			9				3				25
26	Feb	9	(h)	READING	W 6-0	Simms (4), Hoar, Higginbotham	5000	1		11				8		7		6	2	10			4	5						9	3				26
27	Feb	12	(a)	Southend United	D 1-1	Simms	7000	1		11				8		7		6	2	10			4	5						9	3				27
28	Feb	26	(a)	Merthyr Town	L 1-4	Simms	15000				10			8		7		6	2				4	5					11	9	3			1	28
29	Mar	5	(h)	MERTHYR TOWN	W 1-0	Simms	8000	1		11				8		7		6	2	10				5						9	3	4			29
30	Mar	12	(a)	Plymouth Argyle	L 0-1	-	10000	1		11				8		7		6	2	10			4			5				9	3				30
31	Mar	19	(h)	PLYMOUTH ARGYLE	D 1-1	Simms	9000	1		11				8		7		6	2	10						5				9	3	4			31
32	Mar	25	(a)	Watford	L 0-1	-	11772	1		11						7		6	2	10			4	5				8		9	3				32
33	Mar	26	(h)	EXETER CITY	W 3-0	Simms (2), Mathieson	8000	1		11						7		6	2	10			4				5	8		9	3				33
34	Mar	28	(h)	WATFORD	W 1-0	Mathieson	12908	1		11				8		7		6	2	10			4	5						9	3				34
35	Mar	29	(a)	Bristol Rovers	L 0-5	-	6000	1	4	11						5		6	2	10						3		8		9	3				35
36	Apr	2	(a)	Exeter City	L 0-1	-	8000	1		11		8							2	10	7		4			5	3			9		6			36
37	Apr	9	(h)	MILLWALL	D 0-0	-	6000	1				10	6	7	8				2				4	5			9		11		3				37
38	Apr	16	(a)	Millwall	D 0-0	-	20000	1		11		8				7			2	10			4	6						9	3		5		38
39	Apr	23	(h)	NEWPORT COUNTY	D 2-2	Butcher (2)	5000	1		11		8				7			2	10		5	4	6						9	3				39
40	Apr	30	(a)	Newport County	L 0-2	-	8000	1		11		8				7			2	10			4	5						9	3	6			40
41	May	2	(h)	SOUTHEND UNITED	W 4-0	Simms (2), Hoar, Bookman		1		11		8				7			2	10			4	5						9	3	6			41
42	May	7	(a)	Gillingham	D 0-0	-	6000	1		11		8				7	2			10			4	5						9	3	6			42
				Final League Position: 9th		1 Own goal	**Apps**	38	1	40	5	16	8	27	6	39	3	24	37	29	1	1	36	35	1	11	7	3	2	40	37	10	1	4	
							Goals	-	-	4	1	3	-	3	4	5	-	-	-	11	-	-	-	-	-	-	-	-	-	29	-	-	-	-	

1920/1921 FA CUP

Round	Month	Day	Venue	Opponents	W/L/D Score	Scorers	Attendance	Bailey H	Bayliss LR	Bookman LO	Bradley JL	Butcher G	Cockerill HL	Higginbotham H	Hill FWP	Hoar SW	Hull F	Lamb JW	Lennon GF	Mathieson A	McKechnie J	Millar RM	Molyneux W	Parker TB	Pett EF	Roe A	Semple J	Shankland J	Sidney H	Simms E	Tirrell A	Walsh W	Walker Jimmy	Watson J	Round
Q6	Dec	18	(a)	Rotherham County	W 3-1	Simms (3)	6000	1		11				8		7		6	2	10			4	5						9	3				Q6
1	Jan	8	(h)	BIRMINGHAM	W 2-1	Simms, Bookman	12700	1		11				8		7		6	2	10			4	5						9	3				1
2	Jan	29	(a)	South Shields	W 4-0	Higginbotham, Butcher (2), Simms	21003	1		11		10		8		7		6	2				4	5						9	3				2
3	Feb	19	(h)	PRESTON NORTH END	L 2-3	Higginbotham (2)	17754	1		11		10		8		7		6	2				4	5						9	3				3
							Apps	4		4		2		4		4		4	4	2			4	4						4	4				
							Goals	-		1		2		3		-		-	-	-			-	-						5	-				

▶ Now making a name for himself in the Luton side after being gassed in the war, Leagrave born Sid Hoar was working his way towards a big money move to Arsenal, for whom he played in the 1927 F.A.Cup final.

▶ **The 1920/21 team** – Back row (left to right): Bailey, Watson, Abbott. Second row (left to right): C.Green (Secretary), H.Smart (Director), Mathieson, Reynolds, Semple, Lennon, Tirrell, Bookman, Hull, Cockerell, Higginbotham, Lawson (Trainer). Third row (left to right): Molyneux, Bayliss, Lamb, Parker, Cockerill, Roe, Hoar. Front row (left to right): Pett, Bradley, Hill, Simms, Davis, Wilkins, Atkin.

TIMELINE...

19 February 1921 17,754 cram into Kenilworth Road for a Third Round F.A.Cup tie against Preston.

1921/1922 FOOTBALL LEAGUE DIVISION THREE (SOUTH)

Match No	Month	Day	Venue	Opponents	W,L,D	Score	Scorers	Attendance	Bailey H	Bassett EJ	Bookman LO	Butcher G	Foster JH	Graham RC	Higginbotham H	Hoar SW	Lennon GF	Mathieson A	Millar RM	Molyneux W	Parker TB	Reid S	Roe A	Simms E	Stephenson John	Tirrell A	Walker Jimmy	Walsh W	Match No
1	Aug	27	(a)	Norwich City	W	1-0	Mathieson	12000	1		11	8				7	2	10		4	5			9		3		6	1
2	Aug	29	(h)	SOUTHAMPTON	D	0-0	-	10578	1		11	8				7	2	10		4				9		3	5	6	2
3	Sep	3	(h)	NORWICH CITY	W	2-1	Simms, Hoar	9798	1		11	8				7	2	10		4				9		3	5	6	3
4	Sep	5	(a)	Southampton	L	1-2	Simms	11000	1		11					7	2	10	6				8	9		3	5		4
5	Sep	10	(h)	NEWPORT COUNTY	W	4-0	Mathieson (2), Higginbotham, Simms	8353	1		11				8	7	2	10		4			6	9		3	5		5
6	Sep	14	(h)	EXETER CITY	W	4-0	Simms (3), Hoar	7304	1		11		5	2	8	7		10		4			6	9		3			6
7	Sep	17	(a)	Newport County	D	2-2	Simms (2)	7000	1		11				8	7	2	10		4			6	9		3	5		7
8	Sep	24	(h)	PLYMOUTH ARGYLE	W	1-0	Higginbotham	9886	1		11				8	7	2	10		4			6	9		3	5		8
9	Oct	1	(a)	Plymouth Argyle	L	0-2	-	19000	1		11	8				7	2	10		4			6	9		3	5		9
10	Oct	8	(h)	MERTHYR TOWN	W	3-0	Matthieson, Simms, Higginbotham	8631	1		11				8	7	2	10		4			6	9		3	5		10
11	Oct	15	(a)	Merthyr Town	L	0-2	-	12000	1		11			3	8	7	2	10		4			6	9			5		11
12	Oct	22	(h)	PORTSMOUTH	W	1-0	Walsh	8484	1	7		8	4		10	11	2						6			3	5	9	12
13	Oct	29	(a)	Portsmouth	D	1-1	Robson (og)	16004	1			8	4			7	2	10					6	9		3	5		13
14	Nov	5	(h)	SOUTHEND UNITED	W	3-0	Foster, Tirrell, Simms	8173	1	7		8	4			11	2	10					6	9		3	5		14
15	Nov	12	(a)	Southend United	W	1-0	Hoar	6000	1	7		8	4		10	11	2						6	9		3	5		15
16	Nov	19	(h)	SWANSEA TOWN	W	3-0	Hoar (2), Butcher	10253	1	7		8			10	9	2			4			6			3	5		16
17	Nov	26	(a)	Swansea Town	D	1-1	Butcher	15000	1	7		8			11	9	2			4			6			3	5		17
18	Dec	10	(a)	Exeter City	W	1-0	Butcher	5000	1	7		8	4		11		2	10					6	9		3	5		18
19	Dec	17	(h)	MILLWALL	W	1-0	Tirrell	8962	1	7		8			10								6	9		3	5		19
20	Dec	24	(a)	Millwall	D	1-1	Butcher	11000	1	7	11	10	4		8		2						6			3	5		20
21	Dec	26	(a)	Swindon Town	D	1-1	Walsh	12134	1	7	11	10	5		8		2						6			3		9	21
22	Dec	27	(h)	SWINDON TOWN	W	2-1	Higginbotham, Butcher	15743	1	7	11	10			8		2	9		4			6			3	5		22
23	Dec	31	(h)	GILLINGHAM	W	7-0	Simms (3), Bassett, Butcher (2), Higginbotham	7680	1	7	11	10	4		8				6					9	2	3	5		23
24	Jan	14	(a)	Gillingham	W	1-0	Simms	7000	1	7	11				8		2	10		4			6	9		3	5		24
25	Jan	21	(a)	Reading	L	1-2	Simms	5000	1	7	11				8		2	10		4			6	9		3	5		25
26	Feb	4	(a)	Bristol Rovers	L	0-2	-	8000	1		11	10	4		8	7	2		6				5	9		3			26
27	Feb	11	(h)	BRISTOL ROVERS	L	1-2	Simms	9530	1		11	10	4		8	7	2	10	6				5	9		3			27
28	Feb	18	(a)	Brentford	W	2-0	Bassett, Simms	10000	1	7	11	10	4		8		2						6	9		3	5		28
29	Feb	25	(h)	BRENTFORD	W	3-0	Higginbotham, Bethune (og), Simms	8970	1	7	11	10	4		8		2						6	9		3	5		29
30	Mar	6	(h)	READING	L	0-1	-	4404	1		11	10	4		8	7							6	9	2	3	5		30
31	Mar	11	(h)	ABERDARE ATHLETIC	L	1-2	Mathieson	7661	1		11	10	4		8	7	2	10					6			3	5		31
32	Mar	18	(a)	Brighton & Hove Albion	D	1-1	Bassett	8000	1	7		10			8	11	2			6	9				4	3	5		32
33	Mar	25	(h)	BRIGHTON & HOVE ALBION	W	2-0	Butcher, Higginbotham	5694	1	7		10			8	11	2			6	9				4	3			33
34	Apr	1	(h)	WATFORD	D	1-1	Reid	7691	1	7		10			8	11	2			6		9				3	4	5	34
35	Apr	8	(a)	Watford	L	1-4	Reid	7000	1	7	11		4		8		2	10				9	6			3	5		35
36	Apr	14	(a)	Queens Park Rangers	L	0-1	-	11000	1		11	10				7	2					9	6			3	5		36
37	Apr	15	(h)	CHARLTON ATHLETIC	W	2-0	Mathieson, Butcher	6524	1		11	10	5			7	2	9		4		8	6			3	5		37
38	Apr	17	(h)	QUEENS PARK RANGERS	W	3-1	Higginbotham (3)	9407	1		11		5		8	7	2	10		4		9	6			3			38
39	Apr	22	(a)	Charlton Athletic	W	1-0	Higginbotham	3000	1		11	10	4		8	7	2					9	6			3	5		39
40	Apr	29	(a)	Northampton Town	L	0-2	-	7000	1		11		4		8	7	2	10				9	6			3	5		40
41	May	1	(a)	Aberdare Athletic	L	0-2	-	10000	1	7		10	4		8	11	2					9	6		3		5		41
42	May	6	(h)	NORTHAMPTON TOWN	W	3-0	Walker (2), Higginbotham	7279	1	7		10	5		8	11	2			6		4				3	9		42
				Apps					42	21	32	30	23	2	30	33	39	25	8	20	1	10	35	25	6	39	34	7	
				Goals					-	3	-	9	1	-	12	5	-	6	-	-	-	-	2	18	-	2	2	2	

Final League Position: 4th   2 Own Goals

1921/1922 FA CUP

Round	Month	Day	Venue	Opponents	W,L,D	Score	Scorers	Attendance	Bailey H	Bassett EJ	Bookman LO	Butcher G	Foster JH	Graham RC	Higginbotham H	Hoar SW	Lennon GF	Mathieson A	Millar RM	Molyneux W	Parker TB	Reid S	Roe A	Simms E	Stephenson John	Tirrell A	Walker Jimmy	Walsh W	Round
1	Jan	7	(a)	Portsmouth	D	1-1	Bassett	22437	1	7	11	10	4		8		2						6	9		3	5		1
Rep	Jan	11	(h)	PORTSMOUTH	W	2-1	Higginbotham, Hoar	10480	1	7		10	4		8	11	2						6	9		3	5		Rep
2	Jan	28	(a)	Aston Villa	L	0-1	-	53832	1	7		10	4		8	11	2						6	9		3	5		2
				Apps					3	3	1	3	3	-	3	2	3						3	3		3	3		
				Goals					-	1	-	-	-	-	1	1	-							-		-	-		

The 1921/22 team – Back row (left to right): Bookman, Tirrell, Walker, Bailey, Foster, Roe, Lawson (Trainer), Millar. Front row (left to right): Bassett, Higginbotham, Simms, Butcher, Lennon, Hoar.

TIMELINE...

22 October 1921 Three Luton players appear in an international match. Ernie Simms is capped by England while in the opposing Northern Ireland side are Allan Mathieson and Louis Bookman.
11 March 1922 The Main Stand at Kenilworth Road is burnt down in mysterious circumstances.

1922/1923 FOOTBALL LEAGUE DIVISION THREE (SOUTH)

Match No	Month	Day	Venue	Opponents	W,L,D	Score	Scorers	Attendance	Bailey H	Bird SA	Bonsall C	Brown AC	Butcher G	Clarkson W	Cottingham T	Foster JH	Gibbon T	Graham RC	Henderson WJ	Higginbotham H	Hoar SW	Hoten RV	Irvine TB	Jennings W	Lennon GF	Millar RM	Molyneux W	Mosley HT	Reader AR	Reid S	Roe A	Stephenson John	Thompson R	Tirrell A	Walker Jimmy	Match No
1	Aug	26	(h)	CHARLTON ATHLETIC	D	2-2	Higginbotham, Hoar	11337	1			9	10							8	11			4	2			7		6				3	5	1
2	Aug	28	(a)	Brentford	L	2-3	Thompson (2)	10000	1				10	11					3	8	7			4	2					6			9		5	2
3	Sep	2	(a)	Charlton Athletic	L	1-2	Hoar	8000									1			8	7			4	2			11	10	6			9	3	5	3
4	Sep	4	(h)	BRENTFORD	W	4-0	Higginbotham, Hoar (2), Thompson	7361									1			8	7				2	6		11	10	4			9	3	5	4
5	Sep	9	(h)	BRIGHTON & HOVE ALBION	D	1-1	Reid	8651							8		1			9	7				2	6		11	10	4				3	5	5
6	Sep	16	(a)	Brighton & Hove Albion	W	1-0	Butcher	8000					10	11		4	1			8	7				2					9	6			3	5	6
7	Sep	23	(h)	SWINDON TOWN	W	3-2	Reid (2), Foster	8284					10	11		4	1			8	7				2					9	6			3	5	7
8	Sep	30	(a)	Swindon Town	D	1-1	Higginbotham	7000					10	11		4	1			8	7				2					9	6			3	5	8
9	Oct	7	(h)	ABERDARE ATHLETIC	W	4-1	Higginbotham, Thompson (2), Reid	8756						11		4	1			8	7				2					10	6		9	3	5	9
10	Oct	14	(a)	Aberdare Athletic	L	1-2	Reid	7000						11		4	1			8	7				2					10	6		9	3	5	10
11	Oct	21	(h)	PLYMOUTH ARGYLE	W	2-1	Thompson, Higginbotham	10420						11		4	1			8	7				2					10	6		9	3	5	11
12	Oct	28	(a)	Plymouth Argyle	L	0-4	-	10000						11		4	1			8	7				2				10	9	6			3	5	12
13	Nov	4	(a)	Newport County	W	3-0	Higginbotham (2), Butcher	7000					10	11		4	1			8	7				2					9	6			3	5	13
14	Nov	11	(h)	NEWPORT COUNTY	W	1-0	Tirrell	7957					10	11		4	1			8	7				2					9	6			3	5	14
15	Nov	18	(a)	Watford	L	1-2	Clarkson	10000					10	11		4	1			8	7				2					9	6			3	5	15
16	Nov	25	(h)	WATFORD	L	0-1	-	11222					10	11		4	1			8					2				9	7	6			3	5	16
17	Dec	2	(h)	BRISTOL CITY	D	1-1	Higginbotham	8147					10	11		4	1			8					2					9	6		7	3	5	17
18	Dec	9	(a)	Bristol City	L	0-1	-	15000					8	11			1					10			2		4			9	6		7	3	5	18
19	Dec	16	(a)	Portsmouth	W	2-1	Walker, Thompson	10185		1			8	11								10					4			9	6	2	7	3	5	19
20	Dec	23	(h)	PORTSMOUTH	L	0-2	-	7810					8	11			1					10					4			9	6	2	7	3	5	20
21	Dec	25	(a)	Queens Park Rangers	L	0-4	-	16000					8	11			1					10					4			9	6	2	7	3	5	21
22	Dec	26	(h)	QUEENS PARK RANGERS	W	1-0	Higginbotham	11829						11			1			8	7				2		4		10	9	6			3	5	22
23	Dec	30	(h)	MILLWALL	D	2-2	Molyneux, Reid	6864						11			1			8	7				2		4		10	9	6			3	5	23
24	Jan	6	(a)	Millwall	D	0-0	-	20000					8	11			1				7	10		5	2		4			9	6			3		24
25	Jan	20	(h)	SWANSEA TOWN	W	6-1	Reid (3), Higginbotham, Hoar, Clarkson	6322					10	11			1			8	7			5	2		4			9	6			3		25
26	Jan	27	(a)	Swansea Town	L	0-1	-	20000					8	11			1				7	10		5	2		4			9	6			3		26
27	Feb	3	(h)	BRISTOL ROVERS	W	1-0	Reid	7333					10	11			1			8	7			5	2		4			9	6			3		27
28	Feb	10	(a)	Bristol Rovers	D	1-1	Reid	9000					10	11			1			8	7			5	2		4			9	6			3		28
29	Feb	17	(h)	READING	L	1-2	Butcher	6907					8	11			1				7		10		2		4			9	6			3	5	29
30	Feb	24	(a)	Reading	L	0-3	-	7000					8	11			1				7		10		2		4			9	6			3	5	30
31	Mar	3	(h)	SOUTHEND UNITED	W	2-0	Reid, Hoten	6614					8	11			1				7	10		5	2		4			9	6			3		31
32	Mar	10	(a)	Southend United	W	3-1	Hoten, Reid (2)	7296					8	11			1				7	10		5	2		4			9	6			3		32
33	Mar	17	(a)	Merthyr Town	W	1-0	Clarkson	6000					8	11			1				7	10		5	2		4			9	6			3		33
34	Mar	24	(h)	MERTHYR TOWN	W	2-1	Hoten, Reid	6188					8	11			1				7	10		5	2		4			9	6			3		34
35	Mar	30	(a)	Gillingham	L	0-1	-	8000					8	11			1	7				10		5	2		4			9	6			3		35
36	Mar	31	(h)	Exeter City	W	2-1	Hoar, Tirrell	7000					8	11			1				7	10		5	2		4			9	6			3		36
37	Apr	2	(h)	GILLINGHAM	W	2-0	Reid, Hoten	8950					8	11		2	1				7	10		5			4			9	6			3		37
38	Apr	7	(h)	EXETER CITY	W	6-0	Roe, Hoten (3), Butcher (2)	6076					8	11		2	1				7	10		5			4			9	6			3		38
39	Apr	14	(a)	Northampton Town	L	0-2	-	10000					8	11		2	1					10		5			4			9	6	7		3		39
40	Apr	21	(h)	NORTHAMPTON TOWN	W	2-1	Reid (2)	7771					8	11		2	1					10		5			4			9	6		7	3		40
41	Apr	28	(a)	Norwich City	W	2-1	Jennings, Butcher	6000					8	11			1	4			7	10		5	2					9	6			3		41
42	May	5	(h)	NORWICH CITY	W	4-0	Butcher, Bonsall, Hoten, Hoar	5807			11		8				1	4			7	10			2					9	6			3	5	42
				Final League Position: 5th				**Apps**	2	1	1	1	33	32	1	14	39	9	1	23	36	12	8	30	31	2	23	3	7	33	30	4	17	40	29	
								Goals	-	-	1	-	7	3	-	1	-	-	-	10	7	8	-	1	-	-	1	-	-	18	1	-	7	2	1	

1922/1923 FA CUP

Round	Month	Day	Venue	Opponents	W,L,D	Score	Scorers	Attendance	Bailey H	Bird SA	Bonsall C	Brown AC	Butcher G	Clarkson W	Cottingham T	Foster JH	Gibbon T	Graham RC	Henderson WJ	Higginbotham H	Hoar SW	Hoten RV	Irvine TB	Jennings W	Lennon GF	Millar RM	Molyneux W	Mosley HT	Reader AR	Reid S	Roe A	Stephenson John	Thompson R	Tirrell A	Walker Jimmy	Round
1	Jan	13	(a)	Bury	L	1-2	Tirrell (pen)	16327					10	11			1			8	7			5	2		4				6			3	9	1
								Apps	-	-	-	-	1	1	-	-	1	-	-	1	1	-	-	1	1	-	1	-	-	-	1	-	-	1	1	
								Goals	-	-	-	-	-	-	-	-	-	-	-	-	-	-	-	-	-	-	-	-	-	-	-	-	-	1	-	

◗ **The 1922/23 team** – Back row (left to right): Dormer, Mosley, Molyneux. Second row (left to right): Brown, Parker, Graham, Bailey, Gibbon, Bird. Third row (left to right): W.Soper (Director), W.Allen (Director), H.Smart (Director), Pakes (Trainer), Millar, Stephenson, Foster, Jennings, Higginbotham, Reader, Irvine, S.Godfrey (Director), J.Smith (Director), E.Mouse (Director). Fourth row (left to right): C.Green (Secretary), Hoar, Reid, Thompson, Tirrell, Butcher, Clarkson, Lennon, Lawson (Trainer). Front row (left to right): Walker, Roe.

TIMELINE...

26 August 1922 At Kenilworth Road a magnificent new Main Stand is formally opened by J.P.McKenna, President of the Football League.

1923/1924 FOOTBALL LEAGUE DIVISION THREE (SOUTH)

Match No	Month	Day	Venue	Opponents	W,L,D Score	Scorers	Attendance	Anderson R	Bonsall C	Butcher G	Clarke PR	Danskin C	Foster JH	Gibbon T	Graham RC	Green J	Henderson WJ	Hoar SW	Hoten RV	Jennings W	Kerr A	Millar RM	Molyneux W	Orr J	Pearson J	Prentice H	Reid S	Roe A	Shepherd John	Till J	Tirrell A	Walker Jimmy	Match No
1	Aug	25	(a)	Swansea Town	L 0-1	-	18000					11	4	1	2	8		7	10	5	9	6									3		1
2	Aug	27	(h)	NORTHAMPTON TOWN	D 1-1	Green	9674					11	4	1	2	8		7	10	5	9	6				3							2
3	Sep	1	(h)	SWANSEA TOWN	L 1-2	Kerr	9387		11	8			4	1				7	10	5	9	6								2	3		3
4	Sep	3	(a)	Northampton Town	L 0-2	-	9968			8				1		9		7	11	10	5		4					6		2	3		4
5	Sep	8	(a)	Brentford	L 1-2	Reid	8000		11	8			4	1				7	10	5							9	6		2	3		5
6	Sep	15	(h)	BRENTFORD	W 2-1	Kerr (2)	7508		11					1		8		7	10	5	9									3	2	4	6
7	Sep	22	(a)	Portsmouth	L 0-3	-	11375					11		1		8		7	10	5	9									3	2	4	7
8	Sep	29	(h)	PORTSMOUTH	W 4-1	Kerr (3), Hoten	8516	2		8		11		1				7	10	5	9	6								3		4	8
9	Oct	6	(a)	Exeter City	L 1-2	Kerr	6000	2		8				1	11			7	10	5	9	6								3		4	9
10	Oct	13	(h)	EXETER CITY	W 1-0	Hoten	8125	2		8				1	11			7	10	5	9	6								3		4	10
11	Oct	20	(a)	Aberdare Athletic	W 1-0	Hoten	6000	2		11				1	8			7	10	5	9	6								3		4	11
12	Oct	27	(h)	ABERDARE ATHLETIC	W 1-0	Hoten	7154	2		11				1	8			7	10	5	9	6								3		4	12
13	Nov	3	(h)	WATFORD	D 0-0	-	9560	2		11				1	8			7	10	5	9	6								3		4	13
14	Nov	10	(a)	Watford	D 0-0	-	9407	2		11				1	8			7	10	5	9	6								3		4	14
15	Nov	17	(a)	Millwall	W 1-0	Kerr	15000	2		11				1	8			7	10	5	9	6								3		4	15
16	Nov	24	(h)	MILLWALL	W 2-0	Hoar, Kerr	7134	2		11				1	8			7	10	5	9	6								3		4	16
17	Dec	1	(h)	BOURNEMOUTH	W 6-2	Hoar (2), Kerr (4)	7155	2		11				1	8			7	10	5	9	6								3		4	17
18	Dec	8	(a)	Bournemouth	W 3-2	Kerr, Green, Butcher	3000	2		11				1	8			7	10	5	9	6								3		4	18
19	Dec	15	(h)	READING	W 2-0	Hoten, Green	7656	2		11				1	8			7	10	5	9	6								3		4	19
20	Dec	22	(a)	Reading	W 1-0	Hoar	4406	2		11					8			7	10	5	9	6		1						3		4	20
21	Dec	25	(h)	BRIGHTON & HOVE ALBION	D 0-0	-	13059	2		11					8			7	10	5	9	6		1						3		4	21
22	Dec	26	(a)	Brighton & Hove Albion	L 0-4	-	15457	2					5		8				11		9	6		1		7	10			3		4	22
23	Dec	29	(h)	SOUTHEND UNITED	D 4-4	Millar, Kerr, Hoar (2)	6966	2			10		5					7	11		9	6		1					1	3		4	23
24	Jan	5	(a)	Southend United	D 1-1	Foster	7000	2	11				4		8				10		9	6		1			7			3		5	24
25	Jan	19	(a)	Gillingham	D 0-0	-	5000	2	11						8				10	4	9	6		1			7			3		5	25
26	Jan	26	(h)	GILLINGHAM	D 1-1	Bonsall	6763	2	11						8				10	5	9	6		1						3		4	26
27	Feb	2	(a)	Queens Park Rangers	W 2-0	Green (2)	9000	4	11							8		7	10		9							6		3		5	27
28	Feb	9	(h)	QUEENS PARK RANGERS	W 2-0	Kerr (2)	5711	4	11							8		7	10		9							6		3		5	28
29	Feb	16	(a)	Plymouth Argyle	D 0-0	-	6000	4				11				8		7	10		9							6		3		5	29
30	Feb	23	(h)	PLYMOUTH ARGYLE	L 0-2	-	8379	4				11				8		7	10		9							6		3		5	30
31	Mar	1	(a)	Newport County	L 0-1	-	9000	2				11				8		7	10		9							6		3		5	31
32	Mar	8	(h)	NEWPORT COUNTY	W 2-0	Walker, Hoar	6407	2	11						4			7	10		9							6		3		5	32
33	Mar	15	(h)	MERTHYR TOWN	D 1-1	Butcher	6076	2	11						4			7	10		9							6		3		5	33
34	Mar	22	(a)	Merthyr Town	D 0-0	-	11000	8	10					1	2			7	9	4								6		3		5	34
35	Mar	29	(h)	CHARLTON ATHLETIC	L 0-1	-	5070		10						1	2		7	11	4	8						9	6		3		5	35
36	Apr	5	(a)	Charlton Athletic	D 1-1	Kerr	2000			8					1	2		7	11	5	9	6					10			3		4	36
37	Apr	12	(h)	NORWICH CITY	W 2-1	Reid, Kerr	3963	2		8					1	3		7	11	5	9	6					10					4	37
38	Apr	18	(h)	BRISTOL ROVERS	D 0-0	-	7151	2		8					1			7	11	5	9	6					10			3		4	38
39	Apr	19	(a)	Norwich City	L 0-2	-	7000	2		8					1	3		7	11	5	9	6					10					4	39
40	Apr	21	(a)	Bristol Rovers	D 1-1	Kerr	6000	2		8						3		7	11	5	9	6		1			10					4	40
41	Apr	26	(h)	SWINDON TOWN	W 3-2	Butcher, Reid (2)	3801	2		8						3		7	11	5	9	6		1			10					4	41
42	May	3	(a)	Swindon Town	L 2-3	Reid (2)	4716	2		8						6			10	5	7	11		1			9				3		4	42
				Apps				35	7	30	1	10	10	30	16	26	1	38	42	32	39	29	1	9	1	1	13	11	3	34	6	37	
				Goals				-	1	3	-	-	1	-	-	5	-	7	5	-	20	1	-	-	-	-	6	-	-	-	-	1	

Final League Position: 7th

1923/1924 FA CUP

Round	Month	Day	Venue	Opponents	W,L,D Score	Scorers	Attendance	Anderson R	Bonsall C	Butcher G	Clarke PR	Danskin C	Foster JH	Gibbon T	Graham RC	Green J	Henderson WJ	Hoar SW	Hoten RV	Jennings W	Kerr A	Millar RM	Molyneux W	Orr J	Pearson J	Prentice H	Reid S	Roe A	Shepherd John	Till J	Tirrell A	Walker Jimmy	Round
1	Jan	12	(a)	Arsenal	L 1-4	Green	37500	2		10						8		7	11	5	9	6		1						3		4	1
				Apps				1		1						1		1	1	1	1	1		1						1		1	
				Goals												1																

The Match Card for the 4-4 draw against Southend.

The 1923/24 team – Back row (left to right): E.Mouse (Director), Westgarth (Trainer), Walker, Anderson, Gibbon, Till, Millar, Graham, E.Gibbs (Director). Front row (left to right): Hoar, Butcher, Jennings, Kerr, Hoten, Danskin.

1924/1925 FOOTBALL LEAGUE DIVISION THREE (SOUTH)

Match No	Month	Day	Venue	Opponents	W,L,D	Score	Scorers	Attendance	Anderson R	Brookes GH	Brown TH	Butcher G	Cockle ES	Dennis GT	Graham RC	Hoar SW	Hoten RV	Jennings W	Johnson Joe	Keen WJ	Kerr A	Mackey JA	Millar RM	Mills J	Neal S	Reid S	Richards AC	Roe A	Shankly J	Thirlaway WJ	Till J	Tricker RW	Walker Jimmy	Match No
1	Aug	30	(h)	GILLINGHAM	D	0-0	-	8000	2	1	11					7	10	5	3					6	9				8				4	1
2	Sep	1	(h)	MILLWALL	D	1-1	Hoar	8000	2	1			8	11		7	10	5	3	9				6									4	2
3	Sep	6	(a)	Bournemouth	L	1-2	Cockle	6000	2	1			8	11		7	10	5		9				6							3		4	3
4	Sep	8	(h)	EXETER CITY	D	1-1	Shankly	6000	2	1			8	11		7		5		9				6						10	3		4	4
5	Sep	13	(h)	BRIGHTON & HOVE ALBION	W	3-1	Kerr (2), Mills	7000		1			8	11		7		5	2		9			6						10	3		4	5
6	Sep	15	(a)	Northampton Town	L	0-1	-	5340		1			8	11	3	7		5	2		9			6						10			4	6
7	Sep	20	(a)	Plymouth Argyle	L	0-4	-	12000		1			8	11	3	7		5	2		9			6						10			4	7
8	Sep	22	(h)	NORTHAMPTON TOWN	W	2-0	Dennis, Shankly	5000		1	11			10	3			5	2		9	7		6					8				4	8
9	Sep	24	(h)	BRISTOL CITY	W	3-0	Hoar, Dennis, Shankly	11000		1	11			10	3	7		5	2		9			6					8				4	9
10	Sep	27	(a)	Swindon Town	L	1-4	Shankly	7886		1	11			10	3	7		5	2		9			6					8				4	10
11	Oct	4	(a)	Reading	L	0-3	-			1	11			10	3	7		5	2		9			6					8				4	11
12	Oct	11	(h)	ABERDARE ATHLETIC	D	0-0	-	6000		1			9	11	3	7	10	5	2					6					8				4	12
13	Oct	18	(a)	Norwich City	D	1-1	Dennis	9000	2	1			8	11	3	7	10	5			9			6									4	13
14	Oct	25	(a)	Charlton Athletic	L	0-2	-	5000	2	1	7		8	11	3		10	5			9			6									4	14
15	Nov	1	(h)	QUEENS PARK RANGERS	W	3-0	Mills, Butcher, Dennis	4000	2	1	11	8		10	3	7		5			9			6									4	15
16	Nov	8	(a)	Merthyr Town	D	0-0	-	5000	2	1	11	8		10	3	7		5			9			6									4	16
17	Nov	22	(a)	Swansea Town	L	1-4	Reid	15000	2	1	11	8		10	3	7		5						6		9							4	17
18	Nov	29	(a)	Millwall	D	2-2	Butcher, Kerr	16000	2	1		7	8	11	3			5			9			6		10							4	18
19	Dec	6	(a)	Bristol Rovers	D	1-1	Kerr	8000	2	1		7	8	11	3			5			9			6		10							4	19
20	Dec	13	(h)	NEWPORT COUNTY	D	2-2	Shankly, Reid	3000	2	1				11	3			5			9					10	7	6	8				4	20
21	Dec	20	(a)	Southend United	L	1-2	Reid	5000	2	1			8	11	3			5			9			6		10	7						4	21
22	Dec	25	(a)	Watford	D	1-1	Reid	7000	2	1			8	11				5				7	6			10						9	4	22
23	Dec	26	(h)	WATFORD	L	0-3	-	14000	2	1			8	11	3			5			9	7	6			10							4	23
24	Dec	27	(a)	Gillingham	L	1-4	Reid	1000	2	1			8	11				5			9	7	6			10							4	24
25	Jan	3	(h)	BOURNEMOUTH	L	0-2	-	5000	2	1		8		11								7	4	6	5						3	9		25
26	Jan	17	(a)	Brighton & Hove Albion	L	1-2	Mackey	7246	2	1	11			10				5				7	4	6					8		3			26
27	Jan	24	(h)	PLYMOUTH ARGYLE	D	1-1	Shankly	5000	2	1	11			10				5					9	6					8		3		4	27
28	Feb	7	(h)	SWINDON TOWN	D	2-2	Dennis (2)	5000	2	1				11				5					9	6		10			8		3		4	28
29	Feb	14	(a)	Aberdare Athletic	D	1-1	Dennis	3000	2	1	11			10				5					9	6					8		3		4	29
30	Feb	21	(h)	NORWICH CITY	D	0-0	-	5000	2	1	11			10				5					9	6					8	7	3		4	30
31	Feb	28	(h)	CHARLTON ATHLETIC	W	1-0	Reid	5000	2	1				11				5					9	6		10			8	7	3		4	31
32	Mar	4	(a)	Bristol City	L	0-2	-	6000	2	1				11				5						6		10			8	7	3	9	4	32
33	Mar	7	(a)	Queens Park Rangers	L	1-2	Reid	7000	2	1				11				5					9	6		10			8	7	3		4	33
34	Mar	14	(h)	MERTHYR TOWN	W	6-0	Reid, Shankly (2), Jennings, Dennis, Kerr	5000	2	1				11				5			9			6		10			8	7	3		4	34
35	Mar	21	(h)	READING	W	1-0	Reid	3000	2	1				11				5					9	6		10			8	7	3		4	35
36	Mar	28	(h)	SWANSEA TOWN	D	0-0	-	7000	2	1				11				5					9	6		10			8	7	3		4	36
37	Apr	4	(a)	Exeter City	W	1-0	Dennis	5000	2	1				11				5					9	6		10			8	7	3		4	37
38	Apr	10	(a)	Brentford	L	0-3	-	8000	2	1				11				5					9	6		10			8	7	3		4	38
39	Apr	11	(h)	BRISTOL ROVERS	D	1-1	Dennis	6000	2	1				11				5					9	6		10			8	7	3		4	39
40	Apr	13	(h)	BRENTFORD	W	3-1	Dennis (2), Shankly	6000	2	1				11				5						6		10			8	7	3	9	4	40
41	Apr	18	(a)	Newport County	D	1-1	Shankly	7000		1				11	2			5					9	6		10			8	7	3		4	41
42	Apr	25	(h)	SOUTHEND UNITED	W	4-0	Reid (3), Shankly	5000		1				11	2			5						6		10			8	7	3	9	4	42
								Apps	30	42	15	12	7	41	21	14	6	35	11	3	29	10	28	31	2	26	2	6	28	13	22	4	24	
								Goals	-	-	-	2	1	12	-	2	-	1	-	-	5	1	-	2	-	12	-	-	11	-	-	-	-	

Final League Position: 16th

1924/1925 FA CUP

Round	Month	Day	Venue	Opponents	W,L,D	Score	Scorers	Attendance	Anderson R	Brookes GH	Brown TH	Butcher G	Cockle ES	Dennis GT	Graham RC	Hoar SW	Hoten RV	Jennings W	Johnson Joe	Keen WJ	Kerr A	Mackey JA	Millar RM	Mills J	Neal S	Reid S	Richards AC	Roe A	Shankly J	Thirlaway WJ	Till J	Tricker RW	Walker Jimmy	Round
1	Jan	10	(a)	West Bromwich Albion	L	0-4	-	30287	2	1		10		11	3							7	4	5	6	8						9		1
								Apps	1	1	-	1	-	1	1	-	-	-	-	-	-	1	1	1	1	1	-	-	-	-	-	1	-	
								Goals	-	-	-	-	-	-	-	-	-	-	-	-	-	-	-	-	-	-	-	-	-	-	-	-	-	

◗ Trainer Fred Westgarth takes something from the eye of Will Jennings.

◗ **The 1924/25 team** – Back row (left to right): Walker, Till, Graham, Brookes, Mills, Jennings, Roe. Front row (left to right): Hoten, Kerr, Dennis, Reid.

TIMELINE...
16 February 1925 The Town appoint their first manager, George Thompson.

1925/1926 FOOTBALL LEAGUE DIVISION THREE (SOUTH)

Match No	Month	Day	Venue	Opponents	W,L,D Score	Scorers	Attendance	Agnew W	Anderson R	Bedford SG	Dennis GT	Graham RC	Jennings W	Littlewood SC	Love T	Millar RM	Miller J	Mingay HJ	Moffatt H	Neal S	Purdy A	Reid S	Rennie A	Richards D	Robinson F	Shankly J	Thompson JW	Thomson NS	Till J	Walker Jimmy	Match No
1	Aug	29	(a)	Merthyr Town	L 1-2	Reid	8057		2		11	5				6	7	1				10					9	8	3	4	1
2	Aug	31	(h)	BOURNEMOUTH	W 4-1	Thompson (2), Shankly, Reid	7880		2		11	3	5			6	7	1				10				8	9			4	2
3	Sep	5	(h)	NEWPORT COUNTY	W 4-2	Shankly (2), Dennis (pen), Thompson	6816		2		11	3	5			6		1	7			10				8	9			4	3
4	Sep	9	(a)	Bournemouth	D 2-2	Thompson, Dennis	5612		2		11	3	5			6		1	7			10				8	9			4	4
5	Sep	12	(a)	Watford	L 0-2	-	13035		2		11	3	5			6		1	7			10				8	9			4	5
6	Sep	14	(h)	READING	L 0-1	-	7289		2		11	3	5					1	7		4	9				8	10			6	6
7	Sep	19	(a)	Queens Park Rangers	L 0-1	-	5198				11	2	5			6		1	7							8	9	10	3	4	7
8	Sep	26	(h)	BRISTOL ROVERS	W 1-0	Reid	7100				11	3	5			6		1	7		4	10				8	9		2		8
9	Sep	30	(a)	Reading	L 0-3	-	5621			4	11	3	5			6		1	7							8	9	10	2		9
10	Oct	3	(a)	Swindon Town	L 0-2	-	7482				11	3	5			6		1	7		4	10				8	9		2		10
11	Oct	10	(h)	EXETER CITY	D 1-1	Shankly	7046				11	3	5			6	7	1			4	10				8	9		2		11
12	Oct	17	(h)	BRIGHTON & HOVE ALBION	D 3-3	Littlewood, Millar, Shankly	7522		2			6		9		10	7	1			4		5			8	11		3	4	12
13	Oct	24	(a)	Aberdare Athletic	W 5-2	Graham (2), Till, Thompson, Shankly	4266				10	6	5	9			7	1			4		5			8	11		3		13
14	Oct	31	(h)	CRYSTAL PALACE	W 3-2	Shankly (3)	7980				10	6	5	9			7	1			4		5			8	11		3		14
15	Nov	7	(a)	Brentford	L 0-1	-	7533				10	6	2	5	9		7	1			4		5			8	11	10	3		15
16	Nov	14	(h)	NORWICH CITY	W 3-2	Thompson, Littlewood, Miller	6380				10	6	5	9			7	1			4		5			8	11		2		16
17	Nov	21	(a)	Southend United	L 0-2	-	6706				10	6	5	9		6		1	7				5			8	11		2		17
18	Dec	5	(a)	Bristol City	L 1-5	Miller	10208				11	6	2	5	9	6	7				4						10		3		18
19	Dec	19	(a)	Millwall	L 0-7	-	10418		4			6	2		9	6		9			7			5			11	10	3		19
20	Dec	25	(a)	Gillingham	L 1-2	Thompson	6350	9			10	6	2						7	5	1	8		4			11		3		20
21	Dec	26	(h)	GILLINGHAM	W 5-3	Dennis (2), Thompson (2), Reid	9898	10			11	6	2						7	5	1	8		4			9		3		21
22	Dec	28	(h)	PLYMOUTH ARGYLE	D 1-1	Dennis (pen)	9717	10			11	6	2						7	5	1	8		4			9		3		22
23	Jan	2	(h)	MERTHYR TOWN	W 4-0	Thompson (2), Dennis (pen), Agnew	5858	10			11	6	2						7	5	1			4			9	8	3		23
24	Jan	16	(a)	Newport County	L 1-2	Thompson	4498	10			11	6	2						7	5	1			4			9	8	3		24
25	Jan	23	(h)	WATFORD	W 5-0	Agnew (2), Dennis, Thompson, Thomson	7233	10			11	6	2						7	5	1			4			9	8	3		25
26	Jan	30	(h)	QUEENS PARK RANGERS	W 4-0	Thompson, Thomson, Moffatt, Dennis	6750	10			11	6	2						7	5	1			4			9	8	3		26
27	Feb	6	(a)	Bristol Rovers	D 2-2	Thompson (2)	5896	10			11	6	2						7	5	1			4			9	8	3		27
28	Feb	13	(h)	SWINDON TOWN	W 4-1	Thompson (2), Dennis (pen), Agnew	8588	10			11	6	2						7	4	1			5			9	8	3		28
29	Feb	20	(a)	Exeter City	D 2-2	Thomson, Dennis (pen)	6540	10			11	6	2						7	4	1			5			9	8	3		29
30	Feb	22	(h)	NORTHAMPTON TOWN	W 3-2	Dennis (2 pens), Moffatt	5549	10			11	6	2						7	4	1			5			9	8	3		30
31	Feb	27	(a)	Brighton & Hove Albion	L 0-2	-	7721	10			11	6	2						7	4	1			5			9	8	3		31
32	Mar	6	(h)	ABERDARE ATHLETIC	W 2-1	Thompson, Thomson	7746	10			11	6	2						7	4	1			5			9	8	3		32
33	Mar	13	(a)	Crystal Palace	L 0-3	-	12306	10			11	6	2						7	4	1			5			9	8	3		33
34	Mar	20	(h)	BRENTFORD	W 4-2	Thompson (2), Agnew, Moffatt	6072	10			11	6	2						7	4	1			5			9	8	3		34
35	Mar	27	(a)	Norwich City	L 0-2	-	5763	10			11	6	2						7	4	1			5			9	8	3		35
36	Apr	2	(h)	CHARLTON ATHLETIC	W 1-0	Miller	8509	10				6	2				7	1	11	4				5			9	8	3		36
37	Apr	3	(h)	SOUTHEND UNITED	W 2-0	Robinson, Thomson	7239	10				6	2				1	7	4					5	11		9	8	3		37
38	Apr	5	(a)	Charlton Athletic	L 1-2	Dennis (pen)	4493	10			11	6	2				1	7	4					5			9	8	3		38
39	Apr	10	(a)	Plymouth Argyle	L 3-4	Dennis, Agnew, Thomson	12641	10			11	6	2						7	4	1			5			9	8	3		39
40	Apr	17	(h)	BRISTOL CITY	W 4-1	Thompson (2), Moffatt, Agnew	7336	10			11	6	2				1	7	4					5			9	8	3		40
41	Apr	24	(a)	Northampton Town	W 1-0	Dennis	6697	10			11	6	2				1	7	4					5			9	8	3		41
42	May	1	(h)	MILLWALL	D 2-2	Thompson (2)	9303	10			11	6	2				1	7	4					5			9	8	3		42
				Apps				23	9	1	36	41	17	6	2	39	10	18	33	25	24	13	15	18	1	18	42	26	37	8	
				Goals				7	-	-	15	2	-	2	-	1	3	-	4	-	-	4	-	-	1	9	25	6	1	-	

Final League Position: 7th

1925/1926 FA CUP

Round	Month	Day	Venue	Opponents	W,L,D Score	Scorers	Attendance	Agnew W	Anderson R	Bedford SG	Dennis GT	Graham RC	Jennings W	Littlewood SC	Love T	Millar RM	Miller J	Mingay HJ	Moffatt H	Neal S	Purdy A	Reid S	Rennie A	Richards D	Robinson F	Shankly J	Thompson JW	Thomson NS	Till J	Walker Jimmy	Round
1	Nov	28	(h)	FOLKESTONE	W 3-0	Reid, Littlewood, Shankly	7019				11	3	6	9		4	7				1	8		5			10		2		1
2	Dec	12	(a)	Aberdare Athletic	L 0-1	-	6500		2		11	6				4			9		1	8		5			10	7	3		2
				Apps				-	1	-	2	2	1	1	-	2	1	-	1	-	2	2	-	2	-	-	2	1	2	-	
				Goals				-	-	-	-	-	-	1	-	-	-	-	-	-	-	1	-	-	-	1	-	-	-	-	

▶ **The 1925/26 team** – Back row (left to right): Robinson, Graham, Purdy, Mingay, Till, Walker, Anderson. Middle row (left to right): C.Green (Secretary), Rogers, Richards, Thomson, Bedford, Neil, Thompson, Millar, Littlewood, Barr (Trainer). Front row (left to right): Miller, Shanley, Jennings, G. Thompson (Manager), Moffatt, Reid, Dennis.

1926/1927 FOOTBALL LEAGUE DIVISION THREE (SOUTH)

Match No	Month	Day	Venue	Opponents	W,L,D Score	Scorers	Attendance	Agnew W	Black JR	Clark J	Dennis GT	Fraser CR	Gordon J	Graham RC	Harper WG	Kingham HR	Millar RM	Mingay HJ	Moir RM	Panther FG	Pointon J	Reid S	Rennie A	Richards D	Thompson JW	Thomson NS	Till J	Woods Harry	Yardley J	Match No
1	Aug	28	(a)	Bristol Rovers	W 2-1	Thompson (2)	13705	10		11				2			6	1			7	5	4	9	8	3				1
2	Aug	30	(h)	BRENTFORD	W 2-1	Millar, Thomson	9090	10		11				2			6	1			7	5	4	9	8	3				2
3	Sep	4	(h)	SWINDON TOWN	D 1-1	Thompson	11386	10		11				2			6	1			7	5	4	9	8	3				3
4	Sep	11	(a)	Exeter City	W 2-1	Graham (pen), Thompson	8444	10		11				2			6	1			7	5	4	9	8	3				4
5	Sep	13	(h)	NORTHAMPTON TOWN	W 2-0	Graham (pen), Thomson	8856			11				2			6	1			7	5	4	9	8	3		10		5
6	Sep	18	(h)	MERTHYR TOWN	W 2-1	Thompson, Woods	9920			11			5	2			6	1			7		4	9	8	3		10		6
7	Sep	25	(a)	Southend United	L 1-2	Thompson	9211			11				2			6	1	5		7		4	9	8	3		10		7
8	Oct	2	(h)	GILLINGHAM	W 2-1	Thompson (2)	9138		7	11			5	2			6	1					4	9	8	3		10		8
9	Oct	9	(h)	NORWICH CITY	D 2-2	Clark, Dennis	8775		7	11			5	2			6	1					4	9	8	3		10		9
10	Oct	16	(a)	Newport County	L 2-3	Woods, Reid	6821		7	11	10		4	2			6	1				5	9			3		8		10
11	Oct	23	(h)	ABERDARE ATHLETIC	D 3-3	Pointon (2), Dennis	7329			11	10		4	2			6	1			7	9	5			3		8		11
12	Oct	30	(a)	Watford	L 1-2	Thomson	12199			11	10		4	2	1		6				7	5	9		8	3				12
13	Nov	6	(h)	CRYSTAL PALACE	W 1-0	Woods	7343	10	4	11				2	1		6				7	5	9			3		8		13
14	Nov	13	(a)	Coventry City	L 1-4	Clark	6349		4	11	10				1		6				7	5	9	2		3		8		14
15	Nov	20	(h)	QUEENS PARK RANGERS	W 2-0	Reid, Woods	5075	10	4	11					1		6				7	9	5	2		3		8		15
16	Dec	4	(h)	BRISTOL CITY	D 0-0	-	8601	10	4	11				2	1		6				7	5	9			3		8		16
17	Dec	18	(h)	PLYMOUTH ARGYLE	D 3-3	Woods (2), Reid	8175		4	11				2	1		6				7	5	9			8	3	10		17
18	Dec	25	(h)	MILLWALL	W 6-0	Black, Thomson, Reid (3), Woods	9447		4	11				2	1		6				7	9	5			8	3	10		18
19	Dec	27	(a)	Millwall	L 0-7	-	20936		4	11				2	1		6				7	9	5			8	3	10		19
20	Dec	28	(a)	Northampton Town	L 1-2	Woods	8700		4	11				2	1		6				7	5	9			8	3	10		20
21	Jan	1	(a)	Brentford	D 2-2	Thomson, Panther	9116	10	4	7				2	1		6			9		5				11	8		21
22	Jan	15	(h)	BRISTOL ROVERS	D 1-1	Panther	6723	10	4	11				2	1		6			9	7	5				3		8		22
23	Jan	22	(a)	Swindon Town	L 0-2	-	7567	10	4	11			6	2	1					8	7	9	5			3				23
24	Jan	26	(a)	Bournemouth	L 0-2	-	4833	10		11			6	4	1					9	7	5				3			8	24
25	Jan	29	(h)	EXETER CITY	D 2-2	Pointon, Graham (pen)	5631	10		11			6	4	1					9	7	5				3			8	25
26	Feb	5	(a)	Merthyr Town	L 1-4	Reid	1530		4	11				2	1		6				7	10	5	9		3		8		26
27	Feb	12	(h)	SOUTHEND UNITED	D 0-0	-	4334	8		11			4	2	1		6				7	5	9			3		10		27
28	Feb	19	(a)	Gillingham	D 0-0	-	3979			11			3	1		2	6				7	5	9						10	28
29	Feb	26	(a)	Norwich City	L 2-3	Reid, Pointon	7270		4	11				2	1		6				7	8	5	9		3		10		29
30	Mar	3	(a)	Charlton Athletic	D 2-2	Thompson, Reid	3129		4	11				2	1		6				7	8	5	9		3		10		30
31	Mar	5	(h)	NEWPORT COUNTY	W 4-1	Reid (2), Woods, Thompson	5240		4	11				2	1		6				7	8	5	3	9			10		31
32	Mar	12	(a)	Aberdare Athletic	W 1-0	Thompson	2653		4	11				2	1		6				7	8	5	3	9			10		32
33	Mar	19	(h)	WATFORD	D 2-2	Black, Thompson	10561		4	11				2	1		6				7	8	5	3	9			10		33
34	Mar	26	(a)	Crystal Palace	D 1-1	Reid	9264		4	7	11			2	1		6					8	5	2	9	3		10		34
35	Apr	2	(h)	COVENTRY CITY	W 4-1	Reid, Dennis (2, 1 pen), Thompson	6960		4	7	11				1		6					8	5	2	9	3		10		35
36	Apr	9	(a)	Queens Park Rangers	L 0-1	-	4484		4	7	11				1		6					8	5	2	9	3		10		36
37	Apr	15	(a)	Brighton & Hove Albion	D 1-1	Thompson	12581		4	7	11				1		6					8	5	2	9	3		10		37
38	Apr	16	(h)	CHARLTON ATHLETIC	W 1-0	Thompson	7502		4	7	11				1		6					8	5	2	9	3		10		38
39	Apr	18	(h)	BRIGHTON & HOVE ALBION	W 4-0	Reid (3), Thompson	7353		4		11				1		6				7	8	5	2	9	3		10		39
40	Apr	23	(a)	Bristol City	L 0-6	-	12826		4		11		6		1						7	8	5	2		3		10	8	40
41	Apr	30	(h)	BOURNEMOUTH	W 4-0	Rennie, Reid, Thompson, Dennis	6709		4		11				1		6				7	8	5	2	9	3		10		41
42	May	7	(a)	Plymouth Argyle	L 0-1	-	8142		4		11				1		6				7	8	5	2	9	3		10		42
				Apps				12	27	29	19	4	10	30	31	1	38	11	1	5	33	26	35	29	30	17	37	31	6	
				Goals				-	2	2	5	-	-	3	-	-	1	-	-	-	2	17	1	1	15	5	-	9	-	

Final League Position: 8th

1926/1927 FA CUP

Round	Month	Day	Venue	Opponents	W,L,D Score	Scorers	Attendance	Agnew W	Black JR	Clark J	Dennis GT	Fraser CR	Gordon J	Graham RC	Harper WG	Kingham HR	Millar RM	Mingay HJ	Moir RM	Panther FG	Pointon J	Reid S	Rennie A	Richards D	Thompson JW	Thomson NS	Till J	Woods Harry	Yardley J	Round
1	Nov	27	(h)	LONDON CALEDONIANS	W 4-2	Reid (2), Clark, Pointon	10923	10	2	11				1			4				7	8	6	5			3	9		1
2	Dec	11	(h)	NORTHFLEET UNITED	W 6-2	Woods (3), Reid (2), Rennie	9641		10	11				2	1		4				7	8	6	5			3	9		2
3	Jan	8	(a)	Chelsea	L 0-4	-	41441		6				2	1			4				11	9	5		7	10	3	8		3
				Apps				1	3	1	1	-	-	2	3	-	3	-	-	-	3	3	3	2	1	1	3	3	-	
				Goals				-	-	1	-	-	-	-	-	-	-	-	-	-	1	4	1	-	-	-	-	3	-	

▶ An aerial view of the ground in 1927.

▶ The Oak Road end of the ground in the 1920's.

▶ The Main Stand enclosure looking towards the Kenilworth Road end.

TIMELINE...

26 October 1925 Manager George Thompson is sacked.

1927/1928 FOOTBALL LEAGUE DIVISION THREE (SOUTH)

Match No	Month	Day	Venue	Opponents	W,L,D Score	Scorers	Attendance	Abbott H	Banks JA	Black JR	Briggs H	Davies AS	Dennis GT	Fraser CR	Fulton JJ	Galloway SR	Gordon J	Graham RC	Harkins J	Kingham HR	Lumsden R	Millar RM	Muir J	Nunn AS	Panther FG	Pointon J	Ramage J	Reid S	Rennie A	Reynolds JW	Richards D	Till J	Woods Harry	Yardley J	Match No
1	Aug	27	(a)	Southend United	L 0-1	-	11186	1		4			11			9						6				7		8	5		2	3	10		1
2	Aug	29	(h)	NORWICH CITY	L 1-3	Rennie	9157	1		4			11									6			9	7		8	5		2	3	10		2
3	Sep	3	(h)	BRIGHTON & HOVE ALBION	L 2-5	Panther, Banks	9468	1	10	4	11							2							9	7		8	5			3			3
4	Sep	5	(a)	Norwich City	L 0-3	-	13640		10		11			6	5		4	3				2	1			7								8	4
5	Sep	10	(a)	Bournemouth	D 2-2	Yardley, Galloway	6040		10		11			6	5	9	4	3				2	1			7								8	5
6	Sep	17	(h)	BRENTFORD	W 5-2	Yardley (3), Reid, Pointon	9182			4			10	6	5			3				2	1	11		7		9						8	6
7	Sep	24	(a)	Watford	L 0-1	-	12903	1		4			10	6	5			3						11		7		9						8	7
8	Oct	1	(a)	Millwall	L 2-3	Rennie, Harkins	7645			4				6	5			3	10			2	1	11		7			9					8	8
9	Oct	8	(h)	CRYSTAL PALACE	W 6-1	Black, Rennie (2), Harkins, Pointon, Yardley	8844			4				6	5			3	10			2	1	11		7			9					8	9
10	Oct	15	(a)	Exeter City	L 2-3	Rennie, Nunn	6827			4				6	5			3	10			2	1	11		7			9					8	10
11	Oct	22	(h)	NEWPORT COUNTY	D 1-1	Harkins	5192					11		6	5			3	10			2	4	1		7			9					8	11
12	Oct	29	(a)	Swindon Town	L 2-4	Pointon, Rennie	7580				11			6	5		4	3				2				7			9				10	8	12
13	Nov	5	(h)	QUEENS PARK RANGERS	L 0-1	-	7695		10		11			6	5		4	3				2				7			9					8	13
14	Nov	12	(a)	Coventry City	L 2-4	Reid, Yardley	10141			4			11	6				3				2				7		9	5				10	8	14
15	Nov	19	(h)	GILLINGHAM	W 6-1	Dennis (pen), Woods, Reid, Rennie, Pointon, Yardley	4527	1		4			11	6				3				2				7		9	5				10	8	15
16	Dec	3	(h)	MERTHYR TOWN	W 5-1	Reid (4), Dennis	5040	1		4			11	6				3				2				7		9	5				10	8	16
17	Dec	17	(h)	BRISTOL ROVERS	W 2-0	Pointon, Woods	5946	1		4			11	6				3				2				7		9	5				10	8	17
18	Dec	24	(a)	Charlton Athletic	L 3-4	Yardley, Pointon, Rennie	7265	1		4			11	6				3				2				7		8	5				10	9	18
19	Dec	26	(h)	Northampton Town	L 5-6	Yardley, Reid (4)	10153	1		4			11	6				3				2				7		9	5				10	8	19
20	Dec	31	(h)	SOUTHEND UNITED	D 0-0	-	5402	1		4			11	6				3				2				7		9	5				10	8	20
21	Jan	7	(a)	Brighton & Hove Albion	L 1-3	Pointon	5707	1	9	4			11	6				3				2				7			5				10	8	21
22	Jan	21	(h)	BOURNEMOUTH	D 3-3	Yardley, Woods, Fraser	6453	1		4			11	6				3				2				7		9	5		3		10	8	22
23	Jan	28	(a)	Brentford	L 2-4	Yardley (2)	3291	1		4			11	6				3				2				7	5	9			3		10	8	23
24	Feb	4	(h)	WATFORD	W 3-2	Rennie, Yardley, Woods	8012	1		4			11	6				2								7	5	9			3		10	8	24
25	Feb	11	(h)	MILLWALL	D 1-1	Yardley	8738	1		4				6				2		11						7	5	9			3		10	8	25
26	Feb	18	(a)	Crystal Palace	L 2-3	Rennie (2)	13370	1		4			11	6				2								7	5		9		3		10	8	26
27	Feb	25	(h)	EXETER CITY	W 2-1	Rennie, Nunn	8309	1		4				6										11		7	5		9		3		10	8	27
28	Mar	3	(a)	Newport County	L 2-7	Rennie, Woods	3995	1		4				6										11		7	5		9		3		10	8	28
29	Mar	10	(h)	SWINDON TOWN	W 2-1	Yardley, Woods	6973	1					11					2						6		7	5		9	4	3		10	8	29
30	Mar	17	(a)	Queens Park Rangers	L 2-3	Yardley, Dennis	11217	1					11					2						6		7	5		9	4	3		10	8	30
31	Mar	19	(h)	NORTHAMPTON TOWN	W 2-0	Yardley, Woods	8194	1	7	4				6	5			2						11					9		3		10	8	31
32	Mar	24	(h)	COVENTRY CITY	W 3-1	Rennie, Yardley, Nunn	8054	1	7	4				6	5			2						11					9		3		10	8	32
33	Mar	31	(a)	Gillingham	W 4-0	Dennis (2), Rennie (2)	4045	1	7	4			11		5			2				6							9		3		10	8	33
34	Apr	6	(h)	TORQUAY UNITED	W 5-0	Rennie (3), Woods, Dennis	10397	1	7	4			11		5			2				6							9		3		10	8	34
35	Apr	7	(h)	PLYMOUTH ARGYLE	D 1-1	Banks	10451	1	9	4			11		5			2				6				7					3		10	8	35
36	Apr	9	(a)	Torquay United	W 4-0	Yardley (2), Pointon, Dennis	2994	1		4			11		5			2				6				7		8			3		10	9	36
37	Apr	14	(a)	Merthyr Town	D 0-0	-	2089	1	7	4			11		5			2				6							9		3		10	8	37
38	Apr	21	(h)	WALSALL	W 4-1	Rennie (2), Yardley, Dennis	6118	1	7	4			11		5			2				6							9		3		10	8	38
39	Apr	23	(a)	Walsall	L 1-4	Rennie	3666	1	7	4			11					2									5		9		3		10	8	39
40	Apr	28	(a)	Bristol Rovers	W 2-1	Woods, Yardley	5639	1		4			11		5			2				6				7			9		3		10	8	40
41	May	2	(a)	Plymouth Argyle	L 0-4	-	4719	1					11		5			2			4	6				7			9		3		10	8	41
42	May	5	(h)	CHARLTON ATHLETIC	W 2-1	Rennie, Yardley	5982	1					11		5			2				6				7			9		3		10	8	42
				Apps				32	13	34	2	4	30	25	21	2	4	33	4	22	1	16	10	14	3	32	9	13	36	2	21	8	32	39	
				Goals				-	2	1	-	-	8	1	-	1	-	-	3	-	-	-	-	3	1	8	-	11	23	-	-	-	9	23	

Final League Position: 13th

1927/1928 FA CUP

Round	Month	Day	Venue	Opponents	W,L,D Score	Scorers	Attendance	Abbott H	Banks JA	Black JR	Briggs H	Davies AS	Dennis GT	Fraser CR	Fulton JJ	Galloway SR	Gordon J	Graham RC	Harkins J	Kingham HR	Lumsden R	Millar RM	Muir J	Nunn AS	Panther FG	Pointon J	Ramage J	Reid S	Rennie A	Reynolds JW	Richards D	Till J	Woods Harry	Yardley J	Round
1	Nov	30	(h)	CLAPTON ORIENT	W 9-0	Dennis (2), Woods, Yardley (4), Reid (2)	9639	1		4			11	6				3				2				7		9	5				10	8	1
2	Dec	10	(h)	NORWICH CITY	W 6-0	Reid (3), Woods, Yardley, Dennis	10750	1		4			11	6				3				2				7		9	5				10	8	2
3	Jan	14	(a)	Bolton Wanderers	L 1-2	Reid	20266	1		4			11	6				3				2				7		9	5				10	8	3
				Apps				3	-	3	-	-	3	3	-	-	-	3	-	-	-	3	-	-	-	3	-	3	3	-	-	-	3	3	
				Goals				-	-	-	-	-	3	-	-	-	-	-	-	-	-	-	-	-	-	-	-	6	-	-	-	-	2	5	

▶ **The 1927/28 team** – Back row (left to right): Black, Fulton, Graham, Abbott, Richards, C.Green (Secretary), Millar. Front row (left to right): Banks, Yardley, Rennie, Woods, Dennis, Ramage.

TIMELINE...

14 September 1927 Ex-player John McCartney takes over the managerial position at Kenilworth Road.
26 December 1927 In a fierce blizzard at Northampton, the Town go 5-1 up at half-time with the wind, only to eventually lose the game 5-6!

1928/1929 FOOTBALL LEAGUE DIVISION THREE (SOUTH)

Match No	Month	Day	Venue	Opponents	W,L,D Score	Scorers	Attendance	Abbott H	Banes CS	Bedford L	Black JR	Boylen RH	Clark AW	Curwen W	Daly J	Dennis GT	Forbes AS	Fraser CR	Fulton JJ	Graham RC	Harris B	Kingham HR	Millar RM	Rennie A	Richards D	Roe TW	Vaughan W	Walters AV	Woods Harry	Yardley J	Match No
1	Aug	25	(h)	BRIGHTON & HOVE ALBION	W 1-0	Yardley	10526	1			4				7	11			5			2	6	9	3				10	8	1
2	Aug	30	(a)	Northampton Town	D 2-2	Rennie (2)	12220	1			4				7	11			5			2	6	9	3				10	8	2
3	Sep	1	(a)	Exeter City	D 1-1	Yardley	7375	1			4				7	11			5			2	6	9	3				10	8	3
4	Sep	3	(h)	NORTHAMPTON TOWN	W 4-0	Dennis, Rennie (2), Yardley	10931	1			4				7	11			5			2	6	9	3				10	8	4
5	Sep	8	(h)	SOUTHEND UNITED	W 4-2	Millar, Rennie (2), Yardley	10600	1			4				7	11			5			2	6	9	3				10	8	5
6	Sep	15	(a)	Merthyr Town	W 4-3	Rennie (2), Bedford, Yardley	6016	1		11	4				7				5			2	6	9	3				10	8	6
7	Sep	22	(h)	BOURNEMOUTH	W 2-1	Rennie, Black	10675	1		11	4				7	5						2	6	9	3				10	8	7
8	Sep	29	(a)	Brentford	W 1-0	Rennie	13758	1		11	4				7				5			2	6	9	3				10	8	8
9	Oct	6	(h)	BRISTOL ROVERS	W 4-2	Rennie (2), Woods, Bedford	11650	1		11	4				7				5			2	6	9	3				10	8	9
10	Oct	13	(h)	COVENTRY CITY	D 1-1	Rennie	12509	1		11	4				7				5			2	6	9	3				10	8	10
11	Oct	20	(a)	Watford	L 2-3	Yardley, Bedford	20395	1		11	4				7				5			2	6	9	3				10	8	11
12	Oct	27	(h)	WALSALL	W 3-1	Rennie, Woods	10458	1		11	4				7	6			5		3	2		9					10	8	12
13	Nov	3	(a)	Newport County	W 2-1	Rennie (2)	4177	1		11	4				7	6			5		3	2		9					10	8	13
14	Nov	10	(h)	CRYSTAL PALACE	W 5-3	Rennie, Bedford (2), Yardley (2)	9606	1		11	4				7	6			5		3	2		9					10	8	14
15	Nov	17	(a)	Swindon Town	L 2-4	Rennie, Yardley	6992	1		11					7	6		4	5	3		2		9					10	8	15
16	Dec	1	(a)	Gillingham	L 0-1	-	4661	1		11			5		7	6		4		3		2		9					10	8	16
17	Dec	15	(a)	Fulham	L 2-4	Bedford, Daly	11069	1		11			5		7	6				3		2	4	9			8			10	17
18	Dec	22	(h)	QUEENS PARK RANGERS	W 3-2	Rennie (2), Bedford	9112	1		11	4				7				5	3		2	6	9			8			10	18
19	Dec	25	(h)	NORWICH CITY	W 2-1	Rennie (2)	14146	1		11	4				7				5	3		2	6	9			8			10	19
20	Dec	26	(a)	Norwich City	L 0-3	-	12418	1		11	4				7			5		3		2	6	9					10	8	20
21	Dec	29	(a)	Brighton & Hove Albion	L 0-1	-	6824	1		11	4				7			6	5	3		2					8	9	10		21
22	Jan	5	(h)	EXETER CITY	W 4-0	Clark, Rennie (3)	6882	1		11	4		10		7			6	5	3		2		9						8	22
23	Jan	19	(a)	Southend United	L 0-5	-	6153	1			4		5		7	11				3		2	6	9					10	8	23
24	Jan	26	(h)	MERTHYR TOWN	W 2-0	Roe (2)	7485		1	11	4				7				5	3		2	6	9		10				8	24
25	Feb	2	(a)	Bournemouth	D 3-3	Roe, Rennie, Yardley	3726		1	11	4				7				5			2	6	9	3	10				8	25
26	Feb	9	(h)	BRENTFORD	W 2-1	Yardley, Bedford	8148		1	11	4				7				5			2	6	9	3	10				8	26
27	Feb	16	(a)	Bristol Rovers	D 1-1	Rennie	6749		1	11			4		7				5			2	6	9	3	10				8	27
28	Feb	23	(a)	Coventry City	D 1-1	Rennie	13900		1	11			4		7				5			2	6	9	3	10				8	28
29	Mar	2	(h)	WATFORD	D 2-2	Bedford, Vaughan	15199		1	11			4		7				5			2	6	9	3		10			8	29
30	Mar	9	(a)	Walsall	D 0-0	-	6925		1	11			4		7				5	3		2	6	9		10				8	30
31	Mar	11	(h)	PLYMOUTH ARGYLE	D 2-2	Rennie, Yardley	8289		1	11			4		7				5	3		2	6	9		10				8	31
32	Mar	16	(h)	NEWPORT COUNTY	W 5-2	Roe (3), Bedford, Yardley	8782		1	11			4	3	7				5			2	6	9		10				8	32
33	Mar	23	(a)	Crystal Palace	L 0-3	-	22981		1	11			4		7				5	3		2	6	9		10				8	33
34	Mar	29	(a)	Charlton Athletic	L 1-4	Rennie	12814		1	11			4		7				5	3		2	6	9		10				8	34
35	Mar	30	(h)	SWINDON TOWN	W 5-3	Yardley (2), Rennie (2), Roe	9772		1	11			4		7				5	3			6	9		10				8	35
36	Apr	1	(h)	CHARLTON ATHLETIC	W 3-0	Rennie, Boylen, Vaughan	13214		1	11		7	4						5			2	6	9	3		10			8	36
37	Apr	6	(a)	Torquay United	D 2-2	Rennie (2)	3909		1	11	4	7							5			2	6	9	3		10			8	37
38	Apr	13	(h)	GILLINGHAM	W 8-0	Rennie (5), Yardley, Woods, Bedford	7278		1	11			4		7				5			2	6	9	3				10	8	38
39	Apr	20	(a)	Plymouth Argyle	L 0-2	-	8484		1	11			4		7				5			2	6	9	3				10	8	39
40	Apr	27	(h)	FULHAM	L 1-3	Rennie	13469		1	11	4				7				5			2	6	9	3				10	8	40
41	Apr	29	(h)	TORQUAY UNITED	L 1-2	Yardley	3155		1	11	4				7			5				2	6	9	3				10	8	41
42	May	4	(a)	Queens Park Rangers	D 1-1	Rennie	13449		1	11	4				7				5			2	6	9	3	10				8	42
				Final League Position: 7th			**Apps**	23	19	36	27	2	16	1	40	13	1	7	36	12	19	27	31	41	27	17	3	1	23	40	
							Goals	-	-	11	1	1	1	-	1	1	-	-	-	-	1	-	-	43	-	7	2	-	3	17	

1928/1929 FA CUP

Round	Month	Day	Venue	Opponents	W,L,D Score	Scorers	Attendance	Abbott H	Banes CS	Bedford L	Black JR	Boylen RH	Clark AW	Curwen W	Daly J	Dennis GT	Forbes AS	Fraser CR	Fulton JJ	Graham RC	Harris B	Kingham HR	Millar RM	Rennie A	Richards D	Roe TW	Vaughan W	Walters AV	Woods Harry	Yardley J	Round
1	Nov	24	(h)	SOUTHEND UNITED	W 5-1	Rennie (4), Bedford	12489	1		11					7	4			5	6	3	2		9					10	8	1
2	Dec	8	(a)	Fulham	D 0-0	-	19788	1		11	4				7	6			5	3		2		9			8			10	2
Rep	Dec	13	(h)	FULHAM	W 4-1	Yardley (2), Rennie, Bedford	11250	1		11	4				7	6			5	3		2		9		10				8	Rep
3	Jan	12	(h)	CRYSTAL PALACE	D 0-0	-	14736	1		11	4		10		7			6	5	3		2		9						8	3
Rep	Jan	16	(a)	Crystal Palace	L 0-7	-	17000	1			4		10		7	11			5	3	6			9					2	8	Rep
						Apps	5	-	4	4	-	2	-	5	4	-	1	4	3	5	3	1	5	-	2	-	-	2	5	
						Goals	-	-	2	-	-	-	-	-	-	-	-	-	-	-	-	-	5	-	-	-	-	-	2	

▶ **The 1928/29 team** – Back row (left to right): Clark, Graham, Banes, Harris, Millar. Front row (left to right): Daly, Roe, Rennie, Yardley, Bedford, Fulton.

TIMELINE...

May 1929 Andy Rennie nets 43 goals from only 41 League games – not bad for a converted centre-half.

1929/1930 FOOTBALL LEAGUE DIVISION THREE (SOUTH)

Match No	Month	Day	Venue	Opponents	W,L,D Score	Scorers	Attendance	Baker A	Banes CS	Bedford L	Birch W	Black JR	Boylen RH	Clark AW	Daly J	Drinnan JMcK	Fraser CR	Fulton JJ	Harford GB	Hutchinson A	Kingham HR	McInnes WA	Millar RM	Morgan FG	Rennie A	Richards D	Sheldon W	Smeaton AR	Smith E	Walker Robert	Woods Harry	Yardley J	Young JW	Match No
1	Aug	31	(a)	Exeter City	D 2-2	Bedford, Drinnan	8520		11					4	7	10	6		1			2			5	9				3		8		1
2	Sep	2	(h)	NORWICH CITY	D 1-1	Rennie	11097		7					4		10	6	5	1			2	11			9				3		8		2
3	Sep	7	(h)	SOUTHEND UNITED	L 0-3	-	9992		11		4				7		6		1			2			5	9	3				10	8		3
4	Sep	9	(a)	Norwich City	D 1-1	Bedford	9086		11		4				7		6	5	1			2				9	3				10	8		4
5	Sep	14	(a)	Watford	W 4-0	Yardley, Rennie (3)	16945		11		4				7		6	5	1			2				9	3				10	8		5
6	Sep	16	(h)	GILLINGHAM	W 2-0	Rennie, Yardley	7168		11						7		6	4	1			2			5	9	3				10	8		6
7	Sep	21	(a)	Bournemouth	L 1-5	Woods	7268		11						7		6	4	1			2			5	9	3				8			7
8	Sep	28	(h)	WALSALL	L 2-3	Rennie, Yardley	8700		11					5	7		6	4	1			2				9	3				10	8		8
9	Oct	5	(a)	Queens Park Rangers	L 0-1	-	12273		11					5	7		6	4	1			2				9	3				10	8		9
10	Oct	12	(h)	FULHAM	W 4-1	Drinnan (2), Yardley, Rennie	10053							5	7	10	6	4	1			2				9	3					8		10
11	Oct	19	(h)	NEWPORT COUNTY	W 4-2	Daly, Clark, Rennie, McInnes	8825							4	7	10	6	5	1			2	11			9	3					8		11
12	Oct	26	(a)	Torquay United	D 2-2	Yardley, Drinnan	4755							4	7	10	6	5	1			2	11			9	3					8		12
13	Nov	2	(h)	MERTHYR TOWN	W 4-0	Drinnan (2), Yardley, Bedford	7988			11	8			4	7	10		5	1			2					3	6				9		13
14	Nov	9	(a)	Plymouth Argyle	L 1-6	Clark	15073			11				4	7	10	6	5	1			2					3	6		8		9		14
15	Nov	16	(h)	SWINDON TOWN	D 1-1	Bedford	2547			11	8			4	7	10	6	5	1								2		3			9		15
16	Nov	23	(a)	Brighton & Hove Albion	L 1-4	Clark	4827			11	8			4	7	10	6	5	1								2		3			9		16
17	Dec	7	(a)	Brentford	L 0-2	-	7167							9	7	10	5	4	1		2	11	6				3					8		17
18	Dec	21	(a)	Coventry City	L 1-5	Hutchinson	10865	1			8				7		4			9		11	6				3		5	2		10		18
19	Dec	25	(h)	NORTHAMPTON TOWN	W 1-0	Brett (og)	9473	1							7		6				2	11					3	5			4	10	9	8	19
20	Dec	26	(a)	Northampton Town	L 1-4	Clark	19251	1						4	7		6				2	11					3	5			2	10	9	8	20
21	Dec	28	(h)	EXETER CITY	L 0-4	-	5285	1							7		6				2	11					3	5			4	10	9	8	21
22	Jan	4	(a)	Southend United	D 1-1	Yardley	5859	1			8		7	5		10	6	4				11					2			3			9		22
23	Jan	18	(h)	WATFORD	W 2-0	Birch, Yardley	9920	1			8		7	5		10	6	4				11					2			3			9		23
24	Jan	25	(h)	BOURNEMOUTH	W 1-0	Yardley	6971	1			8		7	5		10	6	4				11					2			3			9		24
25	Feb	1	(a)	Walsall	L 0-1	-	6143	1			8		7	5		10	6	4				11					2			3			9		25
26	Feb	8	(h)	QUEENS PARK RANGERS	W 2-1	Rennie, Fraser	7049	11			1			5	7	10	6	4							9		2			3			8		26
27	Feb	15	(a)	Fulham	D 1-1	Birch	13739	11			1			5	7	10	6	4							9		2			3			10		27
28	Feb	22	(a)	Newport County	D 0-0		3879	1			8			5	7	10	6	4				11					2			3					28
29	Mar	1	(h)	TORQUAY UNITED	W 3-1	Rennie, Birch, Daly	7239	1			8			5	7	10	6								9		2			3	4		11		29
30	Mar	8	(a)	Merthyr Town	L 1-3	Drinnan	1838	1			8			5	7	10	6	4									2			3			11		30
31	Mar	10	(a)	CLAPTON ORIENT	L 1-2	Drinnan	2612	1			8			5	7	10	6								9		2			3	4		11		31
32	Mar	15	(h)	PLYMOUTH ARGYLE	W 5-2	Rennie (3), Yardley (2)	9051	1						5	7	10	4					11	6		9		2						8		32
33	Mar	22	(a)	Swindon Town	D 1-1	Rennie	3710	1						5	7	10	4					11	6		9		2			3			8		33
34	Mar	24	(a)	BRISTOL ROVERS	W 3-0	Drinnan (2), Daly	3589	1						5	7	10	4					11	6		9		2			3			8		34
35	Mar	29	(h)	BRIGHTON & HOVE ALBION	W 1-0	Yardley	7199	1						5	7	10	4					11	6		9		2			3			8		35
36	Apr	5	(a)	Bristol Rovers	D 2-2	Rennie, Yardley	4786	1						5	7	10	4					2	11	6	9		3						8		36
37	Apr	12	(h)	BRENTFORD	W 2-1	Clark, Rennie	11150	1					7	5		10	4				11	2		6	9		3						8		37
38	Apr	18	(h)	CRYSTAL PALACE	D 2-2	Yardley, Drinnan	9135	1					7	5		10	4				11			6	9		2			3			8		38
39	Apr	19	(a)	Clapton Orient	L 1-6	Yardley	6228	1			8		7	5		10	4				11	2		6						3			9		39
40	Apr	21	(a)	Crystal Palace	L 1-4	Rennie	15167	1						5		10	4				7	2		6	9					3			8		40
41	Apr	26	(h)	COVENTRY CITY	D 1-1	Drinnan	4819							5		10	4	1				11	6		9	2		7		3			9		41
42	May	3	(a)	Gillingham	L 0-2	-	4831	1			8		7	5		10		4					6				2	11		3			8		42

Final League Position: 13th   1 Own Goal

| | | | | | | | Apps | 1 | 24 | 13 | 15 | 3 | 9 | 34 | 30 | 31 | 39 | 24 | 18 | 5 | 21 | 22 | 13 | 4 | 27 | 38 | 2 | 6 | 24 | 5 | 11 | 40 | 3 | |
| | | | | | | | Goals | - | - | 4 | 3 | - | - | 5 | 3 | 12 | 1 | - | - | 1 | - | 1 | - | - | 17 | - | - | - | - | - | 1 | 15 | - | |

1929/1930 FA CUP

Round	Month	Day	Venue	Opponents	W,L,D Score	Scorers	Attendance	Baker A	Banes CS	Bedford L	Birch W	Black JR	Boylen RH	Clark AW	Daly J	Drinnan JMcK	Fraser CR	Fulton JJ	Harford GB	Hutchinson A	Kingham HR	McInnes WA	Millar RM	Morgan FG	Rennie A	Richards D	Sheldon W	Smeaton AR	Smith E	Walker Robert	Woods Harry	Yardley J	Young JW	Round
1	Nov	30	(h)	QUEENS PARK RANGERS	L 2-3	Yardley (2)	10235		11	8				4	7	10	6	5	1						2				3			9		1

| | | | | | | | Apps | - | 1 | 1 | - | - | 1 | 1 | 1 | 1 | 1 | 1 | 1 | | | | | | 1 | | | | 1 | - | | 1 | - | |
| | | | | | | | Goals | - | - | - | - | - | - | - | - | - | - | - | - | | | | | | - | | | | - | - | | 2 | - | |

The 1929/30 team – Back row (left to right): Fulton, Richards, Banes, Smith, Fraser. Front row (left to right): Boylen, Birch, Yardley, Drinnan, McInnes, Clark.

TIMELINE...

31 December 1929 Manager John McCartney resigns, citing ill health.
1 January 1930 George Kay appointed manager.

1930/1931 FOOTBALL LEAGUE DIVISION THREE (SOUTH)

Match No	Month	Day	Venue	Opponents	W,L,D Score	Scorers	Attendance	Armstrong JW	Banes CS	Brown WI	Bryce RS	Clark AW	Dent F	Edwards GG	Fraser CR	Gale EWA	Hale A	Harford GB	Heslop AS	Hodgson T	Kingham HR	McGinnigle H	McNestry G	Muir JB	Page JE	Rennie A	Richards D	Richmond J	Rickett WJ	Slicer J	Smith E	Yardley J	Match No
1	Aug	30	(h)	BRENTFORD	D 1-1	Page	11686		1			5						6					2	4	7	9	3		8		10	11	1
2	Sep	3	(a)	Exeter City	D 1-1	Slicer	4627	10	1			5						6					2	4	7	9	3			8		11	2
3	Sep	6	(a)	Crystal Palace	L 1-5	McNestry	15237	10	1			5						6					2	9	7		3	4		8		11	3
4	Sep	8	(h)	BRIGHTON & HOVE ALBION	D 2-2	Rennie (2)	7849		1		10	5						6					2	4	7	9	3			8		11	4
5	Sep	13	(h)	SOUTHEND UNITED	W 2-1	Yardley, Clark	6347		1		8	5						6					2	4	7	9	3					10	5
6	Sep	17	(a)	Brighton & Hove Albion	L 0-2	-	4088				11	5						6	1				2		7	9	3				4	8	6
7	Sep	20	(a)	Watford	L 0-1	-	8991				9	5			6			4	1				2		7		3				10		7
8	Sep	27	(a)	Bristol Rovers	L 1-5	McNestry	7930				9	5			6			4	1				2		7		3				10	8	8
9	Sep	29	(a)	EXETER CITY	W 3-1	McNestry, Slicer, Dent	1450	8				4	10					6	1				2		5	7				9	3	11	9
10	Oct	4	(h)	NEWPORT COUNTY	W 3-1	Dent (2), Slicer	8097	8	1			4	10					6					2		5	7				9	3	11	10
11	Oct	11	(a)	Gillingham	L 0-4	-	7491		1			5	10					6					2	4	7					9	3	11	11
12	Oct	18	(h)	BOURNEMOUTH	L 2-3	Rennie (2)	7367		1			5	10					6					2		7					9	3 4	11	12
13	Oct	25	(a)	Swindon Town	D 0-0	-	4671		1		11	4	10		6	5				3			2		7					9		8	13
14	Nov	1	(h)	FULHAM	W 5-0	Rennie (2), McNestry, Dent (2)	8389		1		11	4	10		6	5					7	3	2			8				9			14
15	Nov	8	(a)	Coventry City	W 2-1	Rennie (2)	10542		1		11	4	10		6	5					7	3	2			8				9			15
16	Nov	15	(h)	WALSALL	D 0-0	-	7508		1		11	4	10		6	5					7	3	2			8				9			16
17	Nov	22	(a)	Queens Park Rangers	L 1-3	Rennie	6388		1		11	4	10		6	5					7	3	2			8				9			17
18	Dec	6	(a)	Thames	L 0-1	-	469	8	1		11		10				4					3	2			7	6			9			18
19	Dec	20	(a)	Notts County	L 0-1	-	11307	8		10	11				6		4			1		2				5				9			19
20	Dec	25	(h)	TORQUAY UNITED	W 3-1	Rennie (2), Bryce	7553				11		10		6		4			1		2				5			7	9		3	20
21	Dec	26	(a)	Torquay United	D 1-1	Armstrong	6619	8			11				6		4			1		2				5			7	9		3 10	21
22	Dec	27	(a)	Brentford	W 1-0	Clark	7353	8			11	5			4					1		3	2			7			6	9		10	22
23	Jan	3	(h)	CRYSTAL PALACE	L 1-2	Rennie	6051	8			11				6		4			1		2				5			7	9		3 10	23
24	Jan	10	(h)	NORWICH CITY	W 1-0	McNestry	5036	8			11	4	10		6					1		3	2			7				9			24
25	Jan	17	(a)	Southend United	W 2-0	McNestry (2)	4857				7	4			6	5				1		3	2			5				8		11 9	25
26	Jan	28	(h)	WATFORD	W 4-1	Rennie, Bryce, McNestry, Yardley	3603				7	4			6						1		3	2			5	8			11	9	26
27	Jan	31	(h)	BRISTOL ROVERS	W 4-1	Rennie, Yardley, McNestry (2)	7174				7	4		1	6						3	2			5	8				11	9		27
28	Feb	7	(a)	Newport County	L 1-3	McNestry	2868				7	4		1	6						3	2			5	8				11	9		28
29	Feb	14	(h)	GILLINGHAM	W 4-1	Rennie, McNestry (2), Yardley	5837					4			6				1	7	3	2			5	8				11	9		29
30	Feb	21	(a)	Bournemouth	D 0-0	-	4439					4			6				1	7	3	2			5	8				11	9		30
31	Feb	28	(h)	SWINDON TOWN	W 4-0	Rennie, Yardley (2), Heslop	5057					4			6				1	7	3	2			5	8				11	9		31
32	Mar	7	(a)	Fulham	L 1-2	Yardley	7000					4			6				1	7	3	2			5	8				11	9		32
33	Mar	14	(h)	COVENTRY CITY	W 2-0	Brown, McNestry	7134			9	11	4			6				1	7	3	2			5	8				10			33
34	Mar	21	(a)	Walsall	W 1-0	Brown	3937			9	11	4			6				1	7	3	2				8	5			10			34
35	Mar	23	(h)	CLAPTON ORIENT	L 0-1	-	3284			9	11	4			6				1	7	3	2				8	5			10			35
36	Mar	28	(a)	QUEENS PARK RANGERS	W 5-1	Yardley (2), Heslop (2), Slicer	6035					4			5		6		1	7	3	2				8				11	3	9	36
37	Apr	4	(a)	Norwich City	L 0-1	-	7903					4			5		6		1	7	3	2				8				11		9	37
38	Apr	6	(h)	NORTHAMPTON TOWN	W 4-0	Rennie, Clark, Slicer, Yardley	12292					5			6		6		1	7	3	2	4			8				11		9	38
39	Apr	7	(a)	Northampton Town	D 0-0	-	8614					5	8		4		6		1	7	3	2				8				11		9	39
40	Apr	11	(h)	THAMES	W 8-0	McNestry (2), Clark, Yardley (2), Bryce, Heslop, Slicer	6029				10	4			6				1	7	3	2			5	8				11		9	40
41	Apr	18	(a)	Clapton Orient	L 2-3	Slicer, Clark	5078					11	4		6				1	7	3	2	5			8				10		9	41
42	Apr	25	(h)	NOTTS COUNTY	W 3-0	Yardley, Slicer, Heslop	7312					10	4		6				5	1	7	3	2			8				11		9	42

Final League Position: 7th

| | | | | | | | Apps | 10 | 14 | 6 | 25 | 37 | 13 | 2 | 30 | 10 | 16 | 26 | 18 | 26 | 39 | 25 | 41 | 4 | 4 | 36 | 14 | 2 | 1 | 27 | 8 | 28 | |
| | | | | | | | Goals | 1 | - | 2 | 3 | 5 | 5 | - | - | - | 5 | - | 5 | - | - | - | 16 | - | 1 | 17 | - | - | - | 8 | - | 13 | |

1930/1931 FA CUP

Round	Month	Day	Venue	Opponents	W,L,D Score	Scorers	Attendance	Armstrong JW	Banes CS	Brown WI	Bryce RS	Clark AW	Dent F	Edwards GG	Fraser CR	Gale EWA	Hale A	Harford GB	Heslop AS	Hodgson T	Kingham HR	McGinnigle H	McNestry G	Muir JB	Page JE	Rennie A	Richards D	Richmond J	Rickett WJ	Slicer J	Smith E	Yardley J	Round
1	Nov	29	(h)	CLAPTON ORIENT	D 2-2	Rennie, Bryce	9244		1		11	4	10		6					3	2	5	7			9						8	1
Rep	Dec	4	(n)	Clapton Orient	W 4-2	McNestry, Rennie (2), Armstrong	8021	8	1		11	4	10		6					3	2	5	7			9							Rep
2	Dec	13	(a)	Watford	L 1-3	Yardley	17770		1		11		10		6		4			3	2	5	7			9						8	2

First Round Replay played at Highbury

| | | | | | | | Apps | 1 | 3 | - | 3 | 2 | 3 | - | 3 | - | 1 | - | - | 3 | 3 | 3 | 3 | - | - | 3 | - | - | - | - | - | 2 | |
| | | | | | | | Goals | 1 | - | - | 1 | - | - | - | - | - | - | - | - | - | - | - | 1 | - | - | 3 | - | - | - | - | - | 1 | |

▶ **The 1930/31 team** – Back row (left to right): Clark, Kingham, Harford, Hodgson, Fraser. Front row (left to right): Heslop, McNestry, Brown, Rennie, Bryce, Richards.

TIMELINE...

6 December 1930 Only 469 turn up for the Town's game at Thames Association – a record low League attendance.
13 May 1931 Manager George Kay is poached by Southampton.
1 June 1931 Harold Wightman is appointed in his place.

1931/1932 FOOTBALL LEAGUE DIVISION THREE (SOUTH)

Match No	Month	Day	Venue	Opponents	W,L,D Score	Scorers	Attendance	Black AJ	Bryce RS	Chapman JR	Cupit WW	Fraser CR	Gale EWA	Hale A	Harford GB	Heslop AS	Hodgson T	Imrie J	Jones VW	Kean FW	Kingham HR	Loasby H	McGinnigle H	McNestry G	Miller W	Rennie A	Rowe DH	Slicer J	Tait T	Turner George	Wales Abraham	Wilson GG	Yardley J	Match No
1	Aug	29	(a)	Reading	L 1-2	Tait	14591					6		1		7	3			4	2			8	5	10		11	9					1
2	Aug	31	(h)	NORTHAMPTON TOWN	W 1-0	Rennie	11235					6			5		3	1		4	2			7		10		11	9			8		2
3	Sep	5	(h)	SOUTHEND UNITED	L 1-3	Rennie	9179	11					5				3	1	6	4	2	8		7		10			9					3
4	Sep	9	(a)	Gillingham	W 3-1	McNestry, Rennie (2)	5950					6				7	3	1		4	2		5	8		10			9		11			4
5	Sep	12	(a)	Fulham	L 2-3	Rennie (2)	8510					6				7	3	1		4	2		5	8		10			9		11			5
6	Sep	14	(h)	GILLINGHAM	W 2-0	Tait (2)	6333					6				7	3	1		4	2		5	8		10			9		11			6
7	Sep	19	(h)	THAMES	W 2-0	Rennie, Heslop	8239					6				7	3	1		4	2		5	8		10			9		11			7
8	Sep	26	(a)	Brentford	L 0-1	-	12540					6				7	3	1		4	2		5	8		10		11	9					8
9	Sep	28	(a)	Northampton Town	W 2-1	Tait, McNestry	6503						6				3	1		4	2		5	7		10		11	8				9	9
10	Oct	3	(h)	EXETER CITY	W 6-3	Yardley (2), Rennie (3), McNestry	8509						6					1		4	2		5	7		10		11	8		3	9	9	10
11	Oct	10	(a)	Coventry City	L 2-3	Yardley (2)	12371	11					6		3			1		4	2		5	7		10			8				9	11
12	Oct	17	(h)	WATFORD	L 0-1	-	14765						6				3	1		4	2		5	7		10			8				9	12
13	Oct	24	(a)	Crystal Palace	D 1-1	Yardley	15327						6		3		2	1	4				5	7		10		11	8				9	13
14	Oct	31	(h)	BOURNEMOUTH	W 1-0	Slicer	7231						6		3	7	2	1		4			5			10		11	8				9	14
15	Nov	7	(a)	Queens Park Rangers	L 1-3	Tait	10993						6			7	3	1		4	2		5			10		11	8				9	15
16	Nov	14	(h)	BRISTOL ROVERS	W 3-0	Yardley, Heslop, Turner	6244						6			7	3	1		4	2		5	8		10				9		10		16
17	Nov	21	(a)	Torquay United	W 2-1	Rennie, McNestry	3490				8		6				3	1		4	2		5	7		10				11		9		17
18	Dec	5	(a)	Swindon Town	L 2-3	Loasby, Tait	2532						6				3	1		4	2	9	5	7		10			8	11				18
19	Dec	19	(a)	Brighton & Hove Albion	L 2-3	Tait, Slicer	6628						6				3	1	4		2		5	7		10		11	8				9	19
20	Dec	25	(h)	CARDIFF CITY	W 2-1	Tait (2)	11609						6				3	1		4	2		5	7		10			8	11			9	20
21	Dec	26	(a)	Cardiff City	L 1-4	Yardley	13515						6				3	1		4			5	7		10			8	11	2		9	21
22	Jan	2	(h)	READING	W 6-1	Hodgkiss (og), McNestry (2), Yardley (3)	5179						6				3	1		4	2		5	7		10		11	8				9	22
23	Jan	11	(a)	CLAPTON ORIENT	L 1-5	Rennie	1716				7		6					1		4	2		5			10			8	11	3		9	23
24	Jan	16	(a)	Southend United	D 1-1	McNestry	5508						6				3	1		4	2			7	5	10		11	8				9	24
25	Jan	23	(h)	FULHAM	L 1-3	Tait	6315						6				3	1		4	2			7	5	10		11	8				9	25
26	Jan	30	(a)	Thames	W 4-2	Loasby (2), Tait, Cupit	1473				7		6				3	1		4	2	9				5			10	11			8	26
27	Feb	6	(h)	BRENTFORD	D 1-1	Loasby	7402				7		6				3	1		4	2	9	5			10			8	11				27
28	Feb	13	(a)	Exeter City	L 1-2	Loasby	6454				7		6				3	1		4	2	9	5			10			8	11		10		28
29	Feb	20	(h)	COVENTRY CITY	W 3-1	Turner (2), Tait	5412						6				3	1		4	2		5	7		10			8	11		9		29
30	Mar	5	(h)	CRYSTAL PALACE	W 3-0	Loasby, McNestry, Turner	6105						6				3	1		4	2	9	5	7		10			8	11				30
31	Mar	12	(a)	Bournemouth	D 1-1	Loasby	4277						6				3	1		4	2	9	5	7		10			8	11				31
32	Mar	19	(h)	QUEENS PARK RANGERS	W 4-1	Loasby, Bryce, Tait (2)	5768		11		7		6				3	1		4	2	9	5			10			8					32
33	Mar	25	(h)	MANSFIELD TOWN	W 3-1	Rennie, Loasby, Bryce	7621		11		7		6				3	1		4	2	9	5			10			8					33
34	Mar	26	(a)	Bristol Rovers	L 1-3	Bryce	4265		11		7		6				3	1		4	2	9	5			10			8					34
35	Mar	28	(a)	Mansfield Town	L 2-5	Bryce, Loasby	5588		11		7		6				3	1		4	2	9	5			10			8					35
36	Mar	29	(h)	NORWICH CITY	W 7-1	Tait, Loasby (3), Slicer (2), Rennie	2619		7				6				3	1		4	2	9	5			10		11	8					36
37	Apr	2	(h)	TORQUAY UNITED	W 6-1	Slicer, Tait (3), Loasby, Rennie	5778		7				6				3	1		4	2	9	5			10		11	8					37
38	Apr	9	(a)	Clapton Orient	D 0-0	-	5979		7				6				3	1		4	2	9	5			10		11	8					38
39	Apr	13	(a)	Watford	L 1-3	Bryce	4635		7				6					1		4	2	9	5			10		11	8				3	39
40	Apr	16	(h)	SWINDON TOWN	W 6-0	Tait (5), Kean	3982						6					1		4	2	5				10		7	8			9	3	40
41	Apr	23	(a)	Norwich City	D 3-3	McNestry, Rennie, Tait	6247						6					1		4	2	5		7		10	11		9			8	3	41
42	Apr	30	(h)	BRIGHTON & HOVE ALBION	W 3-2	Rennie, McNestry, Tait	6328						6					1		4	2	5		7		10	11		9			8	3	42
				Final League Position: 6th		1 Own Goal	**Apps**	1	9	1	8	39	1	6	1	9	35	41	3	40	39	15	36	28	3	40	2	18	41	16	3	7	20	
							Goals	-	5	-	1	-	-	-	2	-	-	-	-	1	-	14	-	10	-	17	-	5	25	4	-	-	10	

1931/1932 FA CUP

Round	Month	Day	Venue	Opponents	W,L,D Score	Scorers	Attendance	Black AJ	Bryce RS	Chapman JR	Cupit WW	Fraser CR	Gale EWA	Hale A	Harford GB	Heslop AS	Hodgson T	Imrie J	Jones VW	Kean FW	Kingham HR	Loasby H	McGinnigle H	McNestry G	Miller W	Rennie A	Rowe DH	Slicer J	Tait T	Turner George	Wales Abraham	Wilson GG	Yardley J	Round
1	Nov	28	(a)	Swindon Town	W 5-0	McNestry (2), Rennie, Yardley (2)	9266					6					3	1		4	2		5	7		10			8	11			9	1
2	Dec	12	(a)	Lincoln City	D 2-2	Yardley (2)	12613					6					3	1		4	2		5	7		10		11	8				9	2
Rep	Dec	16	(h)	LINCOLN CITY	W 4-1	Tait (2), Yardley, Slicer	9264					6					3	1		4	2		5	7		10		11	8				9	Rep
3	Jan	9	(h)	WOLVERHAMPTON WANDERERS	L 1-2	Yardley	17025					6					3	1		4	2		5	7		10		11	8				9	3
						Apps		-	-	-	4	-	-	-	-	-	4	4	-	4	4	-	4	4	-	4	-	3	4	1	-	-	4	
						Goals		-	-	-	-	-	-	-	-	-	-	-	-	-	-	-	-	2	-	1	-	1	2	-	-	-	6	

▶ **The 1931/32 team** – Back row (left to right): McGinnigle, Pakes (Trainer), Kingham, Hodgson, Imrie, Hale, H.Wightman(Manager), Fraser. Front row (left to right): McNestry, Tait, Kean, Yardley, Rennie, Black.

1932/1933 FOOTBALL LEAGUE DIVISION THREE (SOUTH)

Match No	Month	Day	Venue	Opponents	W,L,D	Score	Scorers	Attendance	Alderson T	Brown WI	Coote SA	Corkindale WJ	Diaper AW	Fraser CR	Harford GB	Hayhurst A	Hodgson T	Hutchison Davie	Imrie J	Kean FW	Kingham HR	Mackey TS	McGinnigle H	Mills AS	Nelson A	Pacey HJ	Rennie A	Roberts J	Rowe DH	Tait T	Weaver RS	Whalley R	Match No
1	Aug	27	(h)	NORTHAMPTON TOWN	W	2-1	Mills, Rowe	11414						6			3	8	1	4	2		5	7			10		11	9			1
2	Aug	29	(a)	Clapton Orient	D	0-0	-	7528						6			3	8	1	4	2		5	7			10	11		9			2
3	Sep	3	(a)	Bristol City	L	2-5	Tait (2)	9044						6			3	8	1	4	2		5	7			10		11	9			3
4	Sep	5	(h)	CLAPTON ORIENT	W	4-1	Tait (2), Mills (2)	4496						6	1		3	8		4	2		5	7			10	11		9			4
5	Sep	10	(h)	COVENTRY CITY	W	4-1	Rennie, Rowe, Fraser, Tait	7829						6	1			8		4	2	3	5	7			10		11	9			5
6	Sep	17	(a)	Brentford	L	0-1	-	15409						6	1			8		4	2	3	5	7			10		11	9			6
7	Sep	24	(h)	TORQUAY UNITED	W	2-1	Hutchison (2)	8424						6	1			8		4	2	3	5	7			10		11	9			7
8	Oct	1	(a)	Exeter City	L	0-2	-	6681		9		11		6	1					4	2	3	5	7			10						8
9	Oct	8	(h)	GILLINGHAM	W	2-1	Mills, Whalley	6244		9				6	1					4	2	3	5	7	8		10					11	9
10	Oct	15	(h)	NEWPORT COUNTY	D	2-2	Kean, Nelson	6504		9				6	1					4	2	3	5	7	8		10					11	10
11	Oct	22	(a)	Watford	L	1-4	Hutchison	12130		9				6	1			8		4	2	3	5	7			10					11	11
12	Oct	29	(h)	CARDIFF CITY	W	8-1	Tait (3), Mills (2), Nelson, Hutchison, Fraser	6002						6				10	1	4	2	3	5	7	8				11	9			12
13	Nov	5	(a)	Reading	L	1-4	Tait	9861						6				10	1	4	2	3	5	7	8				11	9			13
14	Nov	12	(h)	NORWICH CITY	D	1-1	Kean	5501						6				10	1	4	2	3	5	7	8				11	9			14
15	Nov	19	(a)	Brighton & Hove Albion	L	0-2	-	4102			5			6					1	4	2	3		7			10		11	9			15
16	Dec	3	(a)	Aldershot	D	2-2	Tait (2)	3993						6					1	4	2	3	5	7	8		10		11	9			16
17	Dec	17	(a)	Southend United	L	1-2	Roberts	6057						6					1	4	2	3	5	7	8		10	11		9			17
18	Dec	24	(h)	CRYSTAL PALACE	D	1-1	Rennie	7042	9					6					1	4	2	3	5	7	8		10	11					18
19	Dec	26	(a)	Bournemouth	W	2-0	Alderson (2)	7342	9					6					1	4	2	3	5	7	8		10	11					19
20	Dec	27	(h)	BOURNEMOUTH	L	1-2	Alderson	10428	9					6					1	4	2	3	5	7	8		10	11					20
21	Dec	31	(a)	Northampton Town	L	0-1	-	8321	8					6					1	4	2	3	5			7	10	11		9			21
22	Jan	7	(h)	BRISTOL CITY	W	5-4	Rennie (3), Mills, Tait	6080	10					6	1		3			4	2		5	7			9	11		8			22
23	Jan	21	(a)	Coventry City	L	0-4	-	11010	10					6	1			8		4	2	3	5	7				11		9			23
24	Feb	1	(h)	BRENTFORD	D	5-5	Nelson (2), Tait (3)	3044	10	4				6	1						2	3	5	7	8			11		9			24
25	Feb	4	(a)	Torquay United	L	1-3	Nelson	2745	10	4				6	1						2	3	5	7	8			11		9			25
26	Feb	11	(h)	EXETER CITY	W	4-0	Alderson, Mills, Tait (2)	6388	10	4				6	1			8			2	3	5	7				11		9			26
27	Feb	22	(a)	Gillingham	D	1-1	Roberts	2152	10	6			4		1						2	3	5			7	9	11		8			27
28	Mar	11	(a)	Cardiff City	L	2-3	Mills, Tait	5919	10	4				6	1						2	3	5	7			9	11		8			28
29	Mar	13	(h)	BRISTOL ROVERS	D	1-1	Hutchison	2272	10	6					1	2		8		4		3	5	7				11		9			29
30	Mar	18	(h)	READING	D	1-1	Rennie	6219	10					6	1			8		4	2	3	5	7			9	11					30
31	Mar	25	(a)	Norwich City	L	1-2	Weaver	14098						6	1			8		4	2	3	5	11	10	7					9		31
32	Apr	1	(h)	BRIGHTON & HOVE ALBION	D	0-0	-	4240					4	6	1			8			2	3	5		10	7		11			9		32
33	Apr	5	(a)	Newport County	L	2-3	Rowe, Hutchison	2344					4	6	1			8			2	3	5			7	10		11		9		33
34	Apr	8	(a)	Bristol Rovers	D	0-0	-	6127		4				6	1			8			2	3	5	7	10		9		11				34
35	Apr	14	(h)	SWINDON TOWN	W	6-2	Rennie (3), Nelson, Mills (2)	5535		4				6	1			8			2	3	5	7	10		9		11				35
36	Apr	15	(h)	ALDERSHOT	W	2-1	Alderson, Rennie	5128	10	4				6	1			8			2	3	5				9		11				36
37	Apr	17	(a)	Swindon Town	D	1-1	Rennie	4693		4				6	1			8			2	3	5	7	10		9		11			10	37
38	Apr	18	(h)	QUEENS PARK RANGERS	W	3-1	Mills, Rowe (2)	2402		4				6	1			10			2	3	5	7			9		11	8			38
39	Apr	22	(a)	Queens Park Rangers	L	1-3	Hutchison	2837		4				6	1			10			2	3	5	7			9		11	8			39
40	Apr	26	(h)	WATFORD	W	3-2	Hutchison, Rowe (2)	4140						6	1			8		4	2	3	5	7			10		11	9			40
41	Apr	29	(h)	SOUTHEND UNITED	D	3-3	Rowe, Mills (2)	2969						6	1			8		4	2	3	5	7			10		11	9			41
42	May	6	(a)	Crystal Palace	L	0-3	-	6554			2			6	1			8		4		3	5	7			10		11	9			42
								Apps	14	12	1	1	3	40	20	1	6	26	22	32	40	38	40	37	21	4	31	17	21	28	3	4	
								Goals	5	-	-	-	-	2	-	-	-	8	-	2	-	-	-	14	6	-	11	2	8	18	1	1	

Final League Position: 14th

1932/1933 FA CUP

Round	Month	Day	Venue	Opponents	W,L,D	Score	Scorers	Attendance	Alderson T	Brown WI	Coote SA	Corkindale WJ	Diaper AW	Fraser CR	Harford GB	Hayhurst A	Hodgson T	Hutchison Davie	Imrie J	Kean FW	Kingham HR	Mackey TS	McGinnigle H	Mills AS	Nelson A	Pacey HJ	Rennie A	Roberts J	Rowe DH	Tait T	Weaver RS	Whalley R	Round
1	Nov	26	(h)	KINGSTONIAN	D	2-2	Rennie, Tait	7701				7		6		5		8	1	4	2	3					9		11	10			1
Rep	Nov	30	(a)	Kingstonian	W	3-2	McGinnigle, Rennie, Tait	6227		7				6					1	4	2	3	5	8			9		10			11	Rep
2	Dec	10	(a)	Stockport County	W	3-2	Kean, Rennie, Tait	9892		7				6					1	4	2	3	5	8			9		10				2
3	Jan	14	(a)	Barnsley	D	0-0	-	15106	10					6	1					4	2	3	5	7			9	11		8			3
Rep	Jan	18	(h)	BARNSLEY	W	2-0	Rennie (2)	10074	10					6	1					4	2	3	5	7			9	11		8			Rep
4	Jan	28	(h)	TOTTENHAM HOTSPUR	W	2-0	Alderson, Tait	17213	9					6	1					4	2	3	5	7				11		10			4
5	Feb	18	(a)	Halifax Town	W	2-0	Nelson, Tait	29325	8					6	1					4	2	3	5		7			11		10			5
6	Mar	4	(a)	Everton	L	0-6	-	55431						6	1					4	2	3	5	7			9	11		10			6
								Apps	4	2		1		8	5	1		1	3	8	8	7	4	5	2		7	5	2	8		1	
								Goals	1	-		-		-	-	-		-	-	1	-	-	1	1	1		5	-	-	5		-	

▶ **The 1932/33 team** – (Left to right): Harford, Mackey, Kean, McGinnigle, Fraser, Mills, Nelson, Tait, Brown, Alderson, Roberts.

TIMELINE...

4 March 1933 The Town reach the F.A.Cup quarter-finals for the first time but sadly go down 0-6 to Everton at Goodison Park.

1933/1934 FOOTBALL LEAGUE DIVISION THREE (SOUTH)

Match No	Month	Day	Venue	Opponents	W.L.D Score	Scorers	Attendance	Anderson SJ	Bell S	Bell T	Brown WI	Fraser CR	Gibson John	Harford GB	Holbeach F	Hutchison Davie	Kean FW	Kingham HR	Kirkwood D	Kitchen H	Lawson H	Mackey TS	Martin GS	McGinnigle H	Mittel JL	Pearson GW	Pease WH	Reece HJ	Rennie A	Rennie J	Tait T	Match No
1	Aug	26	(a)	Northampton Town	W 3-2	Tait (3)	16823					6	3				4	2					8	5	1	11	7		10		9	1
2	Aug	28	(h)	CHARLTON ATHLETIC	W 2-1	Rennie, Tait	11904					6					4	2				3	8	5	1	11	7		10		9	2
3	Sep	2	(h)	TORQUAY UNITED	W 10-2	Rennie (4), T Bell (2), Martin (2), Kean, Pease	10475			9		6					4	2				3	8	5	1	11	7		10			3
4	Sep	4	(a)	Charlton Athletic	L 0-2	-	8089			9		6					4	2				3	8	5	1	11	7		10			4
5	Sep	9	(a)	Queens Park Rangers	L 1-2	Pease	10110					6				10	4	2				3	8	5	1	11	7		9			5
6	Sep	13	(a)	Crystal Palace	D 2-2	Pease (2)	9457			9		6					4	2				3	8	5	1	11	7		10			6
7	Sep	16	(h)	NEWPORT COUNTY	D 1-1	T Bell	10072			9		6					4	2				3	8	5	1	11	7		10			7
8	Sep	23	(a)	Norwich City	L 0-4	-	12599					6					4	2				3	8	5	1	11	7		10		9	8
9	Sep	30	(h)	BRISTOL CITY	W 3-0	T Bell (2), Martin	8831	11		9	4	6		1				2				3	8	5			7		10			9
10	Oct	7	(a)	Clapton Orient	D 1-1	Martin	10182	11		9		6	3	1			4	2				5	8				7		10			10
11	Oct	14	(h)	SWINDON TOWN	L 2-3	Anderson, Tait	7756	11				6	3	1			4	2				5	8				7		10		9	11
12	Oct	21	(h)	WATFORD	W 2-1	Anderson, Martin	10674	11				6		1			4	2				3	8	5			7		10		9	12
13	Oct	28	(a)	Reading	L 1-4	Kirkwood	8110					6		1			4	2	8			3	9	5		11			10		9	13
14	Nov	4	(h)	COVENTRY CITY	L 0-1	-	7690					6		1			4	2	8			3	9	5		11			10		9	14
15	Nov	11	(a)	Southend United	W 1-0	Hutchison	5828	11		9		6		1		8	4	2				3	10	5			7					15
16	Nov	18	(h)	BRISTOL ROVERS	D 2-2	T Bell, Anderson	6778	11		9		6		1		8	4	2				3	10	5						7		16
17	Dec	2	(h)	GILLINGHAM	W 4-2	Rennie (2), Anderson, McGinnigle (pen)	5447	11				6		1			4	2				3	8	5			7		10		9	17
18	Dec	9	(a)	Exeter City	L 2-4	Rennie (2)	4257	11			4	6		1		10		2			7	3		5					9		8	18
19	Dec	16	(h)	CARDIFF CITY	W 3-1	McGinnigle (pen), Rennie, Martin	5984			9	4	6		1		10						2	8	5		11	7	3	10			19
20	Dec	23	(a)	Bournemouth	L 3-4	Pease, Martin, Pearson	4081				4	6		1		10		2				3	8	5		11	7		9	6		20
21	Dec	25	(a)	Aldershot	D 0-0	-	4668				4			1		10		2				3	8	5		11	7		9	6		21
22	Dec	26	(h)	ALDERSHOT	D 1-1	Rennie	8301							1		8	4	2				3	8	5		11	7		10	6	9	22
23	Dec	30	(h)	NORTHAMPTON TOWN	W 3-1	Hutchison (2, 1 pen), Martin	7696			9				1	7	10		2				3	8	5				11		6		23
24	Jan	6	(a)	Torquay United	W 1-0	Rennie	2548			9		6		1			4	2				3	8	5			7	11	10			24
25	Jan	20	(a)	QUEENS PARK RANGERS	W 4-2	Martin, T Bell (2), Hutchison	8096			9		6		1		11	4	2				3	8	5			7		10			25
26	Jan	27	(a)	Newport County	W 2-1	T Bell, Hutchison	5524			9		6		1		11	4	2				3	8	5			7		10			26
27	Feb	3	(h)	NORWICH CITY	L 2-3	Pease (2)	7651			9		6	6	1		11	4	2				3	8	5			7		10			27
28	Feb	10	(a)	Bristol City	D 0-0	-	8697					6		1		11	4	2				3	8	5			7		10			28
29	Feb	17	(h)	CLAPTON ORIENT	W 2-0	Martin, T Bell	7106			9		6		1		11	4	2				3	8	5			7		10			29
30	Feb	24	(a)	Swindon Town	L 1-3	Hutchison	7689			9		6		1		11	4	2				3	8	5			7		10			30
31	Mar	3	(a)	Watford	W 1-0	Pease	10204			9		6		1		11	4					2	8	5			7	3	10			31
32	Mar	10	(h)	READING	W 3-1	Rennie, T Bell, Hutchison (pen)	7568			9		6		1		11	4					2	8	5			7	3	10			32
33	Mar	17	(a)	Coventry City	D 2-2	Kean, Rennie	12455			9		6		1		11	4					2	8	5			7	3	10			33
34	Mar	24	(h)	SOUTHEND UNITED	W 3-1	Rennie (2), Hutchison	6313			9		6		1		11	4					2	8	5			7	3	10			34
35	Mar	30	(a)	Brighton & Hove Albion	D 1-1	Martin	10134			9		6		1		11	4					2	8	5			7	3	10			35
36	Mar	31	(h)	Bristol Rovers	W 1-0	Hutchison	8234			9		6		1		11	4					2	8	5			7	3	10			36
37	Apr	2	(h)	BRIGHTON & HOVE ALBION	L 1-2	Rennie	10133			9		6		1	7	11	4					2	8	5				3	10			37
38	Apr	7	(h)	CRYSTAL PALACE	W 2-1	Tait, T Bell	6841			9		6		1		11	4					2	8	5				3	10		7	38
39	Apr	14	(h)	Gillingham	D 1-1	Kitchen	4729	11		9		6		1		10	4			8		2		5				3			7	39
40	Apr	21	(h)	EXETER CITY	W 3-2	Anderson, Tait, Hutchison	5836	11		9	7	6		1		10	4					2		5				3			8	40
41	Apr	28	(a)	Cardiff City	W 4-0	Hutchison (2), Brown, Martin	3080			9	7	6		1		11	4					2	10	5				3			8	41
42	May	5	(h)	BOURNEMOUTH	W 2-0	S Bell (2)	5614		10	9	7	6		1		11	4					2		5				3			8	42
				Final League Position: 6th			**Apps**	10	1	28	8	37	3	34	2	27	38	29	2	1	1	41	36	40	8	14	33	15	35	4	15	
							Goals	5	2	12	1	-	-	-	-	12	2	-	1	1	-	-	12	2	-	1	8	-	17	-	7	

1933/1934 FA CUP

Round	Month	Day	Venue	Opponents	W.L.D Score	Scorers	Attendance	Anderson SJ	Bell S	Bell T	Brown WI	Fraser CR	Gibson John	Harford GB	Holbeach F	Hutchison Davie	Kean FW	Kingham HR	Kirkwood D	Kitchen H	Lawson H	Mackey TS	Martin GS	McGinnigle H	Mittel JL	Pearson GW	Pease WH	Reece HJ	Rennie A	Rennie J	Tait T	Round
3	Jan	13	(h)	ARSENAL	L 0-1	-	18626			9		6		1		11	4	2				3	8	5			7		10			3
							Apps	-	-	1	-	1	-	1	-	1	1	1	-	-	-	1	1	1	-	-	1	-	1	-	-	
							Goals	-	-	-	-	-	-	-	-	-	-	-	-	-	-	-	-	-	-	-	-	-	-	-	-	

1933/1934 DIVISION THREE (SOUTH) CUP

Round	Month	Day	Venue	Opponents	W,L,D Score	Scorers	Attendance	Anderson SJ	Bell S	Bell T	Brown WI	Fraser CR	Gibson John	Harford GB	Holbeach F	Hutchison Davie	Kean FW	Kingham HR	Kirkwood D	Kitchen H	Lawson H	Mackey TS	Martin GS	McGinnigle H	Mittel JL	Pearson GW	Pease WH	Reece HJ	Rennie A	Rennie J	Tait T	Round
2	Feb	28	(a)	Aldershot	L 3-4	Bell T (2), Martin		-	-	9	7	6	-	1	-	11	4	2	-	-	-	3	8	5	-	-	-	-	10	-	-	2
						Apps		-	-	1	1	1	-	1	-	1	1	1	-	-	-	1	1	1	-	-	-	-	1	-	-	
						Goals		-	-	2	-	-	-	-	-	-	-	-	-	-	-	-	1	-	-	-	-	-	-	-	-	

▶ **The 1933/34 team** – Back row (left to right): McGinnigle, Pakes (Trainer), Mackey, Harford, Reece, Fraser. Front row (left to right): Pease, Martin, Bell, Kean, Rennie, Hutchison.

TIMELINE...

13 January 1934 Another record Kenilworth Road crowd – this time 18,626 – sees the Town lose narrowly 0-1 to mighty Arsenal.

1934/1935 FOOTBALL LEAGUE DIVISION THREE (SOUTH)

Match No	Month	Day	Venue	Opponents	W,L,D Score	Scorers	Attendance	Ball JT	Beck W	Bell S	Bell T	Brown WI	Coen JL	Colquhoun DM	Cook C	Crompton W	Fraser CR	Hutchison D	Kean FW	Kidd GI	Kingham HR	Mackey TS	Martin GS	McGinnigle H	Payne J	Pease WH	Preedy CJF	Reece HJ	Rennie A	Roberts F	Russell CJ	Smith Tom	Stephenson GH	Taylor Joe	Thayne W	Match No
1	Aug	25	(h)	SOUTHEND UNITED	D 1-1	S Bell	12255			9							6		4			2	8	5			1		7		11		10		3	1
2	Aug	27	(a)	Cardiff City	L 0-1	-	18608			9							6		4			2	8	5			1		7		11		10		3	2
3	Sep	1	(a)	Bristol Rovers	D 1-1	S Bell	11980			9							6		4			2	8	5			1		7		11		10		3	3
4	Sep	3	(h)	CARDIFF CITY	W 4-0	Martin (2), S Bell, Cook	9392			10					9		6		4			2	8	5			1		7				11		3	4
5	Sep	8	(h)	CHARLTON ATHLETIC	L 1-2	Russell (pen)	11226								9		6		4			2	8	5			1		7		11		10		3	5
6	Sep	15	(a)	Crystal Palace	L 1-2	S Bell	13416			8			1		9		6		4			2		5					7		11		10		3	6
7	Sep	22	(h)	QUEENS PARK RANGERS	D 1-1	Rennie	7233			8			1		9		6	11	4			2		5					7				10		3	7
8	Sep	29	(a)	Torquay United	L 2-6	T Bell, Stephenson	3612		6	8	9	4	1					7				2		5							11		10		3	8
9	Oct	6	(h)	SWINDON TOWN	W 2-0	S Bell, Stephenson	7801			8	9	4	1				6					2		5					7		11		10		3	9
10	Oct	13	(a)	Aldershot	W 1-0	Stephenson	4931			8	9	4	1				6					2		5					7		11		10		3	10
11	Oct	20	(a)	Exeter City	W 2-1	T Bell (2)	4040			8	9	4	1				6					2		5					7		11		10		3	11
12	Oct	27	(h)	BRISTOL CITY	D 1-1	Ball	8956	9		8		4	1			7	6					2		5							11		10		3	12
13	Nov	3	(a)	Bournemouth	W 3-1	Martin, Stephenson, Brown	5939	9		10		4	1			7	6					2	8	5									11		3	13
14	Nov	10	(h)	WATFORD	D 2-2	Stephenson, Ball	11260	9		8		4	1			7	6					2		5							11		10		3	14
15	Nov	17	(a)	Clapton Orient	D 1-1	S Bell	8455	9		8		4	1			7	6					2		5							11		10		3	15
16	Nov	24	(h)	MILLWALL	W 2-1	Martin, Ball	8936	9		8		4	1			7	6					2		5							11		10		3	16
17	Dec	1	(a)	Reading	L 0-1	-	9513	9		8		4	1			7	6					2		5							11		10		3	17
18	Dec	15	(a)	Millwall	W 4-1	Ball (2), Roberts, S Bell	5279	9		8		4	1			7	6					2								11			10		3	18
19	Dec	22	(h)	COVENTRY CITY	W 4-0	Ball (2, 1 pen), Crompton, S Bell	9231	9		8		4	1			7	6					2								11			10		3	19
20	Dec	25	(h)	BRIGHTON & HOVE ALBION	W 4-0	S Bell (3), Ball	12964	9		8		4	1			7						2								11		5	10		3	20
21	Dec	26	(a)	Brighton & Hove Albion	L 1-4	Ball	13577	9	6	8		4	1			7						2								11		5	10		3	21
22	Dec	29	(a)	Southend United	D 3-3	S Bell, Crompton, Roberts	5394	9		8		4	1			7	6					2								11		5	10		3	22
23	Jan	5	(h)	BRISTOL ROVERS	W 6-2	S Bell (3), Ball (2), Roberts	8574	9		8		4	1			7	6					2								11		5	10		3	23
24	Jan	19	(a)	Charlton Athletic	L 2-4	Ball, Roberts	12222	9		8		4	1			7						2								11		5	10		3	24
25	Jan	30	(h)	CRYSTAL PALACE	D 2-2	S Bell, Wilde (og)	3410	9		8		4	1			7						2								11		5	10		3	25
26	Feb	2	(a)	Queens Park Rangers	L 0-3	-	6201	9		8		4	1			7	6					2								11		5	10		3	26
27	Feb	9	(h)	TORQUAY UNITED	W 3-1	Stephenson, Crompton, Ball	6886	9		8		4	1			7						2								11		5	10	6	3	27
28	Feb	16	(a)	Swindon Town	W 1-0	S Bell	5428	9		8		4	1			7	6					2								11		5	10		3	28
29	Feb	23	(h)	ALDERSHOT	W 6-1	Roberts, S Bell, Ball (2), Stephenson (2)	6536	9		8		4	1			7	6					2								11		5	10		3	29
30	Mar	2	(h)	EXETER CITY	W 4-0	Ball (3, 1 pen), Stephenson	8383	9		8		4	1			7						2								11		5	10	6	3	30
31	Mar	9	(a)	Bristol City	W 2-0	Ball, Roberts	6749	9					1	4		7						2	3	8						11		5	10		3	31
32	Mar	16	(h)	BOURNEMOUTH	W 4-0	Roberts (2), Crompton, Ball	8497	9					1	4		7						2	3	8						11		5	10		3	32
33	Mar	23	(a)	Watford	D 2-2	Ball (2)	10828	9					1	4		7						2	3	8						11		5	10		3	33
34	Mar	30	(h)	CLAPTON ORIENT	W 3-0	Ball (2), Stephenson	7966	9					1	4		7						2	3	8						11		5	10		3	34
35	Apr	6	(a)	Gillingham	D 1-1	Ball	4139	9					1	4		7						2	3	8						11		5	10		3	35
36	Apr	13	(h)	READING	L 2-4	Crompton, Stephenson	11960	9					1	4		7						2	3	8						11		5	10		3	36
37	Apr	19	(a)	Newport County	W 4-2	Martin, Crompton, Stephenson, Ball	4052	9					1	4		7						2	8					3		11		5	10		3	37
38	Apr	20	(a)	Northampton Town	L 1-2	Ball	7240	9					1	4		7						2	8					3		11		5	10		3	38
39	Apr	22	(h)	NEWPORT COUNTY	W 4-1	Crompton (3), Martin	8759	9					1	4		7						2	8					3		11		5	10		3	39
40	Apr	23	(h)	NORTHAMPTON TOWN	D 2-2	Ball (2)	8168	9					1	4		7				6		2	8					3		11		5	10		3	40
41	May	1	(h)	GILLINGHAM	D 2-2	Ball, Martin	3996	9					1	4		7						2	8	5						11		3	10	6	3	41
42	May	4	(a)	Coventry City	L 0-1	-	6843	9					1	4		7						2	8	5						10		3	11		3	42
				Final League Position: 4th		1 Own Goal	**Apps**	31	2	29	6	23	37	12	4	26	25	2	7	2	23	33	28	14	2	0	5	14	11	25	8	23	40	1	29	
							Goals	30	-	18	3	1	-	-	1	9	-	-	-	-	-	-	7	-	-	-	-	-	1	8	1	-	12	-	-	

1934/1935 FA CUP

Round	Month	Day	Venue	Opponents	W,L,D Score	Scorers	Attendance	Ball JT	Beck W	Bell S	Bell T	Brown WI	Coen JL	Colquhoun DM	Cook C	Crompton W	Fraser CR	Hutchison D	Kean FW	Kidd GI	Kingham HR	Mackey TS	Martin GS	McGinnigle H	Payne J	Pease WH	Preedy CJF	Reece HJ	Rennie A	Roberts F	Russell CJ	Smith Tom	Stephenson GH	Taylor Joe	Thayne W	Round
3	Jan	12	(a)	Chelsea	D 1-1	Bell S	46492	9		8		4	1			7	6				3									10		2	11		5	3
Rep	Jan	16	(h)	CHELSEA	W 2-0	Ball, Roberts	23041	9		8		4	1			7	6						5						3	10		2	11		5	Rep
4	Jan	26	(a)	Burnley	L 1-3	Stephenson	26727	9		8		4	1			7	6						3							10		2	11		5	4
							Apps	3	-	3	-	3	3	-	-	3	3	-	-	-	1	-	2	-	-	-	-	-	1	3	-	3	3	-	2	
							Goals	1	-	1	-	-	-	-	-	-	-	-	-	-	-	-	-	-	-	-	-	-	-	1	-	-	1	-	-	

1934/1935 DIVISION THREE (SOUTH) CUP

Round	Month	Day	Venue	Opponents	W.L.D Score	Scorers	Attendance	Ball JT	Beck W	Bell S	Bell T	Brown WI	Coen JL	Colquhoun DM	Cook C	Crompton W	Fraser CR	Hutchison D	Kean FW	Kidd GI	Kingham HR	Mackey TS	Martin GS	McGinnigle H	Payne J	Pease WH	Preedy CJF	Reece HJ	Rennie A	Roberts F	Russell CJ	Smith Tom	Stephenson GH	Taylor Joe	Thayne W	Round
1	Sep	26	(a)	Gillingham	W 3-1	Pease, Bell S, Stephenson	1000	6	8	9	4	1									3					7	2				11		10		5	1
2	Oct	18	(a)	Queens Park Rangers	L 1-2	Bell S			7	9	4	1					6					2	3	8					10		11		11		5	2
						Apps		1	2	2	2	2	-	-	-	-	1	-	-	-	1	2	1	1	-	1	1	-	1	-	1	-	2	-	2	
						Goals		-	-	2	-	-	-	-	-	-	-	-	-	-	-	-	-	-	-	1	-	-	-	-	-	-	1	-	-	

▶ **The 1934/35 team** – Back row (left to right): Thayne, Coote, Taylor, Willoughby, Mackey, Kingham, Russell. Second row (left to right): Pease, Beck, Cook, Coen, McGinnigle, Martin, Rennie, Fraser. Third row (left to right): Reece, E.Mouse (Director), Kean, C.Jeyes (Director), Brown, S.Godfrey (Director), Payne, S.Wilkinson (Director). Front row (left to right): Pembleton (Trainer), S.Bell, Hackett, T.Bell, Hutchison, Stephenson.

TIMELINE...
16 January 1935 Kenilworth Road is dangerously crowded as the Town beat Chelsea 2-0 in a replayed Cup tie in front of 23,041 – another record.

1935/1936 FOOTBALL LEAGUE DIVISION THREE (SOUTH)

Match No	Month	Day	Venue	Opponents	W,L,D Score	Scorers	Attendance	Andrews H	Ball JT	Beresford FE	Booton H	Boyd WG	Coen JL	Colquhoun DM	Cook C	Crompton W	Crook MS	Dolman HW	Fellowes WJ	Finlayson Jock	Godfrey W	Gooney WH	Hodge J	Hubbard AA	Kidd GI	Kingham HR	Mackey TS	Martin GS	McGinnigle H	Nelson JH	Payne J	Rich LT	Roberts F	Sloan FJ	Smith Tom	Stephenson GH	Thayne W	Turner George	Match No
1	Aug	31	(a)	Clapton Orient	L 0-3	-	12494		9	8			1	4		7								6	2		3			5			10			11			1
2	Sep	4	(a)	Bournemouth	L 1-2	Crompton	9018		9	8			1	4		7								6	2	3				5			10			11			2
3	Sep	7	(h)	SOUTHEND UNITED	L 1-2	Ball	14379	8	9				1			7	2		5	4				6		3							10			11			3
4	Sep	9	(h)	BOURNEMOUTH	D 0-0		9350		9	8			1			7				4				6	2					5			10		3	11			4
5	Sep	14	(a)	Northampton Town	D 0-0		13595		9	8			1			7				4				6	2					5			10		3	11			5
6	Sep	16	(h)	QUEENS PARK RANGERS	W 2-0	Beresford, Stephenson	8220			8			1	4	9	7				6					2					5			10		3	11			6
7	Sep	21	(a)	CRYSTAL PALACE	W 6-0	Turner, Stephenson, Crook, Cook (3)	13206						1	4	9		7			6					2					5			10		3	11		8	7
8	Sep	28	(a)	Reading	L 1-2	Ball	11254		9	8			1			7			5	4							2		6				10		3	11			8
9	Oct	5	(h)	CARDIFF CITY	D 2-2	Ball, Finlayson	12288		9	8			1			7			5	4					2				6				10		3	11			9
10	Oct	12	(a)	Gillingham	W 1-0	Roberts	8252		9				1			7			6	4							2	8		5			10		3	11			10
11	Oct	19	(h)	BRIGHTON & HOVE ALBION	W 2-1	Fellowes, Martin	10679		9				1			7			6	4							2	8		5			10		3	11			11
12	Oct	26	(a)	Exeter City	W 2-1	Ball, Crompton	4902		9				1			7			6	4							2	8		5			10		3	11			12
13	Nov	2	(h)	NEWPORT COUNTY	W 7-0	Crompton (2), Roberts (2), Ball (2), Finlayson (pen)	10085		9				1			7			6	4							2	8		5			10		3	11			13
14	Nov	9	(a)	Watford	W 3-1	Crompton, Roberts, Ball	14906		9				1			7			6	4							2	8		5			10		3	11			14
15	Nov	16	(h)	SWINDON TOWN	W 2-1	Finlayson, Stephenson	12213		9				1			7			6	4							2	8		5			10		3	11			15
16	Nov	23	(a)	Aldershot	W 1-0	Stephenson	5019		9				1			7			6	4							2	8		5			10		3	11			16
17	Dec	7	(a)	Millwall	D 0-0		3449		9				1			7			6	4							2	8		5			10		3	11			17
18	Dec	14	(h)	BRISTOL CITY	W 1-0	Roberts (og)	11134						1			7			6	4							2	8		5			10		3	11	9		18
19	Dec	25	(a)	Notts County	W 3-0	Boyd, Martin, Stephenson	12186			7		9	1						6	4							2	8		5			10		3	11			19
20	Dec	26	(h)	NOTTS COUNTY	W 1-0	Roberts	18100			7		9	1						6	4							2	8		5			10		3	11			20
21	Dec	28	(h)	CLAPTON ORIENT	W 5-3	Boyd (5)	13545					9	1	4		7			6								2	8		5			10		3	11			21
22	Jan	4	(a)	Southend United	W 1-0	Boyd	8585					9	1			7			6	4							2	8		5			10		3	11			22
23	Jan	18	(h)	NORTHAMPTON TOWN	D 3-3	Boyd, Martin, Roberts	12781			7		9	1						6	4								8	2	5			10		3	11			23
24	Jan	29	(a)	Crystal Palace	L 1-5	Ball	6804		9				1			7			6	4							2	8		5			10		3	11			24
25	Feb	1	(h)	READING	W 2-1	Crompton, Roberts	15852					9	1			7			6	4							2	8		5			10		3	11			25
26	Feb	8	(a)	Cardiff City	W 3-2	Stephenson, Boyd (2)	12142			7		9	1						6	4							2	8		5			10		3	11			26
27	Feb	15	(h)	GILLINGHAM	L 1-2	Martin	12276					9	1			7			6	4							2	8	5				10		3	11			27
28	Feb	22	(a)	Brighton & Hove Albion	D 1-1	Martin	10111				2	9	1			7			6	4								8		5			10		3	11			28
29	Feb	29	(h)	WATFORD	W 2-1	Stephenson (2)	13226				2	9	1						6	4								8		5		7	10		3	11			29
30	Mar	7	(a)	Bristol City	W 2-1	Rich, Stephenson	8173		9		2		1						6	4								8		5		7	10		3	11			30
31	Mar	14	(h)	EXETER CITY	W 3-1	Rich (2), Stephenson	12710		9		2		1						6	4								8		5		7	10		3	11			31
32	Mar	21	(a)	Swindon Town	L 0-3	-	7839		9		2		1						5	4	6							8				7	10		3	11			32
33	Mar	25	(h)	TORQUAY UNITED	W 1-0	Martin	9693		9		2		1						6	4								8		5		7	10		3	11			33
34	Mar	28	(h)	ALDERSHOT	D 2-2	Roberts, Boyd	12770				2	9	1						6	4										5		7	10	8	3	11			34
35	Apr	4	(a)	Torquay United	L 1-2	Cook	3675						1		9						6		4		2			8		5		7	10		3	11			35
36	Apr	10	(a)	Bristol Rovers	D 2-2	Martin, Rich	16030						1	9							6		4		2			8		5		7	10		3	11			36
37	Apr	11	(h)	MILLWALL	D 0-0		12527											1		4	6				2			8		5	9	7	10		3	11			37
38	Apr	13	(h)	BRISTOL ROVERS	W 12-0	Payne (10), Roberts, Martin	14296			7								1		4					2			8		5	9		10		3	11			38
39	Apr	18	(a)	Newport County	W 2-0	Payne (2)	6356			7								1		4		6			2			8		5	9		10		3	11			39
40	Apr	25	(h)	COVENTRY CITY	D 1-1	Payne	23559											1		4	7	6			2			8		5	9		10		3	11			40
41	Apr	27	(a)	Coventry City	D 0-0		42809											1		4	7	6			2			8		5	9		10		3	11			41
42	May	2	(a)	Queens Park Rangers	D 0-0	-	17951											1		4	7	6			2					5	9		10	8	3	11			42
Apps								1	19	12	7	13	36	4	4	21	5	6	31	33	5	4	4	2	7	9	25	31	3	37	9	9	39	2	39	40	1	4	
Goals								-	8	1	-	11	-	-	4	6	1	-	1	3	-	-	-	-	-	-	-	8	-	-	13	4	9	-	-	10	-	1	

Final League Position: 2nd   1 Own Goal

1935/1936 FA CUP

Round	Month	Day	Venue	Opponents	W,L,D Score	Scorers	Attendance	Andrews H	Ball JT	Beresford FE	Booton H	Boyd WG	Coen JL	Colquhoun DM	Cook C	Crompton W	Crook MS	Dolman HW	Fellowes WJ	Finlayson Jock	Godfrey W	Gooney WH	Hodge J	Hubbard AA	Kidd GI	Kingham HR	Mackey TS	Martin GS	McGinnigle H	Nelson JH	Payne J	Rich LT	Roberts F	Sloan FJ	Smith Tom	Stephenson GH	Thayne W	Turner George	Round
3	Jan	11	(a)	West Ham United	D 2-2	Ball, Roberts	42000		9				1			7			6	4							2	8		5			10		3	11			3
Rep	Jan	15	(h)	WEST HAM UNITED	W 4-0	Ball, Crompton, Roberts, Stephenson	17527		9				1			7			6	4							2	8		5			10		3	11			Rep
4	Jan	25	(a)	Manchester City	L 1-2	Martin	65978		9				1			7			6	4							2	8		5			10		3	11			4
Apps								-	3	-	-	-	3	-	-	3	-	-	3	3	-	-	-	-	-	-	3	3	-	3	-	-	3	-	3	3	-	-	
Goals								-	2	-	-	-	-	-	-	1	-	-	-	-	-	-	-	-	-	-	-	1	-	-	-	-	2	-	-	1	-	-	

1935/1936 DIVISION THREE (SOUTH) CUP

Round	Month	Day	Venue	Opponents	W.L.D Score	Scorers	Attendance	Andrews H	Ball JT	Beresford FE	Booton H	Boyd WG	Coen JL	Colquhoun DM	Cook C	Crompton W	Crook MS	Dolman HW	Fellowes WJ	Finlayson Jock	Godfrey W	Gooney WH	Hodge J	Hubbard AA	Kidd GI	Kingham HR	Mackey TS	Martin GS	McGinnigle H	Nelson JH	Payne J	Rich LT	Roberts F	Sloan FJ	Smith Tom	Stephenson GH	Thayne W	Turner George	Round
1	Sep	25	(a)	Swindon Town	L 3-5	Stephenson (3)	3057						1	4	9		7							3	6		2		5				8			10	11		1
							Apps	-	-	-	-	-	1	1	1	-	1	-	-	-	-	-	-	1	1	-	1	-	1	-	-	-	1	-	-	1	1	-	
							Goals	-	-	-	-	-	-	-	-	-	-	-	-	-	-	-	-	-	-	-	-	-	-	-	-	-	-	-	3	-	-	

▶ The programme for the game against Bristol Rovers in 1936. Joe Payne, who netted ten in the 12-0 thrashing of the Pirates, is not mentioned on the line-up page!

▶ The 1935/36 team – Back row (left to right): Mackey, Smith, Dolman, Nelson, Finlayson, Stephenson. Front row (left to right): Hodge, Martin, Fellowes, Roberts, Payne.

TIMELINE...

9 October 1935 Manager Harold Wightman resigns.

13 April 1936 Converted wing-half Joe Payne bags ten goals in the 12-0 mauling of Bristol Rovers at Kenilworth Road. Paynes Football League record stands to this day.

25 April 1936 The Kenilworth Road attendance record is broken yet again when 23,559 see the Town (and Payne) draw 1-1 with fellow promotion chasers Coventry.

Match No	Month	Day	Venue	Opponents	W,L,D Score	Scorers	Attendance	Ball JT	Beresford FE	Booton H	Coen JL	Crompton W	Dawes AG	Dolman HW	Fellowes WJ	Finlayson Jock	Godfrey W	Hancock E	Hodge J	Hubbard AA	King TP	Kingham HR	Lutterloch HR	Mackey TS	Martin GS	McGinnigle H	Mills HM	Nelson JH	Parris JE	Payne J	Rich LT	Roberts F	Sloan FJ	Smith Tom	Stephenson GH	Stevens RF	Match No
1	Aug	29	(h)	SOUTHEND UNITED	W 1-0	Payne	14461					7		1	4		6							8	2		5			9		10		3	11		1
2	Aug	31	(a)	Walsall	W 1-0	Stephenson	9025							1	6	4			7						2	8	9	5				10		3	11		2
3	Sep	5	(a)	Cardiff City	L 0-3		17915							1	6	4			7						2	8	9	5				10		3	11		3
4	Sep	7	(h)	WALSALL	W 2-0	Ball, Payne	11395	9						1	6	4			7						2		5					10		3	11		4
5	Sep	12	(h)	CRYSTAL PALACE	W 5-2	Fellowes, Ball, Payne (3)	14187	9						1	6	4			7						2		5			8		10		3	11		5
6	Sep	16	(a)	Torquay United	D 2-2	Stephenson, Payne	5075	9						1	6	4			7						2		5			8		10		3	11		6
7	Sep	19	(a)	Exeter City	W 4-2	Payne (2), Ball, Stephenson	6550	9						1	6	4			7						2		5			8		10		3	11		7
8	Sep	26	(h)	READING	W 4-0	Payne (3), Stephenson	16759	9						1	6	4			7						2		5			8		10		3	11		8
9	Oct	3	(a)	Queens Park Rangers	L 1-2	Payne	20437	9						1	6	4			7						2		5			8		10		3	11		9
10	Oct	10	(h)	BRISTOL CITY	W 4-0	Stephenson, Ball (2), Hodge	13616	9						1	6	4			7						2		5			8		10		3	11		10
11	Oct	17	(h)	WATFORD	W 4-1	Payne (3), Ball	20955	9						1	6	4			7						2		5			8		10		3	11		11
12	Oct	24	(a)	Brighton & Hove Albion	L 1-2	Payne	14652	9						1	6	4			7						2		5			8		10		3	11		12
13	Oct	31	(h)	BOURNEMOUTH	W 1-0	Payne	11581	9			1				6	4									2		5			8		10		3	11		13
14	Nov	7	(a)	Northampton Town	L 1-3	Payne	18885	9			1				6	4			7						2		5			8		10		3		11	14
15	Nov	14	(h)	BRISTOL ROVERS	W 2-0	Payne, Ball	13138	9						1	6	4			7						2		5			8		10		3	11		15
16	Nov	21	(a)	Millwall	W 2-0	Payne, Roberts	32629	9						1	6	4									2		5			8	7	10		3	11		16
17	Dec	5	(a)	Aldershot	W 3-2	Rich, Payne, Ball	3884	9						1	6	4									2		5			8	7	10		3	11		17
18	Dec	19	(a)	Newport County	L 1-2	Stephenson	7654	9						1	6	4									2		5			8	7	10		3	11		18
19	Dec	25	(h)	NOTTS COUNTY	W 2-1	Roberts, Payne	17569						10	1	6	4									2		5			9	7	8		3	11		19
20	Dec	26	(a)	Southend United	L 0-3		11869						10	1	6	4									2		5			9	7	8		3		11	20
21	Dec	28	(a)	Notts County	L 1-2	Rich	16987						10	1	6	4			11	3							5			9	7	8		2			21
22	Jan	2	(h)	CARDIFF CITY	W 8-1	Payne (4, 1 pen), Dawes, Stephenson (3)	12368						8	1	6	4		7		3						5	5			9		10		2	11		22
23	Jan	9	(a)	Crystal Palace	W 4-0	Payne (2), Dawes, Roberts	15211						8	1	6	4		7					2				5			9		10		3	11		23
24	Jan	23	(h)	EXETER CITY	D 2-2	Payne, Stephenson	10208						8	1	6			7					2	4			5			9		10		3	11		24
25	Feb	6	(h)	QUEENS PARK RANGERS	L 0-1		13767						8	1	6						4						5			9		10		3	11		25
26	Feb	10	(a)	Reading	D 2-2	Payne (2)	8210						11	1	6	4		7					2				5			9		10	8	3			26
27	Feb	13	(a)	Bristol City	W 3-2	Dawes, Payne (2)	17193						8	1	6	4		7					2				5			9		10		3	11		27
28	Feb	20	(a)	Watford	W 3-1	Dawes, Payne, Roberts	27632						8	1	6	4		7					2				5			9		10		3	11		28
29	Feb	27	(h)	BRIGHTON & HOVE ALBION	W 2-1	Payne, Stephenson	19488						8	1	6	4		7					2				5			9		10		3	11		29
30	Mar	6	(a)	Bournemouth	L 1-2	Stephenson	9432						9	1	6	4		7					2				5			9		10	8	3	11		30
31	Mar	13	(h)	NORTHAMPTON TOWN	W 3-2	Payne (2, 1 pen), Roberts	19579						8	1	6	4		7					2				5		11	9		10		3	11		31
32	Mar	20	(a)	Bristol Rovers	L 0-4		13517						8	1	6	4		7				2					5			9		10		3	11		32
33	Mar	26	(a)	Clapton Orient	W 2-0	Payne, Stephenson	17430				1				6	4						2					5		7	9		10		3	11		33
34	Mar	27	(h)	MILLWALL	W 5-0	Hancock, Payne, Roberts, Stephenson, Finlayson	18523				1				6	4						2					5			9		10	8	3	11		34
35	Mar	29	(h)	CLAPTON ORIENT	W 2-0	Payne, Roberts	18279				1				6	4		7				2					5			9		10	8	3	11		35
36	Apr	3	(a)	Swindon Town	D 2-2	Payne, Stephenson	10432				1				6	4		8				2					5			9	7	10		3	11		36
37	Apr	7	(h)	GILLINGHAM	W 5-2	Payne (4), Finlayson	13386				1		8		6	4		7				2					5			9		10		3	11		37
38	Apr	10	(h)	ALDERSHOT	W 5-2	Dawes (2), Payne (2, 1 pen), Roberts	15505				1		8		6	4		7				2					5			9		10		3	11		38
39	Apr	17	(a)	Gillingham	L 0-1		7327				1		8		6	4		7				2					5			9		10		3	11		39
40	Apr	21	(h)	SWINDON TOWN	W 5-1	Payne (3), Dawes, Stephenson	11668				1		8		6	4		7				2					5			9		10		3	11		40
41	Apr	24	(h)	NEWPORT COUNTY	W 5-0	Payne (3), Stephenson, Dawes	14469				1		8		6	4		7				2					5			9		10		3	11		41
42	May	1	(h)	TORQUAY UNITED	W 2-0	Payne (2)	20755				1		8		6	4		7				2					5			9		10		3	11		42

Final League Position: 1st

| | | | | | | | Apps | 15 | - | 12 | 1 | 21 | 30 | 41 | 40 | 1 | 18 | 16 | 2 | 11 | - | 2 | 29 | 3 | 1 | 2 | 41 | 2 | 39 | 42 | 10 | 42 | 2 | 42 | 37 | 2 | |
| | | | | | | | Goals | 8 | - | - | - | - | 8 | - | 1 | 2 | - | 1 | 1 | - | - | - | - | - | - | - | - | - | - | 55 | 2 | 8 | - | - | 17 | - | |

Round	Month	Day	Venue	Opponents	W,L,D Score	Scorers	Attendance	Ball JT	Beresford FE	Booton H	Coen JL	Crompton W	Dawes AG	Dolman HW	Fellowes WJ	Finlayson Jock	Godfrey W	Hancock E	Hodge J	Hubbard AA	King TP	Kingham HR	Lutterloch HR	Mackey TS	Martin GS	McGinnigle H	Mills HM	Nelson JH	Parris JE	Payne J	Rich LT	Roberts F	Sloan FJ	Smith Tom	Stephenson GH	Stevens RF	Round
3	Jan	16	(h)	BLACKPOOL	D 3-3	Payne (2), Stephenson	13892							1	6	4		7					2				5			9		10		3	11		3
Rep	Jan	20	(a)	Blackpool	W 2-1	Sloan, Roberts	16700							1	6	4			7				2				5			9		10	8	3	11		Rep
4	Jan	30	(h)	SUNDERLAND	D 2-2	Roberts (2)	20205							1	6	4			7				2				5			9		10		3	11		4
Rep	Feb	3	(a)	Sunderland	L 1-3	Payne	53235							1	6	4							2				5			9	7	10	8	3	11		Rep

| | | | | | | | Apps | - | - | - | - | - | 4 | 4 | 4 | - | 1 | 2 | - | - | - | - | 4 | - | - | - | 4 | - | 4 | 1 | 4 | 3 | 4 | 4 | - | |
| | | | | | | | Goals | - | - | - | - | - | - | - | - | - | - | - | - | - | - | - | - | - | - | - | - | - | - | 3 | - | 3 | 1 | - | 1 | - | |

1936/1937 DIVISION THREE (SOUTH) CUP

Round	Month	Day	Venue	Opponents	W/L/D	Score	Scorers	Attendance	Ball JT	Beresford FE	Booton H	Coen JL	Crompton W	Dawes AG	Dolman HW	Fellowes WJ	Finlayson Jock	Godfrey W	Hancock E	Hodge J	Hubbard AA	King TP	Kingham HR	Lutterloch HR	Mackey TS	Martin GS	McGinnigle H	Mills HM	Nelson JH	Parris JE	Payne J	Rich LT	Roberts F	Sloan FJ	Smith Tom	Stephenson GH	Stevens RF	Round
1	Sep	30	(h)	BOURNEMOUTH	W	3-1	Beresford, Roberts, Stephenson	2605	9	8				1	6					7	3			5	2				4				10			11		1
2	Oct	28	(h)	ALDERSHOT	W	1-0	Stephenson	1660	9	8	2	1			6	4				7				5									10		3	11		2
3	Nov	11	(h)	NOTTS COUNTY	L	2-4	Beresford, Stevens	1484	9	10	2	1			6	4				7		3							5		8						11	3
							Apps		3	3	2	2	-	1	3	2	-	-	-	3	1	1	-	2	1	-	-	-	2	-	1	-	2	-	1	2	1	
							Goals		-	2	-	-	-	-	-	-	-	-	-	-	-	-	-	-	-	-	-	-	-	-	-	-	1	-	-	2	1	

▶ New manager Ned Liddell is welcomed to Kenilworth Road by Chairman Charles Jeyes and other Board members in August 1936.

▶ The virtually ever-present half back line on the road to promotion. Jock Finlayson, Jack Nelson and Bill Fellowes.

TIMELINE...

13 August 1936 Ned Liddell is appointed manager at Kenilworth Road.
1 May 1937 The Town finally clinch the championship of Division Three (South) and with it promotion to Division Two – Joe Payne bags 55 League goals during the season which is a record for the Division.

▶ Payne on target during the 8-1 home win over Cardiff.

▶ Jack Nelson leads the team out at Kenilworth Road.

▶ Payne heads home against Newport.

▶ The crowd surges onto the Kenilworth Road pitch after the promotion clinching 2-0 win over Torquay.

The Town's promotion winning squad line up with the Division Three (South) championship shield. Back row (left to right): King, Dolman, Mackey, Coen, Smith. Middle row (left to right): Pakes (Trainer), Finlayson, Nelson, Fellowes, N.Liddell (Manager). Front row (left to right): Hancock, Dawes, Payne, Roberts, Stephenson.

A selection of programme covers from the promotion season.

1937/1938 FOOTBALL LEAGUE DIVISION TWO

Match No	Month	Day	Venue	Opponents	W,L,D	Score	Scorers	Attendance	Carte R	Coen JL	Connelly E	Dawes AG	Dolman HW	Dreyer G	Fellowes WJ	Ferguson C	Finlayson Jock	Griffiths EO	Hancock E	Hogg F	King TP	Lewis J	Loughran JL	Lutterloch HR	Mackey TS	Nelson JH	Parris JE	Payne J	Redfern WJ	Roberts F	Smith Tom	Stephenson GH	Stevens RF	Strathie J	Vinall EJ	Match No
1	Aug	28	(a)	Stockport County	L	1-2	Dawes	19077		1		9			6		4		8		2					5	7			10	3	11				1
2	Sep	1	(h)	ASTON VILLA	W	3-2	Dawes, Payne, Hancock	25349		1		8			6		4		7		2					5		9		10	3	11				2
3	Sep	4	(h)	MANCHESTER UNITED	W	1-0	Dawes	20610		1		8			6		4		7		2					5		9		10	3	11				3
4	Sep	6	(a)	Aston Villa	L	1-4	Stephenson	30439		1		8			6		4		7		2					5		9		10	3	11				4
5	Sep	11	(a)	Sheffield United	L	0-2	-	20283		1		8			6		4		7		2					5		9		10	3	11				5
6	Sep	15	(a)	Newcastle United	W	3-1	Payne, Stevens, Griffiths	17622		1		8			6		4	7			2				3	5		9		10			11			6
7	Sep	18	(h)	TOTTENHAM HOTSPUR	L	2-4	Redfern (2)	23788		1					6		4	7			2				3	5		9	8	10			11			7
8	Sep	25	(a)	Burnley	L	2-3	Payne (2)	14073					1		6		4	7			2					5		9	8	10	3		11			8
9	Oct	2	(h)	BURY	L	0-1	-	17650					1		6		4		7		2					5		9	8	10	3	11				9
10	Oct	9	(a)	Coventry City	L	1-2	Roberts	30549		1	8				6		4	7			2					5		9		10	3	11				10
11	Oct	16	(a)	Bradford Park Avenue	D	1-1	Dawes	15397		1		8			6		4	7			2					5				10	3	11			9	11
12	Oct	23	(h)	WEST HAM UNITED	D	2-2	Dawes, Vinall	17757		1		8			6		4	7			2					5				10	3	11			9	12
13	Oct	30	(a)	Southampton	W	6-3	Parris, Ferguson, Vinall (2), Roberts (2)	20544		1	8				6	7	4				2					5	11			10	3				9	13
14	Nov	6	(h)	BLACKBURN ROVERS	W	4-1	Ferguson (2), Parris, Dawes (pen)	16776		1		8			6	7	4				2					5	11			10	3				9	14
15	Nov	13	(a)	Sheffield Wednesday	L	0-4	-	16815		1	8				6	7	4				2					5	11			10	3				9	15
16	Nov	20	(h)	CHESTERFIELD	D	1-1	Fellowes	17088		1	8				6		4							2		5	11	9		10	3				7	16
17	Nov	27	(a)	Plymouth Argyle	W	4-2	Roberts (2), Payne, Vinall	18969		1	7				6		4								2	5		8		10	3	11			9	17
18	Dec	4	(h)	FULHAM	W	4-0	Payne, Dawes, Vinall	13529		1	7				6		4								2	5		8		10	3	11			9	18
19	Dec	11	(a)	Swansea Town	D	1-1	Payne	7454		1	7				6		4								2	5		8		10	3	11			9	19
20	Dec	18	(h)	NORWICH CITY	D	1-1	Vinall	14492		1	7				6		4								2	5		8		10	3	11			9	20
21	Dec	25	(h)	BARNSLEY	W	4-0	Roberts (2), Dawes (2)	15829		1	7	8			6		4								2	5				10	3	11			9	21
22	Dec	27	(a)	Barnsley	L	1-3	Roberts	8242		1	7	8			6		4								2	5				10	3	11			9	22
23	Jan	1	(h)	STOCKPORT COUNTY	W	6-4	Vinall (2), Dawes (2), Stephenson, Roberts	14138		1	7	8			6		4								2	5				10	3	11			9	23
24	Jan	15	(a)	Manchester United	L	2-4	Ferguson, Redfern	16845		1						7	4						6		2	5			8	10	3	11			9	24
25	Jan	29	(a)	Tottenham Hotspur	L	0-3	-	29806		1	8					7	4						6		2	5				10	3	11			9	25
26	Feb	2	(h)	SHEFFIELD UNITED	L	2-3	Vinall, Payne	8414		1				5	6	7	4								2			8		10	3	11			9	26
27	Feb	5	(h)	BURNLEY	W	3-1	Stephenson, Mackey (2)	14957		1					6	7	4								2	5		8		10	3	11			9	27
28	Feb	16	(a)	Bury	W	4-3	Payne (3), Redfern	4689	2	1	10				6	7	4						3			5		9	8			11				28
29	Feb	19	(h)	COVENTRY CITY	L	1-4	Payne (pen)	17188	2	1					6	7	4						3			5		9	8	10		11				29
30	Feb	26	(h)	BRADFORD PARK AVENUE	W	4-2	Vinall (2), Payne (2, 1 pen)	14494		1						7	4						6	2	3	5		8		10		11			9	30
31	Mar	5	(a)	West Ham United	D	0-0	-	22955		1						7	4					5	6	2	3			8		10		11			9	31
32	Mar	12	(h)	SOUTHAMPTON	L	1-3	Ferguson	14428		1						7	4					5	6	2	3			8		10		11			9	32
33	Mar	19	(a)	Blackburn Rovers	D	2-2	Hancock, Stephenson	11957		1	8				6		4		7						2	5				10	3	11			9	33
34	Mar	26	(h)	SHEFFIELD WEDNESDAY	D	2-2	Roberts, Connelly	13216		1	8				6		4		7						2	5				10	3	11			9	34
35	Apr	2	(a)	Chesterfield	L	2-5	Stephenson, Ferguson	9212		1	8				6	7	4								2	5				10	3	11			9	35
36	Apr	9	(h)	PLYMOUTH ARGYLE	D	1-1	Ferguson	11516	2	1	8				6	7	4									5				10	3	11			9	36
37	Apr	15	(a)	Nottingham Forest	L	0-1	-	17644		1	8				6	7	4						3			5				10		11		2	9	37
38	Apr	16	(a)	Fulham	L	1-4	Smith	17226	2	1	7				6		4									5			9	10	3	11			8	38
39	Apr	18	(h)	NOTTINGHAM FOREST	D	2-2	Vinall, Finlayson	13561			8		1		6	7	4								2	5				10	3	11			9	39
40	Apr	23	(h)	SWANSEA TOWN	W	5-1	Stephenson, Connelly (2), Ferguson (2)	12433			8		1		6	7	4								2	5				10	3	11			9	40
41	Apr	30	(a)	Norwich City	W	4-0	Roberts (2), Finlayson, Vinall	10071			8		1		6	7	4								2	5				10	3	11			9	41
42	May	7	(h)	NEWCASTLE UNITED	W	4-1	Redfern (2), Finlayson, Stephenson	15344					1		6	7	4								2	5			8	10	3	11			9	42
				Apps					4	26	9	23	16	1	38	20	39	6	8	4	18	2	9	8	17	37	5	22	8	37	37	35	3	1	29	
				Goals					-	-	3	11	-	-	1	9	3	1	2	-	-	-	-	-	2	-	2	15	6	12	1	7	1	-	13	

Final League Position: 12th

1937/1938 FA CUP

Round	Month	Day	Venue	Opponents	W,L,D	Score	Scorers	Attendance	Carte R	Coen JL	Connelly E	Dawes AG	Dolman HW	Dreyer G	Fellowes WJ	Ferguson C	Finlayson Jock	Griffiths EO	Hancock E	Hogg F	King TP	Lewis J	Loughran JL	Lutterloch HR	Mackey TS	Nelson JH	Parris JE	Payne J	Redfern WJ	Roberts F	Smith Tom	Stephenson GH	Stevens RF	Strathie J	Vinall EJ	Round
3	Jan	8	(a)	Scarborough	D	1-1	Ferguson	11162		1		8			6	7	4								2	5				10	3	11			9	3
Rep	Jan	12	(h)	SCARBOROUGH	W	5-1	Vinall (2), Ferguson, Dawes, Stephenson	11750		1		8			6	7	4								2	5				10	3	11			9	Rep
4	Jan	22	(h)	SWINDON TOWN	W	2-1	Ferguson, Stephenson	25746		1		8			6	7	4								2	5				10	3	11			9	4
5	Feb	12	(h)	MANCHESTER CITY	L	1-3	Payne	21290		1					6	7	4							2		5		9		10	3	11			8	5
				Apps					-	4	-	3	-	-	4	4	4	-	-	-	-	-	-	1	3	4	-	1	-	4	4	4	-	-	4	
				Goals					-	-	-	1	-	-	-	3	-	-	-	-	-	-	-	-	-	-	-	1	-	-	-	2	-	-	2	

◗ The 1937/38 team – Back row (left to right): N.Liddell (Manager), Finlayson, King, Coen, Smith, Fellowes, Pakes (Trainer). Front row (left to right): Hancock, Dawes, Payne, Roberts, Stephenson, Nelson.

TIMELINE...

Summer 1937 The Town extend the Kenilworth Road terracing and the Main Stand in readiness for Division Two.
1 Sept 1937 25,349 see the Town beat Aston Villa 3-2 in the first game back in Division Two.
22 January 1938 The Town beat Swindon in the F.A.Cup in front of a new record 25,746.
26 February 1938 Manager Ned Liddell resigns to take up the chief scout post at Chelsea.
11 March 1938 Joe Payne is sold to Chelsea.

1938/1939 FOOTBALL LEAGUE DIVISION TWO

Match No	Month	Day	Venue	Opponents	W,L,D Score	Scorers	Attendance	Billington HJR	Burgess WW	Carroll JT	Carte R	Clark C	Coen JL	Connelly E	Dolman HW	Dreyer G	Dunsmore TH	Ferguson C	Finlayson Jock	King TP	Loughran JL	Mayberry S	Nelson JH	Redfern WJ	Roberts F	Smith Tom	Stephenson GH	Stevens RF	Strathie J	Vinall EJ	Match No
1	Aug	27	(a)	West Bromwich Albion	L 0-3	-	24377			7				8	1		3		4	6			5	10	2		11			9	1
2	Aug	31	(h)	NEWCASTLE UNITED	W 2-1	Stephenson, Nelson	17689							8	1		3	7	4	6			5	10	2		11			9	2
3	Sep	3	(h)	NORWICH CITY	W 2-1	Vinall (pen), Ferguson	16547							8	1		3	7	4	6			5	10	2		11			9	3
4	Sep	5	(a)	Coventry City	L 0-1	-	19844				2			8	1		3	7	4	6			5	10			11			9	4
5	Sep	10	(a)	Manchester City	W 2-1	Connelly, Vinall	31316				2			8	1		3	7	4	6			5	10			11			9	5
6	Sep	17	(a)	Plymouth Argyle	L 1-4	Connelly	15083							8	1		3	7	4	6			5	10	2		11			9	6
7	Sep	24	(h)	SHEFFIELD UNITED	W 2-0	Vinall, Connelly	17436							8	1		3	7	4	6			5	10	2		11			9	7
8	Oct	1	(a)	Burnley	L 2-3	Vinall (2)	11699							8	1		3	7	4	6			5	10	2		11			9	8
9	Oct	8	(h)	TOTTENHAM HOTSPUR	D 0-0	-	21061							8	1		3	7	4	6			5	10	2		11			9	9
10	Oct	15	(h)	BRADFORD PARK AVENUE	D 2-2	Connelly (2)	14955							8	1		3	7	4	6			5	10	2		11			9	10
11	Oct	22	(a)	Swansea Town	W 3-2	Clark (2), Connelly	8658					7	1	10			3		4	6			5	8	11	2				9	11
12	Oct	29	(h)	BLACKBURN ROVERS	D 1-1	Clark	16819					7	1	10			3		4	6			5	8		2	11			9	12
13	Nov	5	(a)	Tranmere Rovers	W 3-2	Billington (2), Redfern	11409	9				7	1	10			3		4	6			5	8	2		11				13
14	Nov	12	(h)	WEST HAM UNITED	L 1-2	Stephenson	18331	9				7	1	10			3		4	6			5	8	2		11				14
15	Nov	19	(a)	Bury	W 5-2	Billington (2), Stephenson (2), Redfern	8658	9				7	1	10			3		4	6			5	8	2		11				15
16	Nov	26	(h)	SHEFFIELD WEDNESDAY	L 1-5	Billington	15936	9				7	1	10			3		4	6			5	8	2		11				16
17	Dec	3	(a)	Fulham	L 1-2	Redfern	19443	9				7	1	10			3		4		6		5	8	2			11			17
18	Dec	10	(h)	CHESTERFIELD	W 5-0	Billington (4), Stephenson	12744	9				7	1	10			3		4		6			8	2		11				18
19	Dec	17	(a)	Millwall	L 1-2	Billington	19733	9				7	1	10			3		4		6		5	8	2		11				19
20	Dec	24	(a)	WEST BROMWICH ALBION	W 3-1	Redfern (2), Stephenson	8887	9				7	1	10		5	3		4		6			8	2		11				20
21	Dec	26	(a)	Nottingham Forest	W 4-2	Billington, Connelly, Clark, Redfern	12688	9				7	1	10		5	3		4		6			8	2		11				21
22	Dec	27	(h)	NOTTINGHAM FOREST	W 1-0	Redfern (pen)	17125	9					1	10		5	3		4		6			8	2	7	11				22
23	Dec	31	(a)	Norwich City	L 1-2	Clark	9336	9				7	1	10		5	3		4		6			8	2		11				23
24	Jan	14	(h)	MANCHESTER CITY	W 3-0	Billington, Connelly (2)	16163	9		7			1	10		5	3		4	6				8	2		11				24
25	Jan	21	(h)	PLYMOUTH ARGYLE	L 3-4	Connelly, Billington (2)	13120	9		7			1	10		5	3		4	6				8	2		11				25
26	Jan	28	(a)	Sheffield United	D 2-2	Billington (2)	25315	9		7			1	10		5	3		4	6				8	2		11				26
27	Feb	4	(h)	BURNLEY	W 1-0	Marshall (og)	13547	9		7			1	10		5	3		4	6				8	2		11				27
28	Feb	11	(a)	Tottenham Hotspur	W 1-0	Stephenson	30704	9		7			1	10		5	3		4	6				8	2		11				28
29	Feb	18	(a)	Bradford Park Avenue	L 1-2	Stephenson	8215	9		7			1	10		5	3		4	6				8	2		11				29
30	Feb	25	(h)	SWANSEA TOWN	W 6-3	Billington (4), Clark, Stephenson	11264	9				7	1	10		5	3		4	6				8	2		11				30
31	Mar	11	(h)	TRANMERE ROVERS	W 3-0	Stephenson, Roberts, Billington	12788	9	7				1	10		5	3		4	6				8	2		11				31
32	Mar	16	(a)	Blackburn Rovers	L 0-2	-	8872	9	7				1	10		5	3		4	6				8	2		11				32
33	Mar	18	(a)	West Ham United	W 1-0	Redfern	18628		7				1	10		5	3		4	6				8	2		11			9	33
34	Mar	25	(h)	BURY	W 2-1	Redfern, Connelly	11943		7				1	10		5	3		4	6				8	2		11			9	34
35	Apr	1	(a)	Sheffield Wednesday	L 1-4	Finlayson	28051			7			1	10		5	3		4	6				8	2		11	7		9	35
36	Apr	7	(h)	SOUTHAMPTON	W 6-2	Billington (3), Redfern (2), Connelly	15946	9		7			1	10		5	3		4	6				8	2		11				36
37	Apr	8	(h)	FULHAM	W 2-1	Connelly, Billington	16322	9		7			1	10		5	3		4	6				8	2		11				37
38	Apr	10	(a)	Southampton	W 4-0	Stephenson, Billington (3)	15114	9		7			1	10		5	3		4	6				8	2		11				38
39	Apr	15	(a)	Chesterfield	W 2-1	Redfern (2)	14925	9		7			1	10		5	3		4	6				8	2		11				39
40	Apr	22	(h)	MILLWALL	D 0-0	-	20109	9		7			1	10		5	3		4	6				8	2		11				40
41	Apr	29	(a)	Newcastle United	L 0-2	-	10341	9		7			1	10		5	3		4	6				8	2		11				41
42	May	6	(h)	COVENTRY CITY	L 1-3	Stephenson	13128	9	7				1	10		3	3		4	2	1			8	6		11	5			42
				Final League Position: 7th		1 Own Goal	**Apps**	27	5	13	2	14	31	41	10	22	40	9	42	26	16	1	19	33	37	16	40	2	1	15	
							Goals	28	-	-	-	6	-	13	-	-	-	1	1	-	-	-	1	13	1	-	12	-	-	5	

1938/1939 FA CUP

Round	Month	Day	Venue	Opponents	W,L,D Score	Scorers	Attendance	Billington HJR	Burgess WW	Carroll JT	Carte R	Clark C	Coen JL	Connelly E	Dolman HW	Dreyer G	Dunsmore TH	Ferguson C	Finlayson Jock	King TP	Loughran JL	Mayberry S	Nelson JH	Redfern WJ	Roberts F	Smith Tom	Stephenson GH	Stevens RF	Strathie J	Vinall EJ	Round
3	Jan	7	(a)	Liverpool	L 0-3	-	40341	9				7	1	10		5	3		4	2				8	6		11				3
							Apps	1	-	-		1	1	1		1	1		1	1				1	1		1				
							Goals	-	-	-		-	-	-		-	-		-	-				-	-		-				

SEE PAGE 293 FOR RESULTS IN THE FA CUP FOR 1945/46

▶ **The 1938/39 team** – Back row (left to right): Pembleton (Trainer), Finlayson, Smith, Dolman, Dunsmore, Loughran, McBain (Manager). Front row (left to right): Carroll, Connelly, Vinall, Roberts, Stephenson, Nelson.

TIMELINE...

1 June 1938 Neil McBain is appointed manager.

Summer 1938 The Oak Road end of the ground is covered for the first time.

6 May 1939 The Town finish seventh after a strong push for promotion to the top flight. Sadly, this is to be last season of competitive football for seven years. Local boy Hugh Billington nets 28 goals in only 27 starts.

5 June 1939 McBain resigns citing the ill-health of his wife.

Match No	Month	Day	Venue	Opponents	W,L,D Score	Scorers	Attendance	Bates WH	Beach DF	Billington HJR	Brice GHJ	Bywater NL	Connelly E	Cooke WH	Daniel MJ	Driver A	Duggan EJ	Duke GE	Duncan D	Gager HE	Gardiner D	Goodyear GW	Hacking R	Kettley SC	Lake LE	Morrison M	Sanderson JR	Shanks WG	Soo FC	Steen AW	Streten BR	Wallbanks WH	Waugh WL	Match No
1	Aug	31	(h)	SHEFFIELD WEDNESDAY	W 4-1	Daniel (3), Waugh	21105		2	9			10	6	8			1		5								3		4	7		11	1
2	Sep	4	(a)	Bradford Park Avenue	L 1-2	Daniel	16931		2	9			10	6	8			1		5								3		4	7		11	2
3	Sep	7	(a)	Fulham	L 1-2	Billington	26038			9			10	6	8			1		5								3	2	4	7		11	3
4	Sep	11	(h)	MILLWALL	W 3-0	Billington (2), Connelly	15676		3	9			10	6	8			1		5									2	4	7		11	4
5	Sep	14	(h)	BURY	W 2-0	Connelly, Billington	17864		3	9			10	6	8			1		5									2	4	7		11	5
6	Sep	21	(a)	Nottingham Forest	L 2-4	Billington (2)	24237		3	9			10	6	8			1		5									2	4	7		11	6
7	Sep	28	(a)	Plymouth Argyle	L 1-2	Gager	27535		2		9		10	6	8			1		5								3	2	4	7		11	7
8	Oct	5	(h)	LEICESTER CITY	L 1-2	Gager	18073		2		5		10	6				1		9								3	2	4	7		11	8
9	Oct	7	(a)	Millwall	L 0-2	-	9845	7	3				10	4		9		1										8	2	6			11	9
10	Oct	12	(a)	Chesterfield	L 1-2	Driver	13190		3			1		6		9				5	10	8			2					6			11	10
11	Oct	19	(h)	SOUTHAMPTON	D 2-2	Connelly, Daniel	17668		3			1	10		8	9				5	6				2					4	7		11	11
12	Oct	26	(a)	Newport County	W 3-1	Duggan (2), Daniel	11480		3	9	5	1			4	10	8		11						2					6			7	12
13	Nov	2	(h)	BARNSLEY	W 3-1	Billington (2), Duggan	21723		3	9	5	1			4	10	8		11						2					6			7	13
14	Nov	9	(a)	Burnley	D 1-1	Driver	26007		3	9		1			4	10	8		11	5					2					6			7	14
15	Nov	16	(h)	TOTTENHAM HOTSPUR	W 3-2	Duggan, Duncan, Billington	26362		3	9		1			4	10	8		11	5					2					6			7	15
16	Nov	23	(a)	Swansea Town	L 0-2	-	11768		3	9		1			4	10	8		11	5					2					6			7	16
17	Nov	30	(h)	NEWCASTLE UNITED	W 4-3	Waugh, Driver, Billington, Daniel	25410		3	9		1	2		8	10			11	5	6									4			7	17
18	Dec	7	(a)	West Bromwich Albion	W 2-1	Duncan, Billington	20685			9		1	2		8	10			11	5	6									4			7	18
19	Dec	14	(h)	BIRMINGHAM	L 1-3	Billington	21760		3	9		1	2		8	10			11	5	6									4			7	19
20	Dec	21	(a)	Coventry City	D 0-0	-	13047		3	9		1	2	10					11	5	6	8								4			7	20
21	Dec	25	(a)	West Ham United	L 1-2	Duncan	19948			9		1	2	10	8				11	5	6						3			4			7	21
22	Dec	26	(h)	WEST HAM UNITED	W 2-1	Billington, Waugh	22320		3	9		1	2	10	8				11	5	6	4								4			7	22
23	Dec	28	(a)	Sheffield Wednesday	D 1-1	Daniel	29497		3	9		1	2		8	10			11	5	6									4			7	23
24	Jan	4	(h)	FULHAM	W 2-0	Billington, Cooke (pen)	17341			9	5		2		8	10	1		11		6						3			4			7	24
25	Jan	18	(a)	Bury	L 0-3	-	16083			9		1	2		8	10				5	6						3	11		4			7	25
26	Jan	29	(h)	NOTTINGHAM FOREST	W 3-2	Billington, Duncan, Driver	4209			9			2			10			11	5	6	8					3			4			7	26
27	Feb	1	(a)	PLYMOUTH ARGYLE	L 3-4	Billington, Connelly, Cooke (pen)	15165			9			2	10		8			11	5	6						3			4			7	27
28	Feb	15	(h)	CHESTERFIELD	D 1-1	Daniel	15175			9	5		2		10		8				6						3	7		4	1		11	28
29	Feb	22	(a)	Southampton	W 3-1	Duggan (2), Driver	11710						2		10	9	8			5	6						3	7		4	1		11	29
30	Mar	15	(a)	Burnley	L 1-3	Driver	18462			9			2			10	8			5	6						3	7		4	1		11	30
31	Mar	22	(a)	Tottenham Hotspur	L 1-2	Duggan	36160		2				10	3			8		11	5	6						3	7		4	1		11	31
32	Mar	29	(h)	SWANSEA TOWN	W 3-0	Duggan (2), Billington	13486		3	9		1	10				8		11	5	6							7		4			11	32
33	Apr	4	(a)	Manchester City	L 0-2	-	53692		3	9			10	2	8				11	5										6	1		7	33
34	Apr	5	(a)	Newcastle United	L 2-7	Driver (2)	40372			5			10	2	6	9			11				8				3			4	1		7	34
35	Apr	7	(h)	MANCHESTER CITY	D 0-0	-	22976			10	5		8	2	6	9			11						4		3				1		7	35
36	Apr	12	(h)	WEST BROMWICH ALBION	W 2-0	Connelly, Billington	14920			10	5		8	2	6	9							4		3			7			1		11	36
37	Apr	19	(a)	Birmingham	L 0-1	-	27316			10	5		8	2	6	9							4		3			7			1		11	37
38	Apr	26	(h)	COVENTRY CITY	D 1-1	Waugh	13686			10			8	2		9			11	5	6				4		3				1		7	38
39	May	3	(a)	Leicester City	L 1-2	Driver	18578			9	5			8	10				11	2	6				4		3				1		7	39
40	May	10	(a)	Barnsley	L 0-4	-	15264			9	5			8	10				11	2	6				3	1	3				1		7	40
41	May	24	(h)	BRADFORD PARK AVENUE	W 3-0	Billington (2), Driver	10805			5	9	1	8			6				2	10				3			7		4			11	41
42	May	31	(h)	NEWPORT COUNTY	W 6-3	Connelly, Wallbanks, Waugh, Billington (3)	7814			5	9		8			6				2	10				3					4		1	7	42

Final League Position: 13th

| | | | | | | | Apps | 1 | 23 | 36 | 13 | 19 | 23 | 33 | 29 | 29 | 10 | 10 | 23 | 34 | 22 | 10 | 1 | 1 | 28 | 1 | 6 | 8 | 38 | 10 | 12 | 1 | 41 | |
| | | | | | | | Goals | - | - | 23 | - | - | 6 | 2 | 9 | 10 | 9 | - | 4 | 2 | - | - | - | - | - | - | - | - | - | - | - | 1 | 5 | |

Round	Month	Day	Venue	Opponents	W,L,D Score	Scorers	Attendance	Bates WH	Beach DF	Billington HJR	Brice GHJ	Bywater NL	Connelly E	Cooke WH	Daniel MJ	Driver A	Duggan EJ	Duke GE	Duncan D	Gager HE	Gardiner D	Goodyear GW	Hacking R	Kettley SC	Lake LE	Morrison M	Sanderson JR	Shanks WG	Soo FC	Steen AW	Streten BR	Wallbanks WH	Waugh WL	Round
3	Jan	11	(h)	NOTTS COUNTY	W 6-0	Billington (5), Daniel	21842			9		1	2	8	10				11	5	6						3			4			7	3
4	Jan	25	(h)	SWANSEA TOWN	W 2-0	Daniel, Roberts (og)	24327			9		1	2	8	10				11	5	6						3			4			7	4
5	Feb	8	(h)	BURNLEY	D 0-0	-	22640		3	9		1	2	8	10				11	5	6									4			7	5
Rep	Feb	11	(a)	Burnley	L 0-3	-	28330		3	9		1	2	8		10	7		11	5	6									4				Rep

1 Own Goal

| | | | | | | | Apps | - | 2 | 4 | | 4 | 4 | 4 | 3 | 1 | 1 | | 4 | 4 | 4 | | | | | | 2 | | | 4 | | | 3 | |
| | | | | | | | Goals | - | - | 5 | | - | 1 | 2 | 2 | - | - | | - | - | - | | | | | | - | | | - | | | - | |

The 1946/47 team – Back row (left to right): Pembleton (Trainer), Soo, Lake, Bywater, Cooke, Gardiner, Duggan. Front row (left to right): Waugh, Daniel, Billington, Driver, Duncan, Gager.

TIMELINE...

31 August 1946 Peacetime football returns with a 4-1 home win over Sheffield Wednesday. Mel Daniel nets the first post-war hat-trick.
16 November 1946 A League clash with Tottenham draws in a record 26,362 to Kenilworth Road.
30 November 1946 The Town win 4-3 against promotion chasing Newcastle at Kenilworth Road after being 0-3 down at the interval.

1947/1948 FOOTBALL LEAGUE DIVISION TWO

Match No	Month	Day	Venue	Opponents	W/L/D Score	Scorers	Attendance	Billington HJR	Brennan RA	Collins WH	Connelly E	Cooke WH	Daniel MJ	Driver A	Duggan EJ	Duncan D	Gager HE	Gardiner D	Hall LF	Hughes WM	Lake LE	Nelson SE	O'Brien J	Ottewell S	Owen SW	Shanks WG	Small PV	Soo FC	Streten BR	Wallbanks WH	Waugh WL	Wilson James	Match No
1	Aug	23	(a)	Coventry City	L 1-4	Driver	25550	9			10			8	11	5	6		3	2								4	1		7		1
2	Aug	27	(a)	Brentford	W 3-0	Billington (3)	17022	9			10			8	11	5			3	2					6			4	1		7		2
3	Aug	30	(h)	NEWCASTLE UNITED	W 2-1	Driver, Connelly	24570	9			10			8	11	5			3	2					6			4	1		7		3
4	Sep	3	(h)	BRENTFORD	W 3-0	Billington (3)	20921	9			10			8	11	5			3	2					6			4	1		7		4
5	Sep	6	(a)	Birmingham City	L 1-2	Soo (pen)	40032	9			10			8	11	5			3	2					6			4	1		7		5
6	Sep	8	(a)	Leicester City	L 2-3	Duggan (2)	22573	9					7	10	8	5			3	2					6			4	1		11		6
7	Sep	13	(h)	WEST BROMWICH ALBION	D 1-1	Connelly	21019				8	2		9	10	11	5		3						6			4	1		7		7
8	Sep	17	(h)	LEICESTER CITY	W 2-1	Duggan (2)	17597				8	2		9	10	11	5		3						6			4	1		7		8
9	Sep	20	(a)	Barnsley	L 0-3	-	17670				10	2		8	11	5			3						6			4	1		7		9
10	Sep	27	(h)	PLYMOUTH ARGYLE	D 0-0	-	19244	9				2	10		8		5		3						6	7		4	1		11		10
11	Oct	4	(a)	Bradford Park Avenue	D 2-2	Billington, Daniel	21568	9				2	10		8		5		3						6	7		4	1		11		11
12	Oct	11	(a)	Cardiff City	L 0-1	-	39505	9			10	2			8		5		3						6	7		4	1		11		12
13	Oct	18	(a)	Sheffield Wednesday	L 0-1	-	40299	9			10	2			8	7	5		3						6			4	1		11		13
14	Oct	25	(h)	TOTTENHAM HOTSPUR	D 0-0	-	26496	9	10			2			8	11	5		3						6			4	1		7		14
15	Nov	1	(a)	Millwall	L 1-3	Daniel	25290		7		10	2	8		9		5		3						6			4	1		11		15
16	Nov	8	(h)	CHESTERFIELD	W 2-1	Daniel (2)	18352		7		10	2			9		5		3						6			8	1		11		16
17	Nov	15	(a)	West Ham United	D 0-0	-	30535	8	7		10	2			9		5		3						6				1		11		17
18	Nov	22	(h)	BURY	D 1-1	Duggan	17249	8	7		10	2			9		5		3						6				1		11		18
19	Nov	29	(a)	Southampton	L 1-3	Soo	20133		7		10				9		5		3						6			8	1		11		19
20	Dec	6	(h)	DONCASTER ROVERS	W 2-1	Brennan, Driver	15556	9	7			2		8			5		3				11	10	6			4	1				20
21	Dec	13	(a)	Nottingham Forest	W 2-1	Brennan, Soo (pen)	12977	9	8			2					5		3				11	10	6	7		4	1				21
22	Dec	20	(h)	COVENTRY CITY	L 2-3	Brennan, Billington	15687	9	8			2					5		3				11	10	6	7		4	1				22
23	Dec	26	(a)	Leeds United	W 2-0	O'Brien, Billington	28597	9	8			2					5		3				11	10	6	7		4	1				23
24	Dec	27	(h)	LEEDS UNITED	W 6-1	O'Brien, Ottewell, Duggan, Brennan (2), Soo (pen)	16964		8			2			9		5		3				11	10	6	7		4	1				24
25	Jan	3	(a)	Newcastle United	L 1-4	O'Brien	64931		8			2			9		5		3				11	10	6			4	1				25
26	Jan	17	(h)	BIRMINGHAM CITY	L 0-1	-	19697	9	8			2					6		5	3		7	11	10				4	1				26
27	Jan	31	(a)	West Bromwich Albion	L 0-1	-	27047	9	10			2					5		3				11	8	6			4	1		7		27
28	Feb	14	(a)	Plymouth Argyle	W 3-1	Ottewell, Daniel, Billington	22175	9	7			2	8				6		5	3				10				4	1		11		28
29	Feb	21	(h)	BRADFORD PARK AVENUE	D 3-3	Billington, Brennan, Ottewell	11418	9	7			2	8				6		5	3				10				4	1		11		29
30	Feb	28	(h)	CARDIFF CITY	D 1-1	Daniel	22112		7			2	8		9		6		5	3				10				4	1		11		30
31	Mar	6	(h)	SHEFFIELD WEDNESDAY	D 1-1	Billington	16888	9	7			2	8				6		5	3				10				4	1		11		31
32	Mar	20	(h)	MILLWALL	L 1-2	Daniel	14128		8			3	11	10			6		5	2				9				4	1		7		32
33	Mar	26	(h)	FULHAM	L 0-3	-	18033		10				8		9		6		5	3			11					4	1		7	2	33
34	Mar	27	(a)	Chesterfield	L 0-2	-	10682						11		9			4	5	3				10	6	7		8	1				34
35	Mar	29	(a)	Fulham	D 1-1	Daniel	20151	10				2	8		9			4	5	3					6	7			1		11		35
36	Apr	3	(h)	WEST HAM UNITED	D 0-0	-	15059	10				2	8		9			4	5	3					6	7			1		11		36
37	Apr	5	(a)	Tottenham Hotspur	W 1-0	Daniel	23807	8				2	10		9			4	5	3					6	7			1		11		37
38	Apr	10	(a)	Bury	D 2-2	Brennan, Ottewell	15648	8				2	10		9			4	5	3				9	6	7			1		11		38
39	Apr	14	(h)	BARNSLEY	W 2-1	Daniel, Duggan	13594	8				2	10		9		6		5	3						7			1		11		39
40	Apr	17	(h)	SOUTHAMPTON	L 0-2	-	17202	8				2	10		9			4	5	3					6				1		11		40
41	Apr	24	(a)	Doncaster Rovers	W 2-0	Brennan (2)	7263	8			10	2			9			4	5	3					6				1	7	11		41
42	May	1	(h)	NOTTINGHAM FOREST	W 2-1	Brennan (2, 1 pen)	15126		8	4	10				9				5	3					6				1	7	11	2	42
				Apps				23	27	1	15	33	22	12	24	9	25	26	16	31	17	1	9	15	27	10	5	33	42	3	33	3	
				Goals				12	11	-	2	-	10	3	7	-	-	-	-	-	-	-	3	4	-	-	-	4	-	-	-	-	

Final League Position: 13th

1947/1948 FA CUP

Round	Month	Day	Venue	Opponents	W/L/D Score	Scorers	Attendance	Billington HJR	Brennan RA	Collins WH	Connelly E	Cooke WH	Daniel MJ	Driver A	Duggan EJ	Duncan D	Gager HE	Gardiner D	Hall LF	Hughes WM	Lake LE	Nelson SE	O'Brien J	Ottewell S	Owen SW	Shanks WG	Small PV	Soo FC	Streten BR	Wallbanks WH	Waugh WL	Wilson James	Round
3	Jan	10	(a)	Plymouth Argyle	W 4-2	Brennan (2), Billington (2)	34689	9	8								6	5		3	2		11	10	7			4	1				3
4	Jan	24	(h)	COVENTRY CITY	W 3-2	Soo, Waugh, Ottewell	23982	9	8			2					6	5		3			11	10				4	1		7		4
5	Feb	7	(a)	Queens Park Rangers	L 1-3	Waugh	30564	9	8			2					6	5		3			11	10				4	1		7		5
				Apps				3	3			2					3	3		3	1		3	3	1			3	3		2		
				Goals				2	2															1				1			2		

▶ **The 1947/48 team** – Back row (left to right): Garner, Bywater, Morton, Palmer, Hughes. Second row (left to right): Walker, Mackey (Trainer), Ruffett, Gardiner, Sanderson, Duncan (Manager), Driver, Mitchell (Director), Soo, Duggan, Lake, Hall, Kettley, Hann (Trainer), Cooke. Third row (left to right): Hewson (Director), Daniel, Wright (Director), Billington, Jeyes (Chairman), Gager, England (Director), Connelly, Woods (Director), Richardson (Director). Front row (left to right): High, Warner, Shanks, Thompson, Waugh, Owen, Wallbanks.

TIMELINE...

24 May 1947 Manager George Martin is poached by Newcastle with Dally Duncan given the player-manager role at Kenilworth Road.
Summer 1947 Welsh International full-back Billy Hughes arrives from Birmingham for a Luton record £11,000.
25 October 1947 Tottenham smash the Kenilworth Road gate record again with 26,496 squeezing in.
March 1948 Hugh Billington and Billy Hughes are sold to Chelsea for a combined £20,000.

1948/1949 FOOTBALL LEAGUE DIVISION TWO

Match No	Month	Day	Venue	Opponents	W,L,D	Score	Scorers	Attendance	Aherne T	Arnison JW	Brennan RA	Burtenshaw CE	Burtenshaw WF	Collins WH	Cooke WH	Daniel MJ	Duggan EJ	Duke GE	Gardiner D	Gripton EW	Hall LF	Kiernan T	Lake LE	Lindsay D	Morton RH	Mulvaney J	Nelson SE	O'Brien J	Owen SW	Ruffett RD	Shanks WG	Small PV	Streten BR	Taylor Jack	Watkins C	Waugh WL	Wilson James	Match No
1	Aug	21	(h)	QUEENS PARK RANGERS	D	0-0	-	23764		8			10	2					4	6	5			3	7							1				11		1
2	Aug	23	(a)	Cardiff City	D	3-3	Duggan, Nelson, Arnison	35687		8				4	2		10		6		5			3	7		7					1				11		2
3	Aug	28	(a)	Leeds United	L	0-2	-	25463		8				4	2		10		6		5			3	7		7					1				11		3
4	Aug	30	(h)	CARDIFF CITY	W	3-0	Arnison (3)	20185		8					2		10		6		5			3					6			7	1			11		4
5	Sep	4	(a)	Bradford Park Avenue	L	1-4	Arnison	18697		10					2		8		4		5			3					6			7	1			11		5
6	Sep	6	(h)	BLACKBURN ROVERS	W	2-0	Brennan, Duggan	18642		8					2		10		6		5			3					6			7	1			11		6
7	Sep	11	(h)	SOUTHAMPTON	D	1-1	Small	20257		8				4			10		6		5			3								7	1			11	2	7
8	Sep	18	(a)	Barnsley	W	2-1	Small, Arnison	20922		8				4	3		10		6		5			3								7	1			11	2	8
9	Sep	20	(a)	Blackburn Rovers	L	1-4	Duggan	18478		8				4	3		10		6		5											7	1			11	2	9
10	Sep	25	(h)	GRIMSBY TOWN	D	1-1	Arnison	18173		8				4	3		10		6		5										7		1			11	2	10
11	Oct	2	(a)	Nottingham Forest	L	0-2	-	22695		9	7				3		10		4		5								6		7		1			11	2	11
12	Oct	9	(h)	LEICESTER CITY	D	1-1	Duggan	16663		9	7				3		10	10	8		5								6				1		10	11	2	12
13	Oct	16	(a)	Brentford	L	0-2	-	23211		9	7				3		10		4		5								6		8		1		10	11	2	13
14	Oct	23	(h)	TOTTENHAM HOTSPUR	D	1-1	Arnison (pen)	24859		9	7				3		10		4		5								6		8		1		10	11	2	14
15	Oct	30	(a)	West Ham United	W	1-0	Arnison	28132		9	7				3				6		5	4									8		1		10	11	2	15
16	Nov	6	(h)	BURY	W	1-0	Arnison	16764		9	7				3				6		5	4									8		1		10	11	2	16
17	Nov	13	(a)	West Bromwich Albion	L	1-2	Watkins	32589		9	7				3				6		5	8			4								1		10	11	2	17
18	Nov	20	(h)	CHESTERFIELD	W	1-0	Arnison	17808		9	7				3				6		5	8			4								1		10	11	2	18
19	Nov	27	(a)	Lincoln City	D	4-4	Waugh (2), Kiernan (2)	10817		9	7				3				6		5	8			4								1		10	11	2	19
20	Dec	4	(h)	SHEFFIELD WEDNESDAY	W	2-1	Kiernan, Arnison	18558		9	7				3				6		5	8			4								1		10	11	2	20
21	Dec	11	(a)	Coventry City	L	0-2	-	19951		9	10				3				6		5								7				1		10	11	2	21
22	Dec	18	(h)	Queens Park Rangers	W	3-0	Arnison (2), Brennan	16557		9	7				3				6		5												1		10	11	2	22
23	Dec	25	(h)	PLYMOUTH ARGYLE	W	3-1	Arnison (2), Kiernan	17109		9	7				3				6		5												1		10	11	2	23
24	Dec	27	(a)	Plymouth Argyle	D	1-1	Wilson	32241		9	7				3				6		5												1		10	11	2	24
25	Jan	1	(h)	LEEDS UNITED	D	0-0	-	15310			7				3			9	6		5												1		10	11	2	25
26	Jan	15	(h)	BRADFORD PARK AVENUE	L	0-1	-	16071		9	7				3				6		5												1		10	11	2	26
27	Jan	22	(a)	Southampton	D	1-1	Kiernan	24815			9				3				6		5	8											1		10	11	2	27
28	Feb	5	(h)	BARNSLEY	W	1-0	Small	16386			9	11			3				6		5	8										7	1		10		2	28
29	Feb	26	(h)	NOTTINGHAM FOREST	W	4-3	Brennan, Arnison, Small, Thomas (og)	17777		9	10				3				6		5	8			2							7	1		4	11		29
30	Mar	5	(a)	Leicester City	D	1-1	Owen	26321		9	10				3						5	8			2				6			7	1		4	11		30
31	Mar	12	(h)	BRENTFORD	W	2-1	Brennan (2, 1 pen)	16682		9	10				3						5	8			2				6			7	1		4	11		31
32	Mar	19	(a)	Tottenham Hotspur	L	1-2	Brennan	41839	3	9	10				2						5								6			7	1		4	11		32
33	Mar	26	(h)	WEST HAM UNITED	L	0-1	-	15587		9	10				3						5	8			2				6			7	1		4	11		33
34	Apr	2	(a)	Bury	L	1-3	Brennan	11461	3		9				2						5	8			6	11		4				7	1			11		34
35	Apr	9	(h)	WEST BROMWICH ALBION	L	0-1	-	16651	3		9	7			2				4		5	8							6				1		10	11		35
36	Apr	15	(a)	Fulham	L	1-4	Owen	35622			9	7			2			1	4	5	8		3						6						10	11		36
37	Apr	16	(h)	Chesterfield	L	0-1	-	10938			9	7			2			1	4	5	8	5	3						6						10	11		37
38	Apr	18	(h)	FULHAM	L	1-3	Brennan	20125			9	7			2			1	4	5	8	5	3						6						10	11		38
39	Apr	23	(a)	LINCOLN CITY	W	6-0	C Burtenshaw, Mulvaney (2), Brennan (2, 1 pen), Taylor	12643			10	7			3			1	6						9				5					8	4	11	2	39
40	Apr	30	(a)	Sheffield Wednesday	D	0-0	-	18228		9	7				3			1	6			4							5					8	10	11	2	40
41	May	3	(a)	Grimsby Town	L	1-2	Brennan	13809		9	7				3			1	6			4			11				5					8	10	11	2	41
42	May	7	(h)	COVENTRY CITY	W	2-0	Daniel, Morton	13705		9					3	11			6						4				5					7	1	10		42
				Final League Position: 10th			**1 Own Goal**	**Apps**	3	30	42	8	1	6	37	2	14	6	37	3	36	23	6	7	17	5	3	2	20	1	6	16	36	3	27	38	27	
								Goals	-	17	11	1	-	-	-	-	1	4	-	-	5	-	-	1	2	1	-	2	-	-	4	1	1	2	1		

1948/1949 FA CUP

Round	Month	Day	Venue	Opponents	W,L,D	Score	Scorers	Attendance	Aherne T	Arnison JW	Brennan RA	Burtenshaw CE	Burtenshaw WF	Collins WH	Cooke WH	Daniel MJ	Duggan EJ	Duke GE	Gardiner D	Gripton EW	Hall LF	Kiernan T	Lake LE	Lindsay D	Morton RH	Mulvaney J	Nelson SE	O'Brien J	Owen SW	Ruffett RD	Shanks WG	Small PV	Streten BR	Taylor Jack	Watkins C	Waugh WL	Wilson James	Round
3	Jan	8	(h)	WEST HAM UNITED	W	3-1	Kiernan, Arnison, Watkins	22229		9	7				3				6		5	8			4								1		10	11	2	3
4	Jan	29	(h)	WALSALL	W	4-0	Brennan (3), Watkins	26422			9				3				6		5	8			4						7		1		10	11	2	4
5	Feb	12	(h)	LEICESTER CITY	D	5-5	Kiernan (2), Small, Brennan, Watkins	26280			9				3				6		5	8							7			7	1		10	11	2	5
Rep	Feb	19	(a)	Leicester City	L	3-5	Brennan (2), Arnison	38322		9	10				3				6		5					2			7			7	1		4	11	3	Rep
								Apps		2	4				4				4		4	3			3	1			3			3	4		4	4	3	
								Goals		2	6											3										1			3			

◗ **The 1948/49 team** – Back row (left to right) Mulvaney, Daniel, Shanks, Streten, Arnison, Duke, Small, Ruffett, Eames. Middle row (left to right): C.Burtenshaw, O'Brien, Duggan, Collins, Gardiner, Lake, Waugh, Brennan, W.Burtenshaw. Front row (left to right): Gripton, Pemberton, Wilson, Cooke.

TIMELINE...

May 1949 Bobby Brennan is sold to Birmingham for £20,000.

1949/1950 FOOTBALL LEAGUE DIVISION TWO

Match No	Month	Day	Venue	Opponents	W,L,D	Score	Scorers	Attendance	Aherne T	Arnison JW	Burtenshaw CE	Cooke WH	Gardiner D	Glover A	Hall LF	Hughes I	James PGB	Jinks JT	Kiernan T	Lake LE	Morton RH	Mulvaney J	Northover SC	Owen SW	Shanks WG	Slatter LAH	Small PV	Stobbart GC	Streten BR	Taylor Jack	Walsh Peter	Watkins C	Waugh WL	Wilson James	Wyldes JR	Match No
1	Aug	20	(h)	WEST HAM UNITED	D	2-2	Owen, Taylor	17003	3	9		2	6											5	8		7		1	10		4	11			1
2	Aug	24	(h)	COVENTRY CITY	W	2-0	Watkins, Arnison	16070	3	9		2	6											5	8		7		1	10		4	11			2
3	Aug	27	(a)	Sheffield United	D	2-2	Waugh, Arnison	27572	3	9		2	6											5	8		7		1	10		4	11			3
4	Aug	29	(a)	Coventry City	L	0-1	-	22338	3	9	11	2	6											5	8		7		1	10		4				4
5	Sep	3	(h)	GRIMSBY TOWN	D	0-0	-	16717	3			2	6								4			5	9	11	7		1	10		8				5
6	Sep	7	(a)	Bradford Park Avenue	L	0-1	-	11201	3	9	11	2	6										8	5	7				1	10		4				6
7	Sep	10	(a)	Queens Park Rangers	L	0-3	-	20674	3	9	11	2	6											5	8				1	10		4	7			7
8	Sep	17	(h)	PRESTON NORTH END	D	1-1	Waters (og)	20135	3	8		2	6	7				9						5					1	10		4	11			8
9	Sep	24	(a)	Swansea Town	D	0-0	-	24297	3	8		2	6	7	5			9											1	10		4	11			9
10	Oct	1	(h)	LEEDS UNITED	W	1-0	Taylor	15291	3	8		2	6	7	5			9											1	10		4	11			10
11	Oct	8	(h)	LEICESTER CITY	W	1-0	Walsh	20816		8		2	6	7										5				10	1		9	4	11	3		11
12	Oct	15	(a)	Bury	L	2-5	James, Walsh	17651	3	8		2	6	7			11							5				10	1		9	4				12
13	Oct	22	(h)	TOTTENHAM HOTSPUR	D	1-1	Stobbart	27319	3	8		2	6	7			11							5				10	1		9	4				13
14	Oct	29	(a)	Cardiff City	D	0-0	-	24011	3	8		2	6	7										5				10	1	11	9	4				14
15	Nov	5	(h)	BLACKBURN ROVERS	W	5-2	Stobbart (4), Bell (og)	9513	3			2	6	7										5				8	1	10	9	4			11	15
16	Nov	12	(a)	Brentford	L	0-1	-	20520				2	6	7							4			5	8				1		9	4		3	11	16
17	Nov	19	(h)	HULL CITY	L	0-3	-	22269	3			2	6	10										5	8				1		9	4	7		11	17
18	Nov	26	(a)	Sheffield Wednesday	D	1-1	Watkins	29432	3			2	6	7							4			5	8			9	1			10	11			18
19	Dec	3	(h)	PLYMOUTH ARGYLE	D	1-1	Waugh	13273	3			2	6	7							4			5	8			9	1			10	11			19
20	Dec	10	(a)	Chesterfield	W	1-0	Stobbart	7937	3			2	6	7					8					5	10			9	1			4	11			20
21	Dec	17	(a)	West Ham United	D	0-0	-	16445	3			2	6	7					8					5	10			9	1			4	11			21
22	Dec	24	(h)	SHEFFIELD UNITED	L	1-3	Stobbart	15594	3			2	6	7					8					5	10			9	1			4	11			22
23	Dec	26	(h)	SOUTHAMPTON	D	1-1	Cooke (pen)	18765	3			2	6	7					8					5	10			9	1			4	11			23
24	Dec	27	(a)	Southampton	L	1-2	Kiernan	26928	3	10		2							8		6			5			7	9	1			4	11			24
25	Dec	31	(a)	Grimsby Town	L	1-6	Morton	15991	3			2		7					8		6			5	10			9	1			4	11			25
26	Jan	14	(h)	QUEENS PARK RANGERS	L	1-2	Watkins	16291	3			2	6	7	5	1			8					4						9	10	4	11			26
27	Jan	21	(a)	Preston North End	W	1-0	Shanks	23532	3			2	6	7		1			8					5	9						10	4	11			27
28	Feb	4	(h)	SWANSEA TOWN	L	1-2	Stobbart	15205	3			2	6			1			8				10	5	9			7				4	11			28
29	Feb	18	(a)	Leeds United	L	1-2	Small	37263	3			2	6	7		1			8		4			5	10		9	7					11			29
30	Feb	25	(a)	Leicester City	L	2-3	Watkins, Wyldes	26385	3			2	6	7		1			8		4			5				9				10			11	30
31	Mar	4	(h)	BURY	W	2-1	Glover, Wyldes	14365	3			2	6	7		1		9	8		4			5	10										11	31
32	Mar	11	(a)	Tottenham Hotspur	D	0-0	-	53145	3			2	6	7		1	9		8					5	6			10				4			11	32
33	Mar	18	(h)	CARDIFF CITY	D	0-0	-	15071	3			2	6	7		1			8					5	6			10				4			11	33
34	Mar	25	(a)	Blackburn Rovers	D	0-0	-	17255	3			2	6	7		1		9	8					5	6			10				4			11	34
35	Apr	1	(h)	SHEFFIELD WEDNESDAY	D	0-0	-	15273	3			2	11	7		1			8					5	6			9				10	4			35
36	Apr	7	(h)	BARNSLEY	W	3-1	Kiernan (2), Gardiner	15149	3			2	11	7		1			8					5	6			9				10	4			36
37	Apr	8	(a)	Plymouth Argyle	D	0-0	-	16977	3			2		7		1			8					5	6			9				10	4			37
38	Apr	10	(a)	Barnsley	L	0-1	-	9476				2		7		1			8	3				5	6			9				10	4			38
39	Apr	15	(h)	BRENTFORD	W	1-0	Stobbart	13991	3			2	11	7		1			8					5	6			9				10	4			39
40	Apr	22	(a)	Hull City	D	1-1	Glover	28205	3			2	11	7		1			8					5	6			9				10	4			40
41	Apr	29	(h)	CHESTERFIELD	D	1-1	Kiernan	7420				2	11	7		1			8					5	6			9				10	4	3		41
42	May	6	(h)	BRADFORD PARK AVENUE	W	3-1	Cooke (pen), Taylor, Farr (og)	11232				2		7		1			8					5	6			9				10		3	11	42
			Final League Position: 17th				3 Own Goals	**Apps**	37	13	3	42	33	32	3	17	2	4	24	1	10	3	1	40	30	1	7	30	25	21	8	39	23	4	9	
								Goals	-	2	-	2	1	2	-	-	1	-	4	-	1	-	-	1	1	-	1	9	-	3	2	4	2	-	2	

1949/1950 FA CUP

Round	Month	Day	Venue	Opponents	W,L,D	Score	Scorers	Attendance	Aherne T	Arnison JW	Burtenshaw CE	Cooke WH	Gardiner D	Glover A	Hall LF	Hughes I	James PGB	Jinks JT	Kiernan T	Lake LE	Morton RH	Mulvaney J	Northover SC	Owen SW	Shanks WG	Slatter LAH	Small PV	Stobbart GC	Streten BR	Taylor Jack	Walsh Peter	Watkins C	Waugh WL	Wilson James	Wyldes JR	Round
3	Jan	7	(h)	GRIMSBY TOWN	L	3-4	Kiernan (2), Waugh	18843	3			2	10	7	5				8					6				9	1			4	11			3
								Apps	1	-	-	1	1	1	1	-	-	-	1	-	-	-	-	1	-	-	-	1	1	-	-	1	1	-	-	
								Goals	-	-	-	-	-	-	-	-	-	-	2	-	-	-	-	-	-	-	-	-	-	-	-	-	1	-	-	

The **1949/50 team** – Back row (left to right): Hann (Trainer), Watkins, Cooke, Streten, Aherne, Gardiner, Wilson. Front row (left to right): Small, Shanks, Arnison, Duncan (Manager), Taylor, C.Burtenshaw, Owen.

TIMELINE...

22 October 1949 Tottenham attract 27,319 to Kenilworth Road – yet another record.

1950/51 FOOTBALL LEAGUE DIVISION TWO

Match No	Month	Day	Venue	Opponents	W,L,D	Score	Scorers	Attendance	Aherne T	Armison JW	Cooke WH	Davie WC	Gardiner D	Glover A	Hall LF	Havenga WS	Hughes I	Jinks JT	Jones LC	Kiernan T	Lake LE	McAuley PJ	Moore BJ	Morton RH	Owen SW	Pemberton JT	Shanks WG	Stobbart GC	Streten BR	Taylor Jack	Turner Gordon	Watkins C	Whent JR	Wilson James	Wyldes JR	Match No
1	Aug	19	(h)	BRENTFORD	W	2-0	Taylor, Whent	17721	3		2			7			1								5		6	9		8		4	10		11	1
2	Aug	24	(a)	West Ham United	L	1-2	Glover	20560	3		2			7			1								5		6	9		8		4	10		11	2
3	Aug	26	(a)	Blackburn Rovers	L	0-1	-	25114	3		2			7			1					4			5		6	9		8			10		11	3
4	Aug	30	(h)	WEST HAM UNITED	D	1-1	Wyldes	12366	3		2			7			1								5		6	9		8		4	10		11	4
5	Sep	2	(h)	SOUTHAMPTON	L	0-1	-	16942	3		2			7			1								5		6	9		8		4	10		11	5
6	Sep	6	(h)	HULL CITY	L	1-2	Jinks	14905			2			7			1	9			3				5		6	8		10		4			11	6
7	Sep	9	(a)	Barnsley	L	1-6	Jinks	22052			2			7			1	9			3				5		6	8		10		4			11	7
8	Sep	16	(h)	SHEFFIELD UNITED	D	0-0	-	14768	3		2				11		1	9				8			5		6	7				4				8
9	Sep	23	(a)	Manchester City	D	1-1	Taylor	42312	3		2				11	5	1	9				8					6	7		10		4				9
10	Sep	30	(a)	Leeds United	L	1-2	Kiernan	21209	3		2				11	5	1	9		10		8					6	7				4				10
11	Oct	7	(h)	PRESTON NORTH END	L	1-2	Glover	16637	3		2			7	11		1					8		9	5		6			10		4				11
12	Oct	14	(a)	Notts County	D	2-2	Morton, Stobbart	34054	3		2			7			1					8		10	5		6	9				4			11	12
13	Oct	21	(h)	QUEENS PARK RANGERS	W	2-0	Stobbart, Wyldes	15692	3		2			7			1					8		10	5		6	9				4			11	13
14	Oct	28	(a)	Bury	L	1-4	Wyldes	13486	3	10	2			7			1								5		6	9		8		4			11	14
15	Nov	4	(h)	LEICESTER CITY	L	0-2	-	12967	3		2					5	1			8				4			6	7		9			10		11	15
16	Nov	11	(a)	Chesterfield	D	1-1	Wyldes	10996	3		2				7		1							4	5		8	10		6			9		11	16
17	Nov	18	(h)	GRIMSBY TOWN	W	4-0	Whent (2), Shanks, Taylor	12144	3		2				7		1							4	5		8	10		6			9		11	17
18	Nov	25	(a)	Birmingham City	L	0-3	-	18606			2				7		1			3				4	5		8	10		6			9		11	18
19	Dec	2	(h)	CARDIFF CITY	D	1-1	Havenga	13062	3		2				7	11	1							4	5		8	10		6			9			19
20	Dec	9	(a)	Coventry City	L	1-4	Stobbart	22044	3		2					11								6	5	10	8	7	1		4			9		20
21	Dec	16	(a)	Brentford	L	0-1	-	9808	3		2	10		6		11								4	5		8	7	1				9			21
22	Dec	23	(h)	BLACKBURN ROVERS	D	1-1	Davie	11632	3		2	10		6		11								4	5		8	7	1				9			22
23	Dec	25	(a)	Swansea Town	W	2-0	Shanks, Havenga	16862	3			10		7		11								4	5		8	9	1	6				2		23
24	Dec	26	(h)	SWANSEA TOWN	W	3-1	Havenga (3, 1 pen)	17245	3			10		7		11								4	5		8	9	1	6				2		24
25	Dec	30	(a)	Southampton	D	1-1	Stobbart	21094	3			10		7		11								4	5		8	9	1	6				2		25
26	Jan	13	(h)	BARNSLEY	D	1-1	Shanks	15032	3			10		7		11								4	5		8	9	1	6				2		26
27	Jan	20	(a)	Sheffield United	L	1-2	Glover	26364	3			10		7		11								4	5		8	9	1	6				2		27
28	Feb	3	(h)	MANCHESTER CITY	D	2-2	Davie, Moore	12087	3		2	10		7		11							9	4	5		8		1	6						28
29	Feb	17	(h)	LEEDS UNITED	L	2-3	Stobbart, Glover	13323	3		2	10		7		11								6	5		8	9	1		4					29
30	Feb	24	(a)	Preston North End	L	0-1	-	31096	3		2	10		7		11								6	5		8	9	1		4					30
31	Mar	3	(h)	NOTTS COUNTY	D	1-1	Moore	17398	3		2	10		7		11							9	6	5		8		1		4					31
32	Mar	10	(a)	Queens Park Rangers	D	1-1	Davie	13708	3		2	10		11									9	6	5		8	7	1		4					32
33	Mar	17	(h)	BURY	W	4-2	Moore (2), Watkins, McAuley	11576	3		2	10		11								6	9		5			7	1		8					33
34	Mar	23	(a)	Doncaster Rovers	L	2-5	Moore, Davie	22613	3		2	10		11									9	6	5		8	7	1		4					34
35	Mar	24	(a)	Leicester City	L	1-3	Stobbart	23560	3		2	10											9	6	5		8	7	1		4			11	35
36	Mar	26	(h)	DONCASTER ROVERS	W	3-1	Stobbart, Moore, Davie (pen)	14486	3		2	10											9	6	5	11		7	1		8					36
37	Mar	31	(h)	CHESTERFIELD	W	3-0	Taylor, Moore, Davie	13055			2	10									3		9		5	11	6	7	1	8		4				37
38	Apr	7	(a)	Grimsby Town	W	2-0	Taylor, Pemberton	12435			2	10									3		9		5	11	6	7	1	8		4				38
39	Apr	14	(h)	BIRMINGHAM CITY	D	1-1	Pemberton	16324			2	10									3		9		5	11	6	7	1	8		4				39
40	Apr	21	(a)	Cardiff City	L	1-2	Stobbart	28022	3		2	10											9		5	11	6	7	1	8		4				40
41	Apr	28	(h)	COVENTRY CITY	D	1-1	Davie	11336			3	10											9		5	11	6	7	1	8		4				41
42	May	5	(a)	Hull City	L	3-5	Stobbart, Davie, Wyldes	17478			3	10		5									9				6	7	1	8		4			11	42
								Apps	34	1	36	22	3	24	4	16	19	5	2	8	7	8	13	24	39	7	34	39	23	25	2	35	11	5	16	
								Goals	-	-	-	8	-	4	-	5	-	2	-	1	-	1	7	1	-	2	3	9	-	5	-	1	3	-	5	

Final League Position: 19th

1950/51 FA CUP

Round	Month	Day	Venue	Opponents	W,L,D	Score	Scorers	Attendance	Aherne T	Armison JW	Cooke WH	Davie WC	Gardiner D	Glover A	Hall LF	Havenga WS	Hughes I	Jinks JT	Jones LC	Kiernan T	Lake LE	McAuley PJ	Moore BJ	Morton RH	Owen SW	Pemberton JT	Shanks WG	Stobbart GC	Streten BR	Taylor Jack	Turner Gordon	Watkins C	Whent JR	Wilson James	Wyldes JR	Round
3	Jan	6	(h)	PORTSMOUTH	W	2-0	Davie, Havenga	21631	3		2	10		7		11								4	5		8	9	1			6				3
4	Jan	27	(h)	BRISTOL ROVERS	L	1-2	Watkins	26586	3		2	10		7										4	5		8	9	1			6			11	4
								Apps	2	-	2	2	-	2	-	1								2	2		2	2	2			2			1	
								Goals	-	-	-	1	-	-	-	1								-	-		-	-	-			1			-	

▶ **The 1950/51 team** – Back row (left to right): Cooke, Aherne, Hughes, Morton, Shanks. Front row (left to right): Glover, J.Taylor, Stobbart, Owen, Whent, Wyldes.

1951/52 FOOTBALL LEAGUE DIVISION TWO

Match No	Month	Day	Venue	Opponents	W,L,D Score	Scorers	Attendance	Aherne T	Cooke WH	Cullen MJ	Davie WC	Davies RA	Dunne S	Hall LF	Havenga WS	Jones LC	McJarrow H	Mitchell AJ	Moore BJ	Morton RH	Owen SW	Pemberton JT	Sexton DJ	Shanks WG	Smith RS	Stobbart GC	Stone PJ	Streten BR	Taylor Jack	Turner Gordon	Watkins C	Wyldes JR	Match No
1	Aug	18	(h)	SWANSEA TOWN	D 2-2	Taylor, Mitchell	15606	3	2		10	7						11	9		5					6		1	8		4		1
2	Aug	20	(a)	Sheffield United	L 0-3	-	24012	3	2		10	7						11			5					6		1	8		4		2
3	Aug	25	(a)	Bury	W 1-0	Stobbart	11196	3	2		10	7						11			5					6		1	8		4		3
4	Aug	29	(h)	SHEFFIELD UNITED	W 2-1	Stobbart, Taylor	16642	3	2		10	7						11			5					6		1	8		4		4
5	Sep	1	(a)	Leicester City	D 3-3	Taylor (3)	25735	3	2		10	7						11			5					6		1	8		4		5
6	Sep	5	(a)	Barnsley	W 2-1	Taylor, Mitchell	13109	3	2		10	7						11			5					6		1	8		4		6
7	Sep	8	(h)	NOTTS COUNTY	W 6-0	Taylor (2), Mitchell, Davie, Stobbart (2)	24511	3	2		10	7						11			5					6		1	8		4		7
8	Sep	15	(a)	Queens Park Rangers	D 0-0	-	17391	3	2		10	7						11			5					6		1	8		4		8
9	Sep	22	(h)	BLACKBURN ROVERS	D 1-1	Mitchell	20022	3	2		10	7						11			5					6		1	8		4		9
10	Sep	29	(a)	Hull City	W 2-1	Stobbart, Mitchell	29646	3	2		10	7		5				11								6		1	8		4		10
11	Oct	6	(a)	Nottingham Forest	L 0-2	-	31257	3	2		10	7		5			6	11								9		1	8		4		11
12	Oct	13	(h)	BRENTFORD	L 0-2	-	18521	3	2		10	7					6	11			5					9		1	8		4		12
13	Oct	20	(a)	Doncaster Rovers	D 1-1	Davies	18801	3	2		10	7						11	8		5			6		9		1			4		13
14	Oct	27	(h)	EVERTON	D 1-1	Davies	16667	3	2		10	7						11	8		5					9		1		6			14
15	Nov	3	(a)	Southampton	W 3-2	Taylor (2), Mitchell	20002	3	2		10	7						11		4	5					9		1	8	6			15
16	Nov	10	(h)	SHEFFIELD WEDNESDAY	W 5-3	Mitchell (2), Davies, Taylor, Morton	19091	3	2		10	7						11		4	5					9		1	8	6			16
17	Nov	17	(a)	Leeds United	D 1-1	Stobbart	27405	3	2		10	7						11		4	5					9		1	8	6			17
18	Nov	24	(h)	ROTHERHAM UNITED	D 1-1	Taylor	23565	3	2		10	7						11		4	5					9		1	8	6			18
19	Dec	1	(a)	Cardiff City	L 0-3	-	26106	3	2		10							11	9	4	5					7		1	8	6			19
20	Dec	8	(h)	BIRMINGHAM CITY	L 2-4	Taylor, Stobbart	15937	3	2		10							11	9	4	5					9		1	8	6			20
21	Dec	15	(a)	Swansea Town	W 3-0	Stobbart (2), Havenga	14896	3	2				7			7		11		4	5					9		1	8	10			21
22	Dec	22	(h)	BURY	W 2-1	Taylor, Stobbart	12931	3	2				7					11		4	5					9		1	8	10			22
23	Dec	25	(a)	West Ham United	L 0-3	-	20403	3	2				7			7		11		4	5					9		1	8	10			23
24	Dec	26	(h)	WEST HAM UNITED	W 6-1	Mitchell, Taylor, Turner (3), Stobbart	19476	3					2					11	9	4	5					7		1	8	10	6		24
25	Dec	29	(h)	LEICESTER CITY	L 1-2	Watkins	17992	3					2					11	9	4	5					7		1	8	10	6		25
26	Jan	5	(a)	Notts County	L 4-5	Taylor (2), Turner, Moore	22808	3					2					11	9	4	5					7		1	8	10	6		26
27	Jan	19	(h)	QUEENS PARK RANGERS	L 0-1	-	15242	3					7	2				11	9	4	5					9		1	8	10	6		27
28	Jan	26	(a)	Blackburn Rovers	L 1-2	Mitchell	25156	3					7	2				11	9	4	5					9		1	8	10	6		28
29	Feb	9	(h)	HULL CITY	D 1-1	Moore	16550	3	2				8					11	9	4						7	5	1		10	6		29
30	Feb	16	(h)	NOTTINGHAM FOREST	D 3-3	McJarrow (2), Mitchell	18369	3	2				7				9	11		4	5					10		1	8		6		30
31	Mar	1	(a)	Brentford	D 3-3	Taylor (2), Davies	21218	3	2				7					11	9	4	5					10		1	8		6		31
32	Mar	12	(h)	DONCASTER ROVERS	L 1-4	Morton	5635	3					2	5				11	9					10	4	7		1	8		6		32
33	Mar	15	(a)	Everton	W 3-1	Mitchell (2), Taylor	37889	3					2					11	9	5				10	4	7		1	8		6		33
34	Mar	22	(h)	SOUTHAMPTON	W 2-1	Moore, Mitchell (pen)	15551	3					2					11	9	5				10	4	7		1	8		6		34
35	Apr	2	(a)	Sheffield Wednesday	L 0-4	-	23862	3					2				8	11	9	5				10	4	7		1			6		35
36	Apr	5	(h)	LEEDS UNITED	W 2-1	Moore (2)	11460	3					2					11	9	5				10	7			1			6		36
37	Apr	12	(a)	Rotherham United	W 1-0	Mitchell	17309	3					2					11	9	4	5			10	7			1			6		37
38	Apr	14	(h)	COVENTRY CITY	W 2-1	Moore, Sexton	15216	3					2					11	9	4	5			10	7			1		8	6		38
39	Apr	15	(a)	Coventry City	L 2-5	Moore, Wyldes	26160	3					2						9	4	5			10	7			1		8	6	11	39
40	Apr	19	(h)	CARDIFF CITY	D 2-2	McJarrow, Moore	14186	3								2	10	11	9	4	5					7		1	8		6		40
41	Apr	26	(a)	Birmingham City	L 1-3	Warhurst (og)	28816	3		7						2	10	11	9	4	5			6		8		1					41
42	May	3	(h)	BARNSLEY	W 4-2	Stobbart, Mitchell, McJarrow (2)	8789		3	7						2	10	11	9	4	5					8		1			6		42
				Final League Position: 8th		1 Own Goal	**Apps**	41	27	2	20	25	13	3	2	3	5	41	20	28	35	2	6	18	1	38	1	42	36	11	41	1	
							Goals	-	-	1	4	-	-	-	1	-	5	16	8	2	-	-	1	-	-	12	-	-	20	4	1	1	

1951/52 FA CUP

Round	Month	Day	Venue	Opponents	W,L,D Score	Scorers	Attendance	Aherne T	Cooke WH	Cullen MJ	Davie WC	Davies RA	Dunne S	Hall LF	Havenga WS	Jones LC	McJarrow H	Mitchell AJ	Moore BJ	Morton RH	Owen SW	Pemberton JT	Sexton DJ	Shanks WG	Smith RS	Stobbart GC	Stone PJ	Streten BR	Taylor Jack	Turner Gordon	Watkins C	Wyldes JR	Round
3	Jan	12	(h)	CHARLTON ATHLETIC	W 1-0	Turner	25554	3	2			7	2					11		4	5					9		1	10	8	6		3
4	Feb	2	(h)	BRENTFORD	D 2-2	Turner, Taylor	25320	3	2			9						11		4	5					7		1	10	8	6		4
Rep	Feb	6	(a)	Brentford	D 0-0	-	31143	3	2			9						11		4	5					7		1	10	8	6		Rep
Rep 2	Feb	18	(n)	Brentford	W 3-2	Taylor, Moore, Morton	37269	3	2			7		5				11	9	4						10		1	8		6		Rep 2
5	Feb	23	(h)	SWINDON TOWN	W 3-1	Taylor (2), Davies	27553	3	2			7		5				11	9	4						10		1	8		6		5
6	Mar	8	(h)	ARSENAL	L 2-3	Moore, Mitchell (pen)	28433	3	2			7						11	9	4	5					10		1	8		6		6
							Apps	6	5	-	-	6	1	2	-	-	-	6	3	6	4	-	-	-	-	6	-	6	6	6	3	-	
							Goals	-	-	-	-	1	-	-	-	-	-	1	2	1	-	-	-	-	-	-	-	-	4	2	-	-	

4th Round 2nd Replay played at Highbury

◗ **The 1951/52 team** – Back row (left to right): Hann (Trainer), Arnison, Wyldes, Hawkes, Morton, Groves, Davies, Wheeler, A.Taylor, Havenga, Kelly (Coach), Mackey (Trainer). Middle row (left to right): Duncan (Manager), Cooke, Shanks, Smith, Pemberton, Stibbards, Turner, Hall, Dunne, Streten, Davie, Moore, Jones, Sexton, Coley (Secretary). Front row (left to right): Hewson (Director), J.Taylor, Wright (Director), Aherne, Mitchell (Director), Owen, Woods (Director), Stobbart, England (Director), Watkins, Richardson (Director).

TIMELINE...

8 March 1952 The Town reach the F.A.Cup quarter-finals for the second time in their history but unluckily go down 2-3 to Arsenal in front of another record Kenilworth Road crowd of 28,433.

1952/53 FOOTBALL LEAGUE DIVISION TWO

Match No	Month	Day	Venue	Opponents	W.L.D Score	Scorers	Attendance	Aherne T	Baynham RL	Cooke WH	Cullen MJ	Davies RA	Dunne S	Hall LF	Jones LC	McJarrow H	Mitchell AJ	Moore BJ	Morton RH	Owen SW	Pemberton JT	Pye J	Scott JC	Sexton DJ	Shanks WG	Smith RS	Streten BR	Taylor AA	Turner Gordon	Watkins C	Match No
1	Aug	23	(a)	Plymouth Argyle	L 1-2	Moore	28836	3				2			8		11	9	4	5		10	7				1		6		1
2	Aug	27	(h)	BIRMINGHAM CITY	L 0-1	-	20231	3		2	11				8			9	4	5		10	7				1		6		2
3	Aug	30	(h)	ROTHERHAM UNITED	W 2-1	Turner (2)	14427	3		2	7	11		5				9	4						10		1	8	6		3
4	Sep	3	(a)	Birmingham City	D 2-2	Turner, Moore	17478	3			7	11		5				9	4						10		1	8	6		4
5	Sep	6	(a)	Fulham	L 0-2	-	28680	3			7	11	2						4	5	9				10		1	8	6		5
6	Sep	10	(h)	SWANSEA TOWN	W 3-1	Turner (2), Pye	13218	3	1		7	11	2						4	5	9				10			8	6		6
7	Sep	13	(h)	WEST HAM UNITED	D 0-0	-	16009	3			7	11	2					10	4	5	9						1	8	6		7
8	Sep	18	(a)	Swansea Town	L 2-4	Scott, Moore	17358	3			7		2				11	9	4	5		10	8				1		6		8
9	Sep	20	(a)	Leicester City	D 1-1	Turner	24052	3			7		2				11		4	5	9				10		1	8	6		9
10	Sep	27	(h)	NOTTS COUNTY	W 5-1	Moore (2), Pye (2), Mitchell	13557	3			7		2				11	8	4	5		9					1		10		10
11	Oct	4	(a)	Southampton	W 3-1	Moore, Pye (2)	17539	3			7		2				11	8	4	5		9					1		10		11
12	Oct	11	(a)	Huddersfield Town	L 0-3	-	26345	3			7		2				11	8	4	5		9					1		10		12
13	Oct	18	(h)	SHEFFIELD UNITED	W 4-1	Moore, Pye, Mitchell, Watkins	18185	3			7		2				11	8	4	5		9					1		10		13
14	Oct	25	(a)	Barnsley	W 3-2	Pye (2), Watkins	11423	3			7		2				11	8	4	5		9					1		10		14
15	Nov	1	(h)	LINCOLN CITY	W 4-0	Pye (2), Moore (2)	17538	3			7		2				11	8	4	5		9					1		10		15
16	Nov	8	(a)	Hull City	W 2-0	Pye, Mitchell	22484	3			7		2				11	8	4	5		9					1		10		16
17	Nov	15	(h)	BLACKBURN ROVERS	W 6-0	Pye (3), Mitchell, Davies, Moore	16276	3			7					2	11	8	4	5	3	9					1		10		17
18	Nov	22	(a)	Nottingham Forest	L 3-4	Mitchell (2), Pye	22924	3			7						11	8	4	5		9					1		10		18
19	Nov	29	(h)	EVERTON	W 4-2	Moore, Pye, Mitchell, Clinton (og)	15160	3			7		2				11	8	4	5		9					1		10		19
20	Dec	13	(h)	DONCASTER ROVERS	L 1-2	Mitchell	15258	3			7		2				11	8	4	5		9					1		10		20
21	Dec	20	(h)	PLYMOUTH ARGYLE	W 1-0	Davies	13055	3	1		7		2				11	8	4	5		9							10		21
22	Dec	26	(h)	LEEDS UNITED	W 2-0	McCabe (og), Pye	19480	3	1		7		2				11	8	4	5		9							10		22
23	Dec	27	(a)	Leeds United	D 2-2	Pye, Pemberton	31634	3	1		7		2					8	4	5	11	9							10		23
24	Jan	3	(a)	Rotherham United	W 3-1	Moore, Pye (2)	16850	3	1		7		2					8	4	5		9							10		24
25	Jan	17	(h)	FULHAM	W 2-0	Jones, Moore	21409	3	1			7				2		8	4	5		9						11	10		25
26	Jan	24	(a)	West Ham United	W 1-0	Mitchell	23667	3	1		7					2	11	8	4	5		9	6						10		26
27	Feb	7	(h)	LEICESTER CITY	W 2-0	Turner, Mitchell (pen)	22489	3	1		7				5	2	11	8	4	5		9							10	6	27
28	Feb	19	(a)	Notts County	W 2-1	Pye (2)	8648	3	1		7		2			10	11	8	4	5		9								6	28
29	Feb	21	(h)	SOUTHAMPTON	L 1-2	Cullen	19424	3	1		7				2	9	11	8	4	5									10		29
30	Feb	28	(h)	HUDDERSFIELD TOWN	L 0-2	-	25841	3					2		3			8	4	5	11	9		10		1			6		30
31	Mar	7	(a)	Sheffield United	D 1-1	Turner	38839		1		7			5	2		11		4	6	3	9						8			31
32	Mar	14	(h)	BARNSLEY	W 6-0	Watkins, Yeull (og), Cullen (2), Turner (2)	15315		1		7		2		5		11		4	6	3	9						8			32
33	Mar	21	(a)	Lincoln City	W 2-1	Turner, Pye	15510		1		7			5	2		11		4	6	3	9						8			33
34	Mar	28	(h)	HULL CITY	W 3-2	McJarrow (2), Turner	13747		1		7			5	2	10	11		4	6	3	9						8			34
35	Apr	3	(a)	Bury	L 0-1	-	15648		1		7					10	11		4	6	3	9						8			35
36	Apr	4	(h)	Blackburn Rovers	D 1-1	Mitchell	23920		1			7	2	5			11	8	4	6	3	9							10		36
37	Apr	6	(a)	BURY	W 4-1	Turner, McJarrow (2), Hart (og)	16360		1			7		5		10	11		4	6	3	9						8	6		37
38	Apr	11	(h)	NOTTINGHAM FOREST	W 3-0	Davies, Watkins, Mitchell	18599		1			7				2	11		4	5	3	9			6			8	10		38
39	Apr	16	(a)	Everton	D 1-1	Davies	32948		1			7				2	11		4	5	3	9			6			8	10		39
40	Apr	22	(a)	Brentford	D 1-1	Pye	16347		1			7	2				11		4	5	3	9			6			8	10		40
41	Apr	25	(h)	BRENTFORD	L 0-1	-	15826		1		7		2				11	9	4	5	3	10			6			8			41
42	Apr	30	(a)	Doncaster Rovers	L 0-1	-	9415		1				2			10	11	7	4	5	3	9				6		8			42
				Final League Position: 3rd		**4 Own Goals**	**Apps**	28	22	2	16	29	25	10	16	9	33	30	42	38	15	39	1	3	26	1	20	1	21	35	
							Goals	-	-	-	3	4	-	-	1	4	12	13	-	-	1	24	1	-	-	-	-	-	13	4	

1952/53 FA CUP

Round	Month	Day	Venue	Opponents	W.L.D Score	Scorers	Attendance	Aherne T	Baynham RL	Cooke WH	Cullen MJ	Davies RA	Dunne S	Hall LF	Jones LC	McJarrow H	Mitchell AJ	Moore BJ	Morton RH	Owen SW	Pemberton JT	Pye J	Scott JC	Sexton DJ	Shanks WG	Smith RS	Streten BR	Taylor AA	Turner Gordon	Watkins C	Round
3	Jan	10	(h)	BLACKBURN ROVERS	W 6-1	Taylor (2), Pye (3), Moore	21034	3	1		7				2			8	4	5		9			6			11	10		3
4	Jan	31	(a)	Manchester City	D 1-1	Pye	38411	3	1		7			5	2		11	8	4			9			6				10		4
Rep	Feb	4	(h)	MANCHESTER CITY	W 5-1	Turner (3), Mitchell, Little (og)	21991	3	1		7			5	2		11	8	4			9						10	6		Rep
5	Feb	14	(h)	BOLTON WANDERERS	L 0-1	-	23735	3	1		7				2		11	8	4			9						10	6		5
						1 Own Goal	**Apps**	4	4	-	3	1	-	2	4	-	3	4	4	2	-	4	-	-	2	-	-	1	2	4	
							Goals	-	-	-	-	-	-	-	1	-	1	1	-	-	-	4	-	-	-	-	-	2	3	-	

▶ **The 1952/53 team** – Back row (left to right): Morton, Smith, Cooke, Streten, Sexton, Baynham, Dallas, Williams, Taylor, Thompson, Allen, Coley (Secretary), Crarer (Medical Officer). Middle row (left to right): Kelly (Assistant Manager), Hann (Trainer), Mackey (Trainer), Aherne, Shanks, Pemberton, Richardson (Director), Scott, Hall, Moore, Jones, McJarrow, Davies, Turner, Wright (Director), Kelly, Bradley, Duncan (Manager). Front row (left to right): Cullen, Hewson (Director), Watkins, England (Director), Mitchell, Jeyes (Chairman), Owen, Mitchell (Director), Pye, Woods (Director), Dunne.

1953/54 FOOTBALL LEAGUE DIVISION TWO

Match No	Month	Day	Venue	Opponents	W.L.D Score	Scorers	Attendance	Adam J	Aherne T	Baynham RL	Bennett EW	Cullen MJ	Cummins GP	Davies RA	Downie JD	Dunne S	Groves J	Hall LF	Jones LC	MacEwan MP	McJarrow H	Mitchell AJ	Moore BJ	Morton RH	Owen SW	Pemberton JT	Pye J	Scott JC	Shanks WG	Streten BR	Taylor AA	Turner Gordon	Watkins C	Match No
1	Aug	19	(h)	OLDHAM ATHLETIC	D 4-4	Downie (3), Pemberton (pen)	22822	11	2	1			10	7	8			5					9	4		3			6					1
2	Aug	22	(h)	EVERTON	D 1-1	McJarrow	20217		3				10	7	8	2					9			5					6	1	11		4	2
3	Aug	26	(h)	NOTTINGHAM FOREST	L 0-1	-	17522							7	10	2			3				9	5					6	1	11	8	4	3
4	Aug	29	(a)	Plymouth Argyle	D 2-2	Turner, Moore	22574					7			10	2			3				9	4	5					1	11	8	6	4
5	Sep	2	(a)	Nottingham Forest	L 1-2	Turner	17172					7			10	2			3				9	4	5					1	11	8	6	5
6	Sep	5	(h)	SWANSEA TOWN	W 2-0	Downie, Mitchell	17479						8		10	2			3			11		4	5		9			1		7	6	6
7	Sep	9	(a)	Birmingham City	L 1-5	Downie	18881						8		10	2			3			11		4	5		9			1		7	6	7
8	Sep	12	(a)	Rotherham United	L 1-2	Mitchell	15726						8		10	2			3			11			5			9	6	1		7	4	8
9	Sep	16	(h)	BIRMINGHAM CITY	W 2-0	Cummins, Downie (pen)	12231		3	1		7	8	11	10	2								5					9		4			6	9
10	Sep	19	(h)	LEICESTER CITY	D 2-2	Downie, Dunn (og)	19138		3	1			8	11	10	2											7		9		4			6	10
11	Sep	26	(a)	Stoke City	D 1-1	Scott	24083		3	1			8		10	2						11						9	7		4			6	11
12	Oct	3	(h)	FULHAM	L 1-2	Cummins	18619			1			10		8	2						11			5	3		9	7		4			6	12
13	Oct	10	(h)	HULL CITY	W 3-1	Turner (2), Watkins	14754		3				10			2						11		4	5		9		7	1		8	6	13
14	Oct	17	(a)	Notts County	W 2-1	Cummins, Mitchell	12208		3		7		10			2						11		4	5		9			1		8	6	14
15	Oct	24	(h)	LINCOLN CITY	W 1-0	Davies	15578		3				10	7	8	2						11		4	5		9			1			6	15
16	Oct	31	(a)	Bristol Rovers	D 3-3	Pye (2), Mitchell	20021		3				10	7	8	2	5					11		4			9			1			6	16
17	Nov	7	(h)	BRENTFORD	D 1-1	Mitchell	15167		3				10	7	8	2						11		4	5		9			1			6	17
18	Nov	14	(a)	Derby County	W 2-1	Mitchell (2)	15934		3				10	7		2						11	9	4	5					1		8	6	18
19	Nov	21	(a)	BLACKBURN ROVERS	W 2-1	Watkins, Mitchell	16269		3				10	7		2						11	9	4	5					1		8	6	19
20	Nov	28	(a)	Doncaster Rovers	W 3-1	Pye, Mitchell, Graham (og)	18273		3				10	7		2						11		4	5		9			1		8	6	20
21	Dec	5	(h)	BURY	W 3-2	Morton, Turner, Pye	15309		3				10	7		2						11		4	5		9			1		8	6	21
22	Dec	12	(a)	Oldham Athletic	W 2-1	Turner (2)	14128		3				10	7		2						11		4	5		9			1		8	6	22
23	Dec	19	(a)	Everton	L 1-2	Cummins	33544		3				10	7		2						11			5			9	4	1		8	6	23
24	Dec	25	(a)	West Ham United	L 0-1	-	19721		3				10	7		2						11		4	5			9		1		8	6	24
25	Dec	26	(h)	WEST HAM UNITED	W 3-1	Turner (2), Mitchell	20133		3				10	7						2		11	9		5				4	1		8	6	25
26	Jan	2	(h)	PLYMOUTH ARGYLE	W 2-1	Moore, Turner	9694		3				10	7						2		11	9	4	5					1		8	6	26
27	Jan	16	(a)	Swansea Town	D 1-1	Moore	16785		3				10	7						2		11	9	4	5					1		8	6	27
28	Jan	23	(h)	ROTHERHAM UNITED	D 1-1	Turner	17300		3				10	7						2		11	9	4	5					1		8	6	28
29	Feb	6	(a)	Leicester City	L 1-2	Turner	31892		3				10	7		2				9		11		4				5		1		8	6	29
30	Feb	13	(h)	STOKE CITY	L 0-1	-	17055		3				10	7		2				9		11		4	5					1		8	6	30
31	Feb	20	(a)	Fulham	L 1-5	Downie	26982		3					4	10	2						11	7		9	5				1		8	6	31
32	Feb	27	(a)	Hull City	W 2-1	Shanks, Downie	21555		3			7	11	10					5	2				4					9	1		6	8	32
33	Mar	6	(h)	NOTTS COUNTY	W 2-1	Downie, Davies	14623		3			7	11	10					5	2				4					9	1		6	8	33
34	Mar	13	(a)	Lincoln City	D 1-1	Turner	11195		3			7	11	10						2				4					9	1		6	8	34
35	Mar	20	(h)	BRISTOL ROVERS	D 1-1	Downie	12195	11	3					7	10	2								4	5	8			6	1			9	35
36	Mar	27	(a)	Blackburn Rovers	L 0-2	-	24331		3				8	7	10	2								4	5				6	1			9	36
37	Apr	3	(h)	DONCASTER ROVERS	W 2-0	Turner, Davies	10838		3				10	7	8	2						11		4	5				6	1			9	37
38	Apr	10	(a)	Brentford	W 1-0	Turner	14204		3				10	7	8	2						11		4	5				6	1			9	38
39	Apr	16	(h)	LEEDS UNITED	D 1-1	Mitchell	16129		3				10	7	8	2						11		4	5				6	1			9	39
40	Apr	17	(h)	DERBY COUNTY	W 2-1	Morton, Downie	12874		3				8	7	10	2						11		4	5				6	1			9	40
41	Apr	19	(a)	Leeds United	L 1-2	Turner	13930	11	3					7		2		10		9					5	6					4		8	41
42	Apr	24	(a)	Bury	W 1-0	Mitchell	11018		3				10	7	6	2						11		5					8	4			9	42

Final League Position: 6th   2 Own Goals

| | | | | | | | Apps | 3 | 35 | 5 | 1 | 8 | 33 | 31 | 26 | 25 | 1 | 4 | 22 | 3 | 1 | 30 | 11 | 40 | 25 | 4 | 14 | 12 | 25 | 37 | 4 | 32 | 30 | |
| | | | | | | | Goals | - | - | - | - | - | 4 | 3 | 12 | - | - | - | - | - | 1 | 12 | 3 | 2 | - | 1 | 4 | 1 | 1 | - | - | 16 | 2 | |

1953/54 FA CUP

Round	Month	Day	Venue	Opponents	W.L.D Score	Scorers	Attendance	Adam J	Aherne T	Baynham RL	Bennett EW	Cullen MJ	Cummins GP	Davies RA	Downie JD	Dunne S	Groves J	Hall LF	Jones LC	MacEwan MP	McJarrow H	Mitchell AJ	Moore BJ	Morton RH	Owen SW	Pemberton JT	Pye J	Scott JC	Shanks WG	Streten BR	Taylor AA	Turner Gordon	Watkins C	Round
3	Jan	9	(a)	Blackpool	D 1-1	Cummins	25242		3				10	7					2			11	9	4	5					1		8	6	3
Rep	Jan	13	(h)	BLACKPOOL	D 0-0	-	23472		3				10	7					2			11	9	4	5					1		8	6	Rep
Rep 2	Jan	18	(n)	Blackpool	D 1-1	Cummins	31663		3				10	7					2			11	9	4	5					1		8	6	Rep 2
Rep 3	Jan	25	(n)	Blackpool	L 0-2	-	25855		3				10	7		2						11	9	4	5					1		8	6	Rep 3

3rd Round 2nd Replay played at Villa Park
3rd Round 3rd Replay played at Molineux

| | | | | | | | Apps | - | 4 | - | - | - | 4 | 4 | - | 1 | - | - | 3 | - | - | 4 | 4 | 4 | 4 | - | - | - | - | 4 | - | 4 | 4 | |
| | | | | | | | Goals | - | - | - | - | - | 2 | - | - | - | - | - | - | - | - | - | - | - | - | - | - | - | - | - | - | - | - | |

▌ **The 1953/54 team** – Back row (left to right): Morton, Dunne, Streten, Jones, Watkins. Front row (left to right): Turner, Cummins, Owen, Pye, Downie, Mitchell.

TIMELINE...

7 October 1953 The Town's first floodlights are switched on for a friendly game against Fenerbahce of Turkey.

Match No	Month	Day	Venue	Opponents	W,L,D Score	Scorers	Attendance	Adam J	Aherne T	Allen DS	Baynham RL	Cullen MJ	Cummins GP	Davies RA	Dunne S	Groves J	Hall LF	Jones LC	Kelly TWJ	MacEwan MP	Mitchell AJ	Morton RH	Owen SW	Pearce RS	Pemberton JT	Pye J	Shanks WG	Smith RS	Streten BR	Turner Gordon	Watkins C	Match No
1	Aug	21	(h)	NOTTINGHAM FOREST	W 3-0	Davies, Turner, Pye	19832	11	3					7	2	10							4		5	9	6		1	8		1
2	Aug	24	(a)	Bury	L 1-2	Turner	15545	11	3				9	7	2	10							4		5		6		1	8		2
3	Aug	28	(a)	Ipswich Town	L 1-3	Adam	20665	11	3				9	7	2	10							4		5			6	1	8		3
4	Sep	1	(h)	BURY	W 3-2	Mitchell (pen), Turner, Adam	13654	11	3						2	10					7		4		5	9		6	1	8		4
5	Sep	4	(h)	BIRMINGHAM CITY	W 1-0	Adam	16347	11	3						2	10					7		4		5	9	6		1	8		5
6	Sep	8	(a)	Lincoln City	W 2-1	Pye (2)	13450	11	3					7	2	10							4		5	9	6		1	8		6
7	Sep	11	(a)	Middlesbrough	W 2-0	Davies, Turner	16071	11	3					7	2	10							4		5	9	6		1	8		7
8	Sep	15	(h)	LINCOLN CITY	W 2-1	Turner (2)	11972	11	3					7	2	10							4		5	9	6		1	8		8
9	Sep	18	(h)	STOKE CITY	W 3-1	Adam (2), Watkins	17325	11	3				9	7	2								4		5		6		1	8	10	9
10	Sep	25	(a)	Rotherham United	L 0-2		17114	11	3				9	7	2								4		5		6		1	8	10	10
11	Oct	2	(h)	DERBY COUNTY	W 2-0	Turner, Pye	17156	11	3					7	2								4		5	9	6		1	8	10	11
12	Oct	9	(a)	Bristol Rovers	L 2-3	Turner, Kelly	30654	11	3					7	2				9				4		5		6		1	8	10	12
13	Oct	16	(h)	PLYMOUTH ARGYLE	W 3-1	Davies, Turner, Adam	15059	11	3					7	2	10	5		9				4				6		1	8		13
14	Oct	23	(a)	Fulham	L 1-3	Turner	30632	11	3					7	2	10	5		9				4				6		1	8		14
15	Oct	30	(h)	SWANSEA TOWN	L 1-2	Turner	15555	11	3					7	2	10	5			9			4				6		1	8		15
16	Nov	6	(a)	Notts County	D 3-3	Morton (2), Adam	10395	11	3				10	7	2							9	5		4		6		1	8		16
17	Nov	13	(h)	LIVERPOOL	W 3-2	Morton (2), Adam	15887	11	3		1		10	7	2							9	5		4		6			8		17
18	Nov	20	(a)	West Ham United	L 1-2	Morton	23034	11	3		1		10	7	2							9	5		4		6			8		18
19	Nov	27	(h)	BLACKBURN ROVERS	W 7-3	Pemberton, Adam, Turner (3), Davies (2)	17314	11	3		1		10	7	2							9	5		4		6			8		19
20	Dec	4	(a)	Port Vale	D 1-1	Davies	14052	11	3		1		10	7	2							9	5		4		6			8		20
21	Dec	11	(h)	DONCASTER ROVERS	W 3-0	Turner (2), Morton	14541		3		1	11	10	7	2							9	5		4		6			8		21
22	Dec	18	(h)	Nottingham Forest	W 5-1	Pemberton, Cummins, Turner (2), Davies	11943		3		1	11	10	7	2							9	5		4		6			8		22
23	Dec	25	(h)	HULL CITY	D 1-1	Turner	15853		3		1	11	10	7	2							9	5		4		6			8		23
24	Dec	27	(a)	Hull City	W 4-0	Morton (2), Cullen, Turner	39890		3		1	11	10	7	2							9	5		4		6			8		24
25	Jan	1	(h)	IPSWICH TOWN	W 3-2	Davies, Morton, Cummins	16581		3		1	11	10	7	2							9	5		4		6			8		25
26	Jan	22	(h)	MIDDLESBROUGH	W 2-0	Turner, Davies	13372		3		1	11	10	7	2							9	5		4		6			8		26
27	Feb	5	(a)	Stoke City	D 0-0	-	21156		3		1	11	10	7	2							9	5		4		6			8		27
28	Feb	12	(h)	ROTHERHAM UNITED	W 4-0	Turner (2), Groves, Williams (og)	18450		3		1	11		7	2	10						9	5		4		6			8		28
29	Mar	2	(a)	Derby County	D 0-0	-	5987		3	7	1	11	10		2							9	5		4		6			8		29
30	Mar	5	(a)	Plymouth Argyle	L 1-2	Morton	25975	11	3		1	7	10		2			5				9			4		6			8		30
31	Mar	12	(h)	FULHAM	W 3-0	Turner (2), Groves	17966		3		1	11	10	7	2	9							5		4		6			8		31
32	Mar	19	(a)	Swansea Town	L 1-2	Turner	19422		3		1	11	10	7	2	9							5		4		6			8		32
33	Mar	26	(h)	NOTTS COUNTY	W 3-1	Morton (2), Cummins	16917	11	3		1		10	7	2							9	5		4		6			8		33
34	Apr	2	(a)	Liverpool	D 4-4	Turner (2), Morton (2)	30710	11	3		1		10	7	2							9	5		4		6			8		34
35	Apr	8	(h)	LEEDS UNITED	D 0-0	-	25775	11	3		1		10	7	2							9	5		4		6			8		35
36	Apr	9	(h)	WEST HAM UNITED	W 2-0	Turner, Cummins	27148		3		1	11	10		2	9							5	7	4		6			8		36
37	Apr	11	(a)	Leeds United	L 0-4		29583		3		1	11	10	7	2	9							5		4		6			8		37
38	Apr	16	(a)	Blackburn Rovers	D 0-0	-	35912	11	3		1		10	7	2							9	5		4		6			8		38
39	Apr	20	(a)	Birmingham City	L 1-2	Turner	34612		3		1		10	7	2					11		9	5		4		6			8		39
40	Apr	23	(h)	PORT VALE	W 4-2	Turner (2), Davies, MacEwan	16704		3					7	2					9			4		5	11	6		1	8	10	40
41	Apr	27	(h)	BRISTOL ROVERS	W 2-0	Watkins (2)	20120		3					7	2					9			4		5	11	6		1	8	10	41
42	Apr	30	(a)	Doncaster Rovers	W 3-0	MacEwan (2), Pemberton	12585		3					7	2					9			4		5	11	6		1	8	10	42
				Final League Position: 2nd		1 Own Goal	**Apps**	25	42	1	23	16	28	33	42	13	3	1	3	6	2	39	36	1	27	8	39	2	19	42	11	
							Goals	9	-	-	-	1	4	10	-	2	-	-	1	3	1	14	-	-	3	4	-	-	-	32	3	

1954/55 FA CUP

Round	Month	Day	Venue	Opponents	W,L,D Score	Scorers	Attendance	Adam J	Aherne T	Allen DS	Baynham RL	Cullen MJ	Cummins GP	Davies RA	Dunne S	Groves J	Hall LF	Jones LC	Kelly TWJ	MacEwan MP	Mitchell AJ	Morton RH	Owen SW	Pearce RS	Pemberton JT	Pye J	Shanks WG	Smith RS	Streten BR	Turner Gordon	Watkins C	Round
3	Jan	8	(h)	WORKINGTON	W 5-0	Turner (2), Cummins, Cullen (2)	18853		3		1	11	10	7	2							9	5		4		6			8		3
4	Jan	29	(a)	Rotherham United	W 5-1	Turner (3), Cummins, Cullen	21231		3		1	11	10	7	2							9	5		4		6			8		4
5	Feb	19	(h)	MANCHESTER CITY	L 0-2	-	23104		3		1	11	10	7	2							9	5		4		6			8		5
							Apps	-	3	-	3	3	3	3	3	-	-	-	-	-	-	3	3	-	3	-	3	-	-	3	-	
							Goals	-	-	-	-	3	2	-	-	-	-	-	-	-	-	-	-	-	-	-	-	-	-	5	-	

▶ **The 1954/55 team** – Back row (left to right): Cummins, Collier, Morton, Streten, Watkins, Baynham, Shanks, Dallas. Second row (left to right): Mackey (Trainer), Taylor, Arnison, Davies, McEwan, Scott, Kelly, Thompson, Wright (Trainer), Kelly (Assistant Manager). Third row (left to right): Coley (Secretary), Cullen, Smith, Adam, Turner, Allen, Dunne, Pemberton, Groves, Duncan (Manager). Front row (left to right): Hodgson (Director), Wright (Director), Aherne, England (Director), Pye, Mitchell (Chairman), Owen, Richardson (Director), Mitchell, Hewson (Director), Crarer (Medical Officer).

TIMELINE...

30 April 1955 The Town win 3-0 at Doncaster to clinch promotion to Division One on goal average.

▶ Gordon Turner bangs in a goal during the 2-1 win over Lincoln on the way to promotion.

▶ Gordon Turner hit home 32 goals during the promotion season. He went on to become the Town's record League goalscorer with 243 to his name.

▶ Bob Morton had stints in both the half-back and forward line to help the cause in 1954/55 before going on to become the club's record League appearance holder with 495 games to his credit.

LUTON TOWN FOOTBALL CLUB

LUTON TOWN F.C.

Club's Promotion Celebration

TUESDAY, 9th AUGUST, 1955

consisting of

RIVER TRIP (Marlow to Windsor)

STOLL THEATRE (Kismet)

DINNER (Piccadilly Hotel)

▶ The programme for the Town's promotion celebration 'bash'. A river excursion, followed by a trip to the theatre and then a five course dinner!

1955/56 FOOTBALL LEAGUE DIVISION ONE

Match No	Month	Day	Venue	Opponents	W,L,D Score	Scorers	Attendance	Adam J	Aherne T	Baynham RL	Cullen MJ	Cummins GP	Davies RA	Dunne S	Gregory AC	Groves J	Jones LC	Kelly TWJ	MacEwan MP	McGuffie AS	McLeod GJ	Morton RH	Owen SW	Pearce RS	Pemberton JT	Pounder JA	Shanks WG	Streten BR	Taylor AA	Thompson A	Turner Gordon	Match No
1	Aug	20	(a)	Charlton Athletic	D 2-2	Turner, MacEwan	28460		3	1		10	7	2					9			4	5				6		11		8	1
2	Aug	24	(a)	Preston North End	L 1-2	MacEwan	30770		3	1		10	7	2					9			4	5				6		11		8	2
3	Aug	27	(h)	TOTTENHAM HOTSPUR	W 2-1	Cummins, Turner	21143		3	1		10		2					9			4	5	7			6		11		8	3
4	Aug	31	(h)	PRESTON NORTH END	W 2-1	Cullen, MacEwan	24174		3	1	7	10		2					9	11		4	5				6				8	4
5	Sep	3	(a)	Everton	W 1-0	MacEwan	44237		3	1	7	10		2					9	11		4	5				6				8	5
6	Sep	5	(a)	Burnley	L 1-3	Turner	19350		3	1	7	10		2					9	11		4	5				6				8	6
7	Sep	10	(h)	NEWCASTLE UNITED	W 4-2	Turner, MacEwan, Morton, Lackenby (og)	25814	11	3	1	7	10		2					9			4	5				6				8	7
8	Sep	17	(a)	Birmingham City	D 0-0	-	31013	11	3	1	7	10		2					9			4	5				6				8	8
9	Sep	24	(h)	WEST BROMWICH ALBION	L 0-2	-	24440	11	3	1	7	10		2					9			4	5				6				8	9
10	Oct	1	(a)	Manchester United	L 1-3	Cummins	34661	11	3		7	10		2	8				9			4	5				6	1				10
11	Oct	8	(h)	BLACKPOOL	W 3-1	Turner (2), MacEwan	24493	11	3	1	7	10		2					9			4	5				6				8	11
12	Oct	15	(a)	Huddersfield Town	W 2-0	Turner, Adam	19621	11	3	1	7	10		2					9			4	5				6				8	12
13	Oct	22	(h)	ARSENAL	D 0-0	-	24009	11	3	1	7	10		2					9			4	5				6				8	13
14	Oct	29	(a)	Bolton Wanderers	L 0-4	-	26794	11	3	1	7	10	9	2								4	5				6				8	14
15	Nov	5	(h)	WOLVERHAMPTON WANDERERS	W 5-1	Morton (2), Cullen, Turner (2)	27911	11	3	1	7	10		2					9			4	5				6				8	15
16	Nov	12	(a)	Aston Villa	L 0-1	-	29761	11		1	7	10		2		3			9			4	5				6				8	16
17	Nov	19	(h)	SUNDERLAND	W 8-2	Cullen (2), Adam, Morton (3), Turner (2)	25802	11	3	1	7	10		2					9			4	5				6				8	17
18	Nov	26	(a)	Portsmouth	D 0-0	-	27758	11	3	1	7	10		2					9			4	5				6				8	18
19	Dec	3	(h)	CARDIFF CITY	W 3-0	Turner, Morton, Adam	21827	11	3	1	7			2								9	5	10	4		6				8	19
20	Dec	10	(a)	Manchester City	L 2-3	Morton, Ewing (og)	15499	11	3	1	7			2					9			8	5	10	4		6					20
21	Dec	17	(h)	CHARLTON ATHLETIC	W 2-1	MacEwan, Hammond (og)	19686	11	3	1	7			2					9			8	5	10	4		6					21
22	Dec	24	(a)	Tottenham Hotspur	L 1-2	Turner	41168	11	3	1	7			2								9	5	10	4		6				8	22
23	Dec	26	(a)	Sheffield United	W 4-0	Cullen, Turner, Pearce, Morton	29563		3	1	7		11	2								9	5	10	4		6				8	23
24	Dec	27	(h)	SHEFFIELD UNITED	W 2-1	Pearce, Davies	23522		3	1	7		11	2								9	5	10	4		6				8	24
25	Dec	31	(h)	EVERTON	D 2-2	Turner, Adam	23226	11	3	1	7	10		2								9	5		4		6				8	25
26	Jan	14	(a)	Newcastle United	L 0-4	-	21464		3	1	7	10		2			5					9	11		4		6				8	26
27	Jan	21	(h)	BIRMINGHAM CITY	L 0-1	-	18970		3	1	7	10		2			5					9	11		4		6				8	27
28	Feb	4	(a)	West Bromwich Albion	L 1-3	Turner	25190	11	3	1	7	10		2			5					9			4		6				8	28
29	Feb	11	(h)	MANCHESTER UNITED	L 0-2	-	16368			1	11			2			10	3				9	7		4		6					29
30	Feb	18	(a)	Blackpool	L 2-3	MacEwan, Davies	18562			1	7		11	2			5	3	9			10			4		6				8	30
31	Feb	25	(h)	HUDDERSFIELD TOWN	L 1-2	Turner	15431	11		1	7	10		2			5	3				9			4		6				8	31
32	Mar	7	(a)	Sunderland	W 2-1	Davies, Daniel (og)	21317	11		1	7		10	2	9		5	3							4		6				8	32
33	Mar	10	(h)	BOLTON WANDERERS	D 0-0	-	20432	11		1	7			2	9		5	3						10	4		6				8	33
34	Mar	17	(a)	Wolverhampton Wanderers	W 2-1	Davies, Gregory	32339	11		1			7	2	9		5	3						10	4		6				8	34
35	Mar	24	(h)	ASTON VILLA	W 2-1	Pearce (2)	17126	11		1	7			2	9		5						10	8	4		6			3		35
36	Mar	30	(h)	CHELSEA	D 2-2	Davies, Gregory	24276	11		1			7	2	9		5	3					10		4		6				8	36
37	Mar	31	(a)	Arsenal	L 0-3	-	45968	11		1	7			2	9		10	3					5		4		6				8	37
38	Apr	2	(a)	Chelsea	D 0-0	-	26364	11		1	7			2	9		10	3					5	8	4		6					38
39	Apr	7	(h)	PORTSMOUTH	W 1-0	Turner	17839	11		1				2	9		10	3					5		4	7	6				8	39
40	Apr	14	(a)	Cardiff City	L 0-2	-	16086	11		1	7			2	8	3	10	4					5	9			6					40
41	Apr	21	(h)	MANCHESTER CITY	W 3-2	Turner (pen), Ewing (og), Groves	18074	11	3	1	7			2		10						9	5		4		6				8	41
42	Apr	28	(h)	BURNLEY	L 2-3	Morton, Adam	15999	11	3	1	7			2		10						9	5	8	4		6					42
				Final League Position: 10th		**5 Own Goals**	**Apps**	30	29	41	30	24	16	40	7	12	14	14	17	3	1	39	27	19	20	1	40	1	3	1	33	
							Goals	5	-	-	5	2	5	-	2	1	-	-	8	-	-	10	-	4	-	-	-	-	-	-	19	

1955/56 FA CUP

Round	Month	Day	Venue	Opponents	W,L,D Score	Scorers	Attendance	Adam J	Aherne T	Baynham RL	Cullen MJ	Cummins GP	Davies RA	Dunne S	Gregory AC	Groves J	Jones LC	Kelly TWJ	MacEwan MP	McGuffie AS	McLeod GJ	Morton RH	Owen SW	Pearce RS	Pemberton JT	Pounder JA	Shanks WG	Streten BR	Taylor AA	Thompson A	Turner Gordon	Round
3	Jan	11	(h)	LEICESTER CITY	L 0-4	-	23221		3	1	7	10		2								9	5	11	4		6				8	3
							Apps	-	1	1	1	1	-	1	-	-	-	-	-	-	-	1	1	1	1	-	1	-	-	-	1	
							Goals	-	-	-	-	-	-	-	-	-	-	-	-	-	-	-	-	-	-	-	-	-	-	-	-	

▶ **The 1955/56 team** – Back row (left to right): Smith, Groves, Pearce, Dallas, McLeod, Brown, Jones, Kelly. Second row (left to right): Coley (Secretary), Crarer (Medical Officer), Taylor, Collier, Baynham, Streten, Pemberton, Mackey (Trainer), Wright (Trainer), Duncan (Manager). Third row (left to right): Hodgson (Director), Wright (Director), Dunne, Richardson (Director), Aherne, Owen, Mitchell (Chairman), Morton, England (Director), Hewson (Director). Front row (left to right): Allen, Davies, Turner, Cullen, Cummins, Shanks, Hawkes, Thompson.

TIMELINE...

20 August 1955 Gordon Turner scores the Town's first goal in Division One in an opening day 2-2 draw at Charlton.
19 November 1955 The Hatters humble League leaders Sunderland 8-2 at Kenilworth Road.

1956/57 FOOTBALL LEAGUE DIVISION ONE

Match No	Month	Day	Venue	Opponents	W,L,D Score	Scorers	Attendance	Adam J	Aherne T	Baynham RL	Brown AD	Cullen MJ	Cummins GP	Davies RA	Dunne S	Gregory AC	Groves J	Jones LC	Kelly TWJ	Legate RA	McLeod GJ	McNally JB	Morton RH	Owen SW	Pearce RS	Pemberton JT	Pounder JA	Shanks WG	Smith RS	Streten BR	Thompson A	Turner Gordon	Match No
1	Aug	18	(h)	SUNDERLAND	W 6-2	Turner (4), Groves, Cullen	23049	11	3			7			2		10						9	5	4			6		1		8	1
2	Aug	22	(h)	WOLVERHAMPTON WANDERERS	W 1-0	Morton	26715	11	3			7			2		10						9	5	4			6		1		8	2
3	Aug	25	(a)	Charlton Athletic	W 2-1	Morton, Cullen	19014	11	3			7			2		10						9	5	4			6		1		8	3
4	Aug	29	(a)	Wolverhampton Wanderers	L 4-5	Cullen, Turner (3)	46781	11	3			7			2								9	5	4		10	6		1		8	4
5	Sep	1	(h)	MANCHESTER CITY	W 3-2	Pemberton, Turner, Adam	21648	11	3			7	10		2								9	5		4		6		1		8	5
6	Sep	5	(h)	ASTON VILLA	D 0-0	-	21171	11	3			7	10		2								9	5	4			6		1		8	6
7	Sep	8	(a)	Blackpool	L 0-4	-	32112	11	3			7			2		10						9	5	4			6		1		8	7
8	Sep	15	(h)	EVERTON	W 2-0	Turner, Pearce	18076	11	3			7			2		10						9	5	4			6		1		8	8
9	Sep	22	(a)	Tottenham Hotspur	L 0-5	-	58960	11	3			7			2		10						9	5	4			6		1		8	9
10	Sep	29	(h)	LEEDS UNITED	D 2-2	Turner (2)	20949			1		11	10	7	2		6	3					9	5	4							8	10
11	Oct	6	(a)	Newcastle United	D 2-2	Turner (2)	36941	11		1			10	7	2		6	3					9	5	4							8	11
12	Oct	13	(h)	SHEFFIELD WEDNESDAY	W 2-0	Turner (pen), Legate	19202			1		7	10		2		6	3		11			9	5	4							8	12
13	Oct	20	(a)	Birmingham City	L 0-3	-	31783			1		7	10		2		6	3		11			9	5	4							8	13
14	Oct	27	(h)	WEST BROMWICH ALBION	L 0-1	-	16786	11				7	10			9		3				2		5	4			6		1		8	14
15	Nov	3	(a)	Burnley	D 1-1	Groves	22891					7	10		2		11	3					9	5	4			6		1		8	15
16	Nov	10	(h)	PRESTON NORTH END	D 1-1	Cullen	18721					7	10		2			3		11			9	5	4			6		1		8	16
17	Nov	17	(a)	Chelsea	L 1-4	Gregory	30823					7	10		2	11		3					9	5	4			6		1		8	17
18	Nov	24	(h)	CARDIFF CITY	W 3-0	Morton (2), Gregory	13674		3	1		7	10		2	11							9	5	4			6				8	18
19	Dec	1	(a)	Manchester United	L 1-3	Gregory	34954		3	1		7	10		2	11				5			9		4			6				8	19
20	Dec	8	(a)	ARSENAL	L 1-2	Groves	19792		3	1		7			2	11	10						9	5	4			6				8	20
21	Dec	15	(a)	Sunderland	L 0-1	-	28473	11	3			7	10		2								9	5	4			6		1		8	21
22	Dec	22	(h)	CHARLTON ATHLETIC	W 4-2	Turner (3, 1 pen), Cullen	9922		3	1		7	10		2			11					9	5	4			6				8	22
23	Dec	29	(a)	Manchester City	L 2-3	Turner (2)	27253		3	1		7	10		2			11					9	5	4			6				8	23
24	Jan	12	(h)	BLACKPOOL	L 0-2	-	16589			1		7	10	11	2			3					9	5	4			6				8	24
25	Jan	19	(a)	Everton	L 1-2	Shanks	29017			1			10	7	2			3					9	5	4			6	11			8	25
26	Feb	2	(h)	TOTTENHAM HOTSPUR	L 1-3	Turner (pen)	22586			1			10	7	2			3					9	5	4			6	11			8	26
27	Feb	9	(a)	Leeds United	W 2-1	Brown, McLeod	25646		3	1	8	7	10		2						9		11	5	4			6					27
28	Feb	16	(h)	NEWCASTLE UNITED	W 4-1	Turner (3), Groves	21007		3	1		7	10		2		11				9			5	4			6				8	28
29	Feb	23	(a)	West Bromwich Albion	L 0-4	-	21835		3	1		7	10		2		11				9			5	4			6				8	29
30	Mar	9	(a)	Arsenal	W 3-1	Brown (2), Turner (pen)	41288			1	8	7	10		2		11	3			9			5	4			6					30
31	Mar	13	(a)	Portsmouth	D 2-2	Turner, Morton	22438			1	8	7	10		2			3					11	5	4			6				9	31
32	Mar	16	(h)	BURNLEY	L 0-2	-	16420			1	8	7	10	11	2			3						5	4			6				9	32
33	Mar	20	(h)	PORTSMOUTH	W 1-0	Brown	14601			1	8	7	10	11	2			3						5	4			6				9	33
34	Mar	23	(a)	Preston North End	L 0-2	-	23361			1	8	7	10	11	2									5	4			6			3	9	34
35	Mar	30	(h)	CHELSEA	L 0-4	-	15083			1	8		10	7	2	11		3						5	4			6				9	35
36	Apr	3	(h)	BIRMINGHAM CITY	D 0-0	-	12881			1			10	8	2	9		3			11			5	4	7		6					36
37	Apr	6	(a)	Cardiff City	D 0-0	-	18730			1			10	8	2	9		3			11			5	4	7		6					37
38	Apr	13	(h)	MANCHESTER UNITED	L 0-2	-	21244	11		1		7	10	8		9		3			5	2			4			6					38
39	Apr	19	(a)	Bolton Wanderers	D 2-2	Turner (2)	18666	11		1		7	10			9		3			5	2			4			6				8	39
40	Apr	20	(a)	Sheffield Wednesday	L 0-3	-	21794	11		1		7	10			9		3			5	2			4			6	8				40
41	Apr	22	(h)	BOLTON WANDERERS	W 1-0	Turner	13396	11		1			10		7	9		3			5	2			4			6				8	41
42	Apr	27	(a)	Aston Villa	W 3-1	Turner (2), Brown	28524	11		1	8	7	10					3			5	2			4			6				9	42
							Apps	18	18	23	16	23	17	16	29	13	18	20	8	3	15	16	40	34	26	17	2	28	8	19	1	34	
							Goals	1	-	-	5	5	-	-	-	3	4	-	-	1	1	-	5	-	1	1	-	1	-	-	-	30	

Final League Position: 16th

1956/57 FA CUP

Round	Month	Day	Venue	Opponents	W,L,D Score	Scorers	Attendance	Adam J	Aherne T	Baynham RL	Brown AD	Cullen MJ	Cummins GP	Davies RA	Dunne S	Gregory AC	Groves J	Jones LC	Kelly TWJ	Legate RA	McLeod GJ	McNally JB	Morton RH	Owen SW	Pearce RS	Pemberton JT	Pounder JA	Shanks WG	Smith RS	Streten BR	Thompson A	Turner Gordon	Round
3	Jan	5	(h)	ASTON VILLA	D 2-2	Davies, Turner (pen)	20108					7		11	2					5	9	3	10		4			6		1		8	3
Rep	Jan	7	(a)	Aston Villa	L 0-2	-	28356					7		11	2					5	9	3	10		4			6		1		8	Rep
							Apps	-	-	-	-	2	-	2	2	-	-	-	-	2	2	2	2	-	2	-	-	2	-	2	-	2	
							Goals	-	-	-	-	-	-	1	-	-	-	-	-	-	-	-	-	-	-	-	-	-	-	-	-	1	

1956/57 SOUTHERN PROFESSIONAL FLOODLIT CUP

Round	Month	Day	Venue	Opponents	W,L,D Score	Scorers	Attendance	Adam J	Aherne T	Baynham RL	Brown AD	Cullen MJ	Cummins GP	Davies RA	Dunne S	Gregory AC	Groves J	Jones LC	Kelly TWJ	Legate RA	McLeod GJ	McNally JB	Morton RH	Owen SW	Pearce RS	Pemberton JT	Pounder JA	Shanks WG	Smith RS	Streten BR	Thompson A	Turner Gordon	Round
1	Sep	26	(h)	CHELSEA	W 4-2	Turner (3, 1 pen), Cummins	6861			1		7	10	2	11		3	6					4	5	9							8	1
2	Nov	7	(h)	WATFORD	W 4-3	Cummins (2, 1 pen), Groves, Morton	3935					7	10	2	11	9	3	6				8	4	5						1			2
SF	Mar	26	(a)	Brentford	W 4-0	Pounder (2), Gregory, Smith	7200			1		7		2		9	3	6				8	4	5			11		10				SF
F	Apr	15	(a)	Reading	W 2-1	Adam, Turner	15599	11		1							3	6	2		5		4		9	7		10				8	F
						Apps		1	-	3	-	3	2	3	2	2	4	4	1	-	1	2	4	3	2	1	1	1	1	1	-	2	
						Goals		1	-	-	-	-	3	-	-	1	1	-	-	-	-	-	1	-	-	-	2	-	1	-	-	4	

▶ The 1956/57 team – Back row (left to right): Daniel, Groves, Collier, Streten, Macklin, Baynham, Pearce, Legate, Kelly. Middle row (left to right): Wright (Trainer), Thompson, Davies, Owen, McLeod, Dunne, Pemberton, Cummins, McNally, Mackey (Trainer). Front row (left to right): Adam, Turner, K.Hawkes, Smith, Cullen, Shanks, B.Hawkes, Pounder, Aherne, Morton.

TIMELINE...

Summer 1956 The Oak Road end terracing is doubled in height.

25 August 1956 Following three straight wins at the start of the season the Town are proudly top of Division One for the first time in their history.

15 April 1957 The Town win the Southern Professional Floodlit Cup at the first time of asking.

1957/58 FOOTBALL LEAGUE DIVISION ONE

Match No	Month	Day	Venue	Opponents	W,L,D Score	Scorers	Attendance	Adam J	Baynham RL	Brown AD	Cullen MJ	Cummins GP	Dunne S	Gregory AC	Groves J	Hawkes KK	Jones LC	Kelly TWJ	Marsh WE	McGuffie AS	McLeod GJ	McNally JB	Morton RH	Owen SW	Pacey D	Pearce RS	Rowland DC	Turner Gordon	Whitby BK	Match No
1	Aug	24	(h)	BOLTON WANDERERS	W 1-0	Turner	17591	11	1	10	7		2		9		3						4	5		6		8		1
2	Aug	26	(a)	Blackpool	W 2-1	Turner (2)	21099	11	1	10	7		2		9		3						4	5		6		8		2
3	Aug	31	(a)	Arsenal	L 0-2	-	49914	11	1	10	7		2		9		3						4	5		6		8		3
4	Sep	4	(h)	BLACKPOOL	W 2-0	Brown, Cullen	19567	11	1	10	7		2		9		3						4	5		6		8		4
5	Sep	7	(h)	WOLVERHAMPTON WANDERERS	W 3-1	Turner (2), Cullen	22030		1	10	7		2		4		3				11		9	5		6		8		5
6	Sep	11	(a)	Leeds United	W 2-0	Morton, Turner	21972		1	10	7		2		4		3				11		9	5		6		8		6
7	Sep	14	(a)	Aston Villa	L 0-2	-	28962		1	10	7		2		4		3				11		9	5		6		8		7
8	Sep	18	(h)	LEEDS UNITED	D 1-1	Morton	16887		1	10	7		2		4		3				11		9	5		6		8		8
9	Sep	21	(h)	EVERTON	L 0-1	-	19797		1	10	7		2		4						11	3	9	5		6		8		9
10	Sep	28	(a)	Sunderland	L 0-3	-	36724	7	1	10			2		4		3				11		9	5		6		8		10
11	Oct	5	(h)	BURNLEY	W 3-2	Turner (2), Brown	15179	7	1	9		10	2				3				11		4	5		6		8		11
12	Oct	12	(a)	Preston North End	L 0-1	-	25403	7	1	9		10	2				3				11		4	5		6		8		12
13	Oct	19	(h)	SHEFFIELD WEDNESDAY	W 2-0	McLeod, Brown	14473	7	1	9		10	2				3				11		4	5		6		8		13
14	Oct	26	(a)	Manchester City	D 2-2	Pearce, Turner	30654	7	1	9		10	2				3				11		4	5		6		8		14
15	Nov	2	(h)	BIRMINGHAM CITY	W 3-0	Turner (2), MacLeod	17316	7	1	9		10					3				11	2	4	5		6		8		15
16	Nov	9	(a)	Chelsea	W 3-1	Turner (3)	34102	7	1	9		10	2				3				11		4	5		6		8		16
17	Nov	16	(h)	NEWCASTLE UNITED	L 0-3	-	19703	7	1	9		10	2				3				11		4	5		6		8		17
18	Nov	23	(a)	Tottenham Hotspur	L 1-3	Cummins	41242	7	1	9		10	2				3				11		4	5		6		8		18
19	Nov	30	(h)	NOTTINGHAM FOREST	W 3-1	Turner (3)	18391	7	1	9		10	2				3				11		4	5		6		8		19
20	Dec	7	(a)	Portsmouth	L 0-5	-	17782	7	1	9		10	2				3				11		4	5		6		8		20
21	Dec	14	(h)	WEST BROMWICH ALBION	W 5-1	Turner (2), Adam, Brown, Kennedy (og)	15365	7	1	9			2		10	3					11		4	5		6		8		21
22	Dec	21	(a)	Bolton Wanderers	W 2-1	Turner, Groves	16754	7	1	9			2		10	3					11		4	5		6		8		22
23	Dec	25	(a)	Manchester United	L 0-3	-	39594	7	1	9			2	8	10	3		5			11				4	6				23
24	Dec	26	(h)	MANCHESTER UNITED	D 2-2	Brown, Groves	26478	7		9	10		2		8	3		5	1		11				4	6				24
25	Dec	28	(h)	ARSENAL	W 4-0	Brown (3), Groves	27493	7	1	9			2		10	3					11		4	5		6		8		25
26	Jan	11	(a)	Wolverhampton Wanderers	D 1-1	Brown	30805	7	1	9			2		10	3					11		4	5		6		8		26
27	Jan	18	(h)	ASTON VILLA	W 3-0	Adam, Turner, MacLeod	16619	7	1	9			2		10	3					11		4	5		6		8		27
28	Feb	1	(a)	Everton	W 2-0	Gregory, Turner	26908	7	1				2	9	10	3					11			5	6			8		28
29	Feb	8	(h)	SUNDERLAND	W 7-1	Turner (4), Groves, Brown (2)	15932	7	1	9			2		10	3					11			5	4	6		8		29
30	Feb	15	(a)	Burnley	W 2-1	Turner, Brown	16869	7	1	9			2		10	3					11			5	4	6		8		30
31	Feb	22	(h)	PRESTON NORTH END	L 1-3	Adam	22549	7	1	9			2		10	3		5			11		4			6		8		31
32	Mar	1	(a)	Sheffield Wednesday	L 1-2	Turner	17747	7	1	9		10	2		4	3		5			11					6		8		32
33	Mar	8	(h)	MANCHESTER CITY	L 1-2	Pacey	16019	7	1	9			2		4	3					11			5		6	10	8		33
34	Mar	15	(a)	Birmingham City	D 1-1	Turner (pen)	25225	7	1		10		2		9	3				4	11			5		6		8		34
35	Mar	22	(h)	TOTTENHAM HOTSPUR	D 0-0	-	22384	7	1		10		2		9	3				4	11			5		6		8		35
36	Mar	29	(a)	Newcastle United	L 2-3	Whitby, Turner	16775		1	9	10		2			3				4	11			5		6		8	7	36
37	Apr	5	(h)	CHELSEA	L 0-2	-	15285		1	9	10		2			3				4	11			5		6		8	7	37
38	Apr	7	(h)	LEICESTER CITY	W 2-1	Gregory (2)	14795	11	1			10	2	9	6	3				4				5				8	7	38
39	Apr	8	(a)	Leicester City	L 1-4	Gregory	32480	11	1		7	10	2	9	6	3		5		4								8		39
40	Apr	12	(a)	Nottingham Forest	L 0-1	-	22085		1		11	10	2	9		3		4			6			5				8	7	40
41	Apr	19	(h)	PORTSMOUTH	W 2-1	McLeod, Turner	12942		1		7		2		10	3		4		9	6			5				8	11	41
42	Apr	26	(a)	West Bromwich Albion	L 2-4	Turner (2, 1 pen)	20158		1		7	10	2	9	4	3		5			6							8	11	42
				Final League Position: 8th		1 Own Goal	**Apps**	32	41	33	17	15	41	6	31	22	19	8	1	9	34	2	27	36	12	29	1	40	6	
							Goals	3	-	12	2	1	-	4	4	-	-	-	-	-	4	-	2	-	1	1	-	33	1	

1957/58 FA CUP

Round	Month	Day	Venue	Opponents	W,L,D Score	Scorers	Attendance	Adam J	Baynham RL	Brown AD	Cullen MJ	Cummins GP	Dunne S	Gregory AC	Groves J	Hawkes KK	Jones LC	Kelly TWJ	Marsh WE	McGuffie AS	McLeod GJ	McNally JB	Morton RH	Owen SW	Pacey D	Pearce RS	Rowland DC	Turner Gordon	Whitby BK	Round
3	Jan	4	(a)	Stockport County	L 0-3	-	18200	7	1	9			2		10	3					11		4	5		6		8		3
							Apps	1	1	1	-	-	1	-	1	1	-	-	-	-	1	-	1	1	-	1	-	1	-	
							Goals	-	-	-	-	-	-	-	-	-	-	-	-	-	-	-	-	-	-	-	-	-	-	

1957/58 SOUTHERN PROFESSIONAL FLOODLIT CUP

Round	Month	Day	Venue	Opponents	W.L.D Score	Scorers	Attendance	Adam J	Baynham RL	Brown AD	Cullen MJ	Cummins GP	Dunne S	Gregory AC	Groves J	Hawkes KK	Jones LC	Kelly TWJ	Marsh WE	McCuffie AS	McLeod GJ	McNally JB	Morton RH	Owen SW	Pacey D	Pearce RS	Rowland DC	Turner Gordon	Whitby BK	Round
1	Oct	28	(a)	Southampton	W 2-0	Turner, Cummins	6712	11	1	9	.	7	.	.	.	3	.	.	.	.	10	2	4	5	.	6	.	8	.	1
2	Dec	10	(a)	Brentford	D 0-0	-	4350	11	1	9	.	7	2	.	.	3	.	.	.	.	10	.	4	5	.	6	.	8	.	2
Rep	Jan	29	(h)	BRENTFORD	W 7-1	Turner (2), McLeod (2), Groves, Adam, Brown	4010	11	1	9	.	.	2	.	7	3	.	.	.	.	10	.	4	5	6	.	.	8	.	Rep
SF	Mar	25	(a)	Reading	D 3-3	Turner (2), Groves	10881	11	1	.	9	.	2	.	7	3	.	.	.	4	10	.	.	5	6	.	.	8	.	SF
Rep	Mar	31	(h)	READING	L 0-1	-	4606	.	1	.	9	.	2	.	10	3	.	.	.	4	11	.	.	5	6	.	.	8	7	Rep
							Apps	4	5	3	2	2	4	.	3	4	1	.	.	2	5	1	3	5	3	2	.	5	1	
							Goals	1	.	1	.	1	.	.	2	.	.	.	.	.	2	.	.	.	.	.	.	5	.	

▶ **The 1957/58 team** – Back row (left to right): Groves, Dunne, Baynham, Jones, Pearce. Front row (left to right): Cullen, Turner, Owen, Brown, Morton, McLeod.

TIMELINE...

25 December 1957 The Town play a game on Christmas Day for the last time. They go down 0-3 at Manchester United.

1958/59 FOOTBALL LEAGUE DIVISION ONE

Match No	Month	Day	Venue	Opponents	W,L,D	Score	Scorers	Attendance
1	Aug	23	(h)	WEST BROMWICH ALBION	D	1-1	Turner (pen)	24425
2	Aug	26	(a)	Leeds United	D	1-1	Turner	25498
3	Aug	30	(a)	Birmingham City	W	1-0	Groves	31943
4	Sep	3	(h)	LEEDS UNITED	D	1-1	Brown	13497
5	Sep	6	(h)	WEST HAM UNITED	W	4-1	Turner (2), Brown, Pacey	25715
6	Sep	10	(a)	Manchester City	D	1-1	Groves	30771
7	Sep	13	(h)	BOLTON WANDERERS	D	0-0		19699
8	Sep	17	(h)	MANCHESTER CITY	W	5-1	Turner (2), Adam, Brown (2)	18160
9	Sep	20	(a)	Burnley	D	2-2	Cummins, Turner	23760
10	Sep	27	(h)	PRESTON NORTH END	W	4-1	Adam (2), Cummins, Bingham	23056
11	Oct	4	(a)	Leicester City	L	1-3	McLeod	32019
12	Oct	11	(a)	Nottingham Forest	L	1-3	Turner	30337
13	Oct	18	(h)	CHELSEA	W	2-1	Brown, Cummins	24864
14	Oct	25	(a)	Portsmouth	D	2-2	Hawkes, Brown	24831
15	Nov	1	(h)	ASTON VILLA	W	2-1	Turner (2)	18714
16	Nov	8	(a)	Newcastle United	L	0-1		53488
17	Nov	15	(h)	TOTTENHAM HOTSPUR	L	1-2	Bingham	23592
18	Nov	22	(a)	Manchester United	L	1-2	Cummins	42428
19	Nov	29	(h)	WOLVERHAMPTON WANDERERS	L	0-1		20648
20	Dec	6	(a)	Blackpool	L	0-3		14140
21	Dec	13	(h)	BLACKBURN ROVERS	D	1-1	Bingham	13475
22	Dec	26	(h)	ARSENAL	W	6-3	Adam, Gregory, Bingham (2), Brown (2)	21870
23	Dec	27	(a)	Arsenal	L	0-1		56277
24	Jan	3	(h)	BIRMINGHAM CITY	L	0-1		15538
25	Jan	31	(a)	Bolton Wanderers	L	2-4	Bingham, Brown	27787
26	Feb	7	(h)	BURNLEY	W	6-2	Brown (3), Pacey, Morton (2)	15753
27	Feb	21	(a)	Leicester City	W	4-3	Gregory, Morton, Brown, Cummins	15786
28	Mar	7	(a)	Chelsea	D	3-3	Turner (2), McGuffie	29175
29	Mar	21	(a)	Aston Villa	L	1-3	Bingham	27401
30	Mar	27	(h)	EVERTON	L	0-1		22954
31	Mar	28	(h)	NEWCASTLE UNITED	W	4-2	Brown (2), Gregory, Pacey	20880
32	Mar	30	(a)	Everton	L	1-3	Morton	32620
33	Apr	4	(a)	Tottenham Hotspur	L	0-3		37093
34	Apr	6	(a)	Preston North End	D	0-0		10548
35	Apr	9	(h)	NOTTINGHAM FOREST	W	5-1	Brown (4), Bingham	22352
36	Apr	11	(a)	Manchester United	D	0-0		27025
37	Apr	13	(a)	West Ham United	D	0-0		26784
38	Apr	15	(a)	West Bromwich Albion	L	0-2		19173
39	Apr	18	(a)	Wolverhampton Wanderers	L	0-5		40981
40	Apr	20	(a)	Blackburn Rovers	L	1-3	Brown	18092
41	Apr	22	(h)	PORTSMOUTH	W	3-1	Pacey, Turner, Cummins	11592
42	Apr	25	(h)	BLACKPOOL	D	1-1	Turner	17720

Final League Position: 17th

Appearances / Goals (League):

Player	Apps	Goals
Adam J	29	4
Baynham RL	38	–
Bingham WL	36	8
Brown AD	39	20
Collier AS	3	–
Cummins GP	31	6
Daniel AW	1	–
Dixon MJ	1	–
Dunne S	29	–
Gregory AC	15	3
Groves J	30	2
Hawkes B	3	–
Hawkes KK	40	1
Kelly TWJ	12	–
Kilgannon J	1	–
Marsh WE	1	–
McGuffie AS	3	1
McLeod GJ	1	–
McNally JB	15	1
Morton RH	35	4
Owen SW	31	–
Pacey D	36	4
Turner Gordon	31	14
Walker Jackie	–	–
Whitby BK	1	–

1958/59 FA CUP

Round	Month	Day	Venue	Opponents	W,L,D	Score	Scorers	Attendance
3	Jan	10	(h)	LEEDS UNITED	W	5-1	Bingham (2), Morton, Gregory (2)	18534
4	Jan	24	(a)	Leicester City	D	1-1	Bingham	36984
Rep	Jan	28	(h)	LEICESTER CITY	W	4-1	Brown (3), Gregory	27277
5	Feb	14	(a)	Ipswich Town	W	5-2	Pacey, Morton (2), Bingham, Gregory	26700
6	Feb	28	(a)	Blackpool	D	1-1	Bingham	30634
Rep	Mar	4	(h)	BLACKPOOL	W	1-0	Brown	30069
SF	Mar	14	(n)	Norwich City	D	1-1	Brown	65000
Rep	Mar	18	(n)	Norwich City	W	1-0	Bingham	49500
F	May	2	(n)	Nottingham Forest	L	1-2	Pacey	100000

Semi Final played at White Hart Lane, replay played at St Andrews. Final played at Wembley.

Appearances / Goals (FA Cup):

Player	Apps	Goals
Baynham RL	9	–
Bingham WL	9	6
Brown AD	9	5
Cummins GP	9	–
Gregory AC	9	4
Groves J	9	–
Hawkes KK	9	–
McNally JB	9	–
Morton RH	9	3
Owen SW	9	–
Pacey D	9	2

1958/59 SOUTHERN PROFESSIONAL FLOODLIT CUP

Round	Month	Day	Venue	Opponents	W,L,D Score	Scorers	Attendance	Adam J	Baynham RL	Bingham WL	Brown AD	Collier AS	Cummins GP	Daniel AW	Dixon MJ	Dunne S	Gregory AC	Groves J	Hawkes B	Hawkes KK	Kelly TWJ	Kilgannon J	Marsh WE	McGuffie AS	McLeod GJ	McNally JB	Morton RH	Owen SW	Pacey D	Turner Gordon	Walker Jackie	Whitby BK	Round
1	Nov	3	(a)	Portsmouth	W 2-0	Turner (2),	5066	11	1		9		10				2	7	6	3							4		5	8			1
2	Feb	18	(h)	SOUTHAMPTON	W 4-0	Morton (2), Cummins, Gregory (pen)	2803		1		9		10				2	7	6	3					4		11		5	8			2
SF	Apr	1	(a)	Crystal Palace	L 0-1	-	15731					1	10		9	2					5	11			4		6		8		3	7	SF
						Apps		1	2	-	2	1	3	-	1	1	2	2	2	2	1	1	-	-	2	-	3	-	3	2	1	1	
						Goals		-	-	-	-	-	1	-	-	-	1	-	-	-	-	-	-	-	-	-	2	-	-	2	-	-	

▶ The FA Cup finalists line up with their straw boaters.

TIMELINE...

27 September 1958 Following an unbeaten ten game start to the season, the Town sit proudly on top of Division One.

16 October 1958 Manager Dally Duncan leaves to take up the hot seat at Blackburn.

4 March 1959 Kenilworth Road houses its all-time record crowd with 30,069 managing to see Allan Brown shoot the Town through to the F.A.Cup semi-finals for the first time.

2 May 1959 The Hatters, having fought their way through to the F.A.Cup final lose 1-2 to Nottingham Forest at Wembley.

5 May 1959 Ex-skipper Syd Owen, the current holder of the Footballer of the Year award, is announced as the new Luton manager having been appointed shortly before the Cup final.

▶ **The team in their Wembley strip** – Back row (left to right): Frank King (Trainer), Hawkes, Groves, Baynham, Pacey, McNally. Front row (left to right): Bingham, Brown, Morton, Owen, Cummins, Gregory.

The Town's Syd Owen and his Forest counterpart Jack Burkitt exchange banners before kick-off on the big day at Wembley.

THE FOOTBALL ASSOCIATION CHALLENGE CUP COMPETITION

FINAL TIE

LUTON TOWN

v

NOTTINGHAM FOREST

SATURDAY, MAY 2nd, 1959   KICK-OFF 3 pm

EMPIRE STADIUM

WEMBLEY

OFFICIAL PROGRAMME   ONE SHILLING

Dave Pacey (out of picture) nets the Hatter's consolation goal.

The FA Cup final programme.

Match No	Month	Day	Venue	Opponents	W,L,D Score	Scorers	Attendance	Baynham RL	Bingham WL	Brown AD	Collier AS	Collins MJA	Cummins GP	Daniel AW	Dixon MJ	Dunne S	Gregory AC	Groves J	Hawkes B	Hawkes KK	Kelly TWJ	Kilgannon J	McBride J	McCann A	McCreadie WH	McNally JB	Morton RH	Noake DJ	Pacey D	Tracey MG	Turner Gordon	Warner J	Match No
1	Aug	22	(a)	Everton	D 2-2	Brown, Bingham	38539	1	7	9			10			2	11	6			3						8		4	5			1
2	Aug	26	(h)	BLACKPOOL	L 0-1	-	19095	1	7	9			10			2	11	6			3	5					8		4				2
3	Aug	29	(h)	LEEDS UNITED	L 0-1	-	15822	1	7	9			10			2	11	6			3	5					8		4				3
4	Aug	31	(a)	Blackpool	D 0-0	-	22008	1	7	8			10			2		6			3	5					11		4	9			4
5	Sep	5	(h)	BOLTON WANDERERS	D 0-0	-	15604	1	7	8			10			2		6			3	5					11		4		9		5
6	Sep	9	(h)	MANCHESTER CITY	L 1-2	Brown	13122	1	7	8			10			2		6			3	5					11		4		9		6
7	Sep	12	(a)	Fulham	L 2-4	Bingham (2)	30012	1	7	8			10			2		6			3	5					11		4		9		7
8	Sep	16	(a)	Manchester City	W 2-1	Bingham (2)	29309	1	7	9			10			2		6	11		3	5			4		8						8
9	Sep	19	(h)	NOTTINGHAM FOREST	W 1-0	Brown	16634	1	7	9			10			2	11	6	10		3	5							4		8		9
10	Sep	26	(a)	Sheffield Wednesday	L 0-2	-	24775	1	7	9			10			2	11	6	11		3	5							4		8		10
11	Oct	3	(h)	WOLVERHAMPTON WANDERERS	L 1-5	Dixon	22908	1					10		9	2	11	6	7		3	5							4		8		11
12	Oct	10	(a)	West Ham United	L 1-3	Turner	23266	1	7	10			11			2		6			3	5							4	9	8		12
13	Oct	17	(h)	CHELSEA	L 1-2	Brown	18831	1	7	9			10			2		6		5	3	11							4		8		13
14	Oct	24	(a)	West Bromwich Albion	L 0-4	-	22352	1	7	9			8			2		5			3		11						4	6	10		14
15	Oct	31	(h)	BURNLEY	D 1-1	Brown	15638		7	4	1			3		2		6		5							8			9	10	11	15
16	Nov	7	(a)	Birmingham City	D 1-1	Bingham	19007	1	7	4			10	3		2		6		5							8			9			16
17	Nov	14	(h)	TOTTENHAM HOTSPUR	W 1-0	Cummins	22528	1	7	6			10	3		2	11	4		5		8								9			17
18	Nov	21	(a)	Manchester United	L 1-4	Kilgannon	40807	1	7	6			10	3		2	11	4		5		8								9			18
19	Nov	28	(h)	PRESTON NORTH END	L 1-3	Bingham	17174		7	6	1		10	3		2	11	4		5		8					9						19
20	Dec	5	(a)	Leicester City	D 3-3	Bingham, Pacey, Brown	16682		7	9	1			3		2	11	4		5							8		6		10		20
21	Dec	12	(h)	NEWCASTLE UNITED	L 3-4	Bingham (2), Gregory	14524		7	9	1		10	3		2	11	4		5							8		6				21
22	Dec	19	(a)	Everton	W 2-1	Gregory (2)	9799	1	7	9				3		2	11	4		5							10		6		8		22
23	Dec	26	(h)	Arsenal	W 3-0	Gregory (2), Turner	31331	1	7	9				3		2	11	4		5							10		6		8		23
24	Dec	28	(h)	ARSENAL	L 0-1	-	27055	1	7	9				3		2	11	4		5							10		6		8		24
25	Jan	2	(a)	Leeds United	D 1-1	Turner	19921	1	7	9				3		2	11	4		5									6		8		25
26	Jan	23	(h)	FULHAM	W 4-1	Morton, Brown, Bingham, Turner	17876	1	7	9				3		2	11	4		5							10		6		8		26
27	Feb	6	(a)	Nottingham Forest	L 0-2	-	22808	1	7	9				3		2	11	4		5							10		6		8		27
28	Feb	13	(h)	SHEFFIELD WEDNESDAY	L 0-1	-	14392	1	7	4			10			2				5						3		11	6	9	8		28
29	Feb	23	(a)	Wolverhampton Wanderers	L 2-3	Bingham, Groves	30059	1	7	4						2	11	10		5					9	3			6		8		29
30	Feb	27	(h)	LEICESTER CITY	W 2-0	Turner, McBride	18691	1	7	4						2	11	10		5			9			3			6		8		30
31	Mar	5	(a)	Chelsea	L 0-3	-	33679		7	4	1					2		10		5			9			3			6	11	8		31
32	Mar	9	(a)	Bolton Wanderers	D 2-2	McBride, Turner	14791	1	7	6			10			2			3				9					4	5	11	8		32
33	Mar	12	(h)	WEST BROMWICH ALBION	D 0-0	-	18285	1	7	6			10			2			3				9					4	5	11	8		33
34	Mar	19	(a)	Newcastle United	L 2-3	Bingham (2)	29269	1	7	6			10			2			3				9					4	11	5	8		34
35	Mar	26	(h)	BIRMINGHAM CITY	D 1-1	McBride (pen)	13620	1	7	6			10			2			3				9					4	11	5	8		35
36	Apr	2	(a)	Tottenham Hotspur	D 1-1	McBride	39462	1	7	6			10			2			3				9					4	11	5	8		36
37	Apr	9	(h)	MANCHESTER UNITED	L 2-3	Cummins (2)	21242	1	7	6			10			2			3				9					4	11	5	8		37
38	Apr	15	(a)	Blackburn Rovers	W 2-0	McBride, Bingham	22714	1	7	6			10			2			3				9					4	11	5	8		38
39	Apr	16	(a)	Burnley	L 0-3	-	20893	1	7	6			10			2			3				9					4	11	5	8		39
40	Apr	18	(h)	BLACKBURN ROVERS	D 1-1	Bingham	14167	1	11			4				3				5			9	7		2							40
41	Apr	23	(h)	WEST HAM UNITED	W 3-1	McBride, Cummins, Lansdowne (og)	11404	1					11	3						5			9					4	6	7	8		41
42	Apr	30	(a)	Preston North End	L 0-2	-	29781	1	7	6			10	3		2				5			9					4			8		42
				Final League Position: 22nd		1 Own Goal	**Apps**	37	40	39	5	1	30	16	1	41	18	33	5	22	31	12	13	1	1	6	33	7	32	6	31	1	
							Goals	-	16	7	-	-	4	-	1	-	5	1	-	-	-	1	6	-	-	-	1	-	1	-	6	-	

1959/60 FA CUP

Round	Month	Day	Venue	Opponents	W,L,D Score	Scorers	Attendance	Baynham RL	Bingham WL	Brown AD	Collier AS	Collins MJA	Cummins GP	Daniel AW	Dixon MJ	Dunne S	Gregory AC	Groves J	Hawkes B	Hawkes KK	Kelly TWJ	Kilgannon J	McBride J	McCann A	McCreadie WH	McNally JB	Morton RH	Noake DJ	Pacey D	Tracey MG	Turner Gordon	Warner J	Round
3	Jan	9	(a)	Exeter City	W 2-1	Turner (2)	20193	1	7	9				3		2	11	4		5							10		6		8		3
4	Jan	30	(a)	Huddersfield Town	W 1-0	Gregory	22500	1	7	9				3		2	11	4		5							10		6		8		4
5	Feb	20	(h)	WOLVERHAMPTON WANDERERS	L 1-4	Turner	25619	1	7	4						2		10	11	5						3	9		6		8		5
							Apps	3	3	3	-	-	2	-	-	3	2	3	1	3	-	-	-	-	-	1	3	-	3	-	3	-	
							Goals	-	-	-	-	-	1	-	-	-	1	-	-	-	-	-	-	-	-	-	-	-	-	-	3	-	

1959/60 SOUTHERN PROFESSIONAL FLOODLIT CUP

Round	Month	Day	Venue	Opponents	W,L,D Score	Scorers	Attendance	Baynham RL	Bingham WL	Brown AD	Collier AS	Collins MJA	Cummins GP	Daniel AW	Dixon MJ	Dunne S	Gregory AC	Groves J	Hawkes B	Hawkes KK	Kelly TWJ	Kilgannon J	McBride J	McCann A	McCreadie WH	McNally JB	Morton RH	Noake DJ	Pacey D	Tracey MG	Turner Gordon	Warner J	Round
2	Oct	26	(h)	FULHAM	D 1-1	Warner	5008	7	4	1			3			2		6			5	8					9				10	11	2
Rep	Nov	23	(n)	Fulham	L 0-1		10100		6	1			10	3		2		4			5	8					9		11		7		Rep
					Apps			-	1	2	2	-	1	2	-	2	-	2	-	-	2	2	-	-	-	-	2	-	1	-	2	1	
					Goals			-	-	-	-	-	-	-	-	-	-	-	-	-	-	-	-	-	-	-	-	-	-	-	-	1	

Replay played at Brentford

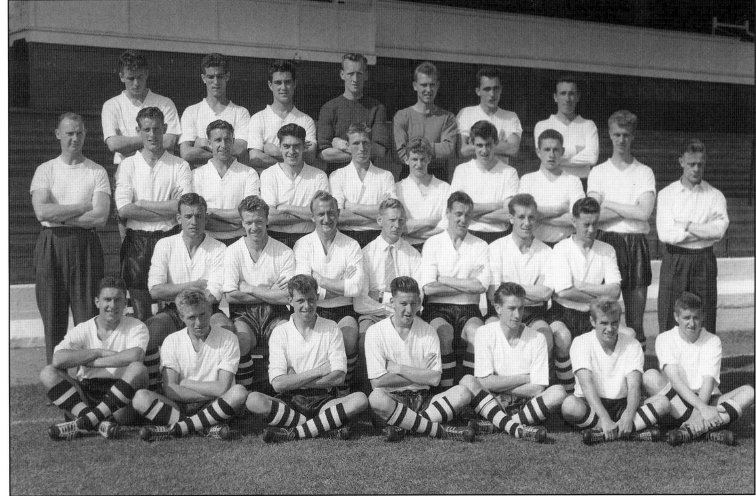

▶ **The 1959/60 team** – Back row (left to right): Dixon, Collins, Brice, Baynham, Collier, Folwell, Kelly. Second row (left to right): King (Trainer), Groves, Morton, Turner, Pacey, Kilgannon, Walker, Raffell, G.King, Shanks (Coach). Third row (left to right): K.Hawkes, Bingham, Dunne, S.Owen (Manager), Brown, McNally, Cummins. Front row (left to right): B.Hawkes, A.McCann, D.King, Parrin, Rowlands, H.McCann, Lesnick.

TIMELINE...

16 April 1960 Syd Owen is sacked as the Town drop back to Division Two.

Match No	Month	Day	Venue	Opponents	W,L,D Score	Scorers	Attendance	Ashworth A	Baynham RL	Bingham WL	Bramwell J	Brogan D	Brown AD	Chandler RAS	Collier AS	Collins MJA	Cummins GP	Daniel AW	Dixon MJ	Dunne S	Fairchild MP	Fleming JP	Groves J	Hawkes KK	Imlach JJS	Kelly TWJ	Legate RA	McBride J	McCann A	McGuffie AS	McNally JB	Morton RH	Noake DJ	O'Hara MJ	Pacey D	Spencer L	Standen JA	Tracey MG	Turner Gordon	Walden HB	Match No
1	Aug	20	(a)	Huddersfield Town	D 1-1	Turner	18156		1	7			5					3		2		10			11			9			4				6				8		1
2	Aug	24	(h)	PORTSMOUTH	W 1-0	Turner	17514		1	7			5					3		2		10			11			9			4				6				8		2
3	Aug	27	(h)	SUNDERLAND	D 3-3	Pacey, McBride, Bingham	17632		1	7			5					3		2		10			11			9			4				6				8		3
4	Aug	31	(a)	Portsmouth	L 2-3	Turner, Bingham	15176		1	7			5					3		2		10			11			9			4				6				8		4
5	Sep	3	(a)	Plymouth Argyle	D 1-1	Brown	21408		1	7			10					3		2					11	5		9			4				6				8		5
6	Sep	7	(a)	Liverpool	D 2-2	Turner, Bingham	27339		1	7			10					3		2					11	5		9			4				6				8		6
7	Sep	10	(h)	NORWICH CITY	L 0-2	-	22252		1	7			10					3		2					11	5		9			4				6				8		7
8	Sep	14	(h)	LIVERPOOL	W 2-1	Brown, McBride	10055		1	7	3		10							2			5		11			9			4				6				8		8
9	Sep	17	(a)	Charlton Athletic	L 1-4	Brown	11778		1	7	3		10							2			5		11			9			4				6				8		9
10	Sep	24	(h)	SHEFFIELD UNITED	L 1-4	Turner	13726		1	7	3		9							2			5		11			10			4				6				8		10
11	Oct	1	(a)	Stoke City	L 0-3	-	9395		1	7	3		6			11	5			2			4					9							10				8		11
12	Oct	8	(h)	BRISTOL ROVERS	W 4-2	Tracey, McBride, Turner, Sampson (og)	9373		1	7	3		6		1					2			5					9			4							11	8		12
13	Oct	15	(a)	Derby County	L 1-4	Ashworth	13447	10			3		4		1					2			5							6	10							11	7		13
14	Oct	22	(h)	LEYTON ORIENT	L 0-1	-	11037	9			3		10		4								5							6	2							11	7		14
15	Oct	29	(a)	Scunthorpe United	L 0-1	-	8643	9			3		10										5							6	2							11	7		15
16	Nov	5	(h)	IPSWICH TOWN	W 3-2	Turner (2), Ashworth	11221	8			3		10										5							6	2		4				7	1	11		16
17	Nov	12	(a)	Brighton & Hove Albion	L 0-1	-	14186	8			3		10										5							6	2		4				7	1	11		17
18	Nov	19	(a)	MIDDLESBROUGH	W 6-1	Brown (2), Spencer, Tracey, Turner (2 pens)	12579	8			3		10										5							6	2		4			7	1	11		18
19	Dec	3	(h)	SOUTHAMPTON	W 4-1	Turner (2), Tracey, Brown	12927	8			3		10										5							6	2		4			7	1	11		19
20	Dec	10	(a)	Rotherham United	L 2-5	Turner (2)	6297	8			3		10										5							6	2	4				7	1	11		20
21	Dec	17	(h)	HUDDERSFIELD TOWN	W 1-0	Turner	11219	8			3		11									10	5							6	2	4				1	7			21
22	Dec	26	(h)	LINCOLN CITY	W 3-0	Fleming (2), Ashworth	15283	8			3		10									11	5							6	2		4				1	7			22
23	Dec	27	(a)	Lincoln City	D 1-1	Ashworth	10345	8			3		10									11	5							6	2		4				1	7			23
24	Dec	31	(a)	Sunderland	L 1-7	Turner	28695	8			3		10									11	5							6	2		4				1	7			24
25	Jan	14	(h)	PLYMOUTH ARGYLE	W 3-2	Turner, Brown, Williams (og)	13873	8			3		10									11	5							6	2		4				1	7			25
26	Jan	21	(a)	Norwich City	L 1-2	Turner	21290	8			3		10									11					5			6	2		4				1		9	7	26
27	Feb	11	(a)	Sheffield United	L 1-2	Turner	16716	8			3		10							2		11	6				5				4	7				1		9		27
28	Feb	23	(h)	STOKE CITY	W 4-1	Turner (4, 1 pen)	12142	8	1		3						10			2		11	6				5				4					1		9	7	28
29	Feb	25	(a)	Bristol Rovers	L 1-4	Mabbutt (og)	13105	8	1		3						10			2		11	6				5				4					1		9	7	29
30	Mar	4	(h)	DERBY COUNTY	D 1-1	Fleming	13001	8	1		3											11	10				5				4	2			6	1		9	7	30
31	Mar	8	(a)	Leeds United	W 2-1	Ashworth, Turner	9995	8	1		3											11	6				5		7	10	4	2				1		9		31
32	Mar	11	(a)	Leyton Orient	L 1-2	McGuffie	11918	8	1		3											11	6				5		7	10	4	2				1		9		32
33	Mar	18	(h)	ROTHERHAM UNITED	W 2-1	McGuffie, Fleming	10179		1		3						10					11	6				5		7	8	2	4				1		9		33
34	Mar	25	(a)	Ipswich Town	W 1-0	McGuffie	21744		1		3						10					11	6				5		7	8	2	4				1		9		34
35	Mar	31	(h)	SWANSEA TOWN	D 2-2	Turner (pen), Nurse (og)	14286		1		3						10					11	6				5			8	2	4	7			1		9		35
36	Apr	1	(h)	LEEDS UNITED	D 1-1	Turner (pen)	11137		1		3						10					11	6				5			8	2	4	7			1		9		36
37	Apr	3	(a)	Swansea Town	L 1-3	Groves	14884		1		3			7								10	11	6			5			8	2	4				1		9		37
38	Apr	8	(a)	Middlesbrough	L 1-2	Legate	13017	8	1		3					5							10				11			2	4	7			6			9		38
39	Apr	15	(h)	BRIGHTON & HOVE ALBION	W 3-1	McGuffie, Legate, Ashworth	9104	8	1		3												6			5	11			10	2	9	7		4					39
40	Apr	22	(a)	Southampton	L 2-3	Morton, Fairchild	7016	8	1		3										7		6			5	11			10	2	9			4					40
41	Apr	26	(h)	CHARLTON ATHLETIC	W 4-1	Ashworth (2), Legate (2)	7149	8	1		3			7		5							6				11			10	2	9			4					41
42	Apr	29	(h)	SCUNTHORPE UNITED	D 0-0	-	8373	8	1		3					5			9				7				11			10	2	4			6					42
				Final League Position: 13th		4 Own Goals	**Apps**	25	25	11	30	4	24	2	2	4	6	7	1	16	1	18	37	6	8	17	5	12	5	24	26	27	10	2	29	7	13	17	37	4	
							Goals	8	-	3	-	-	7	-	-	-	-	-	-	-	1	4	1	-	-	-	4	3	-	4	-	-	1	-	1	1	-	3	26	-	

1960/61 FA CUP

Round	Month	Day	Venue	Opponents	W,L,D Score	Scorers	Attendance	Ashworth A	Baynham RL	Bingham WL	Bramwell J	Brogan D	Brown AD	Chandler RAS	Collier AS	Collins MJA	Cummins GP	Daniel AW	Dixon MJ	Dunne S	Fairchild MP	Fleming JP	Groves J	Hawkes KK	Imlach JJS	Kelly TWJ	Legate RA	McBride J	McCann A	McGuffie AS	McNally JB	Morton RH	Noake DJ	O'Hara MJ	Pacey D	Spencer L	Standen JA	Tracey MG	Turner Gordon	Walden HB	Round
3	Jan	7	(h)	NORTHAMPTON TOWN	W 4-0	Turner (2), Brown, Ashworth	26220	8			3		10										11		5					6	2		7				1		9		3
4	Feb	1	(h)	MANCHESTER CITY	W 3-1	Ashworth (2), Fleming	15583	8			3		10									5	11		6					10	4	2	7				1		9		4
5	Feb	18	(a)	Barnsley	L 0-1	-	32923	8			3		10									5	11		6						4	2	7				1		9		5
						Apps	3	-	-	3	-	2										2	3	-	3					2			1	1	3	3	-	1	-	3	3	-	
						Goals	3	-	-	-	-	1										1																	2	-	

1960/61 LEAGUE CUP

Round	Month	Day	Venue	Opponents	W,L,D Score	Scorers	Attendance	Ashworth A	Baynham RL	Bingham WL	Bramwell J	Brogan D	Brown AD	Chandler RAS	Collier AS	Collins MJA	Cummins GP	Daniel AW	Dixon MJ	Dunne S	Fairchild MP	Fleming JP	Groves J	Hawkes KK	Imlach JJS	Kelly TWJ	Legate RA	McBride J	McCann A	McGuffie AS	McNally JB	Morton RH	Noake DJ	O'Hara MJ	Pacey D	Spencer L	Standen JA	Tracey MG	Turner Gordon	Walden HB	Round
2	Oct	19	(a)	Liverpool	D 1-1	Brogan	10502					10	4					3					5		11			9	6	2				1				7	8		2
Rep	Oct	25	(h)	LIVERPOOL	L 2-5	Turner, Brogan	6125					10	4					3					5					9	6	2		11		1				7	8		Rep
						Apps		-	-	-	2	2	-	-	-	-	2	-	-	-	-	2	-	1	-	-	2	2	2	-	1	-	2	-	-	-	2	2	-	
						Goals		-	-	-	2	-	-	-	-	-	-	-	-	-	-	-	-	-	-	-	-	-	-	-	-	-	-	-	-	-	-	1	-	

▶ The 1960/61 team – Back row (left to right): Folwell, Underwood, Groves, Collins, Baynham, Ker, McNally, McCreadie, Tracey. Second row (left to right): Fielding (Coach), Pacey, McCann, Noake, Raffell, Kilgannon, McBride, Brown, Turner, Bingham, Cummins, King (Trainer). Third row (left to right): Lesnick, Spencer, Hawkes, Dunne, S.Bartram (Manager), Morton, Kelly, Imlach, McGuffie. Front row (left to right): Andrews, Buckland.

TIMELINE...

18 July 1960 Ex-Charlton goalkeeper Sam Bartram is appointed manager at Kenilworth Road.
1 Feb 1961 The Hatters beat Manchester City 3-1 in a re-arranged FA Cup tie at Kenilworth Road four days after the previous match was abandoned with City leading 6-2!

1961/62 FOOTBALL LEAGUE DIVISION TWO

Match No	Month	Day	Venue	Opponents	W/L/D Score	Scorers	Attendance	Ashworth A	Baynham RL	Bramwell J	Chandler RAS	Clarke A	Collins MJA	Cope R	Daniel AW	Fairchild MP	Fleming JP	Groves J	Jardine F	Kelly TWJ	Legate RA	Lornie J	Lownds MU	McGuffie AS	McKechnie TS	McNally JB	Morton RH	Pacey D	Reed BEF	Standen JA	Turner Gordon	Walden HB	Match No
1	Aug	19	(h)	PRESTON NORTH END	W 4-1	Ashworth (2), Turner, Groves	14109	10	1	3				5			11	6				9				2		4			8	7	1
2	Aug	23	(a)	Derby County	L 0-2	-	18705	10	1	3				5			11	6				9				2		4			8	7	2
3	Aug	26	(a)	Plymouth Argyle	W 3-0	Turner (2), Walden	15299	8	1	3							11	6		5					10	2		4			9	7	3
4	Aug	30	(h)	DERBY COUNTY	W 4-2	McKechnie (2), Walden, Ashworth	15380	8	1	3							11	6		5					10	2		4			9	7	4
5	Sep	2	(h)	HUDDERSFIELD TOWN	L 3-4	McKechnie, Lornie, Coddington (og)	14436	8	1	3								6		5		11			10	2		4			9	7	5
6	Sep	9	(a)	Swansea Town	L 2-3	Turner (pen), Fleming	11813	8	1	3				5			11	6							10	2		4			9	7	6
7	Sep	16	(h)	SOUTHAMPTON	L 1-4	Turner	13209	8	1	3				5			11	6							10			4	2		9	7	7
8	Sep	20	(a)	Middlesbrough	W 4-2	McKechnie (2), Turner (2, 1 pen)	15878	8	1	3				5			11	6							10	2		4			9	7	8
9	Sep	23	(a)	Charlton Athletic	W 1-0	Turner	10176	8	1	3				5			11	6							10	2		4			9	7	9
10	Sep	27	(h)	MIDDLESBROUGH	W 3-2	Ashworth, Turner, McKechnie	11276	8	1	3				5			11	6							10	2		4			9	7	10
11	Sep	30	(a)	Newcastle United	L 1-4	McGuffie	22452	8	1	3				5			11	6						10		2		4			9	7	11
12	Oct	7	(h)	BURY	W 4-0	Turner (2), Ashworth (2)	10315	8		3				5			11	6							10	2		4		1	9	7	12
13	Oct	14	(a)	Brighton & Hove Albion	L 1-2	Lornie	14186	8		3			5				11	6				10				2		4		1	9	7	13
14	Oct	21	(h)	SCUNTHORPE UNITED	L 1-2	Ashworth	9766	8		3			5				11	6						9	10	2		4		1		7	14
15	Oct	28	(a)	Norwich City	W 4-0	Ashworth (2), Legate, Scott (og)	18845	9		3				5			7	6			11				10	2		4		1	8		15
16	Nov	4	(h)	LEEDS UNITED	W 3-2	Legate (2), Fleming	10341	10		3				5			7	6			11					2	8	4		1	9		16
17	Nov	11	(a)	Liverpool	D 1-1	Turner	34924	10		3				5			7	6			11					2	8	4		1	9		17
18	Nov	18	(h)	STOKE CITY	D 0-0	-	15163	10		3				5			11	6								2	8	4		1	9	7	18
19	Nov	25	(a)	Sunderland	D 2-2	Ashworth, Pacey	32763	10		3				5			11	6								2	8	4		1	9	7	19
20	Dec	2	(h)	ROTHERHAM UNITED	W 4-3	Ashworth, McKechnie, Walden, McGuffie	9886	9		3				5				6			8			11	10	2		4		1		7	20
21	Dec	9	(a)	Bristol Rovers	L 0-1	-	9688	9		3				5			11	8							10	2		4		1		7	21
22	Dec	16	(a)	Preston North End	L 0-2	-	8702	8		3				5			11	10				9				2		4		1		7	22
23	Dec	23	(h)	PLYMOUTH ARGYLE	L 0-2	-	8410	8		3	9			5			11	6							10	2		4		1		7	23
24	Dec	26	(a)	Walsall	L 0-2	-	9609	9		3				5				10	11						8	2		4		1		7	24
25	Jan	13	(a)	Huddersfield Town	W 2-1	McKechnie, Morton	11140	8		3	9			5				6			5	11			10	2	8	4		1		7	25
26	Jan	20	(h)	SWANSEA TOWN	W 5-1	Fleming, Lownds, Turner (2), Pacey	8107			3							11	6			5	10	4		8	2				1	9	7	26
27	Feb	3	(a)	Southampton	L 0-3	-	13037	8		3				5			11	10				4				2				1	9	7	27
28	Feb	10	(h)	CHARLTON ATHLETIC	L 1-6	Turner	9827	8		3		7		5				4			11				10	2		6		1	9		28
29	Feb	17	(h)	NEWCASTLE UNITED	W 1-0	Turner	9040		1	3		7		5			7	4					10		9	2		6			8	11	29
30	Feb	24	(a)	Bury	L 1-2	McNally	6133		1	3		7		5			7	4					10		9	2		6			8	11	30
31	Mar	3	(h)	BRIGHTON & HOVE ALBION	W 2-1	McKechnie, Pacey	7005		1	3	7			5	2			6						11	10		4	8			9		31
32	Mar	10	(a)	Scunthorpe United	L 0-2	-	7911	8	1	3	7			5											10	2		6			9	11	32
33	Mar	17	(h)	NORWICH CITY	L 1-2	McKechnie	9736	8	1	3				5								11			10	2		6			9	7	33
34	Mar	24	(a)	Leeds United	L 1-2	McNally	13078	8		3							11	4			5				10	2		6		1	9	7	34
35	Mar	31	(h)	LIVERPOOL	W 1-0	Pacey	9086	9		3							11	4			5				10	2	7	6		1	8		35
36	Apr	7	(a)	Stoke City	L 1-2	Morton	7530	9		3							11	4			5				10	2	7	6		1	8		36
37	Apr	11	(h)	WALSALL	W 2-0	Turner (2)	6123	9		3		7					11	4			5				10	2		6		1	8		37
38	Apr	14	(h)	SUNDERLAND	L 1-2	Pacey	9571	9		3		7					11	4			5				10	2		6		1	8		38
39	Apr	20	(a)	Leyton Orient	D 0-0	-	21312	9		3		7					11				5				10	2		4	6		1	8		39
40	Apr	21	(a)	Rotherham United	D 1-1	Turner	3492	8		3							11				5			10		2		4	6		1	9	7	40
41	Apr	23	(h)	LEYTON ORIENT	L 1-3	Morton	13681	8	9	3		7					11				5				10	2		4	6	1			41
42	Apr	28	(h)	BRISTOL ROVERS	W 2-0	Turner, Ashworth	6555	8		3		7					11	6			5					2		4	10	1	9		42
				Final League Position: 13th		2 Own Goals	**Apps**	38	23	42	4	5	3	25	1	-	33	34	3	14	7	5	3	7	33	40	27	30	1	20	33	31	
							Goals	12	-	-	-	-	-	-	-	-	3	1	-	-	3	2	1	2	10	2	3	5	-	-	20	3	

1961/62 FA CUP

Round	Month	Day	Venue	Opponents	W/L/D Score	Scorers	Attendance	Ashworth A	Baynham RL	Bramwell J	Chandler RAS	Clarke A	Collins MJA	Cope R	Daniel AW	Fairchild MP	Fleming JP	Groves J	Jardine F	Kelly TWJ	Legate RA	Lornie J	Lownds MU	McGuffie AS	McKechnie TS	McNally JB	Morton RH	Pacey D	Reed BEF	Standen JA	Turner Gordon	Walden HB	Round
3	Jan	6	(a)	Ipswich Town	D 1-1	Chandler	18450	8	1	3	9			5							11					10	2	4	6				7	3
Rep	Jan	10	(h)	IPSWICH TOWN	D 1-1	Pacey	23818	8	1	3	9			5							11					10	2	4	6				7	Rep
Rep 2	Jan	15	(n)	Ipswich Town	L 1-5	Ashworth	29348	8	1	3	9										5	11				10	2	4	6				7	Rep 2
				3rd Round 2nd Replay played at Highbury			**Apps**	3	3	3	3	-	-	2	-	-	-	-	-	-	1	3	-	-	-	3	3	3	3	-	-	-	3	
							Goals	1	-	-	1	-	-	-	-	-	-	-	-	-	-	-	-	-	-	-	-	1	-	-	-	-	-	

1961/62 LEAGUE CUP

Round	Month	Day	Venue	Opponents	W/L/D Score	Scorers	Attendance	Ashworth A	Baynham RL	Bramwell J	Chandler RAS	Clarke A	Collins MJA	Cope R	Daniel AW	Fairchild MP	Fleming JP	Groves J	Jardine F	Kelly TWJ	Legate RA	Lornie J	Lownds MU	McGuffie AS	McKechnie TS	McNally JB	Morton RH	Pacey D	Reed BEF	Standen JA	Turner Gordon	Walden HB	Round
1	Sep	13	(h)	NORTHAMPTON TOWN	W 2-1	Turner, Foley (og)	7482		1	3			5				11	6				9			10		4		2		8	7	1
2	Oct	4	(h)	ROTHERHAM UNITED	D 0-0	-	6544	8		3			5		7		10		11			9				2	4	6		1				2
Rep	Oct	10	(a)	Rotherham United	L 0-2	-	5176	8		3			5				11	6							10	2	4			1		9	7	Rep
				1 Own Goal			Apps	2	1	3	.	.	2	1	.	1	2	3	1	.	.	2	.	.	2	2	3	1	1	2	2	2	
							Goals	-	-	-	.	.	-	-	.	-	-	-	-	.	.	-	.	.	-	-	-	-	-	-	1	-	

▶ **The 1961/62 team** – Back row (left to right): Wilsher, Lornie, Ker, Baynham, O'Hara, Bramwell, Reed. Second row (left to right): Collins, Morton, Kelly, Pacey, McNally, McGuffie, Groves. Third row (left to right): Jardine, McKechnie, Fleming, Turner, Fairchild, Walden, Riddick. Front row (left to right): Daniel, Legate, Ashworth.

TIMELINE...

23 April 1962 In a home game against Leyton Orient, ex-England international goalkeeper Ron Baynham plays at centre-forward for the Town.
14 June 1962 Sam Bartram leaves Kenilworth Road by 'mutual consent'.

1962/63 FOOTBALL LEAGUE DIVISION TWO

Match No	Month	Day	Venue	Opponents	W.L.D Score	Scorers	Attendance	Baynham RL	Bramwell J	Brennan MH	Chandler RAS	Clapton DR	Clarke A	Cope R	Daniel AW	Davies RT	Fairchild MP	Fleming JP	Goldie J	Groves J	Jardine F	Kelly TWJ	Lornie J	Lownds MU	McGuffie AS	McKechnie TS	McNally JB	Morton RH	Pacey D	Riddick GG	Standen JA	Turner Gordon	Walden HB	Match No
1	Aug	18	(a)	Bury	L 0-1	-	8313	1	3									11				5	9		10		2	4	6			8	7	1
2	Aug	22	(a)	Southampton	D 2-2	Fleming, Pacey	14863	1	3									11	9			5	10				2	4	6			8	7	2
3	Aug	25	(h)	ROTHERHAM UNITED	L 2-3	Lornie (2)	8615	1	3				4					11	9			5	10				2		6			8	7	3
4	Aug	29	(h)	SOUTHAMPTON	W 3-2	Walden, Goldie, Fleming	7124	1							3			11	9			5	10			4	8		2				7	4
5	Sep	1	(a)	Charlton Athletic	L 0-2	-	14012	1	3						2			8	9		11	5	10					4	6				7	5
6	Sep	5	(h)	PRESTON NORTH END	L 0-2	-	6702	1	3									11	9			5	10				2	4	6			8	7	6
7	Sep	8	(h)	STOKE CITY	D 0-0	-	6819	1	3									8				5	11				2	4	6			9	7	7
8	Sep	11	(a)	Preston North End	L 1-3	Turner	12216	1	3					7				8				5					10	2	4	6			9	11	8
9	Sep	15	(a)	Sunderland	L 1-3	Turner	36399	1	3					7				8				5					10	2	4	6			9	11	9
10	Sep	22	(h)	LEEDS UNITED	D 2-2	Turner, McNally	8916	1	3			7		5				8									10	2	4	6		1	9	11	10
11	Sep	29	(a)	Swansea Town	L 0-1	-	9441		3			7						8							6		10	2	4	5		1	9	11	11
12	Oct	6	(h)	PORTSMOUTH	D 3-3	Lornie, McKechnie, Walden	8078		3			7						8					9		6		10	2	4	5	1			11	12
13	Oct	13	(a)	Cardiff City	L 0-1	-	15901	1	3			7						8					9		6		10	2	4	5				11	13
14	Oct	27	(a)	Middlesbrough	W 2-0	Turner, McGuffie	13835	1	3							8		11		6					10			2	4	5			9	7	14
15	Nov	3	(h)	DERBY COUNTY	L 1-2	Turner	7582	1	3							8		11						6	10			2	4	5			9	7	15
16	Nov	10	(a)	Newcastle United	L 1-3	McGuffie	27428	1	3							8	7			6					10			2	4	5			9	11	16
17	Nov	17	(h)	WALSALL	W 4-3	Davies (2), Walden, Jardine	5489	1	3							9				6	11				10	8		2	4	5				7	17
18	Nov	24	(a)	Norwich City	D 3-3	Davies (2), Jardine	16376	1	3							9				6	11				10	8		2	4	5				7	18
19	Dec	1	(h)	GRIMSBY TOWN	D 2-2	Davies (2)	7202	1	3							9				6	11				10			2	4	5				7	19
20	Dec	8	(a)	Plymouth Argyle	L 1-3	McGuffie	9029	1	3							9				6	11				10			2	4	5			8	7	20
21	Dec	15	(h)	BURY	W 2-1	Turner, Davies	6042	1	3					5		9					11				10			2	4	6			8	7	21
22	Dec	21	(a)	Rotherham United	L 1-2	Walden	8198	1	3					5		9					11							2	4	6	10		8	7	22
23	Dec	26	(h)	CHELSEA	L 0-2	-	11867	1	3							9					11	5						2	4	6	10		8	7	23
24	Feb	23	(a)	Portsmouth	L 1-3	Turner	12428	1	3							9						5	11		4	10		2		6			8	7	24
25	Mar	9	(a)	Huddersfield Town	L 0-2	-	10279	1						7		3		9			4	11	5		10			2		6			8		25
26	Mar	16	(h)	HUDDERSFIELD TOWN	W 3-2	Jardine, Turner, Coddington (og)	5428	1		9					3	8					11	5		6				2		4			10	7	26
27	Mar	23	(a)	Derby County	L 0-1	-	10756	1		9					3	8					11	5		6				2		4			10	7	27
28	Mar	25	(h)	MIDDLESBROUGH	W 4-3	Goldie, Turner (2), Lornie	6431	1	3							2			9			5	11		6					4			10	7	28
29	Mar	30	(h)	NEWCASTLE UNITED	L 2-3	Davies (2)	7163	1	3							2	8	7	9			5	11		6					4			10		29
30	Apr	1	(a)	Chelsea	L 1-3	Turner	21211	1	3			7				2	8					5	11		6				4	9			10		30
31	Apr	6	(a)	Walsall	D 1-1	Morton	8960	1	3					7		2	8				10	5					11	4	6				8		31
32	Apr	12	(a)	Scunthorpe United	L 0-2	-	7739	1	3							2	9	7				11	5				10	4	6				8		32
33	Apr	13	(h)	NORWICH CITY	W 4-2	Davies (4)	9536	1	3							2	9	7				11	5				10	4	6				8		33
34	Apr	15	(h)	SCUNTHORPE UNITED	W 1-0	Turner	9091	1	3							2	9	7				11	5				10	4	6				8		34
35	Apr	20	(a)	Grimsby Town	L 1-3	Davies	9504	1	3							2	9	7				11	5				10	4	6				8		35
36	Apr	24	(h)	CARDIFF CITY	L 2-3	Daniel (pen), Davies	7237	1	3		10				2	9	7					11	5					4	6				8		36
37	Apr	27	(h)	PLYMOUTH ARGYLE	W 3-0	Pacey, Brennan, Davies	6853	1	3	8		7				2	9						5				10	4	6	11					37
38	May	1	(h)	SWANSEA TOWN	W 3-1	Davies (3)	7642	1	3	8		7				2	9						5	11			10	4	6						38
39	May	4	(a)	Leeds United	L 0-3	-	23900	1	3	8		7				2	9						5	11	6		10	4							39
40	May	11	(h)	CHARLTON ATHLETIC	W 4-1	Davies (2), Turner (2)	10867	1	6			7				2	9					11					10	3	4				8		40
41	May	13	(h)	SUNDERLAND	L 0-3	-	16419	1	6			7				2	9						5				10	3	4				8		41
42	May	18	(a)	Stoke City	L 0-2	-	34168	1	3							9					6	11	5				10	7	2	4			8		42
				Final League Position: 22nd		1 Own Goal	**Apps**	39	38	4	3	10	4	3	19	29	7	15	7	9	18	29	14	7	21	20	29	34	38	3	3	32	27	
							Goals	-	1	-	-	-	-	-	1	21	-	2	2	-	3	-	4	-	3	1	1	2	-	-	-	14	4	

1962/63 FA CUP

Round	Month	Day	Venue	Opponents	W.L.D Score	Scorers	Attendance	Baynham RL	Bramwell J	Brennan MH	Chandler RAS	Clapton DR	Clarke A	Cope R	Daniel AW	Davies RT	Fairchild MP	Fleming JP	Goldie J	Groves J	Jardine F	Kelly TWJ	Lornie J	Lownds MU	McGuffie AS	McKechnie TS	McNally JB	Morton RH	Pacey D	Riddick GG	Standen JA	Turner Gordon	Walden HB	Round
3	Jan	26	(h)	SWINDON TOWN	L 0-2	-	10840	1	3			7				9					11	5					2	4	6	10			8	3
							Apps	1	1	-	-	1	-	-	-	1	-	-	-	-	1	1	-	-	-	-	1	1	1	1	-	-	1	
							Goals	-	-	-	-	-	-	-	-	-	-	-	-	-	-	-	-	-	-	-	-	-	-	-	-	-	-	

1962/63 LEAGUE CUP

Round	Month	Day	Venue	Opponents	W,L,D Score	Scorers	Attendance	Baynham RL	Bramwell J	Brennan MH	Chandler RAS	Clapton DR	Clarke A	Cope R	Daniel AW	Davies RT	Fairchild MP	Fleming JP	Goldie J	Groves J	Jardine F	Kelly TWJ	Lornie J	Lownds MU	McGuffie AS	McKechnie TS	McNally JB	Morton RH	Pacey D	Riddick GG	Standen JA	Turner Gordon	Walden HB	Round
2	Sep	24	(a)	Southport	W 3-1	Fleming, Turner, Walden	5375		3								7	8	10						6		2	4	5		1	9	11	2
3	Oct	16	(a)	Barnsley	W 2-1	Turner, Fairchild	10335	1	3								7	8			10				6		2	4	5			9	11	3
4	Nov	14	(a)	Manchester City	L 0-1	-	8682	1	3									11		6					10	8	2	4	5			9	7	4
							Apps	2	3								2	3	1	1	1				3	1	3	3	3		1	3	3	
							Goals										1	1														2	1	

▶ The 1962/63 team –
Back row (left to right):
Hargreaves, Lownds,
McKechnie, Baynham,
Ross, Ker, Turner, Riddick,
Lornie, Fairchild, Fleming.
Middle row (left to right):
Brennan, Groves, Cope,
Pacey, Daniel, Goldie,
Caleb, Morton, Scott. Front
row (left to right): Jardine,
Walden, Clarke, Reed,
Bramwell, McNally, Kelly,
McGuffie.

TIMELINE...

29 June 1962 Ex-Hatters coach Jack Crompton accepts the role of manager at Kenilworth Road but resigns a week later for health reasons.
24 July 1962 Bill Harvey accepts the post of manager.
18 May 1963 The Town lose 0-2 at Stoke to confirm relegation back to Division Three.

1963/64 FOOTBALL LEAGUE DIVISION THREE

Match No	Month	Day	Venue	Opponents	W,L,D Score	Scorers	Attendance	Baynham RL	Bramwell J	Caleb GS	Daniel AW	Davies RT	Fairchild MP	Fincham GR	Jardine F	Lownds MU	McBain A	McGuffie AS	McKechnie TS	Morton RH	O'Rourke J	Pacey D	Reid J	Riddick GG	Salisbury G	Smith HR	Tinsley C	Turner Gordon	Walden HB	Weir J	Whittaker RH	Match No
1	Aug	24	(h)	WALSALL	W 1-0	Turner	9046	1	3		2	9		5	11					4		6				10		8	7			1
2	Aug	28	(a)	Crewe Alexandra	L 0-1	-	8909	1	3		2	9		5	11					4		6				10		8	7			2
3	Aug	31	(a)	Reading	D 1-1	Salisbury	7751	1	3		2	9		5	11					4		6				10		8	7			3
4	Sep	6	(a)	Barnsley	L 1-3	Riddick	5388	1	3		2		9	5	11					4		6		10				8	7			4
5	Sep	11	(h)	CREWE ALEXANDRA	D 3-3	Turner (2), Daniel (pen)	5865	1	3		2		9	5	11					4		6		10				8	7			5
6	Sep	14	(h)	COVENTRY CITY	L 1-3	Daniel (pen)	14511	1	6		2			5	11		3	4				10						8	7	11		6
7	Sep	18	(h)	CRYSTAL PALACE	L 0-4	-	6152	1	3					9	5		2	10		4		6						8	7	11		7
8	Sep	21	(a)	Mansfield Town	D 1-1	Gill (og)	9565	1	3						5	6			8	2		4						9	7	11		8
9	Sep	28	(h)	BRENTFORD	L 0-2	-	7379	1	3					7	5	6					2	4			10	8		9		11		9
10	Oct	2	(a)	Crystal Palace	D 1-1	Jardine	16304	1	3					5	11	6				9	2	4			10			8				10
11	Oct	5	(a)	Shrewsbury Town	L 0-1	-	5887	1	3					5	11	6				9	2	4			10			8				11
12	Oct	9	(h)	PORT VALE	W 1-0	McKechnie	5914	1	3					5		6			10	9	2	4			8				7	11		12
13	Oct	12	(h)	BOURNEMOUTH	W 1-0	Salisbury (pen)	6361	1	3					7		6			9		2	4			8				7		10	13
14	Oct	14	(a)	Port Vale	L 0-1	-	11449	1	3					7		6			9		2	4			8				7		10	14
15	Oct	19	(a)	Watford	L 0-2	-	13239	1	3							6			9		2	4			8	10				11		15
16	Oct	23	(h)	BRISTOL CITY	L 1-4	Walden	5107	1	3							6			10		2	4			8	9			7	11		16
17	Oct	26	(h)	SOUTHEND UNITED	W 4-1	Turner (3, 1 pen), Weir	5337	1	3					7		6			10		2	4			8			9	7	11		17
18	Oct	29	(a)	Bristol City	L 1-5	Turner	10269	1	3							6			10		2	4			8			9		11		18
19	Nov	2	(a)	Peterborough United	D 0-0	-	10687	1	3					5		6			9		2	4			8				7	10		19
20	Nov	9	(h)	OLDHAM ATHLETIC	L 1-2	Turner	6222	1	3					5		6					2	4				8		9	7	10		20
21	Nov	23	(h)	QUEENS PARK RANGERS	D 4-4	Turner (2), McKechnie, Smith	6598	1	3					7	5			4	10		2				8			9	7			21
22	Nov	30	(a)	Wrexham	L 0-2	-	6381	1	3					5		6	11				2	4	10		8				9			22
23	Dec	14	(a)	Walsall	L 0-4	-	3893	1	3					7					11		2	4			8				9			23
24	Dec	21	(h)	READING	W 2-1	McKechnie, Turner	4346		3					5		6			10	2	9	4	8				1			11		24
25	Dec	26	(a)	Millwall	L 0-3	-	7625		3					5	11	10			6	2	9	4	1									25
26	Dec	28	(h)	MILLWALL	L 1-3	Jardine	7180		3					5	11				6	2	9	4	1					8	7			26
27	Jan	11	(a)	Barnsley	L 2-3	Turner, O'Rourke	4555	1	6					5			3			2	9		4					8	7	11		27
28	Jan	18	(a)	Coventry City	D 3-3	McKechnie (2), Turner	20921	1	3					5				6	8	2		4	9						7	11		28
29	Jan	25	(h)	COLCHESTER UNITED	W 3-1	Walden, O'Rourke, Turner (pen)	4726	1	3					5					8	2	6	4	9						7	11		29
30	Feb	1	(a)	MANSFIELD TOWN	L 0-2	-	6307	1	3					5					8	2	6	4	9						7	11		30
31	Feb	8	(a)	Brentford	W 6-2	O'Rourke (4), Walden (2)	9003	1	3	5								6	8	2	9	4	10	11					7	11		31
32	Feb	15	(h)	SHREWSBURY TOWN	W 2-0	McKechnie (pen), O'Rourke	6282	1	3	5								6	8	2	9	4	10	11					7			32
33	Feb	22	(a)	Bournemouth	L 1-3	Reid	9298	1	3	5								6	8	2	9	4	10	11					7			33
34	Feb	29	(h)	HULL CITY	W 2-1	McKechnie, O'Rourke	5267	1	3	5								6	8	2	9	4	10					7		11		34
35	Mar	7	(a)	Southend United	W 1-0	O'Rourke	5486	1	3	5								6	8	2	9	4	10						7		11	35
36	Mar	14	(h)	PETERBOROUGH UNITED	L 2-3	Pacey, O'Rourke	6279	1	3	5								6	8	2	9	4			10				7		11	36
37	Mar	21	(a)	Hull City	L 0-2	-	3576	1	3	5								6	8	2	4				10				7		11	37
38	Mar	26	(a)	Notts County	D 1-1	McKechnie	4406	1	3	5								6	8	2		4			10				7		11	38
39	Mar	28	(h)	BRISTOL ROVERS	W 4-2	O'Rourke (3), Turner	6612	1	3									6		2	9	4	5					8	7		11	39
40	Mar	30	(h)	NOTTS COUNTY	W 2-0	O'Rourke (2)	8387	1	3									6		2	9	4	5					8	7		11	40
41	Apr	11	(h)	WREXHAM	W 3-1	Turner (pen), Lownds, O'Rourke	7094	1	3							6				2	9	4	5					8	7		11	41
42	Apr	13	(a)	Bristol Rovers	W 2-1	O'Rourke (2)	8094	1	3				5					6		2	9	4							7		11	42
43	Apr	18	(a)	Colchester United	D 1-1	O'Rourke	3913	1	3					5				6	8	2	9	4							7		11	43
44	Apr	22	(a)	Oldham Athletic	W 1-0	Lownds	6367	1	3					5				6	8	2	9	4							7		11	44
45	Apr	25	(h)	WATFORD	W 2-1	O'Rourke (2)	19799	1	3					5				6		2	9	4							7		11	45
46	Apr	29	(a)	Queens Park Rangers	D 1-1	O'Rourke	5005	1	3					5				6	8	2	9	4	7		10						11	46
				Final League Position: 18th		1 Own Goal	**Apps**	43	46	8	6	3	13	35	16	29	22	12	32	33	23	42	22	11	12	10	3	27	34	12	12	
							Goals	-	-	-	2	-	-	-	2	2	-	-	8	-	22	1	1	1	2	1	-	16	4	1	-	

Round	Month	Day	Venue	Opponents	W,L,D Score	Scorers	Attendance	Baynham RL	Bramwell J	Caleb GS	Daniel AW	Davies RT	Fairchild MP	Fincham GR	Jardine F	Lownds MU	McBain A	McGuffie AS	McKechnie TS	Morton RH	O'Rourke J	Pacey D	Reid J	Riddick GG	Salisbury G	Smith HR	Tinsley C	Turner Gordon	Walden HB	Weir J	Whittaker RH	Round
1	Nov	16	(a)	Bridgwater Town	W 3-0	McKechnie (2), Turner	4453	1	3				7	5	11			6	10	2		4				8		9				1
2	Dec	7	(h)	READING	W 2-1	Fairchild, Turner (pen)	9090	1	3				7	5				6	10	2		4				8		9		11		2
3	Jan	4	(a)	Fulham	L 1-4	Smith	18089	1	6					5			3		11	2	9	4				8		10	7			3
						Apps		3	3	.	.	.	2	3	1	.	1	2	3	3	1	3	.	.	.	3	.	3	1	1	.	
						Goals		.	.	.	.	.	1	.	.	.	.	.	2	.	.	.	.	.	.	1	.	2	.	.	.	

Round	Month	Day	Venue	Opponents	W,L,D Score	Scorers	Attendance	Baynham RL	Bramwell J	Caleb GS	Daniel AW	Davies RT	Fairchild MP	Fincham GR	Jardine F	Lownds MU	McBain A	McGuffie AS	McKechnie TS	Morton RH	O'Rourke J	Pacey D	Reid J	Riddick GG	Salisbury G	Smith HR	Tinsley C	Turner Gordon	Walden HB	Weir J	Whittaker RH	Round
2	Sep	25	(h)	COVENTRY CITY	L 3-4	Salisbury (2), Fincham (pen)	3821	1	3				7	5	6			9	2			4			10	8				11		2
						Apps		1	1	.	.	.	1	1	1	.	.	1	1	.	.	1	.	.	1	1	.	1	.	1	.	
						Goals		.	.	.	.	.	.	1	.	.	.	.	.	.	.	.	.	.	2	.	.	.	.	.	.	

John O'Rourke, whose 22 goals from 23 games saved the Town from relegation.

The 1963/64 team – Back row (left to right): King (Trainer), Daniel, Morton, Baynham, Fincham, Pacey, Bramwell. Front row (left to right): Walden, Turner, Davies, Salisbury, Jardine.

TIMELINE...

4 September 1963 Welsh striker Ron Davies is sold to Norwich for £35,000.

29 April 1964 After a remarkable nine game unbeaten run the Town avoid relegation at the death buoyed by the goals of youngster John O'Rourke.

1964/65 FOOTBALL LEAGUE DIVISION THREE

Match No	Month	Day	Venue	Opponents	W/L/D	Score	Scorers	Attendance	Barton KR	Baynham RL	Bramwell J	Caleb GS	Chandler RAS	Clarke A	Edwards R	Fincham GR	Gibson Jim	Hails W	Harber WH	Jardine F	Knights AF	Lownds MU	McBain A	McKechnie TS	O'Rourke J	Pacey D	Phillips EJ	Pleat DJ	Reid J	Riddick GG	Riley R	Rioch BD	Tinsley C	Whittaker RH	Match No
1	Aug	22	(a)	Brentford	D	2-2	O'Rourke, McKechnie	10883	1		3					5						6	2	8	9	4			10	7				11	1
2	Aug	26	(h)	COLCHESTER UNITED	W	3-1	McKechnie (2), Riddick	9897	1		3					5						6	2	8		4		7	10	9				11	2
3	Aug	29	(h)	BRISTOL ROVERS	L	0-2	-	9985	1		3					5						6	2	8		4		7	10	9				11	3
4	Aug	31	(a)	Colchester United	W	1-0	Whittaker	5115	1		3					5						6	2	8		4		7	10	9				11	4
5	Sep	5	(a)	Oldham Athletic	W	2-0	Reid (2)	10793	1		3					5						6	2	8	9	4		7	10					11	5
6	Sep	9	(h)	PORT VALE	D	1-1	Pleat	11649	1		3					5						6	2	8		4		7	10	9				11	6
7	Sep	12	(h)	EXETER CITY	L	1-2	O'Rourke	10461	1		3					5						6	2	8	9	4		7	10					11	7
8	Sep	14	(a)	Port Vale	L	0-1	-	6381	1		3					5						6	2	8	9	4		7	10					11	8
9	Sep	19	(a)	Bournemouth	L	0-4	-	8763	1		3					5						6	2	8	9	4		7	10					11	9
10	Sep	26	(h)	PETERBOROUGH UNITED	D	1-1	O'Rourke	9339	1		3					5				6			2	8	9	4		7	10					11	10
11	Oct	1	(h)	CARLISLE UNITED	D	1-1	O'Rourke	7745	1		3					5				6			2	8	9	4		7	10					11	11
12	Oct	3	(a)	Grimsby Town	D	2-2	O'Rourke, Cockerill (og)	8410	1		3					5						6	2	9		4		7	10	8				11	12
13	Oct	9	(a)	Carlisle United	D	1-1	Whittaker	9038	1							5	6			3		4	2	9				7	10	8				11	13
14	Oct	?	(a)	Workington	L	0-1	-	6007	1							5	6			3		4	2	9				7	10	8				11	14
15	Oct	12	(a)	Mansfield Town	L	0-2	-	8083	1							5	6			3		4	2	9				7	10	8				11	15
16	Oct	17	(h)	HULL CITY	L	1-3	Riddick	6020	1			5	9				6			3		4	2					7	10	8				11	16
17	Oct	21	(h)	MANSFIELD TOWN	D	1-1	Pleat	2874	1			5					6			3			2	8		4		7	10	9				11	17
18	Oct	24	(a)	Gillingham	L	0-5	-	9424	1			5	9				6			3			2			4		7	10	8				11	18
19	Oct	28	(h)	SCUNTHORPE UNITED	D	1-1	McKechnie	3876				5					6	7		3			2	9		4			10	8			1	11	19
20	Oct	31	(h)	BRISTOL CITY	D	0-0	-	5385				5					6	7		3			2	9		4			10	8			1	11	20
21	Nov	6	(a)	Queens Park Rangers	L	1-7	Pleat	5175				5	9			5	6	7	11	3			2			4		8	10				1		21
22	Nov	21	(a)	Reading	W	2-1	Harber, Riddick	7568				5					6	8	11	3			4	2				7	10	9			1		22
23	Nov	28	(h)	SOUTHEND UNITED	L	0-1	-	5020				5					6	8	3			4	2					7	10	9		11	1		23
24	Dec	12	(h)	BRENTFORD	W	4-2	McKechnie (2), Whittaker, Riddick	6104	1		3	5											2	9		4		7	6	8		10		11	24
25	Dec	19	(a)	Bristol Rovers	L	2-3	Whittaker (2)	10624	1		3					5							2	9		4		7	6	8		10		11	25
26	Dec	26	(h)	WATFORD	L	2-4	Riddick, Whittaker	11020	1							5				3			2	9		4		7	6	8		10		11	26
27	Dec	28	(a)	Watford	L	0-2	-	6867	3	1		5										6	2	9		4		7	10	8		11			27
28	Jan	2	(h)	OLDHAM ATHLETIC	W	2-0	Pacey, McKechnie	5290	3	1		5							11				2	9		4		7	6	8		10			28
29	Jan	16	(a)	Exeter City	L	1-5	McKechnie	4686	3	1		5	9						11				2	10		4		7	6						29
30	Jan	30	(a)	Barnsley	L	0-3	-	2989	6	1		4								3			2	9		5			10	7		8		11	30
31	Feb	6	(a)	Peterborough United	L	0-2	-	12946		1						5	4		7	3			2	8	9				6			10		11	31
32	Feb	13	(h)	GRIMSBY TOWN	D	1-1	O'Rourke	5160			6					5	8		7	3			2	10	9		5		4				1	11	32
33	Feb	20	(h)	BOURNEMOUTH	L	0-1	-	4554			6						4			3			2	7	9	5			10	8		11	1		33
34	Feb	27	(a)	Hull City	L	1-3	O'Rourke	22986									4			3			2	11	9	5	8	7	6	10			1		34
35	Mar	10	(h)	SHREWSBURY TOWN	L	2-7	O'Rourke, Phillips	4914									4			3			2	11	9	5	10	7	6				1		35
36	Mar	13	(a)	Bristol City	L	0-1	-	11001	2							5	4			3				8	9		10	7	6			11	1		36
37	Mar	20	(h)	QUEENS PARK RANGERS	W	2-0	Pleat, Phillips	3998	2							5	4		11	3					9		10	7	6				1		37
38	Mar	26	(a)	Shrewsbury Town	W	2-0	Harber, Phillips	4800	2							5	4		11	3			10				9	7	6				1		38
39	Apr	3	(h)	READING	W	3-1	Harber, Phillips, Pleat	5479	2							5	4		11	3			10				9	7	6	8			1		39
40	Apr	7	(h)	BARNSLEY	W	5-1	O'Rourke, McKechnie (2), Phillips (2)	6112	2							5	4		11	3			10	8			9	7	6				1		40
41	Apr	10	(a)	Southend United	L	0-5	-	4968	2							5	4		11	3			10	8			9	7	6				1		41
42	Apr	16	(h)	WALSALL	L	1-3	Phillips	9353	2							5	4		11	3			8				9	7	6	10			1		42
43	Apr	17	(h)	GILLINGHAM	L	0-2	-	6102		3	5						4	7			6	2					8		10	9			1	11	43
44	Apr	19	(a)	Walsall	W	1-0	Phillips	7482		3							5	7			2	4	10				8		6	9			1	11	44
45	Apr	24	(a)	Scunthorpe United	L	1-8	O'Rourke	2755		3				2	5	4		7	3		4	2		9			8		10				1	11	45
46	Apr	29	(h)	WORKINGTON	D	0-0	-	2915		3				2	5	4	7	9					8						6			10		11	46

Final League Position: 21st 1 Own Goal

| | | | | | | | | Apps | 11 | 28 | 31 | 12 | 4 | - | 1 | 29 | 16 | 3 | 15 | 29 | 2 | 20 | 38 | 36 | 21 | 27 | 12 | 37 | 46 | 28 | - | 11 | 18 | 31 | |
| | | | | | | | | Goals | - | - | - | - | - | - | - | - | - | - | 3 | - | - | - | - | 10 | 10 | 1 | 8 | 5 | 2 | 5 | - | - | - | 6 | |

1964/65 FA CUP

Round	Month	Day	Venue	Opponents	W,L,D	Score	Scorers	Attendance	Barton KR	Baynham RL	Bramwell J	Caleb GS	Chandler RAS	Clarke A	Edwards R	Fincham GR	Gibson Jim	Hails W	Harber WH	Jardine F	Knights AF	Lownds MU	McBain A	McKechnie TS	O'Rourke J	Pacey D	Phillips EJ	Pleat DJ	Reid J	Riddick GG	Riley R	Rioch BD	Tinsley C	Whittaker RH	Round
1	Nov	14	(h)	SOUTHEND UNITED	W	1-0	Bramwell	6892		1	6	5							8	3		4	2					7	10	9				11	1
2	Dec	5	(h)	GILLINGHAM	W	1-0	Riddick	5964		1		5								3			2	9		4		7	6	8		10		11	2
3	Jan	9	(h)	SUNDERLAND	L	0-3	-	16834	3	1		5								11			2	9		4		7	6	8		10			3
							Apps		1	3	1	3							1	3		1	3	2		2		3	3	3		2		2	
							Goals				1																			1					

1964/65 LEAGUE CUP

Round	Month	Day	Venue	Opponents	W,L,D	Score	Scorers	Attendance	Barton KR	Baynham RL	Bramwell J	Caleb GS	Chandler RAS	Clarke A	Edwards R	Fincham GR	Gibson Jim	Hails W	Harber WH	Jardine F	Knights AF	Lownds MU	McBain A	McKechnie TS	O'Rourke J	Pacey D	Phillips EJ	Pleat DJ	Reid J	Riddick GG	Riley R	Rioch BD	Tinsley C	Whittaker RH	Round
1	Sep	7	(a)	Port Vale	W	1-0	McKechnie	5111			5			7					3	6			2	8						9	4	10	1	11	1
2	Sep	23	(h)	ASTON VILLA	L	0-1	-	9011	1	3				5						6			2	8	9	4		7	10					11	2
							Apps		1	1	1			1					1	2			2	2	1	1		1	1	1	1	1	1	2	
							Goals																	1											

▶ The 1964/65 team – Back row (left to right): Reid, Pacey, Caleb, Fincham, Baynham, Tinsley, Rivers, Bramwell, Riddick, Lownds. Second row (left to right): King (Trainer), Readhead (Secretary), Whittaker, O'Rourke, Knights, Martin (Scout), Hails, McBain, Riley, Harvey (Manager), Bentham (Trainer). Third row (left to right): Crarer (Medical Officer), Richardson (Director), B.England (Director), A.England (Director), Hodgson (Chairman), Bigg, (Director), Hawkins (Director), Mitchell (Director). Front row (left to right): McKechnie, Slough, Rioch, Hyde, Long, Forsyth, Jardine.

TIMELINE...

21 November 1964 Manager Bill Harvey resigns leaving trainer Charlie Watkins to assume the role of caretaker manager.
16 February 1965 The Town turn to ex-manager George Martin to take over the reigns once more.
29 April 1965 The Town are relegated to the football basement.

1965/66 FOOTBALL LEAGUE DIVISION FOUR

Match No	Month	Day	Venue	Opponents	W.L.D Score	Scorers	Attendance	Edwards R	French GE	Fry B	Gibson Jim	Harber WH	Jardine F	Long C	McKechnie TS	Moore John	O'Rourke J	Pleat DJ	Ramage G	Read JA	Reid J	Riddick GG	Rioch BD	Rivers AD	Slough AP	Stark WR	Thomson R	Tinsley C	Whittaker RH	Woods M	Match No
1	Aug	21	(h)	BRADFORD PARK AVENUE	W 3-1	McKechnie (2), Reid	6182		7	4			3		8	6	9			·	10						2	1	11	5	1
2	Aug	23	(a)	Wrexham	L 0-2	-	5466		7	4			3		8	6	9				10						2	1	11	5	2
3	Aug	28	(a)	Aldershot	L 1-3	O'Rourke	5310			4	7		3		8	6	9				10		12				2	1	**11**	5	3
4	Sep	4	(h)	NEWPORT COUNTY	W 2-1	Reid (pen), Moore	4899	4			8		3		11	6				9	10				5	7	2	1			4
5	Sep	11	(a)	Torquay United	L 0-2	-	5156	4			9		3		11	6					10	7			5	8	2	1			5
6	Sep	16	(h)	WREXHAM	W 1-0	Whittaker	4780				7		3			6	9				4		10		5	8	2	1	11		6
7	Sep	18	(h)	CHESTERFIELD	L 1-2	Stark	4905						3			6	9				4	7	8		5	10	2	1	11		7
8	Sep	24	(a)	Rochdale	W 2-1	Read, O'Rourke	3692				7		3			6	9			8	4				5	10	2	1	11		8
9	Oct	7	(h)	DONCASTER ROVERS	W 4-3	O'Rourke (3), Whittaker	5020				7		3			6	9			8	4				5	10	2	1	11		9
10	Oct	9	(h)	BARNSLEY	W 5-4	Read (2), O'Rourke, Whittaker, Stark	5948				7		3			6	9			8	4				5	10	2	1	11		10
11	Oct	16	(a)	Bradford City	D 2-2	Moore, O'Rourke	2635		7			10	3			6	9			8	4				5	12	2	1	11		11
12	Oct	23	(h)	CREWE ALEXANDRA	W 4-0	Leigh (og), O'Rourke (3)	6299		7			10	3			6	9			8	4				5		2	1	11		12
13	Oct	30	(h)	Port Vale	W 2-1	O'Rourke, Whittaker	6058		7	10			3			6	9			8	4				5		2	1	11		13
14	Nov	3	(a)	Tranmere Rovers	L 0-2	-	9278		7	10			3			6	9			8	4				5		2	1	11		14
15	Nov	6	(h)	HALIFAX TOWN	W 4-1	Moore, Whittaker, O'Rourke, Read	7879		7	10			3			6	9			8	4	12					2	1	11	5	15
16	Nov	20	(a)	NOTTS COUNTY	W 5-1	Read (3), O'Rourke, Whittaker	6486	3	10			7				6	9			8	4						2	1	11	5	16
17	Nov	23	(a)	Doncaster Rovers	D 1-1	Whittaker (pen)	4134	3	10			7				6	9			8	4						2	1	11	5	17
18	Nov	27	(a)	Lincoln City	D 2-2	Read, Whittaker	2941	3	10			7				6	9			8	4						2	1	11	5	18
19	Dec	10	(a)	Stockport County	L 1-4	Stark	7778		10				3			6	9	7		8	4					12	2	1	11	5	19
20	Dec	18	(h)	BRADFORD CITY	L 2-3	Read, Rioch	5550						3		9			7		8	4		6			10	2	1	11	5	20
21	Dec	27	(a)	Southport	L 2-3	Whittaker (2)	6638		7	8		10	3			6	9				4						2	1	11	5	21
22	Dec	28	(h)	SOUTHPORT	W 2-0	Read, French	7307		7			10	3			6	9			8	4						2	1	11	5	22
23	Jan	1	(a)	Barnsley	L 0-3	-	5053		7				3		10	6	9			8	4						2	1	11	5	23
24	Jan	8	(h)	CHESTER	W 5-2	French, Read, O'Rourke (3)	6670		7				3			6	9			8	4					10	2	1	11	5	24
25	Jan	15	(a)	Crewe Alexandra	L 0-2	-	3534		7				3			6	9			8	4					10	2	1	11	5	25
26	Jan	29	(a)	Bradford Park Avenue	W 3-1	O'Rourke, Whittaker, Moore	6451		7				3			6	9			8	4					10	2	1	11	5	26
27	Feb	5	(h)	ALDERSHOT	W 3-1	Read, O'Rourke (2)	6822	12	7				3			6	9			8	4					10	2	1	11	5	27
28	Feb	12	(h)	HARTLEPOOLS UNITED	W 2-1	O'Rourke (2)	6131		7				3			6	9			8	4					10	2	1	11	5	28
29	Feb	26	(h)	TORQUAY UNITED	W 3-2	O'Rourke (2), Rioch	9271		7				3			6	9			8	4					10	2	1	11	5	29
30	Mar	5	(a)	Hartlepools United	L 0-2	-	4896						3		8	6	9	7		12	4					10	2	1	11	5	30
31	Mar	12	(a)	Chesterfield	W 3-1	O'Rourke, Riddick, Jardine	4264		7				3			6	9		1	8	4	10					2		11	5	31
32	Mar	19	(h)	ROCHDALE	W 4-1	O'Rourke (3), Riddick	7381		7				3			6	9		1	8	4	10					2		11	5	32
33	Mar	26	(h)	TRANMERE ROVERS	W 2-1	Moore, O'Rourke	8076		7	4			3			6	9		1	10	8						2		11	5	33
34	Apr	8	(a)	Colchester United	D 2-2	Edwards, Whittaker (pen)	10200	8		4		7	3			6	9		1	10	2								11	5	34
35	Apr	9	(h)	DARLINGTON	W 2-0	O'Rourke, Whittaker	9774	8		4		7	3			6	9		1	12	10	2							11	5	35
36	Apr	11	(h)	COLCHESTER UNITED	D 1-1	Riddick	15309	8		4		7	3		12	6	9		1	10	2								11	5	36
37	Apr	16	(a)	Notts County	D 1-1	Reid	4740	3	7			4				6	9		1	10	8			12			2		11	5	37
38	Apr	23	(h)	LINCOLN CITY	D 0-0	-	9621	10	7						9	6				8	4	2		12			3	1	**11**	5	38
39	Apr	25	(a)	Barrow	W 1-0	French	5186	3	7					11	6					8	10	4		9			2	1		5	39
40	Apr	30	(a)	Darlington	L 0-1	-	11155	3	7							6			1	10	8	4		9			2		11	5	40
41	May	7	(h)	STOCKPORT COUNTY	W 2-0	Rioch, Whittaker (pen)	9524		7				3			6	9		1	8	4	10		12			2		11	5	41
42	May	14	(h)	PORT VALE	W 5-0	O'Rourke (2), Whittaker, Riddick (2)	12054		7				3			6	9		1	8	4	10		3			2		11	5	42
43	May	16	(a)	Halifax Town	L 0-3	-	3002	12	7				3			6	9		1	8	4	10		3					**11**	5	43
44	May	19	(h)	BARROW	W 3-2	French, Riddick, O'Rourke	10647		7	4	11		3			6	9		1	8	10			3			2			5	44
45	May	25	(a)	Newport County	L 1-3	Reid	2073		7	12	11		3			6	9		1	8	10			3			2			5	45
46	May	28	(a)	Chester	D 1-1	Stark	4740	8	7		4					6			1	9	10			5	3	11	2				46
				Final League Position: 6th		1 Own Goal	**Apps**	14	32	6	15	13	34	1	8	43	40	3	7	31	43	29	19	14	8	8	31	33	40	34	
							Subs	2	-	1	-	-	-	-	2	-	-	-	2	-	-	1	3	1	2	-	-	-	-	-	
							Goals	1	4	-	-	-	1	-	2	5	32	-	-	12	4	6	3	-	-	4	-	-	15	-	

1965/66 FA CUP

Round	Month	Day	Venue	Opponents	W.L.D Score	Scorers	Attendance	Edwards R	French GE	Fry B	Gibson Jim	Harber WH	Jardine F	Long C	McKechnie TS	Moore John	O'Rourke J	Pleat DJ	Ramage G	Read JA	Reid J	Riddick GG	Rioch BD	Rivers AD	Slough AP	Stark WR	Thomson R	Tinsley C	Whittaker RH	Woods M	Round
1	Nov	13	(a)	Romford	D 1-1	Harris (og)	9592			10	7		3			6	9			8	4						2	1	11	5	1
Rep	Nov	18	(h)	ROMFORD	W 1-0	O'Rourke	11061	3			7	10				6	9			8	4						2	1	11	5	Rep
2	Dec	4	(a)	Corby Town	D 2-2	O'Rourke, Whittaker (pen)	6421	3			7	10				6	9			8	4						2	1	11	5	2
Rep	Dec	7	(h)	CORBY TOWN	L 0-1	-	13284	3			7	10				6	9			8	4						2	1	11	5	Rep
						1 Own Goal	Apps	3	-	1	4	3	1	-	-	4	4	-	-	4	4	-	-	-	-	-	4	4	4	4	
							Goals	-	-	-	-	-	-	-	-	-	2	-	-	-	-	-	-	-	-	-	-	-	1	-	

1965/66 LEAGUE CUP

Round	Month	Day	Venue	Opponents	W.L.D Score	Scorers	Attendance	Edwards R	French GE	Fry B	Gibson Jim	Harber WH	Jardine F	Long C	McKechnie TS	Moore John	O'Rourke J	Pleat DJ	Ramage G	Read JA	Reid J	Riddick GG	Rioch BD	Rivers AD	Slough AP	Stark WR	Thomson R	Tinsley C	Whittaker RH	Woods M	Round
1	Sep	1	(h)	BRIGHTON & HOVE ALBION	D 1-1	Gibson	3758	4			8	11	3			6				9	10			5	7		2	1			1
Rep	Sep	7	(a)	Brighton & Hove Albion	L 0-2	-	11745	4			8				11	6				9	10	3		5	7		2	1			Rep
							Apps	2	-	-	2	1	1	-	1	2	-	-	-	2	2	1	-	2	2	-	2	2	-	-	
							Goals	-	-	-	1	-	-	-	-	-	-	-	-	-	-	-	-	-	-	-	-	-	-	-	

▶ **The 1965/66 team** – Back row (left to right): Pleat, Slough, Edwards, Fry, Tinsley, Whittaker, O'Rourke, Reid, McKechnie. Middle row (left to right): Readhead (Secretary), Watkins (Trainer), Rivers, Caleb, Read, Riddick, Phillips, Gibson, Jardine, Rioch, Moore, Martin (Manager), Bentham (Trainer). Front row (left to right): Hyde, England (Director), Hawkins (Director), Hodgson (Chairman), Harris (Director), Richardson (Director), Long.

TIMELINE...
20 November 1965 Originally signed as a goalkeeper, Tony Read plays up front and nets a hat-trick against Notts County.
28 May 1966 The Town miss out on promotion by one point.

Match No	Month	Day	Venue	Opponents	W,L,D Score	Scorers	Attendance	Adamson T	Allen K	Conboy FJ	Dougan MS	French GE	Jardine F	Johnson B	Kevan DT	King GH	Lunnis RE	Moore John	Pleat DJ	Read JA	Riddick GG	Rioch BD	Rivers AD	Slough AP	Swan RM	Thear AC	Thomson R	Whittaker RH	Yardley G	Match No
1	Aug	20	(h)	HALIFAX TOWN	W 2-0	King, Rioch	6149					3				10		6	9	1	7	8	5	2			4	11		1
2	Aug	27	(a)	Brentford	L 0-1	-	6769					3				10		5	7	1	9	8	4	2			6	11		2
3	Sep	3	(h)	NEWPORT COUNTY	W 3-1	Rivers, Whittaker, Rioch	5377				8	3						4	7	1	9	10	5	2			6	11		3
4	Sep	6	(a)	Rochdale	L 0-3	-	2472				8	3						6	7	1	9	10	5	2		12	4	11		4
5	Sep	10	(a)	Barnsley	L 1-2	Moore	2188				8	3				12		6	7	1	9	10	5	2			4	11		5
6	Sep	17	(h)	STOCKPORT COUNTY	L 0-3	-	5887				8	3				11		6	7	1	5	10	9	4			2			6
7	Sep	24	(h)	ALDERSHOT	W 4-0	Whittaker, Slough, Thear (2)	4471					3	7			11		6		1	5	10		4		9	2	8		7
8	Sep	29	(h)	ROCHDALE	W 3-1	Rioch, Thear (2)	6435					3	7			11		6		1	5	10		4		9	2	8		8
9	Oct	1	(a)	Wrexham	L 0-2	-	6887					3	7			11		6	12	1	5	10		4		9	2	8		9
10	Oct	8	(a)	Southport	L 1-4	Rioch	4485					3	7			11		6		1	5	10		4		9	2	8		10
11	Oct	15	(h)	NOTTS COUNTY	L 2-5	Pleat, Thear	5743		4			3	7					6	8	1	5	10		12		9	2	11		11
12	Oct	20	(h)	BRADFORD CITY	D 0-0	-	4150					3	7			10		5	8	1	6			4		9	2	11		12
13	Oct	22	(a)	Chester	D 0-0	-	5751		4			3		7				8		1	5	10		6		9	2	11		13
14	Oct	24	(a)	Newport County	L 0-2	-	3456		4			3	7					6	7	1	5			8		9	2	11		14
15	Oct	29	(h)	BRADFORD PARK AVENUE	D 2-2	Conboy, Whittaker	4566		4			3	7					5	8	1		10		6			2	11	9	15
16	Nov	5	(a)	Port Vale	L 0-1	-	3502		4			3	7					5	8	1	9	10		6			2	11		16
17	Nov	12	(h)	CREWE ALEXANDRA	W 2-1	Riddick (2)	4785		4			3	7					5	7	1	9	10		6			2	11		17
18	Nov	16	(a)	Bradford City	L 1-2	Pleat	3097		4			3	7					5	7	1	9	10		6			2	11		18
19	Nov	19	(a)	Barrow	L 0-3	-	5061		4			3	7					5	7	1	12	10	8	6		9	2	11		19
20	Dec	3	(a)	Lincoln City	L 1-8	Rioch	3893					3	7			11		5	9	1	4	10	8	6			8			20
21	Dec	10	(h)	CHESTERFIELD	W 3-2	Whittaker, Rioch (2)	5096				5	3	7					6	8	1	9	10		4			2	11		21
22	Dec	17	(a)	Halifax Town	D 1-1	Kevan	3622				5	3	7		8			6		1	9	10		4			2	11		22
23	Dec	26	(a)	Tranmere Rovers	L 0-1	-	6806				5	3	7		9			6		1	8	10		4			2	11		23
24	Dec	27	(h)	TRANMERE ROVERS	W 2-0	Whittaker, Kevan	9123				5	3	7		9			6	12	1	8	10		4			2	11		24
25	Dec	31	(h)	BRENTFORD	W 3-0	French, Whittaker, Pleat	8531				5	3	7		8		2	6	9	1	4	10	12					11		25
26	Jan	14	(h)	BARNSLEY	D 1-1	Pleat	8287				5	3	7		8			6	9		4	10			1		2	11		26
27	Jan	20	(a)	Stockport County	L 0-1	-	9555				5	3	7		8			6	9		4	10			1		2	11		27
28	Feb	4	(a)	Aldershot	L 1-4	Rioch	5378				5	3	7		8			6			9	10		4	1		2	11		28
29	Feb	11	(h)	WREXHAM	W 3-1	Slough, Kevan (2)	6551				5	3	7		8			6	9			10		4	1		2	11		29
30	Feb	18	(a)	Exeter City	L 1-2	Riddick	3744				5	3	7	11	8			6	12		9	10		4	1		2			30
31	Feb	25	(h)	SOUTHPORT	D 0-0	-	6903				5	3	7		9				8	10	4			6	1		2	11		31
32	Mar	4	(a)	Notts County	W 2-1	King, Upton (og)	3909				5	3	7		8	10		9	9		4			6	1		2	11		32
33	Mar	11	(h)	EXETER CITY	W 4-0	Riddick, King, French, Allen	6046		8		5	3	7			9		12	10		4	6			1		2	11		33
34	Mar	18	(h)	CHESTER	W 1-0	Allen	6982		8	4			7			10		6	9					5	1		2	11		34
35	Mar	24	(a)	Hartlepools United	L 1-2	French	8442		8	4		3	7			10		6	9					5	1		2	11		35
36	Mar	25	(a)	York City	L 1-5	French	1912		8	4	9	3	7			10		6						5	1		2	11		36
37	Mar	27	(h)	HARTLEPOOLS UNITED	L 0-2	-	7370		8	4	2		7			10		6	9	12				5	1			11		37
38	Apr	1	(h)	PORT VALE	D 1-1	Moore	5410	2	9	4	5	3		11		10		6	8				12		1			7		38
39	Apr	8	(a)	Crewe Alexandra	L 1-3	King	5124		9	4	5	3	7	11				6				8					2	10		39
40	Apr	12	(h)	SOUTHEND UNITED	W 1-0	Allen	4666		8	4	5	3	7			11		6		1				9			2	10		40
41	Apr	15	(h)	BARROW	W 3-1	Whittaker (2, 1 pen), Allen	5710		8	4	5	3	7			11		6		1				9			2	10		41
42	Apr	22	(a)	Bradford Park Avenue	D 0-0	-	3760		8	4	5	3	7			11		6		1				9			2	10		42
43	Apr	24	(a)	Southend United	L 0-2	-	7303	3	8	4	5		7					6	11	1				9			2	10		43
44	Apr	29	(h)	LINCOLN CITY	W 2-1	Allen, Whittaker (pen)	5382		8	4	5	3	7	11				6		1				9			2	10		44
45	May	6	(a)	Chesterfield	D 0-0	-	3055		8	4	5	3	7	11		10		6		1				9			2			45
46	May	13	(h)	YORK CITY	W 5-1	Allen, Baker (og), Jardine, Rioch (2)	5196		9	4	5	3	7	11				6	10	1		8					2			46

Final League Position: 17th   2 Own Goals

							Apps	2	14	19	26	36	45	8	11	21	1	43	27	35	30	37	11	29	14	12	43	41	1	
							Subs	-	-	-	-	-	-	-	-	1		1	3	1	1	-	2	1	-	1	-	-		
							Goals	-	6	1	-	4	1	-	4	4	-	2	4	-	4	10	1	2	-	5	-	9	-	

1966/67 FA CUP

Round	Month	Day	Venue	Opponents	W/L/D Score	Scorers	Attendance	Adamson T	Allen K	Conboy FJ	Dougan MS	French GE	Jardine F	Johnson B	Kevan DT	King GH	Lunnis RE	Moore John	Pleat DJ	Read JA	Riddick GG	Rioch BD	Rivers AD	Slough AP	Swan RM	Thear AC	Thomson R	Whittaker RH	Yardley G	Round
1	Nov	26	(a)	Exeter City	D 1-1	Whittaker	4704			4			3	7				5	8	1	9	10	6		2			11		1
Rep	Dec	1	(h)	EXETER CITY	W 2-0	Rioch, Pleat	7078			4			3	7	12			5	8	1	9	10	6		2			11		Rep
2	Jan	7	(a)	Bristol Rovers	L 2-3	Kevan (2)	8480				5	7	3		8			6	9	1	4	10	2					11		2
						Apps		-	-	2	1	1	3	2	1	-	-	3	3	3	3	3	3	-	2	-	-	3	-	
						Subs		-	-	-	-	-	-	-	1	-	-	-	-	-	-	-	-	-	-	-	-	-	-	
						Goals		-	-	-	-	-	-	-	2	-	-	-	1	-	-	1	-	-	-	-	-	1	-	

1966/67 LEAGUE CUP

Round	Month	Day	Venue	Opponents	W/L/D Score	Scorers	Attendance	Adamson T	Allen K	Conboy FJ	Dougan MS	French GE	Jardine F	Johnson B	Kevan DT	King GH	Lunnis RE	Moore John	Pleat DJ	Read JA	Riddick GG	Rioch BD	Rivers AD	Slough AP	Swan RM	Thear AC	Thomson R	Whittaker RH	Yardley G	Round
1	Aug	24	(a)	Aldershot	D 2-2	Whittaker, Jardine	3677						3			8		6	7	1	4	10	5	2		9		11		1
Rep	Aug	29	(h)	ALDERSHOT	L 1-2	King	4832						3			8		6	7	1	9	10	5	2	12	4		11		Rep
						Apps		-	-	-	-	-	2	-	-	2	-	2	2	2	2	2	2	2	-	2	-	2	-	
						Subs		-	-	-	-	-	-	-	-	-	-	-	-	-	-	-	-	-	1	-	-	-	-	
						Goals		-	-	-	-	-	1	-	-	1	-	-	-	-	-	-	-	-	-	-	-	1	-	

▶ The 1966/67 team – Back row (left to right): Mooney, Nicholson, Rivers, Read, Thear, Adamson, Moore. Middle row (left to right): Martin (Manager), Jardine, Slough, King, Lamb, Whittaker, N.Rioch, B.Rioch, Watkins (Trainer). Front row (left to right): Johnson, Pleat, Riddick, Thomson, French.

TIMELINE...

July 1966 Terrace favourite John O'Rourke is sold to Middlesbrough.
4 November 1966 George Martin is replaced in the Kenilworth Road hot seat by another ex-Hatter Allan Brown.
3 December 1966 The Town crash 1-8 at bottom club Lincoln.

1967/68 FOOTBALL LEAGUE DIVISION FOUR

Match No	Month	Day	Venue	Opponents	W,L,D	Score	Scorers	Attendance	Allen K	Beavon K	Branston TG	Brown MJ	Buxton IR	Denton PR	Dougan MS	French GE	Green HR	Hare T	Jardine F	Johnson B	McDerment WS	McLeish H	Moore John	Potter GR	Read JA	Rioch BD	Ryan JO	Slough AP	Taylor WD	Tinsley C	Walker DG	Whittaker RH	Match No
1	Aug	19	(a)	Wrexham	D	1-1	Green	9514	8		5					7	9	2	3	12			6		1	10		4				11	1
2	Aug	26	(h)	BARNSLEY	W	2-0	Rioch, Allen	7887	8		5	9				7		2	3		4		6		1	10		6			12	11	2
3	Sep	2	(a)	Swansea Town	D	2-2	Brown, Rioch	6674	10		5	8			12	7	9		2		4		6		1	10		3				11	3
4	Sep	4	(a)	Southend United	L	0-3	–	11355	8	7	5	11					9	2	3		4		6			10		12		1			4
5	Sep	9	(h)	HARTLEPOOLS UNITED	W	1-0	Rioch	8347	9		5		8			7		2	3		4		6		1	10						11	5
6	Sep	16	(a)	Newport County	D	1-1	Slough	4625	8		5					7	9	2	3		4		6		1	10		12				11	6
7	Sep	23	(a)	YORK CITY	W	3-1	Rioch (2), Whittaker (pen)	7977	8		5				4	7		2	3		9		6		1	10						11	7
8	Sep	27	(h)	SOUTHEND UNITED	W	3-1	Moore, Branston, French	13332	9		5		8		4	7		2	3				6		1	10						11	8
9	Sep	30	(a)	Rochdale	D	2-2	Buxton, Rioch	1884	9		5		8		4	7		2	3				6		1	10						11	9
10	Oct	3	(a)	Doncaster Rovers	L	0-2	–	5529	9		5		8		4			2	3		7		6		1	10		12				11	10
11	Oct	7	(a)	Chester	W	3-1	Buxton, Allen (2)	3967	9		5	12	8		2				3		7		6		1	10		4				11	11
12	Oct	14	(h)	CHESTERFIELD	W	1-0	Buxton	10441	9		5		8		2	7			3				6		1	10		4				11	12
13	Oct	21	(a)	Exeter City	W	5-0	Buxton, Slough, Allen (2), Whittaker	3434	9		5		8		2				3				6		1	10	7	4				11	13
14	Oct	25	(h)	DONCASTER ROVERS	W	5-3	Buxton (2), Slough, Rioch, Allen	13925	9		5		8		2				3				6		1	10	7	4				11	14
15	Nov	11	(h)	WORKINGTON	W	4-0	Whittaker (2), Rioch, Slough	10935	9		5		8		2				3				6		1	10	7	4				11	15
16	Nov	15	(h)	SWANSEA TOWN	W	4-0	Buxton (2), Rioch, French	14981	9		5		8		2	7			3				6		1	10		4				11	16
17	Nov	18	(a)	Lincoln City	W	3-2	Whittaker (pen), French, Allen	6052	9		5		8		2	7			3		12		6		1	10		4				11	17
18	Nov	25	(h)	HALIFAX TOWN	W	2-0	Buxton, Moore	11572	9		5		8		2	7			3				6		1	10		4				11	18
19	Dec	2	(a)	Bradford City	L	0-2	–	7957			5		8		2	7			3			9	6		1	10		4				11	19
20	Dec	16	(h)	WREXHAM	W	2-1	Rioch, Branston	9598	9		5		8		2				3		12		6		1	10	7	4				11	20
21	Dec	23	(a)	Barnsley	D	2-2	Rioch, Ryan	8704	9		5		8		2				3		12		6		1	10	7	4				11	21
22	Dec	26	(h)	BRADFORD PARK AVENUE	W	2-0	Branston, Whittaker (pen)	16599	9		5		8		2				3		10		6	12	1		7	4				11	22
23	Dec	30	(a)	Bradford Park Avenue	L	1-2	Green	3674	10		5		8		2		9		3	11	12		6		1		7	4					23
24	Jan	13	(a)	Hartlepools United	L	1-2	Branston	4766	9		5		8		4			2	3				6		1	10	7					11	24
25	Jan	20	(h)	NEWPORT COUNTY	D	1-1	Allen	10992	9		5		8		2	7			3				6		1	10		4				11	25
26	Jan	26	(a)	Port Vale	D	0-0	–	5970	9		5	12	8	7	2				3				6		1	10		4				11	26
27	Feb	3	(a)	York City	D	1-1	Allen	2747	8		5			7	2		9		3				6		1	10						11	27
28	Feb	10	(h)	ROCHDALE	W	4-1	Rioch, Branston, Allen, Buxton	10040	9		5		8		2	7	12		3				6		1	10		4				11	28
29	Feb	17	(a)	Brentford	W	2-0	Slough, Rioch	7726	9		5		8		2	7			3				6		1	10		4				11	29
30	Feb	24	(h)	LINCOLN CITY	W	4-2	Whittaker (2, 1 pen), Allen, Rioch	11159	9		5	12	8		2	7			3				6		1	10		4				11	30
31	Feb	26	(a)	DARLINGTON	W	3-1	Rioch, Allen, Moore	13948	9		5		8		2	7			3		12		6		1	10		4				11	31
32	Mar	2	(a)	Chesterfield	D	0-0	–	14075	9		5		8		2	7			3		12		6		1	10						11	32
33	Mar	9	(h)	PORT VALE	W	2-0	Buxton, Rioch	12749	9		5		8		2	7			3		12		6		1	10						11	33
34	Mar	16	(h)	EXETER CITY	D	0-0	–	12409	9		5		8		2	7			3		4		6		1	10						11	34
35	Mar	20	(a)	Aldershot	W	1-0	Buxton	9724	9		5	12	8		2	11			3				6	4	1	10	7						35
36	Mar	23	(a)	Darlington	W	2-1	Rioch, Green	4336	10		5	7	8		2		9		3				6	4	1	10						11	36
37	Mar	30	(h)	ALDERSHOT	W	3-1	Rioch (2), Brown	10618	9		5	7	8		2	11			3				6	4	1	10							37
38	Apr	6	(a)	Workington	W	1-0	French	2195	4		5	7	8		2	9			3				6		1	10						11	38
39	Apr	12	(h)	NOTTS COUNTY	W	2-0	Allen, French	16631	9		5		8		2	7			3				6		1	10		4				11	39
40	Apr	13	(h)	CHESTER	D	0-0	–	13266	9		5		8		2	7	12		3				6		1	10		4				11	40
41	Apr	15	(a)	Notts County	D	2-2	Allen, Buxton	7920	9		5		8		2	7			3				6		1	10		4				11	41
42	Apr	20	(a)	Halifax Town	W	1-0	Rioch	5091	9		5		8		2	11			3		12		6		1	10		4					42
43	Apr	24	(h)	CREWE ALEXANDRA	W	4-0	Rioch (2), Moore, Slough	18904	9		5		8		2	7			3		12		6		1	10		4				11	43
44	Apr	27	(h)	BRADFORD CITY	L	1-3	Whittaker (pen)	14147	9		5		8		2	7			3				6		1	10		4				11	44
45	May	4	(a)	Crewe Alexandra	L	1-2	Rioch	8634	8		5				2	7	9		3		12		6		1	10		4					45
46	May	11	(h)	BRENTFORD	W	2-1	Rioch, Whittaker	14643	8		5				2	7	9		3				6		1	10		4				11	46
							Apps		45	1	46	8	36	3	41	31	9	12	41	1	13	1	45	3	42	44	10	32	3	1	–	38	
							Subs		–	–	–	4	1	1	–	–	2	–	–	–	1	–	6	1	–	2	1	3	–	–	1	–	
							Goals		14	–	5	2	13	–	–	3	5	–	–	–	–	–	4	–	–	24	1	6	–	–	–	10	

Final League Position: 1st

1967/68 FA CUP

Round	Month	Day	Venue	Opponents	W,L,D Score	Scorers	Attendance	Allen K	Beavon K	Branston TG	Brown MJ	Buxton IR	Denton PR	Dougan MS	French GE	Green HR	Hare T	Jardine F	Johnson B	McDermott WS	McLeish H	Moore John	Potter GR	Read JA	Rioch BD	Ryan JO	Slough AP	Taylor WD	Tinsley C	Walker DG	Whittaker RH	Round
1	Dec	14	(h)	OXFORD CITY	W 2-1	Rioch, Buxton	13394	9				8	2	7			12	3		5		6		1	10		4				11	1
2	Jan	6	(a)	Swindon Town	L 2-3	Allen, Whittaker (pen)	18203	9		5	12	10		7			2	3				6				8	4	1			11	2
						Apps		2	-	1	-	2	-	2	1	-	1	2	-	1	-	2	-	1	1	1	2	1	-	-	2	
						Subs		-	-	-	1	-	-	-	-	-	1	-	-	-	-	1	-	-	-	-	-	-	-	-	-	
						Goals		1	-	-	-	1	-	-	-	-	-	-	-	-	-	-	-	-	1	-	-	-	-	-	1	

1st Round: Following original postponement, re-arranged game played at Luton

1967/68 LEAGUE CUP

Round	Month	Day	Venue	Opponents	W,L,D Score	Scorers	Attendance	Allen K	Beavon K	Branston TG	Brown MJ	Buxton IR	Denton PR	Dougan MS	French GE	Green HR	Hare T	Jardine F	Johnson B	McDermott WS	McLeish H	Moore John	Potter GR	Read JA	Rioch BD	Ryan JO	Slough AP	Taylor WD	Tinsley C	Walker DG	Whittaker RH	Round
1	Aug	23	(h)	CHARLTON ATHLETIC	D 1-1	Allen	9001	8		5					7	9	2	3		4		6		1	10						11	1
Rep	Aug	30	(a)	Charlton Athletic	W 2-1	Rioch (2)	7659	4		5	8				7	9				2		6		1	10		3				11	Rep
2	Sep	13	(a)	Leeds United	L 1-3	Whittaker	11473	8		5	7			9			2	3		4		6		1	10						11	2
						Apps		3	-	3	2	-	-	1	2	2	2	2	-	3	-	3	-	3	3	-	1	-	-	-	3	
						Subs		-	-	-	-	-	-	-	-	-	-	-	-	-	-	-	-	-	-	-	-	-	-	-	-	
						Goals		1	-	-	-	-	-	-	-	-	-	-	-	-	-	-	-	-	2	-	-	-	-	-	1	

▶ John Moore on the receiving end of a champagne shampoo as the Town players celebrate winning the championship of Division Four.

TIMELINE...

17 February 1968 After winning 2-0 at Brentford the Town go top of Division Four – a position they hold until the end of the season.
24 April 1968 The Hatters clinch the championship with a 4-0 thumping of second placed Crewe.

▶ **The 1967/68 team** – Back row (left to right): Brown (Manager), Ryan, Jardine, Slough, Read, Branston Dougan, Moore, Evans (Trainer). Front row (left to right): Hare, French, Buxton, Allen, Rioch, Whittaker, McDerment.

◗ 'Golden boy' Bruce Rioch in match action against Notts County.

◗ John Moore hits home the Town's first goal in the 4-0 rout of Crewe.

◗ Skipper Terry Branston shows off the Division Four trophy.

1968/69 FOOTBALL LEAGUE DIVISION THREE

Match No	Month	Day	Venue	Opponents	W,L,D Score	Scorers	Attendance	Allen K	Bannister J	Branston TG	Brown MJ	Buxton IR	Davie AG	Denton PR	Dougan MS	French GE	Harrison MJ	Jardine F	Keen MT	Lewis B	McDermott WS	Moore John	Porter GR	Read JA	Rioch BD	Ryan JO	Sheffield LJ	Slough AP	Stevenson M	Taylor WD	Whittaker RH	Match No
1	Aug	10	(h)	OLDHAM ATHLETIC	W 4-0	Harrison (pen), Allen, Jardine, Lewis	14747	4		5					2	7	11	3		8		12		1	10		9	6				1
2	Aug	17	(a)	Barrow	D 0-0	-	6628	4		5	7				2			3		8				1	10		9	6			11	2
3	Aug	24	(h)	ROTHERHAM UNITED	W 3-1	Rioch (2), Lewis	14163	4		5					2	7	11	3		8		12		1	10		9	6				3
4	Aug	28	(h)	BARNSLEY	W 5-1	Rioch, Lewis (2), Allen, Branston	15899	4		5					2	7	11	3		8		12		1	10		9	6				4
5	Aug	31	(a)	Gillingham	W 3-1	Lewis (2), Sheffield	8227	4		5					2	11		3		8		12		1	10	7	9	6				5
6	Sep	7	(a)	Orient	D 0-0	-	13719	4							2	11		3		8		6		1	10	7	9	5				6
7	Sep	14	(a)	TRANMERE ROVERS	W 3-1	Sheffield, Lewis, Branston	12965			5					2	7	11	3		8		6		1	10		9	4				7
8	Sep	18	(h)	MANSFIELD TOWN	W 4-2	Harrison (pen), Sheffield, French, Lewis	19315			5					2	7	11	3		8		12		1	10		9	4				8
9	Sep	21	(a)	Brighton & Hove Albion	L 0-1	-	11930	4		5					2	12	11	3		8		2		1	10	7	9	6				9
10	Sep	28	(h)	TORQUAY UNITED	W 1-0	Lewis	14936	12		5					2	7	11	3		8		6		1	10		9	4				10
11	Oct	5	(a)	Watford	L 0-1	-	22133	12		5					2	11		3		8		6		1	10	7	9	4				11
12	Oct	8	(a)	Barnsley	L 1-3	Sheffield	13019			5		8			2	11		3				12			10	7	9	4		1		12
13	Oct	12	(h)	HARTLEPOOL	W 3-0	Sheffield, Rioch, Lewis	13415			5					2		7	3		8		2			10		9	6		1	11	13
14	Oct	19	(a)	Plymouth Argyle	L 0-2	-	12659	4		5	12	7						3		8		2			10		9	6		1	11	14
15	Oct	26	(h)	NORTHAMPTON TOWN	W 2-1	Allen, Sheffield	17818	4	6				1		3	7				8		5			10		9	2			11	15
16	Nov	5	(a)	Walsall	L 0-2	-	5381	4	6				1	7	2			3		8		12			10		9	5			11	16
17	Nov	9	(h)	SWINDON TOWN	W 2-0	Sheffield, Lewis	17250		6	5			1		2	7	11	3		8					10		9	4				17
18	Nov	23	(h)	BOURNEMOUTH	D 1-1	Branston	14150	9	6	5			1		2	7				8					10		12	4			11	18
19	Nov	29	(a)	Stockport County	L 0-2	-	13246	10	3	5		9	1		6	7				8		2			11			6				19
20	Dec	14	(a)	Hartlepool	L 0-1	-	3887	4	3	5		9	1		2	7	11			8								6	10			20
21	Dec	21	(h)	PLYMOUTH ARGYLE	W 2-0	Lewis, Allen	10971	9	3	5			1		2	7	11			8		6			10							21
22	Dec	28	(h)	Northampton Town	W 2-0	Rioch (2)	15161	9	3	5			1		2	7	11			8		6			10							22
23	Jan	8	(a)	Shrewsbury Town	L 1-3	Slough	4729	9	3	5			1		2	7	11			8	12	6			10							23
24	Jan	18	(a)	Swindon Town	D 0-0	-	19105	9	3	5			1		2		11			8		6			10	7						24
25	Jan	25	(h)	WALSALL	W 1-0	Rioch	15205	12	3	5			1		2	7			8	9		6			11							25
26	Jan	29	(a)	Crewe Alexandra	L 0-2	-	5053	10	3	5		9	1		2		11		8	7		6										26
27	Feb	1	(h)	READING	W 2-1	Slough, Lewis (pen)	11871	9	3	5		8	1		2	7	11			10	12	6										27
28	Feb	8	(a)	Bournemouth	W 2-0	Jardine, Sheffield	9253	10	3	5			1		2	7		11	8			6					9	4				28
29	Feb	26	(h)	CREWE ALEXANDRA	W 2-0	Slough, Allen	13384	9	3	5			1		2	7		11	8	10		6						4				29
30	Mar	1	(a)	Oldham Athletic	W 1-0	Lawson (og)	3946	10	3	5			1		2	7		11	8	12		6					9	4				30
31	Mar	5	(h)	SHREWSBURY TOWN	W 2-1	Allen, Keen	14733	10	3	5			1		2	7		11	8			6					9	4				31
32	Mar	12	(a)	Reading	D 1-1	Sheffield	6146	10	3				1		2	7		11	8		4	6					9	5				32
33	Mar	15	(a)	Rotherham United	D 2-2	French, Lewis	9873	8	3				1		2	7		11	10	4		6				12	9	5				33
34	Mar	19	(h)	BRISTOL ROVERS	W 3-0	Sheffield, Allen, Lewis	14506	8	3	5			1		2	7			10			6			11		9	4				34
35	Mar	22	(h)	GILLINGHAM	D 1-1	Sheffield	14562	8	3	5			1		2	7			10			6			11		9	4				35
36	Mar	26	(h)	BARROW	W 5-1	Slough, Allen, Rioch, Lewis (2)	14244	8	3				1		2	7		12	10			6			11		9	4				36
37	Mar	29	(h)	ORIENT	W 2-1	Branston, Sheffield	13915	8	3	5			1		2				10			6	12		11	7	9	4				37
38	Mar	31	(a)	Bristol Rovers	D 0-0	-	8112	8	3				1		2		11	4	10	12		6			7		9	5				38
39	Apr	4	(a)	Torquay United	D 1-1	McDermott	11427	9	3				1		2		11	4	8	7	6			10				5				39
40	Apr	7	(a)	Mansfield Town	L 0-1	-	8681	9					1		2	7	12	3	4	11	6			10				5				40
41	Apr	8	(h)	SOUTHPORT	D 0-0	-	15963			5		12	1		2	7	11	3	10	8		6					9	4				41
42	Apr	12	(a)	BRIGHTON & HOVE ALBION	W 3-0	French, Lewis, Slough	11695		3	5		9			2	7			10	8		6		1	11			4		12		42
43	Apr	14	(a)	Southport	D 1-1	Lewis	3392		3	5		9			2	7			10	8		6		1	11			5				43
44	Apr	18	(a)	Tranmere Rovers	W 2-0	Moore, Rioch	6723	4	3			9			2	7			10	8		6		1	11			5				44
45	Apr	25	(h)	STOCKPORT COUNTY	W 4-1	Lewis (3), Rioch	12055	10	3			9			2	7			4	8		6		1	11			5				45
46	Apr	30	(h)	WATFORD	W 2-1	Buxton, Allen	25253	10	3			9			2	7			4	8		6		1	11			5				46
				Final League Position: 3rd		1 Own Goal	Apps	37	30	35	1	10	27	1	43	35	18	23	14	43	15	29	-	16	37	7	28	46	1	3	7	
							Subs	3	-	-	1	1	-	-	-	1	1	1	-	-	-	6	4	2	-	-	1	1	-	-	1	
							Goals	9	-	4	-	1	-	-	-	3	2	2	1	22	1	1	-	-	10	-	12	5	-	-	-	

1968/69 FA CUP

Round	Month	Day	Venue	Opponents	W/L/D Score	Scorers	Attendance	Allen K	Bannister J	Branston TG	Brown MJ	Buxton IR	Davie AG	Denton PR	Dougan MS	French GE	Harrison MJ	Jardine F	Keen MT	Lewis B	McDerment WS	Moore John	Potter GR	Read JA	Rioch BD	Ryan JO	Sheffield LJ	Slough AP	Stevenson M	Taylor WD	Whittaker RH	Round
1	Nov	16	(h)	WARE TOWN	W 6-1	Potter, Slough (2), Allen (3, 1pen)	10952	12	6	5			1		2	7				8	3		10		11		9	4				1
2	Dec	7	(h)	GILLINGHAM	W 3-1	French, Harrison (2, 1pen)	12035		4	5		9	1		2	7	11			8	3				10			6				2
3	Jan	4	(a)	Manchester City	L 0-1	-	37120	9	3	5			1		2	7	11			8	12	6			10			4				3
							Apps	1	3	3	.	1	3	.	3	3	2	.	.	3	2	1	1	.	3	.	1	3	.	.	.	
							Subs	1	.	.	.	.	.	.	.	.	.	.	.	.	1	.	.	.	.	.	.	.	.	.	.	
							Goals	3	.	.	.	.	.	.	.	1	2	.	.	.	.	.	1	.	.	.	.	2	.	.	.	

1968/69 LEAGUE CUP

Round	Month	Day	Venue	Opponents	W/L/D Score	Scorers	Attendance	Allen K	Bannister J	Branston TG	Brown MJ	Buxton IR	Davie AG	Denton PR	Dougan MS	French GE	Harrison MJ	Jardine F	Keen MT	Lewis B	McDerment WS	Moore John	Potter GR	Read JA	Rioch BD	Ryan JO	Sheffield LJ	Slough AP	Stevenson M	Taylor WD	Whittaker RH	Round
1	Aug	14	(h)	WATFORD	W 3-0	Harrison (2), Lewis	20,167	4		5					2		11	3		8	12			1	10	7	9	6				1
2	Sep	4	(a)	Brighton & Hove Albion	D 1-1	Sheffield	15,200	4							2	11		3		8	6			1	10	7	9	5				2
Rep	Sep	11	(h)	BRIGHTON & HOVE ALBION	W 4-2	Slough (2), Sheffield, Rioch	18,679			5					2	7	11	3		8	6			1	10		9	4				Rep
3	Sep	24	(a)	Everton	L 1-5	Sheffield	30,405			5		10			2	7	11	3		8	6			1		12	9	4				3
							Apps	2	.	3	.	1	.	.	4	3	3	3	.	4	2	.	.	4	3	2	4	4	.	.	.	
							Subs	.	.	.	.	.	.	.	.	.	.	.	.	.	1	.	.	.	.	1	.	.	.	.	.	
							Goals	.	.	.	.	.	.	.	.	.	2	.	.	1	.	.	.	.	1	.	3	2	.	.	.	

▶ **Brian Lewis,** big money signing from Coventry who banged in 22 League goals as the Hatters narrowly failed to win back to back promotions.

▶ **The 1968/69 team** – Back row (left to right): Dougan, Jardine, McDerment, Moore. Middle row (left to right): Whitehouse (Trainer), Whittaker, Allen, Read, Taylor, Slough, J.O.Ryan, Brown (Manager). Front row (left to right): French, Lewis, Branston, Sheffield, Rioch, Harrison.

TIMELINE...

19 December 1968 Allan Brown is sacked for 'disloyalty'.

20 December 1968 Ex-QPR boss Alec Stock takes over at Kenilworth Road.

30 April 1969 The Town beat local rivals Watford in front of the best crowd at Kenilworth Road since 1961 but finish third and fail to win back-to-back promotions.

1969/70 FOOTBALL LEAGUE DIVISION THREE

Match No	Month	Day	Venue	Opponents	W,L,D Score	Scorers	Attendance	Allen K	Bannister J	Branston TG	Busby VD	Collins JW	Davie AG	Dougan MS	French GE	Harrison MJ	Jardine F	Keen MT	Lewis B	Macdonald M	Moore John	Nicholl CJ	Phillips PS	Read JA	Ryan JG	Sheffield LJ	Slough AP	Starling AW	Tees M	Match No
1	Aug	9	(h)	BARROW	W 3-0	Allen, Collins, Keen	12080	10	3	5		7			12			4	8	11	6			1	2	9				1
2	Aug	16	(a)	Bournemouth	W 1-0	Macdonald	9578	10	3	5		7			11			4		8				1	2	9	6			2
3	Aug	23	(h)	ORIENT	W 3-2	Collins, Macdonald, French	13761	10	3	5		7			11			4	12	8				1	2	9	6			3
4	Aug	26	(h)	HALIFAX TOWN	D 1-1	Macdonald	13759	10	3			7			11			4	9	8	6			1	2	12	5			4
5	Aug	30	(a)	Gillingham	W 2-0	Macdonald (pen), Green (og)	7792	10	3			7			11			4		8		5		1	2		6		9	5
6	Sep	6	(h)	BRISTOL ROVERS	W 4-0	Macdonald, Allen, Collins, Tees	15198	10	3			7		2	11			4		8		5		1			6		9	6
7	Sep	13	(a)	Bradford City	D 1-1	Allen	10851	10	3			7	1	2	11			4		8		5					6		9	7
8	Sep	16	(a)	Southport	W 3-0	Macdonald, French, Nicholl	4003	10	3			7	1	2	11			4		8		5					6		9	8
9	Sep	20	(h)	SHREWSBURY TOWN	D 2-2	Collins, Slough	15396	10	3			7	1	2	11			4		8		5					6		9	9
10	Sep	27	(a)	Plymouth Argyle	W 3-1	Tees (2), French	14111	10	3			7	1	2	11			4		8		5					6		9	10
11	Sep	30	(a)	Walsall	W 3-1	Tees (2), Collins	7557	10	3			7	1	2	11		12	4		8		5					6		9	11
12	Oct	4	(h)	STOCKPORT COUNTY	W 2-0	Nicholl, Macdonald (pen)	15944	10	3			7	1		11		2	4		8		5					6		9	12
13	Oct	7	(h)	BOURNEMOUTH	D 0-0	-	18065	10	3			7	1		11		2	4		8		5				12	6		9	13
14	Oct	11	(a)	Doncaster Rovers	L 0-2	-	17380	10	3			7	1		11		2	4		8		5				12	6		9	14
15	Oct	18	(a)	Brighton & Hove Albion	W 2-1	Collins (2)	20016	10	3			7	1		11		2	4		8		5	12				6		9	15
16	Oct	25	(h)	TORQUAY UNITED	D 1-1	Tees	16087	10	3			7	1		11			4	12	8		5			2		6		9	16
17	Nov	1	(a)	Rotherham United	D 1-1	Allen	8911	10	3			7	1		11			4		8		5			2		6		9	17
18	Nov	8	(h)	BARNSLEY	D 1-1	Macdonald	17442	10	3	5			1		7	11		4		8					2		6		9	18
19	Nov	22	(h)	ROCHDALE	W 2-0	Collins, Allen	15876	10	3	5		7			11	12		4		8					2		6		9	19
20	Nov	25	(h)	FULHAM	W 1-0	Macdonald	16485	10	3				1		7	11		4		8		5			2		6		9	20
21	Dec	13	(a)	BRADFORD CITY	W 5-0	Macdonald (3, 1 pen), Tees, Collins	11857	10	3			8	1		11			4	7			5	12		2		6		9	21
22	Dec	26	(a)	Orient	L 0-1	-	17619	10	3			7	1		11			4	12	8		5	9		2		6		9	22
23	Dec	27	(h)	GILLINGHAM	L 1-2	Keen	17402	10	3			8	1		11			4		7		5	9		2		6			23
24	Jan	10	(a)	Shrewsbury Town	L 1-5	Harrison	4406	10	3			8	1			11		4	7			5	12		2		6		9	24
25	Jan	17	(h)	PLYMOUTH ARGYLE	L 0-2	-	12358	10	3			7	1					12		8	6	5			2		4		9	25
26	Jan	24	(a)	Bury	W 3-1	Macdonald, Tees (2)	6813	12	3			7	1					10		8	4	5			2		6		9	26
27	Jan	31	(a)	Stockport County	D 1-1	Tees	3922		3			7	1					10		9	4	5			2		6		8	27
28	Feb	7	(h)	DONCASTER ROVERS	W 4-0	Slough, Macdonald (2, 1 pen), Tees	12828	9	3			7	1					4		10		5			2		6		9	28
29	Feb	10	(a)	Bristol Rovers	L 0-3	-	13304	10	3			12	1					4		8	7	5			2		6		9	29
30	Feb	14	(a)	Barrow	L 1-2	French	3843	10	3	12		8	1		11			4		7		5			2		6		9	30
31	Feb	21	(a)	Torquay United	D 2-2	Harrison, Macdonald	6964						1		7	11	3	10		8	6				2		6		9	31
32	Feb	28	(h)	BRIGHTON & HOVE ALBION	D 1-1	Macdonald (pen)	17584					8	1		7	11	3	10		9	6	5			2		4		12	32
33	Mar	3	(h)	TRANMERE ROVERS	W 2-0	Macdonald, Ryan	11368			5		8	1		11		3	10		7	6				2		4		9	33
34	Mar	11	(a)	Reading	W 1-0	Macdonald	18929	12		5		7	1		11		3	10		8	6				2		4		9	34
35	Mar	14	(h)	MANSFIELD TOWN	D 2-2	Ryan, Harrison	12690	12				8	1			11	3	10		7		5			2				9	35
36	Mar	17	(h)	BURY	D 0-0	-	12751					8	1			11		10		7					2		4		9	36
37	Mar	21	(a)	Tranmere Rovers	L 2-3	Allen, Slough	4035	8	3	5		7			11			10		9	6				2		4		12	37
38	Mar	27	(h)	ROTHERHAM UNITED	W 2-1	Allen, Slough	14315	8	3	5	7				11	12		10		9	6				2		4	1		38
39	Mar	28	(h)	READING	W 5-0	Macdonald (3), Harrison, Busby	14401		3	5	8				11			10		9	6				2		4	1		39
40	Mar	31	(a)	Barnsley	L 1-2	Keen	9988		3	5	8	7			11			10		9	6				2		4	1		40
41	Apr	4	(a)	Halifax Town	D 0-0	-	3482		3	5	8	7			11			10		9	6	12			2		4	1		41
42	Apr	8	(a)	Fulham	W 1-0	Macdonald	18987	10	3	5	8				11			10		9	6				2		7	1		42
43	Apr	11	(h)	WALSALL	W 3-0	Busby, Collins, Macdonald	17173	12	3	5	8	7			11			10		9	6				2		4	1		43
44	Apr	14	(h)	SOUTHPORT	W 1-0	Busby	16756			5	8	7	2		11			10		9	6			1	3		4			44
45	Apr	20	(a)	Mansfield Town	D 0-0	-	10301	10	3	5	8	7			11			10		9	6			1	2		7			45
46	Apr	25	(a)	Rochdale	W 2-1	Busby, Macdonald	5886	12	3	5	8	7			11					9	6			1	2		4		10	46
						Apps		32	40	18	9	39	31	7	38	10	9	45	2	46	22	27	2	9	36	3	45	6	30	
						Subs		6	-	1	-	1	-	-	1	2	1	1	3	-	1	-	-	3	-	-	3	-	2	
						Goals		7	-	-	4	10	-	-	4	4	-	3	-	25	-	2	-	-	2	-	4	-	11	

Final League Position: 2nd
1 Own Goal

1969/70 FA CUP

Round	Month	Day	Venue	Opponents	W,L,D Score	Scorers	Attendance	Allen K	Bannister J	Branston TG	Busby VD	Collins JW	Davie AG	Dougan MS	French GE	Harrison MJ	Jardine F	Keen MT	Lewis B	Macdonald M	Moore John	Nicholl CJ	Phillips PS	Read JA	Ryan JG	Sheffield LJ	Slough AP	Starling AW	Tees M	Round
1	Nov	15	(a)	Bournemouth	D 1-1	Collins	7362	10	3	5		7	1		11		12	4		8					2		6		9	1
Rep	Nov	18	(h)	BOURNEMOUTH	W 3-1	Collins, Tees, Macdonald	13384	10	3	5		7	1		11			4		8					2		6		9	Rep
2	Dec	6	(a)	Hillingdon Borough	L 1-2	Tees	9330	10	3			7	1		11	12		4		8		5			2		6		9	2
						Apps		3	3	2	·	3	3	·	3	0	0	3	·	3	·	1	·	·	3	·	3	·	3	
						Subs		·	·	·	·	·	·	·	·	1	1	·	·	·	·	·	·	·	·	·	·	·	·	
						Goals		·	·	·	·	2	·	·	·	·	·	·	·	1	·	·	·	·	·	·	·	·	2	

1969/70 LEAGUE CUP

Round	Month	Day	Venue	Opponents	W,L,D Score	Scorers	Attendance	Allen K	Bannister J	Branston TG	Busby VD	Collins JW	Davie AG	Dougan MS	French GE	Harrison MJ	Jardine F	Keen MT	Lewis B	Macdonald M	Moore John	Nicholl CJ	Phillips PS	Read JA	Ryan JG	Sheffield LJ	Slough AP	Starling AW	Tees M	Round
1	Aug	13	(a)	Peterborough United	D 1-1	Sheffield	10249	10	3	5					11			4		8	6			1	2	9	7			1
Rep	Aug	19	(h)	PETERBOROUGH UNITED	W 5-2	Branston, Allen, Lewis (2), Macdonald	13105	10	3	5					11			4	7	8				1	2	9	6			Rep
2	Sep	2	(h)	MILLWALL	D 2-2	Macdonald, Sheffield	17372	10	3	5		7			11			4	12	8						9	6			2
Rep	Sep	8	(a)	Millwall	W 1-0	Allen	14125	10	3	5		7	1	2	11			4		8						9	6			Rep
3	Sep	23	(a)	Sheffield United	L 0-3	-	16884	10	3	5		7	1	2	11			4		8						12	6		9	3
						Apps		5	5	5	·	3	2	3	5	·	·	5	1	5	1	·	·	3	2	4	5	·	1	
						Subs		·	·	·	·	·	·	·	·	·	·	·	1	·	·	·	·	·	·	1	·	·	·	
						Goals		2	·	1	·	·	·	·	·	·	·	·	2	2	·	·	·	·	·	2	·	·	·	

◗ Another promotion celebration – this time to Division Two.

TIMELINE...

10 July 1969 'Golden Boy' Bruce Rioch is sold to Aston Villa for £100,000 – a record for a Division Three club.
16 July 1969 £17,500 of this money is spent on unknown Fulham full-back, Malcolm Macdonald.
31 January 1970 TV star Eric Morecambe joins the Board.
25 April 1970 The 25 goals of Macdonald, by now a feared striker, catapult the Town to promotion to Division Two.

▶ The 1969/70 team – Back row (left to right): Busby, Moore, Starling, Allen, Read, Nicholl, Davie, Slough, J.G.Ryan, Phillips. Front row (left to right): Collins, Tees, Jardine, Branston, Keen, Macdonald, Bannister, Dougan.

▶ 'Never afraid to miss', Malcolm Macdonald.

▶ Viv Busby nets the goal against Southport which virtually assures the Town of promotion.

▶ Alan Slough heads home against Shrewsbury.

1970/71 FOOTBALL LEAGUE DIVISION TWO

Match No	Month	Day	Venue	Opponents	W.L.D Score	Scorers	Attendance	Anderson PT	Bannister J	Barber K	Branston TG	Busby VD	Collins JW	Court DJ	Givens DJ	Goodeve KGA	Guild A	Hoy RE	Keen MT	Macdonald M	Moore John	Nicholl CJ	Read JA	Ryan J	Ryan JG	Slough AP	Starling AW	Tees M	Match No
1	Aug	15	(a)	Bolton Wanderers	L 2-4	Keen, Macdonald (pen)	11350				5	11			8			4	10	9	6			7	3	2	1		1
2	Aug	22	(h)	NORWICH CITY	D 0-0	-	16110					12		8	11			4	10	9	6	5	1	7	2	3			2
3	Aug	29	(a)	Birmingham City	D 1-1	Macdonald (pen)	30141	12						8	11			4	10	7	6	5	1		2	3		9	3
4	Sep	1	(h)	OXFORD UNITED	W 4-0	Tees (2), Macdonald (2)	16173							8	11			4	10	7	6	5	1	12	2	3		9	4
5	Sep	5	(h)	MIDDLESBROUGH	W 1-0	Givens	16018							8	11	4			10	7	6	5	1	12	2	3		9	5
6	Sep	12	(a)	Leicester City	L 0-1	-	23397	12						8	11			4	10	9	6	5	1	7	2	3			6
7	Sep	19	(h)	ORIENT	W 4-0	Slough (2), Macdonald (2)	16711					11		8				4	10	9	6	5	1	7	2	3			7
8	Sep	26	(a)	Swindon Town	D 0-0	-	18698					11		8	12			4	10	9	6	5	1	7	2	3			8
9	Sep	29	(a)	Queens Park Rangers	W 1-0	Keen	19268					12		8	11			4	10	9	6	5	1	7	2	3			9
10	Oct	3	(h)	BRISTOL CITY	W 3-0	Macdonald (2), Slough	15992					12		8	11			4	10	9	6	5	1	7	2	3			10
11	Oct	10	(a)	Sheffield Wednesday	W 5-1	Macdonald (3), Givens (2)	15189							8	11			4	10	9	6	5	1	7	2	3			11
12	Oct	17	(h)	BOLTON WANDERERS	W 2-0	Nicholl, Givens	19055							8	11			4	10	9	6	5	1	7	2	3			12
13	Oct	20	(h)	BLACKBURN ROVERS	W 2-0	Givens, Macdonald	16372					12		8	11			4	10	9	6	5	1	7	2	3			13
14	Oct	24	(a)	Charlton Athletic	D 1-1	Givens	12928					12		8	11			4	10	9	6	5	1	7	2	3			14
15	Oct	31	(h)	SUNDERLAND	L 1-2	Macdonald	19202					12		8	11			4	10	9	6	5	1	7	2	3			15
16	Nov	7	(a)	Hull City	W 2-0	Givens, Macdonald	18343							8	11			4	10	9	6	5	1	7	2	3			16
17	Nov	14	(h)	CARLISLE UNITED	D 3-3	Jim Ryan, Slough, Macdonald	14837					12		8	11			4	10	9	6	5	1	7	2	3			17
18	Nov	21	(h)	PORTSMOUTH	W 2-1	John Ryan, Givens	16876	12				11			8			4	10	9	6	5	1	7	2	3			18
19	Nov	28	(a)	Cardiff City	D 0-0	-	26689	3						8	11			4	10	9		5	1	7	2	6			19
20	Dec	5	(h)	SHEFFIELD UNITED	W 2-1	Macdonald, Jim Ryan	19665	3						8	11			4	10	9		5	1	7	2	6			20
21	Dec	12	(a)	Watford	W 1-0	Keen	24456	3					12	8	11			4	10	9		5	1	7	2	6			21
22	Dec	19	(a)	Norwich City	D 1-1	Macdonald	17438	3					4	8	11				10	9		5	1	7	2	6			22
23	Jan	9	(h)	QUEENS PARK RANGERS	D 0-0	-	22024	3				12		8	11			4	10	9		5	1	7	2	6			23
24	Jan	16	(a)	Blackburn Rovers	L 0-1	-	8385	3				12		8	11			4	10	9		5	1	7	2	6			24
25	Feb	6	(a)	Sheffield United	L 1-2	Jim Ryan	30386	3						8	11			4	10	9	6	5	1	7	2	3			25
26	Feb	13	(h)	WATFORD	W 1-0	Macdonald	20099	11						8				4	10	9	6	5	1	7	2	3			26
27	Feb	20	(a)	Portsmouth	W 1-0	Givens	13661	11						8				4	10	9	6	5	1	7	2	3			27
28	Feb	27	(a)	Sunderland	D 0-0	-	12471	11						8				4	10	9	6	5	1	7	2	3			28
29	Mar	6	(h)	CHARLTON ATHLETIC	D 1-1	Busby	15262	11				12		8				4	10	9	6	5	1	7	2	3			29
30	Mar	13	(a)	Carlisle United	L 0-1	-	13681					8			4	12			10	9	6	5	1	7	2	3			30
31	Mar	20	(h)	HULL CITY	W 3-1	Moore, Busby, Macdonald	19566	11				8			4				10	9	6	5	1	7	2	3			31
32	Mar	27	(a)	Middlesbrough	L 1-2	Macdonald	19579	11				8			4				10	9	6	5	1	7	2	3			32
33	Mar	30	(h)	MILLWALL	D 1-1	Keen	17578		3			8			11				10	9	6	5	1	7	2	3			33
34	Apr	3	(h)	BIRMINGHAM CITY	W 3-2	Busby (2), Slough	25172	11				8			4				10	9	6	5	1	7	2	3			34
35	Apr	9	(a)	Bristol City	L 2-3	Busby, Macdonald	18846	11				8			4	12			10	9	6	5	1	7	2	3			35
36	Apr	10	(a)	Millwall	L 0-4	-	13864		3			8		11	12				10	9			1	7	2	5			36
37	Apr	12	(h)	LEICESTER CITY	L 1-3	Sjoberg (og)	24405	11	12			8			4				10	9	6	5		7	2	5			37
38	Apr	17	(h)	SHEFFIELD WEDNESDAY	D 2-2	Anderson, Givens	12308	7	3	1		8			11			4	10	9	6				2	5			38
39	Apr	24	(a)	Orient	W 2-1	Busby (2)	6339	12		1		7			11			4	10	9	6	5			2	3			39
40	Apr	28	(a)	Oxford United	L 1-2	Busby	9531			1		7			11				10	9	6	5		12	2	3			40
41	May	1	(h)	SWINDON TOWN	D 1-1	Givens (pen)	10205	7		1		8			11	3			10	9	6	5			2	6			41
42	May	4	(h)	CARDIFF CITY	W 3-0	Macdonald (3)	10784	7		1		8			11	3			10	9	6	5			2	4			42
							Apps	13	9	3	1	17	1	27	39	2	1	32	42	42	35	38	38	34	42	42	1	3	
							Subs	1	4	-	-	10	1	-	2	2	-	-	-	-	-	-	-	4	-	-	-	2	
							Goals	1	-	-	-	8	-	-	11	-	-	-	4	24	1	1	-	3	1	5	-	2	

Final League Position: 6th
1 Own Goal

1970/71 FA CUP

Round	Month	Day	Venue	Opponents	W.L.D Score	Scorers	Attendance	Anderson PT	Bannister J	Barber K	Branston TG	Busby VD	Collins JW	Court DJ	Givens DJ	Goodeve KGA	Guild A	Hoy RE	Keen MT	Macdonald M	Moore John	Nicholl CJ	Read JA	Ryan J	Ryan JG	Slough AP	Starling AW	Tees M	Round
3	Jan	2	(a)	Nottingham Forest	D 1-1	Macdonald	23230		3					8	11			4	10	9		5	1	7	2	6			3
Rep	Jan	11	(h)	NOTTINGHAM FOREST	L 3-4	Macdonald (3, 1 pen)	23483		3					8	11			4	10	9		5	1	7	2	6			Rep
							Apps	-	2	-	-	-	-	2	2	-	-	2	2	2	-	2	2	2	2	2	-	-	
							Subs	-	-	-	-	-	-	-	-	-	-	-	-	-	-	-	-	-	-	-	-	-	
							Goals	-	-	-	-	-	-	-	-	-	-	-	-	4	-	-	-	-	-	-	-	-	

1970/71 LEAGUE CUP

Round	Month	Day	Venue	Opponents	W,L,D Score	Scorers	Attendance	Anderson PT	Bannister J	Barber K	Branston TG	Busby VD	Collins JW	Court DJ	Givens DJ	Goodeve KGA	Guild A	Hoy RE	Keen MT	Macdonald M	Moore John	Nicholl CJ	Read JA	Ryan J	Ryan JG	Slough AP	Starling AW	Tees M	Round
1	Aug	19	(a)	Gillingham	W 1-0	Macdonald	7328							8	11			4	10	9	6	5	1	7	3	2			1
2	Sep	8	(h)	WORKINGTON	W 3-0	Givens (2), Macdonald	11072							8	11		4		10	7	6	5	1	12	2	3		9	2
3	Oct	6	(h)	ARSENAL	L 0-1	-	27023					12		8	11			4	10	9	6	5	1	7	2	3			3
						Apps		·	·	·	·		·	3	3	·	1	2	3	3	3	3	3	2	3	3	·	1	
						Subs		·	·	·	·	1		·	·	·		·	·	·	·	·	·	1	·	·		·	
						Goals		·	·	·	·		·	·	2	·		·	·	2	·	·	·	·	·	·		·	

▶ The 1970/71 team – Back row (left to right): Hoy, Bannister, Court, Ryan, Nicholl, Starling, Read, Branston, Moore, Jardine, Slough. Front row (left to right): Collins, Tees, Givens, Macdonald, Keen, Phillips, Busby, French.

TIMELINE...

1 August 1970 Mercurial winger Graham French is arrested after a shooting incident at the Unicorn pub the previous day.

4 December 1970 French is sentenced to three years behind bars.

9 March 1971 Following the crash of his Vehicle and General Insurance Company, Chairman Tony Hunt resigns.

7 May 1970 In the wake of the V & G collapse Malcolm Macdonald is sold to Newcastle for £160,000 to 'square the books'.

1971/72 FOOTBALL LEAGUE DIVISION TWO

Match No	Month	Day	Venue	Opponents	W,L,D	Score	Scorers	Attendance	Anderson PT	Barber K	Busby VD	Court DJ	Garner AH	Givens DJ	Goodeve KGA	Halom VL	Hindson G	Hoy RE	Keen MT	Moore John	Nicholl CJ	Read JA	Ryan J	Ryan JG	Shanks D	Slough AP	Wainwright RK	Match No
1	Aug	14	(h)	NORWICH CITY	D	1-1	Givens (pen)	12428	11		8	10		9					4	6	5	1	7	2		3		1
2	Aug	21	(a)	Burnley	L	1-2	Busby	13333	11		8	10		9					4	6	5	1	7	2		3		2
3	Aug	28	(h)	PRESTON NORTH END	D	1-1	Anderson	11772	11		7			10					4	6	5	1	12	2	3	8	9	3
4	Sep	1	(a)	Oxford United	D	1-1	Givens	10490	11		7			10					4	6	5	1		2	3	8	9	4
5	Sep	4	(a)	Orient	D	0-0	-	8703	11		7			10					4	6	5	1		2	3	8	9	5
6	Sep	11	(h)	BIRMINGHAM CITY	D	0-0	-	14678	11		7			10		9			4	6	5	1		2	3	8		6
7	Sep	18	(a)	Millwall	D	2-2	Anderson (2)	12433	11		7			10		9			8	6	5	1		2	3	4	12	7
8	Sep	25	(h)	MIDDLESBROUGH	W	3-2	Halom, Wainwright, Anderson	13001	11					10		9			8	6	5	1		2	3	4	7	8
9	Sep	28	(h)	FULHAM	W	2-0	Wainwright, Halom	14017	11	1				10		9			8	6	5		12	2	3	4	7	9
10	Oct	2	(a)	Hull City	D	0-0	-	13904		1				10		9			8	6	5		11	2	3	4	7	10
11	Oct	9	(h)	SWINDON TOWN	D	0-0	-	13423	11	1	12			10		9			8	6	5			2	3	4	7	11
12	Oct	16	(a)	Norwich City	L	1-3	Slough	22558	7	1				10		9	11		8	6	5			2	3	4		12
13	Oct	19	(a)	Queens Park Rangers	L	0-1	-	15858	7	1				10		9	11		8	6	5			2	3	4		13
14	Oct	23	(h)	CARLISLE UNITED	L	0-2	-	11963	7	1	12			10		9	11		8	6	5			2	3	4		14
15	Oct	30	(a)	Sunderland	D	2-2	Nicholl, Anderson	17979	7					10		9	11		8	6	5	1		2	4	3		15
16	Nov	6	(h)	CHARLTON ATHLETIC	L	1-2	Keen	11011	7					10		9	11		8	6	5	1		2	4	3		16
17	Nov	13	(a)	Watford	L	1-2	Halom	14000	4		7	12		10		9	11		8	6	5	1		2		3		17
18	Nov	20	(a)	Blackpool	W	1-0	Givens	8432	7		8	4		9			11		10	6	5	1		2		3		18
19	Nov	27	(h)	PORTSMOUTH	W	3-2	Keen, Hindson, Anderson	9910	7		8	4		9		12	11		10	6	5	1		2		3		19
20	Dec	4	(a)	Bristol City	D	0-0	-	12921	7			4		10		9	11		8	6	5	1		2		3		20
21	Dec	11	(h)	CARDIFF CITY	D	2-2	Anderson, Givens (pen)	10606	7			4		10		9	11		8	6	5	1		2		3		21
22	Dec	18	(h)	ORIENT	W	2-0	Slough, Givens	9193	7			4		10		9	11		8	6	5	1	12	2		3		22
23	Dec	27	(a)	Sheffield Wednesday	D	2-2	Givens, Anderson	31391	7		8			10		9	11		4	6	5	1		2		3		23
24	Jan	1	(h)	MILLWALL	W	2-1	Nicholl, Anderson	15113	7		8			10		9	11		4	6	5	1		2		3		24
25	Jan	8	(a)	Preston North End	W	1-0	Slough	12844	7		8			10		9	11		4	6	5	1		2		3		25
26	Jan	22	(a)	Fulham	L	1-3	Anderson	11328	7		8			10		9	11		4	6	5	1		2		3		26
27	Jan	29	(h)	QUEENS PARK RANGERS	D	1-1	John Ryan	17280	7		8			10		9	11		4	6	5	1		2		3		27
28	Feb	5	(h)	OXFORD UNITED	L	1-2	Halom	9892	7		8			10		9	11		4	6	5	1	12	2		3		28
29	Feb	12	(a)	Carlisle United	D	0-0	-	8731			7	8		11		10	12		4	6	5	1		2		3	9	29
30	Feb	19	(h)	SUNDERLAND	L	1-2	Nicholl	10994	12		7	10		11		9			4	6	5	1		2		3	8	30
31	Feb	26	(a)	Charlton Athletic	L	0-2	-	7941	7	1	8	10		11		12			4	6	5			2		3	9	31
32	Mar	4	(h)	WATFORD	D	0-0	-	10816	12	1		8		10		9	11		4		5		7	2	3	6		32
33	Mar	18	(h)	BURNLEY	W	1-0	Busby	8490	1		11	8	5	10					4				7	2	3	6		33
34	Mar	25	(a)	Birmingham City	L	0-1	-	34395	9	1	10	8	5	11					4				7	2	3	6		34
35	Mar	31	(a)	Middlesbrough	D	0-0	-	11720	9	1	10	8	5	11		7			4	12				2	3	6		35
36	Apr	1	(h)	SHEFFIELD WEDNESDAY	W	3-1	Halom (3)	9121	9	1	11	8	5	12		7			10	4				2	3	6		36
37	Apr	4	(h)	HULL CITY	L	0-1	-	9763	11	1	10	8	5	9		10			4	12		7		2	3	6		37
38	Apr	8	(h)	BLACKPOOL	L	1-4	Keen	7270		1	10	8	5	11		9			4	12				2	3	6	7	38
39	Apr	15	(a)	Portsmouth	W	3-0	Givens (pen), John Ryan (2)	8552		1			5	9		8	11		4				10	3	2	7		39
40	Apr	18	(a)	Swindon Town	L	1-2	Givens	8960		1			5	9		8	11		4	6			10	3	2	7		40
41	Apr	22	(h)	BRISTOL CITY	D	0-0	-	8329		1			5	9		8	11		4	6			10	3	2	7		41
42	Apr	29	(a)	Cardiff City	D	1-1	Wainwright	12587		1			5	9		8	11		4	6			10	3	2	7		42
				Final League Position: 13th				**Apps**	33	18	18	23	10	41	-	32	22	-	42	36	32	24	7	42	25	42	15	
								Subs	2	-	2	2	-	1	-	2	1	-	-	-	3	-	4	-	-	-	1	
								Goals	10	-	2	-	-	8	-	7	1	-	3	-	3	-	-	3	-	3	3	

1971/72 FA CUP

Round	Month	Day	Venue	Opponents	W,L,D	Score	Scorers	Attendance	Anderson PT	Barber K	Busby VD	Court DJ	Garner AH	Givens DJ	Goodeve KGA	Halom VL	Hindson G	Hoy RE	Keen MT	Moore John	Nicholl CJ	Read JA	Ryan J	Ryan JG	Shanks D	Slough AP	Wainwright RK	Round
3	Jan	15	(a)	West Ham United	L	1-2	Givens	32099	7		8			10		9	11		4	6	5	1		2		3		3
								Apps	1	-	1	-	-	1	-	1	1	-	1	1	1	1	-	1	-	1	-	
								Subs	-	-	-	-	-	-	-	-	-	-	-	-	-	-	-	-	-	-	-	
								Goals	-	-	-	-	-	1	-	-	-	-	-	-	-	-	-	-	-	-	-	

1971/72 LEAGUE CUP

Round	Month	Day	Venue	Opponents	W,L,D Score	Scorers	Attendance	Anderson PT	Barber K	Busby VD	Court DJ	Garner AH	Givens DJ	Goodeve KGA	Halom VL	Hindson G	Hoy RE	Keen MT	Moore John	Nicholl CJ	Read JA	Ryan J	Ryan JG	Shanks D	Slough AP	Wainwright RK	Round
2	Sep	7	(a)	Crystal Palace	L 0-2	-	13838	11		7			10					4	6	5	1		2	3	8	9	2
						Apps		1	.	1	.	.	1	.	.	.	.	1	1	1	1	.	1	1	1	1	
						Subs		.	.	.	.	.	.	.	.	.	.	.	.	.	.	.	.	.	.	.	
						Goals		.	.	.	.	.	.	.	.	.	.	.	.	.	.	.	.	.	.	.	

1971/72 WATNEY CUP

Round	Month	Day	Venue	Opponents	W,L,D Score	Scorers	Attendance	Anderson PT	Barber K	Busby VD	Court DJ	Garner AH	Givens DJ	Goodeve KGA	Halom VL	Hindson G	Hoy RE	Keen MT	Moore John	Nicholl CJ	Read JA	Ryan J	Ryan JG	Shanks D	Slough AP	Wainwright RK	Round
1	Jul	31	(a)	Colchester United	L 0-1	-	8186	7		10	8		9	14				4	11	6	5		2	3	12		1
						Apps		1	.	1	1	.	1	.	.	.	.	1	1	1	1	.	1	.	1	.	
						Subs		.	.	.	.	.	.	1	.	.	.	.	.	.	.	.	.	.	.	1	
						Goals		.	.	.	.	.	.	.	.	.	.	.	.	.	.	.	.	.	.	.	

▶ **The 1971/72 team** – Back row (left to right): Woods, Busby, Garner, Court, Shanks. Middle row (left to right): Whitfield (Trainer), Givens, Nicholl, Read, Wainwright, Anderson, Andrews (Coach). Front row (left to right): Goodeve, Hoy, Moore, John Ryan, Slough, Jim Ryan.

TIMELINE...
27 April 1972 Manager Alec Stock resigns.

1972/73 FOOTBALL LEAGUE DIVISION TWO

Match No	Month	Day	Venue	Opponents	W,L,D Score	Scorers	Attendance	Anderson PT	Aston J	Barber K	Busby VD	Butlin BD	Carrick WF	Faulkner JG	Fern RA	French GE	Garner AH	Goodeve KGA	Hales DD	Halom VL	Harfield L	Hindson G	Horn GR	Litt SE	Moore John	O'Connor PK	Price PT	Ryan J	Ryan JG	Shanks D	Slough AP	Thomson RA	Match No
1	Aug	12	(a)	Cardiff City	L 1-2	Aston (pen)	16364	4	11	1	9			5	8		6			10								7	2			3	1
2	Aug	19	(h)	PRESTON NORTH END	W 1-0	Anderson	11507	4	11	1	9			5	8		6			10								7	2		12	3	2
3	Aug	26	(a)	Orient	W 1-0	Busby	6494	4	11	1	9			5	8		6			10								7	2			3	3
4	Aug	30	(h)	OXFORD UNITED	L 0-1	-	10891	4	11	1	9			5	8		6			10								7	2		12	3	4
5	Sep	2	(h)	HUDDERSFIELD TOWN	W 4-1	Halom (2), Jim Ryan, Aston (pen)	8133		11	1	9			5	8		6			10								7	2		4	3	5
6	Sep	9	(a)	Nottingham Forest	W 1-0	Aston	9133	4	11	1	9			5	8		6			10								7	2	2		3	6
7	Sep	16	(h)	BRIGHTON & HOVE ALBION	W 2-1	Fern, Halom	11627	4	11	1	9			5	8		6			10								7	2		12	3	7
8	Sep	23	(a)	Sheffield Wednesday	L 0-4	-	18913	4	11	1	9			5	8					10					12			7	2		6	3	8
9	Sep	26	(a)	Swindon Town	W 2-0	Halom (2)	8469	4	11		9		1	5	8					10								7	2		6	3	9
10	Sep	30	(h)	BURNLEY	D 2-2	Aston (pen), Halom	12197	4	11		9		1	5	8					10								7	2		6	3	10
11	Oct	7	(h)	BLACKPOOL	D 2-2	Slough, Aston	12073	4	11	1	9			5	8					10								7	2		6	3	11
12	Oct	14	(a)	Sunderland	W 2-0	Halom, Jim Ryan	13394	4	11	1	9			5	8					10	12							7	2		6	3	12
13	Oct	18	(h)	PORTSMOUTH	D 2-2	Halom, Busby	9813	4	11	1	9			5	8					10								7	2		6	3	13
14	Oct	21	(h)	HULL CITY	L 1-2	Halom	11560	4	11	1					8			5		10	12	9						7	2		6	3	14
15	Oct	28	(a)	Bristol City	W 1-0	Faulkner	13562	4						5			6		9	10								7	2		8	3	15
16	Nov	4	(h)	SWINDON TOWN	L 0-1	-	10596	4	11	1				5	12		6			10		9						7	2		8	3	16
17	Nov	11	(a)	Portsmouth	D 2-2	Stephenson (og), Fern	7601		11	1				5	8		6	12		10		9						7	2		4	3	17
18	Nov	18	(a)	Aston Villa	W 2-0	Fern, Aston	29144	4	11	1				5	10		6					9						7	2		8	3	18
19	Nov	25	(h)	CARLISLE UNITED	L 0-1	-	10091	4	11	1				5	8		6	12				9						7	2		10	3	19
20	Dec	9	(h)	QUEENS PARK RANGERS	D 2-2	Butlin, Halom	13670	8	11			9		5	12		6			10								7	2		4	3	20
21	Dec	16	(h)	MILLWALL	D 2-2	Butlin, French	11550	4	11	1		9				8	5			10								7	6	2		3	21
22	Dec	23	(a)	Middlesbrough	W 1-0	Butlin	10122	7	11	1		9			8		5						6						4	2		3	22
23	Dec	26	(h)	SHEFFIELD WEDNESDAY	D 0-0	-	15799	4	11	1	9				8		5						6					7	2			3	23
24	Dec	30	(a)	Preston North End	L 0-2	-	9638	4	11	1	9						5			10			6					7	8	2	12	3	24
25	Jan	6	(h)	ORIENT	D 1-1	Aston	8344	8	11	1	9						5			10			6					7	4	2	12	3	25
26	Jan	20	(a)	Huddersfield Town	W 2-1	Butlin, Lyon (og)	3871		11	1	9						5			10			6					7	8	2	4	3	26
27	Jan	27	(h)	NOTTINGHAM FOREST	W 1-0	Slough	10083		11	1	9						5			8			6					7	4	2	10	3	27
28	Feb	3	(a)	Brighton & Hove Albion	L 0-2	-	11404		11	1	9						5	12		10			6					7	8	2	4	3	28
29	Feb	17	(h)	CARDIFF CITY	D 1-1	Hales	10422		11		9		1				5		8	10			6					7	2		4	3	29
30	Feb	26	(a)	Millwall	L 2-3	Aston (2)	10504		11		10	9		7			5	12					6	1					8	2	4	3	30
31	Mar	3	(a)	Blackpool	D 1-1	Jim Ryan	6947	8	11		10				1		12					9	6					7	2	4		3	31
32	Mar	10	(h)	SUNDERLAND	W 1-0	Shanks	12458	8			12		5	11			6	9		10	1							7	2	4		3	32
33	Mar	24	(h)	BRISTOL CITY	L 1-3	Garner	7102	8	11		9			7				12		10	1		6						4	2		3	33
34	Mar	27	(a)	Fulham	W 1-0	Fern	7442			1			5	11	8		6	9		10								7	2			3	34
35	Mar	31	(a)	Carlisle United	L 0-2	-	5517	4		1			5	11			6	9		10					12			7	2		8	3	35
36	Apr	7	(h)	FULHAM	W 1-0	Jim Ryan	8430	4	11				5	10	8		6			9	1							7	2			3	36
37	Apr	10	(a)	Hull City	L 0-4	-	5278	4	11	1			5	9	8	6				10								7	2			3	37
38	Apr	14	(a)	Queens Park Rangers	L 0-2	-	16471	4	11	1	9			5			8			10								7	6	2		3	38
39	Apr	21	(h)	ASTON VILLA	D 0-0	-	10981	4	11	1	9			5			8	12		10								7	6	2		3	39
40	Apr	23	(h)	MIDDLESBROUGH	L 0-1	-	6177	4		1	9			5	12	11	6			10								7	8	2		3	40
41	Apr	24	(a)	Burnley	L 0-3	-	17689	4		1				5	9			6	11	10								7	8	2		3	41
42	Apr	28	(a)	Oxford United	L 1-2	Slough	6318	8			9			5			6			10	1					11	12	7			4	3	42
				Apps				34	36	33	20	11	4	29	26	8	27	7	5	25	-	20	5	-	11	1	-	39	36	22	21	42	
				Subs				-	-	-	1	-	-	-	4	-	-	4	2	-	1	1	-	1	1	1	1	-	-	-	5	-	
				Goals				1	9	-	2	4	-	1	4	1	1	-	1	10	-	-	-	-	-	-	-	4	-	1	3	-	

Final League Position: 12th   2 Own Goals

1972/73 FA CUP

Round	Month	Day	Venue	Opponents	W,L,D Score	Scorers	Attendance	Anderson PT	Aston J	Barber K	Busby VD	Butlin BD	Carrick WF	Faulkner JG	Fern RA	French GE	Garner AH	Goodeve KGA	Hales DD	Halom VL	Harfield L	Hindson G	Horn GR	Litt SE	Moore John	O'Connor PK	Price PT	Ryan J	Ryan JG	Shanks D	Slough AP	Thomson RA	Round
3	Jan	13	(h)	CREWE ALEXANDRA	W 2-0	Jim Ryan, Butlin	9411		11	1		9					5					12	6	8				7	4	2	10	3	3
4	Feb	3	(a)	Newcastle United	W 2-0	Aston (2)	42170		11	1		9					5			10			6					7	8	2	4	3	4
5	Feb	24	(a)	Bolton Wanderers	W 1-0	Garner	39556		11			9	1				5			10			6					7	8	2	4	3	5
6	Mar	17	(a)	Sunderland	L 0-2	-	53151	8	11	1	9						5	12		10			6					7	2	4		3	6
				Apps				1	4	3	1	3	1	-	-	-	4	-	-	3	-	-	4	1	-	-	-	4	4	4	3	4	
				Subs				-	-	-	-	-	-	-	-	-	-	-	1	-	-	1	-	-	-	-	-	-	-	-	-	-	
				Goals				-	2	-	-	1	-	-	-	-	1	-	-	-	-	-	-	-	-	-	-	1	-	-	-	-	

1972/73 LEAGUE CUP

Round	Month	Day	Venue	Opponents	W,L,D Score	Scorers	Attendance	Anderson PT	Aston J	Barber K	Busby VD	Butlin BD	Carrick WF	Faulkner JG	Fern RA	French GE	Garner AH	Goodeve KGA	Hales DD	Halom VL	Harfield L	Hindson G	Horn GR	Litt SE	Moore John	O'Connor PK	Price PT	Ryan J	Ryan JG	Shanks D	Slough AP	Thomson RA	Round
2	Sep	5	(a)	Birmingham City	D 1-1	Anderson	20962	4	11	1	9			5	8		6		10									7	2		3		2
Rep	Sep	13	(h)	BIRMINGHAM CITY	D 1-1	Aston	13806	4	11	1	9			5	8		6		10									7	2		3		Rep
Rep 2	Sep	19	(n)	Birmingham City	L 0-1	-	11451	4	11	1	9			5	8		6		10									7	2	12	3		Rep 2
						Apps		3	3	3	3			3	3		3		3									3	3		3		
						Subs		-	-	-	-			-	-		-		-									-	-	1	-		
						Goals		1	1	-	-			-	-		-		-									-	-	-	-		

2nd Round 2nd Replay played at The County Ground, Northampton.

1972/73 ANGLO-ITALIAN CUP

Round	Month	Day	Venue	Opponents	W,L,D Score	Scorers	Attendance	Anderson PT	Aston J	Barber K	Busby VD	Butlin BD	Carrick WF	Faulkner JG	Fern RA	French GE	Garner AH	Goodeve KGA	Hales DD	Halom VL	Harfield L	Hindson G	Horn GR	Litt SE	Moore John	O'Connor PK	Price PT	Ryan J	Ryan JG	Shanks D	Slough AP	Thomson RA	Round
PR	Mar	7	(h)	BARI	W 4-0	Shanks (2), Moore, Thomson	4518	8	11		9				12		5					10	1		6			7	2	4	3		PR
PR	Mar	21	(a)	Verona	L 1-2	French	1799		11		12		1	5	8	10		6	9								7	4	2	3		PR
PR	Apr	4	(h)	FIORENTINA	W 1-0	Hindson	2742	4	11					5	9	8	6					10	1					7	12	2	3		PR
PR	May	2	(a)	Lazio	D 2-2	Anderson, John Ryan	4200	9						5			12	6				10	1		11		2	7	8		4	3	PR
						Apps		3	3	-	1	-	1	3	2	2	1	2	1			3	3		2	-		4	3	3	4	1	
						Subs		-	-	-	1	-	-	-	1	-	1	-	-			-	-		-	-	1	-	1	-	-	-	
						Goals		1	-	-	-	-	-	-	-	1	-	-	-			1	-		1	-		1	-	2	-	1	

▶ **The 1972/73 team** – Back row (left to right): Robinson, Hales, Harfield, Hindson, Hatch, Halom, Thomson, Faulkner, Price, Anderson, Jim Ryan, Jones, Sparks. Middle row (left to right): Castiello, Garner, Wainwright, Goodeve, Barber, Carrick, Read, Moore, Slough, Litt, Gilchrist. Front row (left to right): McCrohan (Coach), John Ryan, Aston, Haslam (Manager), Fern, Busby, Whitfield (Trainer).

TIMELINE...

4 May 1972 Harry Haslam is promoted into the managerial chair at Kenilworth Road.
17 March 1973 The Town reach the FA Cup quarter-finals for the fourth time in their history but go down to eventual winners Sunderland at Roker Park.

1973/74 FOOTBALL LEAGUE DIVISION TWO

Match No	Month	Day	Venue	Opponents	W,L,D Score	Scorers	Attendance	Anderson PT	Aston J	Barber K	Butlin BD	Cruse PA	Faulkner JG	Fern RA	Finney T	Garner AH	Hindson G	Holmes W	Horn GR	Husband J	Litt SE	Ryan J	Ryan JG	Shanks D	Sims J	Thomson RA	West A	Match No
1	Aug	25	(a)	Nottingham Forest	L 0-4	-	10792	6	11	1	9	10	5		12	4						7	8	2		3		1
2	Sep	1	(h)	CARLISLE UNITED	W 6-1	Finney (2), Anderson (2), Aston, Butlin	7231	4	11		9		5		10	6			1			7	8	2		3		2
3	Sep	8	(a)	Bristol City	W 3-1	Aston, John Ryan, Finney	12208	4	11		9		5		10	6			1			7	8	2		3		3
4	Sep	11	(a)	Notts County	D 1-1	Finney	8509	4	11		9		5		10	6			1			7	8	2		3		4
5	Sep	15	(h)	PORTSMOUTH	D 3-3	Thomson, Garner, Finney	11552	4	11		9		5		10	6			1			7	8	2		3		5
6	Sep	22	(a)	Sunderland	W 1-0	Butlin	27334	4	11		9		5		10	6			1			7	8	2		3		6
7	Sep	29	(h)	BLACKPOOL	W 3-0	Butlin (2), Anderson	10365	4	11		9		5		10	6		12	1			7	8	2		3		7
8	Oct	6	(a)	Crystal Palace	W 2-1	Anderson, Butlin	20322	4	11		9		5		10	6	7		1				8	2		3		8
9	Oct	13	(h)	SWINDON TOWN	W 2-1	Aston (pen), Anderson	10732	4	11		9	10	5			6	12		1			7	8	2		3		9
10	Oct	20	(a)	Orient	L 0-2	-	11135	4	11	1	9		5			6						7	8	2		3	10	10
11	Oct	27	(h)	HULL CITY	D 2-2	Anderson, Butlin	11408	4	11	1	9		5		8	6						7		2		3	10	11
12	Nov	3	(a)	Middlesbrough	L 1-2	Butlin	22590	4	11	1	9		5		8	6						7		2		3	10	12
13	Nov	10	(h)	BOLTON WANDERERS	W 2-1	Jim Ryan, McAllister (og)	9528	4	11	1	9	12	5		8	6						7		2		3	10	13
14	Nov	14	(a)	Cardiff City	D 0-0	-	5999	4	11				5	12	8	6			1			7		2	9	3	10	14
15	Nov	17	(h)	SHEFFIELD WEDNESDAY	W 2-1	Aston, Sims	9543	4	11				5		8	6			1			7	12	2	9	3	10	15
16	Nov	24	(a)	Preston North End	D 2-2	Aston, Fern	10279	4	11				5	12	8	6			1			7		2	9	3	10	16
17	Dec	1	(h)	WEST BROMWICH ALBION	L 0-2	-	10192		11		12		5		9	6			1	8			4	2		3	10	17
18	Dec	8	(a)	Millwall	W 1-0	Butlin	6976	4	11		9		5			6			1	8		7		2		3	10	18
19	Dec	12	(h)	CARDIFF CITY	W 1-0	Jim Ryan	7139	4	11		9		5			6			1	8		7		2		3	10	19
20	Dec	15	(h)	ASTON VILLA	W 1-0	Anderson	10020	4	11		9		5		8	6			1			7		2		3	10	20
21	Dec	22	(a)	Blackpool	L 0-3	-	7796	4	11		9		5			6			1	8		7		2		3	10	21
22	Dec	26	(h)	FULHAM	D 1-1	Fraser (og)	15259	4	11		9		5			6			1	8		7		2		3	10	22
23	Dec	29	(h)	BRISTOL CITY	W 1-0	Anderson	11398	4	11		9		5			6			1	8		7		2		3	10	23
24	Jan	1	(a)	Carlisle United	L 0-2	-	9245	4	11		9		5			6			1	8		7	12	2		3	10	24
25	Jan	12	(a)	Portsmouth	D 0-0	-	18476	4	11				5		8	6			1			7	4	2		3	10	25
26	Jan	19	(h)	NOTTINGHAM FOREST	D 2-2	Jim Ryan (2, 1 pen)	11888	9	11		12				8	6			1		5	7	4	2		3	10	26
27	Feb	2	(a)	Aston Villa	W 1-0	Jim Ryan (pen)	26180	9			11		5		8	6			1			7	4	2		3	10	27
28	Feb	5	(a)	Notts County	D 1-1	Anderson	4908	4			11		5		9	6			1	8		7		2		3	10	28
29	Feb	23	(h)	CRYSTAL PALACE	W 2-1	Jim Ryan (pen), Butlin	14287	4	11		9				8	6			1		5	7		2		3	10	29
30	Feb	26	(a)	Swindon Town	W 2-0	Butlin (2)	2791	4	11		9		5			6			1	8		7		2		3	10	30
31	Mar	5	(a)	Fulham	L 1-2	Husband	10071	4	11		9		5			6			1	8		7		2		3	10	31
32	Mar	9	(a)	Hull City	W 3-1	West, Anderson, Aston	7027	4	11		9		5			6			1	8		7		2		3	10	32
33	Mar	16	(h)	ORIENT	W 3-1	Husband (3)	17045	4	11		9		5			6			1	8		7		2		3	10	33
34	Mar	23	(a)	Bolton Wanderers	L 0-1	-	15903	4	11		9		5			6			1	8		7		2		3	10	34
35	Mar	30	(h)	MIDDLESBROUGH	L 0-1	-	19812	4	11		9		5			6			1	8		7		2		3	10	35
36	Apr	6	(h)	PRESTON NORTH END	W 4-2	Husband, Butlin (3)	11806	4	11		9		5			6			1	8		7		2		3	10	36
37	Apr	12	(a)	Oxford United	D 1-1	Jim Ryan	13714	4	11		9		5			6	12		1	8		7		2		3	10	37
38	Apr	13	(a)	Sheffield Wednesday	D 2-2	Husband, Butlin	16685	4	11		9		5			6	7		1	8				2		3	10	38
39	Apr	16	(h)	OXFORD UNITED	L 0-1	-	16357	4	11		9		5			6			1	8		7		2		3	10	39
40	Apr	20	(h)	MILLWALL	W 3-0	Faulkner, Anderson, Hindson	15740	4	11		9		5			6	12		1	8		7		2		3	10	40
41	Apr	27	(a)	West Bromwich Albion	D 1-1	Butlin	13164	4	11		9		5			6	12		1	8		7		2		3	10	41
42	May	1	(h)	SUNDERLAND	L 3-4	Husband (2), Butlin	20285	4			9		5		11	6			1	8		7		2		3	10	42

Final League Position: 2nd — 2 Own Goals

							Apps	41	39	5	36	3	40	5	13	42	3	-	37	22	2	40	29	27	3	42	33	
							Subs	-	-	1	1	-	1	1	-	-	4	1	-	-	-	-	2	-	-	-	-	
							Goals	11	6	-	17	-	1	1	5	1	1	-	-	8	-	7	1	-	1	1	1	

1973/74 FA CUP

Round	Month	Day	Venue	Opponents	W,L,D Score	Scorers	Attendance	Anderson PT	Aston J	Barber K	Butlin BD	Cruse PA	Faulkner JG	Fern RA	Finney T	Garner AH	Hindson G	Holmes W	Horn GR	Husband J	Litt SE	Ryan J	Ryan JG	Shanks D	Sims J	Thomson RA	West A	Round
3	Jan	5	(a)	Port Vale	D 1-1	Jim Ryan	8127	4	11		9		5		12	6			1	8		7		2		3	10	3
Rep	Jan	9	(h)	PORT VALE	W 4-2	Aston, Anderson (2), Jim Ryan	5833	9	11				5		8	6			1			7	4	2		3	10	Rep
4	Jan	26	(h)	BRADFORD CITY	W 3-0	Fretwell (og), Butlin, Jim Ryan	12470	9			11		5		8	6			1			7	4	2		3	10	4
5	Feb	16	(h)	LEICESTER CITY	L 0-4	-	25712	4			11		5	9	12	6			1	8		7		2		3	10	5

1 Own Goal

							Apps	4	2	-	3	-	4	1	2	4	-	-	4	2	-	4	2	4	-	4	4	
							Subs	-	1	-	-	-	-	-	1	-	-	-	-	1	-	-	-	-	-	-	-	
							Goals	2	1	-	1	-	-	-	-	-	-	-	-	-	-	3	-	-	-	-	-	

1973/74 LEAGUE CUP

Round	Month	Day	Venue	Opponents	W,L,D Score	Scorers	Attendance	Anderson PT	Aston J	Barber K	Butlin BD	Cruse PA	Faulkner JG	Fern RA	Finney T	Garner AH	Hindson G	Holmes W	Horn GR	Husband J	Litt SE	Ryan J	Ryan JG	Shanks D	Sims J	Thomson RA	West A	Round
2	Oct	10	(h)	GRIMSBY TOWN	D 1-1	Hindson	9656	4	11		9		5		10	6	7			1			8	2		3		2
Rep	Oct	16	(a)	Grimsby Town	D 0-0	-	13643	4	11		9	10	5			6	7			1			8	2		3		Rep
Rep 2	Oct	23	(a)	Grimsby Town	W 2-0	Finney, Faulkner	15365	4	11	1	9		5		10	6						7		2		3	8	Rep 2
3	Oct	31	(h)	BURY	D 0-0	-	8191	4	11	1	9	12	5		8	6						7		2		3	10	3
Rep	Nov	6	(a)	Bury	W 3-2	Anderson, Shanks, West	7827	4	11	1	9		5		8	6						7		2		3	10	Rep
4	Nov	21	(a)	Millwall	L 1-3	Jones (og)	8777	4	11				5	8		6			1			7		2	9	3	10	4
						1 Own Goal	Apps	6	6	3	5	1	6	1	4	6	2	-	3	-	-	4	2	6	1	6	4	
							Subs	-	-	-	-	1	-	-	-	-	-	-	-	-	-	-	-	-	-	-	-	
							Goals	1	-	-	-	-	1	-	1	-	1	-	-	-	-	-	-	1	-	-	1	

▶ Jim Husband scores one of his hat-trick goals during the important home win over fellow promotion chasers Orient.

TIMELINE...

27 April 1974 Promotion back to Division One is confirmed following a 1-1 draw at West Bromwich.

▶ **The 1973/74 team** – Back row (left to right): Holmes, Anderson, Horn, Barber, Faulkner, Goodeve. Middle row (left to right): McCrohan (Coach), Cruse, John Ryan, Slough, Price, Moore, Thomson, Hindson, Garner, Game (Physiotherapist). Front row (left to right): French, Busby, Jim Ryan, Butlin, Aston, Fern, Shanks.

◗ Promotion for the third time in six years. Happy Hatters celebrate.

◗ Mid-season signings on the road to promotion, Alan West and Jimmy Husband

◗ Peter Anderson heads the only goal of the game against Bristol City.

◗ Top scorer during the promotion campaign – Barry 'Bullet' Butlin.

1974/75 FOOTBALL LEAGUE DIVISION ONE

Match No	Month	Day	Venue	Opponents	W/L/D Score	Scorers	Attendance	Alston A	Anderson PT	Aston J	Barber K	Buckley S	Butlin BD	Chambers BM	Faulkner JG	Fern RA	Fuccillo P	Futcher R	Futcher P	Garner AH	Hindson G	Horn GR	Husband J	King AE	Litt SE	Pollock MA	Ryan J	Ryan JG	Seasman J	Shanks D	Spiring PJ	Thomson RA	West A	Match No
1	Aug	17	(h)	LIVERPOOL	L 1-2	Butlin	21216		4	11			9							6	7	1	8		5			2				3	10	1
2	Aug	19	(a)	West Ham United	L 0-2	-	23182		4	7			9							6	11	1	8		5			2	12			3	10	2
3	Aug	24	(a)	Middlesbrough	D 1-1	Butlin	21478		4	11			9		5					6	7	1	8					2				3	10	3
4	Aug	28	(h)	WEST HAM UNITED	D 0-0	-	16931	12	4	11	1		9		5					6	7		8					2				3	10	4
5	Aug	31	(h)	QUEENS PARK RANGERS	D 1-1	John Ryan	18535	11	4		1		9		5					6	7		8					2				3	10	5
6	Sep	7	(a)	Leeds United	D 1-1	Butlin	26516	11	4		1		9		5					6	7		8					2	12			3	10	6
7	Sep	14	(h)	IPSWICH TOWN	L 1-4	Alston	17577	11	4		1		9		5					6	7		8					2				3	10	7
8	Sep	21	(a)	Arsenal	D 2-2	Alston, Shanks	21649	11	4		1		9		5						7		8				6	2				3	10	8
9	Sep	24	(a)	Coventry City	L 1-2	Jim Ryan (pen)	15643	11	4		1		9		5						7		8				6	2				3	10	9
10	Sep	28	(h)	CARLISLE UNITED	W 3-1	Anderson, Alston, Jim Ryan (pen)	12987	11	4		1				5						7		9				6	2		8		3	10	10
11	Oct	5	(a)	Leicester City	D 0-0	-	19024	11	4		1	3			5						7		9				6	2		8			10	11
12	Oct	12	(h)	BIRMINGHAM CITY	L 1-3	Hindson	15097	11			1	3		4	5						7		9				6	2		8			10	12
13	Oct	16	(h)	MIDDLESBROUGH	L 0-1	-	10464	9	4		1			8						6	11				5		7	2				3	10	13
14	Oct	19	(a)	Manchester City	L 0-1	-	30649	9	4	11	1			8						6					5		7	2				3	10	14
15	Oct	26	(h)	TOTTENHAM HOTSPUR	D 1-1	Aston	22420	9	4	11	1					8				6					5		7	2				3	10	15
16	Nov	2	(a)	Newcastle United	L 0-1	-	30141	9	4	11	1					8				6					5		7	2				3	10	16
17	Nov	9	(h)	SHEFFIELD UNITED	L 0-1	-	12670	9	4	11	1			5		8				6						12	7	2				3	10	17
18	Nov	16	(a)	Stoke City	L 2-4	Anderson, Garner	20646	9	4						5					6		1	8				7	2		11		3	10	18
19	Nov	30	(h)	BURNLEY	L 2-3	Faulkner, Spiring	11816	12	4	11					5					6		1	8				7	2			9	3	10	19
20	Dec	7	(a)	Chelsea	L 0-2	-	19009		4	11		3			5			6				1	8				7	2			9		10	20
21	Dec	14	(a)	Liverpool	L 0-2	-	35151		4	11		3			5			6				1	8				7	2			9		10	21
22	Dec	21	(h)	DERBY COUNTY	W 1-0	Jim Ryan (pen)	12862		4	11		3			5		12	6				1	8				7	2			9		10	22
23	Dec	26	(a)	Ipswich Town	W 1-0	R Futcher	23406		4	11		3			5			9	6			1	8				7	2					10	23
24	Dec	28	(h)	WOLVERHAMPTON WANDERERS	W 3-2	R Futcher (3)	19642		4	11		3			5			9	6			1	8				7	2					10	24
25	Jan	11	(h)	CHELSEA	D 1-1	Husband	23096		4	11		3			5			9	6			1	8				7	2					10	25
26	Jan	18	(a)	Burnley	L 0-1	-	17237		4	11		3			5			9	6			1	8				7	2					10	26
27	Feb	1	(a)	Sheffield United	D 1-1	Anderson	17270		4	11		3			5			9	6			1	8				7	2					10	27
28	Feb	8	(h)	NEWCASTLE UNITED	W 1-0	R Futcher	18019		4	11		3			5			9	6			1	8				7	2					10	28
29	Feb	22	(h)	STOKE CITY	D 0-0	-	19894		4	11		3			5			9	6			1	8				7	2					10	29
30	Feb	25	(a)	Everton	L 1-3	Aston	35714		4	11		3			5			9	6			1	8				7	2					10	30
31	Mar	1	(a)	Queens Park Rangers	L 1-2	Alston	19583	8	4	11		3			5			9	6			1					7	2					10	31
32	Mar	8	(h)	COVENTRY CITY	L 1-3	Aston	14423	8	4	11		3			5			9	6			1					7	2					10	32
33	Mar	15	(a)	Carlisle United	W 2-1	Aston, R Futcher	8339	12	4	11		3			5			9	6			1	8				7	2					10	33
34	Mar	22	(h)	LEEDS UNITED	W 2-1	Aston, Anderson	23048		4	11		3			5			9	6			1	8				7	2					10	34
35	Mar	25	(h)	ARSENAL	W 2-0	Jim Ryan (pen), R Futcher	22120		4	11		3			5			9	6			1	8				7	2					10	35
36	Mar	29	(a)	Derby County	L 0-5	-	24619		4	11		3			5			9	6			1	8				7	2	12				10	36
37	Mar	31	(a)	Wolverhampton Wanderers	L 2-5	Seasman, Jim Ryan	22689		4	11		3			5			9	6			1	8				7	2	8	12			10	37
38	Apr	5	(a)	Tottenham Hotspur	L 1-2	West	25796		4	11		3			5			9	6			1	8				7	2			12		10	38
39	Apr	9	(h)	EVERTON	W 2-1	Anderson (2)	13437	9	4	11	1	3			5				6				8				7	2					10	39
40	Apr	12	(h)	LEICESTER CITY	W 3-0	Alston, Weller (og), Husband	18298	9	4	11	1	3			5				6				8				7	2					10	40
41	Apr	19	(a)	Birmingham City	W 4-1	Jim Ryan, Alston (2), Husband	28755	9	4	11	1	3			5				6				8				7	2					10	41
42	Apr	26	(h)	MANCHESTER CITY	D 1-1	Jim Ryan	20768	9	4	11	1	3			5				6				8	12			7	2					10	42
							Apps	18	40	32	26	24	9	6	34	3	-	16	19	9	17	16	33	-	12	-	30	38	1	15	5	17	42	
							Subs	3	-	-	-	-	-	-	-	1	1	-	-	-	-	-	-	1	-	1	1	-	1	1	2	-	-	
							Goals	7	6	5	-	-	3	-	-	-	-	7	-	1	1	-	3	-	-	-	7	1	1	1	1	-	1	

Final League Position: 20th

1 Own Goal

1974/75 FA CUP

Round	Month	Day	Venue	Opponents	W/L/D Score	Scorers	Attendance	Alston A	Anderson PT	Aston J	Barber K	Buckley S	Butlin BD	Chambers BM	Faulkner JG	Fern RA	Fuccillo P	Futcher R	Futcher P	Garner AH	Hindson G	Horn GR	Husband J	King AE	Litt SE	Pollock MA	Ryan J	Ryan JG	Seasman J	Shanks D	Spiring PJ	Thomson RA	West A	Round
3	Jan	4	(h)	BIRMINGHAM CITY	L 0-1	-	17543		4	11		3			5			9	6			1	8			12	7	2					10	3
							Apps	-	1	1	-	1	-	-	1	-	-	1	1	-	-	1	1	-	-	-	1	1	-	-	-	-	1	
							Subs	-	-	-	-	-	-	-	-	-	-	-	-	-	-	-	-	1	-	-	-	-	-	-	-	-	-	
							Goals	-	-	-	-	-	-	-	-	-	-	-	-	-	-	-	-	-	-	-	-	-	-	-	-	-	-	

1974/75 LEAGUE CUP

Round	Month	Day	Venue	Opponents	W/L/D	Score	Scorers	Attendance	Alston A	Anderson PT	Aston J	Barber K	Buckley S	Butlin BD	Chambers BM	Faulkner JG	Fern RA	Fuccillo P	Futcher R	Futcher P	Garner AH	Hindson G	Horn GR	Husband J	King AE	Litt SE	Pollock MA	Ryan J	Ryan JG	Seasman J	Shanks D	Spring PJ	Thomson RA	West A	Round
2	Sep	11	(h)	BRISTOL ROVERS	W	1-0	Alston	10073	11	4		1		9							5	7		8					6	2			3	10	2
3	Oct	8	(a)	Sheffield United	L	0-2	-	14150	10	7		1	3								12	11		9	4			6	5	2				8	3
								Apps	2	2	-	2	1	1	-	-	-	-	-	-	1	2	-	2	1	-	-	1	2	2	-	-	1	2	
								Subs	-	-	-	-	-	-	-	-	-	-	-	-	1	-	-	-	-	-	-	-	-	-	-	-	-	-	
								Goals	1	-	-	-	-	-	-	-	-	-	-	-	-	-	-	-	-	-	-	-	-	-	-	-	-	-	

1974/75 TEXACO CUP

Round	Month	Day	Venue	Opponents	W/L/D	Score	Scorers	Attendance	Alston A	Anderson PT	Aston J	Barber K	Buckley S	Butlin BD	Chambers BM	Faulkner JG	Fern RA	Fuccillo P	Futcher R	Futcher P	Garner AH	Hindson G	Horn GR	Husband J	King AE	Litt SE	Pollock MA	Ryan J	Ryan JG	Seasman J	Shanks D	Spring PJ	Thomson RA	West A	Round
G2	Aug	3	(h)	SOUTHAMPTON	D	1-1	Butlin	8445		4				9						12	6	11	1	8		5		7	2				3	10	G2
G2	Aug	7	(a)	West Ham United	W	2-1	Anderson, Husband	14705		4	12			9							6	11	1	8		5		7		2			3	10	G2
G2	Aug	10	(a)	Orient	D	2-2	Butlin, Husband	5443		4	12			9							6	11	1	8		5		7		2			3	10	G2
								Apps	-	3	-	-	-	3	-	-	-	-	-	-	3	3	3	3	-	3	-	3	1	2	-	-	3	3	
								Subs	-	-	2	-	-	-	-	-	-	-	-	1	-	-	-	-	-	-	-	-	-	-	-	-	-	-	
								Goals	-	1	-	-	-	2	-	-	-	-	-	-	-	-	-	2	-	-	-	-	-	-	-	-	-	-	

John Aston is mobbed by his team mates after scoring against Tottenham.

The 1974/75 team – Back row (left to right): Pollock, Anderson, John Ryan, P.Futcher, Price, Husband. Middle row (left to right): Game (Physiotherapist), Thomson, Faulkner, Barber, Horn, Butlin, Garner, Litt, McCrohan (Coach). Front row (left to right): Chambers, West, Haslam (Manager), Hindson, Jim Ryan.

TIMELINE...

26 April 1975 The Town's heroic late run ends in disappointment with relegation back to Division Two.

1975/76 FOOTBALL LEAGUE DIVISION TWO

Match No	Month	Day	Venue	W.L.D Score	Opponents	Scorers	Attendance	Alston A	Anderson PT	Aston J	Barber K	Buckley S	Chambers BM	Faulkner JG	Fuccillo P	Futcher R	Futcher P	Hill RA	Husband J	Jones G	King AE	Litt SE	Pollock MA	Price PT	Ryan J	Ryan JG	Seasman J	Spring PJ	Thomson RA	West A	Match No
1	Aug	16	(h)	W 2-0	HULL CITY	R Futcher, King	10389	9	6	11	1	3		4		10					7	5				2				8	1
2	Aug	23	(a)	L 0-1	West Bromwich Albion	-	14062	8	4	11	1	3		5		9	6				7					2				10	2
3	Aug	30	(h)	W 3-0	CHELSEA	Anderson, Buckley (pen), R Futcher	18565	8	4	11	1	3	12	5		9	6				7					2				10	3
4	Sep	6	(a)	W 2-0	Portsmouth	Alston, King	9835	8	4	11	1	3	10	5		9	6				7					2			11		4
5	Sep	13	(h)	L 0-2	BOLTON WANDERERS	-	11217	8	4	11	1	3		5		9	6		12		7			10		2					5
6	Sep	20	(a)	L 0-1	Notts County	-	11173	8	4	11	1	3		5		9	6		12		7			10		2					6
7	Sep	24	(h)	D 1-1	PLYMOUTH ARGYLE	Husband	9226		4	11	1	3		5		9	6		8		7			10		2	11				7
8	Sep	27	(h)	D 1-1	BLACKBURN ROVERS	Husband	8458		4	11	1	3		5		9	6		8						7	2	11			10	8
9	Oct	4	(a)	L 2-3	Blackpool	Anderson, Spiring	7864		4	11	1	3	12				6								7	2	11	9		10	9
10	Oct	11	(a)	D 1-1	Carlisle United	Seasman	6621	8	4				10	5			6				12				7	2	11	9	3	10	10
11	Oct	18	(h)	W 1-0	FULHAM	Chambers	14086		4				10	5		9	6								7	2	11	8	3	12	11
12	Oct	21	(a)	D 0-0	Nottingham Forest	-	12290		4				10	5		9	6								7	2	8		3	11	12
13	Oct	25	(a)	L 0-2	Sunderland	-	28338		4	11	1		8	5			6				12				7	2	9		3	10	13
14	Nov	1	(h)	D 0-0	BRISTOL CITY	-	11446	9		11	1		4	5			6				12				8			7	3	10	14
15	Nov	4	(h)	W 4-0	YORK CITY	Husband, West, King, Anderson	7982	9		11	1		4	5			6				8					2			3	10	15
16	Nov	8	(a)	L 1-3	Southampton	John Ryan	13885	9		11	1		4	5			6				8				7	2			3	10	16
17	Nov	15	(h)	L 2-3	OLDHAM ATHLETIC	Husband, Chambers	8237			11	1		4	5	9		6				8				7	2			3	10	17
18	Nov	22	(a)	L 0-2	Fulham	-	9626			11	1		4	5			6				8				7	2	9		3	10	18
19	Nov	29	(h)	W 1-0	ORIENT	Husband	7897			11	1	3	4	5			6				8		9		7	2		12		10	19
20	Dec	3	(a)	W 5-1	Charlton Athletic	Anderson (2), Husband (2), Chambers	8703		8	11	1	3	4	5			6				9				7	2				10	20
21	Dec	6	(h)	W 2-1	WEST BROMWICH ALBION	King, Aston	10203			11	1	3	4	5		9	6				8				7	2	12			10	21
22	Dec	20	(h)	W 2-1	Hull City	Husband, King	5449			11	1	3	4	5		9	6				8				7	2				10	22
23	Dec	26	(h)	W 3-2	OXFORD UNITED	R Futcher (2), King	13101			11	1	3	4	5		9	6				8				7	2				10	23
24	Dec	27	(a)	W 1-0	Bristol Rovers	King	11042			11	1	3	4	5		9	6				8				7	2				10	24
25	Jan	17	(h)	W 3-1	PORTSMOUTH	Faulkner, King, R Futcher	10464			11	1	3	4	5		9	6				8				7	2				10	25
26	Jan	27	(a)	L 0-3	Bolton Wanderers	-	22037			11	1	3	4	5		9	6				8					2	7			10	26
27	Jan	31	(h)	D 1-1	NOTTINGHAM FOREST	R Futcher	8503			11	1	3	4	5		9	6		7		8					2				10	27
28	Feb	7	(a)	W 3-2	York City	Chambers, R Futcher, Fuccillo	3507				1	3	4		7	9	6				8		5	11		2				10	28
29	Feb	21	(a)	D 1-1	Oldham Athletic	Husband	8796		12		1	3	4	5	11		6				8		9			2				10	29
30	Feb	24	(a)	L 0-3	Plymouth Argyle	-	13927				1	3	4	5	9		6				8		12			2				10	30
31	Feb	28	(h)	W 2-0	SUNDERLAND	Moncur (og), R Futcher	15338				1	3	4	5	11	9	6				8					2				10	31
32	Mar	2	(h)	W 1-0	SOUTHAMPTON	Husband	13737				1	3	4	5	11	9	6				8					2				10	32
33	Mar	6	(a)	L 0-3	Bristol City	-	15872		12		1	3	4	5	11	9	6				8					2				10	33
34	Mar	13	(h)	W 3-0	CARLISLE UNITED	Husband (2), King	8856				1	3	4	5	9		6				8					2				10	34
35	Mar	20	(a)	L 0-3	Orient	-	5544				1	3	4	5	9		6				8		12			2				10	35
36	Mar	27	(h)	D 1-1	CHARLTON ATHLETIC	John Ryan	9947				1	3	4	5	9		6				8		5			2				10	36
37	Apr	3	(a)	L 0-3	Blackburn Rovers	-	7911				1	3	12			9	6						4	5		2		8		10	37
38	Apr	10	(h)	D 1-1	NOTTS COUNTY	West	8277				1	3	8	4		9	6							5		2				10	38
39	Apr	16	(a)	D 2-2	Chelsea	Husband, Chambers	19873				1	3	8	4	9		6							5		2				10	39
40	Apr	17	(a)	W 3-1	Oxford United	Buckley, Fuccillo, Husband	7881			11	1	3	8	4	9		6						12	5		2				10	40
41	Apr	19	(h)	W 3-1	BRISTOL ROVERS	Price, Chambers, Hill	7646				1	3	4	5	8	9	6	12						7		2		11		10	41
42	Apr	24	(h)	W 3-0	BLACKPOOL	R Futcher (2), Fuccillo	8757				1	3	4	8	9	6		11				5		7		2				10	42
						Apps		8	17	28	42	33	30	35	14	31	41	1	28	1	30	1	3	8	12	41	6	7	9	36	
						Subs			2				3		1				2		2		3	3			1		1	1	
						Goals		1	5	1		2	6	1	3	10		1	14		9			2	2		1			2	

Final League Position: 7th   1 Own Goal

1975/76 FA CUP

Round	Month	Day	Venue	W.L.D Score	Opponents	Scorers	Attendance	Alston A	Anderson PT	Aston J	Barber K	Buckley S	Chambers BM	Faulkner JG	Fuccillo P	Futcher R	Futcher P	Hill RA	Husband J	Jones G	King AE	Litt SE	Pollock MA	Price PT	Ryan J	Ryan JG	Seasman J	Spring PJ	Thomson RA	West A	Round
3	Jan	3	(h)	W 2-0	BLACKBURN ROVERS	R Futcher, Chambers	11195			11	1	3	4	5		9	6				7	8				2				10	3
4	Jan	24	(a)	L 0-2	Norwich City	-	24328			11	1	3	4	5		9	6				7	8				2				10	4
						Apps				2	2	2	2	2		2	2				2					2				2	
						Subs																									
						Goals							1			1															

1975/76 LEAGUE CUP

Round	Month	Day	Venue	Opponents	W,L,D Score	Scorers	Attendance	Alston A	Anderson PT	Aston J	Barber K	Buckley S	Chambers BM	Faulkner JG	Fuccillo P	Futcher R	Futcher P	Hill RA	Husband J	Jones G	King AE	Litt SE	Pollock MA	Price PT	Ryan J	Ryan JG	Seasman J	Spiring PJ	Thomson RA	West A	Round
2	Sep	9	(a)	Darlington	L 1-2	R Futcher	6601	4	11	1	3	10	5		9	6					7				12	2		8			2
						Apps		1	1	1	1	1	1		1	1					1					1		1			
						Subs																			1						
						Goals									1																

▶ **The 1975/76 team** – Back row (left to right): West, Jim Ryan, Aston, Anderson, Chambers. Second row (left to right): Hindson, R.Futcher, Faulkner, Barber, Horn, Buckley, Price, Game (Physiotherapist). Third row (left to right): Thomson, P.Futcher, McCrohan (Coach), Haslam (Manager), Litt, Alston. Front row (left to right): Spiring, Fuccillo, King, Pollock, Seasman, Husband.

TIMELINE...

December 1975 Severe financial problems necessitate the sale of Peter Anderson to Antwerp for a knockdown £55,000.

1976/77 FOOTBALL LEAGUE DIVISION TWO

Match No	Month	Day	Venue	Opponents	W,L,D Score	Scorers	Attendance	Aleksic MA	Aston J	Barber K	Buckley S	Carr D	Chambers BM	Deans JK	Faulkner JG	Fuccillo P	Futcher R	Futcher P	Geddis D	Hill RA	Husband J	Jones G	Knight A	McNicholl JA	Price PT	Ryan JG	Smith Tim	West A	Match No
1	Aug	21	(h)	SHEFFIELD UNITED	W 2-0	Deans (2)	10687		11	1	3		4	9	5	10		6		8	7				2				1
2	Aug	24	(a)	Hull City	L 1-3	Hill	5499		11	1	3		4	9	5	10		6		8	7				2		12		2
3	Aug	28	(a)	Burnley	W 2-1	Deans, Hill	12262		11	1	3		4	9	5	10		6		8	7				2				3
4	Sep	4	(h)	NOTTINGHAM FOREST	D 1-1	Barrett (og)	11231		11	1	3			9	5	10	12	6		8	7				2			4	4
5	Sep	10	(a)	Charlton Athletic	L 3-4	Deans, Aston, Hill	9191		11	1	3			9	5	10	12	6		8	7				2	4			5
6	Sep	18	(h)	FULHAM	L 0-2	-	19929		11	1	3			9	5	10		6		12	7				2	4		8	6
7	Sep	25	(a)	Wolverhampton Wanderers	W 2-1	Husband, Deans	19826			1	3			9	5	10	11	6			7				2	4		8	7
8	Oct	2	(a)	Plymouth Argyle	L 0-1	-	12187			1	3			9	5	10	11	6		12	7				2	4		8	8
9	Oct	9	(h)	HEREFORD UNITED	W 2-0	Husband, P Futcher	9395			1	3		11		5	10	9	6			7				2	4		8	9
10	Oct	16	(a)	Carlisle United	D 1-1	Husband	6972		12	1	3		11		5	10	9	6		8					2	7		4	10
11	Oct	23	(h)	SOUTHAMPTON	L 1-4	Chambers	12123		11	1	3		4	9	5	10		6			7				2			8	11
12	Oct	30	(a)	Blackburn Rovers	L 0-1	-	8674		11	1	3		4		5	10	9	6			7				2			8	12
13	Nov	6	(h)	BRISTOL ROVERS	W 4-2	R Futcher (2), Aston, Husband	7066		11		3		4		5	10	9	6			7		1		2			8	13
14	Nov	13	(a)	Millwall	L 2-4	West, Buckley (pen)	10380		11	1	3		4	12		10	9	6			7	5			2			8	14
15	Nov	20	(h)	CARDIFF CITY	W 2-1	Deans, R Futcher	8845		11	1	3		4	7		10	9	6				5			2			8	15
16	Nov	27	(a)	Notts County	W 4-0	West, Aston, Husband, Buckley	10009		11	1	3		4	7	5	10	9	6			12				2			8	16
17	Dec	4	(h)	BLACKPOOL	D 0-0	-	9183		11		3		4	7	5	10	9	6					1		2			8	17
18	Dec	21	(a)	Bolton Wanderers	L 1-2	Fuccillo	18463	1			3		4	7	5	10	9	6							2	11		8	18
19	Dec	27	(h)	Orient	L 0-1	-	8354	1			3		4		5	10	9	6			7				2	11		8	19
20	Dec	29	(h)	CHELSEA	W 4-0	Fuccillo, Chambers, Husband, Buckley (pen)	17107	1			3		4		5	10	9	6			7				2	11		8	20
21	Jan	1	(a)	Bristol Rovers	L 0-1	-	7185	1			3		4		5	10	9	6			7				2	11		8	21
22	Jan	22	(a)	Sheffield United	W 3-0	R Futcher, Husband (2)	16257	1	11		3		4		5	10	9	6			7				2			8	22
23	Jan	24	(h)	HULL CITY	W 2-1	Aston, Husband	8455	1	11		3		4		5	10	9	6			7				2			8	23
24	Feb	5	(h)	BURNLEY	W 2-0	Price, Aston	8638	1	11		3		4		5	10	9	6			7				2			8	24
25	Feb	12	(a)	Nottingham Forest	W 2-1	R Futcher, Aston	18225	1	11		3		4		5	10	9	6	12		7				2			8	25
26	Feb	15	(h)	BLACKBURN ROVERS	W 2-0	Geddis, R Futcher	9044	1	11		3		4		5	10	9	6	7						2			8	26
27	Feb	19	(h)	CHARLTON ATHLETIC	W 2-0	R Futcher (2)	11625	1	11		3		4		5	10	9	6			7				2			8	27
28	Feb	26	(a)	Fulham	W 2-1	Aston, Husband	11071	1	11		3		4		5	10	9	6			7				2			8	28
29	Mar	5	(h)	WOLVERHAMPTON WANDERERS	W 2-0	Husband, Fuccillo	19200	1	11		3		4		5	10	9	6	12		7				2			8	29
30	Mar	8	(h)	OLDHAM ATHLETIC	W 1-0	Geddis	12301	1	11		3		4		5	10	9	6	12		7				2			8	30
31	Mar	12	(h)	PLYMOUTH ARGYLE	D 1-1	Aston	12793	1	11		3		4		5	10	9	6			7				2			8	31
32	Mar	19	(a)	Hereford United	W 1-0	R Futcher	6737	1	11		3		4		5	10	9	6			7	12			2			8	32
33	Mar	26	(h)	CARLISLE UNITED	W 5-0	Fuccillo, R Futcher, Husband, West, Aston	11735	1	11		3		4		5	10	9	6			7				2			8	33
34	Apr	2	(a)	Southampton	L 0-1	-	19923	1	11		3		4		5	10	9	6	12		7	8			2				34
35	Apr	9	(a)	Chelsea	L 0-2	-	32911	1	11		3		4		5	10		6	9		7	12			2			8	35
36	Apr	11	(h)	ORIENT	D 0-0	-	11066	1	11		3		4		5	10	12	6	9		7	2						8	36
37	Apr	12	(h)	MILLWALL	L 1-2	Fuccillo	10459	1	11		3		4		5	10	9	6	7						2			8	37
38	Apr	16	(a)	Cardiff City	L 2-4	R Futcher, Chambers	10438	1	11		3		4		5	10	9	6	7	12					2			8	38
39	Apr	23	(h)	NOTTS COUNTY	W 4-2	R Futcher (2), Hill, Geddis	9585	1	11		3		4		5	10	9	6	7	8					2				39
40	Apr	30	(a)	Blackpool	L 0-1	-	9257	1	11		3		4		5	10	9	6	7	8	12				2				40
41	May	7	(h)	BOLTON WANDERERS	D 1-1	Geddis	11164	1	11		3		4		5	10			9	8	7			6	2				41
42	May	14	(a)	Oldham Athletic	W 2-1	Fuccillo, Aston	7231	1	11		3	9	4		5	10			8	7	12			6	2				42
				Final League Position: 6th		1 Own Goal	Apps	25	34	15	42	1	37	13	40	42	30	40	9	9	33	4	2	2	41	10	-	33	
							Subs	-	1	-	-	-	-	1	-	-	-	-	3	4	-	2	3	3	-	-	1	-	
							Goals	-	10	-	-	-	3	6	-	6	13	-	4	4	12	-	-	-	1	-	-	3	

1976/77 FA CUP

Round	Month	Day	Venue	Opponents	W,L,D Score	Scorers	Attendance	Aleksic MA	Aston J	Barber K	Buckley S	Carr D	Chambers BM	Deans JK	Faulkner JG	Fuccillo P	Futcher R	Futcher P	Geddis D	Hill RA	Husband J	Jones G	Knight A	McNicholl JA	Price PT	Ryan JG	Smith Tim	West A	Round
3	Jan	8	(a)	Halifax Town	W 1-0	Aston	5519	1	11		3		4		5	10	9	6			7				2			8	3
4	Jan	29	(a)	Chester	L 0-1	-	10608	1	11		3		4		5	10	9	6			7				2			8	4
							Apps	2	2	-	2	-	2	-	2	2	2	2	-	-	2	-	-	-	2	-	0	2	
							Subs	-	-	-	-	-	-	-	-	-	-	-	-	-	-	-	-	-	-	-	-	-	
							Goals	-	1	-	-	-	-	-	-	-	-	-	-	-	-	-	-	-	-	-	-	-	

1976/77 LEAGUE CUP

Round	Month	Day	Venue	Opponents	W.L.D Score	Scorers	Attendance	Aleksic MA	Aston J	Barber K	Buckley S	Carr D	Chambers BM	Deans JK	Faulkner JG	Fuccillo P	Futcher R	Futcher P	Geddis D	Hill RA	Husband J	Jones G	Knight A	McNicholl JA	Price PT	Ryan JG	Smith Tim	West A	Round
2	Aug	31	(a)	Sunderland	L 1-3	Husband	22390	11	1	3		4	9	5	10		6		7		8				2	12			2
						Apps		1	1	1		1	1	1	1		1		1		1				1				
						Subs																				1			
						Goals															1								

▶ **The 1976/77 team** – Back row (left to right): Gregory, Buckley, Smith, Wassell, Deans, Hill, Simon. Second row (left to right): Jones, P.Futcher, Faulkner, Knight, Barber, John Ryan, Price, McNichol, Game (Physiotherapist). Front row (left to right): Fuccillo, Chambers, Carr, McCrohan (Coach), Haslam (Manager), Husband, Aston, Mead.

TIMELINE...

2 April 1977 The Town's run of 12 games without defeat, including 11 wins, ends with a 0-1 reversal at Southampton.

1977/78 FOOTBALL LEAGUE DIVISION TWO

Match No	Month	Day	Venue	Opponents	W,L,D Score	Scorers	Attendance	Aleksic MA	Aston J	Boersma P	Buckley S	Carr D	Faulkner JG	Fuccillo P	Futcher R	Futcher P	Heale GJ	Hill RA	Husband J	Ingram GRA	Jones G	Knight A	McNicholl JA	Price PT	Smith Tim	Sperrin MR	Stein B	West A	Match No
1	Aug	20	(h)	ORIENT	W 1-0	Buckley	8061	1	11	9	3	4	5	10		6		12	7					2	8				1
2	Aug	27	(a)	Oldham Athletic	L 0-1	-	7553	1	11		3	4	5	10		6		8	7					2				9	2
3	Sep	3	(h)	CHARLTON ATHLETIC	W 7-1	Husband (4, 1 pen), Buckley, Hill, Heale	9061	1			3		5	4	9	6	11	8	7					2				10	3
4	Sep	10	(a)	Bristol Rovers	W 2-1	Boersma, Buckley	5836	1		11	3	12	5	4	9	6		8	7					2				10	4
5	Sep	17	(h)	BLACKBURN ROVERS	D 0-0	-	9149	1		10	3	11	5	4	9	6		8	7					2					5
6	Sep	24	(a)	Tottenham Hotspur	L 0-2	-	32814	1		10	3	11	5	4	9	6		8	7					2					6
7	Sep	27	(a)	Brighton & Hove Albion	L 2-3	R Futcher, Husband	25199	1		11	3	4	5	10	9	6		8	7					2					7
8	Oct	1	(h)	NOTTS COUNTY	W 2-0	Fuccillo, Boersma	7593	1		11	3		5	10	9	6		8	7					2				4	8
9	Oct	4	(h)	MILLWALL	W 1-0	Price	9119	1		11	3	12	5	10	9	6		8	7					2				4	9
10	Oct	8	(a)	Cardiff City	W 4-1	Byrne (og), Fuccillo, R Futcher, Hill	8726	1		11	3		5	10	9	6	7	8						2				4	10
11	Oct	15	(h)	FULHAM	W 1-0	Faulkner	12736	1		11	3		5	10	9	6		8	7					2				4	11
12	Oct	22	(a)	Blackpool	L 1-2	Husband	12167	1		11	3		5	10	9	6		8	7					2				4	12
13	Oct	29	(a)	Bolton Wanderers	L 1-2	R Futcher	21973	1			3		5	10	9	6	11	8	7					2				4	13
14	Nov	5	(h)	HULL CITY	D 1-1	Husband	8936	1			3		5	10	9	6	11	8	7					2				4	14
15	Nov	12	(a)	Mansfield Town	L 1-3	Hill	7519	1			3		5	10	9			8	7				6	2			12	4	15
16	Nov	19	(h)	STOKE CITY	L 1-2	Buckley	9384	1			3		5	10	9		11	8	7				6	2			12	4	16
17	Nov	26	(a)	Sunderland	D 1-1	R Futcher	26915	1			3	11	5	10	9			8	7				6	2				4	17
18	Dec	3	(h)	BURNLEY	L 1-2	Hill	6921	1		11	3		5	10	9			8	7				6	2				4	18
19	Dec	10	(a)	Southampton	W 1-0	R Futcher	19907	1		11	3		5	10	9			8	7		6			2				4	19
20	Dec	17	(h)	MANSFIELD TOWN	D 1-1	R Futcher	6401	1		11	3		5	10	9			8	7		6			2			12	4	20
21	Dec	26	(a)	Crystal Palace	D 3-3	Price, Boersma, R Futcher	22405	1		11	3		5	10	9			8			6			2			7	4	21
22	Dec	27	(h)	SHEFFIELD UNITED	W 4-0	R Futcher, Fuccillo (pen), Stein (2)	10885	1		11	3	5		10	9			8			6			2			7	4	22
23	Dec	31	(h)	BRIGHTON & HOVE ALBION	W 1-0	Boersma	13200	1		11	3	5		10	9			8			6			2			7	4	23
24	Jan	2	(a)	Orient	D 0-0	-	9270	1		11	3	5		10	9			8			6			2			7	4	24
25	Jan	14	(h)	OLDHAM ATHLETIC	L 0-1	-	7792	1		11	3		5	10	9			4	7	12	6			2				8	25
26	Jan	21	(a)	Charlton Athletic	D 0-0	-	8267	1		11	3		5	10	9	6		4	7		8			2					26
27	Feb	8	(h)	BRISTOL ROVERS	D 1-1	R Futcher	5913	1		11	3		5	10	9	6		12			8			2			7	4	27
28	Feb	11	(a)	Blackburn Rovers	L 0-2	-	11511	1		11	3		5	10	9	6		8	7					2			12	4	28
29	Feb	22	(h)	TOTTENHAM HOTSPUR	L 1-4	West	17024	1		11	3		5	7	9	6		4			10			2			12	8	29
30	Feb	25	(a)	Notts County	L 0-2	-	8558	1		11	3		5	7	9	6		4			10			2			12	8	30
31	Mar	4	(h)	CARDIFF CITY	W 3-1	Boersma (2), Faulkner	6029	1		11	3		5	10	9	6		4						2			7	8	31
32	Mar	10	(a)	Fulham	L 0-1	-	7796	1		11	3		5	10	9	6		12						2			7	8	32
33	Mar	18	(a)	BLACKPOOL	W 4-0	West, R Futcher, Boersma, Fuccillo	6041	1		11	3		5	10	9	6		4						2			7	8	33
34	Mar	21	(h)	BOLTON WANDERERS	W 2-1	West, Boersma	8306	1		11	3		5	10	9	6		4						2			7	8	34
35	Mar	25	(a)	Sheffield United	L 1-4	Calvert (og)	12587			11	3			10	9	6		4			5	1	12	2			7	8	35
36	Mar	27	(h)	CRYSTAL PALACE	W 1-0	Fuccillo (pen)	9816			11	3			10	9	6		4			5	1	4	2			7	8	36
37	Apr	1	(a)	Hull City	D 1-1	West	4054			11	3			10	9	6		4			2	1	5				7	8	37
38	Apr	8	(h)	SUNDERLAND	L 1-3	Stein	7616			11	3			10	9	6		4				1	5	2		12	7	8	38
39	Apr	15	(a)	Stoke City	D 0-0	-	15546	1		11	3			10	9	6		4			5			2			7	8	39
40	Apr	22	(h)	SOUTHAMPTON	L 1-2	Hill	14302	1		11		3		10	9	6		4		12	5			2			7	8	40
41	Apr	25	(a)	Millwall	L 0-1	-	7593	1		11				10	9	6		4		12	3		5	2			7	8	41
42	Apr	29	(a)	Burnley	L 1-2	Ingram	11648	1		12				10		6	11	4		9	3		5	2			7	8	42
				Final League Position: 13th		**2 Own Goals**	**Apps**	38	2	34	24	25	31	42	39	31	7	37	22	1	19	4	11	40	1	-	18	36	
							Subs		1			2								3	2		1		1	1	6		
							Goals			8	4		2	5	10		1	5	7	1				2			3	4	

1977/78 FA CUP

Round	Month	Day	Venue	Opponents	W,L,D Score	Scorers	Attendance	Aleksic MA	Aston J	Boersma P	Buckley S	Carr D	Faulkner JG	Fuccillo P	Futcher R	Futcher P	Heale GJ	Hill RA	Husband J	Ingram GRA	Jones G	Knight A	McNicholl JA	Price PT	Smith Tim	Sperrin MR	Stein B	West A	Round
3	Jan	7	(h)	OLDHAM ATHLETIC	D 1-1	Fuccillo	9851	1		11	3		5	10	9			8	7		12		6	2			4		3
Rep	Jan	10	(a)	Oldham Athletic	W 2-1	Boersma (2)	13802	1		11	3		5	10	9			4	7		8		6	2					Rep
4	Jan	31	(a)	Millwall	L 0-4	-	8763			11	3		5	10	9	6		4	7		8	1		2					4
							Apps	2		3	3		3	3	3	1		3	3		2	1	2	3			1		
							Subs														1								
							Goals			2				1															

1977/78 LEAGUE CUP

Round	Month	Day	Venue	Opponents	W,L,D	Score	Scorers	Attendance	Aleksic MA	Aston J	Boersma P	Buckley S	Carr D	Faulkner JG	Fuccillo P	Futcher R	Futcher P	Heale GJ	Hill RA	Husband J	Ingram GRA	Jones G	Knight A	McNicholl JA	Price PT	Smith Tim	Sperrin MR	Stein B	West A	Round
2	Aug	30	(a)	Wolverhampton Wanderers	W	3-1	Husband, Boersma, Carr	14682	1		9	3	12	5	4	11			8	7				6	2				10	2
3	Oct	25	(h)	MANCHESTER CITY	D	1-1	R Futcher	16443	1			3		5	10	9	6	11	8	7					2				4	3
Rep	Nov	1	(a)	Manchester City	D	0-0	-	28254	1			3		5	10	9	6	11	8	7					2				4	Rep
Rep 2	Nov	9	(n)	Manchester City	L	2-3	Heale (2)	14043	1			3		5	10	9		11	8					6	2	12	7		4	Rep 2
							Apps		4		1	4		4	4	4	2	3	4	3				2	4		1		4	
							Subs						1													1				
							Goals				1		1			1		2		1										

3rd Round 2nd Replay played at Old Trafford

▶ **The 1977/78 team** – Back row (left to right): Game (Physiotherapist), Carr, Jones, McNichol, Faulkner, Aleksic, Knight, P.Futcher, Price, Buckley, McCrohan (Coach). Front row (left to right): Hill, Husband, Smith, Boersma, Haslam (Manager), West, R.Futcher, Fuccillo, Heale.

TIMELINE...

23 January 1978 Harry Haslam resigns to take up the managerial position at Sheffield United.
24 January 1978 David Pleat takes over as manager.

Match No	Month	Day	Venue	Opponents	W,L,D Score	Scorers	Attendance	Aizlewood M	Aleksic MA	Birchenall AJ	Boersma P	Carr D	Donaghy Mal	Findlay JW	Fuccillo P	Hatton RJ	Heale GJ	Hill RA	Ingram GRA	Jones G	Lawson D	McNicholl JA	Moss DJ	Philipson-Masters F	Price PT	Sherlock SE	Silkman B	Stein B	Stephens KW	Taylor SJ	Turner CJ	Turner WL	West A	Match No
1	Aug	19	(h)	OLDHAM ATHLETIC	W 6-1	Hatton (2), Moss (2), Stein, Fuccillo (pen)	8043	6	1				9		8	10		4					11			3		7	2		5			1
2	Aug	22	(a)	Crystal Palace	L 1-3	Fuccillo (pen)	17880	6	1				4		8	10		7	12				11			3		9	2		5			2
3	Aug	26	(a)	Newcastle United	L 0-1	-	24112	3	1				4			10		7				12	11		6			9	2				8	3
4	Sep	2	(h)	CHARLTON ATHLETIC	W 3-0	Hatton, Stein, Hill	8509	3	1	11			7		8	10		4		2					6			9			5		12	4
5	Sep	9	(a)	Bristol Rovers	L 0-2	-	6505	3	1				7		8			4	10	2			11		6			9			5		12	5
6	Sep	16	(h)	CARDIFF CITY	W 7-1	Moss (2), Hatton, Stein (2), Fuccillo(pen), Dwyer (og)	7752	3	1				7		12	10		4		2			11		6			9			5		8	6
7	Sep	23	(h)	CAMBRIDGE UNITED	D 1-1	Stein	10801	3	1				7		12	10		4		2			11		6			9			5		8	7
8	Sep	30	(a)	Sheffield United	D 1-1	Hatton	15295	3	1				6		7	10		4					11		2			9			5		8	8
9	Oct	7	(h)	WREXHAM	W 2-1	Stein, Fuccillo	8683	3	1				6		8	10		4		12			11		2			9			5		7	9
10	Oct	14	(a)	Blackburn Rovers	D 0-0	-	7450	3	1				6		8	10		4					11		2			9			5		7	10
11	Oct	21	(h)	NOTTS COUNTY	W 6-0	Hatton, Stein (2), West, Moss, Fuccillo(pen)	8561	3	1				6		8	10		4		12			11		2			9			5		7	11
12	Oct	28	(a)	Orient	L 2-3	Fuccillo (2)	7035	3	1				2		8	10		4					11		6			9			5		7	12
13	Nov	4	(h)	LEICESTER CITY	L 0-1	-	10608	3	1			12	2		8	10		4					11		6			9			5		7	13
14	Nov	11	(a)	Oldham Athletic	L 0-2	-	6876	3	1				6		8	10		4					11		2			9	12		5		7	14
15	Nov	18	(h)	NEWCASTLE UNITED	W 2-0	Stein, Turner	10434	3				4	6		8							1	11		2			9			5		7	15
16	Nov	21	(h)	Charlton Athletic	W 2-1	Moss, Hatton	10191	3				4	6		8							1	11		2			9			5		7	16
17	Nov	25	(h)	SUNDERLAND	L 0-3	-	10249	3					6		8			4			5	1	11		2			9					7	17
18	Dec	9	(h)	PRESTON NORTH END	L 1-2	Price	7036	3					6	1	8			4					11		2			9			5		7	18
19	Dec	16	(a)	Brighton & Hove Albion	L 1-3	Moss	16216	3				4	6	1	8				9				11		2			12			5		7	19
20	Dec	26	(a)	Millwall	W 2-0	Moss (2)	6041	3				4	6	1		10		8		12			11		2			9			5		7	20
21	Dec	30	(a)	Fulham	L 0-1	-	8984	3				4	6	1		10		8		12			11		2			9			5		7	21
22	Jan	16	(h)	BRISTOL ROVERS	W 3-2	Moss, Price, Hill	6002	3					6	1		10		8		4			11		5			12	2		9		7	22
23	Feb	3	(a)	Cambridge United	D 0-0	-	8125	3					4	1		10		8					11		5				2	9			7	23
24	Feb	6	(a)	STOKE CITY	D 0-0	-	6462					3	4	1		10		8					11		6				2	9	5		7	24
25	Feb	10	(h)	SHEFFIELD UNITED	D 1-1	Turner	7025	3					4	1		10		8					11		6			9	2	12	5		7	25
26	Feb	24	(h)	BLACKBURN ROVERS	W 2-1	West, Turner	6247	3					8			10		7							6		11	9	2	12	5		4	26
27	Feb	26	(h)	WEST HAM UNITED	L 1-4	Turner	14205	3					8			10		11							6		7	9	2		5		4	27
28	Mar	3	(a)	Notts County	L 1-3	Hatton	7624	3					8	1		10		4							6		11	9	2		5		7	28
29	Mar	10	(h)	ORIENT	W 2-1	Turner, Hill	6003	3					8	1		10		6									11	9	2	12	5		7	29
30	Mar	13	(a)	Burnley	L 1-2	Hatton	7691	3					8	1		10		6									11	9	2		5		7	30
31	Mar	24	(h)	CRYSTAL PALACE	L 0-1	-	11008	8				6	4	1		10		7					11		3				2		9		12	31
32	Mar	28	(a)	Leicester City	L 0-3	-	10464		8				4	1				7					11		3				2		9		12	32
33	Mar	31	(a)	Sunderland	L 0-1	-	23358		6			12	4	1		10		7				5	11		3				2		9			33
34	Apr	7	(h)	BURNLEY	W 4-1	Hatton (2), Stein, Taylor	6466	3				6	4	1		10		7					11	5				9	2		12		8	34
35	Apr	9	(a)	West Ham United	L 0-1	-	25398	3				6	4	1		10		7					11	5				9	2		12		8	35
36	Apr	14	(h)	MILLWALL	D 2-2	Moss (2, 1 pen)	8292	3		11			4	1		10		7						5				9	2		12		8	36
37	Apr	16	(a)	Stoke City	D 0-0	-	19214	3		11			4	1		10		7						5	6				2		9		8	37
38	Apr	21	(h)	BRIGHTON & HOVE ALBION	D 1-1	Williams (og)	13132	3		6			4	1		10		7						5					2		9		8	38
39	Apr	25	(a)	Cardiff City	L 1-2	Roberts (og)	10522	3		11			4	1		10		7						5	6				2		9		8	39
40	Apr	28	(a)	Preston North End	D 2-2	Haslegrove (og), Moss	8946	3		11			4	1		10		7							12				2		9		8	40
41	May	5	(h)	FULHAM	W 2-0	Beck (og), West	9122	3					4	1		10		7					11	5				9	2		6		8	41
42	May	7	(a)	Wrexham	L 0-2	-	7842	3					4	1		10		7						5	6			12	2		9	11	8	42
				Final League Position: 18th		5 Own Goals	Apps	39	14	8	1	13	40	23	16	41	-	38	2	6	5	-	29	10	34	2	3	31	24	15	30	1	37	
							Subs	-	-	-	-	-	2	-	-	-	2	-	1	4	-	1	1	-	-	-	-	3	1	5	-	3	-	
							Goals	-	-	-	-	-	-	-	7	11	-	3	-	-	-	-	13	-	2	-	-	10	-	1	5	-	3	

1978/79 FA CUP

Round	Month	Day	Venue	Opponents	W,L,D Score	Scorers	Attendance	Aizlewood M	Aleksic MA	Birchenall AJ	Boersma P	Carr D	Donaghy Mal	Findlay JW	Fuccillo P	Hatton RJ	Heale GJ	Hill RA	Ingram GRA	Jones G	Lawson D	McNicholl JA	Moss DJ	Philipson-Masters F	Price PT	Sherlock SE	Silkman B	Stein B	Stephens KW	Taylor SJ	Turner CJ	Turner WL	West A	Round
3	Jan	9	(a)	York City	L 0-2	-	6700	3				4	6	1		10	12	8		2						5	11	9					7	3
							Apps	1	-	-	-	1	1	1	-	1	-	1	-	1	-	-	-	-	-	1	1	1	-	-	-	-	1	
							Subs	-	-	-	-	-	-	-	-	-	1	-	-	-	-	-	-	-	-	-	-	-	-	-	-	-	-	
							Goals	-	-	-	-	-	-	-	-	-	-	-	-	-	-	-	-	-	-	-	-	-	-	-	-	-	-	

1978/79 LEAGUE CUP

Round	Month	Day	Venue	Opponents	W.L.D Score	Scorers	Attendance	Aizlewood M	Aleksic MA	Birchenall AJ	Boersma P	Carr D	Donaghy Mal	Findlay JW	Fuccillo P	Hatton RJ	Heale GJ	Hill RA	Ingram GRA	Jones G	Lawson D	McNicholl JA	Moss DJ	Philipson-Masters F	Price PT	Sherlock SE	Silkman B	Stein B	Stephens KW	Taylor SJ	Turner CJ	Turner WL	West A	Round
2	Aug	29	(h)	WIGAN ATHLETIC	W 2-0	Stein (2)	6618	3	1				4		8	10							11		6			9	2		5		7	2
3	Oct	3	(h)	CREWE ALEXANDRA	W 2-1	Hill, Hatton	6602	3	1				6		8	10		4					11		2			9			5		7	3
4	Nov	8	(a)	Aston Villa	W 2-0	Hatton, Stein	32737	3	1				6		8	10		4					11		2			9			5		7	4
5	Dec	13	(a)	Leeds United	L 1-4	Stein	28177	3					6	1	8	10		4					11		2			9			5		7	5
						Apps		4	3	.	.	.	4	1	4	4	.	3	.	.	.	.	4	.	4	.	.	4	1	.	4	.	4	
						Subs		.	.	.	.	.	.	.	.	.	.	.	.	.	.	.	.	.	.	.	.	.	.	.	.	.	.	
						Goals		.	.	.	.	.	.	.	.	2	.	1	.	.	.	.	.	.	.	.	.	4	.	.	.	.	.	

▶ The 1978/79 team – Back row (left to right): Ingram, Stephens, Stein, Moss, Carr, Sherlock. Middle row (left to right): Aizlewood, McNichol, Jones, Aleksic, Turner, Price, Donaghy. Front row (left to right): Gutteridge (Coach), Fuccillo, West, Hatton, Pleat (Manager), Hill, Boersma, Johnson (Physiotherapist).

TIMELINE...

19 August 1978 Seven players make their Luton debut in the opening day 6-1 home win over Oldham.

1979/80 FOOTBALL LEAGUE DIVISION TWO

Match No	Month	Day	Venue	Opponents	W,L,D	Score	Scorers	Attendance	Aizlewood M	Birchenall AJ	Donaghy Mal	Findlay JW	Goodyear C	Grealish AP	Hatton RJ	Hill RA	Ingram GRA	Jones G	Judge AG	Madden N	Moss DJ	Pearson AJ	Price PT	Saxby MW	Stein B	Stephens KW	Turner WL	West A	White SJ	Match No
1	Aug	18	(h)	CAMBRIDGE UNITED	D	1-1	Moss	8202	5	8	1			4	10	7					11		6		9	2	3			1
2	Aug	21	(a)	Bristol Rovers	L	2-3	Moss (2, 1 pen)	5621	12	8	1			4	10	7					11		6	5	9	2	3			2
3	Aug	25	(h)	ORIENT	W	2-1	Hatton, Hill	6705			3	1		4	10	7					11		6	5	9	2		8		3
4	Sep	1	(a)	Leicester City	W	3-1	Moss (2, 1 pen), Hill	16241			3	1		4	10	7					11		6	5	9	2		8		4
5	Sep	8	(h)	SWANSEA CITY	W	5-0	Moss (2, 1 pen), Hatton, West, Hill	10004			3	1		4	10	7					11		6	5	9	2		8		5
6	Sep	15	(a)	Notts County	D	0-0	-	9582			3	1		4	10	7					11		6	5	9	2		8		6
7	Sep	22	(h)	OLDHAM ATHLETIC	D	0-0	-	8711	12		3	1		4	10	7					11		6	5	9	2		8		7
8	Sep	29	(a)	Fulham	W	3-1	Moss (pen), Hill, Hatton	9944			3	1		4	10	7					11		6	5	9	2		8		8
9	Oct	6	(a)	Cardiff City	L	1-2	Hatton	9402			3	1		4	10	7					11		6	5	9	2		8		9
10	Oct	9	(h)	BRISTOL ROVERS	W	3-1	Hatton (3)	8507	12		3	1		4	10	7					11		6	5	9	2		8		10
11	Oct	13	(h)	SUNDERLAND	W	2-0	Moss (2)	13504			3	1		4	10	7					11		6	5	9	2		8		11
12	Oct	20	(a)	West Ham United	W	2-1	Stein, Saxby	25049			3	1		4	7		10				11		6	5	9	2		8		12
13	Oct	27	(h)	PRESTON NORTH END	D	1-1	Moss (pen)	11648			3	1		4	10	7					11		6	5	9	2		8		13
14	Nov	3	(a)	Cambridge United	W	2-1	Hatton, Moss (pen)	8104			3	1		4	10	7					11		6	5	9	2		8		14
15	Nov	10	(h)	QUEENS PARK RANGERS	D	1-1	Saxby	19619			3	1		4	10	7					11		6	5	9	2		8		15
16	Nov	17	(a)	Burnley	D	0-0	-	7119			3	1		4	10	7					11		6	5	9	2		8		16
17	Nov	24	(h)	BIRMINGHAM CITY	L	2-3	Moss (pen), Stein	13720			3	1		4	10	7					11		6	5	9	2		8		17
18	Dec	1	(a)	Shrewsbury Town	W	2-1	Stein, Hatton	8565			3	1		4	10	7					11		6	5	9	2		8		18
19	Dec	8	(h)	NEWCASTLE UNITED	D	1-1	Moss	14845			3	1		4	10	7					11		6	5	9	2		8		19
20	Dec	15	(a)	Wrexham	L	1-3	Hatton	9145	12		3	1		4	10	7					11		6	5	9	2		8		20
21	Dec	21	(h)	CHARLTON ATHLETIC	W	3-0	Stein (2), Hatton	7277			3	1		4	10	7					11		6	5	9	2		8		21
22	Dec	26	(h)	Watford	W	1-0	Stephens	20187			3	1		4	10	7					11		6	5	9	2		8		22
23	Dec	29	(a)	Orient	D	2-2	Moss (2, 1 pen)	9292			3	1		4	10	7					11		6	5	9	2		8	12	23
24	Jan	1	(h)	CHELSEA	D	3-3	Donaghy, Saxby, Moss	19717	4		3	1			10	7					11		6	5	9	2		8		24
25	Jan	12	(h)	LEICESTER CITY	D	0-0	-	14141			3	1		4	10	7					11		6	5	9	2		8		25
26	Feb	2	(h)	NOTTS COUNTY	W	2-1	Saxby, Hatton	9007			3	1		4	10	7					11		6	5	9	2		8	12	26
27	Feb	9	(a)	Oldham Athletic	L	1-2	Moss	7555			3	1		4	10	7					11		6	5	9	2		8	12	27
28	Feb	16	(h)	FULHAM	W	4-0	Moss (3), Stein	9179	2		3	1		4	10	7					11		6	5	9			8		28
29	Feb	23	(a)	Sunderland	L	0-1	-	25387			3	1		4	10	7					11		6	5	9	2		8		29
30	Mar	1	(h)	WEST HAM UNITED	D	1-1	Hill	20040			3	1		4	10	7					11		6	5	9	2		8	12	30
31	Mar	4	(a)	Swansea City	L	0-2	-	12775			3	1		4	10	7					11		6	5	9	2		8		31
32	Mar	8	(a)	Preston North End	D	1-1	Hatton	8203	7		3	1		4	12						11		6	5	9	2		8	10	32
33	Mar	14	(h)	CARDIFF CITY	L	1-2	Moss	9246			3	1		4	10	7					11		6	5	9	2		8	12	33
34	Mar	22	(a)	Queens Park Rangers	D	2-2	Stein, Hill	15054	5		3	1		4	10	7		2				12	6		9			8	11	34
35	Mar	29	(h)	BURNLEY	D	1-1	Hatton	8507			3	1		4	10	7						11	6	5	9	2		8		35
36	Apr	4	(a)	Charlton Athletic	W	4-1	Moss (pen), Grealish, West, Hatton	8971			3	1		4	10	7					11		6	5	9	2		8		36
37	Apr	5	(h)	WATFORD	W	1-0	Hatton	12783	12		3	1		4	10	7					11		6	5	9	2		8		37
38	Apr	7	(a)	Chelsea	D	1-1	Grealish	28460	12		3	1		4	10	7					11		6	5	9	2		8		38
39	Apr	12	(h)	SHREWSBURY TOWN	D	0-0	-	10793			3	1		4	10	7					11		6	5	9	2		8	12	39
40	Apr	19	(a)	Birmingham City	L	0-1	-	23662			3	1		4	10	7					11		6	5	9	2		8	12	40
41	Apr	26	(h)	WREXHAM	W	2-0	Moss, Stein	9049			3	1	5	4	10	7				8	11		6		9	2				41
42	May	3	(a)	Newcastle United	D	2-2	Hatton (2)	13765	7		3			4	10				1		11		6	5	9	2		8		42
				Final League Position: 6th				Apps	5	1	42	41	1	41	40	40	1	1	1	1	40	1	42	39	42	40	2	39	2	
								Subs	5	1	-	-	-	1	-	-	-	-	-	-	-	1	-	-	-	-	-	-	7	
								Goals	-	-	1	-	-	2	18	6	-	-	-	-	24	-	-	4	8	1	-	2	-	

1979/80 FA CUP

Round	Month	Day	Venue	Opponents	W,L,D	Score	Scorers	Attendance	Aizlewood M	Birchenall AJ	Donaghy Mal	Findlay JW	Goodyear C	Grealish AP	Hatton RJ	Hill RA	Ingram GRA	Jones G	Judge AG	Madden N	Moss DJ	Pearson AJ	Price PT	Saxby MW	Stein B	Stephens KW	Turner WL	West A	White SJ	Round
3	Jan	5	(h)	SWINDON TOWN	L	0-2	-	12458			3	1		4	10	7					11		6	5	9	2		8	12	3
								Apps	-	-	1	1	-	1	1	1	-	-	-	-	1	-	1	1	1	1	-	1	-	
								Subs	-	-	-	-	-	-	-	-	-	-	-	-	-	-	-	-	-	-	-	-	1	
								Goals	-	-	-	-	-	-	-	-	-	-	-	-	-	-	-	-	-	-	-	-	-	

1979/80 LEAGUE CUP

Round	Month	Day	Venue	Opponents	W,L,D Score	Scorers	Attendance	Aizlewood M	Birchenall AJ	Donaghy Mal	Findlay JW	Goodyear C	Grealish AP	Hatton RJ	Hill RA	Ingram GRA	Jones G	Judge AG	Madden N	Moss DJ	Pearson AJ	Price PT	Saxby MW	Stein B	Stephens KW	Turner WL	West A	White SJ	Round
1:1	Aug	11	(a)	Gillingham	L 0-3	-	6222	3		8	1		4	10	7					11		6	5	9	2				1:1
1:2	Aug	14	(h)	GILLINGHAM	D 1-1	Aizlewood	5509	3		8	1		4	10	7					11		6	5	9	2				1:2
						Apps		2	.	2	2	.	2	2	2	.	.	.	.	2	.	2	2	2	2	.	.	.	
						Subs		-	-	-	-	-	-	-	-	-	-	-	-	-	-	-	-	-	-	-	-	-	
						Goals		1	-	-	-	-	-	-	-	-	-	-	-	-	-	-	-	-	-	-	-	-	

▶ The 1979/80 team – Back row (left to right): Pearson, Heath, Harriott, Heale, Goodyear, Turner, Sisman, Ollis. Second row (left to right): Coates (Trainer), Donaghy, Aizlewood, Findlay, Jones, Judge, Stephens, Stein, Moore (Coach). Third row (left to right): Fuccillo, Hill, Saxby, Gutteridge (Coach), Pleat (Manager), Smith (Chief Executive), Hatton, Price, Birchenall, Moss. Front row (left to right): Cosby, Johnson, Piotrowski, Murphy, Bunn, Walker, Conquest, Cole, Woodward, Madden, Brammer.

TIMELINE...

3 May 1980 David Pleat's team takes shape with a sixth place finish.

1980/81 FOOTBALL LEAGUE DIVISION TWO

Match No	Month	Day	Venue	Opponents	W,L,D Score	Scorers	Attendance	Aizlewood M	Antic R	Bunn FS	Donaghy Mal	Findlay JW	Fuccillo P	Goodyear C	Grealish AP	Harrow A	Heath SJMP	Hill RA	Ingram GRA	Judge AG	Moss DJ	Price PT	Saxby MW	Smith WH	Stein B	Stephens KW	Turner WL	West A	White SJ	Match No
1	Aug	16	(a)	West Ham United	W 2-1	Moss (2 pens)	28033		10		3	1			4			7			11	6	5		8	2		12	9	1
2	Aug	19	(h)	WATFORD	W 1-0	White	13887		10		3	1			4			7			11	6	5		8	2		12	9	2
3	Aug	23	(h)	DERBY COUNTY	L 1-2	Stein	11025	12	10	9	3	1			4			7			11	6	5		8	2			9	3
4	Aug	30	(a)	Newcastle United	L 1-2	Stein	13175	12	10	9	3	1			4			7			11	6	5		8				9	4
5	Sep	6	(h)	WREXHAM	D 1-1	Bunn	8244		10	9	3	1			4			7			11	6	5		8	2		12		5
6	Sep	13	(a)	Blackburn Rovers	L 0-3	-	9076				3	1			4			7	9		11	6	5		8	2		10	12	6
7	Sep	20	(h)	ORIENT	W 2-1	Stein, Hill	8506		10		3	1			4			7			11	6	5		8	2		9		7
8	Sep	27	(a)	Grimsby Town	D 0-0	-	9044	2	10		3	1			4	12		7			11	6	5		8			9		8
9	Oct	4	(h)	NOTTS COUNTY	L 0-1	-	8786	12			3	1			4	9		7			11	6	5		8	2		10		9
10	Oct	7	(a)	Bristol City	L 1-2	Saxby	7571				3	1			4	9		7			11	6	5		8	2		10		10
11	Oct	11	(a)	Preston North End	L 0-1	-	5637	12			3	1			4	9		7				6	5		8	2		10	11	11
12	Oct	18	(h)	SHREWSBURY TOWN	D 1-1	White	8014		10		3	1		5	4			7			11	6			8	2			9	12
13	Oct	21	(h)	SWANSEA CITY	D 2-2	Stein, Moss	8402		10		3	1		5	4			7			11	6			8	2			9	13
14	Oct	25	(a)	Cambridge United	W 3-1	Moss (pen), Goodyear, Stein	7218		10	12	3	1		5	4			7			11				8	2			9	14
15	Nov	1	(h)	SHEFFIELD WEDNESDAY	W 3-0	Moss (2, 1 pen), White	12092		10		3			5	4			7		1	11	6			8	2			9	15
16	Nov	8	(a)	Queens Park Rangers	L 2-3	Stein, Moss	10082		10		3			5	4			7		1	11	6			8	2			9	16
17	Nov	11	(a)	Watford	W 1-0	White	16993	10			3	1			4			7			11	6	5		8	2		12	9	17
18	Nov	15	(h)	WEST HAM UNITED	W 3-2	Stein (2), Moss	17031	10			3	1			4			7			11	6	5		8	2		12	9	18
19	Nov	22	(a)	Cardiff City	L 0-1	-	6041				3	1			4			7			11	6	5		8	2		12	9	19
20	Nov	29	(h)	BOLTON WANDERERS	D 2-2	Hill, Stein	8302	10			3	1			4			7			11	6	5		8	2		12		20
21	Dec	6	(a)	Oldham Athletic	D 0-0	-	4854	10			3	1			4			7			11	6	5		8	2		12		21
22	Dec	13	(h)	PRESTON NORTH END	W 4-2	Moss (2, 1 pen), Fuccillo, Ingram	7874	10		12	3	1	4					7	9		11	6	5		8					22
23	Dec	19	(a)	Shrewsbury Town	W 1-0	Ingram	4521	10		12	3	1			4			7	9		11				8	2		6		23
24	Dec	26	(h)	CHELSEA	W 2-0	Stein (2)	16006	10			3	1			4			7	9		11	6			8	2		5		24
25	Dec	27	(a)	Bristol Rovers	W 4-2	Stein (3), Hill	7010	10		12	3	1			4			7	9		11	6			8	2		5		25
26	Jan	10	(h)	CARDIFF CITY	D 2-2	Moss, Price	9013	10			3	1			4			7	9		11	6	5		8			2		26
27	Jan	17	(h)	NEWCASTLE UNITED	L 0-1	-	10774	10			3	1	12		4			7	9		11	6			8	2		5		27
28	Jan	31	(a)	Derby County	D 2-2	Moss, Ingram	16479				3	1	10					7	9		11	6			8	2	4	5		28
29	Feb	7	(h)	BLACKBURN ROVERS	W 3-1	Price, Hill, Moss	9350	10			3	1			4			7	9		11	6			8	2		5		29
30	Feb	21	(h)	GRIMSBY TOWN	L 0-2	-	9217	10			3	1			4			7	9		11	6			8	2		5	12	30
31	Mar	1	(a)	Orient	D 0-0	-	7974			12	3	1	10					7	9		11	6	5		8	2				31
32	Mar	7	(a)	Notts County	W 1-0	Stein	8075		10		3	1			4			7			11	6	5		8	2			9	32
33	Mar	14	(h)	BRISTOL CITY	W 3-1	White (2), Moss (pen)	8745		10		3	1			4			7			11	6	5		8	2			9	33
34	Mar	28	(h)	CAMBRIDGE UNITED	D 0-0	-	9412		10		3	1						7			11	6	5		8	2			9	34
35	Mar	31	(a)	Wrexham	D 0-0	-	4157		10		3	1			4			7	12		11	6	5		8	2			9	35
36	Apr	4	(a)	Sheffield Wednesday	L 1-3	Ingram	17196	3	10		9	1			4			7	12		11	6	5		8	2				36
37	Apr	11	(h)	QUEENS PARK RANGERS	W 3-0	Ingram, Stein, Antic	12112		10		3	1			4			7	9		11	6	5		8	2				37
38	Apr	18	(h)	BRISTOL ROVERS	W 1-0	Moss (pen)	9009		10		3	1			4			7	9		11	6	5		8	2				38
39	Apr	20	(a)	Chelsea	W 2-0	Moss, Hill	12868		10		3	1			4			7	9		11	6	5		8	2				39
40	Apr	25	(h)	OLDHAM ATHLETIC	L 1-2	Stein	10305	10			3	1			4			7	9		11	6	5		8	2		12		40
41	Apr	27	(a)	Swansea City	D 2-2	Hill (2)	21354		10		3	1						7			11	6	5		8	2		4	9	41
42	May	2	(a)	Bolton Wanderers	W 3-0	Stein, White, Stephens	7278		10		3	1	4					7			11	6	5		8	2			9	42
						Apps		20	18	3	42	40	4	5	37	3	-	42	15	2	41	41	31	-	42	40	1	16	19	
						Subs		3	6	-	-	-	1	-	-	1	-	-	2	-	-	-	-	-	-	-	-	9	2	
						Goals		-	1	1	-	-	1	1	-	-	-	7	5	-	16	2	1	-	18	1	-	-	7	

Final League Position: 5th

1980/81 FA CUP

Round	Month	Day	Venue	Opponents	W,L,D Score	Scorers	Attendance	Aizlewood M	Antic R	Bunn FS	Donaghy Mal	Findlay JW	Fuccillo P	Goodyear C	Grealish AP	Harrow A	Heath SJMP	Hill RA	Ingram GRA	Judge AG	Moss DJ	Price PT	Saxby MW	Smith WH	Stein B	Stephens KW	Turner WL	West A	White SJ	Round
3	Jan	3	(a)	Orient	W 3-1	Moss (2), Ingram	9891		10		3	1			4			7	9		11	6	5		8			2		3
4	Jan	24	(a)	Newcastle United	L 1-2	Ingram	29202		10		3	1			4			7	9		11	6			8	2		5		4
						Apps		2	-	-	2	2	-		2	-	-	2	2	-	2	2	1	-	2	1	-	2	-	
						Subs		-	-	-	-	-	-		-	-	-	-	-	-	-	-	-	-	-	-	-	-	-	
						Goals		-	-	-	-	-	-		-	-	-	-	2	-	2	-	-	-	-	-	-	-	-	

1980/81 LEAGUE CUP

Round	Month	Day	Venue	Opponents	W,L,D	Score	Scorers	Attendance	Aizlewood M	Antic R	Bunn FS	Donaghy Mal	Findlay JW	Fuccillo P	Goodyear C	Grealish AP	Harrow A	Heath SJMP	Hill RA	Ingram GRA	Judge AG	Moss DJ	Price PT	Saxby MW	Smith WH	Stein B	Stephens KW	Turner WL	West A	White SJ	Round
2:1	Aug	27	(a)	Reading	W	2-0	Moss, Stein	5778		10	9	3	1			4			7			11	6	5		8	2			12	2:1
2:2	Sep	2	(h)	READING	D	1-1	Saxby	5707	6	10		3	1			4		11	7	12				5		8	2			9	2:2
3	Sep	23	(h)	MANCHESTER CITY	L	1-2	Antic	10030		10		3	1			4			7			11	6	5	12	8	2		9		3
							Apps		1	3	1	3	3	.	.	3	.	1	3	.	.	2	2	3	.	3	3	.	1	1	
							Subs		.	.	.	.	.	.	.	.	.	.	.	1	.	.	.	.	.	.	.	.	.	1	
							Goals		.	1	.	.	.	.	.	.	.	.	.	.	.	1	.	1	.	1	.	.	.	.	

▶ The 1980/81 team –
Back row (left to right):
Pearson, Johnson,
Harriott, Small, Walker,
Smith, Goodyear, Turner,
Heath. Second row (left
to right): Coates
(Trainer), White,
Aizlewood, Findlay,
Saxby, Antic, Judge,
Donaghy, Ingram, Moore
(Coach). Third row (left
to right): Stephens, West,
Grealish, Stein, Pleat
(Manager), Price, Smith
(Chief Executive), Moss,
Fuccillo, Hill, Sheridan
(Physiotherapist). Front
row (left to right):
Brammer, Cosby, Foote,
Phelps, Madden,
Woodward, Beasley,
Bunn, Cole, Patterson.

TIMELINE...

2 May 1981 Getting closer! This time a fifth place finish.

1981/82 FOOTBALL LEAGUE DIVISION TWO

Match No	Month	Day	Venue	Opponents	W,L,D Score	Scorers	Attendance	Aizlewood M	Aleksic MA	Antic R	Bunn FS	Donaghy Mal	Findlay JW	Fuccillo P	Goodyear C	Hill RA	Horton B	Ingram GRA	Jennings WJ	Judge AG	Money R	Moss DJ	Saxby MW	Small MA	Stein B	Stephens KW	Turner WL	White SJ	Match No
1	Aug	29	(h)	CHARLTON ATHLETIC	W 3-0	Donaghy, McAllister (og), White	8776	3		10		6	1			7	4	11					5		8	2		9	1
2	Sep	1	(a)	Queens Park Rangers	W 2-1	Aizlewood, Hill	18703	3		10		6	1			7	4	11					5		8	2		9	2
3	Sep	5	(a)	Bolton Wanderers	W 2-1	Stein, Aizlewood	6911	3		10		6	1			7	4	11					5	12	8	2		9	3
4	Sep	12	(h)	SHEFFIELD WEDNESDAY	L 0-3	-	12131	3		10		6	1			7	4						5	12	8	2	11	9	4
5	Sep	19	(a)	Leicester City	W 2-1	White (2)	14159	3		10		6	1			7	4				11		5		8	2		9	5
6	Sep	22	(h)	CARDIFF CITY	L 2-3	Saxby, Antic	9015	3		10		6	1	12		7	4				11		5		8	2		9	6
7	Sep	26	(h)	WATFORD	W 4-1	Moss (2 pens), Stein (2)	12839	3				6	1	10		7	4				11		5		8	2		9	7
8	Oct	3	(a)	Orient	W 3-0	Aizlewood, Hill, White	4944	3		12		6	1	10		7	4				11		5		8	2		9	8
9	Oct	10	(a)	Oldham Athletic	D 1-1	White	8403	3		12		6	1	10		7	4				11		5		8	2		9	9
10	Oct	17	(h)	GRIMSBY TOWN	W 6-0	Fuccillo, Moss (pen), White (4)	9090	3			12	6	1	10		7	4				11		5		8	2		9	10
11	Oct	24	(a)	Wrexham	W 2-0	Donaghy, White	4059					6	1	10	3	7	4				11		5		8	2		9	11
12	Oct	31	(h)	CRYSTAL PALACE	W 1-0	Moss (pen)	11712			12		6	1	10	3	7	4				11		5		8	2		9	12
13	Nov	7	(h)	DERBY COUNTY	W 3-2	Moss, Goodyear, Donaghy	10784	5				6	1	10	3	7	4				11				8	2		9	13
14	Nov	14	(a)	Blackburn Rovers	W 1-0	Moss (pen)	9862	5	1			6		10	3	7	4				11				8	2		9	14
15	Nov	21	(a)	Newcastle United	L 2-3	Moss (pen), Donaghy	21084	3	1	12		6		10	5	7	4				11				8	2		9	15
16	Nov	24	(h)	BOLTON WANDERERS	W 2-0	Stein, Moss	8889	3	1	12		6		10	5	7	4				11				8	2		9	16
17	Nov	28	(h)	ROTHERHAM UNITED	W 3-1	White, Donaghy, Stein	11061	3	1			6		10	5	7	4				11				8	2		9	17
18	Dec	5	(a)	Shrewsbury Town	D 2-2	White, Donaghy	5259	3		12		6		10	5	7	4			1	11				8	2		9	18
19	Dec	28	(a)	Norwich City	W 3-1	Antic, White, Stein	18458	3		7		6	1	10	5		4				11				8	2		9	19
20	Jan	19	(a)	Charlton Athletic	D 0-0	-	7013	3		4		6	1	10	5	7					11				8	2		9	20
21	Jan	30	(h)	LEICESTER CITY	W 2-1	White, Donaghy	11810	3		12		6		10	5	7	4			1	11				8	2		9	21
22	Feb	6	(a)	Sheffield Wednesday	D 3-3	White, Moss (pen), Stein	18252	3		12		6		10	5	7	4			1	11				8	2		9	22
23	Feb	20	(a)	Watford	D 1-1	Stein	22798	3				6	1	10	5	7	4				11				8	2		9	23
24	Feb	27	(h)	OLDHAM ATHLETIC	W 2-0	Moss (2, 1 pen)	11506	3				6	1	10	5	7	4				11				8	2		9	24
25	Mar	2	(h)	CAMBRIDGE UNITED	W 1-0	Horton	10597	3		12		6	1	10	5	7	4				11				8	2		9	25
26	Mar	6	(a)	Grimsby Town	D 0-0	-	7734	3		10		6	1		5	7	4				11				8	2		9	26
27	Mar	12	(h)	WREXHAM	D 0-0	-	10880	3		10	12	6	1		5	7	4				11				8	2		9	27
28	Mar	16	(a)	Barnsley	L 3-4	Stein (2), Law (og)	14044	3		12		6	1	10	5	7	4				11				8	2		9	28
29	Mar	20	(a)	Crystal Palace	D 3-3	Antic, Moss (pen), Stein	12187			10		6	1		5	7	4				11				8	2	3	9	29
30	Mar	27	(a)	Derby County	D 0-0	-	15836					6	1		5	7	4		3		11				8	2	10	9	30
31	Mar	30	(h)	ORIENT	W 2-0	Moss (pen), Hill	9716					6	1		5	7	4		3		11				8	2	10	9	31
32	Apr	3	(h)	BLACKBURN ROVERS	W 2-0	Stein, White	10721					6	1		5	7	4	12	3		11				8	2	10	9	32
33	Apr	10	(a)	Cambridge United	D 1-1	Turner	8815			7		6	1	12	5		4		3		11				8	2	10	9	33
34	Apr	12	(h)	NORWICH CITY	W 2-0	Stein, Jennings	15061					6	1	10	5	7	4	12	3		11				8	2		9	34
35	Apr	17	(h)	NEWCASTLE UNITED	W 3-2	Stein (3, 2 pens)	13041			7		6	1		5	7			3						8	2	11	9	35
36	Apr	20	(a)	CHELSEA	D 2-2	Antic, Donaghy	16185			11		6	1	10	5	7	4		3						8	2		9	36
37	Apr	24	(a)	Rotherham United	D 2-2	Fuccillo, Money	11290			12		6		10	5	7			3		1	11			8	2		9	37
38	Apr	30	(h)	SHREWSBURY TOWN	W 4-1	Stein, Hill, White, Moss	14563			12		6	1	10	5	7			3		11				8	2		9	38
39	May	8	(a)	Chelsea	W 2-1	Antic, Stein	15044			7		6	1	10	5	7	4		3		11				8	2		9	39
40	May	11	(h)	QUEENS PARK RANGERS	W 3-2	Hill, White, Moss (pen)	16657			10		6	1		5	7	4		3		11				8	2		9	40
41	May	15	(h)	BARNSLEY	D 1-1	Stein	14463			12		6	1	10	5	7	4		3		11				8	2		9	41
42	May	17	(a)	Cardiff City	W 3-2	Stein (2), Donaghy	10277			10		6	1		5	7	4		3		11			12	8	2		9	42

Final League Position: 1st   2 Own Goals

	Aizlewood M	Aleksic MA	Antic R	Bunn FS	Donaghy Mal	Findlay JW	Fuccillo P	Goodyear C	Hill RA	Horton B	Ingram GRA	Jennings WJ	Judge AG	Money R	Moss DJ	Saxby MW	Small MA	Stein B	Stephens KW	Turner WL	White SJ
Apps	26	4	17	-	42	34	27	32	38	41	3	-	4	13	36	12	-	42	42	7	42
Subs	-	-	13	2	-	-	2	-	-	-	2	-	-	-	-	-	3	-	-	-	-
Goals	3	-	5	-	9	-	2	1	5	1	-	-	1	-	15	1	-	21	-	1	18

1981/82 FA CUP

Round	Month	Day	Venue	Opponents	W,L,D Score	Scorers	Attendance	Aizlewood M	Aleksic MA	Antic R	Bunn FS	Donaghy Mal	Findlay JW	Fuccillo P	Goodyear C	Hill RA	Horton B	Ingram GRA	Jennings WJ	Judge AG	Money R	Moss DJ	Saxby MW	Small MA	Stein B	Stephens KW	Turner WL	White SJ	Round
3	Jan	2	(h)	SWINDON TOWN	W 2-1	Moss, Horton	9488	3				6	1	10	5	7	4				11				8	2		9	3
4	Jan	23	(h)	IPSWICH TOWN	L 0-3	-	20188	3		12		6	1	10	5	7	4				11				8	2		9	4

	Aizlewood M	Aleksic MA	Antic R	Bunn FS	Donaghy Mal	Findlay JW	Fuccillo P	Goodyear C	Hill RA	Horton B	Ingram GRA	Jennings WJ	Judge AG	Money R	Moss DJ	Saxby MW	Small MA	Stein B	Stephens KW	Turner WL	White SJ
Apps	2	-	-	-	2	2	2	2	2	2	-	-	-	2	-	-	-	2	2	-	2
Subs	-	-	1	-	-	-	-	-	-	-	-	-	-	-	-	-	-	-	-	-	-
Goals	-	-	-	-	-	-	-	-	1	1	-	-	-	-	-	-	-	-	-	-	-

1981/82 MILK CUP (LEAGUE CUP)

Round	Month	Day	Venue	Opponents	W,L,D Score	Scorers	Attendance	Aizlewood M	Aleksic MA	Antic R	Bunn FS	Donaghy Mal	Findlay JW	Fuccillo P	Goodyear C	Hill RA	Horton B	Ingram GRA	Jennings WJ	Judge AG	Money R	Moss DJ	Saxby MW	Small MA	Stein B	Stephens KW	Turner WL	White SJ	Round
2:1	Oct	6	(h)	WREXHAM	L 0-2	-	6146		3			6	1	10		7	4					11	5		8	2		9	2:1
2:2	Oct	27	(a)	Wrexham	W 1-0	White	3453					6	1	10	3	7	4	12				11	5		8	2		9	2:2
						Apps		-	1	-	2	2	2	1	2	2	-	-	-	-	2	2	-	2	2	-	2	
						Subs		-	-	-	-	-	-	-	-	-	-	1	-	-	-	-	-	-	-	-	-	
						Goals		-	-	-	-	-	-	-	-	-	-	-	-	-	-	-	-	-	-	-	1	

▶ Brian Stein nets against Watford on the way to promotion.

TIMELINE...

1 September 1981 The Town christen the QPR artificial surface, the first in the country, but spoil the party when winning 2-1!
5 May 1982 It is third time lucky for Pleat as the championship trophy is awarded to his team which has led the table for virtually the whole of a brilliant campaign.

Luton Town Football Club – The Full Record | 171

▶ **The 1981/82 team** – Back row (left to right): Johnson, Turner, Goodyear, Small, Bunn, Ingram, Heath, Madden. Second row (left to right): Moore (Coach), White, Donaghy, Findlay, Saxby, Judge, Aizlewood, Fuccillo, Hartley (Coach). Third row (left to right): Coates (Trainer), Stephens, Hill, Horton, Pleat (Manager), Antic, Moss, Stein, Dr Berry (Club Doctor), Sheridan (Physiotherapist). Front row (left to right): Lane, Popplewell, Breacker, Mitchell Thomas, Keys, Beasley, North, Mark Thomas, Owen, Daniel, Brammer.

The players celebrate promotion back to the top flight.

David Moss was the Town's dead ball expert during the promotion campaign.

Five Watford players cannot dispossess Ricky Hill!

1982/83 FOOTBALL LEAGUE DIVISION ONE

Match No	Month	Day	Venue	Opponents	W,L,D Score	Scorers	Attendance	Antic R	Aylott TKC	Bunn FS	Daniel RC	Donaghy Mal	Elliott PM	Findlay JW	Fuccillo P	Geddis D	Godden AL	Goodyear C	Hill RA	Horton B	Judge AG	Kellock W	Money R	Moss DJ	Parker GA	Small MA	Stein B	Stephens KW	Thomas MA	Turner WL	Walsh Paul	Watts MR	White SJ	Match No
1	Aug	28	(a)	Tottenham Hotspur	D 2-2	Lacy (og), Stein	35195	10				6		1				5	7	4			3	11			8	2			9			1
2	Aug	31	(h)	WEST HAM UNITED	L 0-2	-	13403	10				6		1				5	7	4			3	11			8	2			9			2
3	Sep	4	(a)	NOTTS COUNTY	W 5-3	Walsh (3), Hill, Moss	9071	10				6		1				5	7	4			3	11	12		8	2			9			3
4	Sep	8	(a)	Aston Villa	L 1-4	Moss (pen)	18823	10				6		1				5	7	4		12		11			8	2		3	9			4
5	Sep	11	(a)	Liverpool	D 3-3	Stein (2), Moss	33694	12				6		1				5	7	4			3	11			8	2		10	9			5
6	Sep	18	(h)	BRIGHTON & HOVE ALBION	W 5-0	Stein (3), Turner, Moss	11342					6						5	7	4	1		3	11			8	2		10	9			6
7	Sep	25	(a)	Stoke City	D 4-4	Walsh, Stein (2), Donaghy	18475	12				6						5	7	4	1		3	11			8	2		10	9			7
8	Oct	2	(h)	MANCHESTER UNITED	D 1-1	Hill	17009	12				6		1				5	7	4			3	11			8	2		10	9			8
9	Oct	9	(a)	Birmingham City	W 3-2	Stein, Walsh, Moss	13772					6		1				5	7	4			3	11			8	2			9			9
10	Oct	16	(h)	IPSWICH TOWN	D 1-1	Stein (pen)	13378					6		1	10			5	7	4			3	11			8	2			9			10
11	Oct	23	(a)	West Bromwich Albion	L 0-1	-	16488					6			10			5	7	4	1		3	11			8	2		12	9			11
12	Oct	30	(h)	NOTTINGHAM FOREST	L 0-2	-	12648	12				6		1				5	7	4		10	3	11				2			9			12
13	Nov	6	(h)	ARSENAL	D 2-2	Moss, Walsh	16597	12				6		1	10			5	7				3	11				2		2	9			13
14	Nov	13	(a)	Sunderland	D 1-1	Moss	14238		12			6							7	4	1	10		11				2		5	9			14
15	Nov	20	(a)	Coventry City	L 2-4	Horton, Stein	9670	10						1				5	7	4			3	11			8	2		6	9			15
16	Nov	27	(h)	SOUTHAMPTON	D 3-3	Hill, Stein, Goodyear	11196	12				6		1				5	7	4			3	11			8	2		10	9			16
17	Dec	4	(a)	Swansea City	L 0-2	-	9556	12				6						5	7	4			3	11				2		10	9			17
18	Dec	11	(h)	MANCHESTER CITY	W 3-1	Walsh, Stein, Hartford (og)	11013					6		1				5	7	4			3	11				2		10	9			18
19	Dec	18	(a)	Everton	L 0-5	-	14986					6		1	12	8		5	7	4			3					2		10	9			19
20	Dec	27	(h)	WATFORD	W 1-0	Goodyear	21145					6			10	8		5	7	4			3					2			9			20
21	Dec	28	(a)	Norwich City	L 0-1	-	20415					6			10	8		5	7	4			3					2		6	9			21
22	Jan	1	(h)	COVENTRY CITY	L 1-2	Donaghy	13072	12				6			10	8		5	7	4			3					2			9			22
23	Jan	4	(a)	West Ham United	W 3-2	Walsh (3)	21435			8		6		1				5	7	4		12		11				2	3	10	9			23
24	Jan	15	(h)	TOTTENHAM HOTSPUR	D 1-1	O'Reilly (og)	21231			8		6		1				5	7	4		12						2	3	10	9	11		24
25	Jan	22	(a)	Brighton & Hove Albion	W 4-2	Hill (2), Stevens (og), Case (og)	11778			8		6		1				5	7	4		12		11				2	3	10	9			25
26	Feb	5	(h)	LIVERPOOL	L 1-3	Stein	18434	12				6		1				5	7	4			3	11			8	2		10	9			26
27	Feb	26	(a)	Ipswich Town	L 0-3	-	18632					6		1	10			5	7	4		12		11				2		3	9		8	27
28	Mar	5	(h)	WEST BROMWICH ALBION	D 0-0	-	10852					6	3	1				5	7	4				11				2		10	9		8	28
29	Mar	12	(a)	Nottingham Forest	W 1-0	Hill	14387					6	3	1				5	7	4				11				2		10	9		8	29
30	Mar	19	(a)	Arsenal	L 1-4	Moss	23987					6	3	1				5	7	4				11				2		10	9		8	30
31	Mar	26	(h)	SUNDERLAND	L 1-3	Horton (pen)	11221	8			12	6	3				1	5	7	4				11				2		10	9			31
32	Apr	2	(h)	NORWICH CITY	L 0-1	-	11211	8			12	10	3				1	5	7	4				11		6		2			9			32
33	Apr	4	(a)	Watford	L 2-5	Aylott, Horton	20120	10	8			6	5				1		7	4			3	11				2			9			33
34	Apr	9	(h)	ASTON VILLA	W 2-1	Aylott, Moss	10924	4	8			6	5				1		7	4			3	11				2		10	9			34
35	Apr	12	(h)	BIRMINGHAM CITY	W 3-1	Hill (2), Horton (pen)	12868	10	8			6	5				1		7				3	11				2	12		9			35
36	Apr	16	(a)	Notts County	D 1-1	Donaghy	8897	10	8			6	5				1		7				3	11				2			9			36
37	Apr	23	(h)	SWANSEA CITY	W 3-1	Walsh (3)	11561		8			6	5				1		7				3	11				2		10	9			37
38	Apr	30	(a)	Southampton	D 2-2	Elliott, Antic	18367	4	8			6	5		12		1		7				3	11				2		10	9			38
39	May	2	(h)	STOKE CITY	D 0-0	-	11877	10	9			6	5				1		7	4			3	11				2		8				39
40	May	7	(h)	EVERTON	L 1-5	Hill	12447	12				6					1	5	7	4			3	11				2		10	9			40
41	May	9	(a)	Manchester United	L 0-3	-	34213	12	8		11	6					1	5	7	4			3			10		2			9			41
42	May	14	(a)	Manchester City	W 1-0	Antic	42843	12	8			6	5				1	2	7	4							11	2		10	9			42
				Apps				11	12	3	1	40	13	26	8	4	12	34	42	40	4	2	31	39	1	-	20	40	4	29	41	1	4	
				Subs				13	-	1	2	-	-	-	1	-	-	1	-	-	-	-	-	-	5	-	-	-	1	1	-	1	-	
				Goals				2	2	-	-	3	1	-	-	-	-	2	9	4	-	-	2	9	-	-	14	-	-	1	13	-	-	

Final League Position: 18th. 5 Own Goals

1982/83 FA CUP

Round	Month	Day	Venue	Opponents	W,L,D Score	Scorers	Attendance	Antic R	Aylott TKC	Bunn FS	Daniel RC	Donaghy Mal	Elliott PM	Findlay JW	Fuccillo P	Geddis D	Godden AL	Goodyear C	Hill RA	Horton B	Judge AG	Kellock W	Money R	Moss DJ	Parker GA	Small MA	Stein B	Stephens KW	Thomas MA	Turner WL	Walsh Paul	Watts MR	White SJ	Round
3	Jan	8	(h)	PETERBOROUGH UNITED	W 3-0	Horton, Hill, Walsh	11151			8		6		1				5	7	4								2	3	10	9	11		3
4	Jan	29	(h)	MANCHESTER UNITED	L 0-2	-	20516					6		1				5	7	4		12	3	11			8	2		10	9			4
				Apps				-	-	1	-	2	-	2	-	-	-	2	2	2	-	-	1	1	-	-	1	2	1	2	2	1	-	
				Subs				-	-	-	-	-	-	-	-	-	-	-	-	-	-	1	-	-	-	-	-	-	-	-	-	-	-	
				Goals				-	-	-	-	-	-	-	-	-	-	-	1	1	-	-	-	-	-	-	-	-	-	-	1	-	-	

1982/83 MILK CUP (LEAGUE CUP)

Round	Month	Day	Venue	Opponents	W.L.D Score	Scorers	Attendance	Antic R	Aylott TKC	Bunn FS	Daniel RC	Donaghy Mal	Elliott PM	Findlay JW	Fuccillo P	Geddis D	Godden AL	Goodyear C	Hill RA	Horton B	Judge AG	Kellock W	Money R	Moss DJ	Parker GA	Small MA	Stein B	Stephens KW	Thomas MA	Turner WL	Walsh Paul	Watts MR	White SJ	Round
2:1	Oct	5	(h)	CHARLTON ATHLETIC	W 3-0	Stein, Fuccillo (2)	7030					6		1	10		5	7	4			3		11			8	2			9			2:1
2:2	Oct	26	(a)	Charlton Athletic	L 0-2	-	5973					6		1			5	7	4			3		11			8		2	10	9			2:2
3	Nov	9	(h)	BLACKPOOL	W 4-2	Kellock (2), Bunn, Moss	6409			12		6			10		5		4	1	7	3		11			8	2			9			3
4	Dec	1	(a)	Tottenham Hotspur	L 0-1	-	27461	12				6		1			5	7	4			3		11			8	2		10	9			4
						Apps		-	-	-	-	4	-	3	2	-	4	3	4	1	1	4	-	4	-	-	4	3	1	2	4	-	-	
						Subs		1	-	1	-	-	-	-	-	-	-	-	-	-	-	-	-	-	-	-	-	-	-	-	-	-	-	
						Goals		-	-	1	-	-	-	-	2	-	-	-	-	-	-	2	-	1	-	-	1	-	-	-	-	-	-	

▶ The 1982/83 team – Back row (left to right): Johnson, Turner, North, Small, Goodyear, Bunn, Kellock, Walsh. Middle row (left to right): Moore (Coach), Money, Saxby, Beasley, Findlay, Judge, Aizlewood, Fuccillo, Hartley (Coach). Front row (left to right): Coates (Trainer), Hill, Donaghy, Stephens, Horton, Pleat (Manager), Moss, Stein, Antic, Sheridan (Physiotherapist).

TIMELINE...

14 May 1983 A 1-0 win at Manchester City ensures Division One survival and sends City down.

1983/84 FOOTBALL LEAGUE DIVISION ONE

Match No	Month	Day	Venue	Opponents	W,L,D	Score	Scorers	Attendance	Antic R	Aylott TKC	Breacker T	Bunn FS	Daniel RC	Donaghy Mal	Elliott PM	Goodyear C	Hill RA	Horton B	Johnson R	Moss DJ	North S	Nwajiobi C	Parker GA	Sealey L	Stein B	Stein M	Stephens KW	Thomas MA	Turner WL	Walsh Paul	Match No
1	Aug	27	(a)	Arsenal	L	1-2	Robson (og)	39347				10		6	5		7	4		11				1	8		2		3	9	1
2	Aug	31	(a)	Leicester City	W	3-0	Bunn, Moss, Hill	12629				10		6	5		7	4		11				1	8		2		3	9	2
3	Sep	3	(h)	SUNDERLAND	W	4-1	Hill, Walsh, Munro (og), Stein	10846				10		6	5		7	4		11				1	8		2		3	9	3
4	Sep	6	(h)	NORWICH CITY	D	2-2	Elliott, Stein	11095	12			10		6	5		7	4		11				1	8		2		3	9	4
5	Sep	10	(a)	Manchester United	L	0-2	-	41013	12			10		6	5		7	4		11				1	8		2		3	9	5
6	Sep	17	(h)	WOLVERHAMPTON WANDERERS	W	4-0	Walsh, Stein, Moss, Horton	10975				10		6	5		7	4		11				1	8		2		3	9	6
7	Sep	24	(a)	Nottingham Forest	L	0-1	-	16296	12			10		6	5		7	4		11				1	8		2		3	9	7
8	Oct	1	(h)	ASTON VILLA	W	1-0	Moss (pen)	12747	12			10		6	5		7	4		11				1	8		2		3	9	8
9	Oct	15	(a)	Everton	W	1-0	Walsh	14327				10		6	5		7	4		11				1	8		2		3	9	9
10	Oct	22	(h)	SOUTHAMPTON	W	3-1	Aylott (2), Stein	12389	12	9		10		6	5		7	4		11				1	8		2		3		10
11	Oct	29	(a)	Liverpool	L	0-6	-	31940	11					6	5		7	4						1	8		2	3	10	9	11
12	Nov	5	(a)	Queens Park Rangers	W	1-0	Elliot	15053		10				6	5		7	4				11		1	8		2		3	9	12
13	Nov	12	(h)	BIRMINGHAM CITY	D	1-1	Stein	11111	12					6	5		7		4			11		1	8		2	3	10	9	13
14	Nov	19	(h)	TOTTENHAM HOTSPUR	L	2-4	Stein, Walsh	17275	11	10				6	5	4	7							1	8		2		3	9	14
15	Nov	26	(a)	Watford	W	2-1	Stein, Bunn	17791		10		11		6	5		7	4						1	8		2		3	9	15
16	Dec	3	(h)	COVENTRY CITY	L	2-4	Pearce (og), Aylott	10698	12	10		11		6	5		7	4						1	8		2		3	9	16
17	Dec	10	(a)	Stoke City	W	4-2	Walsh (3), Daniel	10329		10			11	6	5		7	4						1	8		2	3		9	17
18	Dec	18	(h)	WEST BROMWICH ALBION	W	2-0	Horton (pen), Aylott	11566		10			11	6	5		7	4						1	8		2	3		9	18
19	Dec	26	(a)	Notts County	W	3-0	Aylott (2), Daniel	9789		10			11	6	5		7	4						1	8		2	3		9	19
20	Dec	27	(h)	WEST HAM UNITED	L	0-1	-	16343		10			11	6	5		7	4						1	8		2	3	12	9	20
21	Dec	31	(a)	Sunderland	L	0-2	-	19482	12			10	11	6	5		7	4	2					1	8		2		3	9	21
22	Jan	2	(h)	NOTTINGHAM FOREST	L	2-3	Walsh, Nwajiobi	12126	12			10		6	5		7	4				11		1	8		2	3		9	22
23	Jan	14	(h)	ARSENAL	L	1-2	Kay (og)	16320		10		11		6	5			4				12	7	1	8		2	3		9	23
24	Jan	21	(a)	Wolverhampton Wanderers	W	2-1	Parker, Walsh	11594		10		11		6	5	12		4					7	1	8		2	3		9	24
25	Feb	4	(a)	Aston Villa	D	0-0	-	18656		10		11		6	5			4					7	1	8		2	3		9	25
26	Feb	12	(h)	MANCHESTER UNITED	L	0-5	-	11265	12	10		11		6	5		7	4						1	8		2	3		9	26
27	Feb	18	(h)	LIVERPOOL	D	0-0	-	14877					11	10	5	6	7	4						1	8		2	3		9	27
28	Feb	25	(a)	Southampton	L	1-2	Donaghy	17947					10	6	5	12	7	4				11		1	8		2	3		9	28
29	Mar	3	(h)	QUEENS PARK RANGERS	D	0-0	-	11922		11				10	5	6	7	4						1	8		2	3		9	29
30	Mar	13	(h)	IPSWICH TOWN	W	2-1	Aylott (2, 1 pen)	8776	4	10		11		7	5	6								1	8		2	3		9	30
31	Mar	17	(a)	Norwich City	D	0-0	-	13112	4	10		11		7	5	6								1	8		2	3		9	31
32	Mar	20	(a)	Birmingham City	D	1-1	Stein	9592	4	10		11		7	5	6								1	8		2	3		9	32
33	Mar	24	(h)	LEICESTER CITY	D	0-0	-	10509						7	5	6		4		11			10	1	8		2	3		9	33
34	Mar	31	(a)	Ipswich Town	L	0-3	-	14586	5		10	12		7		6		4		11				1	8		2	3		9	34
35	Apr	7	(h)	EVERTON	L	0-3	-	9224		10	7	11		6	5	12		4						1	8	9	2	3			35
36	Apr	14	(a)	Tottenham Hotspur	L	1-2	Parker	25390	12	9		10		6	5			4		11			7	1	8		2	3			36
37	Apr	17	(a)	West Ham United	L	1-3	Walsh	15430				10		6	5	12		4		11			7	1	8		2	3		9	37
38	Apr	21	(h)	NOTTS COUNTY	W	3-2	Moss, Horton (pen), Bunn	8181	12			10			5	6		4		11			7	1	8		2	3		9	38
39	Apr	28	(h)	WATFORD	L	1-2	Walsh	12594	12			10			5	6		4		11			7	1	8		2	3		9	39
40	May	5	(a)	Coventry City	D	2-2	Antic, Stein	9647	11			10		6		5		4					7	1	8		2	3		9	40
41	May	7	(h)	STOKE CITY	L	0-1	-	9867	11			10		6		5		4				12	7	1	8		2	3		9	41
42	May	12	(a)	West Bromwich Albion	L	0-3	-	12004	12	10		11			2		5	4			6		7	1	8				3	9	42
								Apps	8	20	2	29	7	40	38	13	26	37	2	16	1	2	13	42	42	1	40	26	18	39	
			Final League Position: 16th				4 Own Goals	Subs	14	·	·	1	·	·	·	4	·	·	·	·	·	2	·	·	·	·	·	·	·	1	·	
								Goals	1	8	·	3	2	1	2	·	2	3	·	4	·	1	2	·	9	·	·	·	·	11	

1983/84 FA CUP

Round	Month	Day	Venue	Opponents	W,L,D	Score	Scorers	Attendance	Antic R	Aylott TKC	Breacker T	Bunn FS	Daniel RC	Donaghy Mal	Elliott PM	Goodyear C	Hill RA	Horton B	Johnson R	Moss DJ	North S	Nwajiobi C	Parker GA	Sealey L	Stein B	Stein M	Stephens KW	Thomas MA	Turner WL	Walsh Paul	Round
3	Jan	7	(h)	WATFORD	D	2-2	Nwajiobi, B Stein	15007	12			10		6	5		7	4				11		1	8		2	3		9	3
Rep	Jan	10	(a)	Watford	L	3-4	Donaghy, Walsh (2)	20586		10		11		6	5			4				12	7	1	8		2	3		9	Rep
								Apps	·	1	·	2	·	2	2	·	1	2	·	·	·	1	1	2	2	·	2	2	·	2	
								Subs	1	·	·	·	·	·	·	·	·	·	·	·	·	1	·	·	·	·	·	1	·	·	
								Goals	·	·	·	·	·	1	·	·	·	·	·	·	·	1	·	·	1	·	·	·	·	2	

1983/84 MILK CUP (LEAGUE CUP)

Round	Month	Day	Venue	Opponents	W,L,D	Score	Scorers	Attendance	Antic R	Aylott TKC	Breacker T	Bunn FS	Daniel RC	Donaghy Mal	Elliott PM	Goodyear C	Hill RA	Horton B	Johnson R	Moss DJ	North S	Nwajiobi C	Parker GA	Sealey L	Stein B	Stein M	Stephens KW	Thomas MA	Turner WL	Walsh Paul	Round
2:1	Oct	4	(a)	Rotherham United	W	3-2	Walsh, Bunn, Aylott	4035	10	9		5		4			6	11						1	7		2		3	8	2:1
2:2	Oct	25	(h)	ROTHERHAM UNITED	L	0-2	-	6755	10	9			11	6	5		7	4						1	8		2		3		2:2
							Apps		2	2	-	1	1	2	1	-	2	2	-	-	-	-	-	2	2	-	2	-	2	1	
							Subs		-	-	-	-	-	-	-	-	-	-	-	-	-	-	-	-	-	-	-	-	-	-	
							Goals		-	1	-	1	-	-	-	-	-	-	-	-	-	-	-	-	-	-	-	-	-	1	

▶ **The 1983/84 team** – Back row (left to right): Johnson, Turner, Daniel, Breacker, Beasley, North, Thomas, Parker, Watts. Middle row (left to right): Moore (Coach), Money, Goodyear, Sealey, Elliott, Saxby, Findlay, Aylott, Bunn, Hartley (Coach). Front row (left to right): Coates (Trainer), Stephens, Hill, Donaghy, Moss, Pleat (Manager), Horton, Antic, Stein, Walsh, Sheridan (Physiotherapist).

1984/85 FOOTBALL LEAGUE DIVISION ONE

Match No	Month	Day	Venue	Opponents	W,L,D Score	Scorers	Attendance	Breacker T	Bunn FS	Daniel RC	Dibble A	Donaghy Mal	Droy M	Elliott PM	Elliott S	Findlay JW	Foster S	Grimes A	Harford M	Hilaire V	Hill RA	Moss DJ	Nicholas P	North S	Nwajiobi C	Parker GA	Preece D	Sealey L	Stein B	Stein M	Thomas MA	Todd C	Turner WL
1	Aug	25	(h)	STOKE CITY	W 2-0	S Elliott, Bunn	8626	4	10		1	6			9		3				7	11	5						8		2		
2	Aug	28	(a)	Ipswich Town	D 1-1	Moss	15833	4	10		1	6			9		3				7	11	5	12					8		2		
3	Sep	1	(a)	West Bromwich Albion	L 0-4	-	11653	4	10		1	6			9		3				7	11	5	12					8		2		
4	Sep	4	(h)	LIVERPOOL	L 1-2	Donaghy	14127	4			1	6		5	9		3				7	11		12					8		2		10
5	Sep	8	(h)	SOUTHAMPTON	D 1-1	Moss (pen)	8657		12		1	6		5			3				7	11			9	4			8		2		10
6	Sep	16	(a)	Nottingham Forest	L 1-3	Moss	18605		10		1	6		5			3				7	11			9	12			8		2		4
7	Sep	22	(h)	CHELSEA	D 0-0		16066		10		1	6		5			3				7	11			9				8		2		4
8	Sep	29	(a)	Tottenham Hotspur	L 2-4	Moss, Bunn	30204		9		1	6		5			3		10		7	11				12			8		2		4
9	Oct	6	(a)	Queens Park Rangers	W 3-2	S Elliott, P Elliott, B Stein	12051				1	6		5	9		3				7	11			10				8		2		4
10	Oct	13	(h)	SHEFFIELD WEDNESDAY	L 1-2	Bunn	10285		4		1	6		5	9					10	7	11			10				8		2		3
11	Oct	20	(h)	WATFORD	W 3-2	Bunn (2), S Elliott	12192		10			6		5	9	1				11	7					4			8		2		3
12	Oct	27	(a)	Sunderland	L 0-3	-	15280	12	10			6		5	9	1				11	7					4			8		2		3
13	Nov	3	(h)	NEWCASTLE UNITED	D 2-2	Parker, B Stein	10009	2		11	1	6			9						7			5		10			8			4	3
14	Nov	10	(a)	Norwich City	L 0-3	-	13610	2	9		1	6									7		11	5	12	10			8			4	3
15	Nov	17	(a)	Manchester United	L 0-2	-	41630	2	10		1	6	5		9					11	7				4	12			8				3
16	Nov	24	(h)	WEST HAM UNITED	D 2-2	B Stein, Nwajiobi	10789	2	10			3	5		9	1					7			12	6	11			8				
17	Dec	1	(a)	Arsenal	L 1-3	B Stein	26336	2	10			6			9			5			7				12	11			8		3		4
18	Dec	8	(h)	ASTON VILLA	W 1-0	Preece	7696	2	9			6						5			7		11		4		10	1	8		3		
19	Dec	15	(a)	Leicester City	D 2-2	B Stein, Harford	10476	2				6						5	9		7		11		4		10	1	8		12		3
20	Dec	18	(h)	WEST BROMWICH ALBION	L 1-2	Foster	7286	2				6						5	9				11		12	4	10	1	8		7		3
21	Dec	26	(h)	COVENTRY CITY	W 2-0	B Stein, Daniel	9237	2		11		6						5	9		7				12			1	8		3		4
22	Dec	29	(a)	Liverpool	L 0-1	-	35403	2		11	10	6						5			7				12			1	8		3		4
23	Jan	1	(a)	Everton	L 1-2	Harford	31641	2		12		6						5	9		7	11			10			1	8		3		4
24	Feb	2	(h)	TOTTENHAM HOTSPUR	D 2-2	B Stein, Nwajiobi	17511	2		12		6						5	9		7		4		10	11		1	8		3		
25	Feb	23	(a)	Newcastle United	L 0-1	-	24515	2				6						5	9		7		4		10	11		1	8		3		
26	Mar	2	(h)	SUNDERLAND	W 2-1	Harford, Hill	8019	2				6					5		9		7		4		10	11		1	8		3		
27	Mar	16	(h)	Sheffield Wednesday	D 1-1	Harford	18856	2				6					5		9		7		4		10	11		1	8		3		
28	Mar	19	(a)	Watford	L 0-3	-	14185	2				6					5		9		7		4		12	10	11	1	8		3		
29	Mar	23	(h)	QUEENS PARK RANGERS	W 2-0	Harford (2)	9373	2				6					5		9		7		4		10	11		1	8		3		
30	Mar	30	(h)	IPSWICH TOWN	W 3-1	Harford (2), Nwajiobi	12640	2		11		6					5		9		7		4		10	11		1	8		3		
31	Apr	2	(a)	Southampton	L 0-1	-	14906	2		11		6					5		9		7				10			1	8		3		
32	Apr	8	(a)	Stoke City	W 4-0	Harford (2), Nwajiobi, Moss	7108	2				6							9		7	12	4		10	11		1	8		3		5
33	Apr	16	(h)	NORWICH CITY	W 3-1	Nwajiobi (2), Moss (pen)	8794	2				6					5				7	9	4		10	11		1	8		3		
34	Apr	21	(h)	MANCHESTER UNITED	W 2-1	Harford (2, 1 pen)	10320	2				6					5		9		7		4		10	11		1	8		3		
35	Apr	24	(h)	NOTTINGHAM FOREST	L 1-2	Moss (pen)	10156	2				6					5		9		7	10	4			11		1	8		3		
36	Apr	27	(a)	West Ham United	D 0-0		17303	2	9			6					5				7		4		10	12	11	1	8		3		
37	May	4	(h)	ARSENAL	W 3-1	Harford (2, 1 pen), Nwajiobi	12051	2				6					5		9		7		4		10	12	11	1	8		3		
38	May	6	(a)	Aston Villa	W 1-0	B Stein	14130	2				6					5		9				4		10	7	11	1	8		3		12
39	May	8	(a)	Chelsea	L 0-2	-	13789	2	10			6					5		9				4			7		1	8	12	3		11
40	May	11	(h)	LEICESTER CITY	W 4-0	Nwajiobi, Preece, B Stein, Harford	11802	2				6					5		9		7		4		10		11	1	8		3		
41	May	23	(a)	Coventry City	L 0-1	-	14834	2	12			6					5		9		7		4		10		11	1	8		3		
42	May	28	(h)	EVERTON	W 2-0	Nwajiobi, Hill	11509	2				6					5		9		7	12	4		10		11	1	8		3		
Apps								34	17	4	13	42	2	9	12	3	25	9	22	5	39	17	19	7	21	13	21	26	42	-	35	2	23
Subs								1	3	3	-	-	-	1	-	1	-	3	-	1	-	-	1	-	2	-	8	7	-	-	1	1	1
Goals								-	5	1	-	1	-	1	3	-	1	-	15	-	2	7	-	-	9	1	2	-	9	-	-	-	-

Final League Position: 13th

1984/85 FA CUP

Round	Month	Day	Venue	Opponents	W,L,D	Score	Scorers	Attendance	Breacker T	Bunn FS	Daniel RC	Dibble A	Donaghy Mal	Droy M	Elliott PM	Elliott S	Findlay JW	Foster S	Grimes A	Harford M	Hilaire V	Hill RA	Moss DJ	Nicholas P	North S	Nwajiobi C	Parker GA	Preece D	Sealey L	Stein B	Stein M	Thomas MA	Todd C	Turner WL	Round
3	Jan	5	(h)	STOKE CITY	D	1-1	Foster	7270	2		10		6					5		9		7	11			12			1	8		3		4	3
Rep	Jan	9	(a)	Stoke City	W	3-2	Hill, Harford, Donaghy	9917	2		10		6					5		9		7					11		1	8		3		4	Rep
4	Jan	26	(h)	HUDDERSFIELD TOWN	W	2-0	Donaghy, B Stein	8712	2		10		6					5		9		7				12	11		1	8		3		4	4
5	Mar	4	(h)	WATFORD	D	0-0	-	18506	2		11		6					5		9		7				10			1	8		3		4	5
Rep	Mar	6	(a)	Watford	D	2-2	Nwajiobi, Hill	19867	2		**11**		6					5		9		7				10	12		1	8		3		4	Rep
Rep 2	Mar	9	(h)	WATFORD	W	1-0	Turner	15586	2				6					5		9		7				10	11		1	8		3		4	Rep 2
6	Mar	13	(h)	MILLWALL	W	1-0	B Stein	17470	2				6					5		9		7				10	11		1	8		3		4	6
SF	Apr	13	(n)	Everton	L	1-2	Hill	45289	2				6					5		9		7	12			10	11		1	8		3		4	SF
								Apps	8	-	5	-	8	-	-	-	-	8	-	8	-	8	1	-	-	5	5	-	8	8	-	8	-	8	
								Subs	-	-	-	-	-	-	-	-	-	-	-	-	-	-	1	-	-	2	1	-	-	-	-	-	-	-	
								Goals	-	-	-	-	2	-	-	-	-	1	-	1	-	3	-	-	-	1	-	-	-	2	-	-	-	1	

Semi Final played at Villa Park

1984/85 MILK CUP (LEAGUE CUP)

Round	Month	Day	Venue	Opponents	W,L,D	Score	Scorers	Attendance	Breacker T	Bunn FS	Daniel RC	Dibble A	Donaghy Mal	Droy M	Elliott PM	Elliott S	Findlay JW	Foster S	Grimes A	Harford M	Hilaire V	Hill RA	Moss DJ	Nicholas P	North S	Nwajiobi C	Parker GA	Preece D	Sealey L	Stein B	Stein M	Thomas MA	Todd C	Turner WL	Round
2:1	Sep	25	(a)	Orient	W	4-1	Donaghy, B Stein (2), Parker	3080		9		1	6	5				3		10	7					11	12			8		2		4	2:1
2:2	Oct	9	(h)	ORIENT	W	3-1	Bunn, B Stein, S Elliott	3374		10		1	6	5		9		3		12	7					11				8		2		4	2:2
3	Oct	30	(h)	LEICESTER CITY	W	3-1	Moss, Williams (og), Donaghy	8015	2	10		1	6	5		9					7	11	4			12				8				3	3
4	Nov	20	(a)	Sheffield Wednesday	L	2-4	S Elliott (2)	18313	2	10			6	5		9					7	11	4			12				8		3			4
								Apps	2	4	-	3	4	4	-	3	-	2	-	2	4	2	2	-	-	2	1	-	-	4	-	2	-	4	
								Subs	-	-	-	-	-	-	-	-	-	-	-	-	-	-	-	-	-	3	-	-	-	-	-	-	-	-	
								Goals	-	1	-	-	2	-	-	3	-	-	-	-	-	-	1	-	-	-	1	-	-	3	-	-	-	-	

1 Own Goal

▶ **The 1984/85 team** – Back row (left to right): M.Stein, Johnson, Breacker, S.North, M.North, Parker, Turner, Daniel. Middle row (left to right): Moore (Coach), Nwajiobi, Bunn, Findlay, P.Elliott, Dibble, Goodyear, Thomas, Coates (Trainer). Front row (left to right): Hartley (Coach), S.Elliott, Moss, Hill, Donaghy, Pleat (Manager), B.Stein, Grimes, Hilaire, Sheridan (Physiotherapist).

TIMELINE...

December – January 1984/85 Four big money signings turn the season around after a terrible start.
13 March 1985 The Town's F.A.Cup quarter-final win over Millwall at Kenilworth Road is marred by unprecedented crowd violence which is broadcast the world over.
13 April 1985 The Hatters play in the F.A.Cup semi-final for only the second time in their history but lose 1-2 to Everton in highly controversial circumstances.

1985/86 FOOTBALL LEAGUE DIVISION ONE

Match No	Month	Day	Venue	Opponents	W/L/D Score	Scorers	Attendance	Breacker T	Daniel RC	Dibble A	Donaghy Mal	Elliott PM	Foster S	Grimes A	Harford M	Hill RA	Johnson R	King AE	Newell M	Nicholas P	North M	North S	Nwajiobi C	Parker GA	Preece D	Sealey L	Stein B	Stein M	Thomas MA	Match No
1	Aug	17	(h)	NOTTINGHAM FOREST	D 1-1	B Stein	11318	2		1	6		5		9	7				4			10	12	11		8		3	1
2	Aug	21	(a)	Newcastle United	D 2-2	Nwajiobi, Harford	21933			1	6	5		3	9					4			10	7	11		8		2	2
3	Aug	24	(a)	West Ham United	W 1-0	Harford (pen)	14004			1	6	5			9			2		4			10	7	11		8		3	3
4	Aug	27	(h)	ARSENAL	D 2-2	Nwajiobi, B Stein	10012	2		1	6				9	7				4			10	5	11		8		3	4
5	Aug	31	(a)	Aston Villa	L 1-3	B Stein	10524	2		1	6				9	7	5			4			10	12	11		8		3	5
6	Sep	7	(h)	CHELSEA	D 1-1	Harford	10720			1	6	12	5		9	7	2			4					11		8		3	6
7	Sep	14	(a)	Everton	L 0-2	-	25487	2		1	6		5		9	7				4			10	12	11		8		3	7
8	Sep	21	(h)	QUEENS PARK RANGERS	W 2-0	Harford, Foster	9508	2			6		5		9	7				4			12		11	1	8	10	3	8
9	Sep	28	(a)	Sheffield Wednesday	L 2-3	Harford (2)	17877	2			6	12	5		9	7				4			10		11	1	8		3	9
10	Oct	1	(h)	IPSWICH TOWN	W 1-0	Nwajiobi	8553	2			6		5		9	7				4			10		11	1	8		3	10
11	Oct	5	(h)	MANCHESTER UNITED	D 1-1	B Stein	17454	2			6	12	5			7				4	9		10		11	1	8		3	11
12	Oct	12	(a)	Oxford United	D 1-1	B Stein	10609	2			6		5		9	7				4			10		11	1	8		3	12
13	Oct	19	(h)	SOUTHAMPTON	W 7-0	Nwajiobi, B Stein (3, 1 pen), Hill, Preece, Daniel	8876	2	12		6		5		9	7				4			10		11	1	8		3	13
14	Oct	26	(a)	Liverpool	L 2-3	Foster, Harford	31488	2	4		6		5	12	9	7	3						10		11	1	8			14
15	Nov	2	(h)	BIRMINGHAM CITY	W 2-0	B Stein, Harford	8550	2			6		5		9	7				4			10		11	1	8		3	15
16	Nov	9	(a)	Tottenham Hotspur	W 3-1	Harford, B Stein, Hill	19163	2			6		5		9	7				4			10		11	1	8		3	16
17	Nov	16	(h)	COVENTRY CITY	L 0-1	-	9607	2			6		5		9	7				4			10	12	11	1	8		3	17
18	Nov	23	(a)	Watford	W 2-1	Thomas, Terry (og)	16197	2			6		5		9	7				4			10		11	1	8		3	18
19	Nov	30	(h)	MANCHESTER CITY	W 2-1	B Stein (2)	10096	2	12		6	5			9	7				4			10		11	1	8		3	19
20	Dec	7	(h)	NEWCASTLE UNITED	W 2-0	Harford, M North	10319	2			6		5		9	7			10	4	12				11	1	8		3	20
21	Dec	14	(a)	Nottingham Forest	L 0-2	-	12078	2			6		5		9				10	4	12			7	11	1	8		3	21
22	Dec	21	(h)	WEST HAM UNITED	D 0-0	-	14599	2			6		5		9	7				4	10				11	1	8		3	22
23	Dec	26	(a)	West Bromwich Albion	W 2-1	M North, Harford	12508	2			6		5		9	7				4	10				11	1	8		3	23
24	Dec	28	(a)	Ipswich Town	D 1-1	M North	15607	2			6		5		9					4	10	5			11	1	8		3	24
25	Jan	1	(h)	LEICESTER CITY	W 3-1	Harford (3)	10917	2			6		5		9	7				4	10				11	1	8		3	25
26	Jan	11	(a)	Chelsea	L 0-1	-	21102	2	12		6					7			9	4	10				11	1	8		3	26
27	Jan	18	(h)	ASTON VILLA	W 2-0	Newell, B Stein	10217	2			6		5	11					9	4	10					1	8		3	27
28	Feb	1	(a)	Arsenal	L 1-2	Harford	22459	2			6		5		9				10	4	12				11	1	8		3	28
29	Feb	8	(a)	Southampton	W 2-1	Newell, B Stein	13740	2			6		5		9	7			10	4					11	1	8		3	29
30	Feb	22	(a)	Queens Park Rangers	D 1-1	Newell	13252				6		5		9	7	2		8	4	10				11	1			3	30
31	Mar	1	(h)	SHEFFIELD WEDNESDAY	W 1-0	Harford	10206				6		5		9	7	2		8	4	10				11	1			3	31
32	Mar	15	(h)	OXFORD UNITED	L 1-2	Preece	10633				6		5		9	7			10	4	12				11	1	8		3	32
33	Mar	19	(a)	Manchester United	L 0-2	-	33668	10	11		6					7	2		9	4		5		12		1	8		3	33
34	Mar	22	(h)	EVERTON	W 2-1	Foster, Newell	11039	10			6		5		9	7	2		8	4					11	1			3	34
35	Mar	29	(a)	Leicester City	D 0-0	-	9912	10			6		5		9		2	7	8	4					11	1		12	3	35
36	Apr	1	(h)	WEST BROMWICH ALBION	W 3-0	Newell, Harford (pen), Hill	9226	10			6		5		9	7	2		8	4					11	1		12	3	36
37	Apr	6	(a)	Birmingham City	W 2-0	Harford (2)	8836	10			6		5		9	7	2		8	4					11	1			3	37
38	Apr	12	(h)	TOTTENHAM HOTSPUR	D 1-1	Newell	13141				6		5		9	7	2		10	4					11	1	8		3	38
39	Apr	16	(h)	LIVERPOOL	L 0-1	-	15503	12			6		5		9	7	2		10	4					11	1	8		3	39
40	Apr	19	(a)	Coventry City	L 0-1	-	10161	8			6		5		9	7	2		10	4					11	1		12	3	40
41	Apr	26	(h)	WATFORD	W 3-2	Harford (3)	11810	2			6		5		9	7				4			10		11	1	8		3	41
42	May	3	(a)	Manchester City	D 1-1	Nwajiobi	20361	12			6		5		9	7	2			4			10		11	1	8		3	42
							Apps	34	2	7	42	3	35	2	37	38	15	3	16	41	9	2	20	4	40	35	33	3	41	
							Subs	2	3	-	-	3	-	1	-	-	-	-	-	-	4	-	1	4	1	-	-	3	-	
							Goals	-	1	-	-	-	3	-	22	3	-	-	6	-	3	-	5	-	2	-	14	-	1	

Final League Position: 9th

1 Own Goal

1985/86 FA CUP

Round	Month	Day	Venue	W,L,D Score	Scorers	Attendance	Breacker T	Daniel RC	Dibble A	Donaghy Mal	Elliott PM	Foster S	Grimes A	Harford M	Hill RA	Johnson R	King AE	Newell M	Nicholas P	North M	North S	Nwajiobi C	Parker GA	Preece D	Sealey L	Stein B	Stein M	Thomas MA	Round
3	Jan	6	(a) Crystal Palace	W 2-1	B Stein, Preece	9886	2			6		5		9	7				4	10				11	1	8		3	3
4	Jan	25	(h) BRISTOL ROVERS	W 4-0	Hill, Harford, North, Parkin (og)	12463	2			6		5		9	7				4	10				11	1	8		3	4
5	Feb	15	(h) ARSENAL	D 2-2	Hill, Harford	15799				6		5		9	7	2			4	10		12		11	1	8		3	5
Rep	Mar	3	(a) Arsenal	D 0-0	-	26547				6		5		9	7	2	8		4	10				11	1			3	Rep
Rep 2	Mar	5	(h) ARSENAL	W 3-0	M Stein, Foster, O'Leary (og)	13251				6		5		9	7	2	10		4					11	1		8	3	Rep 2
6	Mar	8	(h) EVERTON	D 2-2	M Stein, Harford	15529				6		5		9	7	2	10		4	12				11	1		8	3	6
Rep	Mar	12	(a) Everton	L 0-1	-	44264		12		6		5	10	9	7	2			4					11	1		8	3	Rep
						Apps	2		-	7	-	7	1	7	7	5	3	-	7	4	-	-	-	7	7	3	3	7	
						Subs		1												1		1							
				2 Own Goals		Goals						1		3	2					1				1		1	2		

1985/86 MILK CUP (LEAGUE CUP)

Round	Month	Day	Venue	W,L,D Score	Scorers	Attendance	Breacker T	Daniel RC	Dibble A	Donaghy Mal	Elliott PM	Foster S	Grimes A	Harford M	Hill RA	Johnson R	King AE	Newell M	Nicholas P	North M	Nwajiobi C	Parker GA	Preece D	Sealey L	Stein B	Stein M	Thomas MA	Round
2:1	Sep	24	(a) Sheffield United	W 2-1	B Stein, Nwajiobi	8943	2			6		5		9	7				4		10		11	1	8		3	2:1
2:2	Oct	8	(h) SHEFFIELD UNITED	W 3-1	Hill, North, Preece	5660	2			6		5			7				4	9	10		11	1	8		3	2:2
3	Oct	29	(h) NORWICH CITY	L 0-2	-	8203	2	4		6		5	12	9	7	3					10	11		1	8			3
						Apps	3	1	-	3	-	3	-	2	3	1	-	-	2	1	3	1	2	3	3	-	2	
						Subs							1															
						Goals									1					1	1		1		1			

▶ **The 1985/86 team** – Back row (left to right): M. Stein, Preece, Parker, Nwajiobi, S. North, M. North, Daniel, Johnson. Middle row (left to right): Moore (Coach), Breacker, Sealey, Elliott, Harford, Dibble, Thomas, Faulkner (Coach). Front row (left to right): Hartley (Coach), Hill, Donaghy, Foster, Pleat (Manager), Nicholas, B.Stein, Grimes, Sheridan (Physiotherapist).

TIMELINE...

17 August 1985 Brian Stein scores the first goal on the Kenilworth Road 'plastic'.
12 March 1986 The Town reach the F.A.Cup quarter-final once more but go down 0-1 at Everton after a replay.

1986/87 FOOTBALL LEAGUE DIVISION ONE

Match No	Month	Day	Venue	Opponents	W,L,D Score	Scorers	Attendance	Breacker T	Cobb G	Dibble A	Donaghy Mal	Foster S	Grimes A	Harford M	Harvey R	Hill RA	Johnson R	McDonough D	McEvoy R	Newell M	Nicholas P	North M	North S	Nwajiobi C	Preece D	Sealey L	Stein B	Stein M	Wilson R	Match No
1	Aug	23	(a)	Leicester City	D 1-1	B Stein	9801	2			6	5				7	3			9	4	12		11		1	8		10	1
2	Aug	26	(h)	SOUTHAMPTON	W 2-1	Wilson, B Stein	8777	2			6	5				7	3			9	4			11		1	8		10	2
3	Aug	30	(h)	NEWCASTLE UNITED	D 0-0	-	9254	2			6	5				7	3			9	4			11		1	8		10	3
4	Sep	3	(a)	Aston Villa	L 1-2	B Stein	13122	2			6	5				7	3			9	4	12		11		1	8		10	4
5	Sep	6	(a)	Chelsea	W 3-1	Newell (2), B Stein	13040				6	5	3			7	2			9	4			11		1	8		10	5
6	Sep	13	(h)	ARSENAL	D 0-0	-	9876				6	5	3			7	2			9	4			11		1	8	12	10	6
7	Sep	20	(a)	West Ham United	L 0-2	-	19133				6	5	3			7	2			9	4				11	1	8	12	10	7
8	Sep	27	(h)	MANCHESTER CITY	W 1-0	B Stein	9371				6	5	3			7	2			9	4				11	1	8	10		8
9	Oct	4	(a)	Tottenham Hotspur	D 0-0	-	22738				6	5	3			7	2			9	4				11	1	8			9
10	Oct	11	(h)	NORWICH CITY	D 0-0	-	10022				6	5	3			7	2	12		9	4	10			11	1	8			10
11	Oct	18	(a)	Manchester United	L 0-1	-	39927	2			6	5	3			7		12		9	4				11	1	8	10		11
12	Oct	25	(h)	LIVERPOOL	W 4-1	Newell (3), Hill	13140				6	5	3			7	2			9	4				11	1	8	10	12	12
13	Nov	1	(h)	QUEENS PARK RANGERS	W 1-0	Neill (og)	9085				6	5	3			7	2	12		9	4				11	1	8	10		13
14	Nov	8	(a)	Wimbledon	W 1-0	M Stein	6181	2			6	5				7	3	11		9	4					1	8	10	12	14
15	Nov	15	(h)	NOTTINGHAM FOREST	W 4-2	M Stein (2), Foster, B Stein	11097				6	5	11		3	7				9	4					1	8	10	12	15
16	Nov	22	(a)	Sheffield Wednesday	L 0-1	-	21171	2			6	5	11		3	7				9	4					1	8	10	12	16
17	Nov	29	(h)	CHARLTON ATHLETIC	W 1-0	M Stein	9273				6	5	3				2	11		9	4					1	8	10	7	17
18	Dec	6	(a)	Oxford United	L 2-4	B Stein, M Stein	8800	7			6	5	3				2	11		9	4					1	8	10		18
19	Dec	13	(h)	EVERTON	W 1-0	Newell	11151	2			6	5	11		3	7				9	4					1	8	10		19
20	Dec	20	(a)	Arsenal	L 0-3	-	28213	2			6		11		3	7				9	4		5			1	8	10		20
21	Dec	26	(h)	WATFORD	L 0-2	-	11140	2			6		11		3	7			12	9	4		5			1	8	10		21
22	Dec	28	(a)	Nottingham Forest	D 2-2	B Stein, Newell	20273	2			6	5	11	10			3			9	4					1	8	12	7	22
23	Jan	1	(a)	Coventry City	W 1-0	B Stein	16667	2			6	5	11	10			3			9	4					1	8		7	23
24	Jan	3	(h)	CHELSEA	W 1-0	Newell	10556	2			6	5	11	10			3			9	4					1	8		7	24
25	Jan	24	(h)	LEICESTER CITY	W 1-0	Newell	9102	2			6	5	11	10		7	3			9	4					1	8		7	25
26	Feb	7	(a)	Newcastle United	D 2-2	Grimes, Breacker	22447	2			6	5	11	10			3			9	4					1	8		7	26
27	Feb	14	(a)	ASTON VILLA	W 2-1	Foster, Harford (pen)	9174	2			6	5	11	10			3			9	4					1	8		7	27
28	Feb	21	(a)	Manchester City	D 1-1	B Stein	17507				6	5	3	10		7	2			9	4					1	8	11		28
29	Feb	28	(h)	WEST HAM UNITED	W 2-1	Nicholas, Grimes	11101				6	5	3	10		7	2			9	4					1	8	11		29
30	Mar	7	(a)	Liverpool	L 0-2	-	32433				6	5	11	10		7	3			9	4					1	8		12	30
31	Mar	14	(h)	MANCHESTER UNITED	W 2-1	Harford, B Stein	12509	2			6		11	10		7	3			9	4		5			1	8			31
32	Mar	21	(a)	Norwich City	D 0-0	-	16142	2			6		11	10		7	3			9	4		5			1	8			32
33	Mar	24	(a)	Southampton	L 0-3	-	12117	2			6		11	10		7	3	12		9	4		5			1	8			33
34	Mar	28	(h)	TOTTENHAM HOTSPUR	W 3-1	Harford, Newell, McDonough	13447	2			6		3	10		7		11		9	4		5			1	8			34
35	Apr	4	(h)	WIMBLEDON	D 0-0	-	9729	2			6			10	3	7		11		9	4		5			1	8			35
36	Apr	11	(a)	Queens Park Rangers	D 2-2	M Stein, Hill	9450	2			6				3	7				9	4		5		11	1	8	10		36
37	Apr	18	(h)	COVENTRY CITY	W 2-0	B Stein, Newell	9380	2			6		3	10		7		12		9	4		5		11	1	8			37
38	Apr	21	(a)	Watford	L 0-2	-	14650	2		1	6		3	10		7				9	4		5		11		8			38
39	Apr	25	(h)	SHEFFIELD WEDNESDAY	D 0-0	-	9278	2			6		3	10		7				9	4		5		11	1	8	12		39
40	May	2	(a)	Charlton Athletic	W 1-0	Harford	5469	2	8		6			10	3	7		12		9	4		5		11	1				40
41	May	5	(h)	OXFORD UNITED	L 2-3	Newell, M Stein	8917		8		6				3	7	2	12		9	4		5		11	1		10		41
42	May	9	(a)	Everton	L 1-3	M Stein	44097				6					7	2	3		9	4		5		11	1	8	10	12	42
							Apps	29	2	1	42	28	31	18	5	30	34	10	-	42	42	2	14	6	14	41	38	17	16	
							Subs					2	2	4				8	1						3			4	5	
							Goals	1				2	2	4		2		1		12	1						12	8	1	

Final League Position: 7th

1 Own Goal

1986/87 FA CUP

Round	Month	Day	Venue	Opponents	W/L/D Score	Scorers	Attendance	Breacker T	Cobb G	Dibble A	Donaghy Mal	Foster S	Grimes A	Harford M	Harvey R	Hill RA	Johnson R	McDonough D	McEvoy R	Newell M	Nicholas P	North M	North S	Nwajiobi C	Preece D	Sealey L	Stein B	Stein M	Wilson R	Round
3	Jan	11	(h)	LIVERPOOL	D 0-0	-	11085			6	5	3		10		7	2			9	4				11	1	8			3
Rep	Jan	26	(a)	Liverpool	D 0-0	-	34822	2		6	5	11		10		7	3			9	4					1	8			Rep
Rep 2	Jan	28	(h)	LIVERPOOL	W 3-0	B Stein, Harford, Newell	14687	2		6	5	11		10		7	3	12		9	4					1	8			Rep 2
4	Jan	31	(h)	QUEENS PARK RANGERS	D 1-1	Harford	12707	2		6	5	11		10		7	3			9	4					1	8			4
Rep	Feb	4	(a)	Queens Park Rangers	L 1-2	Harford	15848	2		6	5	11		10		7	3			9	4					1	8			Rep
Apps								4		5	5	5		5		5	5			5	5				1	5	5			
Subs																		1												
Goals														3						1							1			

The 1986/87 team – Back row (left to right): Tuite, Preece, M.Stein, Nwajiobi, M.North, McEvoy, Johnson. Middle row (left to right): Ryan (Coach), Breacker, Sealey, M.Harford, S.North, Dibble, Newell, Faulkner (Coach). Front row (left to right): R.Harford (coach), Hill, Donaghy, Foster, Moore (Manager), Nicholas, B.Stein, Grimes, Kirby (Physiotherapist).

TIMELINE...

16 May 1986 David Pleat resigns to take up the manager's position at Tottenham.
3 June 1986 Another ex-player, John Moore, takes over the manager's job.
Summer 1986 The Kenilworth Road terrace is covered, the Bobbers Stand is converted to Executive boxes and seats are installed in the Oak Road end.
August 1986 The Town controversially ban away supporters from Kenilworth Road which leads to expulsion from that season's Littlewoods Cup.
9 May 1987 A final position of seventh in Division One is achieved, the highest in the club's history.

1987/88 FOOTBALL LEAGUE DIVISION ONE

Match No	Month	Day	Venue	Opponents	W.L.D Score	Scorers	Attendance	Allinson I	Black K	Breacker T	Cobb G	Dibble A	Donaghy Mal	Foster S	Gray RP	Grimes A	Harford M	Harvey R	Hill RA	James J	Johnson M	Johnson R	McDonough D	McEvoy R	Newell M	North S	Nwajiobi C	Oldfield D	Preece D	Sealey L	Stein B	Stein M	Weir M	Wilson D	Wilson R	Match No
1	Aug	15	(a)	Derby County	L 0-1	-	17204			2			6	5		3	9		4				13	12					11	1	8			7	10	1
2	Aug	18	(h)	COVENTRY CITY	L 0-1	-	7506			2				5		3	9		4				6		8		12		11	1				7	10	2
3	Aug	22	(h)	WEST HAM UNITED	D 2-2	Harford (2)	8073			2	8			5		3	9		4				6	10	12				11	1				7		3
4	Aug	29	(a)	Chelsea	L 0-3	-	16075			2	8		4	5		3			7						9				11	1				7	6	4
5	Aug	31	(h)	ARSENAL	D 1-1	Wilson (pen)	8745			2			6	5		3			4						9				11	1	8	12		7		5
6	Sep	5	(a)	Oxford United	W 5-2	Breacker, Harford, Hill, Nwajiobi, B Stein	6804			2			6	5		3	9		4			12			10		11			1	8	13		7		6
7	Sep	12	(h)	EVERTON	W 2-1	Hill, B Stein	8124			2			6	5		3	9		4			13			10		11			1	8	12		7		7
8	Sep	19	(a)	Charlton Athletic	L 0-1	-	5002			2			6	5			9		4			13	3				11			1	8	10	12	7		8
9	Sep	26	(a)	Queens Park Rangers	L 0-2	-	11175		11	2			6	5		3	9		4											1	8	10	12	7		9
10	Oct	3	(h)	MANCHESTER UNITED	D 1-1	Harford	9137		11	2			6	5		3	9		4				12							1	8	13	10	7		10
11	Oct	10	(a)	Portsmouth	L 1-3	Harford (pen)	12391			2			6	5		3	9		4			10	12						13	1	8		11	7		11
12	Oct	17	(h)	WIMBLEDON	W 2-0	B Stein, Wilson	7018	12	10	2			6	5		3	9					4								1	8		11	7		12
13	Oct	24	(h)	LIVERPOOL	L 0-1	-	11997	10		2			6	5		3	9					4								1	8		11	7		13
14	Nov	7	(h)	NEWCASTLE UNITED	W 4-0	Nwajiobi, B Stein, M Stein (2)	7638	11		2			6	5		3						4					9			1	8	10		7		14
15	Nov	14	(a)	Sheffield Wednesday	W 2-0	Allinson, M Stein	16960	11		2			6	5		3						4					9			1	8	10		7		15
16	Nov	21	(h)	TOTTENHAM HOTSPUR	W 2-0	Allison (2)	10091	11		2			6	5		3					7	4					9			1	8	10		7		16
17	Dec	5	(h)	NORWICH CITY	L 1-2	B Stein	7002	11		2			6	5		3					12	4					9			1	8		10	7		17
18	Dec	12	(a)	Watford	W 1-0	Foster	12152	11		2			6	5		3	9					4								1	8		10	7		18
19	Dec	18	(h)	SOUTHAMPTON	D 2-2	Harford, McDonough	6618	11		2			6	5		3	9				12	4								1	8			7		19
20	Dec	26	(a)	Everton	L 0-2	-	32128	11		2			6	5		3	9				10		13							1	8		12	7		20
21	Dec	28	(h)	CHARLTON ATHLETIC	W 1-0	Wilson	7243	11		2			6	5			9						3							1	8	10		7		21
22	Jan	1	(h)	CHELSEA	W 3-0	M Stein, B Stein, Harford	8018	11		2			6	5			9						3							1	8	10		7		22
23	Jan	2	(a)	West Ham United	D 1-1	M Stein	16716	11		2			6	5			9						3							1	8	10		7		23
24	Jan	16	(a)	DERBY COUNTY	W 1-0	McDonough	7175	11	9	2			6	5									3							1	8	10		7		24
25	Feb	6	(h)	OXFORD UNITED	W 7-4	Harford (2), B Stein, McDonough, M Stein (3)	8063	11		2			6	5		12	9						3							1	8	10		7		25
26	Feb	13	(a)	Arsenal	L 1-2	M Stein	22612	11		2			6	5		3	9						4							1	8	10		7		26
27	Mar	5	(a)	Wimbledon	L 0-2	-	4854	11		2			6			3	9			5	4									1	8	10		7		27
28	Mar	15	(a)	Coventry City	L 0-4	-	13711	11	12	2	13		6	5		3	9					8								1	8	10		7		28
29	Mar	29	(h)	PORTSMOUTH	W 4-1	B Stein, M Stein, Wilson, Mariner (og)	6740	11		2			6	5		3						9	4							1	8	10		7		29
30	Apr	2	(a)	Newcastle United	L 0-4	-	20752	11	12	2			6	5		3	9					8	4						13	1	8	10		7		30
31	Apr	5	(h)	SHEFFIELD WEDNESDAY	D 2-2	McDonough, B Stein	7337	12		2			6	5		3	9					11	4							1	8	10		7		31
32	Apr	12	(a)	Manchester United	L 0-3	-	28830	11	12	2		1	6	5			9						3								8	10		7		32
33	Apr	19	(h)	QUEENS PARK RANGERS	W 2-1	Wilson (pen), Foster	6735			2		1		5			9			6	3	4						11			8	10		7		33
34	Apr	30	(a)	Norwich City	D 2-2	M Stein, Wilson (pen)	13171	9	11	2		1	6			10		4		12	3							13				8		7		34
35	May	2	(h)	WATFORD	W 2-1	Oldfield, Wilson (pen)	10409	8	11	2		1		5		3				10	6	4					9							7		35
36	May	4	(a)	Tottenham Hotspur	L 1-2	Grimes	15437			2	12	1		5		10					6	3					7	8	11				4			36
37	May	7	(a)	Southampton	D 1-1	Wilson	12722	12	11	2	8	1		5		3		13			6	4					10	9						7		37
38	May	9	(a)	Liverpool	D 1-1	Oldfield	30374	8	11	2	12	1		5		4		13			6	3						9	10					7		38
39	May	13	(h)	NOTTINGHAM FOREST	D 1-1	Donaghy	9108			2		1	6	5		3	9				12	4						8	10					7		39
40	May	15	(a)	Nottingham Forest	D 1-1	Oldfield	13106	11	12	2	4	1		5				13			6	3						9	10			8		7		40
				Apps				23	10	40	4	9	32	39	-	31	24	-	16	-	7	21	24	-	4	-	10	6	13	31	28	20	7	38	3	
				Subs				4	-	-	3	-	-	-	-	1	1	-	1	3	2	4	3	-	1	1	2	2	-	-	-	-	-	5	1	
				Goals				3	-	1	-	-	1	2	-	1	9	-	2	-	-	-	4	-	1	1	2	3	-	-	9	11	-	8	-	

Final League Position: 9th   1 Own Goal

1987/88 FA CUP

Round	Month	Day	Venue	Opponents	W/L/D	Score	Scorers	Attendance	Allinson I	Black K	Breacker T	Cobb G	Dibble A	Donaghy Mal	Foster S	Gray RP	Grimes A	Harford M	Harvey R	Hill RA	James J	Johnson M	Johnson R	McDonough D	McEvoy R	Newell M	North S	Nwajiobi C	Oldfield D	Preece D	Sealey L	Stein B	Stein M	Weir M	Wilson D	Wilson R	Round
3	Jan	9	(a)	Hartlepool United	W	2-1	Weir, McDonough	6187	11		2			6	5							3		4							1	8	10	9	7		3
4	Jan	30	(h)	SOUTHAMPTON	W	2-1	Allinson, B Stein	10009	11		2			6	5		12	9				3		4							1	8	10		7		4
5	Feb	20	(a)	Queens Park Rangers	D	1-1	Harford	15856	11		2			6	5		3	9						4							1	8	10		7		5
Rep	Feb	24	(h)	QUEENS PARK RANGERS	W	1-0	Neill (og)	10854	11		2			6	5		3	9						4							1	8	10		7		Rep
6	Mar	12	(h)	PORTSMOUTH	W	3-1	Wilson, M Stein, Harford	12857	11		2			6	5		3	9				8		4							1		10		7		6
SF	Apr	9	(n)	Wimbledon	L	1-2	Harford	25963		12	2		1	6	5		3	9				11		4								8	10		7		SF
							Apps		5	-	6	-	1	6	6	-	4	5	-	-	-	4	-	6	-	-	-	-	-	-	5	5	6	1	6	-	
							Subs		-	1	-	-	-	-	-	-	1	-	-	-	-	-	-	-	-	-	-	-	-	-	-	-	-	-	-	-	
							Goals		1	-	-	-	-	-	-	-	-	3	-	-	-	-	-	1	-	-	-	-	-	-	-	1	1	1	1	-	

Semi Final played at White Hart Lane.

1 Own Goal

1987/88 LITTLEWOODS CUP (LEAGUE CUP)

Round	Month	Day	Venue	Opponents	W/L/D	Score	Scorers	Attendance	Allinson I	Black K	Breacker T	Cobb G	Dibble A	Donaghy Mal	Foster S	Gray RP	Grimes A	Harford M	Harvey R	Hill RA	James J	Johnson M	Johnson R	McDonough D	McEvoy R	Newell M	North S	Nwajiobi C	Oldfield D	Preece D	Sealey L	Stein B	Stein M	Weir M	Wilson D	Wilson R	Round
2:1	Sep	22	(a)	Wigan Athletic	W	1-0	Weir	5018			2			6	5			9	4					3					12	11	1	8		10	7		2:1
2:2	Oct	6	(h)	WIGAN ATHLETIC	W	4-2	Harford (3), McDonough	4240		10	2			6	5		3	9						4							1	8		11	7		2:2
3	Oct	27	(n)	COVENTRY CITY	W	3-1	Harford (2), Weir	11448			2			6	5		3	9				10		4							1	8		11	7		3
4	Nov	17	(a)	Ipswich Town	W	1-0	B Stein	15643	12		2			6	5					3		10			9	13					1	8	11		7		4
5	Jan	19	(h)	BRADFORD CITY	W	2-0	Foster, Harford	11022		11	2			6	5			9						4							1	8	10		7		5
SF1	Feb	10	(a)	Oxford United	D	1-1	B Stein	12943			2			6	5		11	9						3							1	8	10		7		SF1
SF2	Feb	28	(h)	OXFORD UNITED	W	2-0	B Stein, Grimes	13010			2			6	5		3	9				11		3							1	8	10		7		SF2
F	Apr	24	(n)	Arsenal	W	3-2	B Stein (2), Wilson	95732	11		2	1		6	5		13	9	4					3						10		8	12		7		F
							Apps		-	3	8	-	-	8	8	-	4	7	1	2	-	7	-	6	1	-	1	-	2	7	8	4	3	8			
							Subs		-	1	-	-	-	-	-	-	1	-	-	-	-	-	-	-	-	-	-	1	1	-	-	-	-	1	1		
							Goals		-	-	-	-	-	-	1	-	1	6	-	-	-	-	-	1	-	-	-	-	-	-	-	5	2	1			

3rd Round match was a "home" game but played at Filbert Street. Final played at Wembley.

1987/88 SIMOD CUP (FULL MEMBERS CUP)

Round	Month	Day	Venue	Opponents	W/L/D	Score	Scorers	Attendance	Allinson I	Black K	Breacker T	Cobb G	Dibble A	Donaghy Mal	Foster S	Gray RP	Grimes A	Harford M	Harvey R	Hill RA	James J	Johnson M	Johnson R	McDonough D	McEvoy R	Newell M	North S	Nwajiobi C	Oldfield D	Preece D	Sealey L	Stein B	Stein M	Weir M	Wilson D	Wilson R	Round
3	Feb	16	(a)	Everton	W	2-1	Oldfield (2)	5204	6	10	2	7	1			5	8	11	12			3			4				9								3
4	Mar	1	(h)	STOKE CITY	W	4-1	Harford (2), B Stein (2)	4580	11	7	2				6			9	3			5		4						12	1	8	10				4
SF	Mar	8	(h)	SWINDON TOWN	W	2-1	B Stein, M Stein	10027	11	12	2				6		3	9				4		5							1	8	10		7		SF
F	Mar	27	(n)	Reading	L	1-4	Harford	61740	11	12	2				6	5	3	9						13					4		1	8	10		7		F
							Apps		4	2	4	1	1		3	2	1	3	3	1	-	2		2	2	1	-		1	-	3	3	3	-	2	-	
							Subs		-	2	-	-	-		-	-	-	-	-	-	-	1		-	-	-	-		-	1	-	-	-	-	-	-	
							Goals		-	-	-	-	-		-	-	-	3	-	-	-	-		-	-	-	-		2	-	-	3	1	-	-	-	

Final played at Wembley.

TIMELINE...

16 June 1987 John Moore resigns his position to be replaced in the 'hot seat' by his assistant Ray Harford.
27 March 1988 The Town go down 1-4 to Reading in the Simod Cup final at Wembley.
9 April 1988 Defeat for the Hatters in the F.A.Cup semi-final.
24 April 1988 At last! A major trophy is secured with Arsenal seen off 3-2 in the Littlewoods Cup final at Wembley.

1987/88
LITTLEWOODS CUP WINNERS

▶ **The 1987/88 team** – Back row (left to right): Preece, Nwajiobi, Harvey, North, Cobb, Black, M.Stein. Middle row (left to right): Ryan (Coach), Faulkner (Coach), Johnson, Grimes, Sealey, M.Harford, Dibble, McDonough, R.Wilson, Weir, Kirby (Physiotherapist). Front row (left to right): D.Wilson, B.Stein, Foster, R.Harford (Manager), Donaghy, Hill, Breacker.

▶ Brian Stein nets the first goal in the Littlewoods Cup Final.

▶ Danny Wilson nods in number two.

▶ Stein crashes home the last minute winner.

▶ The victorious squad.

1988/89 FOOTBALL LEAGUE DIVISION ONE

Match No	Month	Day	Venue	Opponents	W,L,D Score	Scorers	Attendance	Allinson I	Beaumont D	Black K	Breacker T	Chamberlain A	Cooke R	Donaghy Mal	Dowie I	Dreyer J	Foster S	Grimes A	Harford M	Harvey R	Hill RA	James J	Johnson M	Johnson R	McDonough D	Meade R	Oldfield D	Preece D	Sealey L	Wegerle R	Williams S	Wilson D	Match No
1	Aug	27	(a)	Sheffield Wednesday	L 0-1	-	16433	12		11	2			6		3	5		9								10		1	8	4	7	1
2	Sep	3	(h)	WIMBLEDON	D 2-2	Ryan (og), Black	8067			11				6			5	3	9					2			10	8	1		4	7	2
3	Sep	10	(a)	Southampton	L 1-2	Foster	13214			11				6			5	3	9					2			8	10	1	12	4	7	3
4	Sep	17	(h)	MANCHESTER UNITED	L 0-2		11010			11						3	5		9		10		6	2			8		1	12	4	7	4
5	Sep	24	(a)	Everton	W 2-0	Black, Oldfield	26002	13		11	12			6		3	5		9		10			2			8		1		4	7	5
6	Oct	1	(a)	Nottingham Forest	D 0-0		15340	12		11				6		3	5		9		10			2			8		1		4	7	6
7	Oct	8	(h)	LIVERPOOL	W 1-0	Harford	12117			11				6		3	5		9		10			2			8		1	12	4	7	7
8	Oct	22	(a)	Middlesbrough	L 1-2	Wilson (pen)	17792			11	12					3	5		9		10		6	2	4		8		1	13		7	8
9	Oct	25	(h)	ARSENAL	D 1-1	Black	10548			11	3						5		9		10		6	2	4		12		1	8		7	9
10	Oct	29	(h)	QUEENS PARK RANGERS	D 0-0		8453	9		11						3	5				10		6	2			12		1	8	4	7	10
11	Nov	5	(a)	Millwall	L 1-3	Wilson	12511			11						3	5				10	2	6	12			8		1	9	4	7	11
12	Nov	12	(a)	Coventry City	L 0-1		12625			11							5	3	9		10		6	2			12		1	8	4	7	12
13	Nov	19	(h)	WEST HAM UNITED	W 4-1	Black (2), Wegerle, Wilson	9308			11							5	3	9				6	2			10	4	1	8		7	13
14	Nov	26	(a)	Norwich City	D 2-2	Wegerle (2)	13541			11							5		9	3			6	2			10	4	1	8		7	14
15	Dec	3	(h)	NEWCASTLE UNITED	D 0-0		8338	12		11							5			3	10		6	2			9	4	1	8		7	15
16	Dec	10	(a)	Derby County	W 1-0	Harford	15228			11							5		9	3	10		6	2			12	4	1	8		7	16
17	Dec	17	(h)	ASTON VILLA	D 1-1	Wegerle	8785			11							5		9	3	10		6	2				4	1	8		7	17
18	Dec	26	(a)	Tottenham Hotspur	D 0-0		27337										5		9	3	10		6	2			11	4	1	8		7	18
19	Dec	31	(a)	Wimbledon	L 0-4		4899	12									5		9	3	10		6	2			11		1	8		7	19
20	Jan	2	(h)	SOUTHAMPTON	W 6-1	Black, Harford (2), Hill, Wegerle (2)	8637			11							5		9	3	10		6	2				4	1	8		7	20
21	Jan	14	(a)	Charlton Athletic	L 0-3	-	5212			11	12					13	5			3	10		6				9	2	1	8		7	21
22	Jan	21	(h)	EVERTON	W 1-0	Wegerle	9013			11	2					13	5	3	9		10		6		12			4	1	8		7	22
23	Feb	4	(h)	NOTTINGHAM FOREST	L 2-3	Black, Harford	10465			11	2						5	3	9		10		6				12	4	1	8		7	23
24	Feb	18	(h)	MIDDLESBROUGH	W 1-0	Foster	8187		6	11	2						5	3	9		10							4	1	8		7	24
25	Feb	25	(a)	Arsenal	L 0-2		31026		6	11	2						5		9	3	10						12	4	1	8		7	25
26	Mar	11	(h)	MILLWALL	L 1-2	Wilson (pen)	10722		6	11	2					12	13	3	9		10				5			4	1	8		7	26
27	Mar	14	(a)	Liverpool	L 0-5		31447		6	11	2					12		3	9		10				5		8	4	1			7	27
28	Mar	18	(h)	SHEFFIELD WEDNESDAY	L 0-1		7776		6	11	2					12	5	3	9	13	10						8	4	1			7	28
29	Mar	21	(a)	Queens Park Rangers	D 1-1	Hill	9072		6	11	2					12	5		9	3	10						4	8	1			7	29
30	Mar	25	(a)	Manchester United	L 0-2		36335		6	11	2		12			13	5		9	3	10						4	8	1			7	30
31	Mar	28	(h)	TOTTENHAM HOTSPUR	L 1-3	Foster	11146		6	11	2		12			8	5	3	9		10						7	4	1			7	31
32	Apr	1	(a)	Aston Villa	L 1-2	Hill	15640		6	11	2					13	5	3	9		10						7	12	1	8		4 7	32
33	Apr	15	(h)	COVENTRY CITY	D 2-2	Dreyer, Wilson	8610		6	11	2	1	12			3	5		9		10						9	4		8		7	33
34	Apr	22	(a)	Newcastle United	D 0-0		18636		6	11	2	1				3	5		9		10				13	12		4		8		7	34
35	Apr	29	(h)	DERBY COUNTY	W 3-0	Wilson (pen), Harford, Black	8507		6	11	2	1	12			3	5		9		10							4		8		7	35
36	May	2	(h)	CHARLTON ATHLETIC	W 5-2	Wilson (2), Black, Harford, Wegerle	10024		6	11	2	1	12			3	5		9		10							4		8		7	36
37	May	6	(a)	West Ham United	L 0-1		18686		6	11	2	1	12			3	5		9		10							4		8		7	37
38	May	13	(h)	NORWICH CITY	W 1-0	Wilson (pen)	10862		6	11	2	1				3	5		9		10							4		8		7	38
				Final League Position: 16th		1 Own Goal	**Apps**	1	15	36	19	6	-	6	1	16	36	12	33	11	33	1	16	19	9	2	15	26	32	26	10	37	
							Subs	4	-	1	3	-	6	-	7	2	-	-	-	1	-	-	-	-	2	1	2	6	-	-	4	-	
							Goals	-	-	9	-	-	-	-	-	1	3	-	7	-	3	-	-	-	-	-	1	-	-	8	-	9	

1988/89 FA CUP

Round	Month	Day	Venue	W,L,D Score	Scorers	Attendance	Allinson I	Beaumont D	Black K	Breacker T	Chamberlain A	Cooke R	Donaghy Mal	Dowie I	Dreyer J	Foster S	Grimes A	Harford M	Harvey R	Hill RA	James J	Johnson M	Johnson R	McDonough D	Meade R	Oldfield D	Preece D	Sealey L	Wegerle R	Williams S	Wilson D	Round
3	Jan	7	(a) Millwall	L 2-3	Black, Wilson (pen)	12504			11							5		9	3	10	13	6	2			12	4	1	8		7	3
						Apps			1							1		1	1	1		1	1				1	1	1	1	1		
						Subs															1					1							
						Goals			1																						1		

1988/89 LITTLEWOODS CUP (LEAGUE CUP)

Round	Month	Day	Venue	Opponents	W,L,D Score	Scorers	Attendance	Allinson I	Beaumont D	Black K	Breacker T	Chamberlain A	Cooke R	Donaghy Mal	Dowie I	Dreyer J	Foster S	Grimes A	Harford M	Harvey R	Hill RA	James J	Johnson M	Johnson R	McDonough D	Meade R	Oldfield D	Preece D	Sealey L	Wegerle R	Williams S	Wilson D	Round
2:1	Sep	27	(h)	BURNLEY	D 1-1	R Johnson	6282		11	12				6		3	5		9		10			2			8		1	4		7	2:1
2:2	Oct	11	(a)	Burnley	W 1-0	Hill	14036	13	11	12				6		3	5		9		10			2			8		1	4		7	2:2
3	Nov	2	(a)	Leeds United	W 2-0	Wilson, Oldfield	19450		11							3	5				10	2	6				8		1	9	4	7	3
4	Nov	29	(h)	MANCHESTER CITY	W 3-1	Oldfield, Wegerle (2)	10178		11							3	5		9	3	12		6				10	4	1	8		7	4
5	Jan	18	(h)	SOUTHAMPTON	D 1-1	Hill	11735		11	2				6	9	3	5				10							4	1	8		7	5
Rep	Jan	25	(a)	Southampton	W 2-1	Harford, Hill	18872		11	2				6		3	5		9		10						12	4	1	8		7	Rep
SF1	Feb	12	(a)	West Ham United	W 3-0	Harford, Wegerle, Wilson (pen)	24602		6	11	2					3	5		9		10							4	1	8		7	SF1
SF2	Mar	1	(h)	WEST HAM UNITED	W 2-0	Harford, Wegerle	12020		6	11	2					3	5		9		10							4	1	8		7	SF2
F	Apr	9	(n)	Nottingham Forest	L 1-3	Harford	76130		6	11	2					3	5		9		10				12			4	1	8		7	F
							Apps		9	4	4			3	1	9	9		7		8	1	2	2			6	5	9	9	1	9	
							Subs	1		2											1				1		1						
							Goals												4		3			1			2			4		2	

Final played at Wembley.

1988/89 SIMOD CUP (FULL MEMBERS CUP)

Round	Month	Day	Venue	Opponents	W,L,D Score	Scorers	Attendance	Allinson I	Beaumont D	Black K	Breacker T	Chamberlain A	Cooke R	Donaghy Mal	Dowie I	Dreyer J	Foster S	Grimes A	Harford M	Harvey R	Hill RA	James J	Johnson M	Johnson R	McDonough D	Meade R	Oldfield D	Preece D	Sealey L	Wegerle R	Williams S	Wilson D	Round
3	Jan	10	(a)	Crystal Palace	L 1-4	Dowie	5842				2	1			8	3			9		10	5	6				11	4		12	7		3
							Apps				1	1			1	1			1		1	1	1				1	1			1		
							Subs																							1			
							Goals								1																		

TIMELINE...
9 April 1989 The Town reach the Littlewoods Cup final again but lose 1-3 to Nottingham Forest.

Match No	Month	Day	Venue	Opponents	W/L/D Score	Scorers	Attendance	Allpress T	Beaumont D	Black K	Breacker T	Chamberlain A	Cooke R	Donaghy Mal	Dowie I	Dreyer J	Elstrup L	Farrell S	Gray RP	Harford M	Harvey R	Hughes C	James J	Johnson M	Kennedy M	McDonough D	Nogan K	Pouch N	Preece D	Rees J	Rodger G	Tighe A	Wegerle R	Williams S	Wilson D	Match No
1	Aug	19	(a)	Tottenham Hotspur	L 1-2	Wegerle	17668		6	11	2	1			12	3					13				7	5			10				8	4	9	1
2	Aug	22	(h)	SHEFFIELD WEDNESDAY	W 2-0	Wilson (pen), Black	9503		6	11	2	1				3	12								7	5			10				8	4	9	2
3	Aug	26	(h)	LIVERPOOL	D 0-0	-	11124		6	11	2	1				3	12				13				7	5			10				8	4	9	3
4	Aug	30	(a)	Queens Park Rangers	D 0-0	-	10565		6	11	2	1				3	12								7	5			10				8	4	9	4
5	Sep	9	(h)	CHARLTON ATHLETIC	W 1-0	Wilson (pen)	8859		6	11	2	1				3									7	5			10				8	4	9	5
6	Sep	16	(a)	Coventry City	L 0-1	-	11207		6	11	2	1	13		9	3					12				7	5			10				8	4		6
7	Sep	23	(h)	WIMBLEDON	D 1-1	Wegerle (pen)	8449		6	11	2	1	13		9	3					12				7	5			10				8	4		7
8	Sep	30	(a)	Manchester City	L 1-3	Black	23863		6	11	2	1	12		9	3								13	7	5			10				8	4		8
9	Oct	14	(h)	ASTON VILLA	L 0-1	-	9433		6	11	2	1	12		9	3					13				7				10		5		8	4		9
10	Oct	21	(h)	NORWICH CITY	W 4-1	Black, Dreyer, Wilson, Williams	9038		6	11	2	1				3	12				13				7				10		5		8	4	9	10
11	Oct	28	(a)	Millwall	D 1-1	Elstrup	11140		6	11	2	1			12	3	9				13					5			10				8	4	7	11
12	Nov	4	(h)	DERBY COUNTY	W 1-0	Dowie	8919		6	11	2	1			9	3	8								7	5			10				12	4		12
13	Nov	11	(a)	Crystal Palace	D 1-1	Wilson	11346		6	11	2	1				3	8				12				7	5			10				13	4	9	13
14	Nov	18	(h)	MANCHESTER UNITED	L 1-3	Wilson	11414			11	2	1			9	6	12				3					5			10				8	4	7	14
15	Nov	25	(a)	Southampton	L 3-6	Dreyer, Black, Elstrup	14014			11	2	1			9	6	8				3			12		5			10				13	4	7	15
16	Dec	2	(h)	TOTTENHAM HOTSPUR	D 0-0	-	12620			11	2	1			9	6	13				3				12	5			10					4	7	16
17	Dec	9	(a)	Sheffield Wednesday	D 1-1	James	16339				2	1	12		9	6	10				3		8			5			11					4	7	17
18	Dec	16	(a)	Arsenal	L 2-3	Elstrup (2, 1 pen)	28760			11	2	1	12	5	9	6	10		13				8							4					7	18
19	Dec	26	(h)	NOTTINGHAM FOREST	D 1-1	Cooke	10754			11	2	1	8	5	9	6	10			12	13									4					7	19
20	Dec	30	(h)	CHELSEA	L 0-3	-	10068			11	2	1	7	5	9	6				12	3		8						10	4						20
21	Jan	1	(a)	Everton	L 1-2	Wilson (pen)	21755				2	1		5	9	6			11		12	13	8						10	4					7	21
22	Jan	13	(a)	Liverpool	D 2-2	Black, Nogan	35312			11	2	1		5	9	6					3						8		10	4					7	22
23	Jan	20	(h)	QUEENS PARK RANGERS	D 1-1	Preece	9703			11	2	1			9	6					3		12			5	8		10	4					7	23
24	Feb	14	(a)	Wimbledon	W 2-1	Nogan, Dowie	3618			11	2	1			9	6	12				3					5	8		10	4					7	24
25	Feb	19	(a)	Charlton Athletic	L 0-2	-	6201			11	2	1			9	6	12				3		13			5	8		10	4					7	25
26	Feb	24	(h)	SOUTHAMPTON	D 1-1	Dowie	9417			11	2	1			9	6					3		12			5	8		10	4					7	26
27	Mar	3	(a)	Manchester United	L 1-4	Black	35237			11	2	1	12		9	6					3		13			5	8		10	4					7	27
28	Mar	7	(h)	COVENTRY CITY	W 3-2	Black, Gray, Dowie	8244			11	2	1			9	6			13		3		12			5	8		10	4					7	28
29	Mar	10	(a)	Aston Villa	L 0-2	-	22505	3		11	2	1			9	6							10			5	8	12		4					7	29
30	Mar	17	(h)	MANCHESTER CITY	D 1-1	Wilson (pen)	9765			11	2	1			9	6	12				3					5	8		10	13					7	30
31	Mar	24	(h)	MILLWALL	W 2-1	McCarthy (og), Black	9027			11	2	1			9	6			8		3		12			5			10	4					7	31
32	Mar	31	(a)	Norwich City	L 0-2	-	14451			11	2	1			9	6					12		8	3		5			10	4					7	32
33	Apr	7	(a)	Chelsea	L 0-1	-	13114		13	11	2	1	8		9	6	12							3		5			10	4					7	33
34	Apr	14	(h)	EVERTON	D 2-2	Dowie (2)	9538		12	11	2	1	13		9	6								3		5	8		10	4					7	34
35	Apr	16	(a)	Nottingham Forest	L 0-3	-	17001		12	11	2	1			9	6	13							3		5	8		10	4					7	35
36	Apr	21	(h)	ARSENAL	W 2-0	Dowie, Black	11595		4	11	2	1			9	6	12						13	3		5	8		10						7	36
37	Apr	28	(h)	CRYSTAL PALACE	W 1-0	Dowie	10369		4	11	2	1			9	6	12						13	3		5	8		10						7	37
38	May	5	(a)	Derby County	W 3-2	Breacker, Black (2)	17044		4	11	2	1			9	6	12						13	3		5	8		10						7	38
				Apps				1	16	36	38	38	3	5	26	38	13	-	2	1	17	1	19	7	30	15	10	-	30	8	2	-	13	14	35	
				Subs				-	3	-	-	-	8	-	3	-	10	1	5	3	9	-	1	5	2	-	-	1	2	6	-	-	2	-	-	
				Goals				-	-	11	1	-	1	-	8	2	4	-	1	-	-	-	1	-	-	-	2	-	1	-	-	-	2	1	7	

Final League Position: 17th

1 Own Goal

1989/90 FA CUP

Round	Month	Day	Venue	Opponents	W,L,D Score	Scorers	Attendance	Allpress T	Beaumont D	Black K	Breacker T	Chamberlain A	Cooke R	Donaghy Mal	Dowie I	Dreyer J	Elstrup L	Farrell S	Gray RP	Harford M	Harvey R	Hughes C	James J	Johnson M	Kennedy M	McDonough D	Nogan K	Poutch N	Preece D	Rees J	Rodger G	Tighe A	Wegerle R	Williams S	Wilson D	Round
3	Jan	6	(a)	Brighton & Hove Albion	L 1-4	Wilson	10361		11	2	1				12	6				9	3		**4**	5	8				10						7	3
						Apps			1	1	1					1				1	1		1	1	1				1						1	
						Subs									1																					
						Goals																													1	

1989/90 LITTLEWOODS CUP (LEAGUE CUP)

Round	Month	Day	Venue	Opponents	W,L,D Score	Scorers	Attendance	Allpress T	Beaumont D	Black K	Breacker T	Chamberlain A	Cooke R	Donaghy Mal	Dowie I	Dreyer J	Elstrup L	Farrell S	Gray RP	Harford M	Harvey R	Hughes C	James J	Johnson M	Kennedy M	McDonough D	Nogan K	Poutch N	Preece D	Rees J	Rodger G	Tighe A	Wegerle R	Williams S	Wilson D	Round
2:1	Sep	19	(a)	Mansfield Town	W 4-3	Wegerle (2), Elstrup (2)	5361	6	12	2	1					3	9								7	5			10				8	11	4	2:1
2:2	Oct	3	(h)	MANSFIELD TOWN	W 7-2	Wegerle (2), Preece, Elstrup (3), Dreyer	6519	6	11	2	1					3	9								7				10		5		8		4	2:2
3	Oct	24	(a)	Everton	L 0-3	-	18428	6	11	2	1			13		3	9				7		12			5			10				8		4	3
						Apps		3	2	3	3					3	3				1				2	2			3		1		3	1	3	
						Subs			1					1									1													
						Goals										1	5												1				4			

1989/90 ZENITH DATA SYSTEMS CUP (FULL MEMBERS CUP)

Round	Month	Day	Venue	Opponents	W,L,D Score	Scorers	Attendance	Allpress T	Beaumont D	Black K	Breacker T	Chamberlain A	Cooke R	Donaghy Mal	Dowie I	Dreyer J	Elstrup L	Farrell S	Gray RP	Harford M	Harvey R	Hughes C	James J	Johnson M	Kennedy M	McDonough D	Nogan K	Poutch N	Preece D	Rees J	Rodger G	Tighe A	Wegerle R	Williams S	Wilson D	Round
1	Nov	8	(a)	Oxford United	W 3-2	Dowie (2), Gray	1754	6		2	1	7			9				12		3			5	10				11			13	8		4	1
2	Nov	27	(a)	Crystal Palace	L 1-4	Dowie	3747	5		2	1		12		8	6			13		3		9						7			11	10		4	2
						Apps		1	1		2	2	1		2	1					2		1	1	1				2			1	2		2	
						Subs							1						2													1				
						Goals									3				1																	

TIMELINE...

Summer 1989 The Town sell their 'Crown Jewel' as Kenilworth Road goes to the local authority for £3.25 million.

14 August 1989 The Town smash their incoming transfer fee record when paying a reported £650,000 to Odense for Danish International forward Lars Elstrup.

11 December 1989 Roy Wegerle is sold to QPR for £1 million – a record sale.

3 January 1990 Manager Ray Harford is dismissed to be replaced as caretaker manager by coach Terry Mancini.

11 January 1990 The Hatters promote from within again and give the manager's job to Jim Ryan.

5 May 1990 An improbable last day win at Derby sees the Town avoid the drop.

1990/91 FOOTBALL LEAGUE DIVISION ONE

Match No	Month	Day	Venue	Opponents	W/L/D Score	Scorers	Attendance	Beaumont D	Black K	Breacker T	Chamberlain A	Dowie I	Dreyer J	Elstrup L	Farrell S	Harvey R	Holsgrove P	Hughes C	Jackson M	James J	Johnson M	McDonough D	Nogan K	Pembridge M	Preece D	Rees J	Rodger G	Telfer P	Williams S	Match No
1	Aug	25	(h)	CRYSTAL PALACE	D 1-1	Dowie	9583	5	11	2	1	9	6	7				10		3		4			8	12				1
2	Aug	29	(a)	Arsenal	L 1-2	Elstrup	32723	5	11	2	1	9	6	7		13		10		3		4			8	12				2
3	Sep	1	(a)	Southampton	W 2-1	Elstrup (2)	13538	5		2	1	9	6	7		12		10		3		4	13		8	11				3
4	Sep	4	(h)	MANCHESTER UNITED	L 0-1	-	12576	5	11	2	1	9	6	7		3		10		4	13				8	12				4
5	Sep	8	(h)	LEEDS UNITED	W 1-0	Black	10185	5	11	2	1	9	6	7				10		3	12	13			8	4				5
6	Sep	15	(a)	Queens Park Rangers	L 1-6	Hughes	10196	5	11	2	1	9	6	7				10		3	12	13			8	4				6
7	Sep	22	(a)	COVENTRY CITY	W 1-0	Dowie	8336	5	11	2	1	9	6	7		3		10		12					8	4				7
8	Sep	29	(a)	Norwich City	W 3-1	Elstrup (3)	12794	5	11	2	1	9	6	7		3		10							8				4	8
9	Oct	20	(a)	Sunderland	L 0-2	-	20035	5	11		1	9	6	7		3		10			2	13			8	12			4	9
10	Oct	27	(h)	EVERTON	D 1-1	Elstrup	10047	5	11		1	9	6	7		3		10			2				8	12			4	10
11	Nov	3	(a)	Derby County	L 1-2	Black	15008	5	11		1	9	6	7		3		10			2	13	12		8				4	11
12	Nov	10	(a)	Liverpool	L 0-4	-	35207	5	11		1	9	6	7		3		10			2				8				4	12
13	Nov	17	(h)	MANCHESTER CITY	D 2-2	Dowie, Dreyer (pen)	9564	5	11		1	9	6	7	12	3		10			2	13			8				4	13
14	Nov	24	(h)	ASTON VILLA	W 2-0	Black, Elstrup	10071		11		1	9	6	7		3		10			2	5			8				4	14
15	Dec	1	(a)	Nottingham Forest	D 2-2	Elstrup (2)	16498	12	11		1	9	6	7		3		10			2	5			8				4	15
16	Dec	8	(h)	ARSENAL	D 1-1	Dreyer (pen)	12506		11		1	9	6	7	12	3					2	5			8	10			4	16
17	Dec	16	(a)	Crystal Palace	L 0-1	-	15579	10	11		1	9	6	7	13	3					2	5			8	12			4	17
18	Dec	22	(a)	Tottenham Hotspur	L 1-2	Dowie	27007	13	11		1	9	6	7	12	3		10			2	5			8				4	18
19	Dec	26	(h)	SHEFFIELD UNITED	L 0-1	-	10004	12	11		1	9	6	7	13	3		10			2	5			8				4	19
20	Dec	29	(h)	CHELSEA	W 2-0	Cundy (og), Black	12005		11		1		6	7	9	3			12		2	5			8	10			4	20
21	Jan	1	(a)	Wimbledon	L 0-2	-	4592		11		1		6	7	9	3			12		2	5			8	10			4	21
22	Jan	12	(h)	SOUTHAMPTON	L 3-4	Elstrup, James, Dreyer (pen)	9021	10	11		1		6	7	9	3					2	5		4	8			12		22
23	Jan	19	(a)	Leeds United	L 1-2	Elstrup	27010		11		1		6	7	12	3					2	5		10	8				4	23
24	Feb	2	(h)	QUEENS PARK RANGERS	L 1-2	Black	8479	2	11		1	9	6	7		3			12			5		10	8		5			24
25	Feb	23	(h)	LIVERPOOL	W 3-1	Black, Dowie (2)	12032	4	11		1	9	6	7						3	2			10	8	12	5			25
26	Mar	2	(h)	NOTTINGHAM FOREST	W 1-0	Dowie	9577	4	11		1	9	6	7							2	3		10	8		5			26
27	Mar	5	(a)	Manchester City	L 0-3	-	20404	4	11		1	9	6	7	12						2	3		10	8		5			27
28	Mar	9	(a)	Aston Villa	W 2-1	Mountfield (og), Pembridge	20587	4	11		1	9	6	7							2	3		10	8		5			28
29	Mar	13	(a)	Coventry City	L 1-2	Rodger	9725	4	11		1	9	6	7	12						2	3		10	8		5			29
30	Mar	16	(h)	NORWICH CITY	L 0-1	-	8604	4	11		1	9	6	7	13	12					2	3		10	8		5			30
31	Mar	23	(a)	Manchester United	L 1-4	Preece	41752	4	11		1		6	7	9	3					2			10	8	12	5			31
32	Mar	30	(a)	Sheffield United	L 1-2	Elstrup	18481	4	11		1		6	7	9	3				13	2	12		10	8		5			32
33	Apr	1	(h)	TOTTENHAM HOTSPUR	D 0-0	-	11322	13	11		1		6	7	9	3				12	2			10	8	4	5			33
34	Apr	6	(a)	Chelsea	D 3-3	Elstrup, Farrell, Black	9416	4	11		1		6	7	9	3				13	2	12		10	8		5			34
35	Apr	13	(h)	WIMBLEDON	L 0-1	-	8219	4	11		1		6	7	9	3					2			10	8	12	5			35
36	Apr	20	(h)	SUNDERLAND	L 1-2	Rodger	11157	4	11		1		6	7	9	3					2	13		10	8	12	5			36
37	May	4	(a)	Everton	L 0-1	-	20134	2	11		1		6	7		12						4		10	8	9	5		13	37
38	May	11	(h)	DERBY COUNTY	W 2-0	Harford (og), Elstrup	12889	2	11		1		6	7	9	3				12		5	13	10	8	4				38
				Final League Position: 18th		3 Own Goals	**Apps**	29	37	8	38	26	38	37	11	26	-	17	-	10	24	21	1	18	37	11	14	-	15	
							Subs	4	-	-	-	3	-	-	9	3	1	-	7	2	5	8	-	-	-	10	-	1	1	
							Goals	-	7	-	-	7	3	15	1	-	-	1	-	1	-	-	-	1	1	-	2	-	-	

1990/91 FA CUP

Round	Month	Day	Venue	Opponents	W,L,D	Score	Scorers	Attendance	Beaumont D	Black K	Breacker T	Chamberlain A	Dowie I	Dreyer J	Elstrup L	Farrell S	Harvey R	Holsgrove P	Hughes C	Jackson M	James J	Johnson M	McDonough D	Nogan K	Pembridge M	Preece D	Rees J	Rodger G	Telfer P	Williams S	Round
3	Jan	5	(a)	Sheffield United	W	3-1	Elstrup (2), Farrell	13948	10	11		1		6	7	9	3				2		5		4	8					3
4	Jan	26	(h)	WEST HAM UNITED	D	1-1	Black	12087		11		1	12	6	7	9	3				2		5		10	8	13			4	4
Rep	Jan	30	(a)	West Ham United	L	0-5	-	25659		11		1	9	6	7	12	3				2	13	5		10	8				4	Rep
							Apps		1	3	-	3	1	3	3	2	3	-	-	-	3	-	3	-	3	3	-	-	-	2	
							Subs		-	-	-	1	-	-	1	-	-	-	-	-	-	1	-	-	-	-	1	-	-	-	
							Goals		-	1	-	-	-	-	2	1	-	-	-	-	-	-	-	-	-	-	-	-	-	-	

1990/91 RUMBELOWS CUP (LEAGUE CUP)

Round	Month	Day	Venue	Opponents	W,L,D	Score	Scorers	Attendance	Beaumont D	Black K	Breacker T	Chamberlain A	Dowie I	Dreyer J	Elstrup L	Farrell S	Harvey R	Holsgrove P	Hughes C	Jackson M	James J	Johnson M	McDonough D	Nogan K	Pembridge M	Preece D	Rees J	Rodger G	Telfer P	Williams S	Round
2:1	Sep	25	(h)	BRADFORD CITY	D	1-1	Harvey	5120	5	11	2	1	9	6	7		3		10		12				13	8	4				2:1
2:2	Oct	10	(a)	Bradford City	D	1-1	Black	6180	5	11		1	9	6			3		10		2	12			7	8	13			4	2:2
							Apps		2	2	1	2	2	2	1	-	2	-	2	-	1	-	-	1	-	2	1	-	-	1	
							Subs		-	-	-	-	-	-	-	-	-	-	-	-	1	1	-	1	-	-	-	-	-	
							Goals		-	1	-	-	-	-	-	-	1	-	-	-	-	-	-	-	-	-	-	-	-	-	

Lost 4-5 on penalties aet.

1990/91 ZENITH DATA SYSTEMS CUP (FULL MEMBERS CUP)

Round	Month	Day	Venue	Opponents	W,L,D	Score	Scorers	Attendance	Beaumont D	Black K	Breacker T	Chamberlain A	Dowie I	Dreyer J	Elstrup L	Farrell S	Harvey R	Holsgrove P	Hughes C	Jackson M	James J	Johnson M	McDonough D	Nogan K	Pembridge M	Preece D	Rees J	Rodger G	Telfer P	Williams S	Round
2	Dec	19	(h)	WEST HAM UNITED	W	5-1	Farrell (2), Rees, Elstrup, Black	5759	12	11		1		6	7	9	3				2		5	13	10		8			4	2
3	Feb	18	(a)	Chelsea	D	1-1	Dreyer	3849	4		1	9	6	7	13	3					12	2			10	8	11	5			3
ASF	Feb	26	(a)	Crystal Palace	L	1-3	Rees	7170	4		1	9	6	7	13				12	3	2			10	8	11	5			1	ASF
							Apps		2	1	-	3	2	3	3	1	-	-	1	1	-	2	1	-	3	2	3	2	-	1	
							Subs		1	-	-	-	-	-	-	2	-	-	1	1	-	1	-	-	-	-	-	-	-	-	
							Goals		-	1	-	-	1	1	2	-	-	-	-	-	-	-	-	-	-	2	-	-	-	-	

3rd Round won 4-1 on penalties.

TIMELINE...

11 May 1991 Another last day reprieve with the Town beating Derby again, this time at Kenilworth Road, to secure Division One status.

▶ **The 1988/89 team** – Back row (left to right): Preece, M.Stein, Cobb, Allinson, Harvey, Black, R.Johnson. Middle row (left to right): Galley (Physiotherapist), Faulkner (Coach), Wegerle, Dreyer, Oldfield, Sealey, M.Harford, Chamberlain, M.Johnson, Grimes, McDonough, Ryan (Coach). Front row (left to right): Williams, Wilson, Foster, R.Harford (manager), Donaghy, Hill, Breacker.

▶ **The 1989/90 team** – Back row (left to right): Cooke, O'Brien, James, M.Johnson, Harvey, Mead, Black, Gray. Middle row (left to right): Mancini (Coach), Ryan (Coach), McDonough, Dowie, Rodger, Sealey, Chamberlain, M.Harford, Beaumont, Dreyer, Faulkner (Coach), Galley (Physiotherapist). Front row (left to right): Preece, R.Johnson, Wilson, R.Harford (Manager), Wegerle, Breacker, Williams.

▶ **The 1990/91 team** – Back row (left to right): Cooke, Gray, Johnson, Nogan, Harvey, Rees. Middle row (left to right): Ley (Coach), Moore (Coach), James, Hughes, Dowie, Petterson, Chamberlain, Rodger, McDonough, Faulkner (Coach), Galley (Physiotherapist). Front row (left to right): Beaumont, Breacker, Dreyer, Ryan (Manager), Preece, Black, Elstrup.

▶ **The 1991/92 team** – Back row (left to right): James, Farrell, Beaumont, Rodger, Chamberlain, McDonough, Johnson, Dreyer, Harvey. Front row (left to right): Nogan, Hughes, Rees, Preece, Pembridge, Black.

1991/92 FOOTBALL LEAGUE DIVISION ONE

Match No	Month	Day	Venue	Opponents	W,L,D Score	Scorers	Attendance	Allpress T	Beaumont D	Black K	Campbell J	Chamberlain A	Day M	Dreyer J	Farrell S	Glover L	Gray P	Harford M	Harvey R	Holsgrove P	Hughes C	Jackson M	James J	Kamara C	Linton D	McDonough D	Nogan K	Oakes S	Peake T	Pembridge M	Preece D	Rees J	Rodger G	Salton D	Stein B	Sutton S	Telfer P	Thompson Steve	Varadi I	Williams M	Match No
1	Aug	17	(a)	West Ham United	D 0-0	-	25079		2	11	1		6	7			12	3								4				10	8		5		9						1
2	Aug	21	(a)	Coventry City	L 0-5	-	9848		2	11	1		6	7			12	3								4				10	8		5		9						2
3	Aug	24	(h)	LIVERPOOL	D 0-0	-	11132		2	11	1		6					7	3							4				10	8		5		9						3
4	Aug	27	(a)	Arsenal	L 0-2	-	25898		2	11	1			3	13	7		12								4		6		10	8		5		9						4
5	Aug	31	(a)	Chelsea	L 1-4	Gray	17457		2		1			3	11	7		12								4	13	6		10	8		5		9						5
6	Sep	4	(h)	SOUTHAMPTON	W 2-1	Gray, Harvey	8055		13		1			5	9	7		3			2					4	12	6		10	8				11						6
7	Sep	7	(a)	Wimbledon	L 0-3	-	3231				1			5		7		3	11	2						4	9	6		10	13		5		12						7
8	Sep	14	(h)	OLDHAM ATHLETIC	W 2-1	Harford (2)	9005				1			3	9					2						4	13	6		10	7		5		8		12	11			8
9	Sep	17	(h)	QUEENS PARK RANGERS	L 0-1	-	9185				1			3	9					2						4	13	6		10	7		5		8		12	11			9
10	Sep	21	(a)	Manchester United	L 0-5	-	46491		13		1			3	9					2							12	6		10	7		5		8		4	11			10
11	Sep	28	(h)	NOTTS COUNTY	D 1-1	Gray	7629		6		1			3	8	9				12	2					13				10	7		5				4	11			11
12	Oct	5	(a)	Aston Villa	L 0-4	-	18722		13		1			3	8					11	2		2			9		6		10			5		12		7	4			12
13	Oct	19	(h)	SHEFFIELD WEDNESDAY	D 2-2	Harford, Nogan	9401				1			3	8	9	3	12		2		2			4		6		10	11				13		7				13
14	Oct	26	(a)	Norwich City	L 0-1	-	10514							3				13	4		8		12			9	11	5	10			7		6		2				14
15	Nov	2	(h)	EVERTON	L 0-1	-	8002							5	10	9		8			2	4			12	11	6	3						13		7				15
16	Nov	16	(a)	Tottenham Hotspur	L 1-4	Harford	27543							5	9	3			4	2	4	2					12	11		6				8		7				16
17	Nov	23	(h)	MANCHESTER CITY	D 2-2	Harford, Dreyer	10031							5	9	3			4	2	4	2					11		6	10	12			8		7				17
18	Nov	30	(a)	Sheffield United	D 1-1	Telfer	21804			11				5		9	3			2	4							6	10	12				8	1	7				18
19	Dec	7	(h)	LEEDS UNITED	L 0-2	-	11550			12				5		9	3			2	4						11		6	10	13				8	1	7				19
20	Dec	20	(h)	COVENTRY CITY	W 1-0	Harford	7533							5		9	3			2	4					11		6	10	12				8	1	7				20
21	Dec	26	(h)	ARSENAL	W 1-0	Harford	12665							5		9	3			2	4							6	10	11				8	1	7				21
22	Dec	28	(h)	CHELSEA	W 2-0	Harvey, Dreyer (pen)	10738			13				5		9	3			2	4							6	10	11				8	1	7				22
23	Jan	1	(a)	Nottingham Forest	D 1-1	Pembridge	23809			13				5			3			2	4							6	10	11				8	1	7				23
24	Jan	11	(a)	Liverpool	L 1-2	Tanner (og)	35095							5			3			2	4		9	12				6	10	11				8	1	7				24
25	Jan	18	(h)	WEST HAM UNITED	L 0-1	-	11088			12				5			3			2	4		9	13				6	10	11				8	1	7				25
26	Feb	1	(a)	Sheffield Wednesday	L 2-3	Preece, Oakes	22291							5		9	3			12	2	4					7	6	10	11				8						26
27	Feb	8	(h)	NORWICH CITY	W 2-0	Preece, Harford	8554							5		9	3		8	2	4						7	6	10	12				1						27
28	Feb	15	(a)	Manchester City	L 0-4	-	22137							5		9	3	13		2	4						7	6	10	11				8	1		7			28
29	Feb	22	(h)	SHEFFIELD UNITED	W 2-1	Stein, Harford	9003			13				5		9	3	12		2	4						7	6	10	11				8						29
30	Feb	25	(a)	Crystal Palace	D 1-1	Pembridge (pen)	12109			13				5		9	3	12		2	4						7	6	10	11				8	1					30
31	Feb	29	(a)	Leeds United	L 0-2	-	28227			8				5			7			2	4							6	10	11		13	12	1						31
32	Mar	7	(h)	CRYSTAL PALACE	D 1-1	Oakes	8591		9				1	5			3	12		2	4						7	6	10	11				8						32
33	Mar	11	(h)	TOTTENHAM HOTSPUR	D 0-0	-	11494		9				1	5			3	7		2	4							6	10	11				8						33
34	Mar	14	(a)	Everton	D 1-1	Stein	17388			13				5		9	3			2	4						7	6	10	11	7			8						34
35	Mar	21	(a)	Southampton	L 1-2	Pembridge	14192							5		9	3	12		2	4						6	10	11	7				8					13	35
36	Apr	4	(h)	WIMBLEDON	W 2-1	Varadi, Preece	7753					1		5		9	3			2	4						6	10	11				8				7			36
37	Apr	11	(a)	Oldham Athletic	L 1-5	Harford	13210					1		5		9	3	12		2	4						6	10	11	13				8				7			37
38	Apr	14	(h)	NOTTINGHAM FOREST	W 2-1	Harford, James	8014					1		5		12	9	3	13		2	4					6	10	11				8				7			38
39	Apr	18	(h)	MANCHESTER UNITED	D 1-1	Harford	13410					1		5		12	9	3		2	4						6	10	11				13				7			39
40	Apr	20	(a)	Queens Park Rangers	L 1-2	Pembridge (pen)	10749					1		5		9	3	12		2	4					8	6	10	11				13				7			40
41	Apr	25	(h)	ASTON VILLA	W 2-0	Stein, Pembridge	11178					1		5						2	4					7	6	10	11		3		8				12			41
42	May	2	(a)	Notts County	L 1-2	James	11380					1		5		12	9			2	4					7	6	10	11	13	3		8						42

Final League Position: 20th — 1 Own Goal

							Apps	-	6	4	4	24	4	42	3	1	9	29	31	1	6	7	28	28	2	9	6	15	38	42	34	3	11	2	32	14	17	5	5	-	
							Subs	-	3	-	7	-	-	1	-	5	-	1	-	12	2	-	-	1	-	8	6	-	-	4	2	1	1	7	-	3	-	1	1	1	
							Goals	-	-	-	-	-	-	2	-	-	3	12	2	-	-	2	-	-	-	-	1	2	-	5	3	-	-	3	-	1	-	1	1		

1991/92 FA CUP

Round	Month	Day	Venue	Opponents	W,L,D Score	Scorers	Attendance	Allpress T	Beaumont D	Black K	Campbell J	Chamberlain A	Day M	Dreyer J	Farrell S	Glover L	Gray P	Harford M	Harvey R	Holsgrove P	Hughes C	Jackson M	James J	Kamara C	Linton D	McDonough D	Nogan K	Oakes S	Peake T	Pembridge M	Preece D	Rees J	Rodger G	Salton D	Stein B	Sutton S	Telfer P	Thompson Steve	Varadi I	Williams M	Round
3	Jan	4	(a)	Sheffield United	L 0-4	-	12201				12	1		5			3				2	4						9	6	10	11				8		7				3

							Apps	-	-	-	1	-	1	-	-	-	-	1	-	-	1	-	1	1	-	-	1	1	1	1	-	-	-	1	-	1	-	-	-		
							Subs	-	-	-	1	-	-	-	-	-	-	-	-	-	-	-	-	-	-	-	-	-	-	-	-	-	-	-	-	-	-	-	-	-	
							Goals	-	-	-	-	-	-	-	-	-	-	-	-	-	-	-	-	-	-	-	-	-	-	-	-	-	-	-	-	-	-	-	-	-		

1991/92 RUMBELOWS CUP (LEAGUE CUP)

Round	Month	Day	Venue	Opponents	W,L,D Score	Scorers	Attendance	Allpress T	Beaumont D	Black K	Campbell J	Chamberlain A	Day M	Dreyer J	Farrell S	Glover L	Gray P	Harford M	Harvey R	Holsgrove P	Hughes C	Jackson M	James J	Kamara C	Linton D	McDonough D	Nogan K	Oakes S	Peake T	Pembridge M	Preece D	Rees J	Rodger G	Salton D	Stein B	Sutton S	Telfer P	Thompson Steve	Varadi I	Williams M	Round
2:1	Sep	25	(h)	BIRMINGHAM CITY	D 2-2	Gray, Nogan	6315	6		1	3						9				2						12			10	7		5	13	8		4	11			2:1
2:2	Oct	8	(a)	Birmingham City	L 2-3	Gray (2)	13252	5		1						8	9	3			2						12	6		10	11			13			7	4			2:2
						Apps		2		2	1					1	2	1			2							1		2	2		1	2	1		2	2			
						Subs																					2							2							
						Goals											3										1														

1991/92 ZENITH DATA SYSTEMS CUP (FULL MEMBERS CUP)

Round	Month	Day	Venue	Opponents	W,L,D Score	Scorers	Attendance	Allpress T	Beaumont D	Black K	Campbell J	Chamberlain A	Day M	Dreyer J	Farrell S	Glover L	Gray P	Harford M	Harvey R	Holsgrove P	Hughes C	Jackson M	James J	Kamara C	Linton D	McDonough D	Nogan K	Oakes S	Peake T	Pembridge M	Preece D	Rees J	Rodger G	Salton D	Stein B	Sutton S	Telfer P	Thompson Steve	Varadi I	Williams M	Round
2	Oct	22	(a)	Ipswich Town	D 1-1	Telfer	5750	3		13		1						9		4		8					10			11	12	6	5		2		7				2
						Apps		1				1						1		1		1					1			1		1	1		1		1			1	
						Subs				1																					1										
						Goals																															1				

Lost 1-2 on penalties aet

▸ Luton score in front of the Liverpool Kop.

▸ Mick Harford after scoring against Manchester United at Kenilworth Road.

TIMELINE...

13 May 1991 Jim Ryan is dismissed as manager.
7 June 1991 David Pleat returns to Kenilworth Road as manager.
Summer 1991 The Hatters announce the decisions to return to grass, lift the ban on away supporters and build a new stand on the Maple Road 'triangle'.
30 August 1991 The 'transfer fee received' record is broken again with £1.5 million paid by Nottingham Forest for Kingsley Black.
2 May 1992 After several 'great escapes' the Town lose their Division One status.

1992/93 "NEW" FOOTBALL LEAGUE DIVISION ONE (SECOND TIER)

No	Month	Day	Venue	Opponents	W/L/D Score	Scorers	Att	Benjamin I	Campbell J	Chamberlain A	Claridge S	Dixon K	Dreyer J	Gray P	Greene D	Harvey R	Hughes C	James J	Johnson M	Kamara C	Linton D	Matthew D	Oakes S	Peake T	Petterson A	Preece D	Rees J	Salton D	Telfer P	Williams M	No
1	Aug	15	(a)	Leicester City	L 1-2	Campbell	17424		11	12			6	9			8	3		4	2		7	5	1	10					1
2	Aug	22	(h)	BRISTOL CITY	L 0-3	-	7926		11		7		6	9			8	3	13	4	2		12	5	1	10					2
3	Aug	29	(a)	Charlton Athletic	D 0-0	-	6291				7		6	9			8	3			2		12	5	1	10	11	4			3
4	Sep	2	(a)	Newcastle United	L 0-2	-	27082				12		6	9				3			2		8	5	1	10	11	4			4
5	Sep	5	(h)	TRANMERE ROVERS	D 3-3	Claridge, Linton, Oakes	6801				12		6	9				3			2		8	5	1	10	11	4			5
6	Sep	13	(a)	Brentford	W 2-1	James, Gray	7413				7			9				3	6	8	2			5	1	10	11	4			6
7	Sep	19	(h)	BIRMINGHAM CITY	D 1-1	Claridge (pen)	8481		13		7			9				3	6	8	2		12	5	1	10	11	4			7
8	Sep	26	(a)	Notts County	D 0-0	-	5992		13		7			9				3		8	2		12	5	1	10	11	4			8
9	Oct	3	(h)	PORTSMOUTH	L 1-4	Dreyer	7954		12		7		6	9				3		8	2	5	13		1	10	11	4			9
10	Oct	10	(a)	Barnsley	L 0-3	-	5261				7		6	9				3		8	2	5	13		1	10	11	4			10
11	Oct	17	(h)	DERBY COUNTY	L 1-3	Johnson	8848		12		7			9				3	6	8	2	5	11		1	10		4			11
12	Oct	24	(a)	Peterborough United	W 3-2	Gray (2), Telfer	7125				7			10				3	6	8	2		12	5	1	9		4	11		12
13	Oct	31	(h)	SOUTHEND UNITED	D 2-2	James, Gray	7256				7			10				3	6	8	2		12	5	1	9		4	11		13
14	Nov	3	(a)	Cambridge United	D 3-3	Oakes, Gray (2)	5716				7			10				3	6	8	2		11	5	1	9		4			14
15	Nov	7	(h)	GRIMSBY TOWN	L 1-4	Gray	6928		13	1	7			10				3	5	8	2		11	6		9		4	12		15
16	Nov	14	(a)	Oxford United	L 0-4	-	5759			1	7			10				3	5		2		12	6		11	9	4	8		16
17	Nov	21	(h)	MILLWALL	D 1-1	Gray	8371	8		1			2	10			5	3	12				13	6		11	9	4	7		17
18	Nov	29	(h)	WATFORD	W 2-0	Benjamin, Oakes	8341	8		1			2	10			5	3	4				7	6		11	9			12	18
19	Dec	5	(a)	Bristol Rovers	L 0-2	-	6240	8		1			2	10			5	3	4		13		7	6		11	9			12	19
20	Dec	12	(a)	Wolverhampton Wanderers	W 2-1	Gray (2)	13932		13	1			2	10			5	3	4		12		7	6		11	9		8		20
21	Dec	19	(h)	SUNDERLAND	D 0-0	-	8286	9		1			2	10			5	3	4		13		7	6		11	8				21
22	Dec	28	(a)	West Ham United	D 2-2	Hughes, Dreyer	18786		13	1			2	10			5	3	4				7	6		11	9		8		22
23	Jan	9	(a)	Birmingham City	L 1-2	Hughes	9601			1			2	10			5	3	4				7	6		11	9		8	12	23
24	Jan	16	(h)	NOTTS COUNTY	D 0-0	-	6729	8		1			2	10			5	3	4				12	6		11	9		7	13	24
25	Jan	27	(h)	NEWCASTLE UNITED	D 0-0	-	10237		13	1			2	10			5	3	4				12	6		11	9		7	8	25
26	Jan	30	(a)	Bristol City	D 0-0	-	8877		13	1			2	10			5	3	4				12	6		11	9		7	8	26
27	Feb	6	(h)	LEICESTER CITY	W 2-0	Johnson, Gray	9140	13		1			2	10			5	3	4				9	6		11	12		7	8	27
28	Feb	9	(h)	BRENTFORD	D 0-0	-	7248			1			2	10			5	3	4				9	6		11			7	8	28
29	Feb	13	(a)	Tranmere Rovers	W 2-0	Gray, Johnson	8723			1			2	10			5	3	4				9	6		11			7	8	29
30	Feb	20	(h)	CHARLTON ATHLETIC	W 1-0	Gray	8443			1		8	2	10			5	3	4				9	6		11			7	12	30
31	Feb	27	(h)	BARNSLEY	D 2-2	Dixon, Gray (pen)	7595			1		8	2	10			5	3	4				9	6		11			7	12	31
32	Mar	6	(a)	Portsmouth	L 1-2	Gray	10457			1		8	2	10			12	3	4				9	6		11	5		7	13	32
33	Mar	9	(h)	OXFORD UNITED	W 3-1	Preece, Gray, Oakes	6687			1		8	2	10			5	3	4				9	6		11	12		7		33
34	Mar	13	(a)	Grimsby Town	L 1-3	Gray	5193			1		8	2	10	6		5	3	4				9			11	13		7	12	34
35	Mar	17	(h)	SWINDON TOWN	D 0-0	-	8902			1		8	2	10			12	3	4				9			11	5		7	13	35
36	Mar	20	(h)	BRISTOL ROVERS	D 1-1	Maddison (og)	7717			1		8	2	10			12	3	4				9			11	5		7	13	36
37	Mar	24	(a)	Millwall	L 0-1	-	8287			1		12	2	10		11	8	3	4				9				5		7	13	37
38	Mar	27	(h)	CAMBRIDGE UNITED	W 2-0	Dixon, Oakes	8077			1		8	2	10			7	3	4				9			11	5		3	11	38
39	Apr	3	(a)	Watford	D 0-0	-	10656			1		9	2	10			7		4	8			12	6		11	5		3		39
40	Apr	7	(h)	WOLVERHAMPTON WANDERERS	D 1-1	Gray	7948			1		9	2	10				3	4	7			8			11	5		12	13	40
41	Apr	10	(a)	Swindon Town	L 0-1	-	11004			1		9	2	10			7		4	8			12	6		11			7		41
42	Apr	13	(h)	WEST HAM UNITED	W 2-0	Gray (pen), Williams	10959			1		9	2	10			7	5	4	8			13	6		11			3	12	42
43	Apr	17	(a)	Sunderland	D 2-2	Preece, Telfer	16493			1		9	2	10				5	4	8			12	6		11	7		3	13	43
44	Apr	24	(a)	Derby County	D 1-1	Preece	13741			1		9	2	10				5	4	8				6		11			7	13	44
45	May	1	(h)	PETERBOROUGH UNITED	D 0-0	-	10011			1		9	2	10				3	4	8			5	6					7	13	45
46	May	8	(a)	Southend United	L 1-2	Dixon	11913			1		9	2	10			5	3	4	8			12	6		11			7	13	46
				Final League Position: 20th		1 Own Goal	**Apps**	5	2	32	15	16	38	45	1	1	26	43	38	21	17	3	25	40	14	43	29	15	30	7	
							Subs	5	7	-	1	1	-	-	-	-	3	-	2	-	3	2	19	-	-	3	-	-	2	15	
							Goals	1	1	-	2	3	2	19	-	-	2	-	3	-	1	-	5	-	-	3	-	-	2	1	

1992/93 FA CUP

Round	Month	Day	Venue	Opponents	W/L/D Score	Scorers	Att	Benjamin I	Campbell J	Chamberlain A	Claridge S	Dixon K	Dreyer J	Gray P	Greene D	Harvey R	Hughes C	James J	Johnson M	Kamara C	Linton D	Matthew D	Oakes S	Peake T	Petterson A	Preece D	Rees J	Salton D	Telfer P	Williams M	Round
3	Jan	19	(h)	BRISTOL CITY	W 2-0	Gray, Hughes	6092	8		1			2	10			12	5	3	4			13	6		11	9		7		3
4	Jan	23	(h)	DERBY COUNTY	L 1-5	Telfer	9170	8		1			2	10			13	5	3	4			12	6		11	9		7		4
							Apps	2		2			2	2				2	2	2				2		2	2		2		
							Subs										2						2								
							Goals							1			1												1		

1992/93 COCA-COLA CUP (LEAGUE CUP)

Round	Month	Day	Venue	Opponents	W,L,D	Score	Scorers	Attendance	Benjamin I	Campbell J	Chamberlain A	Claridge S	Dixon K	Dreyer J	Gray P	Greene D	Harvey R	Hughes C	James J	Johnson M	Kamara C	Linton D	Matthew D	Oakes S	Peake T	Petterson A	Preece D	Rees J	Salton D	Telfer P	Williams M	Round
2:1	Sep	23	(h)	PLYMOUTH ARGYLE	D	2-2	Claridge (2)	3702	12	7		9							3	6	8	2		11	5	1	10	13	4			2:1
2:2	Oct	6	(a)	Plymouth Argyle	L	2-3	Claridge, Preece	8946		7		9		13					3	6	8	2		12	5	1	10	11	4			2:2
Apps										2		2							2	2	2	2		1	2	2	2	1	2			
Subs									1					1										1				1				
Goals												3															1					

1992/93 ANGLO-ITALIAN CUP

Round	Month	Day	Venue	Opponents	W,L,D	Score	Scorers	Attendance	Benjamin I	Campbell J	Chamberlain A	Claridge S	Dixon K	Dreyer J	Gray P	Greene D	Harvey R	Hughes C	James J	Johnson M	Kamara C	Linton D	Matthew D	Oakes S	Peake T	Petterson A	Preece D	Rees J	Salton D	Telfer P	Williams M	Round
PR	Sep	15	(a)	Watford	D	0-0	-	5197	13	7		9							3	6	8	2		12	5	1	10	11	4			PR
PR	Sep	29	(h)	BRISTOL CITY	D	1-1	Claridge	2538	10	7		9		6					3		8	2	5	13		1	12	11	4			PR
Apps									1	2		2		1					2	1	2	2	1		1	2	1	2	2			
Subs									1															2			1					
Goals												1																				

▶ The 1992/93 team – Back row (left to right): Salton, Campbell, Linton, Chamberlain, Johnson, Sommer, Greene, Dreyer, Kamara. Middle row (left to right): Moore (Coach), James, Telfer, Allpress, Nogan, Harvey, Peake, Owen (Coach). Front row (left to right): Claridge, Preece, Gray, Pleat (Manager), Hughes, Rees, Oakes.

TIMELINE...

8 May 1993 Although the Hatters lose at Southend, results elsewhere ensure they are safe from relegation.

1993/94 "NEW" FOOTBALL LEAGUE DIVISION ONE (SECOND TIER)

Match No	Month	Day	Venue	Opponents	W,L,D Score	Scorers	Attendance	Aunger G	Benjamin I	Burke M	Campbell J	Davis K	Dickov P	Dixon K	Dreyer J	Greene D	Harper A	Hartson J	Houghton S	Hughes C	James J	Johnson M	Linton D	McLaren P	Oakes S	Peake T	Petterson A	Preece D	Rees J	Sommer J	Telfer P	Thomas MA	Thorpe A	Williams M	Woolgar M	Match No
1	Aug	14	(h)	WATFORD	W 2-1	Telfer, Dixon	9149							9	6					12	3		2		8	5	13	11	10	1	7			4		1
2	Aug	21	(a)	Portsmouth	L 0-1		12248		12					9	6				13	10	3		2		8	5		11		1	7			4		2
3	Aug	28	(h)	NOTTINGHAM FOREST	L 1-2	Hartson	9788							9	6			7	10	8	3		2					11	12	1	4			13		3
4	Sep	11	(h)	BOLTON WANDERERS	L 0-2		7199							9	6			7	10	8	3		2		12			11		1	4			13		4
5	Sep	14	(a)	Tranmere Rovers	L 1-4	Benjamin	5871	7							6					8	3		2		9	5		11	10	1	4			12		5
6	Sep	18	(a)	Middlesbrough	D 0-0	-	12487	7							6				13	10	12	3	2		8	5		11	9	1	4					6
7	Sep	25	(h)	Birmingham City	D 1-1	Telfer	11801								6			7	11	10	3		2		8	5			9	1	4			12		7
8	Oct	2	(h)	BARNSLEY	W 5-0	Hartson, Oakes (2), James, Houghton	6201								6		11	9	12	10	3	13	2		8	5				1	7			4		8
9	Oct	5	(h)	BRISTOL CITY	L 0-2		5956								6		11	9	12	10	3		2		8	5				1	7			4		9
10	Oct	9	(a)	Derby County	L 1-2	Williams	15885						13	11	6		4	9		10	3		2		8	5				1	7			12		10
11	Oct	16	(h)	NOTTS COUNTY	W 1-0	Dickov	6366						13	11	6		4	9		10	3		2		8	5				1	7			12		11
12	Oct	20	(a)	Sunderland	L 0-2	-	13645						13	11	6		4	9			3		2		8	5		10		1	7			12		12
13	Oct	23	(a)	Oxford United	W 1-0	Hughes	5161						12	9			4		8	10	3		2		13	5		11		1	7					13
14	Oct	30	(h)	LEICESTER CITY	L 0-2		8813						11	12	6		4	9	13		3		2		8	5				1	7			12		14
15	Nov	2	(a)	Crystal Palace	L 2-3	Aunger, Hughes	10925	11			12		13	9	6		4			10	3		2		8	5				1	7					15
16	Nov	7	(h)	CHARLTON ATHLETIC	W 1-0	Telfer	6327	11					13	9	6		4			10	3		2		8	5				1	7			12		16
17	Nov	13	(a)	Southend United	L 1-2	Dixon	5567	11					13	9	6		4		12	10			2			5				1	7	3				17
18	Nov	27	(h)	STOKE CITY	W 6-2	Dixon (3), Hughes, Oakes, Hartson	7384				6			11	9		4	12		7			2		8	5			10	1		3	13			18
19	Dec	4	(a)	Charlton Athletic	L 0-1		7570				6			11	9		4	12		10			2		8	5			7	1		3				19
20	Dec	11	(h)	TRANMERE ROVERS	L 0-1		7075				6			11	9		4	13		8			2		12	5		10		1	7	3				20
21	Dec	19	(a)	Watford	D 2-2	Preece, Dreyer (pen)	7567						13	9	6		4		12	10			2		8	5		11		1	7	3				21
22	Dec	27	(h)	Peterborough United	D 0-0		9522						13	9	6		4		10	8	12		2			5		11		1	7	3				22
23	Dec	29	(h)	GRIMSBY TOWN	W 2-1	Harper, Hughes	7234						13	9	6		4	11		10	12		2		8	5				1	7	3				23
24	Jan	1	(a)	West Bromwich Albion	D 1-1	Preece	16138						12	9	6		4		10	8	13		2			5		11		1	7	3				24
25	Jan	15	(a)	Notts County	W 2-1	Dixon (2)	6589						13	9	6		4	12		10	3		2		8	5		11		1	7					25
26	Jan	22	(h)	DERBY COUNTY	W 2-1	Telfer, Oakes	9371						11	9	6		4	12		10	3		2		8	5				1	7					26
27	Feb	5	(h)	OXFORD UNITED	W 3-0	Oakes, Thomas, Thorpe	7366								6		4	9	13		3		2		8	5		10		1	7	11	12			27
28	Feb	12	(a)	Leicester City	L 1-2	James	16194								6		4	9	12	10	3		2		8	5		11		1	7		13			28
29	Feb	22	(h)	PORTSMOUTH	W 4-1	Telfer, Preece, Hughes, Oakes	6533							9	6		4	12		10	3		2		8	5		11		1	7		13			29
30	Feb	26	(h)	SUNDERLAND	W 2-1	Hughes, Oakes	9367							9	6		4	13		10	3		2		8	5		11		1	7		12			30
31	Mar	5	(a)	Nottingham Forest	L 0-2		22249		13					9	6		4		8		3		2	5	12			11		1	7		10			31
32	Mar	8	(h)	MIDDLESBROUGH	D 1-1	Dreyer (pen)	6741			11				9	6	5	4	12	8		3		2					10		1	7			13		32
33	Mar	19	(h)	BIRMINGHAM CITY	D 1-1	Telfer	7690			10					6	5	4	9			3		2		8		1	11			7			12	13	33
34	Mar	26	(a)	Barnsley	L 0-1		6289						6			5	4	9		10	3		2		8			11		1	7					34
35	Mar	30	(a)	Millwall	D 2-2	Dreyer, Hartson	9235						12		6	5	4	9		10	3		2		8			11		1	7		2			35
36	Apr	2	(h)	PETERBOROUGH UNITED	W 2-0	Dixon (2)	8398						13	9	6	5	4		10		3		2		8			11	12	1	7		2			36
37	Apr	4	(a)	Grimsby Town	L 0-2	-	5542	11					13		6	5	12	9					2		8				10	1	7	3				37
38	Apr	12	(h)	WOLVERHAMPTON WANDERERS	L 0-2	-	8545							9		5	4	9	10		3		2		8			11		1	7	13				38
39	Apr	16	(h)	CRYSTAL PALACE	L 0-1	-	9880						13			5	4	9		10	6		2		8			11		1	7	3	12			39
40	Apr	19	(a)	Bristol City	L 0-1	-	5350	10						9		5	4	9	8		3		2					11		1	7	13				40
41	Apr	23	(a)	Wolverhampton Wanderers	L 0-1	-	25479							9		5	4		12	8	6		2					11		1	7	3	10			41
42	Apr	26	(h)	MILLWALL	D 1-1	Preece	8257							9	6	5	4	12					2		8			11		1	7	3	10			42
43	Apr	30	(a)	SOUTHEND UNITED	D 1-1	Hartson	7504								6	5	4	9		10	3		2		8			11		1	7		12	13		43
44	May	3	(h)	WEST BROMWICH ALBION	W 3-2	Preece, James, Hartson	10053								6		4	9		10			2		8	5	12	11	1	1	7	3	13			44
45	May	5	(a)	Bolton Wanderers	L 1-2	Hughes	7102								6		4	9		10	3		2		8	5	1	12			7	11	13			45
46	May	8	(a)	Stoke City	D 2-2	Oakes, Telfer (pen)	15893				1		12		6		4	9		10	3	13	2		8	5					7	11				46
							Apps	5	2	2	4	1	8	27	40	10	40	21	6	42	29	17	32	-	33	36	2	28	8	43	44	17	4	5	-	
							Subs	-	1	1	12	-	7	2	-	-	-	1	13	9	-	4	-	1	1	3	-	3	1	2	-	1	3	10	10	
							Goals	1	1	-	-	-	1	9	3	-	1	6	1	7	3	-	-	-	8	-	-	5	-	-	7	1	1	1	-	

Final League Position: 20th

1993/94 FA CUP

Round	Month	Day	Venue	Opponents	W,L,D	Score	Scorers	Attendance	Aunger G	Benjamin I	Burke M	Campbell J	Davis K	Dickov P	Dixon K	Dreyer J	Greene D	Harper A	Hartson J	Houghton S	Hughes C	James J	Johnson M	Linton D	McLaren P	Oakes S	Peake T	Petterson A	Preece D	Rees J	Sommer J	Telfer P	Thomas MA	Thorpe A	Williams M	Woolgar M	Round
3	Jan	18	(h)	SOUTHEND UNITED	W	1-0	Telfer	7953				12			9	6		4	13		10	3		2		8	5		11		1	7					3
4	Jan	29	(a)	Newcastle United	D	1-1	Thorpe	32216				12			9	6		4				3		2		8	5		11		1	7		10			4
Rep	Feb	9	(h)	NEWCASTLE UNITED	W	2-0	Hartson, Oakes	12503			10					6		4	9	13		3		2		8	5		11		1	7		12			Rep
5	Feb	20	(a)	Cardiff City	W	2-1	Oakes, Preece	17296							12	6		4	9		10	3		2		8	5		11		1	7					5
6	Mar	14	(a)	West Ham United	D	0-0	-	27331		12					9	6	5	4	13		10	3		2		8			11		1	7					6
Rep	Mar	23	(h)	WEST HAM UNITED	W	3-2	Oakes (3)	13166							9	6		4			10	3		2		8	5		11		1	7					Rep
SF	Apr	9	(n)	Chelsea	L	0-2	-	59989							9	6		4	12		10	3		2		8	5		11		1	7					SF
								Apps			1				5	7	1	7	2		5	7		7		7	6		7		7	7		1			
								Subs		1		2			1				3	1														1			
								Goals											1							5			1			1		1			

1993/94 COCA-COLA CUP (LEAGUE CUP)

Round	Month	Day	Venue	Opponents	W,L,D	Score	Scorers	Attendance	Aunger G	Benjamin I	Burke M	Campbell J	Davis K	Dickov P	Dixon K	Dreyer J	Greene D	Harper A	Hartson J	Houghton S	Hughes C	James J	Johnson M	Linton D	McLaren P	Oakes S	Peake T	Petterson A	Preece D	Rees J	Sommer J	Telfer P	Thomas MA	Thorpe A	Williams M	Woolgar M	Round
1:1	Aug	17	(a)	Cambridge United	L	0-1	-	4065		11					6						12	10	2	3		4	5		8	7	1	9					1:1
1:2	Aug	24	(h)	CAMBRIDGE UNITED	L	0-1	-	3861		7		9			6					13	10	8	4	3		12	5		11		1				2		1:2
								Apps		2		1			2						1	2	2	2		1	2		2	1	2	1			1		
								Subs												1	1					1											
								Goals																													

1993/94 ANGLO-ITALIAN CUP

Round	Month	Day	Venue	Opponents	W,L,D	Score	Scorers	Attendance	Aunger G	Benjamin I	Burke M	Campbell J	Davis K	Dickov P	Dixon K	Dreyer J	Greene D	Harper A	Hartson J	Houghton S	Hughes C	James J	Johnson M	Linton D	McLaren P	Oakes S	Peake T	Petterson A	Preece D	Rees J	Sommer J	Telfer P	Thomas MA	Thorpe A	Williams M	Woolgar M	Round
PR	Aug	31	(a)	Watford	L	1-2	Preece	2854							9	6			8	10	4	2	3			12	5		11		1	7			13		PR
PR	Sep	7	(h)	SOUTHEND UNITED	D	1-1	Dixon	1823							9	6	12		8	10	4		3	2			5		11		1		7			13	PR
								Apps							2	2			2	2	2	1	2	1			2		2		2	1	1				
								Subs									1									1									1	1
								Goals							1														1							

TIMELINE...

9 April 1994 After a wonderful FA Cup run, the Town go down 0-2 to Chelsea at Wembley in a drab semi-final.

1994/95 "NEW" FOOTBALL LEAGUE DIVISION ONE (SECOND TIER)

Match No	Month	Day	Venue	Opponents	W,L,D Score	Scorers	Att	Adcock A	Allen P	Biggins W	Chenery B	Davis K	Dixon K	Greene D	Hartson J	Harvey R	Houghton S	Hughes C	James J	Johnson M	Linton D	Marshall D	Matthews R	Oakes S	Peake T	Preece D	Skelton A	Sommer J	Taylor John	Telfer P	Thomas MA	Thorpe A	Waddock G	Williams M	Woodsford J	Match No
1	Aug	13	(h)	WEST BROMWICH ALBION	D 1-1	Oakes	8640						9	5			11		2	3	12	13		8	6	10	4	1		7						1
2	Aug	20	(a)	Derby County	D 0-0	-	13060						9	5				11	2	3	4	8			6	10		1		7						2
3	Aug	27	(h)	SOUTHEND UNITED	D 2-2	Hartson, Hughes	5918						13	5	9			11	2	3		8		4	6	10		1		7	12					3
4	Aug	30	(a)	Tranmere Rovers	L 2-4	Hughes, Hartson	5480							5	9			11	2	3		12		4	6	10	4	1		7						4
5	Sep	3	(a)	Port Vale	W 1-0	Marshall	8541						9	5					2	3		8		11	6	10	4	1		7	12				13	5
6	Sep	10	(h)	BURNLEY	L 0-1	-	6911						13	5					2	3		8		11	6	10		1		7	12		4			6
7	Sep	13	(h)	BOLTON WANDERERS	L 0-3	-	5764						9		11				2	3	12	13		8	6	10		1		7	5		4			7
8	Sep	17	(a)	Watford	W 4-2	Oakes, Dixon, Telfer (2)	8880						9						2	3		11			6	10		1		7	5		4			8
9	Sep	24	(a)	Millwall	D 0-0	-	7150						9		12				2	3		11			6	10		1		7	5		4			9
10	Oct	1	(h)	BRISTOL CITY	L 0-1	-	6633						9		13						12	11			6	10		1		7	5		4			10
11	Oct	9	(a)	Stoke City	W 2-1	Marshall, Preece	11682								9				8	2	3			11	12	6	10	1		7	5		4			11
12	Oct	15	(h)	MIDDLESBROUGH	W 5-1	Wilkinson (og), Marshall (2), Preece, Hartson	8412								9				8	2	3			11	12	6	10	1		7	5		4			12
13	Oct	22	(a)	Sheffield United	W 3-1	Gayle (og), James, Dixon	13317						9						8	2	3			11	12	6	10	1		7	5		4			13
14	Oct	29	(h)	BARNSLEY	L 0-1	-	7212						13		9				8	2	3			11		6	10	1		7	5		4			14
15	Nov	1	(h)	GRIMSBY TOWN	L 1-2	Oakes	5839								9				8	2	3			11	12	6	10	1		7	5		4			15
16	Nov	5	(a)	Wolverhampton Wanderers	W 3-2	Preece, Marshall, Dixon	26749						9		12				2	3		11		8	6	10		1		7	5		4			16
17	Nov	12	(a)	Oldham Athletic	D 0-0	-	7907						9		12				2	3		11		8	6	10		1		7	5		4			17
18	Nov	19	(h)	PORTSMOUTH	W 2-0	Dixon, Preece	8214						9						2	3		11		8	6	10		1		7	5	12	4			18
19	Nov	26	(a)	Swindon Town	W 2-1	Dixon, Oakes	9228						9		12				2	3	11			8	6	10		1		7	5		4			19
20	Dec	3	(h)	SHEFFIELD UNITED	L 3-6	Hartson, Gayle (og), Johnson (pen)	8516						9		13				2	3	11	12		8	6	10		1		7	5		4			20
21	Dec	11	(a)	DERBY COUNTY	D 0-0	-	6400		11				9		13				2	3		12		8	6	10		1		7	5		4			21
22	Dec	18	(a)	West Bromwich Albion	L 0-1	-	14392		4				9		12				2	3		11		8	6	10		1		7	5					22
23	Dec	26	(a)	Reading	D 0-0	-	11623		8				9		12				2	3		11		13	6	10		1		7	5		4			23
24	Dec	27	(h)	SUNDERLAND	W 3-0	Oakes (2), Hartson	8953						9						2	3		11		8	6	10	12	1		7	5		4	13		24
25	Dec	31	(a)	Notts County	W 1-0	Telfer	6249	12					9						2	3		11		8	6	10		1		7	5		4			25
26	Jan	2	(h)	CHARLTON ATHLETIC	L 0-1	-	7642	12	10				9						2	3		11		8	6			1		7	5		4			26
27	Jan	14	(a)	Barnsley	L 1-3	Dixon	4808						9			10			2	3		11		8	6		12	1		7	5		4			27
28	Feb	4	(h)	OLDHAM ATHLETIC	W 2-1	Marshall (2)	6903		10				9						2	3		11		8	6			1		7	5	12	4			28
29	Feb	11	(a)	Grimsby Town	L 0-5	-	4615		10				9						2	3		11			6	7		1		13	5		4		12	29
30	Feb	18	(h)	SWINDON TOWN	W 3-0	Horlock (og), Marshall (2)	6595		9										2	3		11			6	10		1		7	5		4		13	30
31	Feb	21	(a)	Portsmouth	L 2-3	Telfer, James	7373						9			12			2	3		11		8	6	10		1		7	5		4		13	31
32	Feb	25	(a)	Bristol City	D 2-2	Oakes (2)	7939						9						2	3		11		8	6	10		1		7	5	12	4			32
33	Mar	4	(h)	MILLWALL	D 1-1	Marshall	6864		9										2	3		11	13	8	6	10		1		7			4			33
34	Mar	7	(h)	PORT VALE	W 2-1	Telfer, Dixon	5947		9				13						2	3		11	12	8	6	10		1		7			4			34
35	Mar	11	(a)	Southend United	L 0-3	-	4558		12				9						2	3		11	10	8	6			1		7			4			35
36	Mar	18	(h)	TRANMERE ROVERS	W 2-0	James, Biggins	6660		9										2	3		11	12	8	6	10		1		7			4			36
37	Mar	21	(a)	Burnley	L 1-2	Marshall	9551						9			12			2	3		11	8		6	10		1		7	5				13	37
38	Mar	26	(h)	WATFORD	D 1-1	Telfer	7984		1							5			2	3		11	8		6	10			9	7		12	4			38
39	Apr	4	(h)	WOLVERHAMPTON WANDERERS	D 3-3	Telfer (2), Taylor	9651		1							5			2	3		11		8	6	10			9	7			4		12	39
40	Apr	8	(h)	NOTTS COUNTY	W 2-0	Telfer, Oakes (pen)	6428		1							5			2	3	13	11	12	8	6	10			9	7			4			40
41	Apr	11	(a)	Bolton Wanderers	D 0-0	-	13619		1							5			2	3	12	13	11	8	6	10			9	7			4			41
42	Apr	15	(a)	Sunderland	D 1-1	Taylor	17292		1					13		5			2	3		2	11	8	6	10			9	7			4			42
43	Apr	17	(h)	READING	L 0-1	-	8717		1							5			2	3		13	11	8	6	10			9	7			4			43
44	Apr	22	(a)	Charlton Athletic	L 0-1	-	10918		1			2		13						3			12	11	6	10			9	7	5		4			44
45	Apr	30	(a)	Middlesbrough	L 1-2	Taylor	23903		1							5				3		2	11	8	6	10			9	7		12	4			45
46	May	7	(h)	STOKE CITY	L 2-3	Harvey, Waddock	8252		1							3			2				12	8	6	10			9	7	5		4		11	46
				Apps				-	4	6	-	9	23	7	11	9	1	8	42	46	5	36	6	37	46	42	3	37	9	45	33	-	40	-	1	
				Subs				2	-	1	-	-	6	1	9	3	-	1	-	-	5	9	5	6	-	-	2	-	-	1	3	4	-	2	6	
				Goals				-	-	1	-	-	7	-	5	1	-	2	3	1	-	11	-	9	-	4	-	-	3	9	-	-	1	-	-	

Final League Position: 16th   4 Own Goals

1994/95 FA CUP

Round	Month	Day	Venue	Opponents	W/L/D	Score	Scorers	Attendance	Adcock A	Allen P	Biggins W	Chenery B	Davis K	Dixon K	Greene D	Hartson J	Harvey R	Houghton S	Hughes C	James J	Johnson M	Linton D	Marshall D	Matthews R	Oakes S	Peake T	Preece D	Skelton A	Sommer J	Taylor John	Telfer P	Thomas MA	Thorpe A	Waddock G	Williams M	Woodsford J	Round
3	Jan	7	(h)	BRISTOL ROVERS	D	1-1	Hartson	7571	12							9				2	3		11		8	6	10		1		7	5		4			3
Rep	Jan	18	(a)	Bristol Rovers	W	1-0	Marshall	8213				2				9					3		11		8	6	10		1		7	5		4			Rep
4	Jan	28	(h)	SOUTHAMPTON	D	1-1	Biggins	9938			8					9					3		11		2	6	10		1		7	5		4	12		4
Rep	Feb	8	(a)	Southampton	L	0-6	-	15075			9			12						2	3		11		8	6	10		1		7	5	13	4			Rep
								Apps			2	1				4				2	4		4		4	4	4		4		4	4		4			
								Subs	1					1																			1		1		
								Goals			1					1							1														

1994/95 COCA-COLA CUP (LEAGUE CUP)

Round	Month	Day	Venue	Opponents	W/L/D	Score	Scorers	Attendance	Adcock A	Allen P	Biggins W	Chenery B	Davis K	Dixon K	Greene D	Hartson J	Harvey R	Houghton S	Hughes C	James J	Johnson M	Linton D	Marshall D	Matthews R	Oakes S	Peake T	Preece D	Skelton A	Sommer J	Taylor John	Telfer P	Thomas MA	Thorpe A	Waddock G	Williams M	Woodsford J	Round
1:1	Aug	16	(h)	FULHAM	D	1-1	Oakes	3287						9	5			11	4	2	3	12	13		8	6	10		1		7						1:1
1:2	Aug	23	(a)	Fulham	D	1-1	Marshall	5134						9	5			11		2	3	4	8		12	6	10	13	1		7						1:2
								Apps						2	2			2	1	2	2	1	1		1	2	2		2		2						
								Subs														1	1		1			1									
								Goals															1		1												

Lost 3-4 on penalties aet.

Showing off their new kit for 1994/95, Kerry Dixon, Ceri Hughes, Juergen Sommer, Dwight Marshall and Scott Oakes

John Hartson, sold to Arsenal for £2.5 million.

TIMELINE...

Summer 1994 The Kenilworth Road end is fully converted to seating.

13 January 1995 John Hartson becomes the most expensive teenager in football as Arsenal pay £2.5 million for his services.

1995/96 "NEW" FOOTBALL LEAGUE DIVISION ONE (SECOND TIER)

Match No	Month	Day	Venue	Opponents	W,L,D Score	Scorers	Attendance	Alexander G	Chenery B	Davis K	Davis Steve	Douglas S	Evers S	Feuer I	Grant K	Guentchev B	Harvey R	Hughes C	James J	Johnson G	Johnson M	Linton D	Marshall D	Matthews R	McLaren P	Oakes S	Oldfield D	Patterson D	Peake T	Riseth V	Simpson G	Skelton A	Sommer J	Taylor John	Thomas MA	Thorpe A	Tomlinson G	Upson M	Vilstrup J	Waddock G	Wilkinson P	Woodsford J	Match No
1	Aug	13	(h)	NORWICH CITY	L 1-3	Guentchev (pen)	7848	7	1							10	11	5			3						8		6					12	2	9				4			1
2	Aug	19	(a)	Southend United	W 1-0	Thorpe	4630	7			4					10	11	5	2		3		8				6						1	9	13	14				12			2
3	Aug	26	(h)	LEICESTER CITY	D 1-1	Hughes	7612				4					14	11	5	2	10	3	7	8				6	13				1		9		12							3
4	Aug	29	(a)	Grimsby Town	D 0-0		4289	5		1	1					9	11		2	10	3	7	8				6	13						14		12						12	4
5	Sep	2	(h)	DERBY COUNTY	L 1-2	Marshall	6427	5		1	1					8	11		2	10	3		7				6	14						9		12					13		5
6	Sep	9	(a)	Reading	L 1-3	Marshall	8550	6		1	1					12	11		2	10	3		7	8			9													5			6
7	Sep	13	(a)	Millwall	L 0-1		7354				4			1		10	11		12		3		7	8			9	2											6	5			7
8	Sep	16	(h)	SUNDERLAND	L 0-2	-	6955				4			1		12	11	10		3			7	8			9	2						13					6	5			8
9	Sep	23	(a)	Wolverhampton Wanderers	D 0-0	-	23659	7			4			1		10	11	5			3		8					13	2										6	12			9
10	Sep	30	(h)	PORTSMOUTH	W 3-1	S Davis, Marshall, Guentchev (pen)	7795	7			4			1		10	11	5			3	13	8					2						9					6	12			10
11	Oct	7	(a)	Tranmere Rovers	L 0-1		6680	7			4			1		10	11				3		8						2											5			11
12	Oct	14	(h)	WEST BROMWICH ALBION	L 1-2	Harvey	8042	7			4			1			11	6	12		3		8				9		2											5	10		12
13	Oct	22	(a)	Ipswich Town	W 1-0	Oldfield	9157	7			4			1		14	11	5		13	3		10			8	9	12	2										6	12			13
14	Oct	29	(h)	CHARLTON ATHLETIC	L 0-1		6270	7			4			1		13	11	5			3	14	10			8	9		2					12						6			14
15	Nov	4	(a)	Stoke City	L 0-5		9349	7			4			1			11	5		3			10						2					9						6			15
16	Nov	11	(h)	OLDHAM ATHLETIC	D 1-1	Douglas	6047	7			4	10		1			11				3				6	8	12	13	2					9									16
17	Nov	18	(h)	BIRMINGHAM CITY	D 0-0		7920	7				12		1			11	5		4	3		10		6	8			2					9					13				17
18	Nov	21	(a)	Watford	D 1-1	S Davis	10042				4	13		1			11	5			3	7	10		6	8		12	2					9		14							18
19	Nov	25	(a)	Barnsley	L 0-1		6437	12				13		1			11	5			3	7	10		6			4	2							14							19
20	Dec	2	(h)	TRANMERE ROVERS	W 3-2	McLaren, Marshall (2)	6025	2						1			11	5			3	7	10		6		9													4			20
21	Dec	10	(h)	WOLVERHAMPTON WANDERERS	L 2-3	Oakes, Marshall	6997		1	7				1		13	10	5			3		10		6	8	9		2					12						4			21
22	Dec	16	(a)	Portsmouth	L 0-4		7012	7			4			1			11				3		10		6	8			2					9	12	13				5			22
23	Dec	23	(h)	HUDDERSFIELD TOWN	D 2-2	Marshall, Oldfield	7076				5			1		14	12						10		6	7	8	13	2					9	3	11				4			23
24	Jan	13	(h)	SOUTHEND UNITED	W 3-1	Guentchev, Oakes (2)	6566	10			5			1		7	13		2						6	8	12							9	3	11				4			24
25	Jan	20	(a)	Norwich City	W 1-0	Guentchev (pen)	12474	10			5			1		7	11		2						6	8	12							9	3					4			25
26	Jan	31	(h)	SHEFFIELD UNITED	W 1-0	Guentchev	6995	10			5			1		7	14	12							6	8	13		2					9	3	11				4			26
27	Feb	3	(a)	Leicester City	D 1-1	Thorpe	15687	10			5			1			11	8		14		13			6			2	12					9	3	7				4			27
28	Feb	10	(h)	GRIMSBY TOWN	W 3-2	Alexander, Guentchev, Marshall	7158				5			1		7		8	2				13				12		6					9	3	11				4			28
29	Feb	17	(h)	MILLWALL	W 1-0	Thorpe (pen)	7308	10			5			1		7	14	8							6		12							9	3	11				4			29
30	Feb	21	(a)	Derby County	D 1-1	Marshall	14825	10			5			1		12			2						6		7		9						3	11				4			30
31	Feb	24	(a)	Sunderland	L 0-1		16693	10			5			1		7	11	8	2				6				9							13	3	12				4			31
32	Feb	27	(h)	READING	L 1-2	Guentchev (pen)	6683	10			5			1		7			2						6		8		12	5	13			9	3	11		14		4			32
33	Mar	2	(h)	CRYSTAL PALACE	D 0-0	-	8478	10			5			1		7	14		2						6	8	13		9					12	3	11				4			33
34	Mar	9	(a)	Huddersfield Town	L 0-1		11950				5			1		7			2		13				12	8	10	6						9	3	11				4			34
35	Mar	19	(a)	Crystal Palace	L 0-2		14703				5			1		7		12			13					8	10	6						9	3	11				4			35
36	Mar	23	(a)	Sheffield United	L 0-1		14935	10			5			1		7			11							12	8	7	2	6				9	3	14	13			4			36
37	Mar	30	(h)	IPSWICH TOWN	L 1-2	Grant	9151	12			5			1	10	13										8	7	6							3	11	14			4	9		37
38	Apr	2	(a)	West Bromwich Albion	W 2-0	Guentchev, Grant	15130	2			5				10	7	11				13					12	4	6							3	8					9		38
39	Apr	5	(a)	Charlton Athletic	D 1-1	Thorpe	14515	2			5				10	7	8				12					13		6							3	11				4	9		39
40	Apr	9	(h)	STOKE CITY	L 1-2	Grant	7689	2			5				10	7						5				11	9	6						13	3	8	12			4			40
41	Apr	13	(a)	Birmingham City	L 0-4		15426	2			5				10	7	12					5				11	9	6						13	3	8	14			4			41
42	Apr	20	(h)	WATFORD	D 0-0	-	9454	2			5				10	7	13					5				11	9	6							3	8				4			42
43	Apr	23	(a)	Port Vale	L 0-1	-	6054	7			5	9			10							2				11		6							3	12	8			4			43
44	Apr	27	(h)	BARNSLEY	L 1-3	Thorpe	6194	8			5	13		1	10	7	14									6			2					12	3	9				4			44
45	Apr	30	(h)	PORT VALE	W 3-2	Thorpe (2), Guentchev	5443	8		2	1	7	11	1	10	13									6				12					14	3	9				4			45
46	May	5	(a)	Oldham Athletic	L 0-1		6623			2		12		1	10	7						13			6									8	3	9				4			46
							Apps	35	2	6	36	3	1	38	10	25	28	21	23	5	33	6	23	-	9	26	23	21	15	6	-	-	2	18	25	23	1	-	6	32	3	1	
							Subs	2	-	-	5	-	-	-	10	8	2	4	1	2	4	3	-	3	3	11	2	3	5	-	1	4	-	10	2	10	6	-	1	4	-	2	
							Goals	1	-	-	2	1	-	-	3	9	1	1	-	-	-	-	9	-	1	3	2	-	-	-	-	-	-	-	-	7	-	-	-	-	-	-	

Final League Position: 24th

1995/96 FA CUP

Round	Month	Day	Venue	Opponents	W,L,D Score	Scorers	Attendance
3	Jan	6	(a)	Grimsby Town	L 1-7	Marshall	5387

	Alexander G	Chenery B	Davis K	Davis Steve	Douglas S	Evers S	Feuer I	Grant K	Guentchev B	Harvey R	Hughes C	James J	Johnson G	Johnson M	Linton D	Marshall D	Matthews R	McLaren P	Oakes S	Oldfield D	Patterson D	Peake T	Riseth V	Simpson G	Skelton A	Sommer J	Taylor John	Thomas MA	Thorpe A	Tomlinson G	Upson M	Vilstrup J	Waddock G	Wilkinson P	Woodsford J
Match	12						1	7			5			6		11		10	8	9								3	13				4		
Apps	·	·	·	·	·	1	·	1	·	·	1	·	·	1	·	1	·	1	1	1	1	·	·	·	·	·	·	1	·	·	·	·	1	·	·
Subs	1	·	·	·	·	·	·	·	·	·	·	·	·	·	·	·	·	·	·	·	·	·	·	·	·	·	·	·	1	·	·	·	·	·	·
Goals	·	·	·	·	·	·	·	·	·	·	·	·	·	·	·	1	·	·	·	·	·	·	·	·	·	·	·	·	·	·	·	·	·	·	·

1995/96 COCA-COLA CUP (LEAGUE CUP)

Round	Month	Day	Venue	Opponents	W,L,D Score	Scorers	Attendance
1:1	Aug	15	(h)	BOURNEMOUTH	D 1-1	Marshall	2728
1:2	Aug	22	(a)	Bournemouth	L 1-2	M Johnson	4884

1st Round 2nd Leg aet, 1-1 after 90 minutes.

	Alexander G	Chenery B	Davis K	Davis Steve	Douglas S	Evers S	Feuer I	Grant K	Guentchev B	Harvey R	Hughes C	James J	Johnson G	Johnson M	Linton D	Marshall D	Matthews R	McLaren P	Oakes S	Oldfield D	Patterson D	Peake T	Riseth V	Simpson G	Skelton A	Sommer J	Taylor John	Thomas MA	Thorpe A	Tomlinson G	Upson M	Vilstrup J	Waddock G	Wilkinson P	Woodsford J
1:1	7			4					10	11	5			3		8			6					1	9	2	12								
1:2	7			4					10	11	2			3		8	12		6					1	9	14	13				5				
Apps	2	·	·	2	·	·	·	·	2	2	1	·	1	·	2	·	·	2	·	·	·	·	2	2	1	·	·	·	·	·	1	·	·	·	·
Subs	·	·	·	·	·	·	·	·	·	·	1	·	·	·	·	·	1	·	·	·	·	·	·	·	1	2	·	·	·	·	·	·	·	·	·
Goals	·	·	·	·	·	·	·	·	·	·	·	·	·	1	·	1	·	·	·	·	·	·	·	·	·	·	·	·	·	·	·	·	·	·	·

1995/96 ANGLO-ITALIAN CUP

Round	Month	Day	Venue	Opponents	W,L,D Score	Scorers	Attendance
PR	Sep	5	(h)	PERUGIA	L 1-4	Guentchev	2352
PR	Oct	11	(a)	Genoa	L 0-4	-	3759
PR	Nov	8	(a)	Cesena	L 1-2	Marshall	461
PR	Dec	13	(h)	ANCONA	W 5-0	Oakes, Marshall, Taylor, Thorpe, Guentchev (pen)	2091

	Alexander G	Chenery B	Davis K	Davis Steve	Douglas S	Evers S	Feuer I	Grant K	Guentchev B	Harvey R	Hughes C	James J	Johnson G	Johnson M	Linton D	Marshall D	Matthews R	McLaren P	Oakes S	Oldfield D	Patterson D	Peake T	Riseth V	Simpson G	Skelton A	Sommer J	Taylor John	Thomas MA	Thorpe A	Tomlinson G	Upson M	Vilstrup J	Waddock G	Wilkinson P	Woodsford J
PERUGIA		1	4		5				8	11	10	2			7	13		9						3				6				12		14	
Genoa	12	1	4						10	11	2		3	7			5	8	9									14			6		13		
Cesena	7	1	4	12						11						10		5	8		2		9	13				3	6						
ANCONA		1	4	12					11	11					3	7	10	6	8		2						9	14	13		5				
Apps	1	·	4	4	·	1	·	·	2	4	1	2	·	2	3	2	·	3	3	2	2	·	1	·	1	·	1	·	1	·	1	·	1	2	1	·	·
Subs	1	·	·	·	1	·	·	·	1	·	·	·	·	·	1	·	·	·	·	·	·	·	1	·	·	·	1	2	·	·	·	1	·	2	
Goals	·	·	·	·	·	·	·	·	2	·	·	·	·	·	·	2	·	·	1	·	·	·	·	·	·	·	1	·	1	·	·	·	·	·	·

TIMELINE...

11 June 1995 David Pleat leaves again, this time to take up the manager's position at Sheffield Wednesday.
3 July 1995 Terry Westley is elevated into the manager's job.
18 December 1995 After a poor run of results Westley is dismissed.
21 December 1995 It is announced that the new manager will be Lennie Lawrence.
5 May 1996 The Town are relegated back to the 'third tier'.

1996/97 "NEW" FOOTBALL LEAGUE DIVISION TWO (THIRD TIER)

Match No	Month	Day	Venue	Opponents	W,L,D Score	Scorers	Attendance	Alexander G	Davis K	Davis Steve	Douglas S	Evers S	Feuer I	Fotiadis A	Grant K	Guentchev B	Harvey R	Hughes C	James J	Johnson M	Kiwomya A	Linton D	Marshall D	McGowan G	McLaren P	Oldfield D	Patterson D	Showler P	Skelton A	Thomas MA	Thorpe A	Upson M	Waddock G	Match No
1	Aug	17	(h)	BURNLEY	L 1-2	Thorpe	7064	8		14			1	12	10	7			2	6		13				9	5			3	11		4	1
2	Aug	24	(a)	Brentford	L 2-3	Thorpe (pen), Hughes	5409	8		5			1		10	12		7	2							9	6			3	11		4	2
3	Aug	27	(a)	Bristol City	L 0-5	-	7028	12		5			1	13	10	14		8	2							9	6	7		3	11		4	3
4	Aug	31	(h)	ROTHERHAM UNITED	W 1-0	Thomas	5112	8		5			1		10	12		7	2	6						9		11		3	13	14	4	4
5	Sep	7	(a)	Wycombe Wanderers	W 1-0	Oldfield	6471	8		5			1	10		11		7	2	6						9				3	12		4	5
6	Sep	10	(h)	GILLINGHAM	W 2-1	Guentchev, Oldfield	5171	8		5			1	10	12	11		7	2	6						9				3			4	6
7	Sep	14	(h)	CHESTERFIELD	L 0-1	-	5292	8		5			1	10	12	11		7	2	6						9		13		3			4	7
8	Sep	21	(a)	Bury	D 0-0	-	3588	8		5		12	1	10		11		7	2	6						9				3			4	8
9	Sep	28	(h)	BLACKPOOL	W 1-0	Grant	5785	8		5	13		1	12	10	11			2	6						9				3	7		4	9
10	Oct	5	(h)	WALSALL	W 3-1	Thorpe, Showler, Fotiadis	5456	8		5	13		1	9		11	10		2	6						14		12		3	7		4	10
11	Oct	12	(a)	Shrewsbury Town	W 3-0	Showler, Thomas, Grant	3357	8		5	12		1		10	13		7	2	6						13		11		3	9		4	11
12	Oct	15	(a)	Stockport County	D 1-1	Davis	5352	8		5			1		10			7	2	6						12		11		3	9		4	12
13	Oct	19	(h)	PETERBOROUGH UNITED	W 3-0	Davis, Showler (2)	6387	8		5			1	12		14		7	2	6						13	9	11		3	10		4	13
14	Oct	26	(a)	Bournemouth	W 2-0	Thorpe (2, 1 pen)	6086	8			13		1			12		10	2	5						14	9	11	6	3	7		4	14
15	Oct	29	(a)	Watford	D 1-1	Showler	14109	8		5	12		1					7	2	6						9		11		3	10		4	15
16	Nov	2	(a)	Plymouth Argyle	D 3-3	Thorpe (3)	7134	8		5	9		1		12	13		7	2	6						11				3	10		4	16
17	Nov	9	(h)	NOTTS COUNTY	W 2-0	Thorpe, Hughes	6134	8		5	12		1		9	11		7	2	6										3	10		4	17
18	Nov	19	(a)	Preston North End	L 2-3	Davis (2)	7004	8		5	9		1			10		7	2	6			13			12				11	14	3		4	18
19	Nov	23	(h)	BRISTOL ROVERS	W 2-1	Marshall, Thorpe (pen)	5791	8		5			1		12	13		7	2	6			9			4				11	10	3		4	19
20	Nov	30	(a)	Bournemouth	L 2-3	James, Marshall	4322	8		5			1		13	14		7	2	6			11					9	4	3	10		4	20
21	Dec	3	(a)	YORK CITY	W 2-0	Marshall, Thorpe	4987	8		5			1		12			7	2	6		12	11			4		9		3	10		4	21
22	Dec	14	(h)	CREWE ALEXANDRA	W 6-0	Alexander, Thorpe (3, 1 pen), Showler, Oldfield	5977	8		5			1		12				2	6			11		7	13		9		3	10		4	22
23	Dec	18	(a)	Millwall	W 1-0	Hughes	7077	8		5			1			11		7	2	6			9			12				3	10		4	23
24	Dec	26	(a)	Gillingham	W 2-1	Thorpe (2)	8491	8		5			1			9		7	2	6						12				3	10		4	24
25	Jan	18	(h)	WREXHAM	D 0-0	-	6167	8		5			1			14		7	2	6		13	11			4		12		3	10		4	25
26	Jan	27	(h)	WATFORD	D 0-0	-	7977	8		5			1					7	2	6		4	11			12		9		3	10		4	26
27	Feb	1	(a)	Notts County	W 2-1	Hughes, Alexander	4866	8		5			1		13	11		7	2	6			4		12	9				3	10		4	27
28	Feb	8	(h)	PLYMOUTH ARGYLE	D 2-2	Thorpe (2)	6827	8		5		4	1	13		7			2	6		12	11			9				3	10		4	28
29	Feb	15	(a)	Bristol Rovers	L 2-3	Thorpe (pen), Waddock	5612	8		5			1	14		7			2	6		11	13			4		9		3	10	12	4	29
30	Feb	22	(h)	PRESTON NORTH END	W 5-1	Oldfield (3), Waddock, Thomas	6896	8		5			1	12				7	2	6			14		13	9		11		3	10		4	30
31	Mar	1	(a)	York City	D 1-1	Davis	3788	8		5			1					7	2	6			13		12	9		11		3	10		4	31
32	Mar	4	(a)	Chesterfield	D 1-1	Thorpe (pen)	3731	8		5			1	12				7	2	6						9	3	11		3	10		4	32
33	Mar	8	(h)	MILLWALL	L 0-2	-	9109	8		5			1			13		7	2	6			14			12	3	11		3	10		4	33
34	Mar	12	(a)	Wrexham	L 1-2	Davis	3392	8		5			1			12		7	2	6			13			14	9	11		3	10		4	34
35	Mar	15	(a)	Crewe Alexandra	D 0-0	-	4474	8		5			1					7	2	6						11	9	3		3	10		4	35
36	Mar	21	(h)	BRENTFORD	W 1-0	Thorpe	8680	8		5			1			12		7	2	6			13			11				3	10		4	36
37	Mar	29	(a)	Burnley	W 2-0	Thorpe (2)	15490	8		5			1		13				6	11		12	2	7		9				3	10		4	37
38	Apr	2	(h)	BRISTOL CITY	D 2-2	Davis, Thorpe	7550	8		5			1	14	11	7			6				13	2		9				3	10		4	38
39	Apr	5	(a)	Rotherham United	W 3-0	Thorpe (3)	2609	8		5			1	12				7	2	6			14		11	9	14			3	10		4	39
40	Apr	8	(h)	WYCOMBE WANDERERS	D 0-0	-	8117	8		5			1	12				7	2	6			13		11	9				3	10		4	40
41	Apr	12	(a)	Walsall	L 2-3	Kiwomya, Davis	5415	8		5			1	13		14			2	6	11				7	9	12			3	10		4	41
42	Apr	15	(a)	Blackpool	D 0-0	-	4382	8		5			1	8					2	6	11		12		7	9				3	10		4	42
43	Apr	19	(h)	SHREWSBURY TOWN	W 2-0	Thorpe (pen), Marshall	7501	8		5			1	11			13		2	6			12		7	9				3	10		4	43
44	Apr	22	(h)	BURY	D 0-0	-	8281	8		5			1	9				7	2	6	11		13			12				3	10		4	44
45	Apr	26	(a)	Peterborough United	W 1-0	Fotiadis	9499	8		5			1	12				7	2	6	11					13				3	10		4	45
46	May	3	(h)	STOCKPORT COUNTY	D 1-1	Fotiadis	9623	8					1	10	12		11		2	6						13		7	9	5	3		4	46
							Apps	44	-	43	2	1	46	9	8	15	1	36	44	44	5	3	9	2	13	31	8	21	2	42	39	-	38	
							Subs	1	-	1	7	-	-	8	17	12	1	-	-	-	-	4	15	-	11	7	2	2	1	-	2	1	1	
							Goals	2	-	8	-	-	-	3	2	1	-	4	1	-	1	-	4	-	-	6	-	6	-	3	28	-	2	

Final League Position: 3rd

1996/97 PLAY-OFFS

Round	Month	Day	Venue	Opponents	W,L,D Score	Scorers	Attendance	Alexander G	Davis K	Davis Steve	Douglas S	Evers S	Feuer I	Fotiadis A	Grant K	Guentchev B	Harvey R	Hughes C	James J	Johnson M	Kiwomya A	Linton D	Marshall D	McGowan G	McLaren P	Oldfield D	Patterson D	Showler P	Skelton A	Thomas MA	Thorpe A	Upson M	Waddock G	Round
SF1	May	11	(a)	Crewe Alexandra	L 1-2	Oldfield	5467	8		5			1	11	13			2				12			7	9	6			3	10		4	SF1
SF2	May	14	(h)	CREWE ALEXANDRA	D 2-2	Oldfield (2)	8168	8		5			1	12			6					13			7	9	2	11		3	10		4	SF2
							Apps	2	-	2	-	-	2	1	-	-	1	1	-	-	-	-	-	-	2	2	2	1	-	2	2	-	2	
							Subs	-	-	-	-	-	-	1	1	-	-	-	-	-	-	2	-	-	-	-	-	-	-	-	-	-	-	
							Goals	-	-	-	-	-	-	-	-	-	-	-	-	-	-	-	-	-	-	3	-	-	-	-	-	-	-	

1996/97 FA CUP

Round	Month	Day	Venue	Opponents	W,L,D Score	Scorers	Attendance	Alexander G	Davis K	Davis Steve	Douglas S	Evers S	Feuer I	Fotiadis A	Grant K	Guentchev B	Harvey R	Hughes C	James J	Johnson M	Kiwomya A	Linton D	Marshall D	McGowan G	McLaren P	Oldfield D	Patterson D	Showler P	Skelton A	Thomas MA	Thorpe A	Upson M	Waddock G	Round
1	Nov	16	(a)	Torquay United	W 1-0	Hughes	3450	8		5	9		1		10			7	2	6			12					11	3				4	1
2	Dec	7	(h)	BOREHAM WOOD	W 2-1	Marshall (2)	5332	8		5			1	12	13			7	2				11		6	9			3				4	2
3	Jan	21	(h)	BOLTON WANDERERS	D 1-1	Johnson	7414	8		5			1		12			7	2	6		4	11			9			3		10			3
Rep	Jan	25	(a)	Bolton Wanderers	L 2-6	Marshall, Thorpe	9713	8		5			1	13	12			7	2	6		4	11			9			3		10			Rep
						Apps		4		4	1		4		1			4	4	3		2	3			1		1	4	2	2		2	
						Subs								1	2	2							1								1			
						Goals												1		1			3								1			

1996/97 COCA-COLA CUP (LEAGUE CUP)

Round	Month	Day	Venue	Opponents	W,L,D Score	Scorers	Attendance	Alexander G	Davis K	Davis Steve	Douglas S	Evers S	Feuer I	Fotiadis A	Grant K	Guentchev B	Harvey R	Hughes C	James J	Johnson M	Kiwomya A	Linton D	Marshall D	McGowan G	McLaren P	Oldfield D	Patterson D	Showler P	Skelton A	Thomas MA	Thorpe A	Upson M	Waddock G	Round
1:1	Aug	20	(h)	BRISTOL ROVERS	W 3-0	Grant, Thorpe (pen), Oldfield	2643	8		5			1		10	14		7	2	6						9	13	12	3	11			4	1:1
1:2	Sep	4	(a)	Bristol Rovers	L 1-2	Oldfield	2320	8		5			1	12	10			4	2	6		7				9				11			4	1:2
2:1	Sep	17	(h)	DERBY COUNTY	W 1-0	James	4459	8		5			1	12	10	11		7	2	6						9			3				4	2:1
2:2	Sep	25	(a)	Derby County	D 2-2	Grant, Thorpe	13569	8		5			1		10	11		7	2	6						9			3		12		4	2:2
3	Oct	22	(a)	Wimbledon	D 1-1	Hughes	5043	8		5			1		10			10	2	6						9			3		11		4	3
Rep	Nov	12	(h)	WIMBLEDON	L 1-2	Blackwell (og)	8076	8		5	12		1		9	13		7	2	6					14				3		10		4	Rep
						Apps		6		6			6		4	3		6	6	6		1				5		3		6	3		5	
						Subs					1			2		2										1		1	1		1			
						Goals									2			1	1							2					2			

Round 3 Replay aet, 1-1 after 90 minutes.   1 Own Goal

1996/97 AUTO WINDSCREENS SHIELD (ASSOCIATE MEMBERS CUP)

Round	Month	Day	Venue	Opponents	W,L,D Score	Scorers	Attendance	Alexander G	Davis K	Davis Steve	Douglas S	Evers S	Feuer I	Fotiadis A	Grant K	Guentchev B	Harvey R	Hughes C	James J	Johnson M	Kiwomya A	Linton D	Marshall D	McGowan G	McLaren P	Oldfield D	Patterson D	Showler P	Skelton A	Thomas MA	Thorpe A	Upson M	Waddock G	Round
1	Dec	10	(h)	LEYTON ORIENT	W 2-1	S Davis, Grant	1594	13	1	5					10	9		7	2			8	11			12	6	14	3				4	1
2	Feb	4	(a)	Northampton Town	L 0-1	-	4201	8		5		4	1	12	9	11		7		6			10			13	2		3				1	2
						Apps		1	1	2		1	1		2	2		2	1	1		1	2				2		1	1			1	
						Subs		1						1												2		1						
						Goals				1					1																			

TIMELINE...

14 May 1997 The Town enter the play-offs for the first time but go out to a Crewe side who they beat 6-0 earlier in the season.

Luton Town Football Club – The Full Record | 207

1997/98 "NEW" FOOTBALL LEAGUE DIVISION TWO (THIRD TIER)

Match No	Month	Day	Venue	Opponents	W,L,D Score	Scorers	Attendance	Abbey N	Alexander G	Allen C	Allen R	Davies Simon	Davis K	Davis Steve	Dibble A	Doherty G	Douglas S	Evers S	Feuer I	Fotiadis A	Fraser S	George L	Gray P	Harvey R	James J	Johnson M	Kean R	Marshall D	McGowan G	McLaren P	Oldfield D	Patterson D	Peake T	Showler P	Small B	Spring M	Thomas MA	Thorpe A	Waddock G	White A	Match No
1	Aug	9	(a)	Blackpool	L 0-1	-	6547	8				11		5			12		1						6			2	7	9							3	10	4		1
2	Aug	18	(h)	SOUTHEND UNITED	W 1-0	Douglas	5140	8				7		5			12		1	9					6			2	11	13							3	10	4		2
3	Aug	23	(a)	Fulham	D 0-0	-	8142	8				7	1	5			10			14					2	6		11	13	12	9						3		4		3
4	Aug	30	(h)	OLDHAM ATHLETIC	D 1-1	Thorpe	5404					7	1	5			12								2	6		11	13	9			14				3	10	4		4
5	Sep	2	(h)	MILLWALL	L 0-2	-	5781	8					1	5			14	13	12						2	6		11	3	7	9								10	4		5
6	Sep	9	(a)	Northampton Town	L 0-1	-	7246					12	1	5			13	10	8						6			11	2	7	9				3					4		6
7	Sep	13	(a)	Bournemouth	D 1-1	Marshall	4561					7	1	5			13	10	12						6			11	2	8	9				3					4		7
8	Sep	20	(h)	WREXHAM	L 2-5	S Davis, Gray	5241						5	1			10	12					7	3				11	2	8	9		14	6					13	4		8
9	Sep	27	(a)	Bristol City	L 0-3	-	8509					7	1				2				11		3			13			8	9			5	12			10	4	6	9	9
10	Oct	4	(h)	WATFORD	L 0-4	-	9041					11	1				13						7	3	12				2	8	9			5				10	4	6	10	10
11	Oct	11	(h)	PLYMOUTH ARGYLE	W 3-0	Thorpe (2), S Davies	4931	2				12	1			11		13					5						8	9				3	7			10	4	6	11
12	Oct	18	(a)	Wigan Athletic	D 1-1	Oldfield	4466	11				13	1	5									7		2			12		8	9				3	4			10	4	6	12
13	Oct	21	(a)	Carlisle United	W 1-0	White	4341	11					1	5									7		2			13		8	9				3	4			10	12	6	13
14	Oct	25	(h)	BRENTFORD	W 2-0	Alexander, Thorpe	5972	11					1	5									7		2	12		13		8	9				3				10	4	6	14
15	Nov	1	(a)	Wycombe Wanderers	D 2-2	Oldfield, Thorpe	6219	11					1	5									7		2					8	9				3				10	4		15
16	Nov	4	(h)	BURNLEY	L 2-3	Alexander (2)	5315	11					1	5				12					7		2					8	9				3				10	4		16
17	Nov	8	(h)	PRESTON NORTH END	L 1-3	Thorpe	5767	11				14	1					12					7		2			13		8	9				3				10	4	5	17
18	Nov	22	(h)	WALSALL	L 0-1	-	4726	11				6						12	1	7					2					8	9				3	13			10	4		18
19	Nov	29	(a)	York City	W 2-1	Alexander, Thorpe	3636	11	7					5					1						2					8	9				3				10	4		19
20	Dec	2	(h)	GILLINGHAM	D 2-2	S Davis, Thorpe	4408	11	7					5				13	1						2					8	9				3		12		10	4	6	20
21	Dec	13	(a)	Chesterfield	D 0-0	-	4358	11	7				12	5					1						2					8	9				3				10	4	6	21
22	Dec	20	(h)	BRISTOL ROVERS	L 2-4	C Allen, Oldfield	5266	11	7		13			5		4			1	12										8	9	2			3				10		6	22
23	Dec	26	(h)	NORTHAMPTON TOWN	D 2-2	Oldfield, Thorpe	8035	11	7					5					1	12										8	9	2			3				10	4	6	23
24	Dec	28	(a)	Millwall	W 2-0	S Davis, Thorpe	7461	11	7					5					1											8	9	2			3				10	4	6	24
25	Jan	3	(a)	Southend United	W 2-1	Alexander (2)	5056	11	7					5					1											8	9	2			3				10	4	6	25
26	Jan	10	(h)	BLACKPOOL	W 3-0	Thorpe (3)	5574	11	7					5					1											8	9	2			3				10	4	6	26
27	Jan	17	(a)	Oldham Athletic	L 1-2	Alexander	6057	11	7			12		5					1									13		9	2				3		8		10	4	6	27
28	Jan	24	(h)	FULHAM	L 1-4	Thorpe	8366	11	7			12		5					1											8	9	2			3				10	4	6	28
29	Jan	31	(h)	BOURNEMOUTH	L 1-2	Johnson	5466	11	7			14	1					13						3		6		12		8					3				10			29
30	Feb	7	(a)	Wrexham	L 1-2	S Davis	3527	11	7				1	5										3		6		12		8	9	2			3				10	4		30
31	Feb	14	(a)	Watford	D 1-1	Johnson	15182	11	7			14	1					12								6		13		8	9	2			3				10	4	5	31
32	Feb	21	(h)	BRISTOL CITY	D 0-0	-	6405	11	7				1	5				4				12	10					13		8	9	2			3						6	32
33	Feb	24	(h)	WIGAN ATHLETIC	D 1-1	Oldfield	4403	11					1	5				4				12	10					7		8	9	2			3						6	33
34	Feb	28	(a)	Plymouth Argyle	W 2-0	Fotiadis, Evers	4846	2					1	5		13		7		12			10					11		8	9	6			3					4		34
35	Mar	3	(a)	Preston North End	L 0-1	-	6992	2				13	1	5				7		12			10					11		8	9	6					14		3	4		35
36	Mar	7	(h)	WYCOMBE WANDERERS	D 0-0	-	6114	2				13	1	5				7		12			10					11		8	9	6					4		3			36
37	Mar	14	(a)	Burnley	D 1-1	Thomas	9656					12	1	5				7		11			10		2					8	9	6							3		4		37
38	Mar	21	(h)	GRIMSBY TOWN	D 2-2	Evers, S Davis	5722	11					1	5				12	4	7					2					10							3					38
39	Mar	28	(a)	Walsall	W 3-2	Oldfield, Allen, Marshall	3922	11		10			1	5		13		12							2			7		8	9				3					4	6	39
40	Apr	4	(h)	YORK CITY	W 3-0	Alexander, Oldfield, Gray	5541	11	10				1	5				4					12		2			7		8	9	6			3						13	40
41	Apr	7	(a)	Grimsby Town	W 1-0	Allen	4455	11	10				1					14					12		2			7		8	9	5			3					4	6	41
42	Apr	11	(a)	Gillingham	L 1-2	Allen	6846	11	10				1					14					12		2			7		8	9	5			3					4	6	42
43	Apr	14	(h)	CHESTERFIELD	W 3-0	Williams (og), Allen, Oldfield	5884	11	10				1	5				12	4						2			7		8	9				3		8				13	43
44	Apr	18	(a)	Bristol Rovers	L 1-2	Oldfield	8038	11	10				1	5				13	8						2			7		9	6					14	3			4	12	44
45	Apr	25	(a)	Brentford	D 2-2	Marshall, Allen	6598	2		10			1	5				12	7						11					9	6					14	3			4		45
46	May	2	(h)	CARLISLE UNITED	W 3-2	Evers, Oldfield, Allen	6729	11		10			1	5				14	12	4	7	3								8	9	2			13						6	46

Final League Position: 17th   1 Own Goal

		Abbey N	Alexander G	Allen C	Allen R	Davies Simon	Davis K	Davis Steve	Dibble A	Doherty G	Douglas S	Evers S	Feuer I	Fotiadis A	Fraser S	George L	Gray P	Harvey R	James J	Johnson M	Kean R	Marshall D	McGowan G	McLaren P	Oldfield D	Patterson D	Peake T	Showler P	Small B	Spring M	Thomas MA	Thorpe A	Waddock G	White A
	Apps	-	39	14	8	8	32	38	1	1	5	14	13	5	1	1	14	5	23	13	-	19	6	41	45	23	-	15	6	27	27	36	26	
	Subs				12						9	12	9		10			3	1	1	1	10	2				1	1		6	1		1	1
	Goals	-	8	1	6	1	-	5	-	-	1	3	-	1	-	-	2	-	-	3	-	2	-	-	10	-	-	-	-	-	1	14	-	1

1997/98 FA CUP

Round	Month	Day	Venue	Opponents	W/L/D Score	Scorers	Attendance	Abbey N	Alexander G	Allen C	Allen R	Davies Simon	Davis K	Davis Steve	Dibble A	Doherty G	Douglas S	Evers S	Feuer I	Fotiadis A	Fraser S	George L	Gray P	Harvey R	James J	Johnson M	Kean R	Marshall D	McGowan G	McLaren P	Oldfield D	Patterson D	Peake T	Showler P	Small B	Spring M	Thomas MA	Thorpe A	Waddock G	White A	Round
1	Nov	15	(h)	TORQUAY UNITED	L 0-1	-	3446	11		12						14			1	7		3	2							8	9	13			6		10	4	5		1
							Apps	·	1	·	·	·	·	·	·	·	·	·	1	1	·	1	1	·	·	·	·	·	·	1	1	·	·	·	1	·	1	1	1	1	
							Subs	·	·	·	1	·	·	·	1	·	·	·	·	·	·	·	·	·	·	·	·	·	·	·	·	1	·	·	·	·	·	·	·	·	
							Goals	·	·	·	·	·	·	·	·	·	·	·	·	·	·	·	·	·	·	·	·	·	·	·	·	·	·	·	·	·	·	·	·	·	

1997/98 COCA-COLA CUP (LEAGUE CUP)

Round	Month	Day	Venue	Opponents	W/L/D Score	Scorers	Attendance	Abbey N	Alexander G	Allen C	Allen R	Davies Simon	Davis K	Davis Steve	Dibble A	Doherty G	Douglas S	Evers S	Feuer I	Fotiadis A	Fraser S	George L	Gray P	Harvey R	James J	Johnson M	Kean R	Marshall D	McGowan G	McLaren P	Oldfield D	Patterson D	Peake T	Showler P	Small B	Spring M	Thomas MA	Thorpe A	Waddock G	White A	Round
1:1	Aug	12	(a)	Colchester United	W 1-0	Thorpe	2840		8	11	5						2		1							12		6		7	9							3	10	4	1:1
1:2	Aug	26	(h)	COLCHESTER UNITED	D 1-1	Thorpe	2816	1	7		5			5			12										2	6	11	8	9							3	10	4	1:2
2:1	Sep	16	(h)	WEST BROMWICH ALBION	D 1-1	Douglas	3437		2	12	5	1					10	7				13		3				6	11	8	9									4		2:1
2:2	Sep	23	(a)	West Bromwich Albion	L 2-4	Davis, Thorpe	7227			11	5	1					10	2				13	7	3						8	9								12	4	6	2:2
							Apps	1	2	·	3	·	4	2	·	3	2	1	·	·	1	2	1	3	·	2	·	4	4	·	·	·	·	·	2	2	4	1				
							Subs	·	·	1	·	·	·	·	1	·	·	·	2	·	1	·	·	·	·	·	·	·	·	·	·	·	·	·	·	1	·					
							Goals	·	·	·	·	·	1	·	·	1	·	·	·	·	·	·	·	·	·	·	·	·	·	·	·	·	·	·	3	·					

1997/98 AUTO WINDSCREENS SHIELD (ASSOCIATE MEMBERS CUP)

Round	Month	Day	Venue	Opponents	W/L/D Score	Scorers	Attendance	Abbey N	Alexander G	Allen C	Allen R	Davies Simon	Davis K	Davis Steve	Dibble A	Doherty G	Douglas S	Evers S	Feuer I	Fotiadis A	Fraser S	George L	Gray P	Harvey R	James J	Johnson M	Kean R	Marshall D	McGowan G	McLaren P	Oldfield D	Patterson D	Peake T	Showler P	Small B	Spring M	Thomas MA	Thorpe A	Waddock G	White A	Round
2	Jan	13	(h)	BRENTFORD	W 2-1	Thorpe, Oldfield	3106	11	7	8				5				4	1			13									9	2					3	10	12	6	2
3	Jan	27	(a)	Fulham	W 2-1	Marshall, Thorpe	5103		7	10		1		5				4				3						11		8	9	2					13	12	6		3
ASF	Feb	17	(a)	Bournemouth	L 0-1	-	5367		2	7		11						4	1					12						10	8	9	6				3			5	ASF
							Apps	·	2	3	·	3	1	2	·	·	·	3	2	·	·	1	·	·	·	1	·	1	·	2	2	3	3	·	·	·	2	1	·	3		
							Subs	·	·	·	·	·	·	·	·	·	·	·	·	·	1	1	·	1	·	·	·	·	·	·	1	·	·	·	·	·	1	2	·	·		
							Goals	·	·	·	·	·	·	·	·	·	·	·	·	·	·	·	·	·	·	·	·	1	·	·	1	·	·	·	·	·	·	2	·	·		

▶ The 1995/96 team –
Back row (left to right): Chenery,
Power, Simpson, Barber, McLaren,
Matthews, G.Johnson, Greene,
S.Davis, K.Davis, Taylor, Peake,
James. Middle row (left to right):
Green (Director), Bassett (Director),
Goodyear (Physiotherapist), Lowe
(Coach), Harvey, Skelton, Oldfield,
Thomas, Linton, M.Johnson,
Guentchev, Woolgar, Turner (Coach),
Moore (Coach), Shannon (Scout),
Terry (Director). Front row (left
to right): Woodsford, Waddock,
Thorpe, Hughes, McGiven (Assistant
Manager), Kohler (Chairman),
Westley (Manager), Oakes, Jones,
Alexander, Marshall.

▶ The 1996/97 team – Back row (left
to right): Woodsford, Guentchev,
Grant, McLaren, Patterson, Simpson,
Taylor, Chenery. Middle row (left to
right): Goodyear (Physiotherapist),
Oldfield, Linton, Johnson, Feuer,
K.Davis, Thomas, Alexander,
Skelton, Peake (Coach). Front
row (left to right): James, Thorpe,
S.Davis, Lawrence (Manager),
Kohler (Chairman), Turner (Coach),
Waddock, Marshall, Harvey.

1998/99 "NEW" FOOTBALL LEAGUE DIVISION TWO (THIRD TIER)

Match No	Month	Day	Venue	Opponents	W,L,D Score	Scorers	Attendance	Abbey N	Alexander G	Bacque H	Boyce E	Cox J	Davies Simon	Davis K	Davis Steve	Doherty G	Douglas S	Dyche S	Evers S	Fotiadis A	Fraser S	George L	Gray P	Harrison G	Johnson M	Kandol T	Marshall D	McGowan G	McIndoe M	McKinnon R	McLaren P	Nyamah K	Scarlett A	Showler P	Spring M	Thomas M	Thorpe A	White A	Willmott C	Zahana-Oni L	Match No
1	Aug	8	(a)	Wycombe Wanderers	W 1-0	S Davis	5252		2	9				1	5				8			12	10		6		11	13						7		4	3					1
2	Aug	15	(h)	PRESTON NORTH END	D 1-1	Marshall	5392		2	9				1	5				8			13	10		6		11	3			7	12				4			14			2
3	Aug	22	(a)	Reading	L 0-3	-	18108		2					1	5	9			8			13	10				11	3			12	7				4			14	6		3
4	Aug	29	(h)	COLCHESTER UNITED	W 2-0	Douglas, S Davis	5005		2	14				1	5		9		8	13		11	10		6			3				7				4			12			4
5	Aug	31	(h)	Wigan Athletic	W 3-1	S Davis, Evers, Gray	3778		2	13				1	5		9		8			11	10		6			3	12			7				4						5
6	Sep	5	(h)	BURNLEY	W 1-0	Douglas	5554		2					1	5	9			8	12			10		6			3	11			7				4			13			6
7	Sep	8	(a)	Wrexham	D 1-1	McKinnon	2951		2	12				1	5	9			8				10		6			3	11			7				4						7
8	Sep	12	(h)	BRISTOL ROVERS	W 2-0	S Davis, Alexander	5558		2					1	5	9			8	12			10					3	11			7				4			13			8
9	Sep	19	(a)	Blackpool	L 0-1	-	5695		2	14				1	5	9			8				10					3	11	12	13	11				4			13			9
10	Sep	26	(h)	WALSALL	L 0-1	-	5530		2			11		1	5	9			8	10			12		6			3	13		7				4			14			10
11	Oct	3	(a)	Fulham	W 3-1	Gray, Douglas, S Davis	11856		2			12		1	5	9			8	13			10		6				11		7				4	3					11
12	Oct	10	(a)	York City	D 3-3	Douglas, Evers, Gray	3780		2			13		1	5	9			8				10		6				11	7					4	3			12			12
13	Oct	17	(h)	OLDHAM ATHLETIC	W 2-0	Gray, Scarlett	5447		2					1	5	9			8	14			10		6				11	7			12		4	3			13			13
14	Oct	20	(h)	NORTHAMPTON TOWN	W 1-0	Alexander	6087		2					1	5	9			8	13			10		6				11	7					4	3			12			14
15	Oct	24	(a)	Gillingham	L 0-1	-	5602		2					1	5		9		7	12			10		6				11	8					4	3			13			15
16	Nov	7	(a)	Stoke City	L 1-3	Douglas	12964		2					1	5	13	9		8				10		6				11	7	12				4	3					16
17	Nov	21	(a)	Lincoln City	D 2-2	Gray, Doherty	4893						11	1		12	9		8				10		6				2	7	13				4	3			5			17
18	Nov	28	(h)	MANCHESTER CITY	D 1-1	Doherty	9070		2				11	1	5	13	9		8				10		6				3	7	12				4				14			18
19	Dec	12	(a)	Macclesfield Town	D 2-2	Douglas, Gray	2902		2					1	5	13	9		8				10		6				11					7	4	3		12	14			19
20	Dec	19	(h)	MILLWALL	L 1-2	S Davis	5939							1	5		9			7	3	12	10		6				2				8		4			7	11	13		20
21	Dec	28	(a)	Bournemouth	L 0-1	-	8863			13				1	5		7	9				10		6										12	11	4	3		2	5		21
22	Jan	2	(a)	Colchester United	D 2-2	Alexander (pen), White	4694		2					1		12	9		11				10	8	6						7				4				3	5		22
23	Jan	9	(h)	WYCOMBE WANDERERS	W 3-1	Spring, Evers, Douglas	5063							1		12	9	5	7				10	2	6						8		13		4				3		11	23
24	Jan	16	(a)	Preston North End	L 1-2	Fotiadis	11034							1		12	9	5	7	10	13			2	6		11				8				4				3			24
25	Jan	23	(h)	WIGAN ATHLETIC	L 0-4	-	4934							1		12	9	5	8	10				2	6				7	13					4				3		11	25
26	Jan	30	(h)	BOURNEMOUTH	D 2-2	McKinnon, Doherty	5426							1		10	9	5	7					2	6				3		11	8			4				13		12	26
27	Feb	6	(a)	Burnley	W 2-1	Fotiadis, Doherty	10285	1	13							12	9	5	7	10				2	6				3		11	8			4				14			27
28	Feb	13	(h)	WREXHAM	L 1-2	Doherty	4759		3			13		1		9		5	7	10					12						11	8			4				14			28
29	Feb	20	(a)	Bristol Rovers	L 0-1	-	6361		2					1		10	9	5					6	13					4		11	8		7	4				3		12	29
30	Feb	23	(h)	NOTTS COUNTY	L 0-1	-	4021		2			7		1		10	9	5					13	6					3		11	8		14	4				12			30
31	Feb	27	(h)	BLACKPOOL	W 1-0	Douglas	4646		2			13		1			9					11	10	7					12		8	14			4	3		6	5			31
32	Mar	6	(a)	Walsall	L 0-1	-	4508		2					1			9					11	10	7	6				12		8	13			4	3		5				32
33	Mar	9	(h)	FULHAM	L 0-4	-	7424		2			13		1			9					11	10	7	6				8		12				4	3		5				33
34	Mar	13	(a)	STOKE CITY	L 1-2	Alexander (pen)	5221		2					1		12	9					11	10	7	6				8		14				4	3		5	13			34
35	Mar	20	(a)	Chesterfield	L 1-3	Gray	3921		2					1		12	9					14	10	7	6			11			8	13			4	3			5			35
36	Mar	23	(h)	READING	D 1-1	Spring	5527		2					1		11	9						10	7	6			3	12		8				4	3	14		5	13		36
37	Mar	27	(h)	GILLINGHAM	W 1-0	Dyche	6705							1		9	5						7		6			11			8				4	3	10	12	2			37
38	Apr	2	(a)	Oldham Athletic	D 1-1	Gray	4948							1		9	5		13				7		6			11	12		8				4	3	10	14	2			38
39	Apr	6	(h)	YORK CITY	W 2-1	Spring, Douglas	4667							1		9	5		8				7		6	12		11	10						4	3			2			39
40	Apr	10	(a)	Northampton Town	L 0-1	-	6856							1		9	5		8		7				11	10									4	3		6	2	12		40
41	Apr	14	(a)	Manchester City	L 0-2	-	26130							1		9	5			13				6	7	11			10						4	3	12	2		8		41
42	Apr	17	(h)	LINCOLN CITY	L 0-1	-	5122					11		1		12	9	5				13			6				10						4	3	7	2		8		42
43	Apr	24	(a)	Notts County	W 2-1	Thorpe (2)	5583							1		12	9			13	11				6				10	8					4	3	7	5	2			43
44	Apr	27	(h)	CHESTERFIELD	W 1-0	Thorpe	4287							1			9			12	11				6				10	8					4	3	7	5	2			44
45	May	1	(h)	MACCLESFIELD TOWN	L 1-2	Doherty	5738							1		13	9			12	11	14			6				10	8					4	3	7	5	2			45
46	May	8	(a)	Millwall	W 1-0	Thorpe	8494	1								13	9			12	11	14	8		6				10						4	3	7	5	2			46
				Apps				2	28	2	1	3	2	44	20	5	42	14	27	8	5	6	32	14	42	2	3	27	17	29	14	-	2	2	45	26	7	18	13	4	
				Subs				-	1	5	-	5	-	-	-	15	-	-	-	13	3	6	3	-	-	-	2	1	4	5	1	9	4	1	-	6	1	15	1	4	
				Goals				-	4	-	-	-	-	-	6	6	9	1	3	2	-	-	8	-	-	-	1	-	-	-	2	-	-	-	1	-	3	-	4	1	-	

Final League Position: 12th

1998/99 FA CUP

Round	Month	Day	Venue	Opponents	W,L,D Score	Scorers	Attendance	Abbey N	Alexander G	Bacque H	Boyce E	Cox J	Davies Simon	Davis K	Davis Steve	Doherty G	Douglas S	Dyche S	Evers S	Fotiadis A	Fraser S	George L	Gray P	Harrison G	Johnson M	Kandol T	Marshall D	McGowan G	McIndoe M	McKinnon R	McLaren P	Nyamah K	Scarlett A	Showler P	Spring M	Thomas M	Thorpe A	White A	Willmott C	Zahana-Oni L	Round
1	Nov	15	(a)	Boreham Wood	W 3-2	Gray (2), S Davis	1772	2						1	5	13	9		8				10		6		3	12	7	4	11		14								1
2	Dec	5	(h)	HULL CITY	L 1-2	S Davis	5021	2						1	5	9	13		8				10				3	12	7	11		14	4			6					2
						Apps		2						2	2	1	1		2				2		1		2		2	2	1		1			1					
						Subs									1	1												2			1	1								
						Goals									2								2																	

1998/99 WORTHINGTON CUP (LEAGUE CUP)

Round	Month	Day	Venue	Opponents	W,L,D Score	Scorers	Attendance	Abbey N	Alexander G	Bacque H	Boyce E	Cox J	Davies Simon	Davis K	Davis Steve	Doherty G	Douglas S	Dyche S	Evers S	Fotiadis A	Fraser S	George L	Gray P	Harrison G	Johnson M	Kandol T	Marshall D	McGowan G	McIndoe M	McKinnon R	McLaren P	Nyamah K	Scarlett A	Showler P	Spring M	Thomas M	Thorpe A	White A	Willmott C	Zahana-Oni L	Round
1:1	Aug	11	(h)	OXFORD UNITED	L 2-3	Alexander (2 pens)	3165	2	9					1	5				8			13	10		6		11	7	14		12				4	3					1:1
1:2	Aug	18	(a)	Oxford United	W 3-1	Gray, Evers, McLaren	5099	2						1	5		9		8			12	10		6		11	3		13	7				4						1:2
2:1	Sep	15	(a)	Ipswich Town	L 1-2	Douglas	9032	2	13			7		1	5		9		8	12			10		6			3	11						4						2:1
2:2	Sep	22	(h)	IPSWICH TOWN	W 4-2	Fotiadis, Douglas, S Davis, Johnson	5665	2	13			12		1	5		9		8	10					6		11	3		7					4		14				2:2
3	Oct	27	(h)	COVENTRY CITY	W 2-0	Gray, S Davis	9051	2						1	5		9		7	12			10		6			11		8					4	3					3
4	Nov	10	(h)	BARNSLEY	W 1-0	Gray	8453	2						1	5		9		7				10		6		3	11		8	13	12			4		14				4
5	Dec	1	(a)	Sunderland	L 0-3	-	35742	2						1	5	12	9		8				10		6			11		7	13				4	3	14				5
						Apps		-	7	1	-	1	-	7	7	-	6	-	7	1	-		6	-	7	-	3	7	2	4	1	-	-	-	7	3	-	-	-		
						Subs		-	-	2	-	1	-	-	-	1	-	-	-	2	-	2	-	-	-	-	-	-	1	1	3	1	-	-	-	-	3	-	-		
						Goals		-	2	-	-	-	-	-	2	-	2	-	1	1	-		3	-	1	-	-	-	-	1	-	-	-	-	-	-	-	-	-		

1998/99 AUTO WINDSCREENS SHIELD (ASSOCIATE MEMBERS CUP)

Round	Month	Day	Venue	Opponents	W,L,D Score	Scorers	Attendance	Abbey N	Alexander G	Bacque H	Boyce E	Cox J	Davies Simon	Davis K	Davis Steve	Doherty G	Douglas S	Dyche S	Evers S	Fotiadis A	Fraser S	George L	Gray P	Harrison G	Johnson M	Kandol T	Marshall D	McGowan G	McIndoe M	McKinnon R	McLaren P	Nyamah K	Scarlett A	Showler P	Spring M	Thomas M	Thorpe A	White A	Willmott C	Zahana-Oni L	Round
2	Jan	5	(h)	WALSALL	L 0-3	-	1870	1		9	2					13		6	4	11	3		8		12			10		7	14				5						2
						Apps		1		1	1	-	-		-	1		1	1	1	1	-	1	-	-		-	1	-	1	-	-	-	-	1	-	-	-	-		
						Subs		-	-	-	-	-		-	-	1	-	-	-	-	-	-	-	-	1		-	-	-	-	1	-	-	-	-	-	-	-	-		
						Goals		-	-	-	-	-		-	-	-	-	-	-	-	-	-	-	-	-		-	-	-	-	-	-	-	-	-	-	-	-	-		

TIMELINE...

23 March 1999 The club enters administrative receivership.

1999/2000 "NEW" FOOTBALL LEAGUE DIVISION TWO (THIRD TIER)

Match No	Month	Day	Venue	Opponents	W,L,D Score	Scorers	Attendance	Abbey N	Ayres J	Boyce E	Doherty G	Douglas S	Fotiadis A	Fraser S	George L	Gray P	Johnson M	Kandol T	Locke A	McGowan G	McIndoe M	McKinnon R	McLaren P	Midgley N	Read P	Roberts B	Scarlett A	Sodje E	Spring M	Taylor M	Thorpe A	Watts J	White A	Zahana-Oni L	Match No
1	Aug	7	(a)	Notts County	D 0-0		6141	1	12			9		2		10	6						11	8					7	3		5	4		1
2	Aug	14	(h)	BLACKPOOL	W 3-2	George (2), Spring	5176	1		4		9	10	2	11		6				14	12		8					7	3		5		13	2
3	Aug	21	(a)	Reading	W 2-1	Fotiadis, George	8741	1		4			9	2	11	10	6				12			8					7	3		5			3
4	Aug	28	(h)	CARDIFF CITY	W 1-0	Gray	5374	1		4	12	9		2	11	10	6				13	14		8					7	3		5			4
5	Aug	31	(a)	Bournemouth	L 0-1		4797	1		4	12	9		2	11	10	6				13			8					7	3		5			5
6	Sep	4	(h)	BURY	D 1-1	Fotiadis	4633	1		4	12	9		2	11	10	6				13			8					7	3		5			6
7	Sep	11	(a)	WREXHAM	W 3-1	Taylor, Spring, George	5121	1		4		9	10	2	11		6		12		13								7	3	14	5			7
8	Sep	18	(a)	Brentford	L 0-2		7039	1		4		9		2	11		6	10	8										7	3	12	5			8
9	Sep	25	(h)	OXFORD UNITED	W 4-2	George (2), Fraser, Locke	6102	1		4		9		2	11		6		8				12	10					7	3		5			9
10	Oct	2	(a)	Wigan Athletic	L 0-1		6866	1		4		9		2	10		6		11				12	8				13	7	3		5			10
11	Oct	9	(a)	Oldham Athletic	L 1-2	Midgley	4532	1				9		2	10		6	12	11		14			8			4	13	7	3		5			11
12	Oct	16	(h)	GILLINGHAM	W 3-1	George (2, 1 pen), Douglas	6394	1		4		9		2	11		6		12		13			8				10	7	3		5			12
13	Oct	19	(h)	WYCOMBE WANDERERS	D 1-1	Douglas	5820	1		4		9		2	11		6		12					8				10	7	3		5			13
14	Oct	23	(a)	Oxford United	W 1-0	George	5866	1		4		9		2	11		6		13				12	8				10	7	3		5			14
15	Nov	2	(a)	Millwall	L 0-1		6181	1		2	4	9			11		6		12					8				10	7	3		5			15
16	Nov	6	(h)	BURNLEY	W 2-1	Midgley (2)	7205	1		2	4	9			11		6		14	13			12	8				10	7	3		5			16
17	Nov	12	(a)	Cambridge United	L 1-3	George	6211	1		2	4	9			11		6		14	13				8				10	7	3	12	5			17
18	Nov	23	(h)	PRESTON NORTH END	L 0-2		5124	1		14	4	9		2			6		13					8				10	7	3		5	12		18
19	Nov	27	(a)	Bristol Rovers	L 0-3		7805	1		13	4			2	9		6		11					8			3		7		12	5			19
20	Dec	4	(h)	NOTTS COUNTY	D 2-2	Doherty, Thorpe	5195	1		12	4	9		2	11		6							8				13	7	3	10	5			20
21	Dec	17	(a)	Colchester United	L 0-3		3049	1			9			2	11		6						12	8				4	7	3	10	5			21
22	Dec	26	(h)	CHESTERFIELD	D 1-1	Locke	5870	1			9				11	13	6						12	8					7	3	10	5			22
23	Dec	28	(a)	Bristol City	D 0-0		11832	1		2	4	9	12			10	3							8					7	11		5	6		23
24	Jan	3	(h)	SCUNTHORPE UNITED	W 4-1	Douglas, Gray, Spring (2)	5574	1		2	4	9	12		11	10	6							8					7	3		5	6		24
25	Jan	8	(a)	Stoke City	L 1-2	Spring (pen)	10016	1		2	4	9	12		13	10	6							8					7	3		5	6		25
26	Jan	15	(a)	Blackpool	D 3-3	Locke, Gray, Taylor	5262	1		2	4	9	12		11	10	6							8					7	3		5			26
27	Jan	22	(h)	READING	W 3-1	Watts, George (2)	6044	1		2	4	9	12		11	10	6			7	3							8				5			27
28	Jan	30	(a)	Cardiff City	W 3-1	Watts, Spring, George	6185	1		2	4	9	12	6	11	10				3								8	7			5			28
29	Feb	5	(h)	BOURNEMOUTH	L 1-2	Boyce	5961	1		2	4	9	13		11	10	6			3				8				12	7			5			29
30	Feb	8	(h)	STOKE CITY	W 2-1	Gray (2)	5396	1		2	4	9	13		11	10	6							8		12			7			5			30
31	Feb	12	(a)	Bury	L 0-1		3760	1		14	6	9	13			10	3							8		2			7	11		5	4		31
32	Feb	19	(h)	BRISTOL ROVERS	L 1-4	Gray	6520	1		2	4	9	13		11		6							8					7	3		5	12		32
33	Feb	26	(h)	BRENTFORD	L 1-2	Gray	6029			2	4	9	13		11		6							8		1			7	3		5	14		33
34	Mar	4	(a)	Wrexham	L 0-1		2073			12	4	9	11	2	13		6			3				8		1			7	14		5			34
35	Mar	7	(a)	Burnley	W 2-0	White, Gray	12080			2	4	9	12				6			3				8	11	1			7			5	6		35
36	Mar	11	(h)	MILLWALL	L 0-2		6341			2	4	9	14		12		6							8	11	1	3		7	13		5			36
37	Mar	18	(a)	Preston North End	L 0-1		13371			2	4	9	12		13		6						14	8		1			7	11		5	6		37
38	Mar	21	(h)	CAMBRIDGE UNITED	D 2-2	Doherty, McLaren	5379			2	9	13	10		11		6						12	8		1			7	3		5	4		38
39	Mar	25	(a)	Chesterfield	W 3-1	Doherty, Watts, George	2597			2	10	9	13		11		6			7				8		1			12	3		5	4		39
40	Apr	1	(h)	COLCHESTER UNITED	W 3-2	Watts, Doherty, Taylor	5125			2	9				11	10	6							8		1			7	3		5	4		40
41	Apr	8	(a)	Scunthorpe United	W 2-1	Gray, Doherty	3811			2	9				11	10	6		12					8		1			7	3		5	4		41
42	Apr	18	(h)	BRISTOL CITY	L 1-2	Doherty	4771			2	9		13		11	10	6		12		14			8		1			7	3		5	4		42
43	Apr	22	(a)	Gillingham	L 0-2		8667			2	9				11	10	6		17					8		1			7	3		5	4		43
44	Apr	24	(h)	WIGAN ATHLETIC	D 1-1	Gray	5010								9	10	12		3		4	2		8		1			7	11		5	6		44
45	Apr	29	(a)	Wycombe Wanderers	W 1-0	Taylor	5379								9	10	12		3		4	2		8		1			7	11		5	6		45
46	May	6	(h)	OLDHAM ATHLETIC	D 1-1	Gray	5963	12		13					9	10	3				4	2		8		1			7	11		5	6		46
				Apps				32	-	23	40	35	8	20	35	28	44	1	27	10	2	-	25	8	-	14	2	5	44	39	3	45	16	-	
				Subs				1	-	7	-	5	15	-	7	1	-	3	7	3	15	3	4	2	-	1	4	1	2	1	2	1	1	3	1	
				Goals				-	-	1	6	3	2	1	14	11	-	-	3	-	-	-	1	3	-	-	-	-	6	4	1	4	1	-	

Final League Position: 13th

1999/2000 FA CUP

Round	Month	Day	Venue	Opponents	W/L/D Score	Scorers	Attendance	Abbey N	Ayres J	Boyce E	Doherty G	Douglas S	Fotiadis A	Fraser S	George L	Gray P	Johnson M	Kandol T	Locke A	McGowan G	McIndoe M	McKinnon R	McLaren P	Midgley N	Read P	Roberts B	Scarlett A	Sodje E	Spring M	Taylor M	Thorpe A	Watts J	White A	Zahana-Oni L	Round
1	Oct	30	(h)	KINGSTONIAN	W 4-2	Gray, George, Spring, Taylor	4682	1	13	4		9		2	11	10	6				12		8						7	3			5		1
2	Nov	19	(h)	LINCOLN CITY	D 2-2	Doherty (2)	4291	1			10	9		2	11		6		4		13		8					12	7	3			5		2
Rep	Nov	30	(a)	Lincoln City	W 1-0	Douglas	3822	1			10	9		2	11		6		12				8					4	7	3			5		Rep
3	Dec	11	(a)	Fulham	D 2-2	George, Spring	5905	1			10	9		2	11		6		8									4	7	3			5		3
Rep	Dec	21	(h)	FULHAM	L 0-3	-	8170	1	12		10	9		2	11		6		4				8						7	3			5		Rep
						Apps		5		1	4	5		5	5	1	5		3				4					2	5	5			5		
						Subs			2										1		2							1							
						Goals					2	1			2	1													2	1					

1999/2000 WORTHINGTON CUP (LEAGUE CUP)

Round	Month	Day	Venue	Opponents	W/L/D Score	Scorers	Attendance	Abbey N	Ayres J	Boyce E	Doherty G	Douglas S	Fotiadis A	Fraser S	George L	Gray P	Johnson M	Kandol T	Locke A	McGowan G	McIndoe M	McKinnon R	McLaren P	Midgley N	Read P	Roberts B	Scarlett A	Sodje E	Spring M	Taylor M	Thorpe A	Watts J	White A	Zahana-Oni L	Round
1:1	Aug	10	(h)	BRISTOL ROVERS	L 0-2	-	2984	1		3	12	9	13	2	14	10					7		8						4	11			5	6	1:1
1:2	Aug	25	(a)	Bristol Rovers	D 2-2	Kandol, Doherty	4414	1		2	12	9	13		7			10	4		11	8						3					5	6	1:2
						Apps		2		2		2		1	1	1		1	1		2	1	1					1	1	1			2	2	
						Subs					2		2		1																				
						Goals					1							1																	

1999/2000 AUTO WINDSCREENS SHIELD (ASSOCIATE MEMBERS CUP)

Round	Month	Day	Venue	Opponents	W/L/D Score	Scorers	Attendance	Abbey N	Ayres J	Boyce E	Doherty G	Douglas S	Fotiadis A	Fraser S	George L	Gray P	Johnson M	Kandol T	Locke A	McGowan G	McIndoe M	McKinnon R	McLaren P	Midgley N	Read P	Roberts B	Scarlett A	Sodje E	Spring M	Taylor M	Thorpe A	Watts J	White A	Zahana-Oni L	Round
1	Dec	7	(a)	Oxford United	L 0-2	-	1220	1	5	11	10	9		2	7		6		8						12		13	3	4						1
						Apps		1	1	1	1	1		1	1		1		1									1	1						
						Subs																			1		1								
						Goals																													

TIMELINE...
15 October 1999 The club exits administrative receivership.

2000/01 "NEW" FOOTBALL LEAGUE DIVISION TWO (THIRD TIER)

Match No	Month	Day	Venue	Opponents	W,L,D Score	Scorers	Attendance	Abbey N	Ayres J	Baptiste R	Boyce E	Breitenfelder F	Brennan D	Douglas S	Dryden R	Fotiadis A	Fraser S	George L	Helin P	Holmes P	Howard S	Johnson M	Kandol T	Karlsen K	Locke A	Mansell L	McGowan G	McLaren P	Nogan L	Ovendale M	Rowland K	Scarlett A	Shepherd P	Spring M	Stein M	Stirling J	Taylor M	Thomson P	Ward S	Watts J	Whitbread A	Match No
1	Aug	12	(h)	NOTTS COUNTY	L 0-1	-	7059				2					9	13	7				12	3		8			6		1				4	10		11			5		1
2	Aug	19	(a)	Wigan Athletic	L 1-2	Watts	6518				2		14			9	12	7	11		6				4			8		1		13			10		3			5		2
3	Aug	26	(h)	BOURNEMOUTH	W 1-0	Spring (pen)	5221				2		12			9	3	7	8						13			6		1				4	10		11			5		3
4	Aug	28	(a)	Wycombe Wanderers	D 1-1	Kandol	6001				6	12				9	2	7					13					8		1			11	4	10		3			5		4
5	Sep	2	(a)	Rotherham United	D 1-1	Fotiadis	4061				6	13				9	14		11			12			2			8		1			7	4	10		3			5		5
6	Sep	9	(h)	NORTHAMPTON TOWN	L 0-2	-	6712	1			6		7			2	9					12			13			8					11	4	10		3			5		6
7	Sep	12	(h)	WALSALL	D 0-0	-	4362	1			6		7				12	14				13			2			8					11	4	10		3	2		5		7
8	Sep	16	(a)	Swansea City	L 0-4	-	6011				2						12	7							9	3		8					1	4	10	6	11			5		8
9	Sep	23	(h)	SWINDON TOWN	L 2-3	Stein, George	4933				6					2	7	8							9	12							11	4	10		3	13		5		9
10	Sep	30	(a)	Bristol Rovers	D 3-3	Kandol (2), George	7901				2				3	7	14						9		8	12	6	1					13	11		10			5		10
11	Oct	8	(h)	MILLWALL	L 0-1	-	5345				6						7								9	8	2	3					1	4	10		11			5		11
12	Oct	13	(a)	Cambridge United	L 1-2	Stein	6191				6		13				7	12							9	8	2	3	1					4	10		11			5		12
13	Oct	17	(a)	Oxford United	D 0-0	-	4537	1			6	12	13		3										8	9	2		2					4	10		11			5		13
14	Oct	21	(h)	BRENTFORD	W 3-1	Douglas (2), Spring (pen)	5382	1			6	12	14	9		7									8	2								4	10		11	13		5		14
15	Oct	28	(h)	WREXHAM	L 3-4	Stein, Watts, George	5341	1			2	3				9	12	7					6		8										10		11	13		5		15
16	Nov	4	(a)	Bury	D 1-1	Helin	2861	1		12	6			9			7	2	13						3			8							10		11			5		16
17	Nov	11	(h)	BRISTOL CITY	L 0-3	-	6595	1		13	6			9		12	7	8							3		2	5							10		11					17
18	Nov	25	(a)	Port Vale	L 0-3	-	4194	1			2					12	13	9	7						3			8	10								11			5	6	18
19	Dec	2	(a)	Stoke City	W 3-1	McLaren, Thomson (2)	12389	1								12		9	2		3				13	7		8									11	10		5	6	19
20	Dec	16	(h)	COLCHESTER UNITED	L 0-3	-	4791	1								12		9	2		3				7			8	10								4			5	6	20
21	Dec	23	(a)	Reading	L 1-4	Nogan	10771			14						9	12	7	2		3				13			8	10								11				6	21
22	Dec	26	(h)	PETERBOROUGH UNITED	W 3-2	Spring, Holmes, Boyce	7374	1			5					9	3		2	8			13		7				10		12			4			11			5	6	22
23	Dec	30	(h)	WIGAN ATHLETIC	L 0-2	-	5322									9	3		2	8			13		7				10	1				4	13		11	12		5	6	23
24	Jan	1	(a)	Bournemouth	L 2-3	Fotiadis, Locke	5411			13						9	3	12	2	8					7				10	1	14					12	11		5	6	24
25	Jan	12	(h)	WYCOMBE WANDERERS	L 1-2	Locke	4551			5	2			9		3	7			12					8						13			1		14	11	10			6	25
26	Jan	23	(a)	Oldham Athletic	L 0-2	-	3011			2				9		7	13			11				5		8	3		10	1				4	14			12			6	26
27	Feb	10	(a)	Northampton Town	W 1-0	Douglas	6633				6			9	3	12		10	2							7								1	8		4		5	11		27
28	Feb	13	(a)	Notts County	W 3-1	Boyce, George, Fotiadis	4333				6			9	3	13		10	2						12	7								1	8		4		5	11		28
29	Feb	17	(h)	SWANSEA CITY	W 5-3	Mansell (2), Douglas, Rowland, George	7085				6			9	3	12		10	2						13	7					5			1	8		4		5	11		29
30	Feb	21	(h)	Walsall	L 1-3	Spring	4816				6			9	3	13		10	2						12	7					5			1	8		4		5	11	14	30
31	Feb	24	(a)	Swindon Town	W 3-1	Rowland, Boyce, Mansell	7160				6				3	9		10	2						7	13					5			1	8		4	12		11	14	31
32	Mar	3	(h)	BRISTOL ROVERS	D 0-0	-	7405	1			6			12	3			9	2						7						8				4		10	13	11		5		32
33	Mar	6	(h)	CAMBRIDGE UNITED	W 1-0	Taylor	6370	1			6			9	3	12		10	2						7						5				8		4	14	11			13	33
34	Mar	10	(a)	Millwall	L 0-1	-	11691	1			6			9	3	12		10	2						7						5				8		4	13	11			14	34
35	Mar	27	(a)	Peterborough United	D 1-1	Mansell	5425	1			6				3			10	2		9				7						5				8		4	12	11				35
36	Mar	31	(a)	Colchester United	L 1-3	Howard (pen)	4271	1			6			12	3			10	2		9				7						5		8				4		11				36
37	Apr	3	(h)	READING	D 1-1	Harper (og)	6132	1			6			12	3			13	2		9				7						5		8				4	10	11				37
38	Apr	7	(h)	STOKE CITY	L 1-2	Mansell	6456	1			6			12	3			13	2		9				7						5		8				4	10	11				38
39	Apr	10	(h)	OXFORD UNITED	D 1-1	Watts	6010	1			6				3			10	2		9				7						5		8				4	13	12	11		5		39
40	Apr	14	(h)	OLDHAM ATHLETIC	D 0-0	-	4886				6			10	3			7			9					4		8		1			2						11			5		40
41	Apr	16	(a)	Wrexham	L 1-3	Watts	3329				6			10	3			7			9				12	4		8		1			2						11			5		41
42	Apr	21	(a)	BURY	L 1-2	George	4902				6			10	3			10			9					7				1									11			5		42
43	Apr	24	(h)	ROTHERHAM UNITED	L 0-1	-	4854				6			10	3			7			9	5				8							2					12	11			5		43
44	Apr	28	(a)	Bristol City	L 1-3	George	9161				6			13	3			10			9	7				2	5				14								12	11			5		44
45	May	3	(a)	Brentford	D 2-2	Howard, McLaren	3287				6				3			10			9	5			13	7							2					4	11		12			45
46	May	5	(h)	PORT VALE	D 1-1	Howard	5260				6				3			10			9			12		7							2					4	11		5		46
				Final League Position: 22nd		1 Own Goal	**Apps**	20	-	-	42	2	2	15	20	12	10	37	23	12	12	9	6	4	17	17	5	35	7	26	12	5	7	41	19	5	45	4	-	26	9	
							Subs	-	-	3	-	3	7	6	-	10	5	6	-	6	-	-	7	2	8	1	1	-	-	4	-	-	-	-	11	4	-	7	1	2	-	
							Goals	-	-	-	3	-	-	4	-	3	-	7	1	1	3	-	3	-	2	5	-	2	1	-	2	-	-	4	3	-	1	2	-	4	-	

2000/01 FA CUP

Round	Month	Day	Venue	Opponents	W,L,D Score	Scorers	Attendance	Abbey N	Ayres J	Baptiste R	Boyce E	Breitenfelder F	Brennan D	Douglas S	Dryden R	Fotiadis A	Fraser S	George L	Helin P	Holmes P	Howard S	Johnson M	Kandol T	Karlsen K	Locke A	Mansell L	McGowan G	McLaren P	Nogan L	Ovendale M	Rowland K	Scarlett A	Shepherd P	Spring M	Stein M	Stirling J	Taylor M	Thomson P	Ward S	Watts J	Whitbread A	Round
1	Nov	17	(h)	RUSHDEN & DIAMONDS	W 1-0	George	5771	1		2						3	9	7			6							8						4	10		11	12		5		1
2	Dec	9	(a)	Darlington	D 0-0	-	3641	1								2	9				3		7					8	10					4			11	10		5	6	2
Rep	Dec	19	(h)	DARLINGTON	W 2-0	Nogan, McLaren	3563	1		12						9	7	2			3		13					8	10					4			11			5	6	Rep
3	Jan	6	(h)	QUEENS PARK RANGERS	D 3-3	Fotiadis, George, Douglas	8677			5				12		9	3	7	2		8							10	1					4		13	11	11			6	3
Rep	Jan	17	(a)	Queens Park Rangers	L 1-2	Mansell	14395							9		10	3			8			5		7	2		11	1		14			4	13	12			6	Rep
							Apps	3		2			1		3	4	4	3	1		2		2	2	1	1		3	3	2				5	1		4			3	4	
							Subs			1			1			1										1						1			1	2		1			1		
							Goals						1		1			2								1		1	1														

2000/01 WORTHINGTON CUP (LEAGUE CUP)

Round	Month	Day	Venue	Opponents	W,L,D Score	Scorers	Attendance	Abbey N	Ayres J	Baptiste R	Boyce E	Breitenfelder F	Brennan D	Douglas S	Dryden R	Fotiadis A	Fraser S	George L	Helin P	Holmes P	Howard S	Johnson M	Kandol T	Karlsen K	Locke A	Mansell L	McGowan G	McLaren P	Nogan L	Ovendale M	Rowland K	Scarlett A	Shepherd P	Spring M	Stein M	Stirling J	Taylor M	Thomson P	Ward S	Watts J	Whitbread A	Round
1:1	Aug	22	(h)	PETERBOROUGH UNITED	D 0-0	-	3175			2	12				9	3	7		8									6	1					4	10		11			5		1:1
1:2	Sep	5	(a)	Peterborough United	D 2-2	Stein, Scarlett	4286			6				7		2	9		12				14	13				8	1		11			4	10		3			5		1:2
2:1	Sep	19	(a)	Sunderland	L 0-3	-	24668			2						3	12		8				9					6	1		7			4	10		11	13		5		2:1
2:2	Sep	26	(h)	SUNDERLAND	L 1-2	Kandol	5262			2				12		3	7						9		8			6	1					4			11	10		5		2:2
							Apps			4		1			1	4	3		2				2		1			4	4		2			4	3		4	1		4		
							Subs				2						1		1				1															1				
							Goals																1									1			1							

2000/01 LDV VANS TROPHY (ASSOCIATE MEMBERS CUP)

Round	Month	Day	Venue	Opponents	W,L,D Score	Scorers	Attendance	Abbey N	Ayres J	Baptiste R	Boyce E	Breitenfelder F	Brennan D	Douglas S	Dryden R	Fotiadis A	Fraser S	George L	Helin P	Holmes P	Howard S	Johnson M	Kandol T	Karlsen K	Locke A	Mansell L	McGowan G	McLaren P	Nogan L	Ovendale M	Rowland K	Scarlett A	Shepherd P	Spring M	Stein M	Stirling J	Taylor M	Thomson P	Ward S	Watts J	Whitbread A	Round
1	Dec	5	(a)	Peterborough United	L 0-1	-	2075	6						9	3	2						5	7					8	13	1				4	12		11	10				1
							Apps	1						1	1	1		1				1	1					1		1				1			1	1				
							Subs																						1						1							
							Goals																																			

TIMELINE...

4 July 2000 Lennie Lawrence is dismissed.

10 July 2000 Ex-Hatters favourite, Ricky Hill is appointed manager.

15 November 2000 Ricky Hill is sacked - his assistant, Lil Fuccillo, is given the job on a caretaker basis.

7 February 2001 Joe Kinnear is handed the manager's job at Kenilworth Road.

5 May 2001 The Town are relegated to the football basement once more.

The 1997/98 team – Back row (left to right): Kean, Evers, Douglas, McLaren, Davies, Fotiadis, Harvey, Marshall, Goodyear (Physiotherapist). Middle row (left to right): Turner (Coach), Showler, Oldfield, Thomas, Abbey, Feuer, K.Davis, Johnson, Willmott, Alexander, Peake (Coach). Front row (left to right): Thorpe, S.Davis, Terry (Director), Kohler (Chairman), Lawrence (Manager), Bassett (Director), Green (Director), Waddock, James.

The 1998/99 team – Back row (left to right): Marshall, Sweeney, Clarke, Spring, Boyce, Augustine, McGowan, Lawes, Fraser, Douglas, Cox, McIndoe, Scarlett. Middle row (left to right): Goodyear (Physiotherapist), Lowe (Coach), Cherry Newbery (Secretary), Fotiadis, Davies, Showler, Doherty, White, K.Davis, Abbey, James, Willmott, McLaren, Alexander, Lough, Shannon (Scout), Mandy Malins (Fitness Trainer), Moore (Coach). Front row (left to right): George, Gray, S.Davis, Green (Director) Kohler (Chairman), Lawrence (Manager), Bassett (Director), Terry (Director), Thomas, Johnson, Evers.

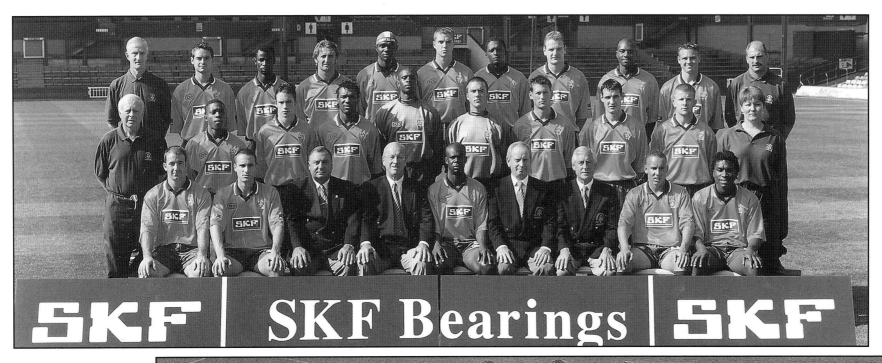

▶ **The 1999/00 team** – Back row (left to right): Moore (Coach), McKinnon, Zahana-Oni, Locke, Sodje, White, Kandol, Doherty, Boyce, Taylor, Goodyear (Physiotherapist). Middle row (left to right): Hartley (Coach), Scarlett, McIndoe, McGowan, Abbey, Tate, McLaren, Spring, Fraser, Mandy Malins (Fitness Trainer). Front row (left to right): Gray, Fotiadis, Green (Director), Bassett (Director), Johnson, Lawrence (Manager), Terry (Director), George, Douglas.

▶ **The 2000/01 team** – Back row (left to right): M.Stein, Scarlett, Fraser, Fotiadis, Taylor, Holmes, Douglas, McGowan, Brennan. Middle row (left to right): Moore (Assistant Manager), Thompson, Stirling, Karlsen, Abbey, Ovendale, Ayres, Breitenfelder, Kandol, Baptiste, B.Stein (Coach). Front row (left to right): George, Boyce, Helin, Spring, Fuccillo (Caretaker Manager), McLaren, Watts, Johnson, Locke.

2001/02 "NEW" FOOTBALL LEAGUE DIVISION THREE (FOURTH TIER)

Match No	Month	Day	Venue	Opponents	W,L,D Score	Scorers	Attendance	Bayliss D	Boyce E	Brennan D	Brkovic A	Coyne C	Crowe D	Douglas S	Dryden R	Emberson C	Forbes A	Fotiadis A	Fraser S	George L	Gillman R	Griffiths C	Hillier I	Holmes P	Howard S	Hughes JP	Johnson M	Kabba S	Locke A	Mansell L	McSwegan G	Nicholls K	Neilson A	Ovendale M	Perrett R	Skelton A	Spring M	Stirling J	Street K	Taylor M	Thomson P	Valois J-L	Match No
1	Aug	11	(a)	Carlisle United	W 2-0	Hughes, Griffiths	4432	2						13		1		14				10			9	4	3		12	7		8			5	6				11			1
2	Aug	18	(h)	CHELTENHAM TOWN	W 2-1	Hughes, Griffiths	6177		6						1	7	12			13		10	2		9	4			14	11		8			5					3			2
3	Aug	25	(a)	Bristol Rovers	L 2-3	Taylor, Mansell	9057	2						14		1	12					10	7		9	4	3	6	13			8						5		11			3
4	Aug	27	(h)	SOUTHEND UNITED	W 2-0	Griffiths, Fotiadis	6496	5					12	6		1		13				10	2		9	4	3			7		8								11			4
5	Sep	1	(a)	Exeter City	D 2-2	Taylor (2)	3088	2					9	6		1		12		13		10		14		7	3		4			8			5			8		11			5
6	Sep	8	(h)	OXFORD UNITED	D 1-1	Nicholls	6736	6						13		1	7					10	12		9							8			5	2	4			11			6
7	Sep	15	(a)	York City	W 2-1	Griffiths, Hillier	3247	6						13		1	7			11		10	14		9		3			12		8			5	2	4			3			7
8	Sep	18	(h)	LINCOLN CITY	D 1-1	Skelton	5066	2				6		9		1	13					11	10	3						12		14			5	7	4			3			8
9	Sep	22	(h)	TORQUAY UNITED	W 5-1	Howard, Griffiths (3), Valois	6392	2				6		14			13					22	10	12	9	7						8		1	5		4			3	11		9
10	Sep	25	(a)	Leyton Orient	W 3-1	Taylor, Valois, Howard	6540	2				6					12					10		7	9					13		8		1	5		4			3	11		10
11	Sep	29	(a)	Plymouth Argyle	L 1-2	Crowe	5782	2				6	10	13			12							7	9					14		8		1	5		4			3	11		11
12	Oct	5	(h)	DARLINGTON	W 5-2	Spring, Howard, Crowe, Nicholls (pen), Valois	7219	2				6	10			1	13						12		9					7		8			5		4			3	11		12
13	Oct	13	(a)	Scunthorpe United	W 2-0	Forbes, Perrett	3959	2	13			6	10			1	14						12		9					7		8			5		4			3	11		13
14	Oct	20	(h)	ROCHDALE	L 0-1	-	7696	12				7				1	13	14					2		9							8			5		4			3	11		14
15	Oct	23	(a)	Halifax Town	W 4-2	Crowe (2), Nicholls, Forbes	2140					7	6			1	12						2		9							8			5		4			3	11		15
16	Oct	27	(h)	SWANSEA CITY	W 3-0	Crowe, Perrett, Forbes	6705					7	6			1	12	13					3		9							8			5	2	4			3	11		16
17	Nov	3	(a)	Mansfield Town	L 1-4	Crowe	5973					7	6			1	12						13		9							8			5	2	4			3	11		17
18	Nov	9	(h)	SHREWSBURY TOWN	W 1-0	Spring	6809					7	6			1							12		9							8			5	2	4			3	11		18
19	Nov	20	(h)	HULL CITY	L 0-1	-	6526	12				7	6			1	13						2		9							8			5		4		14	3	11		19
20	Nov	24	(a)	Macclesfield Town	L 1-4	Howard	2250	5				6	13			1	10	14					12		9							8			2	4	7		3	11		20
21	Dec	8	(a)	Hartlepool United	W 2-1	Crowe, Taylor	3585	5	2			7	6	10			12						3		9							8			5					11			21
22	Dec	15	(h)	RUSHDEN & DIAMONDS	W 1-0	Crowe	7495	5	2			7	6	6								14	13		9							8			5	1	12			4	3		22
23	Dec	22	(h)	HARTLEPOOL UNITED	D 2-2	Howard, Johnson	6739	6	2			7										13	14		9		12					8			5	1				4	3		23
24	Dec	26	(a)	Oxford United	W 2-1	Crowe, Spring	11121	6	2			12	10				7						13		9							8			5	1				4	3		24
25	Dec	29	(a)	Southend United	W 2-1	Crowe, Taylor	5973	6	2			12	10				7						13		9							8			5	1				4	3		25
26	Jan	8	(a)	Kidderminster Harriers	W 4-1	Taylor, Spring (2), Howard	4147	6	2			7	10										12		9	14						8			5	1				4	3		26
27	Jan	12	(a)	Cheltenham Town	D 1-1	Howard	5026	6	2			7	10										3		9	14						8			5	1				4	11	13	27
28	Jan	19	(h)	CARLISLE UNITED	D 1-1	Perrett	6647	6	2			7	10										12		9		13					8			5	1				4	3	11	28
29	Jan	26	(a)	Darlington	L 2-3	Howard, Valois	3564		6			7	10	12			13						2		9	14					1	8			5					4	3	11	29
30	Feb	2	(h)	PLYMOUTH ARGYLE	W 2-0	Nicholls (pen), Howard	9585	6	2			12	10			1	7								9							8			5					4	3	11	30
31	Feb	9	(a)	Rochdale	L 0-1	-	4306	6	2			12	10			1	7								9	13						8			5					4	3	11	31
32	Feb	16	(h)	SCUNTHORPE UNITED	L 2-3	Howard, Taylor	6371	6	12			2	13			1	7								9						10	8			5					4	3	11	32
33	Feb	19	(a)	Bristol Rovers	W 3-0	Howard, Coyne, Nicholls (pen)	5651	6	2			7	12	10		1	13								9							8			5					4	3	11	33
34	Feb	23	(h)	YORK CITY	W 2-1	Howard (2)	6188		2			7	6			1	10								9	12	13						5			8			4		3	11	34
35	Feb	26	(a)	Lincoln City	W 1-0	Taylor	2921					7	6			1	10								9	8	3						2			5			4		11		35
36	Mar	2	(a)	Torquay United	W 1-0	Brkovic	3280		13		6					1									12	13				9		2			5			4		11	14		36
37	Mar	5	(h)	LEYTON ORIENT	W 3-0	Coyne, Crowe, Forbes	6683	12				6	10			1	9								7	13			14	8		2			5			4		3		11	37
38	Mar	9	(a)	Rushden & Diamonds	W 2-1	Crowe, Howard	5876	13				6	10			1	7								9	12	3					8			5			4		11			38
39	Mar	12	(h)	EXETER CITY	W 3-0	Howard (2), Taylor	6327	12				6	10			1	7								9	13						8			5			4		3	11		39
40	Mar	16	(h)	KIDDERMINSTER HARRIERS	W 1-0	Hughes	6488	2	13			6	10			1	12								9	7						8	3	1	5			4		3	11		40
41	Mar	23	(h)	HALIFAX TOWN	W 5-0	Spring, Coyne, Howard, Crowe, Valois	6830	2				6	10			1	12								9	7						8			5			4		3	11		41
42	Mar	30	(h)	Swansea City	W 3-1	Taylor, Holmes, Howard	5436	2	12			6	10			1	14							13	9		3					8			5			4		11	7	12	42
43	Apr	1	(h)	MANSFIELD TOWN	W 5-3	Valois, Crowe, Nicholls (pen), Howard (2)	8231	2				6	10			1	12						7		9		5	13				8			5			4		3	11		43
44	Apr	6	(a)	Hull City	W 4-0	Howard (3), Crowe	9379	2				6	10			1	14						7		9	12	13					8			5			4		3	11		44
45	Apr	13	(h)	MACCLESFIELD TOWN	D 0-0	-	7873	2				6	10			1	13						9	7	12	14						8			5			4		3	11		45
46	Apr	20	(a)	Shrewsbury Town	W 2-0	Rioch (og), Howard	7858	14				6	10			1	7						9	8	12	13						2			5			4		3	11		46
				Final League Position: 2nd		1 Own Goal	**Apps**	15	30	-	17	29	32	2	2	33	15	-	-	2	-	10	11	4	42	12	11	-	1	6	2	42	8	13	39	9	42	1	1	43	-	32	
							Subs	3	7	-	4	2	2	7	1	-	25	8	-	2	-	-	-	-	-	12	-	3	10	7	3	-	2	5	1	-	1	-	-	-	1	2	
							Goals	-	-	-	1	3	15	-	-	-	4	1	-	-	-	7	1	1	24	3	1	-	-	1	-	6	-	-	3	1	6	-	-	11	-	6	

2001/02 FA CUP

Round	Month	Day	Venue	Opponents	W,L,D	Score	Scorers	Attendance	Bayliss D	Boyce E	Brennan D	Brkovic A	Coyne C	Crowe D	Douglas S	Dryden R	Emerson C	Forbes A	Fotiadis A	Fraser S	George L	Gillman R	Griffiths C	Hillier I	Holmes P	Howard S	Hughes JP	Johnson M	Kabba S	Locke A	Mansell L	McSwegan G	Nicholls K	Neilson A	Ovendale M	Perrett R	Skelton A	Spring M	Stirling J	Street K	Taylor M	Thomson P	Valois J-L	Round
1	Nov	17	(a)	Southend United	L	2-3	Forbes, Brkovic	7214		11	7		9	6	1	10	13				12			5	8													2	4		3			1
			Apps							1	1		1		1		1	1	1		1			1	1													1		1	1		
			Subs															1	1																							
			Goals								1						1																									

2001/02 WORTHINGTON CUP (LEAGUE CUP)

Round	Month	Day	Venue	Opponents	W,L,D	Score	Scorers	Attendance	Bayliss D	Boyce E	Brennan D	Brkovic A	Coyne C	Crowe D	Douglas S	Dryden R	Emerson C	Forbes A	Fotiadis A	Fraser S	George L	Gillman R	Griffiths C	Hillier I	Holmes P	Howard S	Hughes JP	Johnson M	Kabba S	Locke A	Mansell L	McSwegan G	Nicholls K	Neilson A	Ovendale M	Perrett R	Skelton A	Spring M	Stirling J	Street K	Taylor M	Thomson P	Valois J-L	Round
1	Aug	21	(a)	Reading	L	0-4	-	5115		2					13	12	1	7					10		14	9	4	6			11		8			5					3			1
			Apps							1							1	1					1			1	1	1			1		1			1					1			
			Subs												1	1										1																	
			Goals																																							

2001/02 LDV VANS TROPHY (ASSOCIATE MEMBERS CUP)

Round	Month	Day	Venue	Opponents	W,L,D	Score	Scorers	Attendance	Bayliss D	Boyce E	Brennan D	Brkovic A	Coyne C	Crowe D	Douglas S	Dryden R	Emerson C	Forbes A	Fotiadis A	Fraser S	George L	Gillman R	Griffiths C	Hillier I	Holmes P	Howard S	Hughes JP	Johnson M	Kabba S	Locke A	Mansell L	McSwegan G	Nicholls K	Neilson A	Ovendale M	Perrett R	Skelton A	Spring M	Stirling J	Street K	Taylor M	Thomson P	Valois J-L	Round
2	Oct	31	(a)	Dagenham & Redbridge	L	2-3	Brennan, Thomson	2433		11				5				9	2	7	6		3	4							8		1						12			10		2
			Apps							1				1				1	1	1	1		1							1		1									1		
			Subs																																		1						
			Goals								1																															1		

▶ Ian Hillier nets the winner at York

▶ Steve Howard congratulates scorer Carl Griffiths during the 5-1 thumping of Torquay.

TIMELINE...

20 April 2002 Despite a run of 13 wins and a draw from the final 14 games the Hatters fail to catch Plymouth and have to settle for runners-up spot.

▶ **The 2001/02 team** – Back row (left to right): Crowe, Valois, Perrett, Ovendale, Emberson, Bayliss, Neilson, Fotiadis. Middle row (left to right): Sewell (Physiotherapist), Harford (Coach), Skelton, Coyne, Howard, Holmes, Hughes, Boyce, Kabba, Stein (Coach), Cherry Newbery (Secretary). Front row (left to right): Brkovic, Mansell, Spring, Johnson, Kinnear (Manager), Watson-Challis (Chairman), Nicholls, Forbes, Hillier, Taylor.

◗ Top scorer Steve Howard with the match ball after netting a hat-trick at Hull.

◗ The players celebrate promotion after winning 3-1 at Swansea.

◗ Kevin Nicholls – led by example.

◗ Dean Crowe, Kevin Nicholls and Jean-Louis Valois celebrate another goal on the road to promotion.

2002/03 "NEW" FOOTBALL LEAGUE DIVISION TWO (THIRD TIER)

Match No	Month	Day	Venue	Opponents	W,L,D Score	Scorers	Attendance	Bayliss D	Barnett L	Beckwith R	Berthelin C	Boyce E	Brkovic A	Coyne C	Crowe D	Davis Sol	Deeney J	Emberson C	Foley K	Forbes A	Fotiadis A	Griffiths C	Hillier I	Hirschfeld L	Holmes P	Howard S	Hughes JP	Igoe S	Johnson M	Judge M	Jupp D	Kimble A	Leary M	Mansell L	Neilson A	Nicholls K	Okai P	Osborn J	Ovendale M	Perrett R	Roberts B	Robinson S	Skelton A	Spring M	Thorpe A	Willmott C	Winters R	Match No
1	Aug	10	(h)	PETERBOROUGH UNITED	L 2-3	Crowe, Brkovic	7860						12	5	13			1			14					9						3			2	8					6		11		4	10	7	1
2	Aug	13	(a)	Blackpool	L 2-5	Howard, Thorpe	6377	6				12	7	5	13			1			14				11	9						3			2	8									4	10		2
3	Aug	17	(a)	Plymouth Argyle	L 1-2	Howard	10973	12				2	11	5	13	3		1								9						14				8					6	7			4	10		3
4	Aug	24	(h)	BARNSLEY	L 2-3	Nicholls (pen), Spring	6230					2	11	5	12	3					13					9										8					6	1	7		4			4
5	Aug	26	(a)	Cardiff City	D 0-0	-	13564					2	7	5	10	3										9	11									8					6	1	12		4			5
6	Aug	31	(h)	CHESTERFIELD	W 3-0	Perrett, Howard, Crowe	6060	5					2	7												9	11								12	8				6	1	13		4			6
7	Sep	7	(a)	Brentford	D 0-0		7145	5					2	7												9	11								13	8				6	1	12		4			7
8	Sep	14	(h)	NOTTS COUNTY	D 2-2	Perrett, Howard,	6456	5						7	13	10	3		12		14					9	11									8				6	1			4			8
9	Sep	17	(h)	MANSFIELD TOWN	L 2-3	Howard, Nicholls	6004	5				2	7	12	10	3			1		14					9	11									8				6		13		4			9
10	Sep	21	(a)	Huddersfield Town	W 1-0	Howard	9249					2		5	10	3		1			12	13		14		9	11									8				6		7		4			10
11	Sep	28	(h)	SWINDON TOWN	W 3-0	Howard, Fotiadis, Robinson (pen)	6393					2		5	13	3		1			10				12	9	11									8				6		7		4			11
12	Oct	5	(a)	Stockport County	W 3-2	Spring (2), Fotiadis	5932				1	2		5	12	3					10		6			9	11									8						7		4			12
13	Oct	12	(h)	CHELTENHAM TOWN	W 2-1	Coyne, Fotiadis	6447				1	2	14	5	13	3					10				12	9	11									8						7		4			13
14	Oct	19	(a)	Oldham Athletic	W 2-1	Fotiadis, Thorpe	6916				1	2	13	5	10	3					9		14		11																	7	8	4	12		14
15	Oct	26	(h)	WIGAN ATHLETIC	D 1-1	Skelton	7364				1	2		5		3					10				11	9										6						7	8	4			15
16	Oct	29	(a)	Crewe Alexandra	W 1-0	Howard	6030				1	2	11	5		3					10		6			9																7	8	4	12		16
17	Nov	2	(a)	Northampton Town	L 0-3	-	5750				1	2	11	5		3							6		13	9									12	14						7	8	4	10		17
18	Nov	9	(h)	PORT VALE	D 0-0	-	6112				1	2		5		3									11	9	12								4	8					6		7			10		18
19	Nov	23	(h)	QUEENS PARK RANGERS	D 0-0		9477				1	2	11	5		3					12		13			9									6	8						7		4	10		19
20	Nov	30	(a)	Tranmere Rovers	W 3-1	Spring, Brkovic, Howard	8273				1	2	11	5		3					14					9	13					12			6	8						7		4	10		20
21	Dec	14	(h)	COLCHESTER UNITED	L 1-2	Fotiadis	5890				1	2	11	5	10						9						12					3			6	8			1			7		4			21
22	Dec	21	(a)	Bristol City	D 1-1	Howard	14057				1	2	11	5	7	3		1			12					9	4					13				8									10		22
23	Dec	26	(h)	CARDIFF CITY	W 2-0	Thorpe, Howard	7805				1	2	11	5	7			1			6					9	4					3				8									10		23
24	Dec	28	(a)	Wycombe Wanderers	W 2-1	Howard (2)	7740				1	2	11	5	7	3		1			14					9	4					13		12		8									10		24
25	Jan	1	(a)	Chesterfield	L 1-2	Brkovic	4638	12			1	2	11	5		3					7		6			9	4									8									10		25
26	Jan	18	(a)	Barnsley	W 3-2	Spring, Thorpe (2)	9079	13						5	14			1			2					9	11													12		3		6	8	7	4		26
27	Jan	25	(h)	WYCOMBE WANDERERS	W 1-0	Spring	7351					2	12	5		3										9	11															3		6	8	7	4		27
28	Feb	1	(a)	Peterborough United	D 1-1	Howard	6760					2	11	5	13											9	8												1			6		7		4	10	12	28
29	Feb	8	(a)	Port Vale	W 2-1	Thorpe, Nicholls (pen)	4714					2	11	5	12											9	7												1			3	8		4	10	6	29
30	Feb	11	(h)	BLACKPOOL	L 1-3	Thorpe	6563					2	11	5	7						12					9													1			3	8		4	10	6	30
31	Feb	15	(h)	NORTHAMPTON TOWN	W 3-2	Hughes (2), Nicholls	7048					2	7	5	10			1			12					11																3	8		4	9	6	31
32	Feb	22	(h)	BRENTFORD	L 0-1	-	6940						7	5	10	3		1			13					11									2	8							12	4	9	6	32
33	Feb	25	(h)	PLYMOUTH ARGYLE	W 1-0	Thorpe	7589						12	5	7	3					2	1				9	11									8									4	10	6	33
34	Mar	1	(a)	Notts County	L 1-2	Thorpe	6778						12	5	7	3					2	1				9	11			13						8									4	10	6	34
35	Mar	4	(a)	Mansfield Town	L 2-3	Thorpe (2)	4829						7	5	10								1	12		11					2					8						13			4	9	6	35
36	Mar	8	(h)	HUDDERSFIELD TOWN	W 3-0	Thorpe, Holmes, Howard	6122						7	5		3		1					13		12	9	11			2						8					6		14		4	10		36
37	Mar	15	(a)	Wigan Athletic	D 1-1	Howard	7087	2					11	5							3	1				9						12				8					6		7		4	10		37
38	Mar	18	(h)	OLDHAM ATHLETIC	D 0-0	-	6142						11	5		3		12					2	1	13	9	7									8					6				4	10		38
39	Mar	22	(a)	CREWE ALEXANDRA	L 0-4	-	6607	13					11	5		3		1		7			2		12	9	14									8					6				4	10		39
40	Apr	5	(h)	TRANMERE ROVERS	D 0-0	-	6326					2	11	5		3		1		12	14				9	13	7									8					6				4	10		40
41	Apr	8	(a)	Cheltenham Town	D 2-2	Hughes, Forbes	3762						5			3		1		10					11	9	7		13							8					6				4		2	41
42	Apr	12	(a)	Queens Park Rangers	L 0-2	-	15786					2			5	3				10					11	9	7								12	8			1					4		6	42
43	Apr	19	(h)	BRISTOL CITY	D 2-2	Howard (2)	6381		1			2			3		12			10					11	9	7			13					5									4		6	43
44	Apr	21	(a)	Colchester United	W 5-0	Howard (3), Griffiths, Nicholls (pen)	3967	12	1			2			3					10					11	9	7		14						5								13	4		6	44
45	Apr	26	(h)	STOCKPORT COUNTY	D 1-1	Howard	6010	12	1			2			13					10					11	9	7								5	8								14	4		6	45
46	May	3	(a)	Swindon Town	L 1-2	Thorpe	6455	5	1			2	11							13	12					9	7									8							3		14	4	10	46

Final League Position: 9th

	Bayliss D	Barnett L	Beckwith R	Berthelin C	Boyce E	Brkovic A	Coyne C	Crowe D	Davis Sol	Deeney J	Emberson C	Foley K	Forbes A	Fotiadis A	Griffiths C	Hillier I	Hirschfeld L	Holmes P	Howard S	Hughes JP	Igoe S	Johnson M	Judge M	Jupp D	Kimble A	Leary M	Mansell L	Neilson A	Nicholls K	Okai P	Osborn J	Ovendale M	Perrett R	Roberts B	Robinson S	Skelton A	Spring M	Thorpe A	Willmott C	Winters R
Apps	7	-	4	9	33	29	38	17	34	-	18	-	3	8	3	12	5	8	41	30	2	-	-	2	8	-	1	21	35	-	-	5	5	19	5	23	5	41	28	12	1
Subs	6	-	-	1	7	2	10	-	-	2	2	2	9	-	10	-	9	-	5	-	5	-	1	3	4	1	5	1	-	1	1	-	1	1	6	3	-	2	1
Goals	-	-	-	-	3	1	2	-	-	-	1	5	1	-	1	22	3	-	-	-	-	-	-	-	-	5	-	2	-	1	1	6	13	-	-

2002/03 FA CUP

Round	Month	Day	Venue	Opponents	W,L,D Score	Scorers	Attendance	Bayliss D	Barnett L	Beckwith R	Berthelin C	Boyce E	Brkovic A	Coyne C	Crowe D	Davis Sol	Deeney J	Emberson C	Foley K	Forbes A	Fotiadis A	Griffiths C	Hillier I	Hirschfeld L	Holmes P	Howard S	Hughes JP	Igoe S	Johnson M	Judge M	Jupp D	Kimble A	Leary M	Mansell L	Neilson A	Nicholls K	Okai P	Osborn J	Ovendale M	Perrett R	Roberts B	Robinson S	Skelton A	Spring M	Thorpe A	Willmott C	Winters R	Round
1	Nov	16	(h)	GUISELEY AFC	W 4-0	Spring, Thorpe, Brkovic (2)	5248					2	11	5		3		1							13	9								12	8					6		7		4	10			1
2	Dec	7	(a)	Wigan Athletic	L 0-3	-	4544					2	10	5				1				9		12	11		8					13	3		6							7		4				2
						Apps						2	2	2		1		2				1		1	1	1							1	1	1					1		1		2	2	1		
						Subs																		1	1		1							1												1	1		
						Goals							2																																1	1		

2002/03 WORTHINGTON CUP (LEAGUE CUP)

Round	Month	Day	Venue	Opponents	W,L,D Score	Scorers	Attendance	Bayliss D	Barnett L	Beckwith R	Berthelin C	Boyce E	Brkovic A	Coyne C	Crowe D	Davis Sol	Deeney J	Emberson C	Foley K	Forbes A	Fotiadis A	Griffiths C	Hillier I	Hirschfeld L	Holmes P	Howard S	Hughes JP	Igoe S	Johnson M	Judge M	Jupp D	Kimble A	Leary M	Mansell L	Neilson A	Nicholls K	Okai P	Osborn J	Ovendale M	Perrett R	Roberts B	Robinson S	Skelton A	Spring M	Thorpe A	Willmott C	Winters R	Round
1	Sep	10	(a)	Watford	W 2-1	Spring, Howard	14171	5				2	7		10	3		1								9	11							13	8					6		12		4				1
2	Oct	2	(a)	Aston Villa	L 0-3	-	20833					2		5	14	3		1			10			13	8	9	11							12						6		7		4				2
						Apps		1				2	1	1	1	2		2			1			1	1	2	2							1						2		1		2				
						Subs								1										1											2								1						
						Goals																				1																			1				

2002/03 LDV VANS TROPHY (ASSOCIATE MEMBERS CUP)

Round	Month	Day	Venue	Opponents	W,L,D Score	Scorers	Attendance	Bayliss D	Barnett L	Beckwith R	Berthelin C	Boyce E	Brkovic A	Coyne C	Crowe D	Davis Sol	Deeney J	Emberson C	Foley K	Forbes A	Fotiadis A	Griffiths C	Hillier I	Hirschfeld L	Holmes P	Howard S	Hughes JP	Igoe S	Johnson M	Judge M	Jupp D	Kimble A	Leary M	Mansell L	Neilson A	Nicholls K	Okai P	Osborn J	Ovendale M	Perrett R	Roberts B	Robinson S	Skelton A	Spring M	Thorpe A	Willmott C	Winters R	Round
1	Oct	22	(a)	Woking	W 2-0	Holmes, Deeney	1216	14				9					5		12		2				8				6	10		3	4	11			13	7	1									1
2	Nov	12	(a)	Stevenage Borough	W 4-3	Thorpe, Brkovic (3)	2601						10				5	1	2		4				11				14	13		3	12	7		8						6			9			2
3	Dec	10	(h)	CAMBRIDGE UNITED	L 1-2	Thorpe	3578					2	11	5	10	3						13	6		14		8						12						1			7		4	9			3
						Apps		1				3	1	1	1	2	1	1			2		2		2		1	1		2	1	2		1		1	2			1	1	1	2				
						Subs			1										1		1				1				1	1		1	1			1					1						
						Goals							3				1								1																				2			

2003/04 "NEW" FOOTBALL LEAGUE DIVISION TWO (THIRD TIER)

Match No	Month	Day	Venue	Opponents	W.L.D Score	Scorers	Attendance	Barnett L	Bayliss D	Beckwith R	Beresford M	Boyce E	Brill D	Brkovic A	Coyne C	Crowe D	Davies C	Davis Sol	Deeney D	Foley K	Forbes A	Hillier I	Holmes P	Howard S	Hughes JP	Hyldgaard M	Judge M	Keane K	Leary M	Mansell L	McSheffrey G	Neilson A	Nicholls K	Okai P	O'Leary S	Perrett R	Pitt C	Robinson S	Showunmi E	Spring M	Thorpe A	Underwood P	Match No
1	Aug	9	(h)	RUSHDEN & DIAMONDS	W 3-1	Thorpe (2), Spring	6878		1			6		12	5					2				9	4											3	7	11		8	10		1
2	Aug	16	(a)	Stockport County	W 2-1	Neilson, Howard	4566		1			6		12	5					2		7		9	4											3	8	11			10		2
3	Aug	23	(h)	GRIMSBY TOWN	L 1-2	Nicholls (pen)	5827		1			6		13	5	12				2				9	4								10			3	7	11		8			3
4	Aug	25	(a)	Brighton & Hove Albion	L 0-2	-	6604	6	1						5	12	3			2				9	4								10					11		7			4
5	Aug	30	(h)	HARTLEPOOL UNITED	W 3-2	Howard (2), McSheffrey	5515	6	1			2		14	5	12		13		7				9	4							10	3					11		8			5
6	Sep	6	(a)	Notts County	D 1-1	Coyne	7505	6	1			2		11	5	12		13		7				9	4							10	3							8			6
7	Sep	13	(a)	Plymouth Argyle	L 1-2	McSheffrey	9894	6	1			2		11	5	12		3		7		13			4						9								10	8		7
8	Sep	16	(h)	PORT VALE	W 2-0	McSheffrey, Foley	5079	6	1			2		11	5			3		7	10				4						9									12	8		8
9	Sep	20	(h)	QUEENS PARK RANGERS	D 1-1	Howard	8339	6	1			2		11	5			3		7				9					4		10								12		8		9
10	Sep	27	(a)	Oldham Athletic	L 0-3	-	6077		1			6	14	7	5			3					2	9	4				8	12	10					13	11						10
11	Oct	1	(a)	Swindon Town	D 2-2	McSheffrey (pen), Forbes	7573		1			2			5			3		7	10				4					12	9					6	11	8					11
12	Oct	6	(h)	TRANMERE ROVERS	W 3-1	Perrett, McSheffrey, Forbes	5002		1			2			5			3		7	10				4						9					6	11	12			8		12
13	Oct	11	(h)	WYCOMBE WANDERERS	W 3-1	McSheffrey (2), Perrett	5695		1			2	1		5			3			10				4					13	9					6	11	7	12		8		13
14	Oct	18	(a)	Brentford	L 2-4	Forbes (2)	5579					2	1		5			3		7	10				4	12					9					6	11				8		14
15	Oct	21	(a)	Bournemouth	L 3-6	Purches (og), Hughes, Forbes	6388		1			2			5			3		7	10				4					13	9					6	11	12			8		15
16	Oct	25	(h)	PETERBOROUGH UNITED	D 1-1	Forbes	6067			6	1	6			5			3		2	10	3								7	9	12				8			4	16
17	Nov	1	(a)	Bristol City	D 1-1	McSheffrey	9735			6	1				5			3			10	13								7	9	2				8	12		4	17
18	Nov	15	(a)	WREXHAM	W 3-2	Forbes, Robinson, Mansell	5505			6	1				5			3		2	10									7	9					8		4	18
19	Nov	22	(a)	Sheffield Wednesday	D 0-0	-	21027			6	1				5						10	2	3	5							12	7	9			8		4	19
20	Nov	29	(h)	CHESTERFIELD	W 1-0	Howard	5453			6	1				5			3			7	2	12	9							10				8		4	20
21	Dec	13	(a)	Blackpool	W 1-0	Robinson	5739			6	1				5			3		2	10			9							12	7				8		4	21
22	Dec	20	(h)	BARNSLEY	L 0-1	-	6162			6	1				5			3		2	10			9								7				8		4	22
23	Dec	26	(a)	Colchester United	D 1-1	Mansell	5083			6	1				5			3		2	10				12						7				8		4	23
24	Dec	28	(h)	NOTTS COUNTY	W 2-0	Forbes, Boyce	7181			6	1				5			3		2	10	13	12	9							7				8	14	4	24
25	Jan	10	(a)	Rushden & Diamonds	D 2-2	Forbes, Holmes	5823			6	1				5			3		2	10	3	4	9							12	7				8		25
26	Jan	17	(h)	STOCKPORT COUNTY	D 2-2	Griffin (og), Howard	5920				1	6				6	3		2	10			4	9							7				8	12	26
27	Feb	7	(h)	COLCHESTER UNITED	W 1-0	Showunmi	5662					6			5	12	3		2			11	9		1						7				8	10	4	27
28	Feb	10	(h)	BRIGHTON & HOVE ALBION	W 2-0	Holmes, Nicholls (pen)	6846					6		14	5	12	3		2			11	9		1				13		7				8	10	4	28
29	Feb	14	(a)	Wycombe Wanderers	D 0-0	-	6407					6		12	5		3				11	9		1		2					7				8	10	4	29
30	Feb	21	(h)	BRENTFORD	W 4-1	Boyce, Showunmi (3)	6273					6			5		3			11	9	13	1		2	4		12		7	14	8	10	30
31	Feb	24	(a)	Grimsby Town	L 2-3	Howard (2)	3143					6		13	5		3			11	9	12	1		2	4				7	8	10	31
32	Feb	28	(a)	Peterborough United	W 2-1	Howard, Brkovic	6628					6		11	5		3				9	4	1		2			12		7	8	10	32
33	Mar	6	(a)	Barnsley	D 0-0	-	8656					6		11	5		3				12	9	4	1		2				7	8	10	33
34	Mar	13	(h)	BLACKPOOL	W 3-2	Boyce, Holmes, Showunmi	6343					6			5		3				11	9	4	1		2				7	8	10	34
35	Mar	16	(a)	Port Vale	L 0-1	-	5048					6		12	5		3				11	9	4	1		2				7	8	10	35
36	Mar	20	(h)	PLYMOUTH ARGYLE	D 1-1	Coyne	8499					6		5	13	12					11	9	4	1		2			3	7	8	10	36
37	Mar	27	(a)	Queens Park Rangers	D 1-1	Showunmi	17695					6		10	5				14	13	12	4	1		2			3	7	8	9	11	37
38	Apr	3	(h)	OLDHAM ATHLETIC	D 1-1	Showunmi	5966					6		11	5		3			7	13	9	1		2			4	12	8	10	38
39	Apr	6	(a)	Hartlepool United	L 3-4	Howard, Leary (2)	4434							11	5		3			7	12	9	1		2	4				8	10	39
40	Apr	10	(a)	Tranmere Rovers	L 0-1	-	7937					6		11	5		3			2	12	9	1		4	7				8	10	40
41	Apr	12	(h)	SWINDON TOWN	L 0-3	-	7008					6			5		3			2	13	9	1		12	4	7		11	8	10	41
42	Apr	17	(h)	BRISTOL CITY	W 3-2	Howard, Boyce, Keane	6944					6		11	5		3			7	10	9	1		2				8	4	12	42
43	Apr	20	(h)	BOURNEMOUTH	D 1-1	Howard	6485					6		11	5		12	3		7	10	9	1		2	13			8	4	14	43
44	Apr	24	(a)	Wrexham	L 1-2	Howard	3239								5		6	3		7	12	9	1		2	4	13		8	11	10	44
45	May	1	(h)	SHEFFIELD WEDNESDAY	W 3-2	Howard (2), O'Leary	7157					6	1		5		3			7	10	9				2	8	11	4	12	45
46	May	8	(a)	Chesterfield	L 0-1	-	6285					6	1		5		3			7	10				2	8	11	4	9	46

							Apps	-	6	13	11	42	4	24	44	-	4	34	-	32	21	8	11	34	20	18	-	14	8	12	18	11	21	-	3	5	11	32	18	24	2	1	
							Subs	-	-	-	-	1	8	-	-	8	2	2	-	1	6	3	5	-	2	-	1	1	6	4	-	3	-	2	1	1	1	-	2	8	-	-	
							Goals	-	-	-	-	4	-	1	2	-	-	-	-	1	9	-	3	15	1	-	-	1	2	2	8	1	2	-	1	-	-	1	2	7	1	2	-	

Final League Position: 10th   2 Own Goals

2003/04 FA CUP

Round	Month	Day	Venue	Opponents	W,L,D	Score	Scorers	Attendance	Barnett L	Bayliss D	Beckwith R	Beresford M	Boyce E	Brill D	Brkovic A	Coyne C	Crowe D	Davies C	Davis Sol	Deeney D	Foley K	Forbes A	Hillier I	Holmes P	Howard S	Hughes JP	Hyldgaard M	Judge M	Keane K	Leary M	Mansell L	McSheffrey G	Neilson A	Nicholls K	Okai P	O'Leary S	Perrett R	Pitt C	Robinson S	Showunmi E	Spring M	Thorpe A	Underwood P	Round
1	Nov	7	(a)	Thurrock	D	1-1	Boyce	1551		1		6	11	5	13				3		10	2								12	7								8	9	4			1
Rep	Nov	18	(h)	THURROCK	W	3-1	Forbes (3)	3667	3	1		6	11	5	13				2		10	12			9						7			14					8		4			Rep
2	Dec	6	(a)	Rochdale	W	2-0	Robinson (pen), Mansell	2807		1		6	11	5					3		10	2			4	9					7								8					2
3	Jan	3	(a)	Bradford City	W	2-1	Forbes (2)	8222		1		6	11	5					3		2	10			12	9					7								8		4			3
4	Jan	24	(h)	TRANMERE ROVERS	L	0-1	-	8767		1		6	11	5	13				3		2	4						12		10	7				8						9			4
							Apps		1	5		5	5	5	3				5		5	4			2	2		1		1	5				1				4	1	4			
							Subs								3							1			1			1		1				1										
							Goals						1									5									1								1					

2003/04 CARLING CUP (LEAGUE CUP)

Round	Month	Day	Venue	Opponents	W,L,D	Score	Scorers	Attendance	Barnett L	Bayliss D	Beckwith R	Beresford M	Boyce E	Brill D	Brkovic A	Coyne C	Crowe D	Davies C	Davis Sol	Deeney D	Foley K	Forbes A	Hillier I	Holmes P	Howard S	Hughes JP	Hyldgaard M	Judge M	Keane K	Leary M	Mansell L	McSheffrey G	Neilson A	Nicholls K	Okai P	O'Leary S	Perrett R	Pitt C	Robinson S	Showunmi E	Spring M	Thorpe A	Underwood P	Round
1	Aug	12	(h)	YEOVIL TOWN	W	4-1	Foley, Thorpe, Pitt, Howard	6337		1			6		5	13			12	2					9	8								3	7		14	11				4	10	1
2	Sep	23	(a)	Charlton Athletic	D	4-4	Foley, Bayliss, McSheffrey, Coyne	10905	6	1		2		11	5	13			3		7	14			9	8				10		12										4		2
							Apps		1	2		1	1	1	2				1	1	1				2	2				1				1	1			1				2	1	
							Subs									2			1			1										1					1							
							Goals			1						1					2				1							1						1				1		

2nd Round lost 7-8 on penalties aet, 3-3 after 90 minutes

2003/04 LDV VANS TROPHY (ASSOCIATE MEMBERS CUP)

Round	Month	Day	Venue	Opponents	W,L,D	Score	Scorers	Attendance	Barnett L	Bayliss D	Beckwith R	Beresford M	Boyce E	Brill D	Brkovic A	Coyne C	Crowe D	Davies C	Davis Sol	Deeney D	Foley K	Forbes A	Hillier I	Holmes P	Howard S	Hughes JP	Hyldgaard M	Judge M	Keane K	Leary M	Mansell L	McSheffrey G	Neilson A	Nicholls K	Okai P	O'Leary S	Perrett R	Pitt C	Robinson S	Showunmi E	Spring M	Thorpe A	Underwood P	Round
1	Oct	14	(a)	Stevenage Borough	W	1-0	Judge	2412	6					1	10	5			3	13	2							12		4	7				11				8	9				1
2	Nov	4	(a)	Rushden & Diamonds	W	2-1	Showunmi, Leary (pen)	2746	6					1	11		10	12	3		5									4	7		2		8					9				2
3	Dec	9	(a)	Southend United	L	0-3	-	2027				1			5	10			3	6	12	2			8	9		14		7									11	13	4			3
							Apps		2			1		2	2	2	1		3	1	2	1			1	1				3	2		1		2				2	2	1			
							Subs											1		1	1							2												1				
							Goals																					1		1										1				

TIMELINE...

23 May 2003 Joe Kinnear is sacked in a bizarre fashion by the new 'consortium' that had taken over the club.
21 June 2003 Mike Newell is appointed manager after a shameful and embarrassing phone vote.
14 July 2003 The Town enter administrative receivership.

◗ **The 2002/03 team** – Back row (left to right): Brkovic, Neilson, Perrett, Ovendale, Berthelin, Emberson, Holmes, Hillier, Bayliss. Middle row (left to right): Sewell (Physiotherapist), Davis, Griffiths, Thorpe, Howard, Coyne, Skelton, Hughes, Fotiadis, Leary, Stein (Coach). Front row (left to right): Boyce, Kimble, Forbes, Nicholls, Harford (Coach), Kinnear (Manager), Spring, Johnson, Mansell, Robinson. Inset: Crowe.

▶ **The 2003/04 team** – Back row (left to right): Mansell, Hillier, Neilson, Bayliss, Spring, Davis, Boyce, Crowe. Middle row (left to right): Julie Frost (Physiotherapist), Nicholls, Hughes, Beckwith, Howard, Brill, Coyne, Showunmi, Stein (Coach). Front row (left to right): Brkovic, Forbes, Perrett, Newell (Manager), Harford (Director of Football), Robinson, Leary, Foley.

2004/05 FOOTBALL LEAGUE ONE (THIRD TIER)

Match No	Month	Day	Venue	Opponents	W,L,D Score	Scorers	Attendance	Andrew C	Barnett L	Bayliss D	Beresford M	Blinkhorn M	Brkovic A	Coyne C	Davies C	Davis Sol	Feeney W	Foley K	Holmes P	Howard S	Hughes JP	Keane K	Leary M	Mansell L	McSheffrey G	Neilson A	Nicholls K	O'Leary S	Perrett R	Robinson S	Royce S	Seremet D	Showunmi E	Underwood P	Vine R	Match No
1	Aug	7	(h)	OLDHAM ATHLETIC	W 2-1	Howard, Underwood	6634			1			13	5	6	3		2		9							8	7		4			12	11	10	1
2	Aug	11	(a)	Swindon Town	W 3-2	Nicholls (pen), Fallon (og), Howard	6286			1			14	5	6	3		2		9					12		8	7		4			13	11	10	2
3	Aug	14	(a)	Barnsley	W 4-3	Howard, Vine, Brkovic, Robinson	10057			1			13	5	6	3		2		9					12		8	7		4			14	11	10	3
4	Aug	21	(h)	TORQUAY UNITED	W 1-0	Howard	6664			1			7	5	6	3				9		2					8			4			12	11	10	4
5	Aug	28	(a)	Blackpool	W 3-1	Howard, Brkovic (2)	5793			1			7	5	6	3				9		2					8			4				11	10	5
6	Aug	30	(h)	BOURNEMOUTH	W 1-0	Nicholls	7404			1			7	5	6	3		2		9							8			4			12	11	10	6
7	Sep	4	(a)	Sheffield Wednesday	D 0-0	–	20806			1			7	5	6	3				9		2					8			4				11	10	7
8	Sep	11	(h)	CHESTERFIELD	W 1-0	Vine	7532			1			7	5	6	3		2		9				12			8			4			13	11	10	8
9	Sep	18	(a)	Stockport County	W 3-1	Robinson, Vine, Brkovic	5128			1			7	5	6	3		2		9		14	13				8			4				11	10	9
10	Sep	25	(h)	PETERBOROUGH UNITED	W 2-1	Vine, Underwood	7694			1			7	5	6	3		2		9					13		8			4		12		11	10	10
11	Oct	2	(a)	Tranmere Rovers	D 1-1	Coyne	10884						7	5	6	3		2		9						9	8			4		1		11	10	11
12	Oct	8	(h)	HARTLEPOOL UNITED	W 3-0	Howard, Brkovic, McSheffrey	7865						7	5	6	3				9					12		8	13		4		1	14	11	10	12
13	Oct	16	(h)	HUDDERSFIELD TOWN	L 1-2	Underwood	8192						7	5	6	3		2			4				12		8	14				1	13	11	10	13
14	Oct	19	(a)	Walsall	L 0-2	–	5963						7	5	6	3		2		9							8	13		4		1	12	11	10	14
15	Oct	23	(a)	Hull City	L 0-3	–	18575					14		5	6	3		2	13	9							8	7		4		1	12	11	10	15
16	Oct	30	(h)	BRADFORD CITY	W 4-0	Brkovic (2), Howard, Underwood	7975					13	7	5	6	3		2		9							8	12	4	1				11	10	16
17	Nov	6	(h)	WREXHAM	W 5-1	Robinson, Davis, O'Leary, Howard, Brkovic	7144						7	5	6	3		2		9					12		8	4	1				13	11	10	17
18	Nov	20	(a)	Milton Keynes Dons	W 4-1	Vine, Howard (3)	6683			1			7	5	6	3		2	13	9		12					8	4						11	10	18
19	Nov	27	(h)	DONCASTER ROVERS	D 1-1	Nicholls	8142			1			7	5	6	3		2	12	9		13					8	4					14	11	10	19
20	Dec	7	(a)	Brentford	L 0-2	–	6393	12		1			7	5	6	3				9		2					8	4					13	11	10	20
21	Dec	11	(h)	PORT VALE	W 1-0	Brkovic	6974	10		1			7	5	6	3		2									8	4					12	11	9	21
22	Dec	18	(a)	Bristol City	W 2-1	Coyne, Showunmi	13414			1			7	5	6	3		2	4								8						10	11	9	22
23	Dec	26	(a)	Chesterfield	W 1-0	Showunmi	7158	10		1			7	5		3		2	4								8		6				9	11		23
24	Dec	28	(h)	COLCHESTER UNITED	D 2-2	Vine (2)	8806			1			7	5	6	3		2	11	9							8	12		4			13		10	24
25	Jan	1	(h)	SHEFFIELD WEDNESDAY	D 1-1	Howard	9500			1			7	5	6	3		2		9							8			4				11	10	25
26	Jan	3	(a)	Peterborough United	D 2-2	Nicholls, Howard	7662	14		1				6		3		2	7	9							8	4	5	12			10	11	13	26
27	Jan	15	(a)	STOCKPORT COUNTY	W 3-0	Coyne, Howard, Nicholls (pen)	6603			1			7	5	6			2	13	9		12				3	8			4			14	11	10	27
28	Jan	22	(a)	Colchester United	D 0-0	–	4309							5	6	3		2	12	9		4					8			7			13	11	10	28
29	Jan	29	(h)	TRANMERE ROVERS	D 1-1	Nicholls (pen)	8594						7	5	6	3		2		9		4					8						11		10	29
30	Feb	5	(a)	Huddersfield Town	D 1-1	Brkovic	12611	13		1			7		6	3		2		9		4				12	8		5	11					10	30
31	Feb	12	(h)	HULL CITY	W 1-0	Brkovic	9500	12		1			7	5	6	11		2								3	8	13		4			9		10	31
32	Feb	15	(a)	Hartlepool United	W 3-2	Coyne, Showunmi, Foley	5542			1			7	5	6	11		2				12				3	8			4			9		10	32
33	Feb	19	(a)	Bradford City	W 1-0	Vine	8702			1			7	5	6	11		2		9						3	8			4			12		10	33
34	Feb	22	(h)	WALSALL	W 1-0	Nicholls (pen)	7236			1			7	5	6	11		2		9						3	8	12		4			13		10	34
35	Feb	26	(a)	Port Vale	L 1-3	Foley	5353			1			7	5	6	11		2	13	9						3	8	4	14				12		10	35
36	Mar	5	(h)	BRISTOL CITY	W 5-0	Brkovic (2), Nicholls (pen), Davis, Holmes	8330	13		1			7		6	3			4	9		2	14				8						12	11	10	36
37	Mar	12	(h)	SWINDON TOWN	W 3-1	Nicholls (pen), Brkovic, Holmes	8173			1			7		6	3	13		4	9		2	14				8			5			12	11	10	37
38	Mar	19	(a)	Oldham Athletic	D 2-2	Underwood, Howard	5809			1			7	5	6	3		2	4	9		13					8						12	11	10	38
39	Mar	25	(a)	BARNSLEY	L 1-3	Showunmi	7548	13		1				5	6	3		4		9		2	12				8						7	11	10	39
40	Mar	28	(a)	Torquay United	W 4-1	Nicholls, Holmes, Howard, Vine	4264						7		6	3		2	4	9				12			8			5				11	10	40
41	Apr	2	(h)	BLACKPOOL	W 1-0	Howard	7816						7		6	3	12	2	4	9			14				8			5			13	11	10	41
42	Apr	9	(a)	Bournemouth	W 1-0	Showunmi	9058						7	12	6	3	13	2	4	9							8			5			14	11	10	42
43	Apr	16	(h)	MILTON KEYNES DONS	W 1-0	Chorley (og)	9000						7	5	6	3	13	2	4	9							8						12	11	10	43
44	Apr	23	(a)	Wrexham	W 2-1	Davies, Coyne	6614						7	5	6	3	12	2	4	9							8			13			11		10	44
45	Apr	30	(h)	BRENTFORD	W 4-2	Brkovic, Nicholls (pen), Showunmi, Robinson	9313						7	5	6	3	10	2		9							8			4			13	11	12	45
46	May	7	(a)	Doncaster Rovers	D 3-3	Perrett, Howard, Nicholls	8928						7	5		3	12	2		9							8		6	4		1	13	11	10	46

Final League Position: 1st   2 Own Goals

	Andrew C	Barnett L	Bayliss D	Beresford M	Blinkhorn M	Brkovic A	Coyne C	Davies C	Davis Sol	Feeney W	Foley K	Holmes P	Howard S	Hughes JP	Keane K	Leary M	Mansell L	McSheffrey G	Neilson A	Nicholls K	O'Leary S	Perrett R	Robinson S	Royce S	Seremet D	Showunmi E	Underwood P	Vine R
Apps	2	–	38	–	39	39	44	45	1	38	13	40	–	11	1	–	1	6	44	12	9	28	2	6	7	37	43	
Subs	6	–	–	2	3	1	–	–	5	1	6	–	6	7	1	4	3	–	5	3	3	–	1	28	–	2		
Goals	–	–	–	–	15	5	1	2	–	2	3	18	–	–	1	–	12	1	1	4	–	6	5	9				

2004/05 FA CUP

Round	Month	Day	Venue	Opponents	W,L,D Score	Scorers	Attendance	Andrew C	Barnett L	Bayliss D	Beresford M	Blinkhorn M	Brkovic A	Coyne C	Davies C	Davis Sol	Feeney W	Foley K	Holmes P	Howard S	Hughes JP	Keane K	Leary M	Mansell L	McSheffrey G	Neilson A	Nicholls K	O'Leary S	Perrett R	Robinson S	Royce S	Seremet D	Showunmi E	Underwood P	Vine R	Round
1	Nov	12	(a)	Southend United	W 3-0	Howard (2), Brkovic	6683						7	5	6	3		2		9			12					8		4	1		13	11	10	1
2	Dec	4	(a)	Wycombe Wanderers	W 3-0	Howard (2), Nicholls	4767	13			1		7	5	6	3				9	2						8			4			12	11	10	2
3	Jan	8	(h)	BRENTFORD	L 0-2	-	6861	12			1		7	5	6	3		2		9							8			4			13	11	10	3
						Apps					2		3	3	3	3		2		3	1						2	1		3	1			3	3	
						Subs		2															1										3			
						Goals							1							4							1									

2004/05 CARLING CUP (LEAGUE CUP)

Round	Month	Day	Venue	Opponents	W,L,D Score	Scorers	Attendance	Andrew C	Barnett L	Bayliss D	Beresford M	Blinkhorn M	Brkovic A	Coyne C	Davies C	Davis Sol	Feeney W	Foley K	Holmes P	Howard S	Hughes JP	Keane K	Leary M	Mansell L	McSheffrey G	Neilson A	Nicholls K	O'Leary S	Perrett R	Robinson S	Royce S	Seremet D	Showunmi E	Underwood P	Vine R	Round
1	Sep	7	(a)	Boston United	L 3-4	Lee (og), Nicholls (pen), Showunmi	2631		1	12	2			5	6	3				9	7						8			4			13	11	10	1
						1 Own Goal	Apps		1		1			1	1	1				1	1						1			1				1	1	
							Subs			1																							1			
							Goals																				1						1			

2004/05 LDV VANS TROPHY (ASSOCIATE MEMBERS CUP)

Round	Month	Day	Venue	Opponents	W,L,D Score	Scorers	Attendance	Andrew C	Barnett L	Bayliss D	Beresford M	Blinkhorn M	Brkovic A	Coyne C	Davies C	Davis Sol	Feeney W	Foley K	Holmes P	Howard S	Hughes JP	Keane K	Leary M	Mansell L	McSheffrey G	Neilson A	Nicholls K	O'Leary S	Perrett R	Robinson S	Royce S	Seremet D	Showunmi E	Underwood P	Vine R	Round
1	Sep	28	(a)	Swansea City	L 0-2	-	3559	10	6	5									4	8	2		11				3	7	12		1		9			1
							Apps	1	1	1									1	1	1		1				1	1			1		1			
							Subs																						1							
							Goals																													

▶ The players celebrate winning the League One title at Wrexham.

TIMELINE...

26 May 2004 The club finally exits administrative receivership.

7 May 2005 A glorious season comes to an end with the Town winning the title by 12 points.

▶ **The 2004/05 team** – Back row (left to right): O'Leary, Bayliss, Neilson, Vine, Leary, Showunmi, Davies, Barnett, Hillier, Mansell. Middle row (left to right): Coleman (Physiotherapist), Blinkhorn, Hughes, Howard, Beckwith, Seremet, Beresford, Brill, Coyne, Underwood, Keane, Bowden (Physiotherapist), Stein (Coach). Front row (left to right): Holmes, Brkovic, Nicholls, Newell (Manager), Tomlins (Chairman), Harford (Director of Football), Perrett, Robinson, Davis.

▶ Chris Coyne is delighted at netting the goal that clinched the championship at Wrexham.

▶ Ahmet Brkovic heads in an important late winner at home to fellow promotion challengers Hull.

▶ The team with the League One trophy.

2005/06 FOOTBALL LEAGUE CHAMPIONSHIP (SECOND TIER)

Match No	Month	Day	Venue	Opponents	W,L/D Score	Scorers	Attendance	Andrew C	Barnett L	Bell D	Beresford M	Brill D	Brkovic A	Coyne C	Davies C	Davis Sol	Edwards C	Feeney W	Foley K	Heikkinen M	Holmes P	Howard S	Keane K	Leary M	Morgan D	Nicholls K	O'Leary S	Perrett R	Robinson S	Showunmi E	Stevens D	Underwood P	Vine R	Match No
1	Aug	6	(a)	Crystal Palace	W 2-1	Howard, Brkovic	21166				1		7		6			10	2	5	12	9			11	8			4	13		3		1
2	Aug	9	(h)	SOUTHAMPTON	W 3-2	Nicholls, Brkovic, Morgan	9447				1		7		6			10	2	5		9			11	8			4	12		3		2
3	Aug	13	(h)	LEEDS UNITED	D 0-0	-	10102				1		7		6			10	2	5		9			11	8			4	12		3		3
4	Aug	20	(a)	Stoke City	L 1-2	Morgan	18653				1		7		6	12	13	10	2	5		9			11	8			4	14		3		4
5	Aug	27	(a)	Leicester City	W 2-0	Brkovic, Nicholls (pen)	22048				1		7	13	6	12	14	10	2			9			11	8			4	9		3		5
6	Aug	29	(h)	MILLWALL	W 2-1	Feeney, Davies	8220				1		7	13	6	12	14	10	2			9			11	8			4	9		3		6
7	Sep	10	(h)	WOLVERHAMPTON WANDERERS	D 1-1	Nicholls	10248				1		7	6		3	2	10		5		9				8		13	4	12	11			7
8	Sep	13	(a)	Queens Park Rangers	L 0-1	-	13492				1		7	5		3	2	10			14	9			12			6	4	13	11			8
9	Sep	17	(a)	Hull City	W 1-0	Howard	19184		12		1		7	5		3	2	10				9			11	8		6	4					9
10	Sep	23	(h)	SHEFFIELD WEDNESDAY	D 2-2	Howard (2)	8267				1		7	5		3	2	10		13		9			11			6	4	12				10
11	Sep	27	(h)	PRESTON NORTH END	W 3-0	Feeney, Brkovic, Howard	7815				1		7	6		3	2	10		5	12	9	14		11				4	13				11
12	Oct	1	(a)	Cardiff City	W 2-1	Morgan, Holmes	14657				1		7	6		3	2	10		5	4	9	13		11	8				14		12		12
13	Oct	15	(a)	Crewe Alexandra	L 1-3	Morgan	6604				1		7	6		3	2	10	12	5	4	9			11	8				13				13
14	Oct	18	(h)	NORWICH CITY	W 4-2	Feeney, Edwards, Holmes, Howard	10248				1		7	6		3	2	10	12	5	8	9			11				4	14				14
15	Oct	22	(a)	PLYMOUTH ARGYLE	D 1-1	Feeney	8714				1		7	6		3	2	10		5	4	9			11					13				15
16	Oct	29	(a)	Coventry City	L 0-1	-	22228		13		1		7	6		3		10	2	5	4	9	12		11					14				16
17	Nov	1	(a)	Sheffield United	L 0-4	-	22554		5		1		11	6			7	10	2	8	4	9	14							13		3	12	17
18	Nov	5	(h)	BURNLEY	L 2-3	Howard, Feeney	8518		5		1		7					10	2	8	4	9			11			6		13		3	12	18
19	Nov	19	(a)	Norwich City	L 0-2	-	25383				1		7					10	2	5		9			11	8		6	4	12		3	13	19
20	Nov	22	(h)	CREWE ALEXANDRA	W 4-1	Vine (2, 1 pen), Morgan, Showunmi	7474		6		1		13				7	10	2	5	8				12				4	9		3	11	20
21	Nov	26	(h)	CRYSTAL PALACE	W 2-0	Heikkinen, Vine	10248				1			6			7	13	2	5	8	14			11				4	10		3	9	21
22	Dec	3	(a)	Reading	L 0-3	-	19478		12		1		7					14	2	5	8	13			11			6	4			3	9	22
23	Dec	11	(a)	Southampton	L 0-1	-	19086				1		7	6			11		2	5	13	9				8			4	10		3	12	23
24	Dec	17	(h)	STOKE CITY	L 2-3	Brkovic, Nicholls (pen)	8296					1	11	6			7		2	5		9				8			4	13		3	10	24
25	Dec	26	(a)	Derby County	D 1-1	Brkovic	26807					1	11	6			7		2	5	8	9			12				4			3	10	25
26	Dec	28	(h)	BRIGHTON & HOVE ALBION	W 3-0	Howard, Feeney, Robinson	9429					1	11	6			7	10	2	5		9			12	8			4	13		3	14	26
27	Dec	31	(a)	Ipswich Town	L 0-1	-	23957		13			1	11	6			7	10	2	5					12				4	14		3	9	27
28	Jan	2	(h)	WATFORD	L 1-2	Edwards	10248		6			1	11				7	13	2	5		9				8			4	12		3	10	28
29	Jan	13	(a)	Wolverhampton Wanderers	L 1-2	Howard	21823				1		11	6			7	12	2	5		9				8			4			3	10	29
30	Jan	21	(h)	QUEENS PARK RANGERS	W 2-0	Heikkinen, Howard	9797		12		1		11	6			7	13	2	5		9			14				4			3	10	30
31	Jan	31	(a)	Sheffield Wednesday	W 2-0	Nicholls (pen), Vine	23965		13		1		11	6			7	12	2	5		9			14				4			3	10	31
32	Feb	4	(h)	HULL CITY	L 2-3	Keane, Coyne	8835			13	1		11	6			7	14	2	5		9	3		12	8			4				10	32
33	Feb	11	(a)	Preston North End	L 1-5	Mears (og)	15237		12	4	1		11	6		14	7		2			9	3		13	8							10	33
34	Feb	14	(h)	CARDIFF CITY	D 3-3	Vine (2), Barker (og)	7826		6		1		7	3					2	4	5	12	9		11	8							10	34
35	Feb	21	(h)	READING	W 3-2	Vine (2), Morgan	8705		6		1		7			3	2	12		4	5	13	9		11	8				14			10	35
36	Feb	25	(a)	Leeds United	L 1-2	Howard	23644		5		1		7	6		3	2	12		4		9			11	8				13		3	10	36
37	Mar	4	(a)	Millwall	L 1-2	Coyne	9871				1		11	6			2	12	7	5	4	9			13	8				14		3	10	37
38	Mar	11	(h)	LEICESTER CITY	L 1-2	Howard	9783		5	12	1		11	6		3	7	13	2	4		9				8				14		11	10	38
39	Mar	18	(h)	DERBY COUNTY	W 1-0	Howard	9163		12		1		11	6		3	7	10	2	5		9					5	4			8	13		39
40	Mar	25	(a)	Brighton & Hove Albion	D 1-1	Robinson	7139		12		1		11	6		3	7	10	2	5		9							4	14	8	13		40
41	Apr	1	(h)	IPSWICH TOWN	W 1-0	Howard	9820				1		13	6		3	7	12	2	8		9			11		5		4	14		10		41
42	Apr	9	(a)	Watford	D 1-1	Brkovic	15922		12		1		11			3	7	10	2			9			14			6	4	8		13		42
43	Apr	15	(h)	COVENTRY CITY	L 1-2	Williams (og)	8752	3	14		1		11	6			7	10	2	5	4		12		13	8						9		43
44	Apr	17	(a)	Plymouth Argyle	W 2-1	Vine, Andrew	13486	14	6	7	1		13				2	10		5	4				11	8					3	12		44
45	Apr	22	(h)	SHEFFIELD UNITED	D 1-1	Brkovic	10248		5	12	1		7				2	10			4	6			11	13			8		3	9		45
46	Apr	29	(a)	Burnley	D 1-1	Vine	12473		5	14	1		7					10	2		12	6	3		11	8			4	13			10	46
				Apps				-	12	2	41	5	39	28	6	17	38	29	35	38	16	40	5	-	25	31	-	9	26	15	-	28	21	
				Subs				1	8	7	-	5	3	2	-	4	4	13	3	1	7	3	5	-	11	1	-	2	-	26	1	1	10	
				Goals				1	-	-	-	-	8	2	1	-	2	6	-	2	2	14	1	-	6	5	-	-	2	1	-	-	10	

Final League Position: 10th   3 Own Goals

2005/06 FA CUP

Round	Month	Day	Venue	Opponents	W,L,D Score	Scorers	Attendance	Andrew C	Barnett L	Bell D	Beresford M	Brill D	Brkovic A	Coyne C	Davies C	Davis Sol	Edwards C	Feeney W	Foley K	Heikkinen M	Holmes P	Howard S	Keane K	Leary M	Morgan D	Nicholls K	O'Leary S	Perrett R	Robinson S	Showunmi E	Stevens D	Underwood P	Vine R	Round
3	Jan	7	(h)	LIVERPOOL	L 3-5	Howard, Robinson, Nicholls (pen)	10170	12	1				11	6			7	13	2	5		9				8			4	14		3	10	3
						Apps		-	-	1	1	1	1	1		1	1	1	1		1			1			1		1			1	1	
						Subs		-	1								1									1			1		1			
						Goals		-	-									1				1				1			1					

2005/06 CARLING CUP (LEAGUE CUP)

Round	Month	Day	Venue	Opponents	W,L,D Score	Scorers	Attendance	Andrew C	Barnett L	Bell D	Beresford M	Brill D	Brkovic A	Coyne C	Davies C	Davis Sol	Edwards C	Feeney W	Foley K	Heikkinen M	Holmes P	Howard S	Keane K	Leary M	Morgan D	Nicholls K	O'Leary S	Perrett R	Robinson S	Showunmi E	Stevens D	Underwood P	Vine R	Round
1	Aug	23	(a)	Leyton Orient	W 3-1	Coyne, Feeney, Alexander (og)	2383		1					5	6	3	7	10			13		2	4	11	8	14	12		9				1
2	Sep	20	(a)	Reading	L 0-1	-	6941	6			1		7	5		3	2	10			4	9	12		11	8								2
						1 Own Goal — Apps		1	-	1	1	1	1	2	1	2	2	2		1	1	1	1	1	2	2								
						Subs		-	-											1		1					1	1						
						Goals		-	-					1			1																	

▶ Past players return in September 2005 to celebrate '100 years at Kenilworth Road'. Back row (left to right): Ron Baynham, Dave Pacey, Alan Daniel, Billy Waugh, Steve Buckley, Mike Cullen, Mike Keen, Max Dougan, Terry Branston, Bernard Moore, Jack Bannister, John Moore, Seamus Dunne, Bobby Thomson, Tony Gregory, Ray Smith, Ken Hawkes, Terry Kelly, Billy Bingham, Kirk Stephens. Front row (left to right): Jimmy Husband, Alan West, Julian James, Kingsley Black, Wally Shanks.

TIMELINE...

1 September 2005 Curtis Davies is sold to West Brom for £3 million – a new Luton record.

2006/07 FOOTBALL LEAGUE CHAMPIONSHIP (SECOND TIER)

Match No	Month	Day	Venue	Opponents	W,L,D Score	Scorers	Attendance	Andrew C	Barnett L	Bell D	Beresford M	Boyd A	Brill D	Brkovic A	Carlisle C	Coyne C	Davis Sol	Edwards C	Emanuel L	Feeney W	Foley K	Heikkinen M	Holmes P	Idrizaj B	Keane K	Kiely D	Langley R	Morgan D	O'Leary S	Parkin S	Perrett R	Robinson S	Runstrom B	Spring M	Talbot D	Vine R	Match No
1	Aug	5	(h)	LEICESTER CITY	W 2-0	Barnett, Edwards	8131		6	1	12						3	7	11	10	2	5					8	13				4				9	1
2	Aug	8	(a)	Sheffield Wednesday	W 1-0	Emanuel	22613		6	1	12					13	3	7	11	10	2	5					8					4				9	2
3	Aug	12	(a)	Norwich City	L 2-3	Vine, Morgan	23863		6	1	14					12	3	7	11	10	2	5					8	13				4				9	3
4	Aug	19	(h)	STOKE CITY	D 2-2	Barnett, Langley (pen)	7727		6	1							5	3	7	11	10	2	4				8	12								9	4
5	Aug	26	(a)	Wolverhampton Wanderers	L 0-1	-	19378										3	7	11	10	2	5					8	12		13		4				9	5
6	Sep	9	(h)	CRYSTAL PALACE	W 2-1	Edwards, Vine	9187										3	7	11	12	2	5					8			10		4				9	6
7	Sep	12	(h)	COLCHESTER UNITED	D 1-1	Parkin	7609										3	7	11		2	5					8			10		4				9	7
8	Sep	16	(a)	Cardiff City	L 1-4	Vine	14108									12	3	7	11		2	5					8	13		10		4				9	8
9	Sep	23	(h)	WEST BROMWICH ALBION	D 2-2	Vine (2)	9332			1				13				7	3	12	2	5					8	11		10		4				9	9
10	Sep	30	(a)	Barnsley	W 2-1	Edwards, Brkovic	10175			1				13				7	3		2	5					8	11		10		4				9	10
11	Oct	14	(h)	BIRMINGHAM CITY	W 3-2	Vine (2, 1 pen), Bell	9275		6	13							3	7	11	14	2	5					12	8		10		4				9	11
12	Oct	17	(a)	Hull City	D 0-0	-	14895		6	7	1						3				2	5					8	11	14	10		4				9	12
13	Oct	21	(h)	LEEDS UNITED	W 5-1	Edwards (2), Vine, Bell, Heikkinen	10260		6	1		13					3	7		10	2	5			14		11	12				4				9	13
14	Oct	29	(a)	Ipswich Town	L 0-5	-	20975		6	8		13		12				7	3	10	2				5		11					4	14			9	14
15	Oct	31	(h)	BURNLEY	L 0-2	-	7664		6	13	1	12		7						2					10		8	11				4				9	15
16	Nov	4	(a)	Preston North End	L 0-3	-	13094		6	13	1	10	12	14				7			2	5			3		8	11				4				9	16
17	Nov	11	(h)	QUEENS PARK RANGERS	L 2-3	Boyd, Brkovic	9007		6	8		10	1	11				7	3	13	2	5						12				4				9	17
18	Nov	18	(h)	DERBY COUNTY	L 0-2	-	9708		6	14		10	1	11				7	3	13	2	5						12			5	4				9	18
19	Nov	25	(a)	Southampton	L 1-2	Perrett	20482		6	13				10				7	3	9	2	8				1		12			5	4				9	19
20	Nov	28	(a)	Plymouth Argyle	L 0-1	-	9965		6	12				11				7	3	10	2					1		13			5	4				9	20
21	Dec	2	(h)	PRESTON NORTH END	W 2-0	Vine, Edwards	7665		6	8				11				7	3	12	2	5				1		10			13	4				9	21
22	Dec	9	(a)	Sunderland	L 1-2	Morgan	30445		6	8		13		11				7	3	12	2	5				1		10				4				9	22
23	Dec	15	(h)	SOUTHEND UNITED	D 0-0	-	7468		6	8				11		13		7	3	12	2	5				1		10				4				9	23
24	Dec	23	(h)	COVENTRY CITY	W 3-1	Brkovic, Vine, Morgan	8299		6	8				11		12		7	3	13	2	5			14	1		10				4				9	24
25	Dec	26	(a)	Colchester United	L 1-4	Vine (pen)	5427		4	8				11		6	13	7	3	12	2	5				1		10								9	25
26	Dec	29	(a)	Birmingham City	D 2-2	Vine, Feeney	24642		4							6	12	7	3	10	2	5	13			1		8								9	26
27	Jan	1	(h)	CARDIFF CITY	D 0-0	-	8004		6	8		13		7					3	12					14	1	4	11		5						9	27
28	Jan	12	(a)	West Bromwich Albion	L 2-3	Keane, Feeney	19927			8		13		7		6	3		11	10					2	1	12	9		5		4					28
29	Jan	20	(h)	BARNSLEY	L 0-2	-	7441			6	7	12		13		5	3		11	10					2	1	8	9			14	4					29
30	Jan	30	(a)	Coventry City	L 0-1	-	18781			7		12	1			5			11		2				6		10			5	4						30
31	Feb	3	(a)	Leicester City	D 1-1	Morgan	20410			7	1	14					3		11		2				6		13	12		5	4	9	8	10		31
32	Feb	17	(a)	Stoke City	D 0-0	-	12375			7	1	10					3		12		2	5			13		14	11		6	4	9	8	10		32
33	Feb	20	(h)	SHEFFIELD WEDNESDAY	W 3-2	Runstrom, Spurr (og), Talbot	8011			7	1	13							3		2	5			6		12	11			4	9	8	10		33
34	Feb	24	(a)	Crystal Palace	L 1-2	Hudson (og)	16177			6	11	1							3						5		7	12			4	9	8	10		34
35	Feb	27	(h)	NORWICH CITY	L 2-3	Runstrom, Talbot	8868			6	11	1							3	12	7	5			2						4	9	8	10		35
36	Mar	3	(h)	WOLVERHAMPTON WANDERERS	L 2-3	Emanuel, Barnett	10002			6	11	1			12				3	13	7	5			2						4	9	8	10		36
37	Mar	10	(a)	Leeds United	L 0-1	-	27138			8	7	1			6		3		11	10		5			2				13		4	9			12		37
38	Mar	13	(h)	HULL CITY	L 1-2	Talbot	7777			10	8	1	12		6		3		11	13	7	5			2			4	14						9		38
39	Mar	17	(h)	IPSWICH TOWN	L 0-2	-	8880			6	11				5	12			3	13	7	5			2						4	14			9		39
40	Mar	31	(a)	Burnley	D 0-0	-	11088	14		6	7			1		5	12	3			13	4			2			11				8		10	9		40
41	Apr	7	(h)	SOUTHAMPTON	L 0-2	-	9171	12					1	7		6			3		4	5			13	2		14	11			8		10	9		41
42	Apr	9	(a)	Queens Park Rangers	L 2-3	Bell (2, 1pen)	14360	9		11			1	7		6			3			5			14	2	12	13	12			4		8	10		42
43	Apr	14	(h)	PLYMOUTH ARGYLE	L 1-2	O'Leary	7601	9		6	11			1		5			3		7				13	2		14	12			4		8	10		43
44	Apr	20	(a)	Derby County	L 0-1	-	28499	9		6	11			1		5			3		2	4			12			13	7					8	10		44
45	Apr	28	(a)	Southend United	W 3-1	Andrew, Spring, Idrizaj	10276	9		6	11			1		5	12		3		2	4		10	14				7					8	13		45
46	May	6	(h)	SUNDERLAND	L 0-5	-	10260	9		6	11			1	13	5			3			4		10	2			12			7			8			46

Final League Position: 23rd   2 Own Goals

							Apps	5	39	28	26	5	9	14	4	11	20	26	39	15	38	37	3	3	17	11	18	21	5	7	8	37	7	14	13	26	
							Subs	2	-	6	-	13	2	6	1	7	4	-	1	14	1	-	-	2	4	-	2	11	15	2	1	3	1	1	-	2	
							Goals	1	3	4	-	1	-	3	-	-	-	6	2	2	-	1	-	1	1	-	1	4	1	1	1	-	2	1	3	12	

2006/07 FA CUP

Round	Month	Day	Venue	Opponents	W,L,D	Score	Scorers	Attendance	Andrew C	Barnett L	Bell D	Beresford M	Boyd A	Brill D	Brkovic A	Carlisle C	Coyne C	Davis Sol	Edwards C	Emanuel L	Feeney W	Foley K	Heikkinen M	Holmes P	Idrizaj B	Keane K	Kiely D	Langley R	Morgan D	O'Leary S	Parkin S	Perrett R	Robinson S	Runstrom B	Spring M	Talbot D	Vine R	Round
3	Jan	6	(a)	Queens Park Rangers	D	2-2	Vine, Feeney	10064	2		1				7		6	3		10								8	11			5	4				9	3
Rep	Jan	23	(h)	QUEENS PARK RANGERS	W	1-0	Rehman (og)	7494		10		9		1	7		6	3	11		2							8	12			5	4					Rep
4	Jan	27	(h)	BLACKBURN ROVERS	L	0-4	-	5887		7		1	9				6	3	11		2					12		8	13	14		5	4			10		4
							1 Own Goal	Apps	1	2	1	2	1	1	2		3	3	2	1	2							3	1			3	3			1	1	
								Subs																		1			2	1						1		
								Goals													1																1	

2006/07 CARLING CUP (LEAGUE CUP)

Round	Month	Day	Venue	Opponents	W,L,D	Score	Scorers	Attendance	Andrew C	Barnett L	Bell D	Beresford M	Boyd A	Brill D	Brkovic A	Carlisle C	Coyne C	Davis Sol	Edwards C	Emanuel L	Feeney W	Foley K	Heikkinen M	Holmes P	Idrizaj B	Keane K	Kiely D	Langley R	Morgan D	O'Leary S	Parkin S	Perrett R	Robinson S	Runstrom B	Spring M	Talbot D	Vine R	Round
1	Aug	22	(a)	Bristol Rovers	D	1-1	Boyd	2882	6	7	1		9		11		5	3	12		13			8		2			10	4							14	1
2	Sep	19	(a)	Brentford	W	3-0	Morgan, Feeney, Vine	3005	6	8	1		9		7		5	3	12	10	13					2			11	4							14	2
3	Oct	24	(a)	Everton	L	0-4	-	27149	6	4	1		13		14			3	7	10	2	5							11	12			8				9	3
								Apps	3	3	3		2		2		2	3	1	2	1	1		1		2			3	2			1				1	
								Subs					1		1				2		2									1							2	
								Goals					1								1								1								1	

1st Round won 5-3 on penalties aet.

◗ The Town move up to fifth in the Championship following a 5-1 win over **Leeds** - a high point. Marcus Heikkinen heads home goal number five.

TIMELINE...

15 March 2007 Manager Mike Newell is dismissed – coach Brian Stein is handed a caretaker role.
27 March 2007 Luton boy Kevin Blackwell is the new manager at Kenilworth Road.
6 May 2007 The Town are relegated from the Championship.

▶ The 2005/06 team – Back row (left to right): Underwood, Keane, Barnett, Leary, Davies, Vine, Foley, Andrew, Edwards, Stevens. Middle row (left to right): Murray (Physiotherapist), Kharine (Coach), Stein (Coach), Hughes, O'Leary, Showunmi, Beckwith, Seremet, Brill, Beresford, Howard, Coyne, Heikkinen, Johnson (Coach), Bowden (Physiotherapist), Catlin (Kit Man). Front row (left to right): Morgan, Holmes, Brkovic, Nicholls, Tomlins (Chairman), Newell (Manager), Perrett, Robinson, Davis, Feeney.

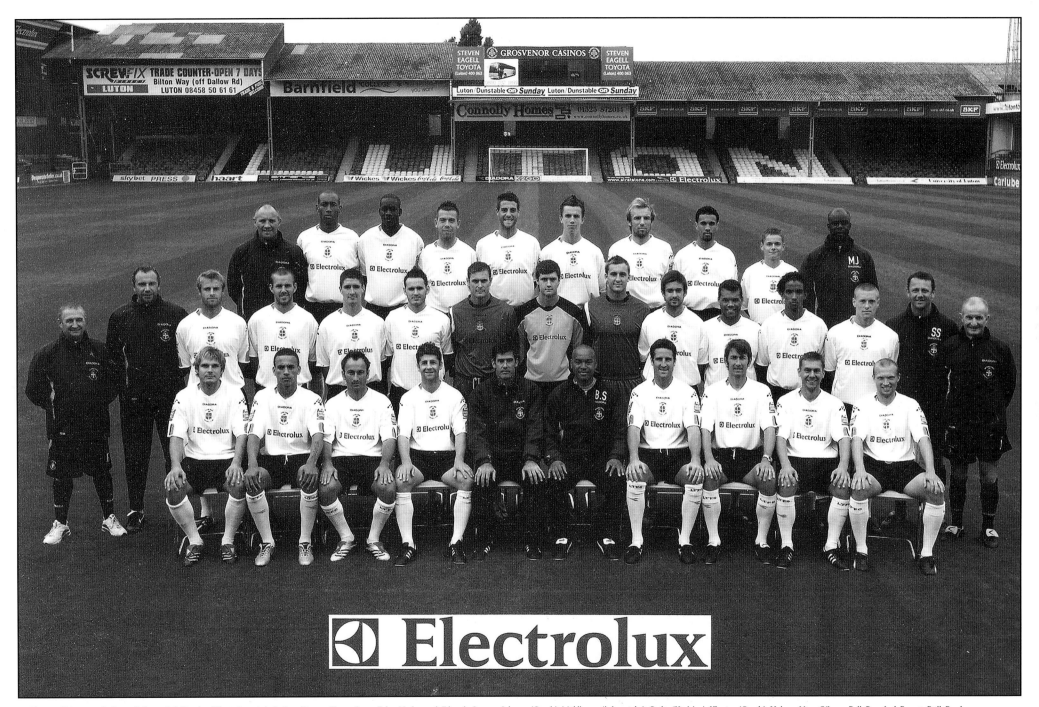

▶ **The 2006/07 team** – Back row (left to right): Bowden (Physiotherapist), Andrew, Barnett, Keane, Leary, Foley, Underwood, Edwards, Stevens, Johnson (Coach). Middle row (left to right): Catlin (Kit Man), Kharine (Coach), Holmes, Vine, O'Leary, Bell, Beresford, Barrett, Brill, Boyd, Emanuel, Langley, Pendleton, Sedgley (Coach), Murray (Physiotherapist). Front row (left to right): Heikkinen, Morgan, Brkovic, Robinson, Newell (Manager), Stein (Assistant Manager), Coyne, Perrett, Davis, Feeney.

2007/08 FOOTBALL LEAGUE ONE (THIRD TIER)

Match No	Month	Day	Venue	Opponents	W,L,D Score	Scorers	Attendance	Alnwick B	Andrew C	Asafu-Adjaye E	Beavan G	Bell D	Brill D	Brkovic A	Charles R	Coyne C	Currie D	Davis Sol	Edwards D	Emanuel L	Fojut J	Forde D	Furlong P	Goodall A	Grant A	Howells J	Hutchison Don	Jackson R	Keane K	Langley R	McVeigh P	Morgan D	O'Leary S	Parkin S	Perry C	Peschisolido P	Robinson S	Spring M	Talbot D	Wilson M	Match No
1	Aug	11	(h)	HARTLEPOOL UNITED	W 2-1	Currie, Goodall	8013						1			6	11		7				9	3			14	2			13				12	5	10	4	8		1
2	Aug	18	(a)	Swindon Town	L 1-2	Edwards	7520						1			6	11		7				9	3				2			12	14			5	10	4	8	13		2
3	Aug	25	(h)	GILLINGHAM	W 3-1	Bell, Furlong, Spring (pen)	6178		13			11				6	7		4			1	9	3				2			12				5			8	10		3
4	Sep	1	(a)	Leeds United	L 0-1	-	26856		14			11				6	7		4			1	9	3					2		13	12			5			8	10		4
5	Sep	8	(h)	BRISTOL ROVERS	L 1-2	Spring (pen)	6131					11				6	7					1	9	3			14	2			13				5	12		4	8	10	5
6	Sep	14	(a)	Tranmere Rovers	L 1-2	Furlong	6525					7		12		6			10		13	1	9	3				2			11				5	14	4	8			6
7	Sep	22	(h)	PORT VALE	W 2-1	Furlong, Bell	6084		14			7				6	12	10				1	9	3				2			13	11			5			4	8		7
8	Sep	29	(a)	Huddersfield Town	L 0-2	-	9028	1	14			7					12			6			9	3				2			10	11			5			4	8		8
9	Oct	2	(a)	Yeovil Town	D 0-0	-	4848	1	9			7				6	11	10			5			3				2										4	8	12	9
10	Oct	6	(h)	DONCASTER ROVERS	D 1-1	Furlong	6513	1	10							6	11		7				9	3				12			13				5			4	8		10
11	Oct	15	(h)	NORTHAMPTON TOWN	W 4-1	Currie, Spring (2 pens), Furlong	5881		12			7	1				11			6			9	3			4	2							5				8	10	11
12	Oct	20	(a)	Crewe Alexandra	L 0-2	-	4490	1	10			7					11			13			9	3				4			12				5		14		8		12
13	Oct	27	(h)	NOTTINGHAM FOREST	W 2-1	Perry, Bell	8524					7	1			6	12	10			5		9	3				2							5		14		8		13
14	Nov	3	(a)	Brighton & Hove Albion	L 1-3	Edwards	5317		9			7	1			6	11	10			5			3			14	13			12				2				4		14
15	Nov	6	(h)	CARLISLE UNITED	D 0-0	-	5462		9			7	1			6	11	10			5												13		2			4	8		15
16	Nov	17	(a)	Walsall	D 0-0	-	5056		9			7	1			6					5						4	3			10				2				8	11	16
17	Nov	24	(h)	SOUTHEND UNITED	W 1-0	Andrew	6820		9			7	1			6	13	11			5					12		3	2		10								8		17
18	Dec	4	(a)	Oldham Athletic	D 1-1	Fojut	4251		10			7	1			6	13	11			5				14			3	2										8		18
19	Dec	14	(a)	Cheltenham Town	L 0-1	-	3702		14			7	1			6	7						9					3	13						5		4		8	10	19
20	Dec	22	(h)	TRANMERE ROVERS	W 1-0	Edwards	6070		12			7	1			6	11		10		5		9	3				2									4		8	13	20
21	Dec	26	(a)	Bristol Rovers	D 1-1	Edwards	7556		9			7	1			6			10		5							3	11								4		8		21
22	Dec	29	(a)	Port Vale	W 2-1	Fojut, Spring	4224		9			7	1				11	4		6			12				14				13				2				8	10	22
23	Jan	1	(h)	YEOVIL TOWN	W 1-0	Andrew	6811		9			7	1				11	4		6			13					3			12				2				8	10	23
24	Jan	12	(h)	SWANSEA CITY	L 1-3	Furlong	6756		9			7	1				11						13	3			8	2	6			12			5				10		24
25	Jan	19	(a)	Leyton Orient	L 1-2	Keane	5516		9				1				11			14				3			6		2		12				5		4		10		25
26	Jan	22	(a)	Bournemouth	L 3-4	Spring (pen), Morgan, Furlong	3489		13				1				11						9	3			6	2			7	12			5		4		8	10	26
27	Jan	26	(h)	LEEDS UNITED	D 1-1	Parkin	9756		10				1				11						9	3				2	6		12	14	13	5			4		8	7	27
28	Jan	29	(h)	SWINDON TOWN	L 0-1	-	5738		10			4	1				11						9	3				2	6		12	14	13	5					8	7	28
29	Feb	2	(a)	Hartlepool United	L 0-4	-	3913		13			11	1					3					9	14			8		6		12			5			4		10	7	29
30	Feb	9	(h)	BOURNEMOUTH	L 1-4	Emanuel	5897		13			7	1	12					11	3	2								6		10		9				4		8	14	30
31	Feb	16	(h)	LEYTON ORIENT	L 0-1	-	6412		10		6	7	1							3	2							12	5		11	9									31
32	Feb	22	(a)	Swansea City	L 0-1	-	14122		14			7	1					3		11							12	13	2		6	9			5		4		8	10	32
33	Feb	26	(h)	MILLWALL	D 1-1	Furlong	6417		13			7	1							3			9	12				2	6		14	11	4		5				8	10	33
34	Mar	1	(h)	WALSALL	L 0-1	-	6157		12			7	1							3			9	13				2	6		7	11	14	5							34
35	Mar	8	(a)	Southend United	L 0-2	-	8241		13			7	1	12						3			9	3				2	6		11		14	5	4				8	10	35
36	Mar	11	(a)	Carlisle United	L 1-2	Bell	5489					4	1		10	3				11			9						6		7		13	5					8	12	36
37	Mar	15	(h)	OLDHAM ATHLETIC	W 3-0	Charles, Spring (pen), Emanuel	5417					4	1		10	3				11			9					13	2	6	7	14	12	5					8		37
38	Mar	22	(h)	CHELTENHAM TOWN	D 1-1	Parkin	6087		14			4	1		10	3				11								2	6		7	13	9	5					8	12	38
39	Mar	24	(a)	Millwall	D 0-0	-	8375		12			11	1		10	3												5	2		7		4	9					8		39
40	Mar	29	(h)	CREWE ALEXANDRA	W 2-1	Spring (2, 1 pen)	5465		12	2			1		10	3												5	6		7		4	9					8		40
41	Apr	1	(a)	Gillingham	L 1-2	Parkin	6412		12	2			1		10	3												5	6		7		4	9					8		41
42	Apr	5	(a)	Northampton Town	L 1-2	Parkin	5132		10	2							12	3		11								5	6		7		4	9					8		42
43	Apr	12	(h)	BRIGHTON & HOVE ALBION	L 1-2	Parkin	6652		10	2							12	3		11								5	6		7		4	9				13	8		43
44	Apr	19	(a)	Nottingham Forest	L 0-1	-	17331		12	2						7		3		11								5	6		10		4	9					8		44
45	Apr	26	(a)	Doncaster Rovers	L 0-2	-	9332		13	2						7		3		11								5	6		10		4	9				12	8		45
46	May	3	(h)	HUDDERSFIELD TOWN	L 0-1	-	6539		10	6						7		3		11					13	14		5	2				9	12					8		46
				Apps				4	19	7	1	32	37	-	6	18	25	15	18	15	15	5	24	25	1	-	15	27	27	-	15	8	10	12	35	2	24	44	16	4	
				Subs				-	20	-	1	-	-	1	1	-	6	-	1	2	1	-	8	4	3	1	6	2	1	1	10	8	6	7	-	2	3	-	11	-	
				Goals				-	2	-	-	4	-	-	1	-	2	-	4	2	2	-	8	1	-	-	1	-	1	-	-	1	-	5	1	-	9	-	-	

Final League Position: 24th

2007/08 FA CUP

Round	Month	Day	Venue	Opponents	W,L,D Score	Scorers	Attendance	Alnwick B	Andrew C	Asafu-Adjaye E	Beavan G	Bell D	Brill D	Brkovic A	Charles R	Coyne C	Currie D	Davis Sol	Edwards D	Emanuel L	Fojut J	Forde D	Furlong P	Goodall A	Grant A	Howells J	Hutchison Don	Jackson R	Keane K	Langley R	McVeigh P	Morgan D	O'Leary S	Parkin S	Perry C	Peschisolido P	Robinson S	Spring M	Talbot D	Wilson M	Round
1	Nov	10	(h)	BRENTFORD	D 1-1	Andrew	4167		12			7	1			6	11		10	5			9	14				3							2		4	8	13		1
Rep	Nov	27	(a)	Brentford	W 2-0	Coyne, Fojut	2643		9			7	1			6	12		8	5							4	3	13		14				2			11	10		Rep
2	Dec	11	(h)	NOTTINGHAM FOREST	W 1-0	Andrew	5758		9			7	1			6	11		10	5					12			3							2		4	8			2
3	Jan	6	(h)	LIVERPOOL	D 1-1	Riise (og)	10226		9			7	1			6	11		4			3												2	5			8	10		3
Rep	Jan	15	(a)	Liverpool	L 0-5		41446		9			7	1				11				13	3					6	2	5		14			12			4	8	10		Rep
						1 Own Goal	Apps		4			5	5			4	4		4	3		1					2	4	2						4		3	5	3		
							Subs		1								1			1	1	1	1					1		2		1					1		
							Goals		2							1					1																			

2007/08 CARLING CUP (LEAGUE CUP)

Round	Month	Day	Venue	Opponents	W,L,D Score	Scorers	Attendance	Alnwick B	Andrew C	Asafu-Adjaye E	Beavan G	Bell D	Brill D	Brkovic A	Charles R	Coyne C	Currie D	Davis Sol	Edwards D	Emanuel L	Fojut J	Forde D	Furlong P	Goodall A	Grant A	Howells J	Hutchison Don	Jackson R	Keane K	Langley R	McVeigh P	Morgan D	O'Leary S	Parkin S	Perry C	Peschisolido P	Robinson S	Spring M	Talbot D	Wilson M	Round
1	Aug	14	(a)	Dagenham & Redbridge	W 2-1	Spring (pen), Talbot	1754						1			6			7	3			12				4	2	5		13	11	9				8	10		1
2	Aug	28	(h)	SUNDERLAND	W 3-0	Bell, Furlong (2)	4401	14				11				6				1	9	3					2	12			13	7			5		4	8	10		2
3	Sep	25	(h)	CHARLTON ATHLETIC	W 3-1	Robinson, Spring, Talbot	4534				7	1	14			12				6			9	3				2			10	11			5		4	8	13		3
4	Oct	31	(h)	EVERTON	L 0-1	-	8944	12				7	1			6	11		10	5			9	3							14	13			2		4	8			4
							Apps					3	3			3	1		2	1		1	3	3			1	3	1		1	3			3		3	4	2		
							Subs		2						1															1					3			1		
							Goals					1											2													1	2	1		

2007/08 JOHNSTONE'S PAINT TROPHY (ASSOCIATE MEMBERS CUP)

Round	Month	Day	Venue	Opponents	W,L,D Score	Scorers	Attendance	Alnwick B	Andrew C	Asafu-Adjaye E	Beavan G	Bell D	Brill D	Brkovic A	Charles R	Coyne C	Currie D	Davis Sol	Edwards D	Emanuel L	Fojut J	Forde D	Furlong P	Goodall A	Grant A	Howells J	Hutchison Don	Jackson R	Keane K	Langley R	McVeigh P	Morgan D	O'Leary S	Parkin S	Perry C	Peschisolido P	Robinson S	Spring M	Talbot D	Wilson M	Round
1	Sep	4	(h)	NORTHAMPTON TOWN	W 2-0	Hutchison, Peschisolido	2532	9			11	1	7							6			3				4		2		12	14		5	13	8			10		1
2	Oct	9	(a)	Gillingham	L 3-4	Furlong (2), Spring (pen)	1417	10				1	12					7	3	6		9					4	2			11			5				8	14		2
							Apps		2			1	2	1					1	1	1		1				2	1	1		1			2		1	1	1	1		
							Subs						1														1				1	1	1							
							Goals															2											1				1			

TIMELINE...

22 November 2007 The club is placed into administration for a third time in less than ten years and take an immediate ten point penalty.

16 January 2008 Kevin Blackwell is dismissed with old favourite Mick Harford taking his place.

26 February 2008 LTFC2020 assume control of the club.

3 May 2008 A second successive relegation for the Hatters.

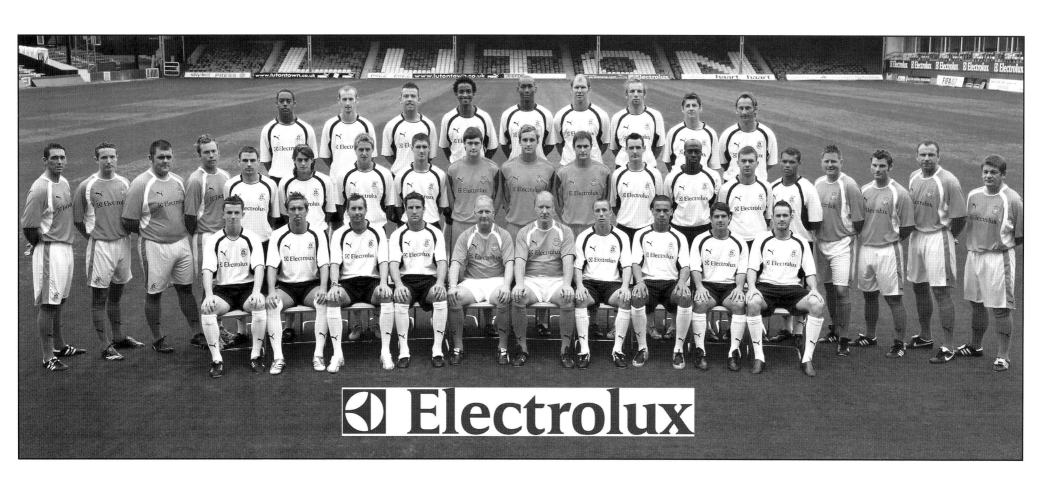

▶ **The 2007/08 team** – Back row (left to right): Asafu-Adjaye, Talbot, Keane, Langley, Andrew, Parkin, Underwood, Robinson, Brkovic. Middle row (left to right): Scott-Stackman (Physiotherapist), Edmondson (Physiotherapist), Bradley (Kit Manager), Gargiulo (Sports Scientist), Goodall, Sinclair, Edwards, O'Leary, Barrett, Brill, Beresford, Spring, Furlong, Davis, Emanuel, Cummins (Director of Youth Football), Lewis (Sports Scientist), Kharine (Coach), Carver (Coach).
Front row (left to right): Foley, Currie, Hutchison, Coyne, Blackwell (Manager), Ellis (Assistant Manager), Perry, Morgan, Peschisolido, Bell.

▶ **The 2008/09 team** – Back row (left to right): Asafu-Adjaye, Beavan, Spillane, Gnakpa, Watson, Emanuel. Middle row (left to right): Scott-Stackman (Physiotherapist), Bannister (Kit Manager), McVeigh, Davis, Pilkington, Brill, Logan, Roper, Hall, Charles, Dunbar (Fitness Coach), Kharine (Coach). Front row (left to right): Plummer, Keane, Nicholls, Harford (Manager), Neill (Assistant Manager), Jarvis, Parkin, Martin.

Match No	Month	Day	Venue	Opponents	W,L,D Score	Scorers	Attendance	Andrews W	Asafu-Adjaye E	Beavan G	Bower M	Brill D	Charles R	Craddock T	Davis Sol	Emanuel L	Gallen K	Gnakpa C	Hall A	Henderson I	Howells J	Jarvis R	Keane K	Klein-Davies J	Livermore D	Logan C	Martin C	McVeigh P	Nicholls K	O'Connor G	Parkin S	Patrick J	Pilkington G	Plummer T	Price L	Pugh M	Roper I	Sinclair S	Spillane M	Talbot D	Wasiu S-A	Watson K	Worley H	Match No
1	Aug	9	(h)	PORT VALE	L 1-3	Parkin	7149					1		3	11		2	4				7		13			10		8		9		6	12		5								1
2	Aug	16	(a)	Gillingham	W 1-0	Parkin	5339					1		3			2	4				11	7				10		8		9		6	13				5			12			2
3	Aug	23	(h)	NOTTS COUNTY	D 1-1	Martin	6085					1		3	11		2	4				7					10		8		9		6	12				5			13			3
4	Aug	30	(a)	Exeter City	W 1-0	Parkin	5328					1	12	3	11		7					4	2				10		8		9		6					5						4
5	Sep	6	(a)	Macclesfield Town	L 1-2	Charles	2349					1	12	3	11		7	13				4	2				9				6	14				5			8			5
6	Sep	13	(h)	ALDERSHOT TOWN	W 3-1	Spillane, Hall, Martin	6462					12			3		2	4				7	8		1	10		9		6	13		11		5			14			6
7	Sep	20	(a)	Rotherham United	L 0-1	-	4095		14			1	12		3		2	4				7	8		1	10		9				11		5			13	6		7
8	Sep	27	(h)	CHESTER CITY	D 1-1	Hall	5731					12		3	11		2	4				7	8		1	10						9		5				6		8
9	Oct	4	(a)	Bradford City	D 1-1	Spillane	13083		2					14	3	11	7	4		12	10	8		1	9	13					5				6		9
10	Oct	11	(h)	DARLINGTON	L 1-2	Gnakpa	5560		2					13			7	4		3	10	8		1	9			11				12		5			6		10
11	Oct	18	(h)	ACCRINGTON STANLEY	L 1-2	Hall	5492	12						10				4		3	7	8		1	9	13		11				5		2			6		11
12	Oct	21	(a)	Grimsby Town	D 2-2	Craddock (2, 1 pen)	4021							10	3		7	4			11	8	2		1	9	12			13	14			5		6			12
13	Oct	25	(a)	Bury	W 2-1	Craddock, Roper	3052	13						10	3		7	4			11	8	2		1	9	12						5		6		14		13
14	Nov	1	(a)	Shrewsbury Town	L 0-3	-	6188	12						10			7				3	8	2		1	9	11			13			5		4			6		14
15	Nov	15	(h)	DAGENHAM & REDBRIDGE	W 2-1	Davis, McVeigh	5402							3		10	2	13		11	12	4		1	9	7	8					5		6			15
16	Nov	22	(a)	Rochdale	L 0-2	-	2901									10	2	4			8	3		1	9	7	11					5		6		13	6		16
17	Nov	25	(a)	BRENTFORD	L 0-1	-	5248	12						3		10	2	4		11	13	8		1	7						5		6	9		17
18	Dec	2	(h)	BOURNEMOUTH	D 3-3	Parry (og), Gallen, McVeigh (pen)	6773							11	10	2	14		3	12	5		1	9	7	8		6				13	4		18
19	Dec	6	(h)	BARNET	W 3-1	McVeigh, Martin, Townsend (og)	5536	13							9	14	12		3	8	4		1	11	7		6				5		2	10		19
20	Dec	13	(a)	Wycombe Wanderers	D 0-0	-	5567	10		12					9				3	8	2		1	11	7						5		6			20
21	Dec	20	(h)	MORECAMBE	D 1-1	Spillane	5664	13	12						9	14	4		3	8	2		1	11	7						5		6	10		21
22	Dec	26	(a)	Chesterfield	D 2-2	Craddock, Roper	4243							10			9	12	4		11	8	2		1	13	7					5		6	14		22
23	Dec	28	(h)	LINCOLN CITY	W 3-2	Martin (2), Roper	6643			6				7		3	10	13			12	8	4		1	9					5		2	11		23
24	Jan	13	(a)	Chester City	D 2-2	Martin, Emanuel	1652			6				10	3	4				11	12	8	7		1	9					5		2			24
25	Jan	17	(a)	Darlington	L 1-5	Martin	3319		2	3				7			14	11	13	8	4		1	9						5		6		12		25
26	Jan	24	(h)	BRADFORD CITY	D 3-3	Hall (2), Wasiu	6053		2					3		10		4	7	14	8		1	11		12		13			5		6	9		26
27	Jan	27	(a)	Bournemouth	D 1-1	Hollands (og)	5230		3	6					12		10		4	13	14	11		1		8		9			5		2	7		27
28	Jan	31	(h)	BURY	L 1-2	Hall	5545		5	6					10	3		4	14	11	7	12		1		8		9					2	13		28
29	Feb	14	(a)	Dagenham & Redbridge	L 1-2	Henderson	2310		3					9			10	12	4	11		7				8		14		1		5		2	13		29
30	Feb	21	(h)	SHREWSBURY TOWN	W 3-1	Craddock, Parkin, Hall	5661		2	6	1	14		10	3		13	7	4		12	8	5			11		9					2			30
31	Feb	24	(a)	Accrington Stanley	D 0-0	-	1033		2	6	1			10	3		13	4		12	8	5			11		9					2			31
32	Feb	28	(a)	Port Vale	W 3-1	Hall, Gallen, Martin	5689		2	6	1			9	3		10	14	4	7		8	5			11						13		2			32
33	Mar	3	(h)	GILLINGHAM	D 0-0	-	5739		2	6	1			10	3		8		4	7			5			11							2			33
34	Mar	7	(h)	EXETER CITY	L 1-2	Craddock	6460		2	6	1	12		10	3		8		4	7	13		5			11		9				14				34
35	Mar	10	(a)	Notts County	W 2-0	Martin, Craddock (pen)	2886		2	6	1			9	3		10		4	7	12		8			11		13					6			35
36	Mar	14	(a)	Aldershot Town	L 1-2	Craddock	3098		2	5	1			9	3	12	10		4	7						11		13		14		6			36
37	Mar	17	(h)	GRIMSBY TOWN	W 2-1	Bower, Hall	5830			5	1			11		3	10		12	13	7	4				9	8		14		6		2			37
38	Mar	21	(h)	MACCLESFIELD TOWN	W 1-0	Craddock (pen)	5363			5	1			7	13	3			4	12		11				10	8		9		6		2			38
39	Mar	28	(a)	Morecambe	W 2-1	Martin, Gallen	2599			5	1			7		3	9		10			12	2		4	11	8				6			39
40	Mar	31	(h)	ROTHERHAM UNITED	L 2-4	Martin, Hall	5975			5	1			7		3	9		10			12	2	4		11	8		12		6			40
41	Apr	11	(a)	Lincoln City	D 0-0	-	4664		2	5	1			7		3	9	13	14				11	4		10		8				12			41
42	Apr	13	(h)	CHESTERFIELD	D 0-0	-	6494		2	5	1			11			7	10	12				4	3		9	8		6		13			42
43	Apr	18	(h)	Barnet	D 1-1	Jarvis	2808		5		1			9	3			10	12	14	7	4	11		8			13		6		2			43
44	Apr	21	(h)	WYCOMBE WANDERERS	L 0-1	-	6553				1			9	3	12	13		4	11		7	5		8		10				6		2			44
45	Apr	25	(h)	ROCHDALE	D 1-1	Craddock (pen)	7025				1			9		8			4	7	3		5		11		10			12		6		2			45
46	May	2	(a)	Brentford	L 0-2	-	10223				1	13		9		12	8		4	7	3		5		11		10					6		14	2		46

Final League Position: 24th   3 Own Goals

							Apps	1	17	3	16	23	-	27	22	17	26	19	35	14	14	31	40	-	8	22	39	9	16	3	15	-	18	-	1	3	18	-	35	4	2	2	6	
							Subs	6	2	1	-	-	10	-	2	3	3	8	7	5	14	4	-	-	1	-	1	4	3	-	8	2	-	5	-	1	1	4	3	3	4	2	
							Goals	-	-	-	1	-	1	10	1	1	3	1	10	1	-	1	-	-	1	-	-	4	-	-	-	-	3	-	3	1	-		

2008/09 FA CUP

Round	Month	Day	Venue	Opponents	W,L,D Score	Scorers	Attendance	Andrews W	Asafu-Adjaye E	Beavan G	Bower M	Brill D	Charles R	Craddock T	Davis Sol	Emanuel L	Gallen K	Gnakpa C	Hall A	Henderson I	Howells J	Jarvis R	Keane K	Klein-Davies J	Livermore D	Logan C	Martin C	McVeigh P	Nicholls K	O'Connor G	Parkin S	Patrick J	Pilkington G	Plummer T	Price L	Pugh M	Roper I	Sinclair S	Spillane M	Talbot D	Wasiu S-A	Watson K	Worley H	Round
1	Nov	8	(h)	ALTRINCHAM	D 0-0	-	3200	10		3								2			11	4	5			1	9	7	8	13									6	14		12		1
Rep	Nov	18	(a)	Altrincham	D 0-0	-	2397								12			2	10		3	13	4			1	9	7	8	11						5			6	14				Rep
2	Nov	29	(a)	Southend United	L 1-3	Spillane	4111	14							3	13		2	10		11	4				1	9	7						12		5			6			8		2
							Apps	1		1					1			3	2		3	2	2			3	3	3	2	1						2			3			1		
							Subs	1							1	1						1								1				1							2		1		
							Goals																																	1					

1st Round Replay won 4-2 on penalties aet.

2008/09 CARLING CUP (LEAGUE CUP)

Round	Month	Day	Venue	Opponents	W,L,D Score	Scorers	Attendance	Andrews W	Asafu-Adjaye E	Beavan G	Bower M	Brill D	Charles R	Craddock T	Davis Sol	Emanuel L	Gallen K	Gnakpa C	Hall A	Henderson I	Howells J	Jarvis R	Keane K	Klein-Davies J	Livermore D	Logan C	Martin C	McVeigh P	Nicholls K	O'Connor G	Parkin S	Patrick J	Pilkington G	Plummer T	Price L	Pugh M	Roper I	Sinclair S	Spillane M	Talbot D	Wasiu S-A	Watson K	Worley H	Round
1	Aug	12	(h)	PLYMOUTH ARGYLE	W 2-0	Jarvis, Plummer	2862			1					3	11		2	4			7	13				10		8	9	6			12				5				14		1
2	Aug	26	(a)	Reading	L 1-5	Charles	7498						13		3	11		2	14			12	5			1	10		8	9	6			7							4			2
							Apps			1					2	2		2	1			1	1			1	2		2	2	2			1				1			1		
							Subs						1						1			1	1											1							1		
							Goals						1									1												1									

2008/09 JOHNSTONE'S PAINT TROPHY (ASSOCIATE MEMBERS CUP)

Round	Month	Day	Venue	Opponents	W,L,D Score	Scorers	Attendance	Andrews W	Asafu-Adjaye E	Beavan G	Bower M	Brill D	Charles R	Craddock T	Davis Sol	Emanuel L	Gallen K	Gnakpa C	Hall A	Henderson I	Howells J	Jarvis R	Keane K	Klein-Davies J	Livermore D	Logan C	Martin C	McVeigh P	Nicholls K	O'Connor G	Parkin S	Patrick J	Pilkington G	Plummer T	Price L	Pugh M	Roper I	Sinclair S	Spillane M	Talbot D	Wasiu S-A	Watson K	Worley H	Round
2	Oct	7	(h)	BRENTFORD	D 2-2	Martin (2)	2029		2				10					7	4		3	8				1	9	14		11				12				13	5				6	2
3	Nov	4	(a)	Walsall	W 1-0	Jarvis	1844			3				10				2			11	8	4			1	9	7						12				5	6			14	13	3
ASF	Dec	16	(h)	COLCHESTER UNITED	W 1-0	Gnakpa	2368	11	2	12								7	10		3	8	4			1	13	14										5	6	9				ASF
AF1	Jan	20	(a)	Brighton & Hove Albion	D 0-0	-	6127		2									7	4		12	8	5			1	9	11				13				3			6	10				AF1
AF2	Feb	17	(h)	BRIGHTON & HOVE ALBION	D 1-1	Craddock	8711	6				1	14	10	3			7	12		13	8	4				11	9										5	2					AF2
F	Apr	5	(n)	Scunthorpe United	W 3-2	Martin, Craddock, Gnakpa	55378	5				1		9	3			12	10			7	4				11	8						13					6			2		F
							Apps	1	5	1		1	1	3	2	1		5	4		3	6	5			4	5	2	1		1	1		1		1		3	6	2		1	1
							Subs		1			1						1	1		2						1	2			1	2		1		1		1				1	1
							Goals							2				2				1					3																

2nd Round won 4-3 on penalties.
Area Final 2nd Leg won 4-3 on penalties.
Final played at Wembley, aet, 2-2 after 90 mins.

TIMELINE...

10 July 2008 The Football League hits the Town with a 20 point penalty for exiting administration without a CVA – this is on a top of an earlier 10 point penalty imposed by the FA for 'financial irregularities.'

11 August 2008 Eight of the 13 players on duty in the home defeat at the hands of Port Vale are making their Luton debut.

5 April 2009 The Hatters win the Johnstone's Paint Trophy at Wembley.

2 May 2009 The Town are relegated from the Football League.

❯ Happy Hatters at Wembley with the Johnstone's Paint Trophy.

▶ Chris Martin nets the Town's first goal in the final at Wembley.

▶ Tom Craddock knocks in number two.

▶ The winners!!!

2009/10 FOOTBALL CONFERENCE PREMIER (NON-LEAGUE)

Match No	Month	Day	Venue	Opponents	W/L/D Score	Scorers	Attendance	Asafu-Adjaye E	Barnes-Homer M	Basham S	Blackett S	Burgess A	Charles R	Craddock T	Donnelly G	Emanuel L	Gallen K	Gnakpa C	Gore S	Hall A	Hatch L	Heslop S	Howells J	Jarvis R	Keane K	Kovacs J	Murray F	Nathaniel T	Nelthorpe C	Newton A	Nicholls K	Nwokeji M	Pilkington G	Pilkington K	Reynolds C	Tyler M	Watkins A	White A	Wright B	Match No
1	Aug	8	(a)	AFC Wimbledon	D 1-1	Craddock (pen)	4488			13	5	11		9	3		10			8			12	14	4					7			6		2	1				1
2	Aug	11	(h)	MANSFIELD TOWN	W 4-1	Pilkington (2), Perry (og), Craddock (pen)	7295			12		11		9			10	14		8			13	4	5		3			7			6		2	1				2
3	Aug	15	(h)	GATESHEAD	W 2-1	Hall, Gallen	6829			12	5	7		9			10	13		8		11		4	2		3						6			1				3
4	Aug	18	(a)	Forest Green Rovers	W 1-0	Craddock	1805			13	3	11		9			10			8			12	4	2		7						6		2	1		5		4
5	Aug	29	(a)	Kettering Town	D 0-0	-	3266			12	11			9	13		10						14	4	2		3			7	8		6			1		5		5
6	Sep	1	(h)	CRAWLEY TOWN	W 3-0	Pilkington (2), Craddock	6389			13				9	14		10	2		12			4	11			3			7	8		6			1		5		6
7	Sep	5	(a)	Salisbury City	D 1-1	Gallen	2044			14	13			11			9	2		12			10	4			3			7	8		6			1		5		7
8	Sep	8	(a)	Oxford United	L 0-2	-	10613				3			11	13		9			10				4	2		12			7	8		6			1		5		8
9	Sep	12	(h)	BARROW	W 1-0	Newton	6264							11			9	2		10	12			4	8		3			7			6			1		5		9
10	Sep	22	(h)	Wrexham	L 0-3	-	3448			12			13	11	14		10	2		8	9			4			3			7			6			1		5		10
11	Sep	26	(a)	Cambridge United	W 4-3	Gallen (2, 1pen), Jarvis, Howells	4870			13				14			10	2		8	9		11	4			3			7			6		12	1		5		11
12	Sep	29	(h)	STEVENAGE BOROUGH	L 0-1	-	8223	2				14		9			12	10					11	4			3			7	8		6			1		5	13	12
13	Oct	3	(h)	TAMWORTH	W 2-1	Hall, Wright	6297	2				14	13				12			4	9		11				3			7	8		6			1		5	10	13
14	Oct	10	(a)	Kidderminster Harriers	W 2-1	Newton, Charles	2927	2					13	9			12			4			14	11			3			7	8		6			1		5	10	14
15	Oct	17	(a)	Altrincham	W 1-0	Craddock (pen)	1762	2					12	9				7		11			3							4	8		6	13		1		5	10	15
16	Oct	20	(h)	YORK CITY	D 1-1	Hall	6387	2					12	9				7		11			3							4	8		6			1		5	10	16
17	Oct	31	(h)	RUSHDEN & DIAMONDS	L 0-2	-	7101	2			12			9			10	13		4			3	11					14	7	8		6			1				17
18	Nov	14	(a)	Grays Athletic	W 2-0	Craddock, Gallen	1668					6		9			10	7					13	4			3			11	8	12	2		1			5		18
19	Nov	21	(h)	CAMBRIDGE UNITED	D 2-2	Gnakpa, Craddock	7458	2			5			9			10	7					12	4			3			11	8	6	6			1				19
20	Dec	2	(h)	KETTERING TOWN	L 0-1	-	6608		12			6		9	13		10	7						4			3			11	8	2	6			1		5		20
21	Dec	28	(h)	EASTBOURNE BOROUGH	W 4-1	Barnes-Homer, Gallen (2), Jarvis	6646	14	9			12		11			10	7		13			3	4	5					2	8		6			1				21
22	Jan	23	(a)	Gateshead	W 1-0	Farman (og)	1218		10		5			9				2		4			11	7			3		13	12		14	6		1				22
23	Jan	27	(a)	Histon	W 2-0	Kovacs, Hall	1543		12					9			10	11		4	13		14	7	2	5	3			7	8		6			1				23
24	Jan	30	(h)	EBBSFLEET UNITED	L 2-3	Hatch, Craddock	6658	13	10					11					12	4	9			2	5	3	14	7		7	8	1	6			1				24
25	Feb	6	(a)	Barrow	W 1-0	Hatch	1579							10				11		4	9			13	5	3	14	7		7	8	12	6			1				25
26	Feb	9	(h)	OXFORD UNITED	W 2-1	Pilkington, Keane	8860		13					11				12		4	9			7			14	2	10				6			1				26
27	Feb	13	(a)	Eastbourne Borough	W 1-0	Hall	2018		9					11				7		4			13	8	5	3		2	10	12			6			1				27
28	Feb	16	(a)	York City	D 0-0	-	3316	14			13			11				12		4	9			7	8	5	3		2	10			6			1				28
29	Feb	20	(h)	AFC WIMBLEDON	L 1-2	Craddock	7736		12					9			10			11	13		14	7	4					3	8		6			1				29
30	Feb	27	(a)	Crawley Town	L 1-2	Barnes-Homer	2118		14					11			9	2		4	13			7	5	3			2	10			6			1				30
31	Mar	2	(h)	Mansfield Town	D 0-0	-	3407		10					13				7		4	9		11		8			14	2		12		6			1				31
32	Mar	6	(a)	Hayes & Yeading	W 3-2	Hatch, Gnakpa (pen), Craddock	1881		10					12				7		4	9		11		8			13	2				6			1				32
33	Mar	9	(h)	FOREST GREEN ROVERS	W 2-1	Craddock (2, 1 pen)	5884	2	10					11			9	7		4			13	12	8	5	3			6			6			1				33
34	Mar	13	(h)	WREXHAM	W 1-0	Craddock	6528	2						9			10	7				4	11	12	8	5	3			13			6			1				34
35	Mar	16	(h)	KIDDERMINSTER HARRIERS	W 3-1	Howells, Gallen (2)	5908	2	12					9			10	7		13		4	11		8								6			1				35
36	Mar	20	(a)	Ebbsfleet United	W 6-1	Gnakpa (3), Gallen, Craddock, Barnes-Homer	2142	2	12		13			9			10	7		4			11		8	5	3						6			1				36
37	Mar	27	(h)	HAYES & YEADING	W 8-0	Gallen (2), Gnakpa (2), Keane, Craddock (2), Howells	6761	2	13					12			10	7		14		4	11		8	5	3						6			1				37
38	Mar	30	(h)	SALISBURY CITY	W 4-0	Gnakpa, Craddock, Howells, Heslop	6692	2			5			9						13	4	11			8		3		14	12			6			1				38
39	Apr	3	(a)	Stevenage Borough	W 1-0	Barnes-Homer	7024	2	13		5			9			10	7				12	4	11	8		3			14			6			1				39
40	Apr	5	(h)	GRAYS ATHLETIC	W 6-0	Craddock (2), Gallen (3), Hatch	7860	2	14					9			10	7			13	4	11		8	5		12					6			1				40
41	Apr	10	(a)	Tamworth	D 1-1	Pilkington	2246	2	12			5					10	14	7			9	4	11	13		3						6			1				41
42	Apr	13	(a)	HISTON	W 6-3	Howells (2), Craddock (3, 1 pen), Gallen	7083	2	12			5		9			10				13	4	11	8			7						6			1				42
43	Apr	17	(h)	ALTRINCHAM	D 0-0	-	7374	2	12			5		9			10			8	13	4	11				3			7			6			1				43
44	Apr	24	(a)	Rushden & Diamonds	D 1-1	Craddock	4820		10			13		9			8				12		7	4		5	3			2	14		6			1				44

Final League Position: 2nd
2 Own Goals

							Apps	18	8	-	13	5	-	40	-	1	30	26	-	27	10	11	21	21	33	17	38	-	-	32	22	-	44	7	3	37	-	16	4	
							Subs	2	14	5	10	1	6	4	4	1	1	9	1	5	10	-	10	6	-	2	-	8	3	-	7	-	2	-	-	-	-	1	1	
							Goals	-	4	-	-	-	1	23	-	-	16	8	-	5	4	1	6	2	2	1	-	-	-	2	-	-	-	6	-	-	1	1	

2009/10 PLAY-OFFS

Round	Month	Day	Venue	Opponents	W/L/D Score	Scorers	Attendance	Asafu-Adjaye E	Barnes-Homer M	Basham S	Blackett S	Burgess A	Charles R	Craddock T	Donnelly G	Emanuel L	Gallen K	Gnakpa C	Gore S	Hall A	Hatch L	Heslop S	Howells J	Jarvis R	Keane K	Kovacs J	Murray F	Nathaniel T	Nelthorpe C	Newton A	Nicholls K	Nwokeji M	Pilkington G	Pilkington K	Reynolds C	Tyler M	Watkins A	White A	Wright B	Round
SF1	Apr	29	(a)	York City	L 0-1	-	6204		12		5			9			10	7		4	11		8		3					2			6			1				SF1
SF2	May	3	(h)	YORK CITY	L 0-1	-	9781		13		5			9			10	7		14	12	4	11		8		3			2			6			1				SF2

							Apps	-	-	-	2	-	-	2	-	-	2	2	-	1	1	1	2	-	2	-	2	-	-	2	-	-	2	-	-	2	-	-	-	
							Subs	-	2	-	-	-	-	-	-	-	-	-	-	1	1	-	-	-	-	-	-	-	-	-	-	-	-	-	-	-	-	-	-	
							Goals	-	-	-	-	-	-	-	-	-	-	-	-	-	-	-	-	-	-	-	-	-	-	-	-	-	-	-	-	-	-	-	-	

2009/10 FA CUP

Round	Month	Day	Venue	Opponents	W,L,D	Score	Scorers	Attendance	Asafu-Adjaye E	Barnes-Homer M	Basham S	Blackett S	Burgess A	Charles R	Craddock T	Donnelly G	Emanuel L	Gallen K	Gnakpa C	Gore S	Hall A	Hatch L	Heslop S	Howells J	Jarvis R	Keane K	Kovacs J	Murray F	Nathaniel T	Nelthorpe C	Newton A	Nicholls K	Nwokeji M	Pilkington G	Pilkington K	Reynolds C	Tyler M	Watkins A	White A	Wright B	Round
Q4	Oct	24	(h)	GRAYS ATHLETIC	W	3-0	Blackett, Rnkovic (og), Hall	2721	12		6	11	9					10	13		8			3				14			7		4	2	1			5			Q4
1	Nov	7	(h)	ROCHDALE	D	3-3	Basham (2), Newton	3167		9	6	8			13			10	7	1				12		4		3			11		2					5			1
Rep	Nov	11	(a)	Rochdale	W	2-0	Gallen (2)	1982	2			11	14		9			10	13	1	4			3	7						12	8	6					5			Rep
2	Nov	28	(a)	Rotherham United	D	2-2	Craddock (pen), Nwokeji	3210			6				9			10	7		14			13		4		3			11	8	12	2	1			5			2
Rep	Dec	8	(h)	ROTHERHAM UNITED	W	3-0	Newton, White, Gnakpa	2518			6				12			9	7		13			14	8	4		3			11	10		2	1			5			Rep
3	Jan	2	(a)	Southampton	L	0-1	-	18786	2			5			9			10	13		4			3	11						7	8	12	6	1				14		3

1 Own Goal

							Apps		2	-	1	5	3	1	3	-	-	6	3	2	3	-	-	3	3	3	-	3	0	-	5	4	-	6	3	1	-	5	-	-	
							Subs		1	-	-	-	-	-	1	2	-	-	3	-	2	-	-	3	-	-	1	-	1	-	2	-	-	-	-	-	1	-	-	1	
							Goals		-	-	2	1	-	-	1	-	-	2	1	-	1	-	-	-	-	-	-	-	-	-	2	-	1	-	-	-	-	1	-	-	

2009/10 FA TROPHY

Round	Month	Day	Venue	Opponents	W,L,D	Score	Scorers	Attendance	Asafu-Adjaye E	Barnes-Homer M	Basham S	Blackett S	Burgess A	Charles R	Craddock T	Donnelly G	Emanuel L	Gallen K	Gnakpa C	Gore S	Hall A	Hatch L	Heslop S	Howells J	Jarvis R	Keane K	Kovacs J	Murray F	Nathaniel T	Nelthorpe C	Newton A	Nicholls K	Nwokeji M	Pilkington G	Pilkington K	Reynolds C	Tyler M	Watkins A	White A	Wright B	Round
1	Dec	12	(a)	Cambridge United	L	1-3	Hatswell (og)	1665	13			6			14	12	9	7							8	4		3			11	10		2	1			5			1

1 Own Goal

							Apps		-	-	1	-	-	-	-	-	1	1	-	-	-	-	-	-	1	1	-	1	-	-	1	1	-	1	1	-	-	1	-	-	
							Subs		1	1	-	-	-	-	1	1	-	-	-	-	-	-	-	-	-	-	-	-	-	-	-	-	-	-	-	-	-	-	-	-	
							Goals		-	-	-	-	-	-	-	-	-	-	-	-	-	-	-	-	-	-	-	-	-	-	-	-	-	-	-	-	-	-	-	-	

2009/10 EXPUNGED RESULTS

Match No	Month	Day	Venue	Opponents	W,L,D	Score	Scorers	Attendance	Asafu-Adjaye E	Barnes-Homer M	Basham S	Blackett S	Burgess A	Charles R	Craddock T	Donnelly G	Emanuel L	Gallen K	Gnakpa C	Gore S	Hall A	Hatch L	Heslop S	Howells J	Jarvis R	Keane K	Kovacs J	Murray F	Nathaniel T	Nelthorpe C	Newton A	Nicholls K	Nwokeji M	Pilkington G	Pilkington K	Reynolds C	Tyler M	Watkins A	White A	Wright B	Match No
(5)	Aug	22	(h)	CHESTER CITY	D	0-0	-	6563			10	3	11		9			4						13	7			12					8	6	2		1	5			(5)
(22)	Dec	5	(a)	Chester City	D	0-0	-	1352	10		6				9	11							8		3						7	13	2				1	5			(22)

Ashley Cain 12, against Chester on 5th December. This was his only appearance for Luton during a loan spell. The appearances in the expunged games do not count towards the player appearance records.

							Apps		-	1	1	2	1	-	2	-	1	1	-	-	-	-	1	-	1	1	-	1	-	-	1	1	-	2	-	1	-	2	-	-	
							Subs		-	-	-	-	-	-	-	-	-	-	-	-	-	-	-	1	-	-	-	1	-	-	-	1	-	-	-	-	-	-	-	
							Goals		-	-	-	-	-	-	-	-	-	-	-	-	-	-	-	-	-	-	-	-	-	-	-	-	-	-	-	-	-	-	-	-	

TIMELINE...

1 October 2009 Mick Harford leaves Kenilworth Road by 'mutual consent' with coach Alan Neilson taking on the caretaker role.

30 October 2009 Former Hatter Richard Money is appointed into the manager's chair.

20 March 2010 The Town net six second half goals at Ebbsfleet.

27 March 2010 The Hatters go one better when scoring seven first half goals at home to Hayes.

3 May 2010 In the play-offs, for the second time in their history, the Town fail to see off York.

▶ **The 2009/10 team** – Back row (left to right): Emanuel, Caines, Atieno, Kovacs, Heslop, Barnes-Homer, Charles, Hatch, Hall, Jarvis, Gnakpa. Middle row (left to right): Prickett (Under-18s Manager), Sanson (Kit Manager), Bedford (Physiotherapist), Poku, Craddock, Newton, Nwokeji, Keane, Gore, Tyler, O'Donnell, Howells, Asafu-Adjaye, Beavan, DeSouza (Under-16 Coach), Broughton (Youth Development Officer), Kharine (Coach), Chatfield (Youth Team Physiotherapist). Front row (left to right): Murray, Nelthorpe, Blackett, Neilson (Assistant Manager), Money (Manager), Watson (Coach), Nicholls, Pilkington, Gallen.

▶ **The 2010/11 team** – Back row (left to right): Poku, Newton, Asafu-Adjaye, Kroca, Gnakpa, J.Walker, O'Donnell, Lawless. Middle row (Left to right): Parsell (Physiotherapist), D.Walker, Graham, Blackett, Tyler, K.Pilkington, Gleeson, Barnes-Homer, Murray, Cook (Kit-man). Front row (left to right): Carden, Watkins, Howells, Kharine (Goalkeeping coach), Brabin (Manager), Neilson (Assistant manager), G.Pilkington, Keane, Willmott.

2010/11 FOOTBALL CONFERENCE PREMIER (NON-LEAGUE)

Match No	Month	Day	Venue	Opponents	W,L,D Score	Scorers	Attendance	Ann A	Asafu-Adjaye E	Atieno T	Barnes-Homer M	Besta P	Blackett S	Carden P	Carney N	Craddock T	Crow D	Drury A	Gallen K	Gleeson D	Gnakpa C	Graham L	Hinton C	Howells J	Keane K	Kroca Z	Lacey A	Lawless A	Morgan-Smith A	Murray A	Murray F	Newton A	O'Donnell JJ	Owusu L	Patrick J	Pilkington G	Pilkington K	Poku G	Tavernier C	Tyler M	Walker D	Walker J	Watkins A	Willmott R	Woodrow C	Match No
1	Aug	14	(h)	ALTRINCHAM	W 2-1	Kroca, Barnes-Homer	6665			9						14	12	7	10	2	13			11	4	5				8	3					6				1						1
2	Aug	17	(a)	Kettering Town	W 3-1	Barnes-Homer (3, 2 pens)	2906			9	14						12	11	10	2	7			13	4	5				8	3					6	1			1						2
3	Aug	21	(a)	Fleetwood Town	W 3-0	Barnes-Homer, Gnakpa, Craddock	2831			9	8					13	10	11		2	7			12	4	5					3					6				1						3
4	Aug	24	(h)	NEWPORT COUNTY AFC	D 1-1	Kroca	6945			9	8					14	13	11	10	2	7			12	4	5					3					6				1						4
5	Aug	28	(a)	Tamworth	L 1-3	Craddock	1694			9	8					10		11	13	2	7			12	4	5					3	14				6	1			1						5
6	Aug	30	(h)	HAYES & YEADING	D 1-1	Drury	6354			9			3				10	7	12	2	13			11	4	5				8						6				1						6
7	Sep	4	(a)	Grimsby Town	L 0-2		3822		14	9	12		3			13	10			2	7				4	5			11	8						6				1						7
8	Sep	11	(h)	CAMBRIDGE UNITED	W 2-0	Drury, Pilkington	6691		10	9			6			14	11			2	7			13		5				8	3	12				4				1						8
9	Sep	17	(h)	AFC WIMBLEDON	W 3-0	Pilkington, Kroca, Barnes-Homer	7283		10	9			6				11				7			8	4	5				3	2					4				1	12					9
10	Sep	21	(h)	Darlington	D 2-2	Gnakpa, Howells	1665		10	9			6			13	11	12		7				8		5				3	2					4				1						10
11	Sep	25	(a)	Gateshead	L 0-1		1075		10	9			6			12				2	7			13	4	5				3	11					8				1	14					11
12	Sep	28	(h)	MANSFIELD TOWN	W 2-0	Crow, Morgan-Smith	6024		14	9							10			2	7			8	4	5		11	12	3	13					6				1						12
13	Oct	2	(a)	Barrow	W 1-0	Barnes-Homer	1416		14	9							10	11		2	7			8	4	5		12		3						6		13		1						13
14	Oct	5	(h)	CRAWLEY TOWN	L 1-2	Drury (pen)	6895		10	9			6				12	11		2	7				4	5				3	8					6				1						14
15	Oct	16	(a)	Eastbourne Borough	W 4-2	Pilkington, Barnes-Homer, Crow (2, 1 pen)	2518			9							10	7		2				8	4	5		11		3						6	12	13		1						15
16	Oct	19	(h)	FOREST GREEN ROVERS	W 6-1	Drury, Morgan-Smith, Crow (2), Barnes-Homer, D Walker	5704			9							10	7		2	12			8	4	5		11		3						6	13	14		1						16
17	Oct	30	(h)	BATH CITY	W 3-1	Crow, Pilkington, Atieno	7003		9	11	12						10	7		2				8	4	5				3						6	13			1						17
18	Nov	11	(a)	Wrexham	L 0-1		2733		12	9							11			2	10			8	4	5		7		3						6	13			1						18
19	Nov	13	(a)	Altrincham	W 1-0	Lawless	1416			9							10	11		2	7			12	4	5		8		3						6	13			1						19
20	Nov	20	(h)	HISTON	W 5-1	Gnakpa, Howells, J Walker, Drury (pen), Atieno	5963	14	13	9		12						7		2				11	4	5		8		3						6		10		1						20
21	Jan	1	(h)	RUSHDEN & DIAMONDS	W 3-0	Barnes-Homer (2), Gnakpa	6928			9							10	8		2	7			3	4	5		13	11							6	14	12		1						21
22	Jan	4	(a)	Hayes & Yeading	W 1-0	Gnakpa	801			9							10	8		2	7			3	4	5		13	11							6	12			1						22
23	Jan	8	(a)	Bath City	D 0-0		2301			9							10	8		2	7			3	4	5		13	11							6	12			1						23
24	Jan	12	(a)	AFC Wimbledon	D 0-0		4287		12	11							10	8		2	7			3	4	5		12	11							6	13			1						24
25	Jan	18	(a)	YORK CITY	W 5-0	Drury, Gnakpa, Owusu, Kroca, Atieno	5997			9							14	10		2	7			3	4	5		8						9		6		8		1			13			25
26	Jan	22	(h)	GATESHEAD	D 2-2	Crow, Gnakpa	5958	2	13	11							10				7			3	4	5		8						9		6	12			1			14			26
27	Jan	25	(h)	GRIMSBY TOWN	W 1-0	Gnakpa	5609			9								11		2	7			3	4	5		8						10		6				1			12			27
28	Feb	1	(h)	DARLINGTON	W 4-0	Gnakpa, Owusu (2), Lawless	5770			9										2	7	14		3	4	5		8		11				10		6				1			12	13		28
29	Feb	12	(h)	FLEETWOOD TOWN	L 1-3	Owusu	6227			9										2	7	12		3	4	5		8	11					10		6	13			1			14			29
30	Feb	18	(a)	Newport County AFC	D 1-1	Willmott	2834						8							2	7	12		13	4	5				3						6				1			9	11		30
31	Mar	1	(a)	Forest Green Rovers	W 1-0	Owusu	1015			9			12			13				7	2			8	4	5				3				10		6				1			11			31
32	Mar	5	(h)	KIDDERMINSTER HARRIERS	D 1-1	Barnes-Homer	6108			9			8							2	7			11	4	5				12	3					6				1			10			32
33	Mar	8	(h)	TAMWORTH	W 2-0	Owusu, Barnes-Homer	5737			9										2	7			11	4	5		8	12	3				10		6				1			13			33
34	Mar	15	(a)	Cambridge United	D 0-0		2831			14			8		9					12	2			3	4	5		13		11				10		6				1				7		34
35	Mar	22	(a)	Rushden & Diamonds	W 1-0	Willmott	2459			9			8				10							3	4	5		11		2						6	13			1			12	7		35
36	Mar	26	(a)	Southport	L 1-2	Barnes-Homer	1695			9			8				12			7	2			3	4	5		13			11	10				6		14		1			9	7		36
37	Mar	29	(h)	BARROW	D 0-0		5528			9			8				10			12				11	4	5				3	2					6				1				7		37
38	Apr	2	(a)	Kidderminster Harriers	D 3-3	Willmott, Gnakpa, J Walker	2756			9								10		2	12			11	4	5		8		3	14					6				1		13	7			38
39	Apr	5	(h)	KETTERING TOWN	D 2-2	Howells, Morgan-Smith	5715			12					14						7	13		3	4	5		8	10		2					6				1		9	11			39
40	Apr	9	(h)	SOUTHPORT	W 6-0	Morgan-Smith, Willmott, Murray, J Walker, Kroca, Gnakpa (pen)	5844			13											12			11	4	5		8	10	3	2					6				1		9	7			40
41	Apr	12	(a)	Crawley Town	D 1-1	Lawless	3326			12			4								7			11		5		8	13	3	2					6				1		9	10			41
42	Apr	16	(a)	Mansfield Town	D 0-0		2203			12										2	7			11	4	5		8	10	3						6				1		9	13			42
43	Apr	19	(a)	York City	L 0-1		2955			7										2	12	5		11	4			10	3	8						6				1	14	9	13			43
44	Apr	23	(h)	EASTBOURNE BOROUGH	W 3-0	Willmott (2), Gnakpa	6171	13												2	7			3	4	5		8			12	10				6				1	14	9	11			44
45	Apr	25	(a)	Histon	W 4-0	Morgan-Smith, Barnes-Homer (2), Gnakpa	1159	3		9			4							2	12	6				5		10	11		8			1			13	14		7						45
46	Apr	30	(h)	WREXHAM	D 1-1	J Walker (pen)	6443	3		9										2					5	13		8			10		6		4		1	11	14	12	7					46
							Apps	-	3	6	39	3	7	8	-	1	17	23	4	33	33	6	-	34	39	45	-	15	15	6	28	14	-	13	-	45	3	2	-	43	1	8	-	12	-	
							Subs	-	2	7	5	3	1	2	-	3	11	-	2	1	9	4	-	8	-	-	1	5	5	1	-	5	-	-	5	-	-	7	-	-	11	12	3	3	-	
							Goals	-	-	3	16	-	-	-	-	2	7	6	-	-	13	-	-	3	-	5	-	3	5	-	1	-	-	6	-	4	-	-	-	-	1	4	-	6	-	

Final League Position: 3rd

2010/11 PLAY-OFFS

Round	Month	Day	Venue	Opponents	W,L,D Score	Scorers	Attendance	Asafu-Adjaye E	Atieno T	Drury A	Gallen K	Gnakpa C	Graham L	Hinton C	Kroca Z	Lawless A	Newton A	Pilkington K	Tyler M	Walker J	Watkins A	Willmott R	Round
SF1	May	5	(a)	Wrexham	W 3-0	Lawless, Gnakpa, Asafu-Adjaye	7211	3	12	2	7	8	4	5		10		6	1	9	11		SF1
SF2	May	10	(h)	WREXHAM	W 2-1	Kroca, J Walker	9078	3	12	2	7	8	4	5		10	13	6	1	9	11		SF2
F	May	21	(n)	AFC Wimbledon	D 0-0		18195	3	12	2	7	8	4	5		10	13	6	1	9		11	F
						Apps		3		3	3	3	3	3		3		3	3	3	3	3	
						Subs			3								2						
						Goals		1				1			1	1				1			

Final played at Eastlands, lost 4-3 on penalties aet.

2010/11 FA CUP

Round	Month	Day	Venue	Opponents	W,L,D Score	Scorers	Attendance	Ann A	Asafu-Adjaye E	Atieno T	Craddock T	Crow D	Drury A	Gleeson D	Gnakpa C	Graham L	Hinton C	Kroca Z	Morgan-Smith A	Murray A	Newton A	Pilkington K	Tavernier C	Walker J	Walker D	Watkins A	Round
Q4	Oct	23	(h)	ST ALBANS CITY	W 4-0	Morgan-Smith (3), Crow	4144	12		9		10		2	7	8	4	5	11		3	6	13	1		14	Q4
1	Nov	6	(a)	Corby Town	D 1-1	Barnes-Homer	2000	5	10	9				2	7	8	4			3		6	12	1	11		1
Rep	Nov	17	(h)	CORBY TOWN	W 4-2	Barnes-Homer, Atieno (2), Gnakpa	3050	5	10	9	11			2	7	8	4			3	14	6	12	1	13		Rep
2	Nov	27	(a)	Charlton Athletic	D 2-2	Drury (2)	8682		12	9		10	8	2	7	3	4	5	11			6		1	13		2
Rep	Dec	9	(h)	CHARLTON ATHLETIC	L 1-3	Kroca	5914		13	9		10	8	2	7	3	4	5	11			6	12	1			Rep
						Apps		2	2	5	1	3	2	5	5	5	5	3	3	2	1	5	2	5	2	1	
						Subs		1	2												1		4		3		
						Goals				2		1	2		1			1									

2010/11 FA TROPHY

Round	Month	Day	Venue	Opponents	W,L,D Score	Scorers	Attendance	Ann A	Asafu-Adjaye E	Atieno T	Barnes-Homer M	Craddock T	Crow D	Drury A	Gleeson D	Gnakpa C	Graham L	Hinton C	Howells J	Keane K	Kroca Z	Lacey A	Lawless A	Morgan-Smith A	Murray F	Newton A	O'Donnell JJ	Owusu L	Pilkington K	Poku G	Tavernier C	Tyler M	Walker J	Watkins A	Willmott R	Round
1	Dec	12	(h)	WELLING UNITED	D 0-0		1639	2	10		8				5	3		6	11				12						4	1	7	9				1
Rep	Dec	14	(a)	Welling United	W 2-1	J Walker, Lawless	404	3	10		8	12			5		6	2					11		14				4	1	7	9		13		Rep
2	Jan	15	(h)	UXBRIDGE	W 4-0	Atieno (2), Watkins (2, 1pen)	1958	14	5	10	8	12			6	2		3											4	7	1	9	11	13	2
3	Feb	4	(h)	GLOUCESTER CITY	W 1-0	Graham	2212	2		10					7	6	8				11			3					1	4	13	9	12	14	3
4	Feb	26	(h)	Guiseley	W 1-0	Barnes-Homer	1152	9		13	12		2		11	4	5		8	7		3							6	1	14		10		4
SF1	Mar	13	(a)	Mansfield Town	L 0-1		3208	9		12			7	2	11	4	5		8	13		3				10			6	1	14				SF1
SF2	Mar	19	(h)	MANSFIELD TOWN	D 1-1	Owusu	6133	9		13			7	2	3	4	5		8	14				11		10			6	1			12		SF2
						Apps		4	3	3	3		1		3	4	2	5	3	4	3	6	2	2	1	3	2		3	4	4	1	3	2	5	1	
						Subs		1				2		3					1						2			1			2		1	1	1	3	
						Goals			2	1			1			1										1		1						2		

Semi Final 2nd Leg aet, 1-0 after 90 mins.

TIMELINE...

28 March 2011 Richard Money departs the hot seat at Kenilworth Road to be replaced by his assistant Gary Brabin.

21 May 2011 The Town reach the play-off final where they go down to AFC Wimbledon on penalties after a disappointing 0-0 stalemate.

2011/12 FOOTBALL CONFERENCE PREMIER (NON-LEAGUE)

Match No	Month	Day	Venue	Opponents	W,L,D Score	Scorers	Attendance
1	Aug	16	(h)	FOREST GREEN ROVERS	D 1-1	Beckwith	6061
2	Aug	20	(h)	SOUTHPORT	W 5-1	Watkins, Antwi, Morgan-Smith, Willmott, Crow	5681
3	Aug	23	(a)	Mansfield Town	D 1-1	Antwi	2592
4	Aug	27	(h)	BRAINTREE TOWN	W 3-1	Morgan-Smith (2), Howells	5703
5	Aug	30	(a)	Hayes & Yeading	D 2-2	Morgan-Smith, Crow	1015
6	Sep	2	(a)	Stockport County	D 1-1	Lawless	3389
7	Sep	10	(h)	DARLINGTON	W 2-0	Crow, Fleetwood	5952
8	Sep	13	(a)	AFC Telford United	W 2-0	Morgan-Smith (2)	2640
9	Sep	17	(h)	LINCOLN CITY	W 1-0	Fleetwood	6316
10	Sep	20	(a)	Bath City	D 1-1	Morgan-Smith	1158
11	Sep	24	(a)	York City	L 0-3		3570
12	Sep	27	(h)	CAMBRIDGE UNITED	L 0-1		6274
13	Oct	1	(h)	BARROW	W 5-1	Willmott (2), Watkins, Dance, Morgan-Smith	5613
14	Oct	8	(a)	Kidderminster Harriers	W 2-1	Willmott (2)	3332
15	Oct	11	(a)	Ebbsfleet United	D 2-2	Morgan-Smith, Dance	1651
16	Oct	15	(h)	GATESHEAD	W 5-1	Howells (2), O'Connor, Hand (2)	6285
17	Oct	18	(h)	WREXHAM	L 0-1		7270
18	Oct	21	(a)	Grimsby Town	W 1-0	Wright	3239
19	Nov	5	(h)	FLEETWOOD TOWN	L 1-2	Kovacs	6361
20	Nov	19	(a)	Cambridge United	D 1-1	Fleetwood	4796
21	Nov	26	(a)	Newport County AFC	W 1-0	Crow	1511
22	Nov	29	(h)	AFC TELFORD UNITED	D 1-1	Willmott	5399
23	Dec	6	(a)	Lincoln City	D 1-1	Crow	2049
24	Dec	17	(a)	Tamworth	W 3-1	Crow (2), Dance	1467
25	Dec	26	(h)	KETTERING TOWN	W 5-0	Howells, O'Connor, Lawless, Fleetwood, Willmott	7164
26	Jan	1	(a)	Kettering Town	W 5-0	Howells, Watkins, Kovacs, Taylor, Fleetwood	3247
27	Jan	7	(h)	NEWPORT COUNTY AFC	W 2-0	O'Connor, Crow	6108
28	Jan	10	(h)	STOCKPORT COUNTY	W 1-0	O'Connor (pen)	5588
29	Jan	21	(a)	Southport	D 3-3	Crow, Watkins, O'Connor	1665
30	Jan	25	(h)	MANSFIELD TOWN	D 0-0		5261
31	Jan	28	(h)	ALFRETON TOWN	W 1-0	Pilkington (pen)	5658
32	Feb	18	(h)	TAMWORTH	W 3-0	Fleetwood, Kovacs, Francis (og)	5833
33	Feb	21	(a)	Barrow	L 0-1		925
34	Mar	3	(h)	BATH CITY	W 2-0	Kovacs, Watkins	5745
35	Mar	7	(a)	Wrexham	L 0-2		4206
36	Mar	13	(a)	Darlington	D 1-1	Fleetwood	1382
37	Mar	20	(a)	Forest Green Rovers	L 0-3		975
38	Mar	24	(h)	GRIMSBY TOWN	D 1-1	Gray	6419
39	Mar	30	(h)	YORK CITY	L 1-2	Gray	5925
40	Apr	7	(a)	Braintree Town	L 1-3	Gray	1703
41	Apr	9	(h)	HAYES & YEADING	W 4-2	Fleetwood (2), Keane, Gray	6003
42	Apr	14	(a)	Alfreton Town	D 0-0		1654
43	Apr	17	(h)	EBBSFLEET UNITED	W 3-0	Fleetwood (2), McAllister	5526
44	Apr	21	(h)	KIDDERMINSTER HARRIERS	W 1-0	Willmott	8415
45	Apr	24	(a)	Gateshead	D 0-0		703
46	Apr	28	(a)	Fleetwood Town	W 2-0	Pond (og), Gray	4446

Final League Position: 5th
2 Own goals

Player appearance totals:

Player	Apps	Subs	Goals
Ann A	-	-	-
Antwi W	12	2	2
Asafu-Adjaye E	7	-	-
Barnes-Homer M	1	-	-
Beckwith D	8	-	1
Blackett S	5	4	-
Boucaud A	4	3	-
Brunt R	1	5	-
Carden P	1	-	-
Carney N	-	-	-
Crow D	23	6	9
Dance J	21	5	3
Fleetwood S	22	15	11
Gleeson D	8	2	-
Gray A	9	2	5
Hand J	11	-	2
Henry C	-	-	-
Howells J	42	-	5
Keane K	33	-	1
Kissock JP	7	14	-
Kovacs J	37	-	4
Lacey A	-	-	-
Lawless A	38	-	2
Longden B	-	-	-
McAdams C	-	-	-
McAllister C	4	-	1
Morgan-Smith A	15	10	9
Murray F	-	-	-
Nash J	-	-	-
O'Connor A	21	2	5
O'Donnell JJ	28	-	-
Osano C	28	13	1
Pilkington G	33	-	1
Pilkington K	12	-	-
Poku G	5	13	-
Samuel C	-	5	-
Smith C	-	1	-
Tavernier C	-	5	-
Taylor G	15	1	1
Tyler M	34	-	-
Walker D	-	2	-
Watkins A	20	1	5
Willmott R	29	14	8
Woolley J	-	10	-
Wright T	1	3	1

2011/12 PLAY-OFFS

Round	Month	Day	Venue	Opponents	W,L,D	Score	Scorers	Attendance	Fleetwood S	Gleeson D	Henry C	Howells J	Keane K	Kissock JP	Lawless A	McAdams C	McAllister C	Morgan-Smith A	O'Connor A	O'Donnell JJ	Taylor G	Tyler M	Walker D	Watkins A	Willmott R	Round
SF1	May	3	(h)	WREXHAM	W	2-0	Gray, Fleetwood	9012	10	9	3	4	13	5	7	12	14		2	6		1	8	11		SF1
SF2	May	7	(a)	Wrexham	L	1-2	Pilkington (pen)	9087	10	9	3	4		5	7	13	14		2	6		1	8	11	12	SF2
F	May	20	(n)	York City	L	1-2	Gray	39265	10	9	3	4	12	5	7	13		14	2	6		1	8	11		F

Final at Wembley

							Apps		3	3	3	3		3	3	3			3	3		3	3	3	
							Subs						2				3	2		1					1
							Goals		1	2															

2011/12 FA CUP

Round	Month	Day	Venue	Opponents	W,L,D	Score	Scorers	Attendance	Ann A	Asafu-Adjaye E	Carney N	Crow D	Dance J	Fleetwood S	Gray A	Hand J	Henry C	Howells J	Keane K	Kissock JP	Kovacs J	Lawless A	Morgan-Smith A	O'Connor A	O'Donnell JJ	Osano C	Taylor G	Watkins A	Willmott R	Woolley J	Round
Q4	Oct	29	(h)	HENDON	W	5-1	O'Connor (2, 1pen), Dance, Wright, Fleetwood	2242	6	5		12	8	9	4	14	3		11					7	2	1	13			10	Q4
1	Nov	12	(h)	NORTHAMPTON TOWN	W	1-0	Watkins	4799				13			8		3	4	11	5	7		9	10	2	6 1		14	12		1
2	Dec	3	(h)	CHELTENHAM TOWN	L	2-4	O'Connor (2)	4516			2	9			3	4	12	5	8					7	6 1			10	11		2

							Apps		1	1	1	1	1	2	3	2	2	2	2		1		3	2	2 3		1	1	1	
							Subs				2					1		1	1					1				1	1	1
							Goals				1	1												4				1	1	

2011/12 FA TROPHY

Round	Month	Day	Venue	Opponents	W,L,D	Score	Scorers	Attendance	Ann A	Asafu-Adjaye E	Beckwith D	Blackett S	Carney N	Crow D	Dance J	Fleetwood S	Gleeson D	Hand J	Henry C	Howells J	Keane K	Kissock JP	Kovacs J	Lacey A	Lawless A	Longden B	McAdams C	McAllister C	Morgan-Smith A	Murray F	O'Connor A	O'Donnell JJ	Osano C	Pilkington K	Samuel C	Smith C	Taylor G	Tyler M	Walker D	Watkins A	Willmott R	Woolley J	Wright T	Round
1	Dec	10	(h)	SWINDON SUPERMARINE	W	2-0	Fleetwood, Wright	1298		5		10		9	2			4	11		6				14			13	7						3	1	8				12	1
2	Jan	18	(a)	Hinckley United	D	0-0		754	10	6				4	9				8		5			7			13	3	2						3	1		11	12		
Rep	Jan	23	(h)	HINCKLEY UNITED	W	3-0	Bragoli (og), Morgan-Smith, Fleetwood	1004		6				9				8		5	14	7	10	4			3	2		13					1			11	12		Rep
3	Feb	7	(a)	Kidderminster Harriers	W	2-1	Howells, Fleetwood	1186		5	6			9				8	11	10		4						14	2					3	1	13	7	12		3
4	Feb	25	(h)	GATESHEAD	W	2-0	Kissock, Keane	2499		2		5		9		13		12	11	4	10		8					14			6				3	1					4
SF1	Mar	10	(a)	York City	L	0-1		3365		2		12		9				8	11	4	5		7						13	6					3	1	10		14	SF1
SF2	Mar	17	(h)	YORK CITY	D	1-1	Willmott	5796						9	10				11	4	5		8						2	6					3	1	12	7		SF2

1 Own goal

							Apps		1	4	2	2		3	1	5	1	2	4	5	2	3	4	2		1	1	2	5	3			5	7	2	5		
							Subs				1			1		1			1				1	1	2	1						1			2	4	1	
							Goals					3			1	1	1																1	1		

TIMELINE...
31 March 2012 Gary Brabin is sacked.
8 April 2012 Paul Buckle is announced as the new manager.
20 May 2012 The Hatters reach the play-offs for the third year running but are beaten by York at Wembley in the final.

▶ **The 2011/12 team** – Back row (left to right): Brunt, Wright, Taylor, Hand, Morgan-Smith, Kidd, Kovacs, Walker, Keane, Lacey, O'Donnell. Middle row (left to right): Parsell (Physiotherapist), Poku, O'Connor, Watkins, Murray, Willmott, Lawless, Tyler, K.Pilkington, Osano, Beckwith, Gleeson, Deeney, Kissock, Cook (Kit-man), Kharine (Goalkeeping coach). Front row (left to right): Howells, Dance, Fleetwood, Carden (Coach), Brabin (Manager), Neilson (Assistant manager), Crow, Asafu-Adjaye, G.Pilkington.

▶ **The 2012/13 team** – Back row (left to right): Shaw, Rendell, Lacey, Walker, Kidd, Tyler, Brill, Beckwith, Rowe-Turner, Ann, Kovacs. Middle row (left to right: Driver (Youth team coach), Fleetwood, Howells, O'Donnell, Spiller, Dance, Kasim, Lawless, Woolley, Robinson, Richards, Parsell (Physiotherapist). Front row (left to right): Gray, Kharine (Goalkeeping coach), Neilson (Assistant manager), Henry, Buckle (Manager), Taylor, Emberson (Coach), Carden (Coach), Watkins.

Match No	Month	Day	Venue	Opponents	W.L.D Score	Scorers	Attendance	Ainge S	Beckwith D	Brill D	Dance J	Essam C	Fleetwood S	Goodman J	Gray A	Griffiths S	Henry R	Howells J	Jibodu J	Kasim Y	Kovacs J	Lacey A	Lawless A	Martin D	McNulty S	Mendy A	Neilson S	O'Donnell JJ	Rendell S	Robinson J	Robinson M	Rowe-Turner L	Shaw J	Smith Jonathan	Taiwo S	Taylor G	Thomas W	Tyler M	Walker D	Wall A	Watkins A	Woolley J	Match No
1	Aug	11	(h)	GATESHEAD	D 2-2	Shaw, Fleetwood	6743						10	9	5	11	4	6		13								7	8				3	12				2	1			14		1
2	Aug	14	(a)	Kidderminster Harriers	W 2-0	Fleetwood (2)	2275						10	12	2		4	6			7							11	8		13	5	9		3		1						2
3	Aug	17	(a)	Hyde	W 2-1	O'Donnell, Fleetwood	1141						10		13		2	12			4	6						11	8		14	5	9		3		1						3
4	Aug	25	(h)	AFC TELFORD UNITED	L 0-1		5970						10		13	6	3	4			2							11	8			5	9		12		1			7		4
5	Aug	27	(a)	Ebbsfleet United	W 3-1	Fleetwood (2), Rendell	2018	6					11	10	4						2							7	8			5	9		3		1			13	12	5
6	Sep	1	(h)	MACCLESFIELD TOWN	W 4-1	Howells, Gray, Rendell, Fleetwood	5803	5				14	7	10	4			6										8	9		3				11		1			12	13	6
7	Sep	4	(h)	CAMBRIDGE UNITED	W 3-2	Kovacs, Gray, Beckwith	6742	5				12	11	10	4			6			7							8	9		3		2		1						13	7
8	Sep	8	(a)	Alfreton Town	L 0-3		1392	5				12	13	9	2	4		14	6		7							11		10	3		1			8						8
9	Sep	15	(h)	WREXHAM	D 0-0		6675	5					11	7	2	3	14	6		4								8	10		12	9			1	13						9
10	Sep	21	(a)	Grimsby Town	L 1-4	Rendell	4074	5				12	11	7	2	3	13	6		4								8	10	14		9			1						10
11	Sep	25	(a)	Tamworth	W 2-1	Kasim, Fleetwood	1137	5				6	13	7	2	8	14			4								11	10	12	3	9			1						11
12	Sep	29	(h)	SOUTHPORT	W 3-1	Fleetwood, Rendell (2, 1pen)	5696	5				6	9	10	2	3		4			7							11	8	14	12	13			1						12
13	Oct	6	(a)	Lincoln City	W 2-1	Farman OG, Shaw	2970	5				6	9	7	2	3	14	4										8	10	11	13	12			1						13
14	Oct	9	(h)	BRAINTREE TOWN	L 2-3	Ainge, Walker	5523	5				6	10	7	2	3	12	4										8		11		9			1	13					14
15	Oct	13	(h)	NUNEATON TOWN	W 2-0	Lawless (2)	6148	5				6		7	2	8	13	4										11	10		3	9			1	12					15
16	Oct	27	(a)	Forest Green Rovers	W 2-1	Fleetwood, Rendell (pen)	2112	5	1				10	7	2	11		6			4							12	8		3	9									16
17	Nov	6	(a)	Hereford United	L 0-1		2108	5	1				9	7	2	11		6	12		4							14	10	13	3		8								17
18	Nov	10	(h)	DARTFORD	L 0-2		6567	5	1				9	7	6	3		2			4							11	10		3		8			12					18
19	Nov	18	(a)	Mansfield Town	D 2-2	Gray (2)	2619	5					12	9	2	11		7			6								10		3		8								19
20	Dec	8	(h)	ALFRETON TOWN	W 3-0	O'Donnell, Smith, Gray	5648	5					12	9	2	4		6			7							11	10		3	13	8			1	14				20
21	Dec	11	(a)	Newport County	L 2-5	Gray, Shaw	2247	5	6				12	9	2	8		7					4					11	10		3	13			1						21
22	Dec	26	(h)	WOKING	W 3-1	Kovacs, Shaw, Rendell (pen)	6744	5					11	7	2	3		6			8		4					12	10	13		9			1						22
23	Jan	1	(a)	Woking	L 1-3	Gray	2961	5					13	9	2	3		6			8	4	11					10			14	7	12		1						23
24	Jan	8	(h)	BARROW	W 6-1	Neilson, Kovacs, Shaw (3), Gray	5165						14	10	2	12		6			7	4	11			13		5	9	8		3		1						24
25	Jan	15	(a)	AFC Telford United	D 0-0		1606						13	10	2	12		6			7	4	11					5	9	8		3		1						25
26	Feb	2	(a)	Barrow	L 0-1		1188						10		2	14			7	11	5	4	12					6	9	8	13			1						26
27	Feb	9	(h)	FOREST GREEN ROVERS	D 1-1	Gray	6374						14	10	2	3		6			4	11	5	12	7	13						9	8		1					27
28	Feb	12	(a)	Dartford	L 0-1		1802							10	2	3		6			11	5	4	7	13	12		9	8		14			1						28
29	Feb	19	(a)	Macclesfield Town	D 1-1	Gray	1984						14	7	2	11		4				5	13			12	10		6	9	8		3		1					29
30	Feb	23	(h)	MANSFIELD TOWN	L 2-3	Rendell, Gray	5968						12	9	2	13		4	11	5		7					3	10			8			6	1					30
31	Feb	26	(a)	Braintree Town	L 0-2		1003	14					11	9	2			7		5	4	13			10			3			8			12	6	1				31
32	Mar	2	(a)	Stockport County	W 1-0	Howells	4074						10	9	2	11	6	7		5	4							3	8		12				14	1				32
33	Mar	5	(a)	Nuneaton Town	D 0-0		1173						10	6	9	2		7		5	4	12	14					3	8						13	1				33
34	Mar	9	(h)	HEREFORD UNITED	D 1-1	Martin	6001							6	9	2	11			7	14	5	4				13	10			8			3		12				34
35	Mar	12	(h)	HYDE	L 1-2	Howells	4847							6	9	2	11			7	13	5	4				4			14		8			3		12	10		35
36	Mar	16	(a)	Wrexham	D 0-0		3907	2						6			7				11	5	4			10				3	8	12			1	13	9			36
37	Mar	19	(h)	STOCKPORT COUNTY	W 1-0	McNulty	5106	2						6	10		7				11	5	4							3	9	8	4			1	12			37
38	Mar	23	(h)	TAMWORTH	D 0-0		5501	2						6	12		7				11	5					13			3	9	8	4			1		10		38
39	Mar	30	(a)	Cambridge United	D 2-2	Shaw, Taiwo (pen)	3217	2						6	10		7					11	5							3	9	8	4		1		12			39
40	Apr	1	(h)	KIDDERMINSTER HARRIERS	L 1-2	Gray	6108	2						6	14	12	7					11	5							8	3	9	13	4						40
41	Apr	6	(a)	Gateshead	L 1-5	Walker	382	2		1				6	9							11	5				13			12	3	8	4			7	10			41
42	Apr	9	(h)	LINCOLN CITY	W 3-0	Martin (2), Gray	5393	6						10	3	2					7	11	5						12	4	9	8					14	13		42
43	Apr	12	(h)	GRIMSBY TOWN	D 1-1	Lawless	5662			1				10	3						7	11	5						8	6	9	2	4				12			43
44	Apr	16	(h)	NEWPORT COUNTY	D 2-2	Gray (2)	5125			1				10	3	13					7	11	5						8	6	9	2	4				12			44
45	Apr	18	(h)	EBBSFLEET UNITED	W 2-0	Wall (2)	5934	14						6	12	11						5					4	10	8	3	2			1	7	9	13		45
46	Apr	20	(a)	Southport	W 3-1	Robinson, Gray (2)	1406	12						6	10	3		13			7	11							8	5	9	2	4				14			46
				Final League Position: 7th		1 Own Goal	**Apps**	19	8	7	-	5	19	11	39	4	33	34	-	5	19	-	35	14	20	16	6	20	28	3	6	32	26	26	8	13	2	39	2	5	2	-	
							Subs	3	-	-	-	4	11	-	5	2	-	7	6	1	-	-	2	-	2	2	-	2	8	4	4	5	5	2	1	4	-	-	10	7	3	4	
							Goals	1	1	-	-	-	10	-	17	-	3	-	1	3	3	1	-	-	1	-	2	8	-	1	-	8	1	1	-	-	-	-	1	-	2	2	-	

Game 41 played at Brunton Park.

2012/13 FA CUP

Round	Month	Day	Venue	Opponents	W,L,D Score	Scorers	Attendance	Ainge S	Beckwith D	Brill D	Dance J	Essam C	Fleetwood S	Goodman J	Gray A	Griffiths S	Henry R	Howells J	Jibodu J	Kasim Y	Kovacs J	Lacey A	Lawless A	Martin D	McNulty S	Mendy A	Neilson S	O'Donnell JJ	Rendell S	Robinson J	Robinson M	Rowe-Turner L	Shaw J	Smith Jonathan	Taiwo S	Taylor G	Thomas W	Tyler M	Walker D	Wall A	Watkins A	Woolley J	Round
Q4	Oct	20	(a)	Cambridge United	W 2-0	Gray, Shaw	2321	13					10		7	2	3				6		4			11		8			14	12	5	9				1					Q4
1	Nov	3	(h)	NUNEATON TOWN	D 1-1	Rendell	3089		1				11		7	2	3				6			4				8	9	12		5				10				13			1
Rep	Nov	13	(a)	Nuneaton Town	W 2-0	Rendell (2, 1pen)	1596				14		9		2	3		6				8	4			11	10				12	5				1	7				13		Rep
2	Dec	1	(h)	DORCHESTER TOWN	W 2-1	Gray, Lawless	3287	5					13		9	2	4			6	12	7	14			11	10				3	8				1						2
3	Jan	5	(h)	WOLVERHAMPTON WANDERERS	W 1-0	Lawless	9638						12		10	2		6				7	4			11	13				5	9	8		3	1					3
4	Jan	26	(a)	Norwich City	W 1-0	Rendell	26521						14		10	2	11	6			7	4			12	13				5	9	8		3	1					4
5	Feb	16	(h)	MILLWALL	L 0-3		9768						12		9	5	3	6			7	4			11	10				13	2				1					5
						Apps		1	1			2	7		7	6		7		6		6	6		6	4		6	4		3	4	6	2		3	6					
						Subs			1		1		4				1				1			1		1	2	2		2											1	1	
						Goals							2								2			4				1				1									

2012/13 FA TROPHY

Round	Month	Day	Venue	Opponents	W,L,D Score	Scorers	Attendance	Ainge S	Beckwith D	Brill D	Dance J	Essam C	Fleetwood S	Goodman J	Gray A	Griffiths S	Henry R	Howells J	Jibodu J	Kasim Y	Kovacs J	Lacey A	Lawless A	Martin D	McNulty S	Mendy A	Neilson S	O'Donnell JJ	Rendell S	Robinson J	Robinson M	Rowe-Turner L	Shaw J	Smith Jonathan	Taiwo S	Taylor G	Thomas W	Tyler M	Walker D	Wall A	Watkins A	Woolley J	Round
1	Nov	27	(a)	Dorchester Town	D 2-2	Martin (og), Fleetwood	688	5			13		12		9	2	4			6		7						11	10				3					1					1
Rep	Dec	4	(h)	DORCHESTER TOWN	W 3-1	O'Donnell, Walker (2)	897	5		1	7		13					12				6	2					11			4	3	9						10		8	14	Rep
2	Dec	15	(a)	Matlock Town	W 2-1	Ainge, Shaw	823	5		1			12	10	2	3		6				7		4				11	8				13	9									2
3	Jan	12	(h)	SKELMERSDALE UNITED	W 2-0	Watkins, Gray	2479	5		1	7		14	12				11	3				2					8				10	4	6					9		13		3
4	Jan	29	(a)	Grimsby Town	L 0-3		2791	13		1			9		2	3		6				7		4				11	10				5	12	8						14		4
						1 Own Goal	**Apps**	4		4	2		1	2	3	4		3	1	5		3	4	2		4	2		1	2		1			
							Subs	1			1		4	1			1				1			1		1			2	1	
							Goals	1			1		1		1			1					1		2		1

2013/14 FOOTBALL CONFERENCE PREMIER (NON-LEAGUE)

Match No	Month	Day	Venue	Opponents	W.L.D Score	Scorers	Attendance	Banton Z	Benson P	Chabata T	Charles A	Cullen M	Davis J	Ferdinand K	Franks F	Gray A	Griffiths S	Guttridge L	Henry R	Howells J	Inniss R	Justham E	Lacey A	Lawless A	Longden B	Martin D	Mawson A	McGeehan C	McNulty S	Mendy A	O'Donnell JJ	Parry A	Rees I	Robinson M	Rooney L	Ruddock P	Shaw J	Smith C	Smith Jonathan	Stevenson J	Taiwo S	Trotman L	Tyler M	Viana D	Wall A	Whalley S	Match No
1	Aug	10	(a)	Southport	L 0-1		2210				13	9				12	3	8		10			6			11				5		14								2	4	1		7		1
2	Aug	13	(h)	SALISBURY CITY	W 2-0	Taiwo (pen), Guttridge	6520		6			10				12	3	8		14			13			11				5							9				2	4	1		7		2
3	Aug	17	(h)	MACCLESFIELD TOWN	D 1-1	Guttridge	6216					13				10	3	8	2	12			6			11				5							9				14	4	1		7		3
4	Aug	24	(a)	Forest Green Rovers	D 0-0		1858					11				10	3	8	2	12			6							5							9		4				1		7		4
5	Aug	26	(h)	CAMBRIDGE UNITED	D 0-0		7517					10				7	3	8	2	12			6			13				5							9		4				1		11		5
6	Aug	31	(a)	Kidderminster Harriers	W 2-0	Howells (2pens)	2866		9							7	3	10	2	11			6			13				5		8								4				1		12		6
7	Sep	7	(h)	GRIMSBY TOWN	D 0-0		6131		9							7	3	10	2	11			6							5		8								4	12		1		14	13	7
8	Sep	13	(a)	Wrexham	L 0-2		3122		9			10				14	3	8	2	11				13						5		6								4			1		12	7	8
9	Sep	17	(h)	DARTFORD	W 3-0	Benson, Guttridge, Lawless	5433		9								3	10	2	11				7	12					5		6								4	8	14	1		13		9
10	Sep	21	(h)	LINCOLN CITY	W 3-2	Cullen (2), Guttridge	6203					9				12	3	10	2	11				7					13	6										4	8	14	1		10		10
11	Sep	24	(a)	Woking	W 4-0	Cullen (2), Lacey, Gray	1955	13				9				7	3	10	2	11			6						12	5		8								4			1		14		11
12	Sep	28	(a)	Hereford United	D 0-0		2386		9			10				12	3	7	2	11			6							5		8								4			1		13		12
13	Oct	5	(h)	FC HALIFAX TOWN	W 4-3	Guttridge, Benson, Gray, Wall	6519		9							10	3	11	2				6	7						5		8	13							4			1		12		13
14	Oct	8	(a)	Aldershot Town	D 3-3	Gray, Parry, Whalley (pen)	2693		9							7	3	10	2	11			6							5		8								4			1		12	13	14
15	Oct	12	(h)	HYDE	W 4-1	Gray (3), Guttridge	7081		9			14				10	3	11	2				6	7						5		8	13							4			1		12		15
16	Oct	19	(a)	Tamworth	W 4-3	Smith, Parry, Benson (2)	2066		9		13					10	3	11	2				6	12						5		8								4			1		7		16
17	Nov	2	(a)	Gateshead	D 0-0		1080		9			12				7	3	10	2	11			6							5		8								4			1		13		17
18	Nov	12	(a)	Braintree Town	W 2-1	Benson, Parry	1518		9			13				10	3		2	11			6	7						5		8								4	12		1				18
19	Nov	16	(a)	Chester FC	D 1-1	Gray	3291		9			11				10	3	11	2	13			6	7						5		8								4			1		14		19
20	Nov	23	(h)	WELLING UNITED	W 2-1	Gray (2)	6592		9							10	3	12	2				6	7						5		8	13							4			1		11		20
21	Nov	26	(h)	SOUTHPORT	W 3-0	McNulty, Smith, Gray	6057		9			14				10	3	8	2				6	7						5		4	12						11				1		13		21
22	Dec	7	(a)	Alfreton Town	W 5-0	Gray (2), Benson, Guttridge, Lawless	1279		9				12			10	3	11	2					7		6				5								8		4			1				22
23	Dec	21	(h)	GATESHEAD	W 4-2	Benson, Lawless (2), Gray	6913		9			6				7	3	10	2					11						5			12	8					4				1				23
24	Dec	26	(a)	Barnet	W 2-1	Benson, Lawless	3608		9			13	6			7	3	10	2					11						5			12	8					4				1				24
25	Dec	28	(h)	KIDDERMINSTER HARRIERS	W 6-0	Guttridge (2), Benson, Howells (2, 1pen), Griffiths	8488		9			13	6			7	3	10	2	12				11						5			4	8									1				25
26	Jan	1	(h)	BARNET	W 2-1	Gray, Benson	7543		9			6				7	3	10	2	11				8						5			4										1				26
27	Jan	4	(a)	Lincoln City	D 0-0		2928		9			6	12			7	3	10	2	11				8						5			4										1				27
28	Jan	25	(h)	NUNEATON TOWN	W 3-0	Gray (3)	7310		9			12				7	3	10	2	11	6			13			8	5					4										1				28
29	Feb	11	(a)	Macclesfield Town	W 2-1	Gray (2)	1705		9							6	7	3	10	2	11						12			4	5												1				29
30	Feb	15	(h)	HEREFORD UNITED	W 7-0	Gray (3), Benson, Howells (pen), Ruddock, Lawless	7111		9							6	7	3	10	2	11					13				4	5			12		8	14						1				30
31	Feb	22	(a)	Nuneaton Town	W 5-0	Benson (2), Gray, Guttridge, Howells	3480		9							6	7	3	10	2	11					13				4	5			14		8	12						1				31
32	Feb	25	(h)	WREXHAM	W 5-0	Guttridge (2), Gray, Benson, Howells (pen)	7526		9							6	7	3	10	2	11					13				4	5			14		8	12						1				32
33	Mar	1	(h)	ALFRETON TOWN	W 3-0	Guttridge, Gray, Benson	8412		9							6	7	3	10	2	11					13				4	5			12		8	14						1				33
34	Mar	8	(a)	Salisbury City	D 0-0		2633		9			13				6	7	3		2	11					10				4	5			12		8							1				34
35	Mar	11	(a)	Cambridge United	D 1-1	Cullen	6050		9			13				6	7	3		2	11					10				4	5		14	12		8							1				35
36	Mar	17	(h)	WOKING	L 0-1		6683		9			14				6	7	3		2	11					10				4	5		13	8		12							1				36
37	Mar	22	(h)	CHESTER FC	W 3-0	Robinson, Gray, Benson	8475		9			12				6	7	3		2	11					8					5		4		13	14	10						1				37
38	Mar	25	(a)	Grimsby Town	W 2-1	Robinson, Benson	3789		9							6	11	3		2						7				4	5		8			10							1				38
39	Mar	29	(a)	FC Halifax Town	L 0-2		3586		9			12				6	7	3		2						11				4	5		8		13	10						1				39
40	Apr	1	(a)	Dartford	W 2-1	Ruddock, Gray	2869		9			12				6	10	3		2	11					7				4	5		8		14	13						1				40
41	Apr	5	(h)	ALDERSHOT TOWN	W 1-0	McGeehan	8558		9			13				6	7	3		2	14					11				4	5		12	10	8							1				41
42	Apr	8	(h)	TAMWORTH	W 2-0	McGeehan, Cullen	8554		9			12				6	7	3		2	11					13				4	5		8	10		14						1				42
43	Apr	12	(h)	BRAINTREE TOWN	L 2-3	Howells (pen), Wall	10020		9			10				6		3		2	11					7				4	5		8	12	14							1		13		43
44	Apr	19	(a)	Welling United	W 2-1	Cullen, Gray	2650					9				6	7	3		2	11				12				4	5		13	11	8	14							1		10		44
45	Apr	21	(h)	FOREST GREEN ROVERS	W 4-1	Gray (2, 1pen), McGeehan, Cullen	10044					9				6	7	3		2	11				12				4	5		8		10	14							1		13		45
46	Apr	26	(a)	Hyde	W 1-0	Wall	2759				13	9				7	3			11			6							4	5		2		10	8			14			1		12		46

Final League Position: 1st

	Banton Z	Benson P	Chabata T	Charles A	Cullen M	Davis J	Ferdinand K	Franks F	Gray A	Griffiths S	Guttridge L	Henry R	Howells J	Inniss R	Justham E	Lacey A	Lawless A	Longden B	Martin D	Mawson A	McGeehan C	McNulty S	Mendy A	O'Donnell JJ	Parry A	Rees I	Robinson M	Rooney L	Ruddock P	Shaw J	Smith C	Smith Jonathan	Stevenson J	Taiwo S	Trotman L	Tyler M	Viana D	Wall A	Whalley S
Apps	-	36	-	1	12	5	-	17	39	46	31	43	28	1	-	18	23	-	3	1	18	46	-	-	18	-	13	2	18	4	-	22	3	3	-	46	-	1	8
Subs	1	-	-	3	17	1	1	-	5	-	1	-	7	-	-	3	8	4	-	-	2	5	-	-	14	4	3	7	-	2	2	2	-	-	-	-	-	9	8
Goals	-	17	-	-	8	-	-	-	30	1	13	-	8	-	-	1	6	-	-	-	3	1	-	-	3	-	2	-	2	-	-	2	-	1	-	-	-	3	1

2013/14 FA CUP

Round	Month	Day	Venue	Opponents	W,L,D Score	Scorers	Attendance	Banton Z	Benson P	Chabata T	Charles A	Cullen M	Davis J	Ferdinand K	Franks F	Gray A	Griffiths S	Guttridge L	Henry R	Howells J	Inniss R	Justham E	Lacey A	Lawless A	Longden B	Martin D	Mawson A	McGeehan C	McNulty S	Mendy A	O'Donnell JJ	Parry A	Rees I	Robinson M	Rooney L	Ruddock P	Shaw J	Smith C	Smith Jonathan	Stevenson J	Taiwo S	Trotman L	Tyler M	Viana D	Wall A	Whalley S	Round
Q4	Oct	26	(a)	Woking	W 1-0	Cullen	1452		9		6	10					12		2	3		1				11			5			13		8					4						7		Q4
1	Nov	9	(a)	Welling United	L 1-2	Benson	1555	14	9			7						10		3		1	6		12	11			5		13	2							4	8							1
							Apps		2		1	2						1	1	2		2	1			2			2			1		1					2	1					1		
							Subs	1									1								1						1	1																
							Goals		1			1																																					

2013/14 FA TROPHY

Round	Month	Day	Venue	Opponents	W,L,D Score	Scorers	Attendance	Banton Z	Benson P	Chabata T	Charles A	Cullen M	Davis J	Ferdinand K	Franks F	Gray A	Griffiths S	Guttridge L	Henry R	Howells J	Inniss R	Justham E	Lacey A	Lawless A	Longden B	Martin D	Mawson A	McGeehan C	McNulty S	Mendy A	O'Donnell JJ	Parry A	Rees I	Robinson M	Rooney L	Ruddock P	Shaw J	Smith C	Smith Jonathan	Stevenson J	Taiwo S	Trotman L	Tyler M	Viana D	Wall A	Whalley S	Round
1	Nov	30	(a)	Staines Town	D 0-0		621	9		2		10	5						3			1								8				4		6	13							11	12	7	1
Rep	Dec	3	(h)	STAINES TOWN	W 2-0	Parry, Whalley	911	12		2		9	5						3			1				6				13		4		8			11								10	7	Rep
2	Dec	14	(h)	WREXHAM	W 2-0	Cullen, Ashton (OG)	1617	12		6		11	5						3			1				2				4		10		8												9	7	2
3	Jan	11	(a)	Cambridge United	D 2-2	Inniss, Wall	3194		6			9	8						3		5	1			2							13		12								4			7	10	11	3
Rep	Jan	14	(h)	CAMBRIDGE UNITED	L 0-1		2312	12		6		11							3		5	1			2					8		9		4											13	10	7	Rep
						1 Own Goal	Apps	1	1	4		5	4						5		2	5			2	2				3		3		4		1	1				1	1			2	4	5	
							Subs	3																						1		1		1			1								1	1		
							Goals					1									1											1														1	1	

TIMELINE…

15 April 2014 Following Cambridge United's defeat at Kidderminster comes confirmation that the Town are champions and finally back in the Football League.
26 April 2014 A victory in the final game of the season at Hyde confirms 101 points, 102 goals scored and a massive 19 points ahead of the second placed club.

▶ **The 2013/14 team** – Back row (left to right): Robinson, Whalley, Wall, Lacey, Rowe-Turner, Woolley, O'Donnell, Fitzsimons, Charles, Smith, Lawless. Middle row (left to right): Richardson (Fitness coach), Hayrettin (Coach), Griffiths, Jibodu, Rendell, Shaw, Tyler, Justham, Longden, Stevenson, Cullen, Parry, Parsell (Physiotherapist), Cook (Kit –man). Front row (left to right): Howells, Martin, Guttridge, Harris (Assistant manager), Henry, Still (Manager), Taiwo, McNulty, Gray.

◗ Ronny Henry holds up the Skrill Premier trophy at the end of a momentous season.

❱ Alex Wall slams home the winner during the thrilling 4-3 victory over Halifax.

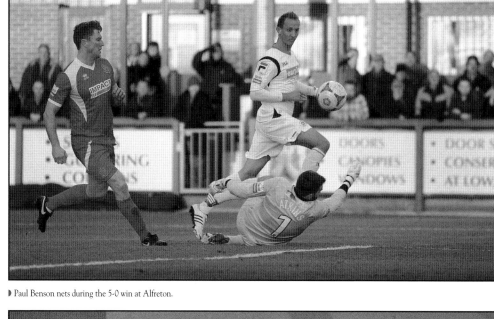

❱ Paul Benson nets during the 5-0 win at Alfreton.

❱ Luke Guttridge scores during the 6-0 home win against Kidderminster to send the Town top.

❱ Atrocious conditions at Kenilworth Road but a vital 2-1 win over Barnet maintains top spot.

▶ Mark Cullen's last minute equaliser at Cambridge in front of 2286 Luton fans.

▶ Andre Gray scores his second goal in the 4-1 win against Forest Green Rovers. His 30th of the season.

▶ The Luton fans celebrate after the Forest Green Rovers clash.

▶ The players join in the celebrations.

1894/95 Southern League (One)

		P	W	D	L	F	A	Pts
1	Millwall Athletic	16	12	4	0	68	19	28
2	LUTON TOWN	16	9	4	3	36	22	22
3	Southampton St Mary's	16	9	2	5	34	25	20
4	Ilford	16	6	3	7	26	40	15
5	Reading	16	6	2	8	33	38	14
6	Chatham	16	4	5	7	22	25	13
7	Royal Ordnance Factories	16	3	6	7	20	30	12
8	Clapton	16	5	1	10	22	38	11
9	Swindon Town	16	4	1	11	24	48	9

1895/96 Southern League (One)

		P	W	D	L	F	A	Pts
1	Millwall Athletic	18	16	1	1	75	16	33
2	LUTON TOWN	18	13	1	4	68	14	27
3	Southampton St Mary's	18	12	0	6	44	23	24
4	Reading	18	11	1	6	45	38	23
5	Chatham	18	9	2	7	43	45	20
6	New Brompton	18	7	4	7	30	37	18
7	Swindon Town	18	6	4	8	38	41	16
8	Clapton	18	4	2	12	30	67	10
9	Royal Ordnance Factories	18	3	3	12	23	44	9
10	Ilford	18	0	0	18	10	81	0

'1897/98 Football League Div Two

		P	W	D	L	F	A	W	D	L	F	A	Pts
1	Burnley	30	14	1	0	64	13	6	7	2	16	11	48
2	Newcastle United	30	14	0	1	43	10	7	3	5	21	22	45
3	Manchester City	30	10	4	1	45	15	5	5	5	21	21	39
4	Newton Heath	30	11	2	2	42	10	5	4	6	22	25	38
5	Woolwich Arsenal	30	10	4	1	41	14	6	1	8	28	35	37
6	Small Heath	30	11	1	3	37	18	5	3	7	21	32	36
7	Leicester Fosse	30	8	5	2	26	11	5	2	8	20	24	33
8	LUTON TOWN	30	10	2	3	50	13	3	2	10	18	37	30
9	Gainsborough Trinity	30	10	4	1	30	12	2	2	11	20	42	30
10	Walsall	30	9	4	2	42	15	3	2	10	16	43	29
11	Blackpool	30	8	4	3	32	15	2	1	12	17	46	25
12	Grimsby Town	30	9	1	5	44	24	1	3	11	8	38	24
13	Burton Swifts	30	7	3	5	25	21	1	2	12	13	48	21
14	Lincoln City	30	6	3	6	27	27	0	2	13	16	55	17
15	Darwen	30	4	1	10	21	32	2	1	12	10	44	14
16	Loughborough	30	5	2	8	15	26	1	0	14	9	61	14

'1898/99 Football League Div Two

		P	W	D	L	F	A	W	D	L	F	A	Pts
1	Manchester City	34	15	1	1	64	10	8	5	4	28	25	52
2	Glossop	34	12	1	4	48	13	8	5	4	28	25	46
3	Leicester Fosse	34	12	5	0	35	12	6	4	7	29	30	45
4	Newton Heath	34	12	4	1	51	14	7	1	9	16	29	43
5	New Brighton Tower	34	13	2	2	48	13	5	5	7	23	39	43
6	Walsall	34	12	5	0	64	11	3	7	7	15	25	42
7	Woolwich Arsenal	34	14	2	1	55	10	4	3	10	17	31	41
8	Small Heath	34	14	1	2	66	17	3	6	8	19	33	41
9	Burslem Port Vale	34	12	2	3	35	12	5	3	9	21	22	39
10	Grimsby Town	34	10	3	4	39	17	5	2	10	32	43	35
11	Barnsley	34	11	4	2	44	18	1	3	13	8	38	31
12	Lincoln City	34	10	5	2	31	16	2	2	13	20	40	31
13	Burton Swifts	34	7	5	5	35	25	3	3	11	16	45	28
14	Gainsborough Trinity	34	8	4	5	40	22	1	1	14	16	50	25
15	LUTON TOWN	34	8	1	8	37	31	2	1	14	24	64	23
16	Blackpool	34	6	3	8	35	30	2	1	14	14	60	20
17	Loughborough	34	5	4	8	31	26	1	2	14	7	66	18
18	Darwen	34	2	4	11	16	32	0	1	16	6	109	9

'1899/1900 Football League Div Two

		P	W	D	L	F	A	W	D	L	F	A	Pts
1	Sheffield Wed.	34	17	0	0	61	7	8	4	5	23	15	54
2	Bolton Wanderers	34	14	2	1	47	7	8	6	3	32	18	52
3	Small Heath	34	15	1	1	58	12	5	5	7	20	26	46
4	Newton Heath	34	15	1	1	44	11	5	3	9	19	16	44
5	Leicester Fosse	34	11	5	1	34	8	6	4	7	19	28	43
6	Grimsby Town	34	10	3	4	46	24	7	3	7	21	22	40
7	Chesterfield Town	34	10	4	3	35	24	6	2	9	30	36	38
8	Woolwich Arsenal	34	13	1	3	47	12	3	3	11	14	31	36
9	Lincoln City	34	11	5	1	31	9	3	3	11	15	34	36
10	New Brighton Tower	34	9	4	4	44	22	4	5	8	22	36	35
11	Burslem Port Vale	34	11	2	4	26	16	3	4	10	13	33	34
12	Walsall	34	10	5	2	35	18	2	3	12	15	37	32
13	Gainsborough Trinity	34	8	4	5	37	24	1	3	13	10	51	25
14	Middlesbrough	34	8	5	4	28	15	0	4	13	11	54	24
15	Burton Swifts	34	8	5	4	31	24	1	1	15	12	60	24
16	Barnsley	34	8	4	5	36	23	0	2	15	10	56	23
17	LUTON TOWN	34	5	3	9	25	25	0	5	12	25	50	18
18	Loughborough	34	1	6	10	12	26	0	0	17	6	74	8

1900/01 Southern League (One)

		P	W	D	L	F	A	Pts
1	Southampton	28	18	5	5	58	26	41
2	Bristol City	28	17	5	6	54	27	39
3	Portsmouth	28	17	4	7	56	32	38
4	Millwall	28	17	2	9	55	32	36
5	Tottenham Hotspur	28	16	4	8	55	33	36
6	West Ham United	28	14	5	9	40	28	33
7	Bristol Rovers	28	14	4	10	46	35	32
8	Queens Park Rangers	28	11	4	13	43	48	26
9	Reading	28	8	8	12	24	25	24
10	LUTON TOWN	28	11	2	15	43	49	24
11	Kettering	28	7	9	12	33	46	23
12	New Brompton	28	7	5	16	34	51	19
13	Gravesend United	28	6	7	15	32	85	19
14	Watford	28	6	4	18	24	52	16
15	Swindon Town	28	3	8	17	19	47	14

1901/02 Southern League (One)

		P	W	D	L	F	A	Pts
1	Portsmouth	30	20	7	3	67	24	47
2	Tottenham Hotspur	30	18	6	6	61	22	42
3	Southampton	30	18	6	6	71	28	42
4	West Ham United	30	17	6	7	45	28	40
5	Reading	30	16	7	7	57	24	39
6	Millwall	30	13	6	11	48	31	32
7	LUTON TOWN	30	11	10	9	31	35	32
8	Kettering	30	12	5	13	44	39	29
9	Bristol Rovers	30	12	5	13	43	39	29
10	New Brompton	30	10	7	13	39	38	27
11	Northampton Town	30	11	5	14	53	64	27
12	Queens Park Rangers	30	8	7	15	34	56	23
13	Watford	30	9	4	17	36	60	22
14	Wellingborough	30	9	4	17	34	72	22
15	Brentford	30	7	6	17	34	61	20
16	Swindon Town	30	2	3	25	17	93	7

1902/03 Southern League (One)

		P	W	D	L	F	A	Pts
1	Southampton	30	20	8	2	83	20	48
2	Reading	30	19	7	4	72	30	45
3	Portsmouth	30	17	7	6	69	32	41
4	Tottenham Hotspur	30	14	7	9	47	31	35
5	Bristol Rovers	30	13	8	9	46	34	34
6	New Brompton	30	11	8	11	37	35	33
7	Millwall	30	14	3	13	52	37	31
8	Northampton Town	30	12	6	12	39	48	30
9	Queens Park Rangers	30	11	6	13	34	42	28
10	West Ham United	30	9	10	11	35	49	28
11	LUTON TOWN	30	10	7	13	43	44	27
12	Swindon Town	30	10	7	13	38	46	27
13	Kettering	30	8	11	11	33	40	27
14	Wellingborough	30	11	3	16	36	56	25
15	Watford	30	6	4	20	35	87	16
16	Brentford	30	2	1	27	16	84	5

1903/04 Southern League (One)

		P	W	D	L	F	A	Pts
1	Southampton	34	22	6	6	75	30	50
2	Tottenham Hotspur	34	16	11	7	54	37	43
3	Bristol Rovers	34	17	8	9	66	42	42
4	Portsmouth	34	17	8	9	41	38	42
5	Queens Park Rangers	34	15	11	8	53	37	41
6	Reading	34	14	13	7	48	35	40
7	Millwall	34	16	8	10	65	42	40
8	LUTON TOWN	34	14	12	8	38	33	40
9	Plymouth Argyle	34	13	10	11	44	34	36
10	Swindon Town	34	10	11	13	30	42	31
11	Fulham	34	9	12	13	34	36	30
12	West Ham United	34	10	7	17	39	44	27
13	Brentford	34	9	9	16	34	60	27
14	Wellingborough	34	11	5	18	44	63	27
15	Northampton Town	34	10	7	17	36	60	27
16	New Brompton	34	6	13	15	26	43	25
17	Brighton & HA	34	6	12	16	45	69	24
18	Kettering	34	6	7	21	39	78	19

1904/05 Southern League (One)

		P	W	D	L	F	A	Pts
1	Bristol Rovers	34	20	8	6	74	36	48
2	Reading	34	18	7	9	57	38	43
3	Southampton	34	18	7	9	54	40	43
4	Plymouth Argyle	34	18	5	11	57	39	41
5	Tottenham Hotspur	34	15	8	11	53	34	38
6	Fulham	34	14	10	10	46	34	38
7	Queens Park Rangers	34	14	8	12	51	46	36
8	Portsmouth	34	16	4	14	61	56	36
9	New Brompton	34	11	11	12	40	41	33
10	Watford	34	15	3	16	41	44	33
11	West Ham United	34	12	8	14	48	42	32
12	Brighton & HA	34	13	6	15	44	45	32
13	Northampton Town	34	12	8	14	43	54	32
14	Brentford	34	10	9	15	33	38	29
15	Millwall	34	11	7	16	38	47	29
16	Swindon Town	34	12	5	17	41	59	29
17	LUTON TOWN	34	12	3	19	45	54	27
18	Wellingborough	34	5	3	26	25	104	13

1905/06 Southern League (One)

		P	W	D	L	F	A	Pts
1	Fulham	34	19	12	3	44	15	50
2	Southampton	34	19	7	8	58	39	45
3	Portsmouth	34	17	9	8	61	35	43
4	LUTON TOWN	34	17	7	10	64	40	41
5	Tottenham Hotspur	34	16	7	11	46	29	39
6	Plymouth Argyle	34	16	7	11	52	33	39
7	Norwich City	34	13	10	11	46	38	36
8	Bristol Rovers	34	15	5	14	56	56	35
9	Brentford	34	14	7	13	43	52	35
10	Reading	34	12	9	13	53	46	33
11	West Ham United	34	14	5	15	42	39	33
12	Millwall	34	11	11	12	38	41	33
13	Queens Park Rangers	34	12	7	15	58	44	31
14	Watford	34	8	10	16	38	57	26
15	Swindon Town	34	8	9	17	31	52	25
16	Brighton & HA	34	9	7	18	30	55	25
17	New Brompton	34	7	8	19	20	62	22
18	Northampton Town	34	8	5	21	32	79	21

1906/07 Southern League (One)

		P	W	D	L	F	A	Pts
1	Fulham	38	20	13	5	58	32	53
2	Portsmouth	38	22	7	9	64	36	51
3	Brighton & HA	38	18	9	11	53	43	45
4	LUTON TOWN	38	18	9	11	52	52	45
5	West Ham United	38	15	14	9	60	41	44
6	Tottenham Hotspur	38	17	9	12	63	45	43
7	Millwall	38	18	6	14	71	50	42
8	Norwich City	38	15	12	11	57	48	42
9	Watford	38	13	16	9	46	43	42
10	Brentford	38	17	8	13	57	56	42
11	Southampton	38	13	9	16	49	56	35
12	Reading	38	14	6	18	57	47	34
13	Leyton	38	11	12	15	38	60	34
14	Bristol Rovers	38	12	9	17	55	54	33
15	Plymouth Argyle	38	10	13	15	43	50	33
16	New Brompton	38	12	9	17	47	59	33
17	Swindon Town	38	11	11	16	43	54	33
18	Queens Park Rangers	38	11	10	17	47	55	32
19	Crystal Palace	38	8	9	21	46	66	25
20	Northampton Town	38	5	9	24	29	88	19

1907/08 Southern League (One)

		P	W	D	L	F	A	Pts
1	Queens Park Rangers	38	21	9	8	82	57	51
2	Plymouth Argyle	38	19	11	8	50	31	49
3	Millwall	38	19	8	11	49	32	46
4	Crystal Palace	38	17	10	11	54	51	44
5	Swindon Town	38	16	10	12	55	40	42
6	Bristol Rovers	38	16	10	12	59	56	42
7	Tottenham Hotspur	38	17	7	14	59	48	41
8	Northampton Town	38	15	11	12	50	41	41
9	Portsmouth	38	17	6	15	63	52	40
10	West Ham United	38	15	10	13	47	48	40
11	Southampton	38	16	6	16	51	60	38
12	Reading	38	15	6	17	55	50	36
13	Bradford Park Avenue	38	12	12	14	53	54	36
14	Watford	38	12	10	16	47	59	34
15	Brentford	38	14	5	19	49	52	33
16	Norwich City	38	12	9	17	46	49	33
17	Brighton & HA	38	12	8	18	46	59	32
18	LUTON TOWN	38	12	6	20	33	56	30
19	Leyton	38	8	11	19	51	73	27
20	New Brompton	38	9	7	22	44	75	25

1908/09 Southern League (One)

		P	W	D	L	F	A	Pts
1	Northampton Town	40	25	5	10	90	45	55
2	Swindon Town	40	22	5	13	96	55	49
3	Southampton	40	19	10	11	67	58	48
4	Portsmouth	40	18	10	12	68	60	46
5	Bristol Rovers	40	17	9	14	60	63	43
6	Exeter City	40	18	6	16	56	65	42
7	New Brompton	40	17	7	16	48	59	41
8	Reading	40	11	18	11	60	57	40
9	LUTON TOWN	40	17	6	17	59	60	40
10	Plymouth Argyle	40	15	10	15	46	47	40
11	Millwall	40	16	6	18	59	61	38
12	Southend United	40	14	10	16	52	54	38
13	Leyton	40	15	8	17	52	55	38
14	Watford	40	14	9	17	51	64	37
15	Queens Park Rangers	40	12	12	16	52	50	36
16	Crystal Palace	40	12	12	16	62	62	36
17	West Ham United	40	16	4	20	56	60	36
18	Brighton & HA	40	14	7	19	60	61	35
19	Norwich City	40	12	11	17	59	75	35
20	Coventry City	40	15	4	21	64	91	34
21	Brentford	40	13	7	20	59	74	33

1909/10 Southern League (One)

		P	W	D	L	F	A	Pts
1	Brighton & HA	42	23	13	6	69	28	59
2	Swindon Town	42	22	10	10	92	46	54
3	Queens Park Rangers	42	19	13	10	56	47	51
4	Northampton Town	42	22	4	16	90	44	48
5	Southampton	42	16	16	10	64	55	48
6	Portsmouth	42	20	7	15	70	63	47
7	Crystal Palace	42	20	6	16	69	50	46
8	Coventry City	42	19	8	15	71	60	46
9	West Ham United	42	15	15	12	69	56	45
10	Leyton	42	16	11	15	60	46	43
11	Plymouth Argyle	42	16	11	15	61	54	43
12	New Brompton	42	19	5	18	76	74	43
13	Bristol Rovers	42	16	10	16	37	48	42
14	Brentford	42	16	9	17	50	58	41
15	LUTON TOWN	42	15	11	16	72	92	41
16	Millwall	42	15	7	20	45	59	37
17	Norwich City	42	13	9	20	59	78	35
18	Exeter City	42	14	6	22	60	69	34
19	Watford	42	10	13	19	51	76	33
20	Southend United	42	12	9	21	51	90	33
21	Croydon Common	42	13	5	24	52	96	31
22	Reading	42	7	10	25	38	73	24

1910/11 Southern League (One)

		P	W	D	L	F	A	Pts
1	Swindon Town	38	24	5	9	80	31	53
2	Northampton Town	38	18	12	8	54	27	48
3	Brighton & HA	38	20	8	10	58	36	48
4	Crystal Palace	38	17	13	8	55	48	47
5	West Ham United	38	17	11	10	63	46	45
6	Queens Park Rangers	38	13	14	11	52	41	40
7	Leyton	38	16	8	14	57	52	40
8	Plymouth Argyle	38	15	9	14	54	55	39
9	LUTON TOWN	38	15	8	15	67	63	38
10	Norwich City	38	15	8	15	46	48	38
11	Coventry City	38	16	6	16	65	68	38
12	Brentford	38	14	9	15	41	42	37
13	Exeter City	38	14	9	15	51	53	37
14	Watford	38	13	9	16	49	65	35
15	Millwall	38	11	9	18	42	54	31
16	Bristol Rovers	38	10	10	18	42	55	30
17	Southampton	38	11	8	19	42	67	30
18	New Brompton	38	11	8	19	34	65	30
19	Southend United	38	10	9	19	47	64	29
20	Portsmouth	38	8	11	19	34	53	27

1911/12 Southern League (One)

		P	W	D	L	F	A	Pts
1	Queens Park Rangers	38	21	11	6	59	35	53
2	Plymouth Argyle	38	23	6	9	63	31	52
3	Northampton Town	38	22	7	9	82	41	51
4	Swindon Town	38	21	6	11	82	50	48
5	Brighton & HA	38	19	9	10	73	35	47
6	Coventry City	38	17	8	13	66	54	42
7	Crystal Palace	38	15	10	13	70	46	40
8	Millwall	38	15	10	13	60	57	40
9	Watford	38	13	10	15	56	68	36
10	Stoke	38	13	10	15	51	63	36
11	Reading	38	11	14	13	43	59	36
12	Norwich City	38	10	14	14	40	60	34
13	West Ham United	38	13	7	18	64	69	33
14	Brentford	38	12	9	17	60	65	33
15	Exeter City	38	11	11	16	48	62	33
16	Southampton	38	10	11	17	46	63	31
17	Bristol Rovers	38	9	13	16	41	62	31
18	New Brompton	38	11	9	18	35	72	31
19	LUTON TOWN	38	9	10	19	49	61	28
20	Leyton	38	7	11	20	27	52	25

1912/13 Southern League (Two)

		P	W	D	L	F	A	Pts
1	Cardiff City	24	18	5	1	54	15	41
2	Southend United	24	14	6	4	43	23	34
3	Swansea Town	24	12	7	5	29	23	31
4	Croydon Common	24	13	4	7	51	29	30
5	LUTON TOWN	24	13	4	7	52	39	30
6	Llanelly	24	9	6	9	33	39	24
7	Pontypridd	24	6	11	7	30	28	23
8	Mid Rhondda	24	9	4	11	33	31	22
9	Aberdare	24	8	6	10	38	40	22
10	Newport County	24	7	5	12	29	36	19
11	Mardy	24	6	3	15	38	38	15
12	Treharris	24	5	2	17	18	60	12
13	Ton Pentre	24	3	3	18	22	69	9

1913/14 Southern League (Two)

		P	W	D	L	F	A	Pts
1	Croydon Common	30	23	5	2	76	14	51
2	LUTON TOWN	30	24	3	3	92	22	51
3	Brentford	30	20	4	6	80	18	44
4	Swansea Town	30	20	4	6	66	23	44
5	Stoke	30	19	2	9	71	34	40
6	Newport County	30	14	8	8	49	38	36
7	Mid Rhondda	30	13	7	10	55	37	33
8	Pontypridd	30	14	5	11	43	38	33
9	Llanelly	30	12	4	14	45	39	28
10	Barry	30	9	8	13	44	70	26
11	Abertillery	30	8	4	18	44	51	20
12	Ton Pentre	30	8	4	18	33	61	20
13	Mardy	30	6	6	18	30	60	18
14	Caerphilly	30	4	7	19	21	103	15
15	Aberdare	30	4	5	21	33	87	13
16	Treharris	30	2	4	24	19	106	8

1914/15 Southern League (One)

		P	W	D	L	F	A	Pts
1	Watford	38	22	8	8	68	46	52
2	Reading	38	21	7	10	68	43	49
3	Cardiff City	38	22	4	12	72	38	48
4	West Ham United	38	18	9	11	58	47	45
5	Northampton Town	38	16	11	11	56	51	43
6	Southampton	38	19	5	14	78	74	43
7	Portsmouth	38	16	10	12	54	42	42
8	Millwall	38	16	10	12	50	51	42
9	Swindon Town	38	15	11	12	77	59	41
10	Brighton & HA	38	16	7	15	46	47	39
11	Exeter City	38	15	8	15	50	41	38
12	Queens Park Rangers	38	13	12	13	55	56	38
13	Norwich City	38	11	14	13	53	56	36
14	LUTON TOWN	38	13	8	17	61	73	34
15	Crystal Palace	38	13	8	17	47	61	34
16	Bristol Rovers	38	14	3	21	53	75	31
17	Plymouth Argyle	38	8	14	16	51	61	30
18	Southend United	38	10	8	20	44	64	28
19	Croydon Common	38	9	9	20	47	63	27
20	Gillingham	38	6	8	24	43	83	20

1919/20 Southern League (One)

		P	W	D	L	F	A	Pts
1	Portsmouth	42	23	12	7	73	27	58
2	Watford	42	26	6	10	69	42	58
3	Crystal Palace	42	22	12	8	69	43	56
4	Cardiff City	42	18	17	7	70	43	53
5	Plymouth Argyle	42	20	10	12	57	29	50
6	Queens Park Rangers	42	18	10	14	62	50	46
7	Reading	42	16	13	13	51	43	45
8	Southampton	42	18	8	16	72	63	44
9	Swansea Town	42	16	11	15	53	45	43
10	Exeter City	42	17	9	16	57	51	43
11	Southend United	42	13	17	12	46	48	43
12	Norwich City	42	15	11	16	64	57	41
13	Swindon Town	42	17	7	18	65	68	41
14	Millwall	42	14	12	16	52	55	40
15	Brentford	42	15	10	17	52	59	40
16	Brighton & Hove Albion	42	14	8	20	60	72	36
17	Bristol Rovers	42	11	13	18	61	78	35
18	Newport County	42	13	7	22	45	70	33
19	Northampton Town	42	12	9	21	64	103	33
20	LUTON TOWN	42	10	10	22	51	76	30
21	Merthyr Town	42	9	11	22	47	78	29
22	Gillingham	42	10	7	25	34	74	27

'1920/21 Football League Div Three

		P	W	D	L	F	A	W	D	L	F	A	Pts
1	Crystal Palace	42	15	4	2	45	17	9	7	5	25	17	59
2	Southampton	42	14	5	2	46	10	5	11	5	18	18	54
3	Queens Park Rangers	42	14	4	3	38	11	8	5	8	23	21	53
4	Swindon Town	42	14	5	2	51	17	7	5	9	22	32	52
5	Swansea Town	42	9	10	2	32	19	9	5	7	24	26	51
6	Watford	42	14	4	3	40	15	6	4	11	19	29	48
7	Millwall	42	11	5	5	25	8	7	6	8	17	22	47
8	Merthyr Town	42	13	5	3	46	20	2	10	9	14	29	45
9	LUTON TOWN	42	14	6	1	51	15	2	6	13	10	41	44
10	Bristol Rovers	42	15	3	3	51	22	3	4	14	17	35	43
11	Plymouth Argyle	42	10	7	4	25	13	1	14	6	10	21	43
12	Portsmouth	42	10	8	3	28	14	2	7	12	18	34	39
13	Grimsby Town	42	12	5	4	32	16	3	4	14	17	43	39
14	Northampton Town	42	11	4	6	32	23	4	4	13	27	52	38
15	Newport County	42	8	5	8	20	23	6	4	11	23	41	37
16	Norwich City	42	9	10	2	31	14	1	6	14	13	39	36
17	Southend United	42	13	2	6	32	20	1	6	14	12	41	36
18	Brighton & HA	42	11	6	4	28	20	3	2	16	14	41	36
19	Exeter City	42	9	7	5	27	15	1	8	12	12	39	35
20	Reading	42	8	4	9	26	22	4	3	14	16	37	31
21	Brentford	42	7	9	5	27	23	2	3	16	15	44	30
22	Gillingham	42	6	9	6	19	24	2	3	16	15	50	28

'1921/22 Division Three (South)

		P	W	D	L	F	A	W	D	L	F	A	Pts
1	Southampton	42	14	7	0	50	8	9	8	4	18	13	61
2	Plymouth Argyle	42	17	4	0	43	4	8	7	6	20	20	61
3	Portsmouth	42	13	5	3	38	18	5	12	4	24	21	53
4	LUTON TOWN	42	16	2	3	47	9	6	6	9	17	26	52
5	Queens Park Rangers	42	13	7	1	36	12	5	6	10	17	32	49
6	Swindon Town	42	10	7	4	40	21	6	6	9	32	39	45
7	Watford	42	9	9	3	34	21	4	9	8	20	27	44
8	Aberdare Ath.	42	11	6	4	38	18	6	4	11	19	33	44
9	Brentford	42	15	2	4	41	17	1	9	11	11	26	43
10	Swansea Town	42	11	8	2	40	19	2	7	12	10	28	41
11	Merthyr Town	42	14	2	5	33	15	3	4	14	12	41	40
12	Millwall	42	6	13	2	22	10	4	5	12	16	32	38
13	Reading	42	10	5	6	28	15	4	5	12	12	32	38
14	Bristol Rovers	42	8	8	5	32	24	6	2	13	20	43	38
15	Norwich City	42	8	10	3	29	17	4	3	14	21	45	37
16	Charlton Athletic	42	10	6	5	28	19	3	5	13	15	37	37
17	Northampton Town	42	13	3	5	30	17	0	8	13	17	54	37
18	Gillingham	42	11	4	6	36	20	3	4	14	11	40	36
19	Brighton & HA	42	9	6	6	33	19	4	3	14	12	32	35
20	Newport County	42	8	7	6	22	18	3	5	13	22	43	34
21	Exeter City	42	7	5	9	22	29	4	7	10	16	30	34
22	Southend United	42	7	5	9	23	23	1	6	14	11	51	27

'1922/23 Division Three (South)

		P	W	D	L	F	A	W	D	L	F	A	Pts
1	Bristol City	42	16	4	1	43	13	8	7	6	23	27	59
2	Plymouth Argyle	42	18	3	0	47	6	5	4	12	14	23	53
3	Swansea Town	42	13	6	2	46	14	9	3	9	32	31	53
4	Brighton & HA	42	15	3	3	39	13	5	8	8	13	21	51
5	LUTON TOWN	42	14	4	3	47	18	7	3	11	21	31	49
6	Millwall	42	9	10	2	27	13	5	8	8	18	27	46
7	Portsmouth	42	10	5	6	34	20	9	3	9	24	32	46
8	Northampton Town	42	13	6	2	40	17	4	5	12	14	27	45
9	Swindon Town	42	14	4	3	41	17	3	7	11	21	39	45
10	Watford	42	10	6	5	35	23	7	4	10	22	31	44
11	Queens Park Rangers	42	10	4	7	34	24	6	6	9	20	25	42
12	Charlton Athletic	42	11	6	4	33	14	3	8	10	22	37	42
13	Bristol Rovers	42	7	9	5	25	19	6	7	8	10	17	42
14	Brentford	42	9	4	8	27	23	4	8	9	14	28	38
15	Southend United	42	10	6	5	35	18	2	7	12	14	36	37
16	Gillingham	42	13	4	4	38	18	2	3	16	13	41	37
17	Merthyr Town	42	10	4	7	27	17	1	10	10	12	31	36
18	Norwich City	42	8	7	6	29	26	5	3	13	22	45	36
19	Reading	42	9	8	4	24	15	1	6	14	12	40	34
20	Exeter City	42	10	4	7	27	18	3	3	15	20	66	33
21	Aberdare Ath.	42	6	8	7	25	23	3	3	15	17	47	29
22	Newport County	42	8	6	7	28	21	0	5	16	12	49	27

'1923/24 Division Three (South)

		P	W	D	L	F	A	W	D	L	F	A	Pts
1	Portsmouth	42	15	3	3	57	11	9	8	4	30	19	59
2	Plymouth Argyle	42	13	6	2	46	15	10	3	8	24	19	55
3	Millwall	42	17	3	1	45	11	5	7	9	19	27	54
4	Swansea Town	42	18	2	1	39	10	4	6	11	21	38	52
5	Brighton & HA	42	16	4	1	56	12	5	5	11	12	25	51
6	Swindon Town	42	14	5	2	38	11	3	8	10	20	33	47
7	LUTON TOWN	42	11	7	3	35	19	5	7	9	15	25	46
8	Northampton Town	42	14	3	4	40	15	3	8	10	24	32	45
9	Bristol Rovers	42	11	7	3	34	15	4	6	11	18	31	43
10	Newport County	42	15	4	2	39	15	2	5	14	17	49	43
11	Norwich City	42	13	5	3	45	18	3	3	15	15	41	40
12	Aberdare Ath.	42	9	9	3	35	18	3	5	13	10	40	38
13	Merthyr Town	42	11	8	2	33	19	0	8	13	12	46	38
14	Charlton Athletic	42	8	7	6	26	20	3	8	10	12	25	37
15	Gillingham	42	11	6	4	27	15	1	7	13	16	43	37
16	Exeter City	42	14	3	4	33	17	1	4	16	4	35	37
17	Brentford	42	9	8	4	33	21	5	0	16	21	50	36
18	Reading	42	12	2	7	35	20	1	7	13	16	37	35
19	Southend United	42	11	7	3	35	19	1	3	17	18	65	34
20	Watford	42	8	8	5	35	18	1	7	13	10	36	33
21	Bournemouth	42	6	8	7	19	19	5	3	13	21	46	33
22	Queens Park Rangers	42	9	6	6	28	26	2	3	16	9	51	31

'1924/25 Division Three (South)

		P	W	D	L	F	A	W	D	L	F	A	Pts
1	Swansea Town	42	17	4	0	51	12	6	7	8	17	23	57
2	Plymouth Argyle	42	17	3	1	55	12	6	7	8	22	26	56
3	Bristol City	42	14	5	2	40	10	8	4	9	20	31	53
4	Swindon Town	42	17	2	2	51	13	3	9	9	15	25	51
5	Millwall	42	12	5	4	35	14	6	8	7	23	24	49
6	Newport County	42	13	6	2	35	12	7	3	11	27	30	49
7	Exeter City	42	13	4	4	37	19	6	5	10	22	29	47
8	Brighton & HA	42	14	3	4	43	17	5	5	11	16	28	46
9	Northampton Town	42	12	3	6	34	18	8	3	10	17	26	46
10	Southend United	42	14	1	6	34	18	5	4	12	17	43	43
11	Watford	42	12	3	6	22	20	5	6	10	16	27	43
12	Norwich City	42	10	8	3	39	18	4	5	12	14	33	41
13	Gillingham	42	11	8	2	25	11	2	6	13	10	33	40
14	Reading	42	9	6	6	28	15	5	4	12	9	23	38
15	Charlton Athletic	42	12	6	3	31	13	1	6	14	15	35	38
16	LUTON TOWN	42	9	10	2	34	15	1	7	13	15	42	37
17	Bristol Rovers	42	10	5	6	26	13	2	8	11	16	36	37
18	Aberdare Ath.	42	13	4	4	40	21	1	5	15	14	46	37
19	Queens Park Rangers	42	10	6	5	28	19	4	2	15	14	44	36
20	Bournemouth	42	8	6	7	20	17	5	2	14	20	41	34
21	Brentford	42	8	7	6	28	26	1	0	20	10	65	25
22	Merthyr Town	42	8	3	10	24	27	0	2	19	11	50	21

'1925/26 Division Three (South)

		P	W	D	L	F	A	W	D	L	F	A	Pts
1	Reading	42	16	5	0	49	16	7	6	8	28	36	57
2	Plymouth Argyle	42	16	2	3	71	33	8	6	7	36	34	56
3	Millwall	42	14	6	1	52	12	7	5	9	21	27	53
4	Bristol City	42	14	3	4	42	15	7	6	8	30	36	51
5	Brighton & HA	42	12	4	5	47	33	7	5	9	37	40	47
6	Swindon Town	42	16	2	3	48	22	4	4	13	21	42	46
7	LUTON TOWN	42	16	4	1	60	25	2	3	16	20	50	43
8	Bournemouth	42	10	5	6	44	30	7	4	10	31	61	43
9	Aberdare Ath.	42	11	6	4	50	24	6	2	13	24	42	42
10	Gillingham	42	11	4	6	36	19	6	4	11	17	30	42
11	Southend United	42	13	2	6	50	20	6	2	13	28	53	42
12	Northampton Town	42	13	3	5	47	26	4	4	13	35	54	41
13	Crystal Palace	42	16	1	4	50	21	3	2	16	25	58	41
14	Merthyr Town	42	13	3	5	51	25	1	8	12	18	50	39
15	Watford	42	12	5	4	47	26	3	4	14	26	63	39
16	Norwich City	42	11	5	5	35	26	4	4	13	23	47	39
17	Newport County	42	11	5	5	39	27	3	5	13	25	47	38
18	Brentford	42	12	4	5	44	32	4	2	15	25	62	38
19	Bristol Rovers	42	9	4	8	44	28	6	2	13	22	41	36
20	Exeter City	42	13	2	6	54	25	2	3	16	18	45	35
21	Charlton Athletic	42	9	7	5	32	23	2	6	13	16	45	35
22	Queens Park Rangers	42	5	7	9	23	32	1	2	18	14	52	21

'1926/27 Division Three (South)

		P	W	D	L	F	A	W	D	L	F	A	Pts
1	Bristol City	42	19	1	1	71	24	8	7	6	33	30	62
2	Plymouth Argyle	42	17	4	0	52	14	8	6	7	43	47	60
3	Millwall	42	16	2	3	55	19	7	8	6	34	32	56
4	Brighton & HA	42	15	4	2	61	24	6	7	8	18	26	53
5	Swindon Town	42	16	3	2	64	31	5	6	10	36	54	51
6	Crystal Palace	42	12	6	3	57	33	6	3	12	27	48	45
7	Bournemouth	42	13	2	6	49	24	5	6	10	29	42	44
8	LUTON TOWN	42	12	9	0	48	19	3	5	13	20	47	44
9	Newport County	42	15	4	2	40	20	4	2	15	17	51	44
10	Bristol Rovers	42	12	4	5	46	28	4	5	12	32	52	41
11	Brentford	42	10	9	2	46	20	3	5	13	24	41	40
12	Exeter City	42	14	4	3	46	18	1	6	14	30	55	40
13	Charlton Athletic	42	13	5	3	44	22	3	3	15	16	39	40
14	Queens Park Rangers	42	9	8	4	41	27	6	1	14	24	44	39
15	Coventry City	42	11	4	6	44	33	4	3	14	27	53	37
16	Norwich City	42	10	5	6	41	25	2	6	13	18	46	35
17	Merthyr Town	42	11	5	5	42	25	2	4	15	21	55	35
18	Northampton Town	42	13	4	4	36	23	2	1	18	23	64	35
19	Southend United	42	12	3	6	44	25	2	3	16	20	52	34
20	Gillingham	42	10	5	6	36	26	1	5	15	18	46	32
21	Watford	42	9	6	6	36	27	3	2	16	21	60	32
22	Aberdare Ath.	42	8	2	11	38	48	1	5	15	24	53	25

'1927/28 Division Three (South)

		P	W	D	L	F	A	W	D	L	F	A	Pts
1	Millwall	42	19	2	0	87	15	11	3	7	40	35	65
2	Northampton Town	42	17	3	1	67	23	6	6	9	35	41	55
3	Plymouth Argyle	42	17	2	2	60	19	6	5	10	25	35	53
4	Brighton & HA	42	14	4	3	51	24	5	6	10	30	45	48
5	Crystal Palace	42	15	3	3	46	23	3	9	9	33	49	48
6	Swindon Town	42	12	6	3	60	26	7	3	11	30	43	47
7	Southend United	42	14	2	5	48	19	6	4	11	32	45	46
8	Exeter City	42	11	6	4	49	27	6	6	9	21	33	46
9	Newport County	42	12	5	4	52	38	6	4	11	29	46	45
10	Queens Park Rangers	42	8	5	8	37	35	9	4	8	35	36	43
11	Charlton Athletic	42	12	5	4	34	27	3	8	10	26	43	43
12	Brentford	42	12	4	5	49	30	4	4	13	27	44	40
13	LUTON TOWN	42	13	5	3	56	27	3	2	16	38	60	39
14	Bournemouth	42	12	6	3	44	24	1	6	14	28	55	38
15	Watford	42	10	5	6	42	34	4	5	12	26	44	38
16	Gillingham	42	10	3	8	33	26	3	8	10	29	55	37
17	Norwich City	42	9	8	4	41	26	1	8	12	25	44	36
18	Walsall	42	9	6	6	52	35	3	3	15	23	66	33
19	Bristol Rovers	42	11	3	7	41	36	3	1	17	26	57	32
20	Coventry City	42	5	8	8	40	36	6	1	14	27	60	31
21	Merthyr Town	42	7	6	8	38	40	2	7	12	15	51	31
22	Torquay United	42	4	10	7	27	36	4	4	13	26	67	30

'1928/29 Division Three (South)

		P	W	D	L	F	A	W	D	L	F	A	Pts
1	Charlton Athletic	42	14	5	2	51	22	9	3	9	35	38	54
2	Crystal Palace	42	14	2	5	40	25	9	6	6	41	42	54
3	Northampton Town	42	14	6	1	68	23	6	6	9	28	34	52
4	Plymouth Argyle	42	14	6	1	51	13	6	6	9	32	38	52
5	Fulham	42	14	3	4	60	31	7	7	7	41	40	52
6	Queens Park Rangers	42	13	7	1	50	22	6	7	8	32	39	52
7	LUTON TOWN	42	16	3	2	64	28	3	8	10	25	45	49
8	Watford	42	15	3	3	55	31	4	7	10	24	43	48
9	Bournemouth	42	14	4	3	54	31	5	5	11	30	46	47
10	Swindon Town	42	12	5	4	48	27	3	8	10	27	45	43
11	Coventry City	42	9	6	6	35	23	5	8	8	27	34	42
12	Southend United	42	10	7	4	44	27	5	4	12	36	48	41
13	Brentford	42	11	4	6	34	21	3	6	12	22	39	38
14	Walsall	42	11	7	3	47	25	2	5	14	26	54	38
15	Brighton & HA	42	14	2	5	39	28	2	4	15	19	48	38
16	Newport County	42	8	6	7	37	28	5	3	13	32	58	35
17	Norwich City	42	12	3	6	49	29	2	3	16	20	52	34
18	Torquay United	42	10	3	8	46	36	4	3	14	20	48	34
19	Bristol Rovers	42	9	6	6	39	28	4	1	16	21	51	33
20	Merthyr Town	42	11	6	4	42	28	0	2	19	13	75	30
21	Exeter City	42	7	6	8	49	40	2	5	14	18	48	29
22	Gillingham	42	7	8	6	22	24	3	1	17	21	59	29

'1929/30 Division Three (South)

		P	W	D	L	F	A	W	D	L	F	A	Pts
1	Plymouth Argyle	42	18	3	0	63	12	12	5	4	35	26	68
2	Brentford	42	21	0	0	66	12	7	5	9	28	32	61
3	Queens Park Rangers	42	13	5	3	46	26	8	4	9	34	42	51
4	Northampton Town	42	14	6	1	53	20	7	2	12	29	38	50
5	Brighton & HA	42	16	2	3	54	20	5	6	10	33	43	50
6	Coventry City	42	14	3	4	54	25	5	6	10	34	48	47
7	Fulham	42	12	6	3	54	33	6	5	10	33	50	47
8	Norwich City	42	14	4	3	55	28	4	6	11	33	49	46
9	Crystal Palace	42	14	5	2	56	26	3	7	11	25	48	46
10	Bournemouth	42	11	6	4	47	24	4	7	10	25	37	43
11	Southend United	42	11	6	4	41	19	4	7	10	28	40	43
12	Clapton Orient	42	10	8	3	38	21	4	5	12	17	41	41
13	LUTON TOWN	42	13	4	4	42	25	1	8	12	22	53	40
14	Swindon Town	42	10	7	4	42	25	3	5	13	31	58	38
15	Watford	42	10	4	7	37	30	5	4	12	23	43	38
16	Exeter City	42	10	6	5	45	29	2	5	14	22	44	35
17	Walsall	42	10	4	7	45	24	3	4	14	26	54	34
18	Newport County	42	9	9	3	48	29	3	1	17	26	56	34
19	Torquay United	42	9	6	6	50	38	1	5	15	14	56	31
20	Bristol Rovers	42	11	3	7	45	31	0	5	16	22	62	30
21	Gillingham	42	9	5	7	38	28	2	3	16	13	52	30
22	Merthyr Town	42	5	6	10	39	49	1	3	17	21	86	21

'1930/31 Division Three (South)

		P	W	D	L	F	A	W	D	L	F	A	Pts
1	Notts County	42	16	4	1	58	13	8	7	6	39	33	59
2	Crystal Palace	42	17	2	2	71	20	5	5	11	36	51	51
3	Brentford	42	14	3	4	62	30	8	3	10	28	34	50
4	Brighton & HA	42	13	5	3	45	20	4	10	7	23	33	49
5	Southend United	42	16	0	5	53	26	6	5	10	23	34	49
6	Northampton Town	42	10	6	5	37	20	8	6	7	40	39	48
7	LUTON TOWN	42	15	3	3	61	17	4	5	12	15	34	46
8	Queens Park Rangers	42	15	0	6	57	23	5	3	13	25	52	43
9	Fulham	42	15	3	3	49	21	3	4	14	28	54	43
10	Bournemouth	42	11	7	3	39	22	4	6	11	33	51	43
11	Torquay United	42	13	5	3	56	26	4	4	13	24	58	43
12	Swindon Town	42	15	5	1	68	29	3	1	17	21	65	42
13	Exeter City	42	12	6	3	55	35	5	2	14	29	55	42
14	Coventry City	42	11	4	6	55	28	5	5	11	20	37	41
15	Bristol Rovers	42	12	3	6	49	36	4	5	12	26	56	40
16	Gillingham	42	10	6	5	40	29	4	4	13	21	47	38
17	Walsall	42	9	5	7	44	38	5	4	12	34	57	37
18	Watford	42	9	4	8	41	29	5	3	13	31	46	35
19	Clapton Orient	42	12	3	6	47	33	2	4	15	16	58	35
20	Thames	42	12	5	4	34	20	1	3	17	20	73	34
21	Newport County	42	10	5	6	45	31	1	1	19	24	80	28
22	Norwich City	42	10	7	4	37	20	0	1	20	10	56	28

'1931/32 Division Three (South)

		P	W	D	L	F	A	W	D	L	F	A	Pts
1	Fulham	42	15	3	3	72	27	9	6	6	39	35	57
2	Reading	42	19	1	1	65	21	4	8	9	32	46	55
3	Southend United	42	12	5	4	41	18	9	6	6	36	35	53
4	Crystal Palace	42	14	7	0	48	12	6	4	11	26	51	51
5	Brentford	42	11	6	4	40	22	8	4	9	28	30	48
6	LUTON TOWN	42	16	1	4	62	25	4	6	11	33	45	47
7	Exeter City	42	16	3	2	53	16	4	4	13	24	46	47
8	Brighton & HA	42	12	4	5	42	21	5	8	8	31	37	46
9	Cardiff City	42	14	2	5	62	29	5	6	10	25	44	46
10	Norwich City	42	12	7	2	51	22	5	5	11	25	45	46
11	Watford	42	14	4	3	49	27	5	4	12	32	52	46
12	Coventry City	42	17	2	2	74	28	1	6	14	34	69	44
13	Queens Park Rangers	42	11	6	4	50	30	4	6	11	29	43	42
14	Northampton Town	42	12	3	6	48	26	4	4	13	21	43	39
15	Bournemouth	42	8	8	5	42	32	5	4	12	28	46	38
16	Clapton Orient	42	7	8	6	41	35	5	3	13	36	55	35
17	Swindon Town	42	12	2	7	47	31	2	4	15	23	53	34
18	Bristol Rovers	42	11	6	4	46	30	2	2	17	19	62	34
19	Torquay United	42	9	6	6	49	39	3	3	15	23	67	33
20	Mansfield Town	42	11	5	5	54	45	0	5	16	21	63	32
21	Gillingham	42	8	6	7	26	26	2	2	17	14	56	28
22	Thames	42	6	7	8	35	35	1	2	18	18	74	23

'1932/33 Division Three (South)

		P	W	D	L	F	A	W	D	L	F	A	Pts
1	Brentford	42	15	4	2	45	19	11	6	4	45	30	62
2	Exeter City	42	17	2	2	57	13	7	8	6	31	35	58
3	Norwich City	42	16	3	2	49	17	6	10	5	39	38	57
4	Reading	42	14	5	2	68	30	5	8	8	35	41	51
5	Crystal Palace	42	14	4	3	51	21	5	4	12	27	43	46
6	Coventry City	42	16	1	4	75	24	3	5	13	31	53	44
7	Gillingham	42	14	4	3	54	24	4	4	13	18	37	44
8	Northampton Town	42	16	5	0	54	11	2	3	16	22	55	44
9	Bristol Rovers	42	13	5	3	38	22	2	9	10	23	34	44
10	Torquay United	42	12	7	2	51	26	4	5	12	21	41	44
11	Watford	42	11	8	2	37	22	5	4	12	29	41	44
12	Brighton & HA	42	13	3	5	42	20	4	5	12	24	45	42
13	Southend United	42	11	5	5	39	27	4	6	11	26	55	41
14	LUTON TOWN	42	12	8	1	60	32	1	5	15	18	46	39
15	Bristol City	42	11	5	5	59	37	1	8	12	24	53	37
16	Queens Park Rangers	42	9	8	4	48	32	4	3	14	24	55	37
17	Aldershot	42	11	6	4	37	21	2	4	15	24	51	36
18	Bournemouth	42	10	7	4	44	27	2	5	14	16	54	36
19	Cardiff City	42	12	4	5	48	30	0	3	18	21	69	31
20	Clapton Orient	42	7	8	6	39	35	1	5	15	20	58	29
21	Newport County	42	9	4	8	42	42	2	3	16	19	63	29
22	Swindon Town	42	7	9	5	36	29	2	2	17	24	76	29

'1933/34 Division Three (South)

		P	W	D	L	F	A	W	D	L	F	A	Pts
1	Norwich City	42	16	4	1	55	19	9	7	5	33	30	61
2	Coventry City	42	16	3	2	70	22	5	9	7	30	32	54
3	Reading	42	17	4	0	60	13	4	8	9	22	37	54
4	Queens Park Rangers	42	17	2	2	42	12	7	4	10	28	39	54
5	Charlton Athletic	42	14	5	2	53	27	8	3	10	30	29	52
6	LUTON TOWN	42	14	3	4	55	28	7	7	7	28	33	52
7	Bristol Rovers	42	14	4	3	49	21	6	7	8	28	26	51
8	Swindon Town	42	13	5	3	42	25	4	6	11	22	43	45
9	Exeter City	42	12	5	4	43	19	4	6	11	25	38	43
10	Brighton & HA	42	12	7	2	47	18	3	6	12	21	42	43
11	Clapton Orient	42	14	4	3	60	25	2	6	13	15	44	42
12	Crystal Palace	42	11	6	4	40	25	5	3	13	31	42	41
13	Northampton Town	42	10	6	5	45	32	4	6	11	26	46	40
14	Aldershot	42	8	6	7	28	27	5	6	10	24	44	38
15	Watford	42	12	4	5	43	16	3	3	15	28	47	37
16	Southend United	42	9	6	6	32	27	3	4	14	19	47	34
17	Gillingham	42	8	8	5	49	41	3	3	15	26	55	33
18	Newport County	42	6	9	6	25	23	2	8	11	24	47	33
19	Bristol City	42	7	8	6	33	22	3	5	13	25	63	33
20	Torquay United	42	10	4	7	32	28	3	3	15	21	65	33
21	Bournemouth	42	7	7	7	41	37	2	2	17	19	65	27
22	Cardiff City	42	6	4	11	32	43	3	2	16	25	62	24

'1934/35 Division Three (South)

		P	W	D	L	F	A	W	D	L	F	A	Pts
1	Charlton Athletic	42	17	2	2	62	20	10	5	6	41	32	61
2	Reading	42	16	5	0	59	23	5	6	10	30	42	53
3	Coventry City	42	14	5	2	56	14	7	4	10	30	36	51
4	LUTON TOWN	42	12	7	2	60	23	7	5	9	32	37	50
5	Crystal Palace	42	15	3	3	51	14	4	7	10	35	50	48
6	Watford	42	14	2	5	53	19	5	7	9	23	30	47
7	Northampton Town	42	14	4	3	40	21	5	4	12	25	46	46
8	Bristol Rovers	42	14	6	1	54	27	3	4	14	19	50	44
9	Brighton & HA	42	15	4	2	51	16	2	5	14	18	46	43
10	Torquay United	42	15	2	4	60	22	3	4	14	21	53	42
11	Exeter City	42	11	5	5	48	29	5	4	12	22	46	41
12	Millwall	42	11	4	6	33	26	6	3	12	24	36	41
13	Queens Park Rangers	42	14	6	1	49	22	2	3	16	14	50	41
14	Clapton Orient	42	13	3	5	47	21	2	7	12	18	44	40
15	Bristol City	42	14	3	4	37	18	1	6	14	15	50	39
16	Swindon Town	42	11	7	3	45	22	2	5	14	22	56	38
17	Bournemouth	42	10	5	6	36	26	5	2	14	18	45	37
18	Aldershot	42	12	6	3	35	20	1	4	16	15	55	36
19	Cardiff City	42	11	6	4	42	27	2	3	16	20	55	35
20	Gillingham	42	10	7	4	36	25	1	6	14	19	50	35
21	Southend United	42	10	4	7	40	29	1	5	15	25	49	31
22	Newport County	42	7	4	10	36	40	3	1	17	18	72	25

'1935/36 Division Three (South)

		P	W	D	L	F	A	W	D	L	F	A	Pts
1	Coventry City	42	19	1	1	75	12	5	8	8	27	33	57
2	LUTON TOWN	42	13	6	2	56	20	9	6	6	25	25	56
3	Reading	42	18	0	3	52	20	8	2	11	35	42	54
4	Queens Park Rangers	42	14	4	3	55	19	8	5	8	29	34	53
5	Watford	42	12	3	6	47	29	8	6	7	33	25	49
6	Crystal Palace	42	15	4	2	64	20	7	1	13	32	54	49
7	Brighton & HA	42	13	4	4	48	25	5	4	12	22	38	44
8	Bournemouth	42	9	6	6	36	26	7	5	9	24	30	43
9	Notts County	42	10	5	6	40	25	5	7	9	20	32	42
10	Torquay United	42	14	4	3	41	27	2	5	14	21	35	41
11	Aldershot	42	9	6	6	29	21	5	6	10	24	40	40
12	Millwall	42	9	8	4	33	21	5	4	12	25	50	40
13	Bristol City	42	11	5	5	32	21	4	5	12	16	38	40
14	Clapton Orient	42	13	2	6	34	15	3	4	14	21	46	38
15	Northampton Town	42	12	5	4	38	24	3	3	15	24	66	38
16	Gillingham	42	9	5	7	34	25	5	4	12	32	52	37
17	Bristol Rovers	42	11	6	4	48	31	3	3	15	21	64	37
18	Southend United	42	8	7	6	38	21	5	3	13	23	41	36
19	Swindon Town	42	10	5	6	43	33	4	3	14	21	40	36
20	Cardiff City	42	11	5	5	37	23	2	5	14	23	50	36
21	Newport County	42	8	4	9	36	44	3	5	13	24	67	31
22	Exeter City	42	7	5	9	38	41	1	6	14	21	52	27

'1936/37 Division Three (South)

		P	W	D	L	F	A	W	D	L	F	A	Pts
1	LUTON TOWN	42	19	1	1	69	16	8	3	10	34	37	58
2	Notts County	42	15	3	3	44	23	8	7	6	30	29	56
3	Brighton & HA	42	15	5	1	49	16	9	0	12	25	27	53
4	Watford	42	14	4	3	53	21	5	7	9	32	39	49
5	Reading	42	14	5	2	53	23	5	6	10	23	37	49
6	Bournemouth	42	17	3	1	45	20	3	6	12	20	39	49
7	Northampton Town	42	15	4	2	56	22	5	2	14	29	46	46
8	Millwall	42	12	4	5	43	24	6	6	9	21	30	46
9	Queens Park Rangers	42	12	2	7	51	24	6	7	8	22	28	45
10	Southend United	42	10	8	3	49	23	7	3	11	29	44	45
11	Gillingham	42	14	5	2	36	18	4	3	14	16	48	44
12	Clapton Orient	42	10	8	3	29	17	4	7	10	23	35	43
13	Swindon Town	42	12	4	5	52	24	2	7	12	23	49	39
14	Crystal Palace	42	11	7	3	45	20	2	5	14	17	41	38
15	Bristol Rovers	42	14	3	4	49	20	2	1	18	22	60	36
16	Bristol City	42	13	3	5	42	20	2	3	16	16	50	36
17	Walsall	42	11	3	7	38	34	2	7	12	25	51	36
18	Cardiff City	42	10	5	6	35	24	4	2	15	19	63	35
19	Newport County	42	7	7	7	37	28	5	3	13	30	70	34
20	Torquay United	42	9	5	7	42	32	2	5	14	15	48	32
21	Exeter City	42	9	5	7	36	37	1	7	13	23	51	32
22	Aldershot	42	5	6	10	29	29	2	3	16	21	60	23

'1937/38 Division Two

		P	W	D	L	F	A	W	D	L	F	A	Pts
1	Aston Villa	42	17	2	2	50	12	8	5	8	23	23	57
2	Manchester United	42	15	3	3	50	18	7	6	8	32	32	53
3	Sheffield United	42	15	4	2	46	19	7	5	9	27	37	53
4	Coventry City	42	12	5	4	31	15	8	7	6	35	30	52
5	Tottenham Hotspur	42	14	3	4	46	16	5	3	13	30	38	44
6	Burnley	42	15	4	2	35	11	2	6	13	19	43	44
7	Bradford Park Avenue	42	13	4	4	51	22	4	5	12	18	34	43
8	Fulham	42	10	7	4	44	23	6	4	11	17	34	43
9	West Ham United	42	13	5	3	34	16	1	9	11	19	36	42
10	Bury	42	12	3	6	43	26	6	2	13	20	34	41
11	Chesterfield	42	12	2	7	39	24	4	7	10	24	39	41
12	LUTON TOWN	42	10	6	5	53	36	5	4	12	36	50	40
13	Plymouth Argyle	42	10	7	4	40	30	4	5	12	17	35	40
14	Norwich City	42	11	5	5	35	28	3	6	12	21	47	39
15	Southampton	42	12	6	3	42	26	3	3	15	13	51	39
16	Blackburn Rovers	42	13	6	2	51	30	1	4	16	20	50	38
17	Sheffield Wednesday	42	10	5	6	27	21	4	5	12	22	35	38
18	Swansea Town	42	12	6	3	31	21	1	6	14	14	52	38
19	Newcastle United	42	12	4	5	38	18	2	4	15	13	40	36
20	Nottingham Forest	42	12	3	6	29	21	2	5	14	18	39	36
21	Barnsley	42	7	11	3	30	20	4	3	14	20	44	36
22	Stockport County	42	8	6	7	24	24	3	3	15	19	46	31

'1938/39 Division Two

		P	W	D	L	F	A	W	D	L	F	A	Pts
1	Blackburn Rovers	42	17	1	3	59	23	8	4	9	35	37	55
2	Sheffield United	42	9	9	3	35	15	11	5	5	34	26	54
3	Sheffield Wednesday	42	14	4	3	47	18	7	7	7	41	41	53
4	Coventry City	42	13	4	4	35	13	8	4	9	27	32	50
5	Manchester City	42	13	3	5	56	35	8	4	9	40	37	49
6	Chesterfield	42	16	1	4	54	20	4	8	9	15	32	49
7	LUTON TOWN	42	13	4	4	47	27	9	1	11	35	39	49
8	Tottenham Hotspur	42	13	6	2	48	27	6	3	12	19	35	47
9	Newcastle United	42	13	3	5	44	21	5	7	9	17	27	46
10	West Bromwich Albion	42	15	3	3	54	22	3	6	12	35	50	45
11	West Ham United	42	10	5	6	36	21	7	5	9	34	31	44
12	Fulham	42	12	5	4	35	20	5	5	11	26	35	44
13	Millwall	42	12	6	3	44	18	2	8	11	20	35	42
14	Burnley	42	13	3	5	32	20	2	6	13	18	36	39
15	Plymouth Argyle	42	9	7	5	24	13	6	1	14	25	42	38
16	Bury	42	9	5	7	48	36	3	8	10	17	38	37
17	Bradford Park Avenue	42	8	6	7	33	35	4	5	12	28	47	35
18	Southampton	42	9	6	6	35	34	4	3	14	21	48	35
19	Swansea Town	42	8	6	7	33	30	3	6	12	17	53	34
20	Nottingham Forest	42	8	6	7	33	29	2	5	14	16	53	31
21	Norwich City	42	10	5	6	39	29	3	0	18	11	62	31
22	Tranmere Rovers	42	6	4	11	26	38	0	1	20	13	61	17

'1946/47 Division Two

		P	W	D	L	F	A	W	D	L	F	A	Pts
1	Manchester City	42	17	3	1	49	14	9	7	5	29	21	62
2	Burnley	42	11	8	2	30	14	11	6	4	35	15	58
3	Birmingham City	42	17	2	2	51	11	8	3	10	23	22	55
4	Chesterfield	42	12	6	3	37	17	6	8	7	21	27	50
5	Newcastle United	42	11	4	6	60	32	8	6	7	35	30	48
6	Tottenham Hotspur	42	11	8	2	35	21	6	6	9	30	32	48
7	West Bromwich Albion	42	12	4	5	53	37	8	4	9	35	38	48
8	Coventry City	42	12	8	1	40	17	4	5	12	26	42	45
9	Leicester City	42	11	4	6	42	25	7	3	11	27	39	43
10	Barnsley	42	13	2	6	48	29	4	6	11	36	57	42
11	Nottingham Forest	42	13	5	3	47	20	2	5	14	22	54	40
12	West Ham United	42	12	4	5	46	31	4	4	13	24	45	40
13	LUTON TOWN	42	13	4	4	50	29	3	3	15	21	44	39
14	Southampton	42	11	5	5	45	24	4	4	13	24	52	39
15	Fulham	42	12	4	5	40	25	3	5	13	23	49	39
16	Bradford Park Avenue	42	7	6	8	29	28	7	5	9	36	49	39
17	Bury	42	11	6	4	62	34	1	6	14	18	44	36
18	Millwall	42	7	7	7	30	30	7	1	13	26	49	36
19	Plymouth Argyle	42	11	3	7	45	34	3	2	16	34	62	33
20	Sheffield Wednesday	42	10	5	6	39	28	2	3	16	28	60	32
21	Swansea Town	42	9	1	11	36	40	2	6	13	19	43	29
22	Newport County	42	9	1	11	41	52	1	2	18	20	81	23

'1947/48 Division Two

		P	W	D	L	F	A	W	D	L	F	A	Pts
1	Birmingham City	42	12	7	2	34	13	10	8	3	21	11	59
2	Newcastle United	42	18	1	2	46	13	6	7	8	26	28	56
3	Southampton	42	15	3	3	53	23	6	7	8	18	30	52
4	Sheffield Wednesday	42	13	6	2	39	21	7	5	9	27	32	51
5	Cardiff City	42	12	6	3	36	18	6	5	10	25	40	47
6	West Ham United	42	10	7	4	29	19	6	7	8	26	34	46
7	West Bromwich Albion	42	11	4	6	37	29	7	5	9	26	29	45
8	Tottenham Hotspur	42	10	6	5	36	24	5	8	8	20	19	44
9	Leicester City	42	10	5	6	36	29	6	6	9	24	28	43
10	Coventry City	42	10	5	6	33	16	4	8	9	26	36	41
11	Fulham	42	6	9	6	24	19	9	1	11	23	27	40
12	Barnsley	42	10	5	6	31	22	5	5	11	31	42	40
13	LUTON TOWN	42	8	8	5	31	25	6	4	11	25	34	40
14	Bradford Park Avenue	42	11	3	7	45	30	5	5	11	23	42	40
15	Brentford	42	10	6	5	31	26	3	8	10	13	35	40
16	Chesterfield	42	8	4	9	32	26	8	3	10	22	29	39
17	Plymouth Argyle	42	8	9	4	27	22	1	11	9	13	36	38
18	Leeds United	42	12	5	4	44	20	2	3	16	18	52	36
19	Nottingham Forest	42	10	5	6	32	23	2	6	13	22	37	35
20	Bury	42	6	8	7	27	28	3	8	10	31	40	34
21	Doncaster Rovers	42	7	8	6	23	20	2	3	16	17	46	29
22	Millwall	42	7	7	7	27	28	2	4	15	17	46	29

'1948/49 Division Two

		P	W	D	L	F	A	W	D	L	F	A	Pts
1	Fulham	42	16	4	1	52	14	8	5	8	25	23	57
2	West Bromwich Albion	42	16	3	2	47	16	8	5	8	22	23	56
3	Southampton	42	16	4	1	48	10	7	5	9	21	26	55
4	Cardiff City	42	14	4	3	45	21	5	9	7	17	26	51
5	Tottenham Hotspur	42	14	4	3	50	18	3	12	6	22	26	50
6	Chesterfield	42	9	7	5	24	18	6	10	5	27	27	47
7	West Ham United	42	13	5	3	38	23	5	5	11	18	35	46
8	Sheffield Wednesday	42	12	6	3	36	17	3	7	11	27	39	43
9	Barnsley	42	10	7	4	40	18	4	5	12	22	43	40
10	LUTON TOWN	42	11	6	4	32	16	3	6	12	23	41	40
11	Grimsby Town	42	10	5	6	44	28	5	5	11	28	48	40
12	Bury	42	12	5	4	41	23	5	1	15	26	53	40
13	Queens Park Rangers	42	11	4	6	31	26	3	7	11	13	36	39
14	Blackburn Rovers	42	12	5	4	41	23	3	3	15	12	40	38
15	Leeds United	42	11	6	4	36	21	1	7	13	19	42	37
16	Coventry City	42	12	3	6	35	20	3	4	14	20	44	37
17	Bradford Park Avenue	42	8	8	5	37	26	5	3	13	28	52	37
18	Brentford	42	7	10	4	28	21	4	4	13	14	32	36
19	Leicester City	42	6	10	5	41	38	4	6	11	21	41	36
20	Plymouth Argyle	42	11	4	6	33	25	1	8	12	16	39	36
21	Nottingham Forest	42	9	6	6	22	14	5	1	15	28	40	35
22	Lincoln City	42	6	7	8	31	35	2	5	14	22	56	28

'1949/50 Division Two

		P	W	D	L	F	A	W	D	L	F	A	Pts
1	Tottenham Hotspur	42	15	3	3	51	15	12	4	5	30	20	61
2	Sheffield Wednesday	42	12	7	2	46	23	6	9	6	21	25	52
3	Sheffield United	42	9	10	2	36	19	10	4	7	32	30	52
4	Southampton	42	13	4	4	44	25	6	10	5	20	23	52
5	Leeds United	42	11	8	2	33	16	6	5	10	21	29	47
6	Preston North End	42	12	5	4	37	21	6	4	11	23	28	45
7	Hull City	42	11	8	2	39	25	6	3	12	25	47	45
8	Swansea Town	42	11	3	7	34	18	6	6	9	19	31	43
9	Brentford	42	11	5	5	21	12	4	8	9	23	37	43
10	Cardiff City	42	13	3	5	28	14	3	7	11	13	30	42
11	Grimsby Town	42	13	5	3	53	25	3	3	15	21	48	40
12	Coventry City	42	8	6	7	32	24	5	7	9	23	31	39
13	Barnsley	42	11	6	4	45	28	2	7	12	19	39	39
14	Chesterfield	42	12	3	6	28	16	3	6	12	15	31	39
15	Leicester City	42	8	9	4	30	25	4	6	11	25	40	39
16	Blackburn Rovers	42	10	5	6	30	15	4	5	12	25	45	38
17	LUTON TOWN	42	8	9	4	28	22	2	9	10	13	29	38
18	Bury	42	10	8	3	37	19	4	1	16	23	46	37
19	West Ham United	42	8	7	6	30	25	4	5	12	23	36	36
20	Queens Park Rangers	42	6	5	10	21	30	5	7	9	19	27	34
21	Plymouth Argyle	42	6	6	9	19	24	2	10	9	25	41	32
22	Bradford Park Avenue	42	7	6	8	34	34	3	5	13	17	43	31

'1950/51 Division Two

		P	W	D	L	F	A	W	D	L	F	A	Pts
1	Preston North End	42	16	3	2	53	18	10	2	9	38	31	57
2	Manchester City	42	12	6	3	53	25	7	8	6	36	36	52
3	Cardiff City	42	13	7	1	36	20	4	9	8	17	25	50
4	Birmingham City	42	12	6	3	37	20	8	3	10	27	33	49
5	Leeds United	42	14	4	3	36	17	6	4	11	27	38	48
6	Blackburn Rovers	42	13	3	5	39	27	6	5	10	26	39	46
7	Coventry City	42	15	3	3	51	25	4	4	13	24	34	45
8	Sheffield United	42	11	4	6	44	27	5	8	8	28	35	44
9	Brentford	42	13	3	5	44	25	5	5	11	31	49	44
10	Hull City	42	12	5	4	47	28	4	6	11	27	42	43
11	Doncaster Rovers	42	9	6	6	37	32	6	7	8	27	36	43
12	Southampton	42	10	9	2	38	27	5	4	12	28	46	43
13	West Ham United	42	10	5	6	44	33	6	5	10	24	36	42
14	Leicester City	42	10	4	7	42	28	5	7	9	26	30	41
15	Barnsley	42	9	5	7	42	22	6	5	10	32	46	40
16	Queens Park Rangers	42	13	5	3	47	25	2	5	14	24	57	40
17	Notts County	42	7	7	7	37	34	6	6	9	24	26	39
18	Swansea Town	42	14	1	6	34	25	2	3	16	20	52	36
19	LUTON TOWN	42	7	9	5	34	23	2	5	14	23	47	32
20	Bury	42	9	4	8	33	27	3	4	14	27	59	32
21	Chesterfield	42	7	7	7	30	28	2	5	14	14	41	30
22	Grimsby Town	42	6	8	7	37	38	2	4	15	24	57	28

'1951/52 Division Two

		P	W	D	L	F	A	W	D	L	F	A	Pts
1	Sheffield Wednesday	42	14	4	3	54	23	7	7	7	46	43	53
2	Cardiff City	42	18	2	1	52	15	2	9	10	20	39	51
3	Birmingham City	42	11	6	4	36	21	10	3	8	31	35	51
4	Nottingham Forest	42	12	6	3	41	22	6	7	8	36	40	49
5	Leicester City	42	12	6	3	48	24	7	3	11	30	40	47
6	Leeds United	42	13	7	1	35	15	5	4	12	24	42	47
7	Everton	42	12	5	4	42	25	5	5	11	22	33	44
8	LUTON TOWN	42	9	7	5	46	35	7	5	9	31	43	44
9	Rotherham United	42	11	4	6	40	25	6	4	11	33	46	42
10	Brentford	42	11	7	3	34	20	4	5	12	20	35	42
11	Sheffield United	42	13	2	6	57	28	5	3	13	33	48	41
12	West Ham United	42	13	5	3	48	29	2	6	13	19	48	41
13	Southampton	42	11	6	4	40	25	4	5	12	21	48	41
14	Blackburn Rovers	42	11	3	7	35	30	6	3	12	19	33	40
15	Notts County	42	11	5	5	45	27	5	2	14	26	41	39
16	Doncaster Rovers	42	9	4	8	29	28	4	8	9	26	32	38
17	Bury	42	13	2	6	43	22	2	5	14	24	47	37
18	Hull City	42	11	5	5	44	23	2	6	13	16	47	37
19	Swansea Town	42	10	4	7	45	26	2	8	11	27	50	36
20	Barnsley	42	8	7	6	39	33	3	7	11	20	39	36
21	Coventry City	42	9	5	7	36	33	5	1	15	23	49	34
22	Queens Park Rangers	42	8	8	5	35	35	3	4	14	17	46	34

'1952/53 Division Two

		P	W	D	L	F	A	W	D	L	F	A	Pts
1	Sheffield United	42	15	3	3	60	27	10	7	4	37	28	60
2	Huddersfield Town	42	14	4	3	51	14	10	6	5	33	19	58
3	LUTON TOWN	42	15	1	5	53	17	7	7	7	31	32	52
4	Plymouth Argyle	42	12	5	4	37	24	8	4	9	28	36	49
5	Leicester City	42	13	6	2	55	29	5	6	10	34	45	48
6	Birmingham City	42	11	3	7	44	38	8	7	6	27	28	48
7	Nottingham Forest	42	11	5	5	46	32	7	3	11	31	35	44
8	Fulham	42	14	1	6	52	28	3	9	9	29	43	44
9	Blackburn Rovers	42	12	4	5	40	20	6	4	11	28	45	44
10	Leeds United	42	13	4	4	42	24	1	11	9	29	39	43
11	Swansea Town	42	10	9	2	45	26	5	3	13	33	55	42
12	Rotherham United	42	9	7	5	41	30	7	2	12	34	44	41
13	Doncaster Rovers	42	9	9	3	26	17	3	7	11	32	47	40
14	West Ham United	42	9	5	7	38	28	4	8	9	20	32	39
15	Lincoln City	42	9	9	3	41	26	2	8	11	23	45	39
16	Everton	42	9	8	4	38	23	3	6	12	33	52	38
17	Brentford	42	8	8	5	38	29	5	3	13	21	47	37
18	Hull City	42	11	6	4	36	19	3	2	16	21	50	36
19	Notts County	42	11	5	5	41	31	3	3	15	19	57	36
20	Bury	42	10	6	5	33	30	3	3	15	20	51	35
21	Southampton	42	5	7	9	45	44	5	6	10	23	41	33
22	Barnsley	42	4	4	13	31	46	1	4	16	16	62	18

'1953/54 Division Two

		P	W	D	L	F	A	W	D	L	F	A	Pts
1	Leicester City	42	15	4	2	63	23	8	6	7	34	37	56
2	Everton	42	13	6	2	55	27	7	10	4	37	31	56
3	Blackburn Rovers	42	15	4	2	54	16	8	5	8	32	34	55
4	Nottingham Forest	42	15	5	1	61	27	5	7	9	25	32	52
5	Rotherham United	42	13	4	4	51	26	8	3	10	29	41	49
6	LUTON TOWN	42	11	7	3	36	23	7	5	9	28	36	48
7	Birmingham City	42	12	6	3	49	18	6	5	10	29	40	47
8	Fulham	42	12	3	6	62	39	5	7	9	36	46	44
9	Bristol Rovers	42	10	7	4	32	19	4	9	8	32	39	44
10	Leeds United	42	12	5	4	56	30	3	8	10	33	51	43
11	Stoke City	42	8	8	5	43	28	4	9	8	28	32	41
12	Doncaster Rovers	42	9	5	7	32	28	7	4	10	27	35	41
13	West Ham United	42	11	6	4	44	20	4	3	14	23	49	39
14	Notts County	42	8	6	7	26	29	5	7	9	28	45	39
15	Hull City	42	14	1	6	47	22	2	5	14	17	44	38
16	Lincoln City	42	11	6	4	46	23	3	3	15	19	60	37
17	Bury	42	9	7	5	39	32	2	7	12	15	40	36
18	Derby County	42	9	5	7	38	35	3	6	12	26	47	35
19	Plymouth Argyle	42	6	12	3	38	31	3	4	14	27	51	34
20	Swansea Town	42	11	5	5	34	25	2	3	16	24	57	34
21	Brentford	42	9	5	7	25	26	1	6	14	15	52	31
22	Oldham Athletic	42	6	7	8	26	31	2	2	17	14	58	25

'1954/55 Division Two

		P	W	D	L	F	A	W	D	L	F	A	Pts
1	Birmingham City	42	14	4	3	56	22	8	6	7	36	25	54
2	LUTON TOWN	42	18	2	1	55	18	5	6	10	33	35	54
3	Rotherham United	42	17	1	3	59	22	8	3	10	35	42	54
4	Leeds United	42	14	4	3	43	19	9	3	9	27	34	53
5	Stoke City	42	12	5	4	38	17	9	5	7	31	29	52
6	Blackburn Rovers	42	14	4	3	73	31	8	2	11	41	48	50
7	Notts County	42	14	3	4	46	27	7	3	11	28	44	48
8	West Ham United	42	12	4	5	46	28	6	6	9	28	42	46
9	Bristol Rovers	42	15	4	2	52	23	4	3	14	23	47	45
10	Swansea Town	42	15	3	3	58	28	2	6	13	28	55	43
11	Liverpool	42	11	7	3	55	37	5	3	13	37	59	42
12	Middlesbrough	42	13	1	7	48	31	5	5	11	25	51	42
13	Bury	42	10	5	6	44	35	5	6	10	33	37	41
14	Fulham	42	10	5	6	46	29	4	6	11	30	50	39
15	Nottingham Forest	42	8	4	9	29	29	8	3	10	29	33	39
16	Lincoln City	42	8	6	7	39	35	5	4	12	29	44	36
17	Port Vale	42	10	6	5	31	21	2	5	14	17	50	35
18	Doncaster Rovers	42	10	5	6	35	34	4	2	15	23	61	35
19	Hull City	42	7	5	9	30	35	5	5	11	14	34	34
20	Plymouth Argyle	42	10	4	7	29	26	2	3	16	28	56	31
21	Ipswich Town	42	10	3	8	37	28	1	3	17	20	64	28
22	Derby County	42	6	6	9	39	34	1	3	17	14	48	23

'1955/56 Division One

		P	W	D	L	F	A	W	D	L	F	A	Pts
1	Manchester United	42	18	3	0	51	20	7	7	7	32	31	60
2	Blackpool	42	13	4	4	56	27	7	5	9	30	35	49
3	Wolverhampton Wndrs	42	15	2	4	51	27	5	7	9	38	38	49
4	Manchester City	42	11	5	5	40	27	7	5	9	42	42	46
5	Arsenal	42	13	4	4	38	22	5	6	10	22	39	46
6	Birmingham City	42	12	4	5	51	26	6	5	10	24	31	45
7	Burnley	42	11	3	7	37	20	7	5	9	27	34	44
8	Bolton Wanderers	42	13	3	5	50	24	5	4	12	21	34	43
9	Sunderland	42	10	8	3	44	36	7	1	13	36	59	43
10	LUTON TOWN	42	12	4	5	44	27	5	4	12	22	37	42
11	Newcastle United	42	12	4	5	49	24	5	3	13	36	46	41
12	Portsmouth	42	9	8	4	46	38	7	1	13	32	47	41
13	West Bromwich Albion	42	13	3	5	37	25	5	2	14	21	45	41
14	Charlton Athletic	42	13	2	6	47	26	4	4	13	28	55	40
15	Everton	42	11	5	5	37	29	4	5	12	18	40	40
16	Chelsea	42	10	4	7	32	26	4	7	10	32	51	39
17	Cardiff City	42	11	4	6	36	32	4	5	12	19	37	39
18	Tottenham Hotspur	42	9	4	8	37	33	6	3	12	24	38	37
19	Preston North End	42	6	5	10	32	36	8	3	10	41	36	36
20	Aston Villa	42	9	6	6	32	29	2	7	12	20	40	35
21	Huddersfield Town	42	9	4	8	32	30	5	3	13	22	53	35
22	Sheffield United	42	8	6	7	31	35	4	3	14	32	42	33

'1956/57 Division One

		P	W	D	L	F	A	W	D	L	F	A	Pts
1	Manchester United	42	14	4	3	55	25	14	4	3	48	29	64
2	Tottenham Hotspur	42	15	4	2	70	24	7	8	6	34	32	56
3	Preston North End	42	15	4	2	50	19	8	6	7	34	37	56
4	Blackpool	42	14	3	4	55	26	8	6	7	38	39	53
5	Arsenal	42	12	5	4	45	21	9	3	9	40	48	50
6	Wolverhampton Wndrs	42	17	2	2	70	29	3	6	12	24	41	48
7	Burnley	42	14	5	2	41	21	4	5	12	15	29	46
8	Leeds United	42	10	8	3	42	18	5	6	10	30	45	44
9	Bolton Wanderers	42	13	6	2	42	23	3	6	12	23	42	44
10	Aston Villa	42	10	8	3	45	25	4	7	10	20	30	43
11	West Bromwich Albion	42	8	8	5	31	25	6	6	9	28	36	42
12	Chelsea	42	7	8	6	43	36	6	5	10	30	37	39
12	Birmingham City	42	12	5	4	52	25	3	4	14	17	44	39
14	Sheffield Wednesday	42	14	3	4	55	29	2	3	16	27	59	38
15	Everton	42	10	5	6	34	28	4	5	12	27	51	38
16	LUTON TOWN	42	10	4	7	32	26	4	5	12	26	50	37
17	Newcastle United	42	10	5	6	43	31	4	3	14	24	56	36
18	Manchester City	42	10	2	9	48	42	3	7	11	30	46	35
19	Portsmouth	42	8	6	7	37	35	2	7	12	25	57	33
20	Sunderland	42	9	5	7	40	30	3	3	15	27	58	32
21	Cardiff City	42	7	6	8	35	34	3	3	15	18	54	29
22	Charlton Athletic	42	7	3	11	31	44	2	1	18	31	76	22

'1957/58 Division One

		P	W	D	L	F	A	W	D	L	F	A	Pts
1	Wolverhampton Wndrs	42	17	3	1	60	21	11	5	5	43	26	64
2	Preston North End	42	18	2	1	63	14	8	5	8	37	37	59
3	Tottenham Hotspur	42	13	4	4	58	33	8	5	8	35	44	51
4	West Bromwich Albion	42	14	4	3	59	29	4	10	7	33	41	50
5	Manchester City	42	14	4	3	58	33	8	1	12	46	67	49
6	Burnley	42	16	2	3	52	21	5	3	13	28	53	47
7	Blackpool	42	11	2	8	47	35	8	4	9	33	32	44
8	LUTON TOWN	42	13	3	5	45	22	6	3	12	24	41	44
9	Manchester United	42	10	4	7	45	31	6	7	8	40	44	43
10	Nottingham Forest	42	10	4	7	41	27	6	6	9	28	36	42
11	Chelsea	42	10	5	6	47	34	5	7	9	36	45	42
12	Arsenal	42	10	4	7	48	39	6	3	12	25	46	39
13	Birmingham City	42	8	6	7	43	37	6	5	10	33	52	39
14	Aston Villa	42	12	4	5	46	26	4	3	14	27	60	39
15	Bolton Wanderers	42	9	5	7	38	35	5	5	11	27	52	38
16	Everton	42	5	9	7	34	35	8	2	11	31	40	37
17	Leeds United	42	10	6	5	33	23	4	3	14	18	40	37
18	Leicester City	42	11	4	6	59	41	3	1	17	32	71	33
19	Newcastle United	42	6	4	11	38	42	6	4	11	35	39	32
20	Portsmouth	42	10	6	5	45	34	2	2	17	28	54	32
21	Sunderland	42	7	7	7	32	33	3	5	13	22	64	32
22	Sheffield Wednesday	42	12	2	7	45	40	0	5	16	24	52	31

'1958/59 Division One

		P	W	D	L	F	A	W	D	L	F	A	Pts
1	Wolverhampton Wndrs	42	15	3	3	68	19	13	2	6	42	30	61
2	Manchester United	42	14	4	3	58	27	10	3	8	45	39	55
3	Arsenal	42	14	3	4	53	29	7	5	9	35	39	50
4	Bolton Wanderers	42	14	3	4	56	30	6	7	8	23	36	50
5	West Bromwich Albion	42	8	7	6	41	33	10	6	5	47	35	49
6	West Ham United	42	15	3	3	59	29	6	3	12	26	41	48
7	Burnley	42	11	4	6	41	29	8	6	7	40	41	48
8	Blackpool	42	12	7	2	39	13	6	4	11	27	36	47
9	Birmingham City	42	14	1	6	54	35	6	5	10	30	33	46
10	Blackburn Rovers	42	12	3	6	48	28	5	7	9	28	42	44
11	Newcastle United	42	11	3	7	40	29	6	4	11	40	51	41
12	Preston North End	42	9	3	9	40	39	8	4	9	30	38	41
13	Nottingham Forest	42	9	4	8	37	32	8	2	11	34	42	40
14	Chelsea	42	13	2	6	52	37	5	2	14	25	61	40
15	Leeds United	42	8	7	6	28	27	7	2	12	29	47	39
16	Everton	42	11	3	7	39	38	6	1	14	32	49	38
17	LUTON TOWN	42	11	6	4	50	26	1	7	13	18	45	37
18	Tottenham Hotspur	42	10	3	8	56	42	3	7	11	29	53	36
19	Leicester City	42	7	6	8	34	36	4	4	13	33	62	32
20	Manchester City	42	8	7	6	40	32	3	2	16	24	63	31
21	Aston Villa	42	8	5	8	31	33	3	3	15	27	54	30
22	Portsmouth	42	5	4	12	38	47	1	5	15	26	65	21

'1959/60 Division One

		P	W	D	L	F	A	W	D	L	F	A	Pts
1	Burnley	42	15	2	4	52	28	9	5	7	33	33	55
2	Wolverhampton Wndrs	42	15	3	3	63	28	9	3	9	43	39	54
3	Tottenham Hotspur	42	10	6	5	43	24	11	5	5	43	26	53
4	West Bromwich Albion	42	12	4	5	48	25	7	7	7	35	32	49
5	Sheffield Wednesday	42	12	7	2	48	20	7	4	10	32	39	49
6	Bolton Wanderers	42	12	5	4	37	27	8	3	10	22	24	48
7	Manchester United	42	13	3	5	53	30	6	4	11	49	50	45
8	Newcastle United	42	10	5	6	42	32	8	3	10	40	46	44
9	Preston North End	42	10	6	5	43	34	6	6	9	36	42	44
10	Fulham	42	12	4	5	42	28	5	6	10	31	52	44
11	Blackpool	42	9	6	6	32	32	6	4	11	27	39	40
12	Leicester City	42	8	6	7	38	32	5	7	9	28	43	39
13	Arsenal	42	9	5	7	39	38	6	4	11	29	42	39
14	West Ham United	42	12	3	6	47	33	4	3	14	28	58	38
15	Everton	42	13	3	5	50	20	0	8	13	23	58	37
16	Manchester City	42	11	2	8	47	34	6	1	14	31	50	37
17	Blackburn Rovers	42	12	3	6	38	29	4	2	15	22	41	37
18	Chelsea	42	7	5	9	44	50	7	4	10	32	41	37
19	Birmingham City	42	9	5	7	37	36	4	5	12	26	44	36
20	Nottingham Forest	42	8	6	7	30	28	5	3	13	20	46	35
21	Leeds United	42	7	5	9	37	46	5	5	11	28	46	34
22	LUTON TOWN	42	6	5	10	25	29	3	7	11	25	44	30

'1960/61 Division Two

		P	W	D	L	F	A	W	D	L	F	A	Pts
1	Ipswich Town	42	15	3	3	55	24	11	4	6	45	31	59
2	Sheffield United	42	16	2	3	49	22	10	4	7	32	29	58
3	Liverpool	42	14	5	2	49	21	7	5	9	38	37	52
4	Norwich City	42	15	3	3	46	20	5	6	10	24	33	49
5	Middlesbrough	42	13	6	2	44	20	5	6	10	39	54	48
6	Sunderland	42	12	5	4	47	24	5	8	8	28	36	47
7	Swansea Town	42	14	4	3	49	26	4	7	10	28	47	47
8	Southampton	42	12	4	5	57	35	6	4	11	27	46	44
9	Scunthorpe United	42	9	8	4	39	25	5	7	9	30	39	43
10	Charlton Athletic	42	12	3	6	60	42	4	8	9	37	49	43
11	Plymouth Argyle	42	13	4	4	52	32	4	4	13	29	50	42
12	Derby County	42	9	6	6	46	35	6	4	11	34	45	40
13	LUTON TOWN	42	13	5	3	48	27	2	4	15	23	52	39
14	Leeds United	42	7	7	7	41	38	7	3	11	34	45	38
15	Rotherham United	42	9	7	5	37	24	3	6	12	28	40	37
16	Brighton & HA	42	9	6	6	33	26	5	3	13	28	49	37
17	Bristol Rovers	42	13	4	4	52	35	2	3	16	21	57	37
18	Stoke City	42	9	6	6	39	26	3	6	12	12	33	36
19	Leyton Orient	42	10	5	6	31	29	4	3	14	24	49	36
20	Huddersfield Town	42	7	5	9	33	33	6	4	11	29	38	35
21	Portsmouth	42	10	6	5	38	27	1	5	15	26	64	33
22	Lincoln City	42	5	4	12	30	43	3	4	14	18	52	24

'1961/62 Division Two

		P	W	D	L	F	A	W	D	L	F	A	Pts
1	Liverpool	42	18	3	0	68	19	9	5	7	31	24	62
2	Leyton Orient	42	11	5	5	34	17	11	5	5	35	23	54
3	Sunderland	42	17	3	1	60	16	5	6	10	25	34	53
4	Scunthorpe United	42	14	4	3	52	26	7	3	11	34	45	49
5	Plymouth Argyle	42	12	4	5	45	30	7	4	10	30	45	46
6	Southampton	42	13	3	5	53	28	5	6	10	24	34	45
7	Huddersfield Town	42	11	5	5	39	22	5	7	9	28	37	44
8	Stoke City	42	13	4	4	34	17	4	4	13	21	40	42
9	Rotherham United	42	9	6	6	36	30	7	3	11	34	46	41
10	Preston North End	42	11	4	6	34	23	4	6	11	21	34	40
11	Newcastle United	42	10	5	6	40	27	5	4	12	24	31	39
12	Middlesbrough	42	11	3	7	45	29	5	4	12	31	43	39
13	LUTON TOWN	42	12	1	8	44	37	5	4	12	25	34	39
14	Walsall	42	11	7	3	42	23	3	4	14	28	52	39
15	Charlton Athletic	42	10	5	6	38	30	5	4	12	31	45	39
16	Derby County	42	10	7	4	42	27	4	4	13	26	48	39
17	Norwich City	42	10	6	5	36	28	4	5	12	25	42	39
18	Bury	42	9	4	8	32	36	8	1	12	20	40	39
19	Leeds United	42	9	6	6	24	19	3	6	12	26	42	36
20	Swansea Town	42	10	5	6	38	30	2	7	12	23	53	36
21	Bristol Rovers	42	11	3	7	36	31	2	4	15	17	50	33
22	Brighton & HA	42	7	7	7	24	32	3	4	14	18	54	31

1962/63 Division Two

		P	W	D	L	F	A	W	D	L	F	A	Pts
1	Stoke City	42	15	3	3	49	20	5	10	6	24	30	53
2	Chelsea	42	15	3	3	54	16	9	1	11	27	26	52
3	Sunderland	42	14	5	2	46	13	6	7	8	38	42	52
4	Middlesbrough	42	12	4	5	48	35	8	5	8	38	50	49
5	Leeds United	42	15	2	4	55	19	4	8	9	24	34	48
6	Huddersfield Town	42	11	6	4	34	21	6	8	7	29	29	48
7	Newcastle United	42	11	8	2	48	23	7	3	11	31	36	47
8	Bury	42	11	6	4	28	20	7	5	9	23	27	47
9	Scunthorpe United	42	12	7	2	35	18	4	5	12	22	41	44
10	Cardiff City	42	12	5	4	50	29	6	2	13	33	44	43
11	Southampton	42	15	3	3	52	23	2	5	14	20	44	42
12	Plymouth Argyle	42	13	4	4	48	24	2	8	11	28	49	42
13	Norwich City	42	11	6	4	53	33	6	2	13	27	46	42
14	Rotherham United	42	11	3	7	34	30	6	3	12	33	44	40
15	Swansea Town	42	13	5	3	33	17	2	4	15	18	55	39
16	Portsmouth	42	9	5	7	33	27	4	6	11	30	52	37
17	Preston North End	42	11	6	4	43	30	2	5	14	16	44	37
18	Derby County	42	10	5	6	40	29	2	7	12	21	43	36
19	Grimsby Town	42	8	6	7	34	26	3	7	11	21	40	35
20	Charlton Athletic	42	8	4	9	33	38	5	1	15	29	56	31
21	Walsall	42	7	7	7	33	37	4	2	15	20	52	31
22	LUTON TOWN	42	10	4	7	45	40	1	3	17	16	44	29

1963/64 Division Three

		P	W	D	L	F	A	W	D	L	F	A	Pts
1	Coventry City	46	14	7	2	62	32	8	9	6	36	29	60
2	Crystal Palace	46	17	4	2	38	14	6	10	7	35	37	60
3	Watford	46	16	6	1	57	28	7	6	10	22	31	58
4	Bournemouth	46	17	4	2	47	15	7	4	12	32	43	56
5	Bristol City	46	13	7	3	52	24	7	8	8	32	40	55
6	Reading	46	15	5	3	49	26	6	5	12	30	36	52
7	Mansfield Town	46	15	8	0	51	20	5	3	15	25	42	51
8	Hull City	46	11	9	3	45	27	5	8	10	28	41	49
9	Oldham Athletic	46	13	3	7	44	35	7	5	11	29	35	48
10	Peterborough United	46	13	6	4	52	27	5	5	13	23	43	47
11	Shrewsbury Town	46	13	6	4	43	19	5	5	13	30	61	47
12	Bristol Rovers	46	9	6	8	52	34	10	2	11	39	45	46
13	Port Vale	46	13	6	4	35	13	3	8	12	18	36	46
14	Southend United	46	9	10	4	42	26	6	5	12	35	52	45
15	Queens Park Rangers	46	13	4	6	47	34	5	5	13	29	44	45
16	Brentford	46	11	4	8	54	36	4	10	9	33	44	44
17	Colchester United	46	10	8	5	45	26	2	11	10	25	42	43
18	LUTON TOWN	46	12	2	9	42	41	4	8	11	22	39	42
19	Walsall	46	7	9	7	34	35	6	5	12	25	41	40
20	Barnsley	46	9	9	5	34	29	3	6	14	34	65	39
21	Millwall	46	9	4	10	33	29	5	6	12	20	38	38
22	Crewe Alexandra	46	10	5	8	29	26	1	7	15	21	51	34
23	Wrexham	46	9	4	10	50	42	4	2	17	25	65	32
24	Notts County	46	7	8	8	29	26	2	1	20	16	66	27

1964/65 Division Three

		P	W	D	L	F	A	W	D	L	F	A	Pts
1	Carlisle United	46	14	5	4	46	24	11	5	7	30	29	60
2	Bristol City	46	14	6	3	53	18	10	5	8	39	37	59
3	Mansfield Town	46	17	4	2	61	23	7	7	9	34	38	59
4	Hull City	46	14	6	3	51	25	9	6	8	40	32	58
5	Brentford	46	18	4	1	55	18	6	5	12	28	37	57
6	Bristol Rovers	46	14	7	2	52	21	6	8	9	30	37	55
7	Gillingham	46	16	5	2	45	13	7	4	12	25	37	55
8	Peterborough United	46	16	3	4	61	33	6	4	13	24	41	51
9	Watford	46	13	8	2	45	21	4	8	11	26	43	50
10	Grimsby Town	46	11	10	2	37	21	5	7	11	31	46	49
11	Bournemouth	46	12	4	7	40	24	6	7	10	32	39	47
12	Southend United	46	14	4	5	48	24	5	4	14	30	47	46
13	Reading	46	12	8	3	45	26	4	6	13	25	44	46
14	Queens Park Rangers	46	15	5	3	48	23	2	7	14	24	57	46
15	Workington	46	11	7	5	30	22	6	5	12	28	47	46
16	Shrewsbury Town	46	10	6	7	42	38	5	6	12	34	46	42
17	Exeter City	46	8	7	8	33	27	4	10	9	18	25	41
18	Scunthorpe United	46	9	8	6	42	27	5	4	14	23	45	40
19	Walsall	46	9	4	10	34	36	6	3	14	21	44	37
20	Oldham Athletic	46	10	3	10	40	39	3	7	13	21	44	36
21	LUTON TOWN	46	6	8	9	32	36	5	3	15	19	58	33
22	Port Vale	46	7	6	10	27	33	2	8	13	14	43	32
23	Colchester United	46	7	6	10	30	34	3	4	16	20	55	30
24	Barnsley	46	8	5	10	33	31	1	6	16	21	59	29

1965/66 Division Four

		P	W	D	L	F	A	W	D	L	F	A	Pts
1	Doncaster Rovers	46	15	6	2	49	21	9	5	9	36	33	59
2	Darlington	46	16	3	4	41	17	9	6	8	31	36	59
3	Torquay United	46	17	2	4	43	20	7	8	8	29	29	58
4	Colchester United	46	13	7	3	45	21	10	3	10	25	26	56
5	Tranmere Rovers	46	15	1	7	56	32	9	7	7	37	34	56
6	LUTON TOWN	46	19	2	2	65	27	5	6	12	25	43	56
7	Chester	46	15	5	3	52	27	5	7	11	27	43	52
8	Notts County	46	9	8	6	32	25	10	4	9	29	28	50
9	Newport County	46	14	6	3	46	24	4	6	13	29	51	48
10	Southport	46	15	6	2	47	20	3	6	14	21	49	48
11	Bradford Park Avenue	46	14	2	7	59	31	7	3	13	43	61	47
12	Barrow	46	12	8	3	48	31	4	7	12	24	45	47
13	Stockport County	46	12	4	7	42	29	6	2	15	29	41	42
14	Crewe Alexandra	46	12	4	7	42	23	4	5	14	19	40	41
15	Halifax Town	46	11	6	6	46	31	4	5	14	21	44	41
16	Barnsley	46	11	6	6	43	24	4	4	15	31	54	40
17	Aldershot	46	12	6	5	47	27	3	4	16	28	57	40
18	Hartlepools United	46	13	4	6	44	22	3	4	16	19	53	40
19	Port Vale	46	12	7	4	38	18	3	2	18	10	41	39
20	Chesterfield	46	8	9	6	37	35	5	4	14	25	43	39
21	Rochdale	46	12	1	10	46	27	4	4	15	25	60	37
22	Lincoln City	46	9	7	7	37	29	4	4	15	20	53	37
23	Bradford City	46	10	5	8	37	34	2	8	13	26	60	37
24	Wrexham	46	10	4	9	43	43	3	5	15	29	61	35

1966/67 Division Four

		P	W	D	L	F	A	W	D	L	F	A	Pts
1	Stockport County	46	16	5	2	41	18	10	7	6	28	24	64
2	Southport	46	19	2	2	47	15	4	11	8	22	27	59
3	Barrow	46	12	8	3	35	18	12	3	8	41	36	59
4	Tranmere Rovers	46	14	6	3	42	20	8	8	7	24	23	58
5	Crewe Alexandra	46	14	5	4	42	26	7	7	9	28	29	54
6	Southend United	46	15	5	3	44	12	7	4	12	26	37	53
7	Wrexham	46	11	12	0	46	20	5	8	10	30	42	52
8	Hartlepools United	46	15	3	5	44	29	7	4	12	22	35	51
9	Brentford	46	13	7	3	36	19	5	6	12	22	37	49
10	Aldershot	46	14	4	5	48	19	4	8	11	24	38	48
11	Bradford City	46	13	4	6	48	31	6	6	11	26	31	48
12	Halifax Town	46	10	11	2	37	27	5	3	15	22	41	44
13	Port Vale	46	9	7	7	33	27	5	8	10	22	31	43
14	Exeter City	46	11	6	6	30	24	3	9	11	20	36	43
15	Chesterfield	46	13	6	4	33	16	4	2	17	27	47	42
16	Barnsley	46	8	7	8	30	28	5	8	10	30	36	41
17	LUTON TOWN	46	15	5	3	47	23	1	4	18	12	50	41
18	Newport County	46	9	9	5	35	23	3	7	13	21	40	40
19	Chester	46	8	5	10	24	32	7	5	11	30	46	40
20	Notts County	46	10	7	6	31	25	3	4	16	22	47	37
21	Rochdale	46	10	4	9	30	27	3	7	13	23	48	37
22	York City	46	11	5	7	45	31	1	6	16	20	48	35
23	Bradford Park Avenue	46	7	6	10	30	34	4	7	12	22	45	35
24	Lincoln City	46	7	8	8	39	39	2	5	16	19	43	31

1967/68 Division Four

		P	W	D	L	F	A	W	D	L	F	A	Pts
1	LUTON TOWN	46	19	3	1	55	16	8	9	6	32	28	66
2	Barnsley	46	17	6	0	43	14	7	7	9	25	32	61
3	Hartlepools United	46	15	7	1	34	12	10	3	10	26	34	60
4	Crewe Alexandra	46	13	10	0	44	18	7	8	8	30	31	58
5	Bradford City	46	14	5	4	41	22	9	6	8	31	29	57
6	Southend United	46	12	8	3	45	21	8	6	9	32	37	54
7	Chesterfield	46	15	4	4	47	20	6	7	10	24	30	53
8	Wrexham	46	17	3	3	47	12	3	10	10	25	41	53
9	Aldershot	46	10	11	2	36	19	8	6	9	34	36	53
10	Doncaster Rovers	46	12	8	3	36	16	6	7	10	30	40	51
11	Halifax Town	46	10	6	7	34	24	5	10	8	18	25	46
12	Newport County	46	11	7	5	32	22	5	6	12	26	41	45
13	Lincoln City	46	11	3	9	41	31	6	6	11	30	37	43
14	Brentford	46	13	4	6	41	24	5	3	15	20	40	43
15	Swansea Town	46	11	8	4	38	25	5	2	16	25	52	42
16	Darlington	46	6	11	6	31	27	6	6	11	16	26	41
17	Notts County	46	10	7	6	27	27	5	4	14	26	52	41
18	Port Vale	46	10	5	8	41	31	2	10	11	20	41	39
19	Rochdale	46	9	8	6	35	32	3	6	14	16	40	38
20	Exeter City	46	9	7	7	30	30	2	9	12	15	35	38
21	York City	46	9	6	8	44	30	2	8	13	21	38	36
22	Chester	46	6	6	11	35	38	3	8	12	22	40	32
23	Workington	46	8	8	7	35	29	2	3	18	19	58	31
24	Bradford Park Avenue	46	3	7	13	18	35	1	8	14	12	47	23

1968/69 Division Three

		P	W	D	L	F	A	W	D	L	F	A	Pts
1	Watford	46	16	5	2	35	7	11	5	7	39	27	64
2	Swindon Town	46	18	4	1	38	7	9	6	8	33	28	64
3	LUTON TOWN	46	20	3	0	57	14	5	8	10	17	24	61
4	Bournemouth	46	16	2	5	41	17	5	7	11	19	28	51
5	Plymouth Argyle	46	10	8	5	34	25	7	7	9	19	24	49
6	Torquay United	46	13	4	6	35	18	5	8	10	19	28	48
7	Tranmere Rovers	46	12	3	8	36	31	7	7	9	34	37	48
8	Southport	46	14	8	1	52	20	3	5	15	19	44	47
9	Stockport County	46	14	5	4	49	25	2	9	12	18	43	46
10	Barnsley	46	13	6	4	37	21	3	8	12	21	42	46
11	Rotherham United	46	12	6	5	40	21	4	7	12	16	29	45
12	Brighton & HA	46	12	7	4	49	21	4	6	13	23	44	45
13	Walsall	46	10	9	4	34	18	4	7	12	16	31	44
14	Reading	46	13	3	7	41	25	2	10	11	26	41	43
15	Mansfield Town	46	14	5	4	37	18	2	6	15	21	44	43
16	Bristol Rovers	46	12	6	5	41	27	4	5	14	22	44	43
17	Shrewsbury Town	46	11	8	4	28	17	5	3	15	23	50	43
18	Orient	46	10	8	5	31	19	4	6	13	20	39	42
19	Barrow	46	11	6	6	30	23	6	2	15	26	52	42
20	Gillingham	46	10	10	3	35	20	3	5	15	19	43	41
21	Northampton Town	46	9	8	6	37	30	5	4	14	17	31	40
22	Hartlepool	46	6	12	5	25	29	4	7	12	15	41	39
23	Crewe Alexandra	46	11	4	8	40	31	2	5	16	12	45	35
24	Oldham Athletic	46	9	6	8	33	27	4	3	16	17	56	35

1969/70 Division Three

		P	W	D	L	F	A	W	D	L	F	A	Pts
1	Orient	46	16	5	2	43	15	9	7	7	24	21	62
2	LUTON TOWN	46	13	8	2	46	15	10	6	7	31	28	60
3	Bristol Rovers	46	15	5	3	51	26	5	11	7	29	33	56
4	Fulham	46	12	9	2	43	26	8	6	9	38	29	55
5	Brighton & HA	46	16	4	3	37	16	7	5	11	20	27	55
6	Mansfield Town	46	14	4	5	46	22	7	7	9	24	27	53
7	Barnsley	46	14	6	3	43	24	5	9	9	25	35	53
8	Reading	46	16	3	4	52	29	5	8	10	35	48	53
9	Rochdale	46	11	6	6	39	24	7	4	12	30	36	46
10	Bradford City	46	11	6	6	37	22	6	6	11	20	28	46
11	Doncaster Rovers	46	13	4	6	31	19	4	8	11	21	35	46
12	Walsall	46	11	4	8	33	31	6	8	9	21	36	46
13	Torquay United	46	9	9	5	36	22	5	8	10	26	37	45
14	Rotherham United	46	10	8	5	36	19	5	6	12	26	35	44
15	Shrewsbury Town	46	10	12	1	35	17	3	6	14	27	46	44
16	Tranmere Rovers	46	10	8	5	38	29	4	8	11	18	43	44
17	Plymouth Argyle	46	10	7	6	32	23	6	4	13	24	41	43
18	Halifax Town	46	10	9	4	31	25	4	6	13	16	38	43
19	Bury	46	13	4	6	47	29	2	7	14	28	51	41
20	Gillingham	46	7	6	10	28	33	6	7	10	24	31	39
21	Bournemouth	46	8	9	6	28	27	4	6	13	20	44	39
22	Southport	46	11	5	7	31	22	3	5	15	17	44	38
23	Barrow	46	7	9	7	28	27	1	5	17	18	54	30
24	Stockport County	46	4	7	12	17	30	2	4	17	10	41	23

1970/71 Division Two

		P	W	D	L	F	A	W	D	L	F	A	Pts
1	Leicester City	42	12	7	2	30	14	11	6	4	27	16	59
2	Sheffield United	42	14	6	1	49	18	7	8	6	24	21	56
3	Cardiff City	42	12	7	2	39	16	8	6	7	25	25	53
4	Carlisle United	42	16	3	2	39	13	4	10	7	26	30	53
5	Hull City	42	11	5	5	31	16	8	8	5	23	25	51
6	LUTON TOWN	42	12	7	2	40	18	6	6	9	22	25	49
7	Middlesbrough	42	13	6	2	37	16	4	8	9	23	27	48
8	Millwall	42	13	5	3	36	12	6	4	11	23	30	47
9	Birmingham City	42	12	7	2	30	12	5	5	11	28	36	46
10	Norwich City	42	11	8	2	34	20	4	6	11	20	32	44
11	Queens Park Rangers	42	11	5	5	39	22	5	6	10	19	31	43
12	Swindon Town	42	12	7	2	38	14	3	5	13	23	37	42
13	Sunderland	42	11	6	4	34	21	4	6	11	18	33	42
14	Oxford United	42	8	8	5	23	23	6	6	9	18	25	42
15	Sheffield Wednesday	42	10	7	4	32	27	2	5	14	19	42	36
16	Portsmouth	42	9	4	8	32	28	1	10	10	14	33	34
17	Orient	42	5	11	5	16	15	4	5	12	13	36	34
18	Watford	42	6	7	8	18	22	4	6	11	20	38	33
19	Bristol City	42	9	6	6	30	28	1	5	15	16	36	31
20	Charlton Athletic	42	7	6	8	28	30	1	8	12	13	35	30
21	Blackburn Rovers	42	5	8	8	20	28	1	7	13	17	41	27
22	Bolton Wanderers	42	6	5	10	22	31	1	5	15	13	43	24

'1971/72 Division Two

		P	W	D	L	F	A	W	D	L	F	A	Pts
1	Norwich City	42	13	8	0	40	16	8	7	6	20	20	57
2	Birmingham City	42	15	6	0	46	14	4	12	5	14	17	56
3	Millwall	42	14	7	0	38	17	5	10	6	26	29	55
4	Queens Park Rangers	42	16	4	1	39	9	4	10	7	18	19	54
5	Sunderland	42	11	7	3	42	24	6	9	6	25	33	50
6	Blackpool	42	12	6	3	43	16	8	1	12	27	34	47
7	Burnley	42	13	4	4	43	22	7	2	12	27	33	46
8	Bristol City	42	14	3	4	43	22	4	7	10	18	27	46
9	Middlesbrough	42	16	4	1	31	11	3	4	14	19	37	46
10	Carlisle United	42	12	6	3	38	22	5	3	13	23	35	43
11	Swindon Town	42	10	6	5	29	16	5	6	10	18	31	42
12	Hull City	42	10	6	5	33	21	4	4	13	16	32	38
13	LUTON TOWN	42	7	8	6	25	24	3	10	8	18	24	38
14	Sheffield Wednesday	42	11	7	3	33	22	2	5	14	18	36	38
15	Oxford United	42	10	8	3	28	17	2	6	13	15	38	38
16	Portsmouth	42	9	7	5	31	26	3	6	12	28	42	37
17	Orient	42	12	4	5	32	19	2	5	14	18	42	37
18	Preston North End	42	11	4	6	32	21	1	8	12	20	37	36
19	Cardiff City	42	9	7	5	37	25	1	7	13	19	44	34
20	Fulham	42	10	7	4	29	20	2	3	16	16	48	34
21	Charlton Athletic	42	9	7	5	33	25	3	2	16	22	52	33
22	Watford	42	5	5	11	15	25	0	4	17	9	50	19

'1972/73 Division Two

		P	W	D	L	F	A	W	D	L	F	A	Pts
1	Burnley	42	13	6	2	44	18	11	8	2	28	17	62
2	Queens Park Rangers	42	16	4	1	54	13	8	9	4	27	24	61
3	Aston Villa	42	12	5	4	27	17	6	9	6	24	30	50
4	Middlesbrough	42	12	6	3	29	15	5	7	9	17	28	47
5	Bristol City	42	10	7	4	34	18	7	5	9	29	33	46
6	Sunderland	42	12	6	3	35	17	5	6	10	24	32	46
7	Blackpool	42	12	6	3	37	17	6	4	11	19	34	46
8	Oxford United	42	14	2	5	36	18	5	5	11	16	25	45
9	Fulham	42	11	6	4	32	16	5	6	10	26	33	44
10	Sheffield Wednesday	42	14	4	3	40	20	3	6	12	19	35	44
11	Millwall	42	12	5	4	33	18	4	5	12	22	29	42
12	LUTON TOWN	42	6	9	6	24	23	9	2	10	20	30	41
13	Hull City	42	9	7	5	39	22	5	5	11	25	37	40
14	Nottingham Forest	42	12	5	4	32	18	2	7	12	15	34	40
15	Orient	42	11	6	4	33	18	1	6	14	16	35	36
16	Swindont Town	42	8	9	4	28	23	2	7	12	18	37	36
17	Portsmouth	42	7	6	8	21	22	5	5	11	21	37	35
18	Carlisle United	42	10	5	6	40	24	1	7	13	10	28	34
19	Preston North End	42	6	8	7	19	25	5	4	12	18	39	34
20	Cardiff City	42	11	4	6	32	21	0	7	14	11	37	33
21	Huddersfield Town	42	7	9	5	21	20	1	8	12	15	36	33
22	Brighton & HA	42	7	8	6	32	31	1	5	15	14	52	29

'1973/74 Division Two

		P	W	D	L	F	A	W	D	L	F	A	Pts
1	Middlesbrough	42	16	4	1	40	8	11	7	3	37	22	65
2	LUTON TOWN	42	12	5	4	42	25	7	7	7	22	26	50
3	Carlisle United	42	13	5	3	40	17	7	4	10	21	31	49
4	Orient	42	9	8	4	28	17	6	10	5	27	25	48
5	Blackpool	42	11	5	5	35	17	6	8	7	22	23	47
6	Sunderland	42	11	6	4	32	15	8	3	10	26	29	47
7	Nottingham Forest	42	12	6	3	40	19	3	9	9	17	24	45
8	West Bromwich Albion	42	8	9	4	28	24	6	7	8	20	21	44
9	Hull City	42	9	9	3	25	15	4	8	9	21	32	43
10	Notts County	42	8	6	7	30	35	7	7	7	25	25	43
11	Bolton Wanderers	42	12	5	4	30	17	3	7	11	14	23	42
12	Millwall	42	10	6	5	28	16	4	8	9	23	35	42
13	Fulham	42	11	4	6	26	20	5	6	10	13	23	42
14	Aston Villa	42	8	9	4	33	21	5	6	10	15	24	41
15	Portsmouth	42	9	8	4	26	16	5	4	12	19	46	40
16	Bristol City	42	9	5	7	25	20	5	5	11	22	34	38
17	Cardiff City	42	8	7	6	27	20	2	9	10	22	42	36
18	Oxford United	42	8	8	5	27	21	2	8	11	8	25	36
19	Sheffield Wednesday	42	9	6	6	33	24	3	5	13	18	39	35
20	Crystal Palace	42	6	7	8	24	24	5	5	11	19	32	34
21	Preston North End	42	7	8	6	24	23	2	6	13	16	39	31
22	Swindon Town	42	6	7	8	22	27	1	4	16	14	45	25

'1974/75 Division One

		P	W	D	L	F	A	W	D	L	F	A	Pts
1	Derby County	42	14	4	3	41	18	7	7	7	26	31	53
2	Liverpool	42	14	5	2	44	17	6	6	9	16	22	51
3	Ipswich Town	42	17	2	2	47	14	6	3	12	19	30	51
4	Everton	42	10	9	2	33	19	6	9	6	23	23	50
5	Stoke City	42	12	7	2	40	18	5	8	8	24	30	49
6	Sheffield United	42	12	7	2	35	20	6	6	9	23	31	49
7	Middlesbrough	42	11	7	3	33	14	7	5	9	21	26	48
8	Manchester City	42	16	3	2	40	15	2	7	12	14	39	46
9	Leeds United	42	10	8	3	34	20	6	5	10	23	29	45
10	Burnley	42	11	6	4	40	29	6	5	10	28	38	45
11	Queens Park Rangers	42	10	4	7	25	17	6	6	9	29	37	42
12	Wolverhampton Wndrs	42	12	5	4	43	21	2	6	13	14	33	39
13	West Ham United	42	10	6	5	38	22	3	7	11	20	37	39
14	Coventry City	42	8	9	4	31	27	4	6	11	20	35	39
15	Newcastle United	42	12	4	5	39	23	3	5	13	20	49	39
16	Arsenal	42	10	6	5	31	16	3	5	13	16	33	37
17	Birmingham City	42	10	4	7	34	28	4	5	12	19	33	37
18	Leicester City	42	8	7	6	25	17	4	5	12	21	43	36
19	Tottenham Hotspur	42	8	4	9	29	27	5	4	12	23	36	34
20	LUTON TOWN	42	8	6	7	27	26	3	5	13	20	39	33
21	Chelsea	42	4	9	8	22	31	5	6	10	20	41	33
22	Carlisle United	42	8	2	11	22	21	4	3	14	21	38	29

'1975/76 Division Two

		P	W	D	L	F	A	W	D	L	F	A	Pts
1	Sunderland	42	19	2	0	48	10	5	6	10	19	26	56
2	Bristol City	42	11	7	3	34	14	8	8	5	25	21	53
3	West Bromwich Albion	42	10	9	2	29	12	10	4	7	21	21	53
4	Bolton Wanderers	42	12	5	4	36	14	8	7	6	28	24	52
5	Notts County	42	11	6	4	33	13	8	5	8	27	28	49
6	Southampton	42	18	2	1	49	16	3	5	13	17	34	49
7	LUTON TOWN	42	13	6	2	38	15	6	4	11	23	36	48
8	Nottingham Forest	42	13	1	7	34	18	4	11	6	21	22	46
9	Charlton Athletic	42	11	5	5	40	34	4	7	10	21	38	42
10	Blackpool	42	9	9	3	26	22	5	5	11	14	27	42
11	Chelsea	42	7	9	5	25	20	5	7	9	28	34	40
12	Fulham	42	9	8	4	27	14	4	6	11	18	33	40
13	Orient	42	10	6	5	21	12	3	8	10	16	27	40
14	Hull City	42	9	5	7	29	23	5	6	10	16	26	39
15	Blackburn Rovers	42	8	6	7	27	22	4	8	9	18	28	38
16	Plymouth Argyle	42	13	4	4	36	20	0	8	13	12	34	38
17	Oldham Athletic	42	11	8	2	37	24	2	4	15	20	44	38
18	Bristol Rovers	42	7	9	5	20	15	4	7	10	18	35	38
19	Carlisle United	42	9	8	4	29	22	3	5	13	16	37	37
20	Oxford United	42	7	7	7	23	25	4	4	13	16	34	33
21	York City	42	8	3	10	28	34	2	5	14	11	37	28
22	Portsmouth	42	4	6	11	15	23	5	1	15	17	38	25

'1976/77 Division Two

		P	W	D	L	F	A	W	D	L	F	A	Pts
1	Wolverhampton Wndrs	42	15	3	3	48	21	7	10	4	36	24	57
2	Chelsea	42	15	6	0	51	22	6	7	8	22	31	55
3	Nottingham Forest	42	14	3	4	53	22	7	7	7	24	21	52
4	Bolton Wanderers	42	15	2	4	46	21	5	9	7	29	33	51
5	Blackpool	42	11	7	3	29	17	6	10	5	29	25	51
6	LUTON TOWN	42	13	5	3	39	17	8	1	12	28	31	48
7	Charlton Athletic	42	14	5	2	52	27	2	11	8	19	31	48
8	Notts County	42	11	5	5	29	20	8	5	8	36	40	48
9	Southampton	42	12	6	3	40	24	5	4	12	32	43	44
10	Millwall	42	9	6	6	31	22	6	7	8	26	31	43
11	Sheffield United	42	9	8	4	32	25	5	4	12	22	38	40
12	Blackburn Rovers	42	12	4	5	31	18	3	5	13	11	36	39
13	Oldham Athletic	42	11	6	4	37	23	3	4	14	15	41	38
14	Hull City	42	9	8	4	31	17	1	9	11	14	36	37
15	Bristol Rovers	42	8	9	4	32	27	4	4	13	21	41	37
16	Burnley	42	8	9	4	27	20	3	5	13	19	44	36
17	Fulham	42	9	7	5	39	25	2	6	13	15	36	35
18	Cardiff City	42	7	6	8	30	30	5	4	12	26	37	34
19	Orient	42	4	8	9	18	23	5	8	8	19	32	34
20	Carlisle United	42	7	7	7	31	33	4	5	12	18	42	34
21	Plymouth Argyle	42	5	9	7	27	25	3	7	11	19	40	32
22	Hereford United	42	6	9	6	28	30	2	6	13	29	48	31

'1977/78 Division Two

		P	W	D	L	F	A	W	D	L	F	A	Pts
1	Bolton Wanderers	42	16	4	1	39	14	8	6	7	24	19	58
2	Southampton	42	15	4	2	44	16	7	9	5	26	23	57
3	Tottenham Hotspur	42	13	7	1	50	19	7	9	5	33	30	56
4	Brighton & HA	42	15	5	1	43	21	7	7	7	20	17	56
5	Blackburn Rovers	42	12	4	5	33	16	4	9	8	23	44	45
6	Sunderland	42	11	6	4	36	17	3	10	8	31	42	44
7	Stoke City	42	13	5	3	38	16	3	5	13	15	33	42
8	Oldham Athletic	42	9	10	2	32	20	4	6	11	22	38	42
9	Crystal Palace	42	9	7	5	31	20	4	8	9	19	27	41
10	Fulham	42	9	8	4	32	19	5	5	11	17	30	41
11	Burnley	42	11	6	4	35	20	4	4	13	21	44	40
12	Sheffield United	42	13	4	4	38	22	3	4	14	24	51	40
13	LUTON TOWN	42	11	4	6	35	20	3	6	12	19	32	38
14	Orient	42	8	11	2	30	20	2	7	12	13	29	38
15	Notts County	42	10	9	2	36	22	1	7	13	18	40	38
16	Millwall	42	8	8	5	23	20	4	6	11	26	37	38
17	Charlton Athletic	42	11	6	4	38	27	2	6	13	17	41	38
18	Bristol Rovers	42	10	7	4	40	26	3	5	13	21	51	38
19	Cardiff City	42	12	6	3	32	23	1	6	14	19	48	38
20	Blackpool	42	7	8	6	35	25	5	5	11	24	35	37
21	Mansfield Town	42	6	6	9	30	34	4	5	12	19	35	31
22	Hull City	42	6	6	9	23	25	2	6	13	11	27	28

'1978/79 Division Two

		P	W	D	L	F	A	W	D	L	F	A	Pts
1	Crystal Palace	42	12	7	2	30	11	7	12	2	21	13	57
2	Brighton & HA	42	16	3	2	44	11	7	7	7	28	28	56
3	Stoke City	42	11	7	3	35	15	9	9	3	23	16	56
4	Sunderland	42	13	3	5	39	19	9	8	4	31	25	55
5	West Ham United	42	12	7	2	46	15	6	7	8	24	24	50
6	Notts County	42	8	10	3	23	15	6	6	9	25	45	44
7	Preston North End	42	7	11	3	36	23	5	7	9	23	34	42
8	Newcastle United	42	13	3	5	35	24	4	5	12	16	31	42
9	Cardiff City	42	12	5	4	34	23	4	5	12	22	47	42
10	Fulham	42	10	7	4	35	19	3	8	10	15	28	41
11	Orient	42	11	5	5	32	18	4	5	12	19	33	40
12	Cambridge United	42	7	10	4	22	15	5	6	10	22	37	40
13	Burnley	42	11	6	4	31	22	3	6	12	20	40	40
14	Oldham Athletic	42	10	7	4	36	23	3	6	12	16	38	39
15	Wrexham	42	10	6	5	31	16	2	8	11	14	26	38
16	Bristol Rovers	42	10	6	5	34	23	4	4	13	14	37	38
17	Leicester City	42	7	8	6	28	23	3	9	9	15	29	37
18	LUTON TOWN	42	11	5	5	46	24	2	5	14	14	33	36
19	Charlton Athletic	42	6	8	7	28	28	5	5	11	32	41	35
20	Sheffield United	42	9	6	6	34	24	2	6	13	18	45	34
21	Millwall	42	7	4	10	22	29	4	6	11	20	32	32
22	Blackburn Rovers	42	5	8	8	24	29	5	2	14	17	43	30

'1979/80 Division Two

		P	W	D	L	F	A	W	D	L	F	A	Pts
1	Leicester City	42	12	5	4	32	19	9	8	4	26	19	55
2	Sunderland	42	16	5	0	47	13	5	7	9	22	29	54
3	Birmingham City	42	14	5	2	37	16	7	6	8	21	22	53
4	Chelsea	42	14	3	4	34	16	9	4	8	32	36	53
5	Queens Park Rangers	42	10	9	2	46	25	8	4	9	29	28	49
6	LUTON TOWN	42	9	10	2	36	17	7	7	7	30	28	49
7	West Ham United	42	13	2	6	37	21	7	5	9	17	22	47
8	Cambridge United	42	11	6	4	40	23	3	10	8	21	30	44
9	Newcastle United	42	13	6	2	35	19	2	8	11	18	30	44
10	Preston North End	42	8	10	3	30	23	4	9	8	26	29	43
11	Oldham Athletic	42	12	5	4	30	21	4	6	11	19	32	43
12	Swansea City	42	13	1	7	31	20	4	8	9	17	33	43
13	Shrewsbury Town	42	12	3	6	41	23	6	2	13	19	30	41
14	Orient	42	7	9	5	29	31	5	8	8	19	23	41
15	Cardiff City	42	11	4	6	21	16	5	4	12	20	32	40
16	Wrexham	42	13	2	6	26	15	3	4	14	14	34	38
17	Notts County	42	4	11	6	24	22	7	4	10	27	30	37
18	Watford	42	9	6	6	27	18	3	7	11	12	28	37
19	Bristol Rovers	42	9	8	4	33	23	2	5	14	17	41	35
20	Fulham	42	6	4	11	19	28	5	3	13	23	46	29
21	Burnley	42	5	9	7	19	23	1	6	14	20	50	27
22	Charlton Athletic	42	6	6	9	25	31	0	4	17	14	47	22

'1980/81 Division Two

		P	W	D	L	F	A	W	D	L	F	A	Pts
1	West Ham United	42	19	1	1	53	12	9	9	3	26	17	66
2	Notts County	42	10	8	3	26	15	8	9	4	23	23	53
3	Swansea City	42	12	5	4	39	19	6	9	6	25	25	50
4	Blackburn Rovers	42	12	8	1	28	7	4	10	7	14	22	50
5	LUTON TOWN	42	10	6	5	35	23	8	6	7	26	23	48
6	Derby County	42	9	8	4	34	26	6	7	8	23	26	45
7	Grimsby Town	42	10	8	3	21	10	5	7	9	23	32	45
8	Queens Park Rangers	42	11	7	3	36	12	4	6	11	20	34	43
9	Watford	42	13	5	3	34	18	3	6	12	16	27	43
10	Sheffield Wednesday	42	14	4	3	38	14	3	4	14	15	37	42
11	Newcastle United	42	11	7	3	22	13	3	7	11	8	32	42
12	Chelsea	42	8	6	7	27	15	6	6	9	19	26	40
13	Cambridge United	42	13	1	7	36	23	4	5	12	17	42	40
14	Shrewsbury Town	42	9	7	5	33	22	2	10	9	13	25	39
15	Oldham Athletic	42	7	9	5	19	16	5	6	10	20	32	39
16	Wrexham	42	5	8	8	22	24	7	6	8	21	21	38
17	Orient	42	9	8	4	34	20	4	4	13	18	36	38
18	Bolton Wanderers	42	10	5	6	40	27	4	5	12	21	39	38
19	Cardiff City	42	7	7	7	23	24	5	5	11	21	36	36
20	Preston North End	42	8	7	6	28	26	3	7	11	13	36	36
21	Bristol City	42	6	10	5	19	15	1	6	14	10	36	30
22	Bristol Rovers	42	4	9	8	21	24	1	4	16	13	41	23

'1981/82 Division Two

		P	W	D	L	F	A	W	D	L	F	A	Pts
1	LUTON TOWN	42	16	3	2	48	19	9	10	2	38	27	88
2	Watford	42	13	6	2	46	16	10	5	6	30	26	80
3	Norwich City	42	14	3	4	41	19	8	2	11	23	31	71
4	Sheffield Wednesday	42	10	8	3	31	23	10	2	9	24	28	70
5	Queens Park Rangers	42	15	4	2	40	9	6	2	13	25	34	69
6	Barnsley	42	13	4	4	33	14	6	6	9	26	27	67
7	Rotherham United	42	13	5	3	42	19	7	2	12	24	35	67
8	Leicester City	42	12	5	4	31	19	6	7	8	25	29	66
9	Newcastle United	42	14	4	3	30	14	4	4	13	22	36	62
10	Blackburn Rovers	42	11	4	6	26	15	5	7	9	21	28	59
11	Oldham Athletic	42	9	9	3	28	23	6	5	10	22	28	59
12	Chelsea	42	10	5	6	37	30	5	7	9	23	30	57
13	Charlton Athletic	42	11	5	5	33	22	2	7	12	17	43	51
14	Cambridge United	42	11	4	6	31	19	2	5	14	17	34	48
15	Crystal Palace	42	9	2	10	25	26	4	7	10	9	19	48
16	Derby County	42	9	8	4	32	23	3	4	14	21	45	48
17	Grimsby Town	42	5	8	8	29	30	6	5	10	24	35	46
18	Shrewsbury Town	42	10	6	5	26	19	1	7	13	11	38	46
19	Bolton Wanderers	42	10	4	7	28	24	3	3	15	11	37	46
20	Cardiff City	42	9	2	10	28	32	3	6	12	17	29	44
21	Wrexham	42	9	4	8	22	22	2	7	12	18	34	44
22	Orient	42	6	8	7	23	24	4	1	16	13	37	39

'1982/83 Division One

		P	W	D	L	F	A	W	D	L	F	A	Pts
1	Liverpool	42	16	4	1	55	16	8	6	7	32	21	82
2	Watford	42	16	2	3	49	20	6	3	12	25	37	71
3	Manchester United	42	14	7	0	39	10	5	6	10	17	28	70
4	Tottenham Hotspur	42	15	4	2	50	15	5	5	11	15	35	69
5	Nottingham Forest	42	12	5	4	34	18	8	4	9	28	32	69
6	Aston Villa	42	17	2	2	47	15	4	3	14	15	35	68
7	Everton	42	13	6	2	43	19	5	4	12	23	29	64
8	West Ham United	42	13	3	5	41	23	7	1	13	27	39	64
9	Ipswich Town	42	11	3	7	39	23	4	10	7	25	27	58
10	Arsenal	42	11	6	4	36	19	5	4	12	22	37	58
11	West Bromwich Albion	42	11	5	5	35	20	4	7	10	16	29	57
12	Southampton	42	11	5	5	36	22	4	7	10	18	36	57
13	Stoke City	42	13	4	4	34	21	3	5	13	19	43	57
14	Norwich City	42	10	6	5	30	18	4	6	11	22	40	54
15	Notts County	42	12	4	5	37	25	3	3	15	18	46	52
16	Sunderland	42	7	10	4	30	22	5	4	12	18	39	50
17	Birmingham City	42	9	7	5	29	24	3	7	11	11	31	50
18	LUTON TOWN	42	7	7	7	34	33	5	6	10	31	51	49
19	Coventry City	42	10	5	6	29	17	3	4	14	19	42	48
20	Manchester City	42	9	5	7	26	23	4	3	14	21	47	47
21	Swansea City	42	10	4	7	32	29	0	7	14	19	40	41
22	Brighton & HA	42	8	7	6	25	22	1	6	14	13	46	40

'1983/84 Division One

		P	W	D	L	F	A	W	D	L	F	A	Pts
1	Liverpool	42	14	5	2	50	12	8	9	4	23	20	80
2	Southampton	42	15	4	2	44	17	7	7	7	22	21	77
3	Nottingham Forest	42	14	4	3	47	17	8	4	9	29	28	74
4	Manchester United	42	14	3	4	43	18	6	11	4	28	23	74
5	Queens Park Rangers	42	14	4	3	37	12	8	3	10	30	25	73
6	Arsenal	42	10	5	6	41	29	8	4	9	33	31	63
7	Everton	42	9	9	3	21	12	7	5	9	23	30	62
8	Tottenham Hotspur	42	11	4	6	31	24	6	6	9	33	41	61
9	West Ham United	42	10	4	7	39	24	7	5	9	21	31	60
10	Aston Villa	42	14	3	4	34	22	3	6	12	25	39	60
11	Watford	42	9	7	5	36	31	7	2	12	32	46	57
12	Ipswich Town	42	11	4	6	34	23	4	4	13	21	34	53
13	Sunderland	42	8	9	4	26	18	5	4	12	16	35	52
14	Norwich City	42	9	8	4	34	20	3	7	11	14	29	51
15	Leicester City	42	11	5	5	40	30	2	7	12	25	38	51
16	LUTON TOWN	42	7	5	9	30	33	7	4	10	23	33	51
17	West Bromwich Albion	42	10	4	7	30	25	4	5	12	18	37	51
18	Stoke City	42	11	4	6	30	23	2	7	12	14	40	50
19	Coventry City	42	8	5	8	33	33	5	6	10	24	44	50
20	Birmingham City	42	7	7	7	19	18	5	5	11	20	32	48
21	Notts County	42	6	7	8	31	36	4	4	13	19	36	41
22	Wolverhampton Wan.	42	4	8	9	15	28	2	3	16	12	52	29

'1984/85 Division One

		P	W	D	L	F	A	W	D	L	F	A	Pts
1	Everton	42	16	3	2	58	17	12	3	6	30	26	90
2	Liverpool	42	12	4	5	36	19	10	7	4	32	16	77
3	Tottenham Hotspur	42	11	3	7	46	31	12	5	4	32	20	77
4	Manchester United	42	13	6	2	47	13	9	4	8	30	34	76
5	Southampton	42	13	4	4	29	18	6	7	8	27	29	68
6	Chelsea	42	13	3	5	38	20	5	9	7	25	28	66
7	Arsenal	42	14	5	2	37	14	5	4	12	24	35	66
8	Sheffield Wednesday	42	12	7	2	39	21	5	7	9	19	24	65
9	Nottingham Forest	42	13	4	4	35	18	6	3	12	21	30	64
10	Aston Villa	42	10	7	4	34	20	5	4	12	26	40	56
11	Watford	42	10	5	6	48	30	4	8	9	33	41	55
12	West Bromwich Albion	42	11	4	6	36	23	5	3	13	22	39	55
13	LUTON TOWN	42	12	5	4	40	22	3	4	14	17	39	54
14	Newcastle United	42	11	4	6	33	26	2	9	10	22	44	52
15	Leicester City	42	10	4	7	39	25	5	2	14	26	48	51
16	West Ham United	42	7	8	6	27	23	6	4	11	24	45	51
17	Ipswich Town	42	8	7	6	27	20	5	4	12	19	37	50
18	Coventry City	42	11	3	7	29	22	4	2	15	18	42	50
19	Queens Park Rangers	42	11	6	4	41	30	2	5	14	12	42	50
20	Norwich City	42	9	6	6	28	24	4	4	13	18	40	49
21	Sunderland	42	7	6	8	20	26	3	4	14	20	36	40
22	Stoke City	42	3	3	15	18	41	0	5	16	6	50	17

'1985/86 Division One

		P	W	D	L	F	A	W	D	L	F	A	Pts
1	Liverpool	42	16	4	1	58	14	10	6	5	31	23	88
2	Everton	42	16	3	2	54	18	10	5	6	33	23	86
3	West Ham United	42	17	2	2	48	16	9	4	8	26	24	84
4	Manchester United	42	12	5	4	35	12	10	5	6	35	24	76
5	Sheffield Wednesday	42	13	6	2	36	23	8	4	9	27	31	73
6	Chelsea	42	12	4	5	32	27	8	7	6	25	29	71
7	Arsenal	42	13	5	3	29	15	7	4	10	20	32	69
8	Nottingham Forest	42	11	5	5	38	25	8	6	7	31	28	68
9	LUTON TOWN	42	12	6	3	37	15	6	6	9	24	29	66
10	Tottenham Hotspur	42	12	2	7	47	25	7	6	8	27	27	65
11	Newcastle United	42	12	5	4	46	31	5	7	9	21	41	63
12	Watford	42	11	6	4	40	22	5	5	11	29	40	59
13	Queens Park Rangers	42	12	3	6	33	20	3	4	14	20	44	52
14	Southampton	42	10	6	5	32	18	2	4	15	19	44	46
15	Manchester City	42	7	7	7	25	26	4	5	12	18	31	45
16	Aston Villa	42	7	6	8	27	28	3	8	10	24	39	44
17	Coventry	42	6	5	10	31	35	5	5	11	17	36	43
18	Oxford United	42	7	7	7	34	27	3	5	13	28	53	42
19	Leicester City	42	7	8	6	35	35	3	4	14	19	41	42
20	Ipswich	42	8	5	8	20	24	3	3	15	12	31	41
21	Birmingham City	42	5	2	14	13	25	3	3	15	17	48	29
22	West Bromwich Albion	42	3	8	10	21	36	1	4	16	14	53	24

'1986/87 Division One

		P	W	D	L	F	A	W	D	L	F	A	Pts
1	Everton	42	16	4	1	49	11	10	4	7	27	20	86
2	Liverpool	42	15	3	3	43	16	8	5	8	29	26	77
3	Tottenham Hotspur	42	14	3	4	40	14	7	5	9	28	29	71
4	Arsenal	42	12	5	4	31	12	8	5	8	27	23	70
5	Norwich City	42	9	10	2	27	20	8	7	6	26	31	68
6	Wimbledon	42	11	5	5	32	22	8	4	9	25	28	66
7	LUTON TOWN	42	14	5	2	29	13	4	7	10	18	32	66
8	Nottingham Forest	42	12	8	1	36	14	6	3	12	28	37	65
9	Watford	42	12	5	4	38	20	6	4	11	29	34	63
10	Coventy City	42	14	4	3	35	17	3	8	10	15	28	63
11	Manchester United	42	13	3	5	38	18	1	11	9	14	27	56
12	Southampton	42	11	5	5	44	24	3	5	13	25	44	52
13	Sheffield Wednesday	42	9	7	5	39	24	4	6	11	19	35	52
14	Chelsea	42	8	6	7	30	30	5	7	9	23	34	52
15	West Ham United	42	10	4	7	33	28	4	6	11	19	39	52
16	Queens Park Rangers	42	9	7	5	31	27	4	4	13	17	37	50
17	Newcastle United	42	10	4	7	33	29	2	7	12	14	36	47
18	Oxford United	42	8	8	5	30	25	3	5	13	14	44	46
19	Charlton Athletic	42	7	7	7	26	22	4	4	13	19	33	44
20	Leicester City	42	9	7	5	39	24	2	2	17	15	52	42
21	Manchester City	42	8	6	7	28	24	0	9	12	8	33	39
22	Aston Villa	42	7	7	7	25	25	1	5	15	20	54	36

'1987/88 Division One

		P	W	D	L	F	A	W	D	L	F	A	Pts
1	Liverpool	40	15	5	0	49	9	11	7	2	38	15	90
2	Manchester United	40	14	5	1	41	17	9	7	4	30	21	81
3	Nottingham Forest	40	11	7	2	40	17	9	6	5	27	22	73
4	Everton	40	14	4	2	34	11	5	9	6	19	16	70
5	Queens Park Rangers	40	12	4	4	30	14	7	6	7	18	24	67
6	Arsenal	40	11	4	5	35	16	7	8	5	23	23	66
7	Wimbledon	40	8	9	3	32	20	6	6	8	26	27	57
8	Newcastle United	40	9	6	5	32	23	5	8	7	23	30	56
9	LUTON TOWN	40	11	6	3	40	21	3	5	12	17	37	53
10	Coventry City	40	6	8	6	23	25	7	6	7	23	28	53
11	Sheffield Wednesday	40	10	2	8	27	30	5	6	9	25	36	53
12	Southampton	40	6	8	6	27	26	6	6	8	22	27	50
13	Tottenham Hotspur	40	9	5	6	26	23	3	6	11	12	25	47
14	Norwich City	40	7	5	8	26	26	5	4	11	14	26	45
15	Derby County	40	6	7	7	18	17	4	6	10	17	28	43
16	West Ham United	40	6	9	5	23	21	3	6	11	17	31	42
17	Charlton Athletic	40	7	7	6	23	21	2	8	10	15	31	42
18	Chelsea	40	7	11	2	24	17	2	4	14	26	51	42
19	Portsmouth	40	4	8	8	21	27	3	6	11	15	39	35
20	Watford	40	4	5	11	15	24	3	6	11	12	27	32
21	Oxford United	40	5	7	8	24	34	1	6	13	20	46	31

'1988/89 Division One

		P	W	D	L	F	A	W	D	L	F	A	Pts
1	Arsenal	38	10	6	3	35	19	12	4	3	38	17	76
2	Liverpool	38	11	5	3	33	11	11	5	3	32	17	76
3	Nottingham Forest	38	8	7	4	31	16	9	6	4	33	27	64
4	Norwich City	38	8	7	4	23	20	9	4	6	25	25	62
5	Derby County	38	9	3	7	23	18	8	4	7	17	20	58
6	Tottenham Hotspur	38	8	6	5	31	24	7	6	6	29	22	57
7	Coventry City	38	9	4	6	28	23	5	9	5	19	19	55
8	Everton	38	10	7	2	33	18	4	5	10	17	27	54
9	Queens Park Rangers	38	9	5	5	23	16	5	6	8	20	21	53
10	Millwall	38	10	3	6	27	21	4	8	7	20	31	53
11	Manchester United	38	10	5	4	27	13	3	7	9	18	22	51
12	Wimbledon	38	10	3	6	30	19	4	6	9	20	27	51
13	Southampton	38	6	7	6	25	26	4	8	7	27	40	45
14	Charlton Athletic	38	6	7	6	25	24	4	5	10	19	34	42
15	Sheffield Wednesday	38	6	6	7	21	25	4	6	9	13	26	42
16	LUTON TOWN	38	8	6	5	32	21	2	5	12	10	31	41
17	Aston Villa	38	7	6	6	25	22	2	7	10	20	34	40
18	Middlesbrough	38	6	7	6	28	30	3	5	11	16	31	39
19	West Ham United	38	3	6	10	19	30	7	2	10	18	32	38
20	Newcastle United	38	3	6	10	19	28	4	4	11	13	35	31

'1989/90 Division One

		P	W	D	L	F	A	W	D	L	F	A	Pts
1	Liverpool	38	13	5	1	38	15	10	5	4	40	22	79
2	Aston Villa	38	13	3	3	36	20	8	4	7	21	18	70
3	Tottenham Hotspur	38	12	1	6	35	24	7	5	7	24	23	63
4	Arsenal	38	14	3	2	38	11	4	5	10	16	27	62
5	Chelsea	38	8	7	4	31	24	8	5	6	27	26	60
6	Everton	38	14	3	2	40	16	3	5	11	17	30	59
7	Southampton	38	10	5	4	40	27	5	5	9	31	36	55
8	Wimbledon	38	5	8	6	22	23	8	8	3	25	17	55
9	Nottingham Forest	38	9	4	6	31	21	6	5	8	24	26	54
10	Norwich City	38	7	10	2	24	14	6	4	9	20	28	53
11	Queens Park Rangers	38	9	4	6	27	22	4	7	8	18	22	50
12	Coventry City	38	11	2	6	24	25	3	5	11	15	34	49
13	Manchester United	38	8	6	5	26	14	5	3	11	20	33	48
14	Manchester City	38	9	4	6	26	21	3	8	8	17	31	48
15	Crystal Palace	38	8	7	4	27	23	5	2	12	15	43	48
16	Derby County	38	9	1	9	29	21	4	6	9	14	19	46
17	LUTON TOWN	38	8	8	3	24	18	2	5	12	19	39	43
18	Sheffield Wednesday	38	8	6	5	21	17	3	4	12	14	34	43
19	Charlton Athletic	38	4	6	9	18	25	3	3	13	13	32	30
20	Millwall	38	4	6	9	23	25	1	5	13	16	40	26

'1990/91 Division One

		P	W	D	L	F	A	W	D	L	F	A	Pts
1	Arsenal	38	15	4	0	51	10	9	9	1	23	8	83
2	Liverpool	38	14	3	2	42	13	9	4	6	35	27	76
3	Crystal Palace	38	11	6	2	26	17	9	3	7	24	24	69
4	Leeds United	38	12	2	5	46	23	7	5	7	19	24	64
5	Manchester City	38	12	3	4	35	25	5	8	6	29	28	62
6	Manchester United	38	11	4	4	34	17	5	8	6	24	28	59
7	Wimbledon	38	8	6	5	28	22	6	8	5	25	24	56
8	Nottingham Forest	38	11	4	4	42	21	3	8	8	23	29	54
9	Everton	38	9	5	5	26	15	4	7	8	24	31	51
10	Tottenham Hotspur	38	8	9	2	35	22	3	7	9	16	28	49
11	Chelsea	38	10	6	3	33	25	3	4	12	25	44	49
12	Queens Park Rangers	38	8	5	6	27	22	4	5	10	17	31	46
13	Sheffield United	38	9	3	7	23	23	4	4	11	13	32	46
14	Southampton	38	9	6	4	33	22	3	3	13	25	47	45
15	Norwich City	38	9	3	7	27	32	4	3	12	14	32	45
16	Coventry City	38	10	6	3	30	16	1	5	13	12	33	44
17	Aston Villa	38	7	9	3	29	25	2	5	12	17	33	41
18	LUTON TOWN	38	7	5	7	22	18	3	2	14	20	43	37
19	Sunderland	38	6	6	7	15	16	2	4	13	23	44	34
20	Derby County	38	3	8	8	25	36	2	1	16	12	39	24

Arsenal deducted 2 points, Manchester United deducted 1 point.

'1991/92 Division One

		P	W	D	L	F	A	W	D	L	F	A	Pts
1	Leeds United	42	13	8	0	38	13	9	8	4	36	24	82
2	Manchester United	42	12	7	2	34	13	9	8	4	29	20	78
3	Sheffield Wednesday	42	13	5	3	39	24	8	7	6	23	25	75
4	Arsenal	42	12	7	2	51	22	7	8	6	30	24	72
5	Manchester City	42	13	4	4	32	14	7	6	8	29	34	70
6	Liverpool	42	13	5	3	34	17	3	11	7	13	23	64
7	Aston Villa	42	13	3	5	31	16	4	6	11	17	28	60
8	Nottingham Forest	42	10	7	4	36	27	6	4	11	24	31	59
9	Sheffield United	42	9	6	6	29	23	7	3	11	36	40	57
10	Crystal Palace	42	7	8	6	24	25	7	7	7	29	36	57
11	Southampton	43	8	5	9	19	29	7	5	9	22	27	55
12	Queens Park Rangers	43	6	10	5	25	21	6	8	8	24	28	54
13	Everton	42	8	8	5	28	19	5	6	10	24	32	53
14	Wimbledon	42	10	5	6	32	20	3	9	9	21	33	53
15	Chelsea	42	7	8	6	31	30	6	6	9	19	30	53
16	Tottenham Hotspur	42	7	3	11	33	35	8	4	9	25	28	52
17	Oldham Athletic	42	11	5	5	46	36	3	4	14	17	31	51
18	Norwich City	42	8	6	7	29	28	3	6	12	18	35	45
19	Coventry City	42	6	7	8	18	15	5	4	12	17	29	44
20	LUTON TOWN	42	10	7	4	25	17	0	5	16	13	54	42
21	Notts. County	42	7	5	9	24	29	3	5	13	16	33	40
22	West Ham United	42	6	6	9	22	24	3	5	13	15	35	38

'1992/93 "New" Division One

		P	W	D	L	F	A	W	D	L	F	A	Pts
1	Newcastle United	46	16	6	1	58	15	13	3	7	34	23	96
2	West Ham United	46	16	5	2	50	17	10	5	8	31	24	88
3	Portsmouth	46	19	2	2	48	9	7	8	8	32	37	88
4	Tranmere Rovers	46	15	4	4	48	24	8	6	9	24	32	79
5	Swindon Town	46	15	5	3	41	23	6	8	9	33	36	76
6	Leicester City	46	14	5	4	43	24	8	5	10	28	40	76
7	Millwall	46	14	6	3	46	21	4	10	9	19	32	70
8	Derby County	46	11	2	10	40	33	8	7	8	28	24	66
9	Grimsby Town	46	12	6	5	33	25	7	1	15	25	32	64
10	Peterborough United	46	7	11	5	30	26	9	3	11	25	37	62
11	Charlton Athletic	46	10	8	5	28	19	6	5	12	21	27	61
12	Wolverhampton Wndrs	46	11	6	6	37	26	5	7	11	20	30	61
13	Barnsley	46	12	4	7	29	19	5	5	13	27	41	60
14	Oxford United	46	8	7	8	29	21	6	7	10	24	35	56
15	Bristol City	46	10	7	6	29	25	4	7	12	20	42	56
16	Watford	46	8	7	8	27	30	6	6	11	30	41	55
17	Southend United	46	9	8	6	33	22	4	5	14	21	42	52
18	Notts. County	46	10	7	6	33	21	2	9	12	22	49	52
19	LUTON TOWN	46	6	13	4	26	26	4	8	11	22	36	51
20	Birmingham City	46	10	4	9	30	32	3	8	12	20	40	51
21	Sunderland	46	9	6	8	34	28	4	5	14	16	36	50
22	Brentford	46	7	6	10	28	30	6	4	13	24	41	49
23	Cambridge United	46	8	6	9	29	32	3	10	10	19	37	49
24	Bristol Rovers	46	6	6	11	30	42	4	5	14	25	45	41

'1993/94 "New" Division One

		P	W	D	L	F	A	W	D	L	F	A	Pts
1	Crystal Palace	46	16	4	3	39	18	11	5	7	34	28	90
2	Nottingham Forest	46	12	9	2	38	22	11	5	7	36	27	83
3	Millwall	46	14	8	1	36	17	5	9	9	22	32	74
4	Leicester City	46	11	9	3	45	30	8	7	8	27	29	73
5	Tranmere Rovers	46	15	3	5	48	23	6	6	11	21	30	72
6	Derby County	46	15	3	5	44	25	5	8	10	29	43	71
7	Wolverhampton Wndrs	46	10	10	3	34	19	7	7	9	26	28	68
8	Notts. County	46	16	3	4	43	26	4	5	14	22	43	68
9	Middlesbrough	46	12	6	5	40	19	6	7	10	26	35	67
10	Stoke City	46	14	4	5	35	19	4	9	10	22	40	67
11	Charlton Athletic	46	14	3	6	39	22	5	5	13	22	36	65
12	Sunderland	46	14	2	7	35	22	5	6	12	19	35	65
13	Bristol City	46	11	7	5	27	18	5	9	9	20	32	64
14	Grimsby Town	46	7	14	2	26	16	6	6	11	26	31	59
15	Bolton Wanderers	46	10	8	5	40	31	5	6	12	23	33	59
16	Southend United	46	10	5	8	34	28	7	3	13	29	39	59
17	Portsmouth	46	10	6	7	29	22	5	7	11	23	36	58
18	Barnsley	46	9	3	11	25	26	7	4	12	30	41	55
19	Watford	46	10	5	8	39	35	5	4	14	27	45	54
20	LUTON TOWN	46	12	4	7	38	25	2	7	14	18	35	53
21	West Bromwich Albion	46	9	7	7	38	31	4	5	14	22	38	51
22	Birmingham City	46	9	7	7	28	29	4	5	14	24	40	51
23	Oxford United	46	10	5	8	33	33	3	5	15	21	42	49
24	Peterborough United	46	6	9	8	31	30	2	4	17	17	46	37

'1994/95 "New" Division One

		P	W	D	L	F	A	W	D	L	F	A	Pts
1	Middlesbrough	46	15	4	4	41	19	8	9	6	26	21	82
2	Reading	46	12	7	4	34	21	11	3	9	24	23	79
3	Bolton Wanderers	46	16	6	1	43	13	5	8	10	24	32	77
4	Wolverhampton Wndrs	46	15	5	3	39	18	6	8	9	38	43	76
5	Tranmere Rovers	46	17	4	2	51	23	5	6	12	16	35	76
6	Barnsley	46	15	6	2	42	19	5	6	12	21	33	72
7	Watford	46	14	6	3	33	17	5	7	11	19	29	70
8	Sheffield United	46	12	9	2	41	21	5	8	10	33	34	68
9	Derby County	46	12	6	5	44	23	6	6	11	22	28	66
10	Grimsby Town	46	12	7	4	36	19	5	7	11	26	37	65
11	Stoke City	46	10	7	6	31	21	6	8	9	19	32	63
12	Millwall	46	11	8	4	36	22	5	6	12	24	38	62
13	Southend United	46	13	2	8	33	25	5	6	12	21	48	62
14	Oldham Athletic	46	12	7	4	34	21	4	6	13	26	39	61
15	Charlton Athletic	46	11	6	6	33	25	5	5	13	25	41	59
16	LUTON TOWN	46	8	6	9	35	30	7	7	9	26	34	58
17	Port Vale	46	11	5	7	30	24	4	8	11	28	40	58
18	West Bromwich Albion	46	13	3	7	33	24	3	7	13	18	33	58
19	Portsmouth	46	9	8	6	31	28	6	5	12	22	35	58
20	Sunderland	46	5	12	6	22	22	7	6	10	19	23	54
21	Swindon Town	46	9	6	8	28	27	3	6	14	26	46	48
22	Burnley	46	8	7	8	36	33	3	6	14	13	41	46
23	Bristol City	46	8	8	7	26	28	3	4	16	16	35	45
24	Notts. County	46	7	8	8	26	28	2	5	16	19	38	40

'1995/96 "New" Division One

		P	W	D	L	F	A	W	D	L	F	A	Pts
1	Sunderland	46	13	8	2	32	10	9	9	5	27	23	83
2	Derby County	46	14	8	1	48	22	7	8	8	23	29	79
3	Crystal Palace	46	9	9	5	34	22	11	6	6	33	26	75
4	Stoke City	46	13	6	4	32	15	7	7	9	28	34	73
5	Charlton Athletic	46	8	11	4	28	23	9	9	5	29	22	71
6	Leicester City	46	9	7	7	32	29	10	7	6	34	31	71
7	Ipswich Town	46	13	5	5	45	30	6	7	10	34	39	69
8	Huddersfield Town	46	14	4	5	42	23	3	8	12	19	35	63
9	Sheffield United	46	9	7	7	29	25	7	7	9	28	29	62
10	Barnsley	46	9	10	4	34	28	5	8	10	26	38	60
11	Port Vale	46	10	5	8	30	29	5	10	8	29	37	60
12	West Bromwich Albion	46	11	5	7	34	29	5	7	11	26	39	60
13	Tranmere Rovers	46	9	9	5	42	29	5	8	10	22	31	59
14	Southend United	46	11	8	4	30	22	4	6	13	22	39	59
15	Birmingham City	46	11	7	5	37	23	4	6	13	24	41	58
16	Norwich City	46	7	9	7	26	24	7	6	10	33	31	57
17	Oldham Athletic	46	10	7	6	33	20	4	7	12	21	30	56
18	Reading	46	8	7	8	28	30	5	10	8	26	33	56
19	Grimsby Town	46	8	10	5	27	25	6	4	13	28	44	56
20	Wolverhampton Wndrs	46	8	9	6	34	28	5	7	11	22	34	55
21	Portsmouth	46	8	6	9	34	32	5	7	11	27	37	52
22	Millwall	46	7	6	10	23	28	6	7	10	20	35	52
23	Watford	46	7	8	8	40	33	3	10	10	22	37	48
24	LUTON TOWN	46	7	6	10	30	34	4	6	13	10	30	45

'1996/97 "New" Division Two

		P	W	D	L	F	A	W	D	L	F	A	Pts
1	Bury	46	18	5	0	39	7	6	7	10	23	31	84
2	Stockport County	46	15	5	3	31	14	8	8	7	28	27	82
3	LUTON TOWN	46	13	7	3	38	14	8	8	7	33	31	78
4	Brentford	46	8	11	4	26	22	12	3	8	30	21	74
5	Bristol City	46	14	4	5	43	18	7	6	10	26	33	73
6	Crewe Alexandra	46	15	4	4	38	15	7	3	13	18	32	73
7	Blackpool	46	13	7	3	41	21	5	8	10	19	26	69
8	Wrexham	46	11	9	3	37	28	6	9	8	17	22	69
9	Burnley	46	14	3	6	48	27	5	8	10	23	28	68
10	Chesterfield	46	10	9	4	25	18	8	5	10	17	21	68
11	Gillingham	46	13	3	7	37	25	6	7	10	23	34	67
12	Walsall	46	12	8	3	35	21	7	2	14	19	32	67
13	Watford	46	10	8	5	24	14	6	11	6	21	24	67
14	Millwall	46	12	4	7	27	22	4	9	10	23	33	61
15	Preston North End	46	14	5	4	33	19	4	2	17	16	36	61
16	Bournemouth	46	8	9	6	24	20	7	6	10	19	25	60
17	Bristol Rovers	46	13	4	6	34	22	2	7	14	13	28	56
18	Wycombe Wanderers	46	13	4	6	31	14	2	6	15	20	42	55
19	Plymouth Argyle	46	7	11	5	19	18	5	7	11	28	40	54
20	York City	46	8	6	9	27	31	5	7	11	20	37	52
21	Peterborough United	46	7	7	9	38	34	4	7	12	17	39	47
22	Shrewsbury Town	46	8	6	9	27	32	3	7	13	22	42	46
23	Rotherham United	46	4	7	12	17	29	3	7	13	22	41	35
24	Notts. County	46	4	9	10	20	25	3	5	15	13	34	35

'1997/98 "New" Division Two

		P	W	D	L	F	A	W	D	L	F	A	Pts
1	Watford	46	13	7	3	36	22	11	9	3	31	19	88
2	Bristol City	46	16	5	2	41	17	9	5	9	28	22	85
3	Grimsby Town	46	11	7	5	30	14	8	8	7	25	23	72
4	Northampton Town	46	14	5	4	33	17	4	12	7	19	20	71
5	Bristol Rovers	46	13	2	8	43	33	7	8	8	27	31	70
6	Fulham	46	12	7	4	31	14	8	3	12	29	29	70
7	Wrexham	46	10	10	3	31	23	8	6	9	24	28	70
8	Gillingham	46	13	7	3	30	18	6	6	11	22	29	70
9	Bournemouth	46	11	8	4	28	15	7	4	12	29	37	66
10	Chesterfield	46	13	7	3	31	19	3	10	10	15	25	65
11	Wigan Athletic	46	12	5	6	41	31	5	6	12	23	35	62
12	Blackpool	46	13	6	4	35	24	4	5	14	24	43	62
13	Oldham Athletic	46	13	7	3	43	23	2	9	12	19	31	61
14	Wycombe Wanderers	46	10	10	3	32	20	4	8	11	19	33	60
15	Preston North End	46	10	6	7	29	26	5	8	10	27	30	59
16	York City	46	9	7	7	26	21	5	10	8	26	37	59
17	LUTON TOWN	46	7	7	9	35	38	7	8	8	25	26	57
18	Millwall	46	7	8	8	23	23	7	5	11	20	31	55
19	Walsall	46	10	8	5	26	16	4	4	15	17	36	54
20	Burnley	46	10	9	4	34	23	3	4	16	21	42	52
21	Brentford	46	9	7	7	33	29	2	10	11	17	42	50
22	Plymouth Argyle	46	10	5	8	36	30	2	8	13	19	40	49
23	Carlisle United	46	8	5	10	27	28	4	3	16	30	45	44
24	Southend United	46	8	7	8	29	30	3	3	17	18	49	43

'1998/99 "New" Division Two

		P	W	D	L	F	A	W	D	L	F	A	Pts
1	Fulham	46	19	3	1	50	12	12	5	6	29	20	101
2	Walsall	46	13	7	3	37	23	13	2	8	26	24	87
3	Manchester City	46	13	6	4	38	14	9	10	4	31	19	82
4	Gillingham	46	15	5	3	45	17	7	9	7	30	27	80
5	Preston North End	46	12	6	5	46	23	10	7	6	32	27	79
6	Wigan Athletic	46	14	5	4	44	17	8	5	10	31	31	76
7	Bournemouth	46	14	7	2	37	11	7	6	10	26	30	76
8	Stoke City	46	10	4	9	32	32	11	2	10	27	31	69
9	Chesterfield	46	14	5	4	34	16	3	8	12	12	28	64
10	Millwall	46	9	8	6	33	24	8	3	12	19	35	62
11	Reading	46	10	6	7	29	26	6	7	10	25	37	61
12	LUTON TOWN	46	10	4	9	25	26	6	6	11	26	34	58
13	Bristol Rovers	46	8	9	6	35	28	5	8	10	30	28	56
14	Blackpool	46	7	8	8	24	24	7	6	10	20	30	56
15	Burnley	46	8	7	8	23	33	5	9	9	31	40	55
16	Notts. County	46	8	6	9	29	27	6	6	11	23	34	54
17	Wrexham	46	8	6	9	21	28	5	8	10	22	34	53
18	Colchester United	46	9	7	7	25	30	3	9	11	27	40	52
19	Wycombe Wanderers	46	8	5	10	31	26	5	7	11	21	32	51
20	Oldham Athletic	46	8	4	11	26	31	6	5	12	22	35	51
21	York City	46	6	8	9	28	33	7	3	13	28	47	50
22	Northampton Town	46	4	12	7	26	31	6	6	11	17	26	48
23	Lincoln City	46	9	4	10	27	27	4	3	16	15	47	46
24	Macclesfield Town	46	7	4	12	24	30	4	6	13	19	33	43

'1999/2000 "New" Division Two

		P	W	D	L	F	A	W	D	L	F	A	Pts
1	Preston North End	46	15	4	4	37	23	13	7	3	37	14	95
2	Burnley	46	16	3	4	42	23	9	10	4	27	24	88
3	Gillingham	46	16	3	4	46	21	9	7	7	33	27	85
4	Wigan Athletic	46	15	3	5	37	14	7	14	2	35	24	83
5	Millwall	46	14	7	2	41	18	9	6	8	35	32	82
6	Stoke City	46	13	7	3	37	18	10	6	7	31	24	82
7	Bristol Rovers	46	13	7	3	34	19	10	4	9	35	26	80
8	Notts. County	46	9	6	8	32	27	9	5	9	29	28	65
9	Bristol City	46	7	14	2	31	18	8	5	10	28	39	64
10	Reading	46	10	9	4	28	18	6	5	12	29	45	62
11	Wrexham	46	9	6	8	23	24	8	5	10	29	37	62
12	Wycombe Wanderers	46	11	4	8	32	24	5	9	9	24	29	61
13	LUTON TOWN	46	10	7	6	41	35	7	3	13	20	30	61
14	Oldham Athletic	46	8	5	10	27	28	8	7	8	23	27	60
15	Bury	46	8	10	5	38	33	5	8	10	23	31	57
16	Bournemouth	46	11	6	6	37	19	5	3	15	22	43	57
17	Brentford	46	8	6	9	27	31	5	7	11	20	30	52
18	Colchester United	46	9	4	10	36	40	5	6	12	23	42	52
19	Cambridge United	46	8	6	9	38	33	4	6	13	26	32	48
20	Oxford United	46	6	5	12	24	38	6	4	13	19	35	45
21	Cardiff City	46	5	10	8	23	34	4	7	12	22	33	44
22	Blackpool	46	4	10	9	26	37	4	7	12	23	40	41
23	Scunthorpe United	46	4	6	13	16	34	5	6	12	24	40	39
24	Chesterfield	46	5	7	11	17	25	2	8	13	17	38	36

'2000/01 "New" Division Two

		P	W	D	L	F	A	W	D	L	F	A	Pts
1	Millwall	46	17	2	4	49	11	11	7	5	40	27	93
2	Rotherham United	46	16	4	3	50	26	11	6	6	29	29	91
3	Reading	46	15	5	3	58	26	10	6	7	28	26	86
4	Walsall	46	15	5	3	51	23	8	7	8	28	27	81
5	Stoke City	46	12	6	5	39	21	9	8	6	35	28	77
6	Wigan Athletic	46	12	9	2	29	18	7	9	7	24	24	75
7	Bournemouth	46	11	6	6	37	23	9	7	7	42	32	73
8	Notts. County	46	10	6	7	37	33	9	6	8	25	33	69
9	Bristol City	46	11	6	6	47	29	7	8	8	23	27	68
10	Wrexham	46	10	6	7	33	28	7	6	10	32	43	63
11	Port Vale	46	9	8	6	35	22	7	6	10	20	27	62
12	Peterborough United	46	12	6	5	38	27	3	8	12	23	39	59
13	Wycombe Wanderers	46	8	7	8	24	23	7	7	9	22	30	59
14	Brentford	46	9	10	4	34	30	5	7	11	22	40	59
15	Oldham Athletc	46	11	5	7	35	26	4	8	11	18	39	58
16	Bury	46	10	6	7	25	22	6	4	13	20	37	58
17	Colchester United	46	10	5	8	32	23	5	7	11	23	36	57
18	Northampton Town	46	9	6	8	26	28	6	6	11	20	31	57
19	Cambridge United	46	8	6	9	32	31	6	5	12	29	46	53
20	Swindon Town	46	6	8	9	30	35	7	5	11	17	30	52
21	Bristol Rovers	46	6	10	7	28	26	6	5	12	25	31	51
22	LUTON TOWN	46	5	6	12	24	35	4	7	12	28	45	40
23	Swansea City	46	5	9	9	26	24	3	4	16	21	49	37
24	Oxford United	46	5	4	14	23	34	2	2	19	30	66	27

'2001/02 "New" Division Three

		P	W	D	L	F	A	W	D	L	F	A	Pts
1	Plymouth Argyle	46	19	2	2	41	11	12	7	4	30	17	102
2	LUTON TOWN	46	15	5	3	50	18	15	2	6	46	30	97
3	Mansfield Town	46	17	3	3	49	24	7	4	12	23	36	79
4	Cheltenham Town	46	11	11	1	40	20	10	4	9	26	29	78
5	Rochdale	46	13	8	2	41	22	8	7	8	24	30	78
6	Rushden & Diamonds	46	14	5	4	40	20	6	8	9	29	33	73
7	Hartlepool United	46	12	6	5	53	23	8	5	10	21	25	71
8	Scunthorpe United	46	14	5	4	43	22	5	9	9	31	34	71
9	Shrewsbury Town	46	13	4	6	36	19	7	6	10	28	34	70
10	Kidderminster Harriers	46	13	6	4	35	17	6	3	14	21	30	66
11	Hull City	46	12	6	5	38	18	4	7	12	19	33	61
12	Southend United	46	12	5	6	36	22	3	8	12	15	32	58
13	Macclesfield Town	46	7	7	9	23	25	8	6	9	18	27	58
14	York City	46	11	5	7	26	20	5	4	14	28	47	57
15	Darlington	46	11	6	6	37	25	4	5	14	23	46	56
16	Exeter City	46	7	9	7	25	32	7	4	12	23	41	55
17	Carlisle United	46	11	5	7	31	21	1	11	11	18	35	52
18	Leyton Orient	46	10	7	6	37	25	3	6	14	18	46	52
19	Torquay United	46	8	6	9	27	31	4	9	10	19	32	51
20	Swansea City	46	7	8	8	26	26	6	4	13	27	51	51
21	Oxford United	46	8	7	8	34	28	3	7	13	19	34	47
22	Lincoln City	46	8	4	11	25	27	2	12	9	19	35	46
23	Bristol Rovers	46	8	7	8	28	28	3	5	15	12	32	45
24	Halifax Town	46	5	9	9	24	28	3	3	17	15	56	36

'2002/03 "New" Division Two

		P	W	D	L	F	A	W	D	L	F	A	Pts
1	Wigan Athletic	46	14	7	2	37	16	15	6	2	31	9	100
2	Crewe Alexandra	46	11	5	7	29	19	14	6	3	47	21	86
3	Bristol City	46	15	5	3	43	15	9	6	8	36	33	83
4	Queens Park Rangers	46	14	4	5	38	19	10	7	6	31	26	83
5	Oldham Athletic	46	11	6	6	39	18	11	10	2	29	20	82
6	Cardiff City	46	12	6	5	33	20	11	6	6	35	23	81
7	Tranmere Rovers	46	14	5	4	38	23	9	6	8	28	34	80
8	Plymouth Argyle	46	11	6	6	39	24	6	8	9	24	28	65
9	LUTON TOWN	46	8	8	7	32	28	9	6	8	35	34	65
10	Swindon Town	46	10	5	8	34	27	6	7	10	25	36	60
11	Peterborough United	46	8	7	8	25	20	6	9	8	26	34	58
12	Colchester United	46	8	7	8	24	24	6	9	8	28	32	58
13	Blackpool	46	10	8	5	35	25	5	5	13	21	39	58
14	Stockport County	46	8	8	7	39	38	7	2	14	26	32	55
15	Notts. County	46	10	7	6	37	32	3	9	11	25	38	55
16	Brentford	46	8	8	7	28	21	6	4	13	19	35	54
17	Port Vale	46	9	5	9	34	31	5	6	12	20	39	53
18	Wycombe Wanderers	46	8	7	8	39	38	5	6	12	20	28	52
19	Barnsley	46	7	8	8	27	31	6	5	12	24	33	52
20	Chesterfield	46	11	4	8	29	28	3	4	16	14	45	50
21	Cheltenham Town	46	6	9	8	26	31	4	9	10	27	37	48
22	Huddersfield Town	46	7	9	7	27	24	4	3	16	12	37	45
23	Mansfield Town	46	9	2	12	38	45	3	6	14	28	52	44
24	Northampton Town	46	7	4	12	23	31	3	5	15	17	48	39

'2003/04 "New" Division Two

		P	W	D	L	F	A	W	D	L	F	A	Pts
1	Plymouth Argyle	46	17	5	1	52	13	9	7	7	33	28	90
2	Queens Park Rangers	46	16	7	0	47	12	6	10	7	33	33	83
3	Bristol City	46	15	6	2	34	12	8	7	8	24	25	82
4	Brighton & HA	46	17	4	2	39	11	5	7	11	25	32	77
5	Swindon Town	46	12	7	4	41	23	8	6	9	35	35	73
6	Hartlepool United	46	10	8	5	39	24	10	5	8	37	37	73
7	Port Vale	46	15	6	2	45	28	6	4	13	28	35	73
8	Tranmere Rovers	46	13	7	3	36	18	4	9	10	23	38	67
9	Bournemouth	46	11	8	4	35	25	6	7	10	21	26	66
10	Luton Town	46	14	6	3	44	27	3	9	11	25	39	66
11	Colchester United	46	11	8	4	33	23	6	5	12	19	33	64
12	Barnsley	46	7	12	4	25	19	8	5	10	29	39	62
13	Wrexham	46	9	6	8	27	21	8	3	12	23	39	60
14	Blackpool	46	9	5	9	31	28	7	6	10	27	37	59
15	Oldham Athletic	46	9	8	6	37	25	3	13	7	29	35	57
16	Sheffield Wednesday	46	7	9	7	25	26	6	5	12	23	38	53
17	Brentford	46	9	5	9	34	38	5	6	12	18	31	53
18	Peterborough United	46	5	8	10	36	33	7	8	8	22	25	52
19	Stockport County	46	6	8	9	31	36	5	11	7	31	34	52
20	Chesterfield	46	9	7	7	34	31	3	8	12	15	40	51
21	Grimsby Town	46	10	5	8	36	26	3	6	14	19	55	50
22	Rushden & Diamonds	46	9	5	9	37	34	4	4	15	23	40	48
23	Notts. County	46	6	9	8	32	27	4	3	16	18	51	42
24	Wycombe Wanderers	46	5	7	11	31	39	1	12	10	19	36	37

'2004/05 League One

		P	W	D	L	F	A	W	D	L	F	A	Pts
1	LUTON TOWN	46	17	4	2	46	16	12	7	4	41	32	98
2	Hull City	46	16	5	2	42	17	10	3	10	38	36	86
3	Tranmere Rovers	46	14	5	4	43	23	8	8	7	30	32	79
4	Brentford	46	15	4	4	34	22	7	5	11	23	38	75
5	Sheffield Wednesday	46	10	6	7	34	28	9	9	5	43	31	72
6	Hartlepool United	46	15	3	5	51	30	6	5	12	25	36	71
7	Bristol City	46	9	8	6	42	25	9	8	6	32	32	70
8	Bournemouth	46	9	7	7	40	30	11	3	9	37	34	70
9	Huddersfield Town	46	12	6	5	42	28	8	4	11	32	37	70
10	Doncaster Rovers	46	10	11	2	35	20	6	7	10	30	40	66
11	Bradford City	46	9	6	8	40	35	8	8	7	24	27	65
12	Swindon Town	46	12	5	6	40	30	5	7	11	26	38	63
13	Barnsley	46	7	11	5	38	31	7	8	8	31	33	61
14	Walsall	46	11	7	5	40	28	5	5	13	25	41	60
15	Colchester United	46	8	6	9	27	23	6	11	6	33	27	59
16	Blackpool	46	8	7	8	28	30	7	5	11	26	29	57
17	Chesterfield	46	9	8	6	32	28	5	7	11	23	34	57
18	Port Vale	46	13	2	8	33	23	4	3	16	16	36	56
19	Oldham Athletic	46	10	5	8	42	34	4	5	14	18	39	52
20	MK Dons	46	8	10	5	33	28	4	5	14	21	40	51
21	Torquay United	46	8	5	10	27	36	4	10	9	28	43	51
22	Wrexham	46	6	8	9	26	37	7	6	10	36	43	53
23	Peterborough United	46	5	6	12	27	35	4	6	13	22	38	39
24	Stockport County	46	3	4	16	26	46	3	4	16	23	52	26

'2005/06 Championship

		P	W	D	L	F	A	W	D	L	F	A	Pts
1	Reading	46	19	3	1	58	14	12	10	1	41	18	106
2	Sheffield United	46	15	5	3	43	22	11	7	5	33	24	90
3	Watford	46	11	7	5	39	24	11	8	4	38	29	81
4	Preston North End	46	11	10	2	31	12	9	10	4	28	18	80
5	Leeds United	46	13	7	3	35	18	8	8	7	22	20	78
6	Crystal Palace	46	13	6	4	39	20	8	6	9	28	28	75
7	Wolverhampton Wndrs	46	9	10	4	24	18	7	9	7	26	24	67
8	Coventry City	46	12	7	4	39	22	4	8	11	23	43	63
9	Norwich City	46	12	4	7	34	25	6	4	13	22	40	62
10	LUTON TOWN	46	11	6	6	45	31	6	4	13	21	36	61
11	Cardiff City	46	10	7	6	32	24	6	5	12	26	35	60
12	Southampton	46	9	10	4	26	17	4	9	10	23	33	58
13	Stoke City	46	7	5	11	24	32	10	2	11	30	31	58
14	PlymouthArgyle	46	10	7	6	26	22	3	10	10	13	24	56
15	Ipswich Town	46	8	8	7	28	32	6	6	11	25	34	56
16	Leicester City	46	8	9	6	30	25	5	6	12	21	34	54
17	Burnley	46	11	6	6	34	22	3	6	14	12	32	54
18	Hull City	46	8	8	7	24	21	4	8	11	25	34	52
19	Sheffield Wednesday	46	7	8	8	22	24	6	5	12	17	28	52
20	Derby County	46	8	10	5	33	27	2	10	11	20	40	50
21	Queens Park Rangers	46	7	7	9	24	26	5	7	11	26	39	50
22	Crewe Alexandra	46	7	7	9	38	40	2	8	13	19	46	42
23	Millwall	46	4	8	11	13	27	4	8	11	22	35	40
24	Brighton & HA	46	4	8	11	21	34	3	9	11	18	37	38

'2006/07 Championship

		P	W	D	L	F	A	W	D	L	F	A	Pts
1	Sunderland	46	15	4	4	38	18	12	3	8	38	29	88
2	Birmingham City	46	15	5	3	37	18	11	3	9	30	24	86
3	Derby County	46	13	6	4	33	19	12	3	8	29	27	84
4	West Bromwich Albion	46	14	4	5	51	24	8	6	9	30	31	76
5	Wolverhampton Wndrs	46	12	5	6	33	28	10	5	8	26	28	76
6	Southampton	46	13	6	4	36	20	8	6	9	41	33	75
7	Preston North End	46	15	4	4	38	17	7	4	12	26	36	74
8	Stoke City	46	12	8	3	35	16	7	8	8	27	25	73
9	Sheffield Wednesday	46	10	6	7	38	36	10	5	8	32	30	71
10	ColchesterUnited	46	15	4	4	46	19	5	5	13	24	37	69
11	Plymouth Argyle	46	10	8	5	36	26	7	8	8	27	36	67
12	Crystal Palace	46	12	3	8	33	22	6	8	9	26	29	65
13	Cardiff City	46	11	7	5	33	18	6	6	11	24	35	64
14	Ipswich Town	46	13	2	8	40	29	5	6	12	24	30	62
15	Burnley	46	10	6	7	35	23	5	6	12	17	26	57
16	Norwich City	46	10	5	8	29	25	6	4	13	27	46	57
17	Coventry City	46	11	4	8	30	25	5	4	14	17	37	56
18	Queens Park Rangers	46	9	6	8	31	29	5	5	13	23	39	53
19	Leicester City	46	6	8	9	26	31	7	6	10	23	33	53
20	Barnsley	46	9	4	10	27	29	6	1	16	26	56	50
21	Hull City	46	8	3	12	33	32	5	7	11	18	35	49
22	Southend United	46	6	6	11	29	38	4	6	13	18	42	42
23	LUTON TOWN	46	7	5	11	33	40	3	5	15	20	41	40
24	Leeds United	46	10	4	9	27	30	3	3	17	19	42	36

'2007/08 League One

		P	W	D	L	F	A	W	D	L	F	A	Pts
1	Swansea City	46	13	5	5	38	21	14	6	3	44	21	92
2	Nottingham Forest	46	13	8	2	37	13	9	8	6	27	19	82
3	Doncaster Rovers	46	14	4	5	34	18	9	7	7	31	23	80
4	Carlisle United	46	17	3	3	39	16	6	8	9	25	30	80
5	Leeds United	46	15	4	4	41	18	12	6	5	31	20	76
6	Southend United	46	12	6	5	35	20	10	4	9	35	35	76
7	Brighton & HA	46	12	6	5	37	25	7	6	10	21	25	69
8	Oldham Athletic	46	10	7	6	32	21	8	6	9	26	25	67
9	Northampton Town	46	12	6	5	38	21	5	9	9	22	34	66
10	Huddersfield Town	46	12	4	7	29	22	8	2	13	21	40	66
11	Tranmere Rovers	46	13	4	6	32	18	5	7	11	20	29	65
12	Walsall	46	7	9	7	27	26	9	7	7	25	20	64
13	Swindon Town	46	12	5	6	41	24	4	8	11	22	32	61
14	Leyton Orient	46	9	6	8	27	29	7	6	10	22	34	60
15	Hartlepool United	46	11	5	7	40	26	4	4	15	23	40	54
16	Bristol Rovers	46	5	10	8	25	30	7	7	9	20	23	53
17	Millwall	46	9	4	10	30	26	5	6	12	15	34	52
18	Yeovil Town	46	9	4	10	19	27	5	6	12	19	32	52
19	Cheltenham Town	46	10	8	5	23	21	3	4	16	19	43	51
20	Crewe Alexandra	46	8	6	9	27	33	4	8	11	20	32	50
21	Bournemouth	46	10	4	9	31	35	7	3	13	31	37	48
22	Gillingham	46	9	9	5	26	22	2	4	17	18	51	46
23	Port Vale	46	5	8	10	26	35	4	3	16	21	46	38
24	LUTON TOWN	46	10	5	8	29	25	1	5	17	14	38	33

Leeds deducted 15 points
Bournemouth & Luton deducted 10 points

'2008/09 League Two

		P	W	D	L	F	A	W	D	L	F	A	Pts
1	Brentford	46	13	8	2	39	15	10	8	5	26	21	85
2	Exeter City	46	13	5	5	36	25	9	8	6	29	25	79
3	Wycombe Wanderers	46	11	9	3	32	16	9	9	5	22	17	78
4	Bury	46	14	4	5	36	19	7	11	5	27	24	78
5	Gillingham	46	12	7	4	38	21	9	5	9	20	34	75
6	Rochdale	46	11	6	6	40	24	8	7	8	30	35	70
7	Shrewsbury Town	46	14	6	3	41	16	3	12	8	20	28	69
8	Dag & Red	46	12	3	8	44	24	7	8	8	33	29	68
9	Bradford City	46	11	10	2	39	18	7	3	13	27	37	67
10	Chesterfield	46	8	8	7	32	28	8	7	8	30	29	63
11	Morecambe	46	9	9	5	29	24	6	9	8	24	32	63
12	Darlington	46	11	6	6	36	23	9	6	8	25	21	62
13	Lincoln City	46	6	11	6	26	22	8	6	9	27	30	59
14	Rotherham United	46	11	6	6	32	21	10	6	7	28	25	58
15	Aldershot Town	46	9	10	4	36	31	5	2	16	23	49	54
16	Accrington Stanley	46	9	5	9	25	24	4	6	13	17	35	50
17	Barnet	46	7	7	9	30	35	4	8	11	26	39	48
18	Port Vale	46	6	6	11	23	33	7	3	13	21	33	48
19	Notts. County	46	6	6	11	22	31	5	8	10	27	38	47
20	Macclesfield Town	46	7	4	12	23	37	6	4	13	22	40	47
21	Bournemouth	46	11	6	6	28	15	6	6	11	31	36	46
22	Grimsby Town	46	6	7	10	31	28	3	7	13	20	41	41
23	Chester City	46	4	7	12	24	34	4	6	13	19	47	37
24	LUTON TOWN	46	7	8	8	34	34	6	9	8	24	31	26

Luton deducted 30 points
Rotherham & Bournemouth deducted 17 points
Darlington deducted 10 points

2009/10 Conference Premier

		P	W	D	L	F	A	W	D	L	F	A	Pts
1	Stevenage Borough	44	16	5	1	44	11	14	4	4	35	13	99
2	LUTON TOWN	44	14	3	5	54	22	12	7	3	30	18	88
3	Oxford United	44	16	4	2	37	10	9	7	6	27	21	86
4	Rushden & Diamonds	44	12	6	4	40	21	10	7	5	37	18	79
5	York City	44	13	7	2	40	15	9	5	8	22	20	78
6	Kettering Town	44	6	8	8	27	23	12	4	6	24	18	66
7	Crawley Town	44	14	3	5	33	24	5	6	11	17	33	66
8	AFC Wimbledon	44	8	5	9	30	19	10	5	7	31	28	64
9	Mansfield Town	44	9	8	5	34	22	8	3	11	35	38	62
10	Cambridge United	44	11	4	7	44	24	4	10	8	21	29	59
11	Wrexham	44	9	7	6	26	17	6	6	10	19	22	58
12	Salisbury City	44	11	5	6	33	21	10	0	12	25	42	58
13	Kidderminster Harriers	44	11	3	8	31	21	4	9	9	26	31	57
14	Altrincham	44	7	7	8	29	25	6	8	8	24	26	54
15	Barrow	44	7	9	6	27	29	6	4	12	23	38	52
16	Tamworth	44	7	6	9	26	30	4	10	8	16	22	49
17	Hayes & Yeading	44	7	7	8	38	38	5	5	12	21	47	48
18	Histon	44	6	9	7	24	28	5	4	13	20	39	46
19	Eastbourne Borough	44	8	7	7	26	29	3	6	13	16	43	46
20	Gateshead	44	10	3	9	24	23	3	4	15	22	46	45
21	Forest Green Rovers	44	9	5	8	27	29	3	4	15	23	47	45
22	Ebbsfleet United	44	7	4	11	25	36	5	4	13	25	46	44
23	Grays Athletic	44	4	5	13	16	41	1	8	13	19	50	26

Salisbury deducted 10 points, and later demoted from the League
Grays deducted 2 points
Gateshead deducted 1 point
Chester City's record expunged during season

2010/11 Conference Premier

		P	W	D	L	F	A	W	D	L	F	A	Pts
1	Crawley Town	46	18	3	2	57	19	13	9	1	36	11	105
2	AFC Wimbledon	46	17	3	3	46	15	10	6	7	37	32	90
3	LUTON TOWN	46	14	7	2	57	17	9	8	6	28	20	84
4	Wrexham	46	13	7	3	36	24	9	8	6	30	25	81
5	Fleetwood Town	46	12	8	3	35	19	10	4	9	33	23	78
6	Kidderminster Harriers	46	13	6	4	40	27	7	11	5	34	33	72
7	Darlington	46	13	6	4	37	14	5	11	7	24	28	71
8	York City	46	14	6	3	31	13	5	8	10	24	37	71
9	Newport County AFC	46	11	7	5	44	29	7	8	8	34	31	69
10	Bath City	46	10	10	3	38	27	6	5	12	26	41	63
11	Grimsby Town	46	7	12	4	37	28	8	5	10	35	34	62
12	Mansfield Town	46	9	6	8	40	37	8	4	11	33	38	61
13	Rushden & Diamonds	46	10	6	7	37	27	6	8	9	28	35	57
14	Gateshead	46	8	9	6	28	28	6	6	11	37	40	57
15	Kettering Town	46	8	8	7	33	32	7	5	11	31	43	53
16	Hayes & Yeading United	46	10	2	11	34	38	5	4	14	23	43	51
17	Cambridge United	46	7	7	9	32	28	4	10	9	21	33	50
18	Barrow	46	9	6	8	31	22	3	8	12	21	45	50
19	Tamworth	46	6	8	9	34	41	6	5	12	28	42	49
20	Forest Green Rovers	46	7	10	6	28	25	3	6	14	25	47	46
21	Southport	46	9	6	8	39	33	2	7	14	17	44	46
22	Altrincham	46	6	8	9	29	38	5	3	15	18	49	44
23	Eastbourne Borough	46	6	5	12	36	46	4	4	15	26	58	39
24	Histon	46	4	3	16	18	45	4	6	13	23	45	28

Kidderminster Harriers deducted 5 points • Histon deducted 5 points • Kettering Town deducted 2 points
Rushden & Diamonds deducted 5 points and later demoted from the League

2011/12 Conference Premier

		P	W	D	L	F	A	W	D	L	F	A	Pts
1	Fleetwood Town	46	13	8	2	50	25	18	2	3	52	23	103
2	Wrexham	46	16	3	4	48	17	14	5	4	37	16	98
3	Mansfield Town	46	14	6	3	50	25	11	8	4	37	23	89
4	York City	46	11	6	6	43	24	12	8	3	38	21	83
5	LUTON TOWN	46	15	4	4	48	15	7	11	5	30	27	81
6	Kidderminster Harriers	46	10	7	6	44	32	12	3	8	38	31	76
7	Southport	46	8	8	7	36	39	13	5	5	36	30	76
8	Gateshead	46	11	8	4	39	26	10	3	10	30	36	74
9	Cambridge United	46	11	6	6	31	16	8	8	7	26	25	71
10	Forest Green Rovers	46	11	5	7	37	25	8	8	7	29	20	70
11	Grimsby Town	46	12	4	7	51	28	7	9	7	28	32	70
12	Braintree Town	46	11	5	7	39	34	6	6	11	37	46	62
13	Barrow	46	12	6	5	39	25	5	3	15	23	51	60
14	Ebbsfleet United	46	7	6	10	34	39	7	6	10	35	45	54
15	Alfreton Town	46	8	6	9	39	48	7	3	13	23	38	54
16	Stockport County	46	8	7	8	35	28	4	8	11	23	46	51
17	Lincoln City	46	8	6	9	32	24	5	4	14	24	42	49
18	Tamworth	46	7	9	7	30	30	4	6	13	17	40	48
19	Newport County AFC	46	8	6	9	22	22	3	8	12	31	43	47
20	AFC Telford United	46	9	6	8	24	26	1	10	12	21	39	46
21	Hayes & Yeading United	46	5	5	13	26	41	6	3	14	32	49	41
22	Darlington	46	8	7	8	24	24	3	6	14	23	49	36
23	Bath City	46	5	4	14	27	41	2	6	15	16	48	31
24	Kettering Town	46	5	5	13	25	47	3	4	16	15	53	30

Darlington deducted 10 points
Kettering Town deducted 3 points

2012/13 Conference Premier

		P	W	D	L	F	A	W	D	L	F	A	Pts
1	Mansfield Town	46	17	3	3	53	17	13	2	8	39	35	95
2	Kidderminster Harriers	46	15	4	4	49	22	13	5	5	33	18	93
3	Newport County AFC	46	13	5	5	43	27	12	5	6	42	33	85
4	Grimsby Town	46	13	5	5	42	19	10	9	4	28	19	83
5	Wrexham	46	11	9	3	45	24	11	5	7	29	21	80
6	Hereford United	46	9	6	8	37	33	10	7	6	36	30	70
7	LUTON TOWN	46	10	7	6	43	26	8	6	9	27	36	67
8	Dartford	46	12	4	7	41	26	7	5	11	26	37	66
9	Braintree Town	46	9	5	9	32	40	10	4	9	31	32	66
10	Forest Green Rovers	46	8	6	9	33	24	10	5	8	30	25	65
11	Macclesfield Town	46	10	6	7	29	28	7	6	10	36	42	63
12	Woking	46	13	3	7	47	34	5	5	13	26	47	62
13	Alfreton Town	46	9	5	9	41	39	7	7	9	28	35	60
14	Cambridge United	46	9	7	7	33	30	6	7	10	35	39	59
15	Nuneaton Town	46	8	9	6	29	25	6	6	11	26	38	57
16	Lincoln City	46	9	5	9	34	36	6	6	11	32	37	56
17	Gateshead	46	9	9	5	35	22	4	7	12	23	39	55
18	Hyde	46	9	5	9	35	31	7	2	14	28	44	55
19	Tamworth	46	9	4	10	25	27	6	6	11	30	42	55
20	Southport	46	7	4	12	32	44	7	8	8	40	42	54
21	Stockport County	46	8	2	13	34	39	5	9	9	23	37	50
22	Barrow AFC	46	5	7	11	20	35	6	6	11	25	48	46
23	Ebbsfleet United	46	5	11	7	31	37	3	4	16	24	52	39
24	AFC Telford United	46	2	9	12	22	42	4	8	11	30	37	35

2013/14 Conference Premier

		P	W	D	L	F	A	W	D	L	F	A	Pts
1	LUTON TOWN	46	18	3	2	64	16	12	8	3	38	19	101
2	Cambridge United	46	16	4	3	49	14	7	9	7	23	21	82
3	Gateshead	46	12	7	4	42	24	10	6	7	30	26	79
4	Grimsby Town	46	11	7	5	40	26	11	5	7	25	20	78
5	FC Halifax Town	46	16	6	1	55	19	6	5	12	30	39	77
6	Braintree Town	46	12	4	7	27	18	9	7	7	30	21	74
7	Kidderminster Harriers	46	15	4	4	45	22	5	8	10	21	37	72
8	Barnet	46	11	6	6	30	26	8	7	8	28	27	70
9	Woking	46	11	4	8	32	30	9	4	10	34	39	68
10	Forest Green Rovers	46	13	6	4	47	22	6	4	13	33	44	67
11	Alfreton Town	46	13	6	4	45	33	8	1	14	24	41	67
12	Salisbury City	46	13	6	4	34	21	6	4	13	24	42	67
13	Nuneaton Town	46	12	4	7	29	25	6	8	9	25	35	66
14	Lincoln City	46	10	7	6	30	19	7	7	9	30	40	65
15	Macclesfield Town	46	11	5	7	35	27	7	2	14	27	36	61
16	Welling United	46	10	5	8	31	24	6	7	10	28	37	60
17	Wrexham	46	11	5	7	31	21	5	6	12	30	40	59
18	Southport	46	13	5	5	33	23	1	6	16	20	48	53
19	Aldershot Town	46	11	6	6	48	32	5	7	11	21	30	51
20	Hereford United	46	9	6	8	24	24	4	6	13	20	39	51
21	Chester FC	46	5	12	6	26	30	7	3	13	23	40	51
22	Dartford	46	8	3	12	32	35	4	5	14	17	39	44
23	Tamworth	46	6	7	10	25	31	4	2	17	18	50	39
24	Hyde	46	0	3	20	18	57	1	4	18	20	62	10

Aldershot deducted 10 points
Alfreton Town deducted 3 points
Salisbury City demoted from the League
Hereford United demoted from the League

◗ John Moore greets his new coaching staff to Kenilworth Road prior to a 1986/87 campaign which turned out to be the club's best ever in the top flight. Left to right: Jim Ryan, John Moore and Ray Harford.

THE PLAYERS

	APPEARANCES						GOALS					
	L	NL	FAC	LC	OTH	TOT	L	NL	FAC	LC	OTH	TOT
Nathaniel Abbey	55	0	8	3	2	68	0	0	0	0	0	0
Harry Abbott	55	0	8	0	0	63	0	0	0	0	0	0
Robert "Bob" Abbott	0	24	0	0	6	30	0	0	0	0	0	0
Jimmy Adam	137	0	1	0	6	144	22	0	0	0	2	24
Terry Adamson	2	0	0	0	0	2	0	0	0	0	0	0
Tony Adcock	2	0	1	0	0	3	0	0	0	0	0	0
William "Billy" Agnew	35	0	1	0	0	36	7	0	0	0	0	7
Tom "Bud" Aherne	267	0	21	0	0	288	0	0	0	0	0	0
Simon Ainge	0	22	0	0	5	27	0	1	0	0	1	2
Mark Aizlewood	98	0	5	7	0	110	3	0	0	1	0	4
Frederick Albone	0	5	0	0	0	5	0	0	0	0	0	0
Tom Alderson	14	0	4	0	0	18	5	0	1	0	0	6
Milija Aleksic	81	0	4	7	0	92	0	0	0	0	0	0
Graham Alexander	150	0	8	17	8	183	15	0	0	2	0	17
Chris Allen	14	0	0	0	3	17	1	0	0	0	0	1
Derrick 'Sos' Allen	1	0	0	0	0	1	0	0	0	0	0	0
Fred Allen	0	8	10	0	2	20	0	2	6	0	0	8
Keith Allen	137	0	7	10	0	154	36	0	4	3	0	43
Paul Allen	4	0	0	0	0	4	0	0	0	0	0	0
Rory Allen	8	0	0	0	0	8	6	0	0	0	0	6
Ian Allinson	32	0	5	1	4	42	3	0	1	0	0	4
Tim Allpress	1	0	0	0	2	3	0	0	0	0	0	0
Thomas Allsopp	0	56	8	0	0	64	0	8	2	0	0	10
Ben Alnwick	4	0	0	0	0	4	0	0	0	0	0	0
Adrian Alston	29	0	0	2	0	31	8	0	0	1	0	9
Peter Anderson	181	0	7	13	7	208	34	0	2	2	2	40
Robert Anderson	74	0	3	0	0	77	0	0	0	0	0	0
Sam Anderson	10	0	0	0	0	10	5	0	0	0	0	5
Calvin Andrew	55	0	7	2	3	67	4	0	2	0	0	6
Harold Andrews	1	0	0	0	0	1	0	0	0	0	0	0
Wayne Andrews	7	0	2	0	1	10	0	0	0	0	0	0
Alasan Ann	0	0	0	0	2	2	0	0	0	0	0	0
Raddy Antic	100	0	2	6	0	108	9	0	0	1	0	10
Will Antwi	0	12	1	0	0	13	0	2	0	0	0	2
Jimmy Armstrong	10	0	1	0	0	11	1	0	1	0	0	2
Joe Arnison	44	0	2	0	0	46	19	0	2	0	0	21
Ed Asafu-Adjaye	26	34	6	0	16	82	0	0	0	0	1	1
James Ashton	0	2	0	0	0	2	0	0	0	0	0	0
Alec Ashworth	63	0	6	2	0	71	20	0	4	0	0	24
John Aston	174	0	12	11	4	201	31	0	4	1	0	36
Taiwo Atieno	0	13	4	0	3	20	0	3	2	0	2	7
Geoff Aunger	5	0	0	0	0	5	1	0	0	0	0	1
Trevor Aylott	32	0	1	2	0	35	10	0	0	1	0	11
James Ayres	0	0	0	0	2	2	0	0	0	0	0	0
Herve Bacque	7	0	0	3	1	11	0	0	0	0	0	0
Harry Bailey	82	0	7	0	0	89	0	0	0	0	0	0
Albert Baker	1	0	0	0	0	1	0	0	0	0	0	0
Jack Ball	65	0	6	0	3	74	46	0	3	0	0	49
Claude Banes	57	0	3	0	0	60	0	0	0	0	0	0
Jimmy Banks	13	0	0	0	0	13	2	0	0	0	0	2
Jack Bannister	83	0	8	5	0	96	0	0	0	0	0	0
Zane Banton	0	1	1	0	4	6	0	0	0	0	0	0
Rocky Baptiste	3	0	0	0	0	3	0	0	0	0	0	0
Keith Barber	142	0	5	10	1	158	0	0	0	0	0	0
Arthur Barker	0	19	1	0	7	27	0	3	0	0	7	10
William E Barnes	0	101	6	0	27	134	0	13	0	0	4	17
Walter T Barnes	6	0	0	0	0	6	0	0	0	0	0	0
Matthew Barnes-Homer	0	67	5	0	9	81	0	20	2	0	1	23
Leon Barnett	59	0	3	4	4	70	3	0	0	0	0	3
Barratt	0	0	0	0	4	4	0	0	0	0	0	0
George "William" Barrett	0	0	6	0	0	6	0	0	0	0	0	0
Ken Barton	11	0	1	0	0	12	0	0	0	0	0	0
Steve Basham	0	5	1	0	0	6	0	0	2	0	0	2
Edward "Ted" Bassett	21	0	3	0	0	24	3	0	1	0	0	4
Herbert Bateman	0	8	2	0	5	15	0	0	0	0	0	0
William "Billy" Bates	1	0	0	0	0	1	0	0	0	0	0	0
David Bayliss	37	0	0	2	1	40	0	0	0	1	0	1
Leonard "Dick" Bayliss	1	0	0	0	0	1	0	0	0	0	0	0
Ron Baynham	388	0	31	5	10	434	0	0	0	0	0	0
Doug Beach	23	0	3	0	0	26	0	0	0	0	0	0
Dave Beaumont	76	0	1	10	4	91	0	0	0	0	0	0
George Beavan	6	0	1	0	2	9	0	0	0	0	0	0
Ken Beaven	1	0	0	0	0	1	0	0	0	0	0	0
William Beck	2	0	0	0	1	3	0	0	0	0	0	0
Dean Beckwith	0	16	3	0	2	21	0	2	0	0	0	2
Robert Beckwith	17	0	0	2	0	19	0	0	0	0	0	0
Lewis Bedford	49	0	5	0	0	54	15	0	2	0	0	17
Sid Bedford	1	0	0	0	0	1	0	0	0	0	0	0
Edmund "Teddy" Bee	0	15	11	0	0	26	0	0	0	0	0	0
David Bell	75	0	7	6	1	89	8	0	0	1	0	9
Sam Bell	30	0	3	0	2	35	20	0	1	0	2	23
Tommy Bell	34	0	1	0	3	38	15	0	0	0	2	17
Gerald Benham	0	1	0	0	2	3	0	1	0	0	0	1
Ian Benjamin	13	0	2	2	0	17	2	0	0	0	0	2
Edgar Bennett	1	0	0	0	0	1	0	0	0	0	0	0
John Bennett	0	33	3	0	0	36	0	0	0	0	0	0
Paul Benson	0	36	2	0	0	38	0	17	1	0	0	18
Frank Beresford	12	0	0	0	3	15	1	0	0	0	2	3
Marlon Beresford	116	0	10	5	1	132	0	0	0	0	0	0
Cedric Berthelin	9	0	0	0	0	9	0	0	0	0	0	0
Pavel Besta	0	6	0	0	3	9	0	0	0	0	0	0
Wayne Biggins	7	0	2	0	0	9	1	0	1	0	0	2
Hugh Billington	86	0	8	0	0	94	63	0	7	0	0	70
William "Billy" Bingham	87	0	12	0	1	100	27	0	6	0	0	33
Edwin Birch	29	17	2	0	7	55	10	8	0	0	4	22
Wallace Birch	15	0	1	0	0	16	3	0	0	0	0	3
Alan Birchenall	10	0	0	0	0	10	0	0	0	0	0	0
Sid Bird	1	0	0	0	0	1	0	0	0	0	0	0
Alf Black	1	0	0	0	0	1	0	0	0	0	0	0
John Black	91	0	10	0	0	101	4	0	0	0	0	4
Kingsley Black	127	0	6	18	5	156	27	0	2	1	1	31
Joseph Blackett	0	34	1	0	14	49	0	2	0	0	2	4
Shane Blackett	0	40	5	0	6	51	0	0	1	0	0	1
Jimmy Blessington	0	81	16	0	7	104	0	19	15	0	4	38
Matthew Blinkhorn	2	0	0	1	0	3	0	0	0	0	0	0
Phil Boersma	36	0	3	1	0	40	8	0	2	1	0	11
Cyril Bonsall	8	0	0	0	0	8	2	0	0	0	0	2
Louis Bookman	72	29	9	0	0	110	4	4	1	0	0	9
Harold Booton	7	0	0	0	2	9	0	0	0	0	0	0
Andre Boucaud	0	7	0	0	0	7	0	0	0	0	0	0
John Boutwood	1	0	0	0	0	1	0	0	0	0	1	1
Mark Bower	16	0	0	0	0	16	1	0	0	0	0	1
Philip Bower	0	0	1	0	0	1	0	0	0	0	0	0
George Bowler	0	2	0	0	0	2	0	0	0	0	0	0

L = League, NL = Non-League (Southern League and Conference Premier): FAC = FA Cup (including 1945/46): LC = Football League Cup, OTH = United League, Western League, Southern Alliance, Division Three (South) Cup, Southern Professional Floodlit Cup, Watney Cup, Anglo-Italian Cup, Texaco Cup, Full Members Cup, Associate Members Cup, FA Trophy and the Play-Offs. The figures do not include games in World War One and World War Two, the three expunged games from 1939/40 nor the expunged games against Chester in 2009/10.

	APPEARANCES							GOALS					
---	L	NL	FAC	LC	OTH	TOT		L	NL	FAC	LC	OTH	TOT
Harry Boxford	0	0	1	0	0	1		0	0	0	0	0	0
Emmerson Boyce	186	0	12	11	3	212		8	0	1	0	0	9
Adam Boyd	18	0	2	3	0	23		1	0	0	1	0	2
William "Bill" Boyd	13	0	0	0	0	13		11	0	0	0	0	11
Robert Boylen	11	0	0	0	0	11		1	0	0	0	0	1
Eli Bradley	0	11	2	0	7	20		0	6	0	0	0	6
James Bradley	5	0	0	0	0	5		1	0	0	0	0	1
John Bradshaw	0	1	0	0	0	1		0	0	0	0	0	0
John Bramwell	187	0	11	8	0	206		0	0	1	0	0	1
Jim Brandham	0	3	0	0	1	4		0	0	0	0	0	0
Terry Branston	101	0	6	11	0	118		9	0	0	1	0	10
John Bratby	0	3	0	0	0	3		0	0	0	0	0	0
Tim Breacker	210	0	21	24	7	262		3	0	0	0	0	3
Freidrich Breitenfelder	5	0	0	0	0	5		0	0	0	0	0	0
Dean Brennan	9	0	1	3	1	14		0	0	0	0	1	1
Matt Brennan	4	0	0	0	0	4		1	0	0	0	0	1
Robert "Bobby" Brennan	69	0	7	0	0	76		22	0	8	0	0	30
Robert Brewis	0	13	0	0	10	23		0	7	0	0	7	14
Gordon Brice	13	0	1	0	0	14		0	0	0	0	0	0
Harold Briggs	2	0	0	0	0	2		0	0	0	0	0	0
Dean Brill	81	7	7	5	9	109		0	0	0	0	0	0
Ahmet Brkovic	194	0	14	8	7	223		31	0	4	0	3	38
John Brock	52	0	6	0	16	74		15	0	1	0	2	18
Dave Brogan	4	0	0	2	0	6		0	0	0	2	0	2
Gilbert Brookes	42	0	1	0	0	43		0	0	0	0	0	0
Albert C Brown	1	0	0	0	0	1		0	0	0	0	0	0
Allan D Brown	151	0	15	2	7	175		51	0	6	0	1	58
Alexander "Sandy" Brown	0	69	5	0	22	96		0	32	1	0	14	47
Archibald Brown	0	3	0	0	0	3		0	0	0	0	0	0
James Brown	13	0	0	0	0	13		1	0	0	0	0	1
Joe Brown	0	3	0	0	0	3		0	0	0	0	0	0
John Brown	0	22	7	0	0	29		0	7	5	0	0	12
Mick Brown	14	0	1	2	0	17		2	0	0	0	0	2
Norman Brown	0	34	2	0	11	47		0	4	1	0	1	6
Tommy Brown	15	0	0	0	0	15		0	0	0	0	0	0
William 'Buster' Brown	49	0	5	0	3	57		4	0	0	0	0	4
William "Roland" Brown	27	28	17	0	8	80		3	8	4	0	6	21
Ryan Brunt	0	5	0	0	1	6		0	0	0	0	0	0
Robert Bryce	34	0	3	0	0	37		8	0	1	0	0	9
Steve Buckley	123	0	5	7	0	135		9	0	0	0	0	9
Frankie Bunn	59	0	3	7	0	69		9	0	0	3	0	12
Robert Burbage	3	4	2	0	0	9		1	2	0	0	0	3
Burgess	0	0	0	0	1	1		0	0	0	0	0	0
Andy Burgess	0	6	3	0	0	9		0	0	0	0	0	0
William Burgess	5	0	0	0	0	5		0	0	0	0	0	0
Mark Burke	3	0	1	0	0	4		0	0	0	0	0	0
John Burley	0	0	8	0	0	8		0	0	0	0	0	0
Charlie Burtenshaw	11	0	0	0	0	11		1	0	0	0	0	1
William "Bill" Burtenshaw	1	0	0	0	0	1		0	0	0	0	0	0
Viv Busby	77	0	1	5	3	86		16	0	0	0	0	16
William "Billy" Bushell	0	69	5	0	0	74		0	4	0	0	0	4
George Butcher	121	0	8	0	0	129		24	0	2	0	0	26
Barry Butlin	57	0	6	6	3	72		24	0	2	0	2	28
Ian Buxton	47	0	3	1	0	51		14	0	1	0	0	15
Norman "Les" Bywater	19	0	4	0	0	23		0	0	0	0	0	0
Graham Caleb	20	0	3	1	0	24		0	0	0	0	0	0
Jamie Campbell	36	0	4	2	3	45		1	0	0	0	0	1
Robson Campbell	0	0	2	0	0	2		0	0	0	0	0	0
Paul Carden	0	11	0	0	0	11		0	0	0	0	0	0
Clarke Carlisle	5	0	0	0	0	5		0	0	0	0	0	0
Newman Carney	0	0	0	0	2	2		0	0	0	0	0	0
David Carr	43	0	4	1	0	48		0	0	0	1	0	1
Willie Carrick	4	0	1	0	1	6		0	0	0	0	0	0
James "Tony" Carroll	13	0	0	0	0	13		0	0	0	0	0	0
Robert Carte	6	0	0	0	0	6		0	0	0	0	0	0
Walter Catlin	1	0	0	0	4	5		1	0	0	0	2	3
Tinashe Chabata	0	0	0	0	2	2		0	0	0	0	0	0
Alec Chamberlain	138	0	7	7	7	159		0	0	0	0	0	0
Brian Chambers	76	0	4	2	0	82		9	0	1	0	0	10
Robin Chandler	13	0	3	0	0	16		0	0	1	0	0	1
Joe Chapman	1	0	0	0	0	1		0	0	0	0	0	0
Ralph Chapman	0	62	4	0	1	67		0	0	0	0	0	0
Anthony Charles	0	4	1	0	3	8		0	0	0	0	0	0
Ryan Charles	17	6	2	1	2	28		2	1	0	1	0	4
Ben Chenery	2	0	1	0	0	3		0	0	0	0	0	0
William "Manny" Chesher	0	7	14	0	0	21		0	0	3	0	0	3
John "Jimmy" Chipperfield	0	2	1	0	1	4		0	3	0	0	1	4
Danny Clapton	10	0	1	0	0	11		0	0	0	0	0	0
Steve Claridge	16	0	0	2	2	20		2	0	0	3	1	6
Clark	0	0	0	0	1	1		0	0	0	0	0	0
Archie Clark	87	0	5	0	0	92		11	0	0	0	0	11
Charlie Clark	14	0	1	0	0	15		6	0	0	0	0	6
John Clark	29	0	1	0	0	30		2	0	1	0	0	3
Alan Clarke	9	0	0	1	0	10		0	0	0	0	0	0
Horace Clarke	0	1	0	0	0	1		0	0	0	0	0	0
John Clarke	1	0	0	0	2	3		0	0	0	0	0	0
Percy Clarke	1	0	0	0	0	1		0	0	0	0	0	0
Walter Clarke	4	0	0	0	4	8		0	0	0	0	0	0
William "Billy" Clarkson	32	0	1	0	0	33		3	0	0	0	0	3
Thomas Clifford	0	23	4	0	4	31		0	0	0	0	0	0
Gary Cobb	9	0	0	0	1	10		0	0	0	0	0	0
Harry Cockerill	8	0	0	0	0	8		0	0	0	0	0	0
Ernie Cockle	7	0	0	0	0	7		1	0	0	0	0	1
Joe Coen	142	0	11	0	5	158		0	0	0	0	0	0
Alan Collier	10	0	0	0	3	13		0	0	0	0	0	0
Alexander Collins	0	9	2	0	0	11		0	0	0	0	0	0
John Collins	42	0	3	3	0	48		10	0	2	0	0	12
Mike Collins	8	0	0	2	0	10		0	0	0	0	0	0
William "Bill" Collins	7	0	0	0	0	7		0	0	0	0	0	0
David Colquhoun	16	0	0	0	1	17		0	0	0	0	0	0
Robert Colvin	0	28	7	0	0	35		0	2	2	0	0	4
Frank Conboy	19	0	2	0	0	21		1	0	0	0	0	1
Eddie Connelly	88	0	2	0	0	90		24	0	0	0	0	24
Joe Conquest	0	0	0	0	1	1		0	0	0	0	0	0
Colin Cook	8	0	0	0	1	9		5	0	0	0	0	5
Richard Cooke	17	0	0	0	2	19		1	0	0	0	0	1
William "Billy" Cooke	210	0	18	0	0	228		4	0	0	0	0	4
Stanley Coote	1	0	0	0	0	1		0	0	0	0	0	0
Ron Cope	28	0	2	1	0	31		0	0	0	0	0	0
William "Billy" Corkindale	1	0	1	0	0	2		0	0	0	0	0	0
Tom Cottingham	1	0	0	0	0	1		0	0	0	0	0	0
James Coupar	26	18	8	0	28	80		9	12	1	0	10	32
David Court	52	0	3	3	1	59		0	0	0	0	0	0
AG Cox	0	5	1	0	3	9		0	0	0	0	0	0

L = League, NL = Non-League (Southern League and Conference Premier): FAC = FA Cup (including 1945/46): LC = Football League Cup, OTH = United League, Western League, Southern Alliance, Division Three (South) Cup, Southern Professional Floodlit Cup, Watney Cup, Anglo-Italian Cup, Texaco Cup, Full Members Cup, Associate Members Cup, FA Trophy and the Play-Offs. The figures do not include games in World War One and World War Two, the three expunged games from 1939/40 nor the expunged games against Chester in 2009/10.

	APPEARANCES							GOALS					
---	L	NL	FAC	LC	OTH	TOT		L	NL	FAC	LC	OTH	TOT
Jimmy Cox	8	0	0	2	0	10		0	0	0	0	0	0
Ernie Coxhead	0	114	6	0	0	120		0	6	0	0	0	6
Chris Coyne	221	0	18	10	3	252		13	0	1	2	0	16
Tom Craddock	27	48	5	0	6	86		10	25	1	0	2	38
Wilf Crompton	48	0	6	0	0	54		15	0	1	0	0	16
Mark Crook	5	0	0	0	1	6		1	0	0	0	0	1
Danny Crow	0	57	6	0	7	70		0	16	1	0	0	17
Dean Crowe	69	0	4	3	3	79		17	0	0	0	0	17
William Crump	25	0	5	0	15	45		0	0	0	1	0	1
Peter Cruse	4	0	0	2	0	6		0	0	0	0	0	0
Mark Cullen	0	29	2	0	5	36		0	8	1	0	1	10
Mick Cullen	112	0	9	0	5	126		16	0	3	0	0	19
George Cummins	184	0	17	0	8	209		21	0	4	0	5	30
William "Billy" Cupit	8	0	0	0	0	8		1	0	0	0	0	1
Darren Currie	31	0	5	2	0	38		2	0	0	0	0	2
William "Billy" Curwen	1	0	0	0	0	1		0	0	0	0	0	0
Joe Daly	70	0	6	0	0	76		4	0	0	0	0	4
James Dance	0	26	2	0	4	32		0	3	1	0	0	4
Alan Daniel	50	0	2	2	2	56		3	0	0	0	0	3
Mel Daniel	53	0	5	0	0	58		20	0	2	0	0	22
Ray Daniel	22	0	6	2	0	30		4	0	0	0	0	4
Charlie Danskin	10	0	0	0	0	10		0	0	0	0	0	0
Alexander Davidson	0	8	0	0	0	8		0	8	0	0	0	8
Thomas Davidson	0	1	0	0	1	2		0	0	0	0	1	1
Alexander "Sandy" Davie	58	0	6	2	0	66		0	0	0	0	0	0
Willie Davie	42	0	2	0	0	44		9	0	1	0	0	10
Albert "Bert" Davies	4	0	0	0	0	4		0	0	0	0	0	0
Curtis Davies	56	0	3	2	1	62		2	0	0	0	0	2
Roy A Davies	150	0	16	0	3	169		26	0	2	0	0	28
Ron T Davies	32	0	1	0	0	33		21	0	0	0	0	21
Samuel Davies	25	0	7	0	27	59		1	0	1	0	4	6
Simon Davies	22	0	1	4	3	30		1	0	0	0	0	1
Joe Davis	0	6	0	0	3	9		0	0	0	0	0	0
Kelvin Davis	92	0	2	7	6	107		0	0	0	0	0	0
Sol Davis	199	0	13	11	6	229		3	0	0	0	0	3
Steve Davis	138	0	6	19	10	173		21	0	2	3	1	27
Edwin 'Teddy' Daw	34	0	4	0	0	38		0	0	0	0	0	0
Albert "Bert" Dawes	44	0	3	0	0	47		19	0	1	0	0	20
Dawson	1	0	0	0	5	6		0	0	0	0	0	0
John Day	0	3	0	0	6	9		0	0	0	0	0	0
Mervyn Day	4	0	0	0	0	4		0	0	0	0	0	0
Albert Deacon	0	0	1	0	0	1		0	0	0	0	0	0
George Deacon	0	0	12	0	0	12		0	0	0	8	0	8
John 'Dixie' Deans	14	0	0	1	0	15		6	0	0	0	0	6
David Deeney	0	0	0	0	2	2		0	0	0	0	0	0
Joe Deeney	0	0	0	0	2	2		0	0	0	0	1	1
Neil Dempsey	0	5	3	0	1	9		0	1	1	0	0	2
George Dennis	139	0	11	0	0	150		41	0	3	0	0	44
Fred Dent	13	0	3	0	0	16		5	0	0	0	0	5
Peter Denton	5	0	0	0	0	5		0	0	0	0	0	0
Albert Diaper	3	0	0	0	0	3		0	0	0	0	0	0
Andy Dibble	31	0	1	6	1	39		0	0	0	0	0	0
John Dickerson	0	2	0	0	0	2		0	0	0	0	0	0
Paul Dickov	15	0	0	0	0	15		1	0	0	0	0	1
Ernest Dimmock	11	2	0	0	6	19		2	0	0	0	3	5
Jack Dimmock	0	2	10	0	0	12		0	0	5	0	0	5
Walter Dimmock	0	28	0	0	12	40		0	0	0	0	0	0

	APPEARANCES							GOALS					
---	L	NL	FAC	LC	OTH	TOT		L	NL	FAC	LC	OTH	TOT
Kerry Dixon	75	0	9	2	2	88		19	0	0	0	1	20
Mike Dixon	3	0	0	0	1	4		1	0	0	0	0	1
Ernest Dobson	0	6	0	0	1	7		0	1	0	0	0	1
James Docherty	30	15	8	0	28	81		0	0	2	0	1	3
Ernest Dodd	0	0	0	0	1	1		0	0	0	0	0	0
George Dodd	0	10	4	0	0	14		0	4	1	0	0	5
Gary Doherty	70	0	8	3	2	83		12	0	2	1	0	15
Humphrey "Bill" Dolman	62	0	4	0	1	67		0	0	0	0	0	0
Mal Donaghy	415	0	36	34	3	488		16	0	3	2	0	21
Michael Donaghy	0	9	1	0	1	11		0	0	0	0	0	0
Robert Donaldson	17	0	1	0	7	25		10	0	0	0	6	16
George Donnelly	0	4	0	0	0	4		0	0	0	0	0	0
Max Dougan	118	0	6	8	0	132		0	0	0	0	0	0
Stuart Douglas	146	0	10	14	2	172		18	0	2	3	0	23
John Dow	56	3	9	0	15	83		3	0	1	0	2	6
Iain Dowie	66	0	3	4	5	78		15	0	0	0	4	19
Johnny Downie	26	0	0	0	0	26		12	0	0	0	0	12
Frederick "Bob" Draper	9	0	1	0	4	14		6	0	0	0	0	6
William "Bill" Draycott	0	1	0	0	0	1		0	0	0	0	0	0
Gordon Dreyer	23	0	1	0	0	24		0	0	0	0	0	0
John Dreyer	214	0	14	14	8	250		13	0	0	1	1	15
Jimmy Drinnan	31	0	1	0	0	32		12	0	0	0	0	12
Allenby Driver	41	0	4	0	0	45		13	0	0	0	0	13
Micky Droy	2	0	0	1	0	3		0	0	0	0	0	0
Andy Drury	0	23	3	0	0	26		0	6	2	0	0	8
Richard Dryden	23	0	1	1	1	26		0	0	0	0	0	0
Edward "Ted" Duggan	48	0	1	0	0	49		20	0	0	0	0	20
George Duke	16	0	2	0	0	18		0	0	0	0	0	0
Douglas 'Dally' Duncan	32	0	4	0	0	36		4	0	0	0	0	4
John Dunn	0	62	8	0	0	70		0	0	0	0	0	0
Seamus Dunne	301	0	14	0	11	326		0	0	0	0	0	0
Tom Dunsmore	40	0	3	0	0	43		0	0	0	0	0	0
Arthur 'Jimmy' Durrant	32	123	24	0	20	199		8	25	10	0	4	47
Sean Dyche	14	0	0	0	1	15		1	0	0	0	0	1
Samuel Eaton	0	56	4	0	0	60		0	14	0	0	0	14
John Eckford	34	0	4	0	0	38		3	0	1	0	0	4
Carlos Edwards	68	0	1	5	0	74		8	0	0	0	0	8
David Edwards	19	0	4	2	1	26		4	0	0	0	0	4
Gerald Edwards	2	0	0	0	0	2		0	0	0	0	0	0
Richard "Dick" Edwards	17	0	3	2	0	22		1	0	0	0	0	1
Frederick Ekins	33	18	9	0	28	88		5	8	1	0	13	27
Arthur Eling	0	2	0	0	0	2		0	0	0	0	0	0
Edward Ellingham	0	0	0	0	6	6		0	0	0	0	0	0
Richard Ellingham	0	0	1	0	0	1		0	0	1	0	0	1
Paul Elliott	66	0	2	5	0	73		4	0	0	0	0	4
Steve Elliott	12	0	0	3	0	15		3	0	0	3	0	6
Albert Else	0	0	0	0	3	3		0	0	0	0	0	0
Lars Elstrup	60	0	3	4	3	70		19	0	2	5	1	27
John Elvey	0	107	10	0	8	125		0	5	0	0	1	6
Lewis Emanuel	77	2	3	3	3	88		5	0	0	0	0	5
Carl Emberson	53	0	3	3	1	60		0	0	0	0	0	0
Connor Essam	0	9	0	0	0	9		0	0	0	0	0	0
Everitt	0	1	0	0	0	1		0	0	0	0	0	0
Sean Evers	52	0	2	9	6	69		6	0	0	1	0	7
Mick Fairchild	21	0	2	4	0	27		1	0	1	1	0	3
Robert "Walter" Fairgrieve	15	0	4	0	0	19		4	0	2	0	0	6
Harry Farr	1	2	1	0	11	15		0	0	0	0	0	0

L = League, NL = Non-League (Southern League and Conference Premier): FAC = FA Cup (including 1945/46): LC = Football League Cup, OTH = United League, Western League, Southern Alliance, Division Three (South) Cup, Southern Professional Floodlit Cup, Watney Cup, Anglo-Italian Cup, Texaco Cup, Full Members Cup, Associate Members Cup, FA Trophy and the Play-Offs. The figures do not include games in World War One and World War Two, the three expunged games from 1939/40 nor the expunged games against Chester in 2009/10.

	APPEARANCES						GOALS					
	L	NL	FAC	LC	OTH	TOT	L	NL	FAC	LC	OTH	TOT
Samuel Farrant	0	3	0	0	4	7	0	0	0	0	0	0
Sean Farrell	25	0	3	0	3	31	1	0	1	0	2	4
John Faulkner	209	0	12	15	3	239	6	0	0	1	0	7
James Fearn	0	1	0	0	0	1	0	0	0	0	0	0
Warren Feeney	77	0	2	4	0	83	8	0	1	2	0	11
William "Bill" Fellowes	110	0	11	0	3	124	3	0	0	0	0	3
Kane Ferdinand	0	1	0	0	1	2	0	0	0	0	0	0
Charlie Ferguson	29	0	4	0	0	33	10	0	3	0	0	13
Rodney Fern	39	0	1	4	3	47	5	0	0	0	0	5
Ian Feuer	97	0	6	7	5	115	0	0	0	0	0	0
A Field	0	0	0	0	1	1	0	0	0	0	0	0
Gordon Fincham	64	0	3	2	0	69	0	0	0	1	0	1
Jake Findlay	167	0	8	12	0	187	0	0	0	0	0	0
John "Jock" Finlayson	154	0	12	0	2	168	9	0	0	0	0	9
John Finlayson	0	19	11	0	2	32	0	4	4	0	0	8
Tom Finney	14	0	3	4	0	21	5	0	0	1	0	6
Harold Fitzpatrick	0	20	4	0	4	28	0	7	0	0	4	11
Tom Fleckney	0	0	0	0	6	6	0	0	0	0	0	0
Stuart Fleetwood	0	67	7	0	14	88	0	21	1	0	5	27
Jim Fleming	66	0	3	5	0	74	9	0	1	1	0	11
Jaroslaw Fojut	16	0	3	2	2	23	2	0	1	0	0	3
Kevin Foley	151	0	8	5	2	166	3	0	0	2	0	5
W Folley	0	2	0	0	2	4	0	0	0	0	0	0
Adrian Forbes	72	0	5	1	1	79	14	0	6	0	0	20
Alec Forbes	1	0	0	0	0	1	0	0	0	0	0	0
Charles Ford	24	0	6	0	15	45	0	0	0	0	2	2
Harry Ford	0	1	0	0	0	1	0	0	0	0	0	0
William "Bill" Ford	23	0	3	0	14	40	7	0	0	0	2	9
David Forde	5	0	0	1	0	6	0	0	0	0	0	0
John Foster	47	0	3	0	0	50	3	0	0	0	0	3
Steve Foster	163	0	27	20	2	212	11	0	2	1	0	14
Andrew Fotiadis	123	0	7	9	7	146	17	0	1	1	0	19
Joseph Frail	0	29	5	0	0	34	0	0	0	0	0	0
Fraser Franks	0	17	0	0	0	17	0	0	0	0	0	0
Charles Fraser	246	0	24	0	2	272	4	0	0	0	0	4
Stuart Fraser	44	0	9	5	4	62	1	0	0	0	0	1
Graham French	182	0	8	10	2	202	21	0	1	0	1	23
Robert Frith	0	59	7	0	14	80	0	0	1	0	0	1
Arthur Fry	0	2	1	0	0	3	0	0	0	0	0	0
Barry Fry	6	0	1	0	0	7	0	0	0	0	0	0
Henry "Harry" Fryer	0	3	0	0	0	3	0	0	0	0	0	0
Pasquale 'Lil' Fuccillo	160	0	7	13	0	180	24	0	1	2	0	27
John Fulton	81	0	5	0	0	86	0	0	0	0	0	0
Paul Furlong	32	0	2	4	1	39	8	0	0	2	2	12
William Furr	0	1	0	0	0	1	0	0	0	0	0	0
Paul Futcher	131	0	6	4	1	142	1	0	0	0	0	1
Ron Futcher	120	0	8	5	0	133	40	0	1	2	0	43
Horace Gager	59	0	5	0	0	64	2	0	0	0	0	2
Hugh Galbraith	3	29	18	0	12	62	0	28	9	0	6	43
Ernie Gale	11	0	0	0	0	11	0	0	0	0	0	0
Leon Gall	0	17	3	0	0	20	0	8	4	0	0	12
Patrick Gallacher	0	21	0	0	23	44	0	1	0	0	3	4
William Gallacher	30	29	12	0	26	97	7	14	6	0	18	45
Kevin Gallen	29	37	6	0	3	75	3	16	2	0	0	21
Septimus "Randolph" Galloway	2	0	0	0	0	2	1	0	0	0	0	1
Doug Gardiner	121	0	13	0	0	134	1	0	0	0	0	1
Alan Garner	88	0	8	11	5	112	3	0	1	0	0	4

	APPEARANCES						GOALS					
	L	NL	FAC	LC	OTH	TOT	L	NL	FAC	LC	OTH	TOT
A Garratt	1	2	0	0	5	8	0	0	0	0	0	0
David Geddis	17	0	0	0	0	17	4	0	0	0	0	4
Philip Gentle	5	0	0	0	0	5	0	0	0	0	0	0
Liam George	102	0	10	9	3	124	21	0	4	0	0	25
Tommy Gibbon	69	0	1	0	0	70	0	0	0	0	0	0
Gibson	0	0	0	0	1	1	0	0	0	3	0	3
Jim Gibson	32	0	4	2	0	38	0	0	0	1	0	1
John "Jock" Gibson	3	0	0	0	0	3	0	0	0	0	0	0
Robert Gillman	0	0	0	0	1	1	0	0	0	0	0	0
Alfred Gittens	0	23	4	0	4	31	0	5	0	0	3	8
Don Givens	83	0	3	4	1	91	19	0	1	2	0	22
Dan Gleeson	0	44	6	0	4	54	0	0	0	0	0	0
Alec Glover	56	0	3	0	0	59	6	0	0	0	0	6
Lee Glover	1	0	0	0	0	1	0	0	0	0	0	0
Claude Gnakpa	27	77	14	2	16	136	1	21	2	0	3	27
Anthony "Tony" Godden	12	0	0	0	0	12	0	0	0	0	0	0
Will Godfrey	6	0	0	0	0	6	0	0	0	0	0	0
Jim Goldie	7	0	0	1	0	8	2	0	0	0	0	2
Alan Goodall	29	0	3	3	1	36	1	0	0	0	0	1
Ken Goodeve	15	0	0	0	4	19	0	0	0	0	0	0
Sidney Goodge	0	2	0	0	0	2	0	0	0	0	0	0
Jake Goodman	0	11	0	0	0	11	0	0	0	0	0	0
Clive Goodyear	90	0	4	5	0	99	4	0	0	0	0	4
George Goodyear	10	0	2	0	0	12	0	0	0	0	0	0
William "Bill" Gooney	4	0	0	0	0	4	0	0	0	0	0	0
John Gordon	14	0	0	0	0	14	0	0	0	0	0	0
Shane Gore	0	1	2	0	0	3	0	0	0	0	0	0
Luke Graham	0	10	0	0	4	14	0	0	0	0	1	1
Robert "Bob" Graham	164	0	11	0	0	175	5	0	0	0	0	5
Anthony Grant	4	0	1	0	0	5	0	0	0	0	0	0
Kim Grant	35	0	2	4	3	44	5	0	0	2	1	8
Andre Gray	0	97	8	0	6	111	0	52	2	0	3	57
Phil Gray	140	0	5	13	3	161	43	0	4	6	0	53
Robert "Paul" Gray	7	0	0	0	3	10	1	0	0	0	1	2
Robert Gray	0	4	0	0	0	4	0	1	0	0	0	1
Anthony "Tony" Grealish	78	0	3	5	0	86	2	0	0	0	0	3
Harry "Rodney" Green	11	0	0	2	0	13	3	0	0	0	0	3
John Green	26	0	1	0	0	27	5	0	1	0	0	6
David Greene	19	0	1	2	1	23	0	0	0	0	0	0
Anthony "Tony" Gregory	59	0	11	0	4	74	17	0	5	0	2	24
Julius Gregory	0	28	3	0	11	42	0	0	0	0	0	0
Carl Griffiths	13	0	0	1	0	14	8	0	0	0	0	8
Edward Griffiths	6	0	0	0	0	6	1	0	0	0	0	1
Scott Griffiths	0	52	0	0	0	52	0	1	0	0	0	1
Ashley Grimes	87	0	11	13	3	114	3	0	0	1	0	4
William Grimes	0	11	0	0	0	11	0	0	0	0	0	0
Ernest "Billy" Gripton	3	0	0	0	0	3	0	0	0	0	0	0
Groom	0	0	1	0	0	1	0	0	0	0	0	0
John Groves	218	0	16	6	11	251	16	0	0	0	3	19
Bontcho Guentchev	62	0	4	7	5	78	10	0	0	0	2	12
Alan Guild	1	0	0	1	0	2	0	0	0	0	0	0
Luke Guttridge	0	32	1	0	0	33	0	13	0	0	0	13
Robert "Bob" Hacking	1	0	0	0	0	1	0	0	0	0	0	0
William "Billy" Hails	3	0	0	0	0	3	0	0	0	0	0	0
Alf 'Pally' Hale	22	0	1	0	0	23	0	0	0	0	0	0
Derek Hales	7	0	1	0	1	9	1	0	0	0	0	1
Asa Hall	42	32	7	2	6	89	10	5	1	0	0	16

L = League, NL = Non-League (Southern League and Conference Premier): FAC = FA Cup (including 1945/46): LC = Football League Cup, OTH = United League, Western League, Southern Alliance, Division Three (South) Cup, Southern Professional Floodlit Cup, Watney Cup, Anglo-Italian Cup, Texaco Cup, Full Members Cup, Associate Members Cup, FA Trophy and the Play-Offs. The figures do not include games in World War One and World War Two, the three expunged games from 1939/40 nor the expunged games against Chester in 2009/10.

	APPEARANCES						GOALS					
	L	NL	FAC	LC	OTH	TOT	L	NL	FAC	LC	OTH	TOT
Edgar Hall	0	6	2	0	0	8	0	0	0	0	0	0
Les Hall	79	0	12	0	0	91	0	0	0	0	0	0
Proctor Hall	0	9	0	0	9	18	0	1	0	0	0	1
Vic Halom	59	0	1	3	0	63	17	0	0	0	0	17
Edward "Ted" Hancock	26	0	1	0	0	27	3	0	0	0	0	3
Jamie Hand	0	13	2	0	0	15	0	2	0	0	0	2
William "Billy" Harber	28	0	4	1	0	33	3	0	0	0	0	3
Tommy Hare	12	0	2	2	0	16	0	0	0	0	0	0
Les Harfield	1	0	0	0	0	1	0	0	0	0	0	0
George Harford	99	0	7	0	1	107	0	0	0	0	0	0
Mick Harford	168	0	27	17	5	217	69	0	10	10	3	92
James Harkins	4	0	0	0	0	4	3	0	0	0	0	3
Alan Harper	41	0	7	0	0	48	1	0	0	0	0	1
William "Bill" Harper	31	0	3	0	0	34	0	0	0	0	0	0
Bernard Harris	19	0	5	0	0	24	0	0	0	0	0	0
Gerry Harrison	14	0	0	0	1	15	0	0	0	0	0	0
Mike Harrison	31	0	3	3	0	37	6	0	2	2	0	10
Andy Harrow	4	0	0	0	0	4	0	0	0	0	0	0
John Hartson	54	0	6	1	2	63	11	0	2	0	0	13
Richard Harvey	161	0	9	11	11	192	4	0	0	1	0	5
Liam Hatch	0	20	0	0	1	21	0	4	0	0	0	4
Robert "Bob" Hatton	82	0	2	6	0	90	29	0	0	2	0	31
Willie Havenga	18	0	1	0	0	19	6	0	1	0	0	7
HG Hawes	0	0	0	0	3	3	0	0	0	0	1	1
Barry Hawkes	8	0	1	0	0	9	0	0	0	0	0	0
Fred Hawkes	2	504	40	0	79	625	1	23	3	0	8	35
Ken Hawkes	90	0	10	0	6	106	1	0	0	0	0	1
Robert "Bob" Hawkes	0	349	35	0	26	410	0	40	3	0	5	48
Thomas Hawkes	3	0	0	0	5	8	0	0	0	0	1	1
Fred Haycock	0	33	3	0	10	46	0	10	1	0	4	15
Albert "Bert" Hayhurst	1	0	1	0	0	2	0	0	0	0	0	0
Gary Heale	7	0	1	3	0	11	1	0	0	2	0	3
Seamus Heath	0	0	0	1	0	1	0	0	0	0	0	0
Westby Heath	0	7	0	0	0	7	0	1	0	0	0	1
George Hedley	0	21	1	0	0	22	0	2	0	0	0	2
Marcus Heikkinen	76	0	1	0	0	77	3	0	0	0	0	3
Petri Helin	23	0	3	0	1	27	1	0	0	0	0	1
Crosby Henderson	0	19	2	0	12	33	0	0	0	0	1	1
Ian Henderson	19	0	0	0	0	19	0	0	0	0	0	0
William "Bill" Henderson	2	0	0	0	0	2	0	0	0	0	0	0
Charlie Henry	0	2	1	0	3	6	0	0	0	0	0	0
Ronnie Henry	0	76	8	0	3	87	0	0	0	0	0	0
Frederick Hensman	0	5	0	0	0	5	0	0	0	0	0	0
Archie Heslop	27	0	0	0	0	27	7	0	0	0	0	7
Simon Heslop	0	11	0	0	2	13	0	1	0	0	1	1
George Hewitt	12	0	5	0	10	27	6	0	2	0	2	10
Harry Higginbotham	80	11	8	0	0	99	25	5	4	0	0	34
Vince Hilaire	6	0	0	3	0	9	0	0	0	0	0	0
Frederick "Percy" Hill	6	13	0	0	0	19	4	4	0	0	0	8
Ricky Hill	436	0	33	38	1	508	54	0	6	5	0	65
Ian Hillier	56	0	5	2	5	68	1	0	0	0	0	1
Jack Hilsdon	0	8	1	0	0	9	0	0	0	0	0	0
Gordon Hindson	68	0	5	4	6	83	3	0	0	1	1	5
Craig Hinton	0	0	0	0	2	2	0	0	0	0	0	0
Lars Hirschfeld	5	0	0	0	0	5	0	0	0	0	0	0
Sid Hoar	160	61	16	0	7	244	26	9	3	0	0	38
Jack Hodge	20	0	2	0	3	25	1	0	0	0	0	1

	APPEARANCES						GOALS					
	L	NL	FAC	LC	OTH	TOT	L	NL	FAC	LC	OTH	TOT
Tommy Hodgson	67	0	7	0	0	74	0	0	0	0	0	0
Fred Hogg	4	0	0	0	0	4	0	0	0	0	0	0
John Hogg	0	44	2	0	16	62	0	0	0	0	0	0
Fred Holbeach	2	0	0	0	0	2	0	0	0	0	0	0
Herbert Holdstock	13	20	6	0	3	42	1	0	1	0	0	2
James Holland	0	5	0	0	2	7	0	1	0	0	0	1
Peter Holmes	105	0	7	9	6	127	11	0	0	0	1	12
William "Billy" Holmes	1	0	0	0	0	1	0	0	0	0	0	0
Paul Holsgrove	2	0	0	0	0	2	0	0	0	0	0	0
FG Holtum	0	0	0	0	2	2	0	0	0	0	0	0
Frank Hood	0	4	0	0	0	4	0	0	0	0	0	0
Graham Horn	58	0	5	3	6	72	0	0	0	0	0	0
Brian Horton	118	0	6	8	0	132	8	0	2	0	0	10
Ralph Hoten	60	0	1	0	0	61	13	0	0	0	0	13
Scott Houghton	16	0	1	3	2	22	1	0	0	0	0	1
Steven Howard	212	0	8	7	1	228	96	0	5	2	0	103
Alfred Howe	0	13	5	0	0	18	0	0	0	0	0	0
Jake Howells	29	191	25	0	31	276	0	25	0	0	1	26
Albert "Jack" Hoy	0	0	8	0	0	8	0	0	0	0	0	0
Roger Hoy	32	0	2	2	1	37	0	0	0	0	0	0
Arthur Hubbard	4	0	0	0	2	6	0	0	0	0	0	0
Ceri Hughes	175	0	11	13	6	205	17	0	2	1	0	20
Iorwerth Hughes	36	0	0	0	0	36	0	0	0	0	0	0
John "Paul" Hughes	79	0	1	5	3	88	7	0	0	0	0	7
William "Billy" Hughes	31	0	3	0	0	34	0	0	0	0	0	0
Hull	0	1	0	0	0	1	0	0	0	0	0	0
Frank Hull	3	0	0	0	0	3	0	0	0	0	0	0
George Humphrey	0	0	7	0	0	7	0	0	0	0	0	0
Albert Hunt	0	3	0	0	0	3	0	0	0	0	0	0
John Hunt	0	0	1	0	0	1	0	0	0	0	0	0
Jimmy Husband	143	0	10	6	3	162	44	0	0	2	2	48
Albert Hutchinson	5	0	0	0	0	5	1	0	0	0	0	1
Davie Hutchison	55	0	2	0	1	58	20	0	0	0	0	20
Don Hutchison	21	0	2	1	2	26	0	0	0	0	1	1
Morten Hyldgaard	18	0	0	0	0	18	0	0	0	0	0	0
Besian Idrizaj	7	0	0	0	0	7	1	0	0	0	0	1
Sammy Igoe	2	0	0	0	0	2	0	0	0	0	0	0
Stuart Imlach	8	0	0	1	0	9	0	0	0	0	0	0
James Imrie	63	0	7	0	0	70	0	0	0	0	0	0
James Inglis	3	0	0	0	0	3	0	0	0	0	0	0
Godfrey Ingram	27	0	4	2	0	33	6	0	2	0	0	8
Ryan Inniss	0	1	0	0	2	3	0	0	0	0	0	0
Tommy Irvine	8	0	0	0	0	8	0	0	0	0	0	0
Cyril Isaacs	0	0	1	0	0	1	0	0	0	0	0	0
John Jack	0	15	2	0	0	17	0	1	0	0	0	1
Bertram "Bert" Jackson	0	14	1	0	8	23	0	0	0	0	0	0
Matthew Jackson	9	0	0	2	1	12	0	0	0	0	0	0
Richard Jackson	29	0	4	3	1	37	0	0	0	0	0	0
Julian James	282	0	23	17	13	335	13	0	0	1	0	14
Percy James	2	0	0	0	0	2	1	0	0	0	0	1
Fred Jardine	220	0	12	11	0	243	9	0	0	1	0	10
Jack Jarvie	0	24	3	0	14	41	0	0	0	0	0	0
Rossi Jarvis	35	27	6	2	7	77	1	2	0	1	1	5
Richard Jarvis	0	62	0	0	8	70	0	0	0	0	0	0
RW Jeakings	0	1	0	0	0	1	0	0	0	0	0	0
WG Jelley	0	0	0	0	1	1	0	0	0	0	0	0
William "Bill" Jennings	114	0	3	0	0	117	2	0	0	0	0	2

L = League, NL = Non-League (Southern League and Conference Premier): FAC = FA Cup (including 1945/46): LC = Football League Cup, OTH = United League, Western League, Southern Alliance, Division Three (South) Cup, Southern Professional Floodlit Cup, Watney Cup, Anglo-Italian Cup, Texaco Cup, Full Members Cup, Associate Members Cup, FA Trophy and the Play-Offs. The figures do not include games in World War One and World War Two, the three expunged games from 1939/40 nor the expunged games against Chester in 2009/10.

| | APPEARANCES | | | | | | | GOALS | | | | | |
---	L	NL	FAC	LC	OTH	TOT		L	NL	FAC	LC	OTH	TOT
William "Billy" J Jennings	2	0	0	0	0	2		1	0	0	0	0	1
Jerome Jibodu	0	0	0	0	1	1		0	0	0	0	0	0
Jimmy Jinks	9	0	0	0	0	9		2	0	0	0	0	2
Brian Johnson	10	0	2	0	0	12		0	0	0	0	0	0
Gavin Johnson	6	0	0	0	0	6		0	0	0	0	0	0
Joe Johnson (1908-13)	0	64	2	0	9	75		0	6	2	0	2	10
Joe Johnson (1924-25)	11	0	0	0	0	11		0	0	0	0	0	0
Marvin Johnson	372	0	21	29	17	439		7	0	1	2	0	10
Rob Johnson	97	0	15	11	3	126		0	0	0	1	0	1
Abe Jones	0	136	5	0	25	166		0	14	0	0	3	17
Arthur E Jones	0	3	0	0	0	3		0	0	0	0	0	0
Basil Jones	0	1	0	0	0	1		0	0	0	0	0	0
Graham Jones	39	0	4	0	0	43		0	0	0	0	0	0
Les Jones	97	0	7	0	5	109		1	0	0	0	0	1
Vince Jones	3	0	0	0	0	3		0	0	0	0	0	0
Alan Judge	11	0	0	1	0	12		0	0	0	0	0	0
Matthew Judge	2	0	1	0	3	6		0	0	0	0	1	1
John Julian	0	0	8	0	0	8		0	0	2	0	0	2
Duncan Jupp	5	0	0	0	0	5		0	0	0	0	0	0
Elliot Justham	0	0	2	0	5	7		0	0	0	0	0	0
Steven Kabba	3	0	0	0	0	3		0	0	0	0	0	0
Chris Kamara	49	0	1	2	2	54		0	0	0	0	0	0
Tresor Kandol	21	0	0	4	1	26		3	0	0	2	0	5
Kent Karlsen	6	0	2	0	1	9		0	0	0	0	0	0
Yaser Kasim	0	11	0	0	0	11		0	1	0	0	0	1
Fred Kean	117	0	13	0	1	131		5	0	1	0	0	6
Robert Kean	1	0	0	0	0	1		0	0	0	0	0	0
Keith Keane	129	105	18	9	24	285		4	3	0	0	1	8
Mike Keen	144	0	6	9	1	160		11	0	0	0	0	11
William "Billy" Keen	3	0	0	0	0	3		0	0	0	0	0	0
George Kellett	0	3	0	0	0	3		0	0	0	0	0	0
William "Billy" Kellock	7	0	1	1	0	9		0	0	0	0	2	2
Terry Kelly	136	0	9	0	4	149		1	0	0	0	0	1
James Kemplay	29	0	5	0	16	50		11	0	1	0	6	18
Mick Kennedy	32	0	1	2	1	36		0	0	0	0	0	0
Andy Kerr	68	0	1	0	0	69		25	0	0	0	0	25
Spencer Kettley	1	0	0	0	0	1		0	0	0	0	0	0
Derek Kevan	11	0	1	0	0	12		4	0	2	0	0	6
George Kidd	9	0	0	0	1	10		0	0	0	0	0	0
Dean Kiely	11	0	0	0	0	11		0	0	0	0	0	0
Tommy Kiernan	55	0	5	0	0	60		10	0	5	0	0	15
John Kilgannon	13	0	0	0	3	16		1	0	0	0	0	1
Alan Kimble	12	0	1	0	3	16		0	0	0	0	0	0
Andy King	36	0	5	1	0	42		9	0	0	0	0	9
Gerry King	22	0	1	2	0	25		4	0	0	0	1	5
Tom King	55	0	2	0	0	57		0	0	0	0	0	0
Henry Kingham	250	0	22	0	3	275		0	0	0	0	0	0
Dan Kirkwood	2	0	0	0	0	2		1	0	0	0	0	1
John Paul Kissock	0	21	3	0	7	31		0	0	0	0	1	1
Harry Kitchen	1	0	0	0	0	1		1	0	0	0	0	1
Andy Kiwomya	5	0	0	0	0	5		1	0	0	0	0	1
Joshua Klein-Davies	1	0	0	0	0	1		0	0	0	0	0	0
Anthony "Tony" Knight	6	0	1	0	0	7		0	0	0	0	0	0
Anthony Knights	2	0	0	2	0	4		0	0	0	0	0	0
Janos Kovacs	0	74	9	0	8	91		0	8	0	0	0	8
Zdenek Kroca	0	45	3	0	7	55		0	5	1	0	1	7
Alex Lacey	0	22	2	0	7	31		0	1	0	0	0	1

| | APPEARANCES | | | | | | | GOALS | | | | | |
---	L	NL	FAC	LC	OTH	TOT		L	NL	FAC	LC	OTH	TOT
Leslie Lake	59	0	4	0	0	63		0	0	0	0	0	0
John Lamb	24	0	4	0	0	28		0	0	0	0	0	0
George Lamberton	0	33	1	0	0	34		0	8	0	0	0	8
Harry Lane	0	1	0	0	4	5		0	0	0	0	0	0
Richard Langley	30	0	3	1	0	34		1	0	0	0	0	1
Albert "Bert" Lashbrooke	0	13	0	0	0	13		0	0	0	0	0	0
Robert "Bob" Latheron	0	33	0	0	13	46		0	0	0	0	1	1
Alex Lawless	0	126	9	0	21	156		0	14	2	0	2	18
Thomas Lawrence	0	0	2	0	0	2		0	0	0	0	0	0
David Lawson	5	0	0	0	0	5		0	0	0	0	0	0
Herbert "Bert" Lawson	1	0	0	0	0	1		0	0	0	0	0	0
Michael Leary	22	0	3	2	5	32		2	0	0	0	1	3
Roly Legate	15	0	3	0	0	18		8	0	0	0	0	8
George Lennon	107	0	8	0	0	115		0	0	0	0	0	0
Brian Lewis	50	0	3	6	0	59		22	0	0	3	0	25
Jack Lewis	2	0	0	0	0	2		0	0	0	0	0	0
Frank Lindley	0	5	0	0	0	5		0	0	0	0	0	0
Albert Lindsay	0	33	1	0	0	34		0	0	0	0	0	0
David Lindsay	7	0	0	0	0	7		0	0	0	0	0	0
William Lindsay	0	69	15	0	6	90		0	2	4	0	1	7
Des Linton	83	0	9	5	7	104		1	0	0	0	0	1
Steve Litt	15	0	1	1	3	20		0	0	0	0	0	0
Tommy Little	22	0	3	0	11	36		9	0	1	0	1	11
Stewart Littlewood	6	0	1	0	0	7		2	0	1	0	0	3
David Livermore	8	0	0	0	0	8		0	0	0	0	0	0
Harry Loasby	15	0	0	0	0	15		14	0	0	0	0	14
Adam Locke	62	0	7	3	2	74		5	0	0	0	0	5
Conrad Logan	22	0	3	1	4	30		0	0	0	0	0	0
David Lomax	0	0	3	0	0	3		0	0	0	0	0	0
Ernest Lomax	0	10	0	0	0	10		0	0	0	0	0	0
John "Charles" Lomax	0	10	0	0	0	10		0	0	7	0	0	7
Chris Long	1	0	0	0	0	1		0	0	0	0	0	0
George Long	0	0	1	0	0	1		0	0	0	0	0	0
Brett Longden	0	0	0	0	4	4		0	0	0	0	0	0
Jack Lornie	19	0	0	2	0	21		6	0	0	0	0	6
Joe Loughran	25	0	0	0	0	25		0	0	0	0	0	0
Thomas Love	2	0	0	0	0	2		0	0	0	0	0	0
Percy Lovell	0	1	0	0	0	1		0	0	0	0	0	0
Mark Lownds	59	0	1	1	0	61		3	0	0	0	0	3
Robert Lumsden	1	0	0	0	0	1		0	0	0	0	0	0
Roy Lunniss	1	0	0	0	0	1		0	0	0	0	0	0
Herbert "Bert" Lutterloch	10	0	0	0	2	12		0	0	0	0	0	0
Malcolm Macdonald	88	0	5	8	0	101		49	0	5	4	0	58
Peter MacEwan	26	0	0	0	0	26		11	0	0	0	0	11
Jim Mackey	10	0	1	0	0	11		1	0	0	0	0	1
Tom Mackey	183	0	20	0	5	208		2	0	0	0	0	2
Madden	0	1	0	0	0	1		0	0	0	0	0	0
Neil Madden	1	0	0	0	0	1		0	0	0	0	0	0
Lee Mansell	47	0	6	2	7	62		8	0	2	0	0	10
Henry Mardle	0	2	0	0	0	2		0	2	0	0	0	2
Eddie Marsh	2	0	0	0	0	2		0	0	0	0	0	0
Dwight Marshall	128	0	9	9	9	155		28	0	5	2	3	38
FR Marshall	3	0	0	0	0	3		1	0	0	0	0	1
Alfred Martin	0	5	0	0	0	5		0	0	0	0	0	0
Chris Martin	40	0	3	2	6	51		11	0	0	0	3	14
David Martin	0	23	2	0	0	25		0	3	0	0	0	3
George Martin	98	0	5	0	2	105		27	0	1	0	1	29

L = League, NL = Non-League (Southern League and Conference Premier): FAC = FA Cup (including 1945/46): LC = Football League Cup, OTH = United League, Western League, Southern Alliance, Division Three (South) Cup, Southern Professional Floodlit Cup, Watney Cup, Anglo-Italian Cup, Texaco Cup, Full Members Cup, Associate Members Cup, FA Trophy and the Play-Offs. The figures do not include games in World War One and World War Two, the three expunged games from 1939/40 nor the expunged games against Chester in 2009/10.

	APPEARANCES						GOALS					
	L	NL	FAC	LC	OTH	TOT	L	NL	FAC	LC	OTH	TOT
Allan Mathieson	54	2	2	0	0	58	17	0	0	0	0	17
Damian Matthew	5	0	0	0	1	6	0	0	0	0	0	0
Rob Matthews	11	0	0	1	0	12	0	0	0	0	0	0
Alfie Mawson	0	1	0	0	0	1	0	0	0	0	0	0
Sam Mayberry	1	0	0	0	0	1	0	0	0	0	0	0
Thomas "Jimmie" Mayes	0	2	0	0	0	2	0	0	0	0	0	0
Colby McAdams	0	0	0	0	3	3	0	0	0	0	0	0
Craig McAllister	0	14	0	0	3	17	0	1	0	0	0	1
Pat McAuley	8	0	0	0	0	8	1	0	0	0	0	1
Alan McBain	60	0	4	2	0	66	0	0	0	0	0	0
Joe McBride	25	0	0	2	0	27	9	0	0	0	0	9
Albert McCann	6	0	0	0	0	6	0	0	0	0	0	0
William "John" McCartney	27	16	7	0	23	73	0	0	1	0	3	4
William "Harvey" McCreadie	1	0	0	0	0	1	0	0	0	0	0	0
Robert McCrindle	0	17	6	0	0	23	0	0	0	0	0	0
William "Bill" McCurdy	31	162	18	0	40	251	0	0	1	0	0	1
William "Billy" McDerment	40	0	4	6	0	50	1	0	0	0	0	1
Alexander McDonald	0	41	1	0	26	68	0	11	0	0	5	16
Darron McDonough	105	0	10	9	3	127	5	0	1	1	0	7
Ricky McEvoy	1	0	0	0	1	2	0	0	0	0	0	0
Jimmy 'Punch' McEwen	30	99	17	0	29	175	1	1	0	0	0	2
Robert McFarlane	0	5	0	0	0	5	0	1	0	0	0	1
Cameron McGeehan	0	18	0	0	0	18	0	3	0	0	0	3
Hugh McGinnigle	159	0	17	0	1	177	2	0	1	0	0	3
Gavin McGowan	60	0	3	7	0	70	0	0	0	0	0	0
Alwyn McGuffie	79	0	3	5	2	89	10	0	0	0	0	10
Michael McIndoe	39	0	4	5	1	49	0	0	0	0	0	0
Tom McInnes	93	0	16	0	44	153	20	0	9	0	14	43
Willy McInnes	22	0	0	0	0	22	1	0	0	0	0	1
Hugh McJarrow	15	0	0	0	0	15	10	0	0	0	0	10
James McKechnie	1	0	0	0	0	1	0	0	0	0	0	0
Tommy McKechnie	131	0	8	7	0	146	31	0	2	1	0	34
James McKee	0	31	2	0	0	33	0	8	1	0	0	9
Ray McKinnnon	33	0	2	6	0	41	2	0	0	0	0	2
Paul McLaren	167	0	11	14	9	201	4	0	1	1	0	6
Hugh McLeish	2	0	0	0	0	2	0	0	0	0	0	0
George McLeod	51	0	3	0	6	60	6	0	0	0	2	8
John "Brendan" McNally	134	0	17	7	5	163	3	0	0	0	0	3
George McNestry	69	0	7	0	0	76	26	0	3	0	0	29
Jim McNichol	15	0	0	2	0	17	0	0	0	0	0	0
Steve McNulty	0	66	2	0	0	68	0	2	0	0	0	2
Gary McSheffrey	23	0	0	1	0	24	9	0	0	1	0	10
Gary McSwegan	3	0	0	0	0	3	0	0	0	0	0	0
Paul McVeigh	38	0	5	4	6	53	3	0	0	0	0	3
Raphael Meade	4	0	0	0	0	4	0	0	0	0	0	0
Arnaud Mendy	0	18	7	0	4	29	0	0	0	0	0	0
Alexander Menzies	0	33	1	0	12	46	0	8	1	0	6	15
Neil Midgley	10	0	0	0	0	10	3	0	0	0	0	3
Milam	0	1	0	0	0	1	0	0	0	0	0	0
Reuben Mileman	0	0	5	0	0	5	0	0	0	0	0	0
Robert "Bob" Millar	205	0	8	0	0	213	4	0	0	0	0	4
Henry Miller	0	0	3	0	0	3	0	0	0	0	0	0
James Miller	10	0	1	0	0	11	3	0	0	0	0	3
William "Bill" Miller	3	0	0	0	0	3	0	0	0	0	0	0
Arthur Mills	37	0	4	0	0	41	14	0	0	0	0	14
Hugh Mills	2	0	0	0	0	2	0	0	0	0	0	0
Joe Mills	31	0	1	0	0	32	2	0	0	0	0	2
Henry Mingay	29	0	0	0	0	29	0	0	0	0	0	0
Albert "Bert" Mitchell	106	0	13	0	0	119	41	0	2	0	0	43
Joseph Mitchell	0	61	7	0	15	83	0	0	0	0	0	0
James "Jackie" Mittell	8	0	0	0	0	8	0	0	0	0	0	0
Hugh Moffatt	33	0	1	0	0	34	4	0	0	0	0	4
Robert Moir	1	0	0	0	0	1	0	0	0	0	0	0
Fred Molyneux	0	1	0	0	1	2	0	2	0	0	0	2
William Molyneux	80	0	5	0	0	85	1	0	0	0	0	1
Richard Money	44	0	1	4	0	49	1	0	0	0	0	1
James Monks	0	1	0	0	1	2	0	0	0	0	0	0
Herbert Moody	0	232	15	0	19	266	0	86	11	0	9	106
John Moody	0	0	5	0	0	5	0	0	0	0	0	0
Bernard Moore	74	0	11	0	0	85	31	0	3	0	0	34
James Moore	19	0	2	0	12	33	0	0	0	0	0	0
John Moore	274	0	15	14	3	306	13	0	0	0	1	14
Thomas Moore	0	5	0	0	0	5	0	2	0	0	0	2
Dean Morgan	88	0	3	9	1	101	11	0	0	1	0	12
Francis "Gerry" Morgan	4	0	0	0	0	4	0	0	0	0	0	0
Amari Morgan-Smith	0	37	4	0	7	48	0	14	3	0	1	18
Frank Morrison	13	0	4	0	0	17	0	0	0	0	0	0
Murdoch Morrison	1	0	0	0	0	1	0	0	0	0	0	0
Robert "Bob" Morton	495	0	48	7	12	562	48	0	4	0	3	55
Herbert Mosley	3	0	0	0	0	3	0	0	0	0	0	0
David Moss	221	0	8	16	0	245	88	0	3	3	0	94
James Muir	10	0	0	0	0	10	0	0	0	0	0	0
John Muir	4	0	0	0	0	4	0	0	0	0	0	0
Jimmy Mulvaney	8	0	1	0	0	9	2	0	0	0	0	2
Edward Munroe	0	0	2	0	0	2	0	0	0	0	0	0
James Murphy	0	0	1	0	0	1	0	0	0	0	0	0
John Murphy	0	11	0	0	0	11	0	2	0	0	0	2
Neil Murphy	0	8	2	0	14	24	0	2	0	0	1	3
Adam Murray	0	7	0	0	0	7	0	0	0	0	0	0
Freddie Murray	0	68	6	0	5	79	0	1	0	0	0	1
Tom Naisby	0	73	5	0	0	78	0	0	0	0	0	0
Locke Narburgh	0	0	6	0	0	6	0	0	4	0	0	4
Jerry Nash	0	0	0	0	2	2	0	0	0	0	0	0
Taylor Nathaniel	0	0	1	0	0	1	0	0	0	0	0	0
Sid Neal	27	0	1	0	0	28	0	0	0	0	0	0
Oscar Neale	0	2	0	0	0	2	0	0	0	0	0	0
Douglas Needham	0	0	2	0	0	2	0	0	0	0	0	0
Ernest Needham	0	4	0	0	0	4	0	0	0	0	0	0
Alan Neilson	57	0	2	3	1	63	1	0	0	0	0	1
Scott Neilson	0	8	0	0	0	8	0	1	0	0	0	1
Arthur Nelson	21	0	5	0	0	26	6	0	1	0	0	7
Jack Nelson	134	0	11	0	3	148	1	0	0	0	0	1
Sammy Nelson	4	0	0	0	0	4	1	0	0	0	0	1
Craig Nelthorpe	0	8	0	0	0	8	0	0	0	0	0	0
Mike Newell	63	0	5	0	0	68	18	0	1	0	0	19
Adam Newton	0	54	6	0	6	66	0	2	2	0	0	4
Peter Nicholas	102	0	12	2	0	116	1	0	0	0	0	1
Chris Nicholl	97	0	4	4	1	106	6	0	0	0	0	6
Kevin Nicholls	194	22	11	8	3	238	30	0	2	1	0	33
Benjamin Nicholson	0	1	0	0	2	3	0	0	0	0	0	0
Mark Nicholson	0	7	4	0	0	11	0	0	0	0	0	0
David Noake	17	0	3	1	0	21	0	0	0	0	0	0
Kurt Nogan	33	0	0	4	2	39	3	0	0	0	1	4
Lee Nogan	7	0	3	0	1	11	1	0	1	0	0	2

L = League, NL = Non-League (Southern League and Conference Premier): FAC = FA Cup (including 1945/46): LC = Football League Cup, OTH = United League, Western League, Southern Alliance, Division Three (South) Cup, Southern Professional Floodlit Cup, Watney Cup, Anglo-Italian Cup, Texaco Cup, Full Members Cup, Associate Members Cup, FA Trophy and the Play-Offs. The figures do not include games in World War One and World War Two, the three expunged games from 1939/40 nor the expunged games against Chester in 2009/10.

	APPEARANCES							GOALS					
---	L	NL	FAC	LC	OTH	TOT		L	NL	FAC	LC	OTH	TOT
Marc North	18	0	5	1	0	24		3	0	1	1	0	5
Stacey North	25	0	0	1	0	26		0	0	0	0	0	0
Stan Northover	1	0	0	0	0	1		0	0	0	0	0	0
Alf Nunn	14	0	0	0	0	14		3	0	0	0	0	3
Chukwuemeka Nwajiobi	72	0	9	6	0	87		17	0	2	1	0	20
Mark Nwokeji	0	7	2	0	0	9		0	0	1	0	0	1
Kofi Nyamah	0	0	1	1	0	2		0	0	0	0	0	0
Phil O'Connor	2	0	0	0	0	2		0	0	0	0	0	0
Scott Oakes	173	0	15	6	6	200		27	0	5	1	1	34
Joe O'Brien	11	0	3	0	0	14		3	0	0	0	0	3
Herbert Oclee	0	0	5	0	0	5		0	0	1	0	0	1
Aaron O'Connor	0	34	3	0	2	39		0	5	4	0	0	9
Garreth O'Connor	3	0	2	0	2	7		0	0	0	0	0	0
JJ O'Donnell	0	30	9	0	12	51		0	2	0	0	1	3
Mike O'Hara	2	0	0	2	0	4		0	0	0	0	0	0
Parys Okai	0	0	1	1	2	4		0	0	0	0	0	0
David Oldfield	146	0	3	17	12	178		22	0	0	4	6	32
Stephen O'Leary	45	0	4	4	3	56		3	0	0	0	0	3
Roger Ord	0	53	11	0	7	71		0	0	0	0	0	0
John O'Rourke	84	0	5	1	0	90		64	0	2	0	0	66
John Orr	9	0	1	0	0	10		0	0	0	0	0	0
Curtis Osano	0	28	2	0	9	39		0	0	0	0	0	0
James Osborn	0	0	0	0	1	1		0	0	0	0	0	0
Sid Ottewell	15	0	3	0	0	18		4	0	1	0	0	5
Mark Ovendale	45	0	2	4	4	55		0	0	0	0	0	0
Syd Owen	388	0	27	0	8	423		3	0	0	0	0	3
Lloyd Owusu	0	13	0	0	2	15		0	6	0	0	1	7
David Pacey	246	0	22	6	6	280		16	0	3	0	0	19
Harry Pacey	4	0	0	0	0	4		0	0	0	0	0	0
John Page	4	0	0	0	0	4		1	0	0	0	0	1
John Palmer	1	0	0	0	0	1		0	0	0	0	0	0
Fred Panther	8	0	0	0	0	8		3	0	0	0	0	3
Garry Parker	42	0	8	4	0	54		3	0	0	1	0	4
Tom Parker	36	40	8	0	0	84		0	0	1	0	0	1
Sam Parkin	50	0	0	3	3	56		10	0	0	0	0	10
Robert Parkinson	0	10	1	0	0	11		0	5	0	0	0	5
John "Eddie" Parris	7	0	0	0	0	7		2	0	0	0	0	2
Andy Parry	0	23	2	0	1	26		0	3	0	0	1	4
Frank Parsons	0	4	0	0	1	5		0	0	0	0	0	0
Horace "Harry" Parsons	0	0	0	0	1	1		0	0	0	0	0	0
Jordan Patrick	2	0	0	0	1	3		0	0	0	0	0	0
Darren Patterson	56	0	3	1	9	69		0	0	0	0	0	0
Horace "Hod" Paul	0	0	5	0	0	5		0	0	0	0	0	0
Joe Payne	72	0	5	0	0	77		83	0	4	0	0	87
Trevor Peake	179	0	13	7	3	202		0	0	0	0	0	0
Reg Pearce	75	0	4	0	4	83		6	0	0	0	0	6
Andy Pearson	2	0	0	0	0	2		0	0	0	0	0	0
Frank Pearson	0	17	0	0	7	24		0	2	0	0	2	4
George Pearson	14	0	0	0	0	14		1	0	0	0	0	1
John Pearson	1	0	0	0	0	1		0	0	0	0	0	0
William "Billy" Pease	33	0	1	0	1	35		8	0	0	0	1	9
Jim Pemberton	92	0	4	0	1	97		8	0	0	0	0	8
Mark Pembridge	60	0	4	2	4	70		6	0	0	0	0	6
Edward Penman	0	8	0	0	0	8		0	0	0	0	0	0
William "Bill" Perkins	26	0	6	0	17	49		0	0	0	0	0	0
Russell Perrett	100	0	4	4	1	109		9	0	0	0	0	9
George Perrins	6	0	0	0	13	19		0	0	0	0	1	1
Christopher Perry	35	0	4	3	2	44		1	0	0	0	0	1
Paolo "Paul" Peschisolido	4	0	0	0	1	5		0	0	0	0	1	1
Ernie Pett	1	0	0	0	0	1		0	0	0	0	0	0
Bertie Pettengell	0	1	0	0	0	1		0	0	0	0	0	0
Andy Petterson	19	0	0	2	2	23		0	0	0	0	0	0
Forbes Phillipson-Masters	10	0	0	0	0	10		0	0	0	0	0	0
Edward "Ted" Phillips	12	0	0	0	0	12		8	0	0	0	0	8
Peter Phillips	5	0	0	0	0	5		0	0	0	0	0	0
John Pickering	0	49	2	0	25	76		0	13	0	0	15	28
George Pilkington	18	122	14	2	16	172		0	11	0	0	1	12
Kevin Pilkington	0	22	6	0	5	33		0	0	0	0	0	0
Courtney Pitt	12	0	0	2	0	14		0	0	0	0	1	1
Peter Platt	0	130	9	0	44	183		0	0	0	0	1	1
David Pleat	70	0	6	3	0	79		9	0	1	0	0	10
MM Plummer	0	3	0	0	6	9		0	0	0	0	4	4
Tristian Plummer	5	0	0	2	1	8		0	0	0	1	0	1
Joe Pointon	65	0	6	0	0	71		12	0	1	0	0	13
Godfrey Poku	0	19	4	0	6	29		0	0	0	0	0	0
Maitland "Matt" Pollock	6	0	1	0	0	7		0	0	0	0	0	0
George Porter	0	1	0	0	0	1		0	1	0	0	0	1
William Porter	0	5	0	0	0	5		0	3	0	0	0	3
George Potter	7	0	1	0	0	8		0	0	1	0	0	1
Edward Potts	0	100	5	0	14	119		0	0	0	0	0	0
John Pounder	3	0	0	0	1	4		0	0	0	0	2	2
Neil Poutch	1	0	0	0	0	1		0	0	0	0	0	0
David Preece	336	0	27	23	9	395		21	0	2	3	1	27
Charlie Preedy	5	0	0	0	0	5		0	0	0	0	0	0
Horace Prentice	1	0	0	0	0	1		0	0	0	0	0	0
William Prentice	0	14	4	0	0	18		0	8	7	0	0	15
Lewis Price	1	0	0	0	1	2		0	0	0	0	0	0
M Price	0	1	0	0	1	2		0	0	0	0	1	1
Paul Price	207	0	9	13	1	230		8	0	0	0	0	8
Robert Pritchard	0	14	0	0	0	14		0	0	0	0	0	0
Marc Pugh	4	0	0	0	0	4		0	0	0	0	0	0
Arthur Purdy	24	0	2	0	0	26		0	0	0	0	0	0
Jesse Pye	61	0	4	0	0	65		32	0	4	0	0	36
Thomas Quinn	0	68	5	0	0	73		0	26	4	0	0	30
William Ralley	21	0	4	0	4	29		0	0	0	0	0	0
George Ramage	7	0	0	0	0	7		0	0	0	0	0	0
John "Jock" Ramage	9	0	0	0	0	9		0	0	0	0	0	0
Bruce Rankin	0	30	1	0	6	37		0	6	1	0	0	7
Walter Rayner	0	2	0	0	0	2		0	0	0	0	0	0
John "Tony" Read	199	0	11	18	1	229		12	0	0	0	0	12
Matthew Read	0	1	0	0	0	1		0	1	0	0	0	1
Paul Read	0	0	0	0	1	1		0	0	0	0	0	0
Thomas Read	0	0	3	0	0	3		0	0	0	0	0	0
Albert "Dickie" Reader	7	0	0	0	0	7		0	0	0	0	0	0
William "Billy" Redfern	41	0	1	0	0	42		19	0	0	0	0	19
Harry Reece	29	0	1	0	1	31		0	0	0	0	0	0
Barry Reed	1	0	0	1	0	2		0	0	0	0	0	0
Ian Rees	0	0	0	0	4	4		0	0	0	0	0	0
Jason Rees	82	0	3	5	6	96		0	0	0	0	2	2
John Reid	111	0	7	3	0	121		7	0	0	0	0	7
Syd Reid	134	0	9	0	0	143		70	0	11	0	0	81
Scott Rendell	0	36	6	0	4	46		0	8	4	0	0	12
Andy Rennie	307	0	26	0	2	335		147	0	15	0	0	162
Joe Rennie	4	0	0	0	0	4		0	0	0	0	0	0

L = League, NL = Non-League (Southern League and Conference Premier): FAC = FA Cup (including 1945/46): LC = Football League Cup, OTH = United League, Western League, Southern Alliance, Division Three (South) Cup, Southern Professional Floodlit Cup, Watney Cup, Anglo-Italian Cup, Texaco Cup, Full Members Cup, Associate Members Cup, FA Trophy and the Play-Offs. The figures do not include games in World War One and World War Two, the three expunged games from 1939/40 nor the expunged games against Chester in 2009/10.

	APPEARANCES						GOALS					
	L	NL	FAC	LC	OTH	TOT	L	NL	FAC	LC	OTH	TOT
Callum Reynolds	0	5	1	0	0	6	0	0	0	0	0	0
Joe Reynolds	2	0	0	0	0	2	0	0	0	0	0	0
Len Rich	19	0	1	0	1	21	6	0	0	0	0	6
Albert Richards	2	0	0	0	0	2	0	0	0	0	0	0
David Richards	147	0	5	0	0	152	0	0	0	0	0	0
Jimmy Richmond	2	0	0	0	0	2	0	0	0	0	0	0
William "Billy" Rickett	1	0	0	0	0	1	0	0	0	0	0	0
Gordon Riddick	102	0	7	5	0	114	16	0	1	0	0	17
Frederick Riddle	0	2	0	0	0	2	0	0	0	0	0	0
Walter Rigate	0	33	1	0	12	46	0	2	1	0	0	3
Robert Riley	0	0	0	1	0	1	0	0	0	0	0	0
Bruce Rioch	149	0	9	9	0	167	47	0	2	3	0	52
Vidar Riseth	11	0	0	0	1	12	0	0	0	0	0	0
Alan Rivers	30	0	0	4	0	34	1	0	0	0	0	1
Ben Roberts	19	0	0	0	0	19	0	0	0	0	0	0
Frederick Roberts	180	0	15	0	3	198	38	0	6	0	1	45
Hugh Roberts	0	38	4	0	0	42	0	5	1	0	0	6
Joe Roberts	17	0	5	0	0	22	2	0	0	0	0	2
Foster Robinson	1	0	0	0	0	1	1	0	0	0	0	1
James Robinson	0	33	1	0	14	48	0	1	0	0	0	1
Jake Robinson	0	7	2	0	0	9	0	0	0	0	0	0
Matthew Robinson	0	37	3	0	5	45	0	3	0	0	0	3
Stephen Robinson	185	0	15	7	4	211	9	0	2	1	0	12
Graham Rodger	28	0	0	2	3	33	2	0	0	0	0	2
Arthur Roe	93	38	7	0	0	138	1	2	0	0	0	3
Tommy Roe	17	0	2	0	0	19	7	0	0	0	0	7
Edgar Rogers	0	2	0	0	2	4	0	0	0	0	0	0
Frank Rollinson	0	59	6	0	14	79	0	28	6	0	9	43
Luke Rooney	0	6	0	0	0	6	0	0	0	0	0	0
Ian Roper	19	0	2	0	3	24	3	0	0	0	0	3
Davie Ross	0	30	1	0	0	31	0	12	0	0	0	12
Doug Rowe	23	0	2	0	0	25	8	0	0	0	0	8
Lathaniel Rowe-Turner	0	37	6	0	5	48	0	0	0	0	0	0
David Rowland	1	0	0	0	0	1	0	0	0	0	0	0
Keith Rowland	12	0	0	0	0	12	2	0	0	0	0	2
Simon Royce	2	0	0	0	0	2	0	0	0	0	0	0
Pelly Ruddock	0	21	0	0	3	24	0	2	0	0	0	2
Ray Ruffett	1	0	0	0	0	1	0	0	0	0	0	0
Bjorn Runstrom	8	0	0	0	0	8	2	0	0	0	0	2
Albert Russell	0	3	0	0	0	3	0	0	0	0	0	0
Cecil "Jack" Russell	8	0	0	0	1	9	1	0	0	0	0	1
John Rutherford	0	29	4	0	0	33	0	5	0	0	0	5
Jim Ryan	174	0	11	12	7	204	21	0	4	0	0	25
John G Ryan	276	0	17	15	6	314	10	0	0	0	1	11
John O Ryan	18	0	1	3	0	22	1	0	0	0	0	1
George Saddington	0	0	1	0	0	1	0	0	0	0	0	0
Gareth Salisbury	12	0	0	1	0	13	2	0	0	2	0	4
Darren Salton	18	0	0	3	3	24	0	0	0	0	0	0
Collin Samuel	0	1	0	0	0	1	0	0	0	0	0	0
Albert Sanders	0	0	14	0	0	14	0	0	1	0	0	1
John Sanderson	6	0	0	0	0	6	0	0	0	0	0	0
Mike Saxby	82	0	2	7	0	91	6	0	0	1	0	7
Arthur Saxton	0	14	3	0	4	21	0	2	5	0	2	9
Andre Scarlett	18	0	2	2	2	24	1	0	0	1	0	2
Joe Schofield	0	7	0	0	6	13	0	1	0	0	0	1
Joe Scott	13	0	0	0	0	13	2	0	0	0	0	2
Les Sealey	207	0	28	21	3	259	0	0	0	0	0	0
John Seasman	8	0	0	0	0	8	2	0	0	0	0	2
John Semple	7	0	0	0	0	7	0	0	0	0	0	0
Dino Seremet	7	0	1	0	1	9	0	0	0	0	0	0
Dave Sexton	9	0	0	0	0	9	1	0	0	0	0	1
Edward Seymour	0	2	0	0	0	2	0	0	0	0	0	0
John Shankland	3	0	0	0	0	3	0	0	0	0	0	0
John Shankly	46	0	2	0	0	48	20	0	1	0	0	21
Don Shanks	90	0	6	9	5	110	2	0	0	1	2	5
Wally Shanks	264	0	11	0	1	276	6	0	0	0	0	6
Albert Sharp	0	31	4	0	0	35	0	0	0	0	0	0
David Sharpe	21	0	4	0	10	35	0	0	0	0	0	0
Ivan Sharpe	0	0	0	0	1	1	0	0	0	0	0	0
Jon Shaw	0	42	4	0	5	51	0	8	1	0	1	10
Laurie Sheffield	35	0	1	9	0	45	12	0	0	5	0	17
Wilf Sheldon	2	0	0	0	0	2	0	0	0	0	0	0
James Shepherd	0	8	0	0	0	8	0	1	0	0	0	1
John "Billy" Shepherd	3	0	0	0	0	3	0	0	0	0	0	0
Paul Shepherd	7	0	0	0	0	7	0	0	0	0	0	0
Steve Sherlock	2	0	1	0	0	3	0	0	0	0	0	0
Paul Showler	27	0	4	4	2	37	6	0	0	0	0	6
Enoch Showunmi	102	0	6	2	4	114	14	0	0	1	1	16
Hilton Sidney	2	0	0	0	0	2	0	0	0	0	0	0
Barry Silkman	3	0	0	0	0	3	0	0	0	0	0	0
Ernie Simms	65	95	18	0	11	189	47	62	13	0	8	130
Gary Simpson	0	0	0	0	1	1	0	0	0	0	0	0
John Sims	3	0	0	1	0	4	1	0	0	0	0	1
Scott Sinclair	0	0	0	0	1	1	0	0	0	0	0	0
Aaron Skelton	25	0	3	1	3	32	2	0	0	0	0	2
Slater	0	0	0	1	0	1	0	0	0	0	0	0
Les Slatter	1	0	0	0	0	1	0	0	0	0	0	0
Christopher Slennett	0	3	0	0	0	3	0	0	0	0	0	0
Jackie Slicer	45	0	3	0	0	48	13	0	1	0	0	14
Frank Sloan	4	0	3	0	0	7	0	0	1	0	0	1
Alan Slough	275	0	16	19	2	312	28	0	2	2	0	32
Bryan Small	15	0	0	0	0	15	0	0	0	0	0	0
Gilbert Small	0	0	2	0	0	2	0	0	0	0	0	0
Mike Small	4	0	0	0	0	4	0	0	0	0	0	0
Peter Small	28	0	3	0	0	31	5	0	1	0	0	6
A Smart	0	0	1	0	0	1	0	0	0	0	0	0
Thomas Smart	0	2	0	0	3	5	0	0	0	0	0	0
Alec Smeaton	6	0	0	0	0	6	0	0	0	0	0	0
Charlie Smith	0	0	0	0	3	3	0	0	0	0	0	0
Edward "Ted" Smith	32	0	1	0	0	33	0	0	0	0	0	0
FG Smith	0	1	0	0	0	1	0	0	0	0	0	0
George Smith	1	0	0	0	0	1	0	0	0	0	0	0
Harold "Ray" Smith	10	0	3	0	0	13	1	0	1	0	0	2
John Smith	0	64	5	0	0	69	0	32	5	0	0	37
Jonathan Smith	0	52	6	0	2	60	0	3	0	0	0	3
Ray Smith	12	0	0	0	1	13	0	0	0	1	0	1
Tim Smith	2	0	0	0	0	2	0	0	0	0	0	0
Tom Smith	157	0	14	0	1	172	1	0	0	0	0	1
William Smith	0	17	0	0	8	25	0	7	0	0	3	10
William "Herbie" Smith	0	0	0	1	0	1	0	0	0	0	0	0
Efetobore Sodje	9	0	3	1	1	14	0	0	0	0	0	0
Juergen Sommer	82	0	11	6	2	101	0	0	0	0	0	0
Hong 'Frank' Soo	71	0	7	0	0	78	4	0	1	0	0	5
Les Spencer	7	0	0	0	0	7	1	0	0	0	0	1

L = League, NL = Non-League (Southern League and Conference Premier): FAC = FA Cup (including 1945/46): LC = Football League Cup, OTH = United League, Western League, Southern Alliance, Division Three (South) Cup, Southern Professional Floodlit Cup, Watney Cup, Anglo-Italian Cup, Texaco Cup, Full Members Cup, Associate Members Cup, FA Trophy and the Play-Offs. The figures do not include games in World War One and World War Two, the three expunged games from 1939/40 nor the expunged games against Chester in 2009/10.

APPEARANCES / GOALS

Name	L	NL	FAC	LC	OTH	TOT		L	NL	FAC	LC	OTH	TOT
Stanley Spencer	0	3	1	0	0	4		0	0	0	0	0	0
Martyn Sperrin	1	0	0	1	0	2		0	0	0	0	0	0
Michael Spillane	39	0	3	1	6	49		3	0	1	0	0	4
Peter Spiring	15	0	0	1	0	16		2	0	0	0	0	2
Matthew Spring	308	0	24	20	5	357		36	0	3	3	1	43
Jim Standen	36	0	3	3	0	42		0	0	0	0	0	0
Harold Stansfield	0	135	9	0	10	154		0	25	0	0	3	28
William "Billy" Stark	10	0	0	0	0	10		4	0	0	0	0	4
Starkie	0	0	0	0	1	1		0	0	0	0	0	0
Alan Starling	7	0	0	0	0	7		0	0	0	0	0	0
Alan Steen	10	0	0	0	0	10		0	0	0	0	0	0
Brian Stein	427	0	31	35	3	496		130	0	6	15	3	154
Mark Stein	84	0	11	8	4	107		22	0	3	1	1	27
Kirk Stephens	227	0	8	13	0	248		2	0	0	0	0	2
George Stephenson	192	0	15	0	5	212		58	0	5	0	6	69
James Stephenson	0	50	2	0	13	65		0	21	0	0	6	27
John Stephenson	10	0	0	0	0	10		0	0	0	0	0	0
Danny Stevens	1	0	0	0	0	1		0	0	0	0	0	0
Edgar Stevens	0	11	0	0	15	26		0	1	0	0	2	3
Ron Stevens	7	0	0	0	1	8		1	0	0	0	1	2
Jim Stevenson	0	5	1	0	0	6		0	0	0	0	0	0
Morris Stevenson	1	0	0	0	0	1		0	0	0	0	0	0
William Stewart	46	17	12	0	30	105		10	6	4	0	18	38
Jude Stirling	10	0	2	0	1	13		0	0	0	0	0	0
George Stobbart	107	0	9	0	0	116		30	0	0	0	0	30
Peter Stone	1	0	0	0	0	1		0	0	0	0	0	0
Stonebridge	0	0	0	0	1	1		0	0	0	0	0	0
George Storey	0	15	1	0	0	16		0	4	1	0	0	5
James Strathie	2	0	0	0	0	2		0	0	0	0	0	0
Leonard Stratton	0	1	0	0	0	1		0	0	0	0	0	0
Albert Street	0	21	2	0	4	27		0	0	0	0	0	0
Kevin Street	2	0	0	0	0	2		0	0	0	0	0	0
Tommy Streeton	0	21	3	0	3	27		0	6	2	0	3	11
Bernard Streten	276	0	22	0	1	299		0	0	0	0	0	0
Percy Summers	0	32	2	0	0	34		0	0	0	0	0	0
Steve Sutton	14	0	0	0	0	14		0	0	0	0	0	0
Ron Swan	14	0	0	0	0	14		0	0	0	0	0	0
Tommy Tait	84	0	12	0	0	96		50	0	7	0	0	57
Solomon Taiwo	0	14	0	0	2	16		0	2	0	0	0	2
Drew Talbot	49	0	7	3	4	63		3	0	0	2	0	5
Christian Tavernier	0	0	1	0	1	2		0	0	0	0	0	0
Arthur A Taylor	8	0	1	0	0	9		0	0	2	0	0	2
Arthur H Taylor	0	0	21	0	0	21		0	0	0	0	0	0
Greg Taylor	0	34	3	0	6	43		0	0	1	0	0	1
John A Taylor	0	0	1	0	0	1		0	0	0	0	0	0
Jack E Taylor	85	0	6	0	0	91		29	0	4	0	0	33
Joe T Taylor	1	0	0	0	0	1		0	0	0	0	0	0
John P Taylor	37	0	0	2	1	40		3	0	0	0	1	4
Matthew Taylor	129	0	10	6	1	146		16	0	1	0	0	17
Steve Taylor	20	0	0	0	0	20		1	0	0	0	0	1
William "Billy" Taylor	6	0	1	0	0	7		0	0	0	0	0	0
Matt Tees	35	0	3	2	0	40		13	0	2	0	0	15
Paul Telfer	144	0	14	5	2	165		19	0	2	0	1	22
William "Billy" Thayne	30	0	2	0	2	34		0	0	0	0	0	0
Anthony "Tony" Thear	13	0	0	2	0	15		5	0	0	0	0	5
William "Billy" Thirlaway	13	0	0	0	0	13		0	0	0	0	0	0
Mitchell Thomas	292	0	25	18	6	341		6	0	0	0	0	6
Wayne Thomas	0	2	0	0	0	2		0	0	0	0	0	0
Alan Thompson	2	0	0	0	0	2		0	0	0	0	0	0
Frederick Thompson	0	34	3	0	0	37		0	0	0	0	0	0
Jimmy Thompson	72	0	2	0	0	74		42	0	0	0	0	42
Robert Thompson	17	0	0	0	0	17		7	0	0	0	0	7
Sydney Thompson	0	16	2	0	12	30		0	4	0	0	2	6
Steve Thompson	5	0	0	2	0	7		0	0	0	0	0	0
Norman Thomson	43	0	1	0	0	44		11	0	0	0	0	11
Peter Thomson	11	0	2	2	2	17		2	0	0	0	1	3
Robert "Bobby" Thomson	74	0	7	3	0	84		0	0	0	0	0	0
Robert "Bobby" A Thomson	110	0	8	10	7	135		1	0	0	0	1	2
Anthony "Tony" Thorpe	164	0	9	10	9	192		70	0	3	6	5	84
Lionel Thring	0	0	5	0	0	5		0	0	4	0	0	4
Thomas Tierney	0	43	8	0	3	54		0	11	3	0	2	16
Aaron Tighe	0	0	0	0	2	2		0	0	0	0	0	0
James Tildesley	0	1	0	0	1	2		0	0	0	0	0	0
Joe Till	138	0	6	0	0	144		1	0	0	0	0	1
Colin Tinsley	55	0	4	3	0	62		0	0	0	0	0	0
Alf Tirrell	122	0	8	0	0	130		4	0	1	0	0	5
Colin Todd	2	0	0	1	0	3		0	0	0	0	0	0
Graeme Tomlinson	7	0	0	0	0	7		0	0	0	0	0	0
Robert Tomlinson	0	12	0	0	0	12		0	5	0	0	0	5
W Toyer	0	0	0	0	1	1		0	0	0	0	0	0
Mike Tracey	23	0	0	2	0	25		3	0	0	0	0	3
Reg Tricker	4	0	1	0	0	5		0	0	0	0	0	0
Luke Trotman	0	0	0	0	1	1		0	0	0	0	0	0
William Trueman	0	9	0	0	0	9		0	0	0	0	0	0
Turner	0	0	0	0	3	3		0	0	0	0	0	0
Chris Turner	30	0	0	4	0	34		5	0	0	0	0	5
Edward "Ted" Turner	0	32	0	0	1	33		0	0	0	0	0	0
George Turner	20	0	1	0	1	22		5	0	0	0	0	5
Gordon Turner	406	0	25	7	12	450		243	0	18	4	11	276
Peter Turner	0	25	3	0	0	28		0	3	3	0	0	6
Wayne Turner	84	0	10	8	0	102		2	0	1	0	0	3
Mark Tyler	0	199	12	0	19	230		0	0	0	0	0	0
Paul Underwood	67	0	4	1	0	72		5	0	0	0	0	5
Matthew Upson	1	0	0	0	1	2		0	0	0	0	0	0
Thomas Urwin	0	40	4	0	0	44		0	1	0	0	0	1
Jean-Louis Valois	34	0	0	0	0	34		6	0	0	0	0	6
Imre Varadi	6	0	0	0	0	6		1	0	0	0	0	1
William "Billy" Vaughan	3	0	0	0	0	3		2	0	0	0	0	2
David Viana	0	0	0	0	3	3		0	0	0	0	0	0
Robert Vickers	0	0	1	0	0	1		0	0	0	0	0	0
Jonny Vilstrup	7	0	0	0	2	9		0	0	0	0	0	0
Edward "Jack" Vinall	44	0	6	0	0	50		18	0	2	0	0	20
Rowan Vine	102	0	5	4	0	111		31	0	1	1	0	33
Gary Waddock	153	0	8	10	7	178		3	0	0	0	0	3
Robin Wainwright	16	0	0	1	1	18		3	0	0	0	0	3
George Walden	0	7	0	0	0	7		0	0	0	0	0	0
Harry Walden	96	0	5	5	0	106		11	0	0	1	0	12
Jon Walders	0	20	1	0	7	28		0	2	0	0	2	4
A Wales	0	0	0	0	4	4		0	0	0	0	1	1
Abraham Wales	3	0	0	0	0	3		0	0	0	0	0	0
Dan Walker	0	25	6	0	5	36		0	3	0	0	2	5
Dennis Walker	1	0	0	0	0	1		0	0	0	0	0	0
Jackie Walker	0	0	0	0	1	1		0	0	0	0	0	0
Jason Walker	0	20	0	0	9	29		0	4	0	0	2	6

L = League, NL = Non-League (Southern League and Conference Premier): FAC = FA Cup (including 1945/46): LC = Football League Cup, OTH = United League, Western League, Southern Alliance, Division Three (South) Cup, Southern Professional Floodlit Cup, Watney Cup, Anglo-Italian Cup, Texaco Cup, Full Members Cup, Associate Members Cup, FA Trophy and the Play-Offs. The figures do not include games in World War One and World War Two, the three expunged games from 1939/40 nor the expunged games against Chester in 2009/10.

APPEARANCES							GOALS					
	L	NL	FAC	LC	OTH	TOT	L	NL	FAC	LC	OTH	TOT
Jimmy Walker	133	0	5	0	0	138	4	0	0	0	0	4
Robbie Walker	0	38	1	0	0	39	0	13	0	0	0	13
Robert "Bob" Walker	5	0	0	0	0	5	0	0	0	0	0	0
Alex Wall	0	22	0	0	5	27	0	5	0	0	1	6
James Wallace	0	1	0	0	0	1	0	0	0	0	0	0
William "Horace" Wallbanks	4	0	0	0	0	4	1	0	0	0	0	1
Paul Walsh	80	0	4	5	0	89	24	0	3	1	0	28
Peter Walsh	8	0	0	0	0	8	2	0	0	0	0	2
William "Billy" Walsh	17	0	0	0	0	17	2	0	0	0	0	2
Albert Walters	1	0	0	0	0	1	0	0	0	0	0	0
Scott Ward	1	0	0	0	0	1	0	0	0	0	0	0
Alfred Warner	0	49	3	0	23	75	0	11	1	0	6	18
John Warner	1	0	0	0	1	2	0	0	0	0	1	1
Sunday-Akanni Wasiu	5	0	0	0	0	5	1	0	0	0	0	1
Adam Watkins	0	42	4	0	12	58	0	5	1	0	3	9
Charlie Watkins	218	0	21	0	0	239	16	0	4	0	0	20
Joseph "Connie" Watkins	0	33	12	0	9	54	0	0	1	0	0	1
Claude Watson	0	3	1	0	0	4	0	0	0	0	0	0
Jim Watson	4	0	0	0	0	4	0	0	0	0	0	0
Kevin Watson	6	0	2	2	1	11	0	0	0	0	0	0
Julian Watts	73	0	8	6	0	87	8	0	0	0	0	8
Mark Watts	1	0	1	0	0	2	0	0	0	0	0	0
William "Billy" Waugh	135	0	12	0	0	147	9	0	3	0	0	12
Robert "Bob" Weaver	3	0	0	0	0	3	1	0	0	0	0	1
Webdale	0	0	0	0	1	1	0	0	0	0	0	0
Roy Wegerle	45	0	1	10	3	59	10	0	0	8	0	18
Jimmy 'Jock' Weir	12	0	1	1	0	14	1	0	0	0	0	1
Mickey Weir	8	0	1	3	0	12	0	0	1	2	0	3
Alan West	285	0	14	15	3	317	16	0	0	1	0	17
George West	0	2	0	0	0	2	0	0	0	0	0	0
Robert Whalley	4	0	1	0	0	5	1	0	0	0	0	1
Shaun Whalley	0	16	1	0	5	22	0	1	0	0	1	2
Jackie Whent	11	0	0	0	0	11	3	0	0	0	0	3
Adrian Whitbread	9	0	4	0	0	13	0	0	0	0	0	0
Brian Whitby	7	0	0	0	2	9	1	0	0	0	0	1
Frank Whitby	0	0	12	0	0	12	0	0	5	0	0	5
Harry Whitby	0	0	10	0	0	10	0	0	7	0	0	7
Alan White	80	16	7	6	5	114	3	0	1	0	0	4
Fred White	0	237	21	0	46	304	0	10	1	0	4	15
Steve White	76	0	3	4	0	83	25	0	0	1	0	26
Harold Whitehead	0	3	2	0	0	5	0	0	0	0	0	0
Ray Whittaker	170	0	11	7	0	188	40	0	3	2	0	45
Sammy Wightman	0	58	2	0	0	60	0	1	0	0	0	1
Arthur Wileman	0	72	9	0	26	107	0	42	5	0	11	58
James Wilkie	0	17	3	0	8	28	0	0	0	0	0	0
Paul Wilkinson	3	0	0	0	0	3	0	0	0	0	0	0
David Williams	0	23	1	0	0	24	0	6	1	0	0	7
Harry Williams	54	90	18	0	25	187	2	2	0	0	1	5
Martin Williams	40	0	1	1	3	45	2	0	0	0	0	2
Richard Williams	30	11	7	0	30	78	0	0	0	0	0	0
Steve Williams	40	0	2	5	2	49	1	0	0	0	0	1
Chris Willmott	27	0	0	0	0	27	0	0	0	0	0	0
Robbie Willmott	0	54	2	0	11	67	0	14	0	0	1	15
Danny Wilson	110	0	8	20	4	142	24	0	3	3	0	30
Gordon Wilson	7	0	0	0	0	7	0	0	0	0	0	0
James "Jim" Wilson	39	0	3	0	0	42	1	0	0	0	0	1
John Wilson	0	0	5	0	0	5	0	0	0	0	0	0
Marc Wilson	4	0	0	0	0	4	0	0	0	0	0	0
Robert Wilson	24	0	0	0	0	24	1	0	0	0	0	1
Thomas Wilson	0	35	3	0	29	67	0	2	0	0	0	2
Robbie Winters	1	0	0	0	0	1	0	0	0	0	0	0
Cauley Woodrow	0	0	0	0	3	3	0	0	0	0	0	0
Harry Woods	97	0	8	0	0	105	22	0	5	0	0	27
Herbert Woods	0	4	0	0	0	4	0	0	0	0	0	0
Matt Woods	34	0	4	0	0	38	0	0	0	0	0	0
Jamie Woodsford	10	0	0	0	2	12	0	0	0	0	0	0
Matthew Woolgar	0	0	0	0	1	1	0	0	0	0	0	0
Jake Woolley	0	5	1	0	5	11	0	0	0	0	0	0
Harry Worley	8	0	0	0	2	10	0	0	0	0	0	0
Albert Worth	0	23	2	0	14	39	0	3	0	0	4	7
Ben Wright	0	5	0	0	0	5	0	1	0	0	0	1
James Wright	0	0	8	0	0	8	0	0	0	0	0	0
Tommy Wright	0	4	1	0	1	6	0	1	1	0	1	3
John "Bobby" Wyldes	26	0	1	0	0	27	8	0	0	0	0	8
George Yardley	1	0	0	0	0	1	0	0	0	0	0	0
Jimmy Yardley	173	0	15	0	0	188	78	0	16	0	0	94
Joe Young	3	0	0	0	0	3	0	0	0	0	0	0
Landry Zahana-Oni	9	0	0	0	0	9	0	0	0	0	0	0

❯ **Last but by no means least.** Landry Zahana-Oni.

L = League, NL = Non-League (Southern League and Conference Premier): FAC = FA Cup (including 1945/46): LC = Football League Cup, OTH = United League, Western League, Southern Alliance, Division Three (South) Cup, Southern Professional Floodlit Cup, Watney Cup, Anglo-Italian Cup, Texaco Cup, Full Members Cup, Associate Members Cup, FA Trophy and the Play-Offs. The figures do not include games in World War One and World War Two, the three expunged games from 1939/40 nor the expunged games against Chester in 2009/10.

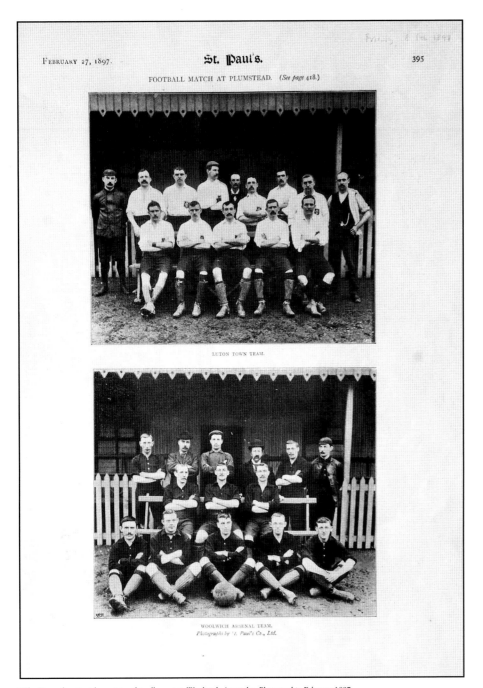

FEBRUARY 27, 1897.

St. Paul's.

395

FOOTBALL MATCH AT PLUMSTEAD. (See page 418.)

LUTON TOWN TEAM.

WOOLWICH ARSENAL TEAM.
Photographs by St. Paul's Co., Ltd.

▶ The Town about to take part in a friendly against Woolwich Arsenal at Plumstead in February 1897.

FOOTBALL!

GRAND OPENING MATCH.

SOUTHERN LEAGUE.

On the TOWN GROUND, LUTON,

SATURDAY, SEPT. 1st, 1900,

LUTON

v.

SOUTHAMPTON

KICK-OFF, 4 P.M.

Admission, 6d.   Stand, 6d.

Cheap Train from St. Albans at 3 p.m., also from Leighton and Dunstable.

S. PRIDE, PRINTER, LUTON.

▶ Back to the Southern League in 1900.

1896/97 UNITED LEAGUE

Match No	Month	Day	Venue	Opponents	W,L,D	Score	Scorers	Attendance
1	Sep	12	(h)	MILLWALL ATHLETIC	L	2-3	Stewart, Gallacher	4000
2	Oct	3	(a)	Woolwich Arsenal	D	2-2	Galbraith, McInnes	10000
3	Oct	17	(a)	Millwall Athletic	L	1-3	Birch	8000
4	Dec	19	(h)	WELLINGBOROUGH	W	7-0	Stewart (2), Galbraith (2), Davies, Docherty, Gallacher	2000
5	Feb	13	(a)	Rushden	W	3-1	McInnes, Galbraith, Ekins	1500
6	Feb	20	(a)	Wellingborough	W	8-0	Coupar (3), Gallacher (2), Galbraith (2), Stewart	
7	Feb	27	(h)	KETTERING TOWN	W	3-0	Davies, Brown (2)	2500
8	Mar	13	(a)	Tottenham Hotspur	W	2-1	Davies (pen), McInnes	6500
9	Mar	20	(h)	WOOLWICH ARSENAL	W	5-2	Gallacher, Stewart, Coupar, Ekins	3000
10	Apr	3	(h)	LOUGHBOROUGH	W	1-0	McCartney	2500
11	Apr	10	(h)	TOTTENHAM HOTSPUR	W	2-1	Ekins	3500
12	Apr	12	(a)	Kettering Town	L	0-1		
13	Apr	16	(h)	RUSHDEN	W	11-0	Birch (3), Gallacher (2), Stewart (2), Coupar (2), Ekins, McInnes	3500
14	Apr	20	(a)	Loughborough	W	5-2	Ekins (4), Stewart	2000

	Pld	W	D	L	F	A	Pts
1 Millwall Athletic	14	11	1	2	43	22	23
2 LUTON TOWN	14	10	1	3	52	16	21
3 Arsenal	14	6	3	5	28	34	15
4 Loughborough	14	6	1	7	29	31	13
5 Rushden	14	6	1	7	25	42	13
6 Kettering Town	14	4	4	6	23	24	12
7 Wellingborough Town	14	3	3	8	17	39	9
8 Tottenham Hotspur	14	1	4	9	25	34	6

In 1896/97 the Town had no alternative but to join the United League as they had resigned from the Southern League and had failed to be elected to the Football League. In subsequent years the United League was used to augment Football League and Southern League games and was regarded as a "first team" competition.

1897/98 UNITED LEAGUE

Match No	Month	Day	Venue	Opponents	W,L,D	Score	Scorers	Attendance
1	Sep	20	(h)	WELLINGBOROUGH	W	4-0	Perrins, Stewart (pen), Coupar, McInnes	
2	Sep	27	(a)	Wellingborough	W	2-0	Gallacher, (og)	
3	Oct	11	(h)	TOTTENHAM HOTSPUR	W	5-0	Gallacher, Little, Stewart (2), Ekins	
4	Oct	18	(h)	KETTERING TOWN	W	3-1	Ekins, McInnes, Stewart	
5	Oct	25	(a)	Millwall Athletic	W	4-0	McCartney, Stewart, Gallacher, McInnes	4000
6	Nov	3	(a)	Southampton	W	2-0	Stewart, Ekins	4000
7	Nov	22	(a)	Rushden	W	3-2	Gallacher (2), Coupar	2000
8	Dec	6	(h)	RUSHDEN	W	5-0	Ekins, Catlin (2), Gallacher, Coupar	
9	Dec	13	(a)	Kettering Town	L	0-1		
10	Dec	28	(h)	LOUGHBOROUGH	W	8-1	Donaldson (3), Stewart (2), Coupar, McInnes, Davies (pen)	2000
11	Jan	24	(h)	MILLWALL ATHLETIC	W	2-0	Gallacher (2)	1550
12	Feb	3	(h)	TOTTENHAM HOTSPUR	D	2-2	McInnes, Stewart	
13	Feb	14	(h)	SOUTHAMPTON	W	2-0	McInnes, Donaldson	
14	Feb	21	(a)	Woolwich Arsenal	D	2-2	Stewart, Durrant	
15	Apr	12	(a)	Loughborough	W	3-1	Gallacher, McCartney, Donaldson	
16	Apr	16	(h)	WOOLWICH ARSENAL	W	2-1	Gallacher, Donaldson	2500

1 Own Goal

	Pld	W	D	L	F	A	Pts
1 LUTON TOWN	16	13	2	1	49	11	28
2 Tottenham Hotspur	16	8	5	3	40	27	21
3 Arsenal	16	8	5	3	35	24	21
4 Kettering Town	16	9	1	6	28	25	19
5 Rushden	16	7	1	8	24	26	15
6 Southampton	16	6	3	7	23	28	13
7 Millwall Athletic	16	4	4	8	27	27	12
8 Wellingborough Town	16	3	3	10	17	41	9
9 Loughborough	16	1	2	13	8	42	4

Southampton two points deducted

1898/99 UNITED LEAGUE

Match No	Month	Day	Venue	Opponents	W,L,D	Score	Scorers	Attendance
1	Sep	1	(h)	WELLINGBOROUGH	D	1-1	Hewitt	
2	Sep	5	(a)	Tottenham Hotspur	L	0-1		4000
3	Sep	19	(h)	TOTTENHAM HOTSPUR	L	3-4	McInnes (2), Clarke	
4	Oct	10	(a)	Woolwich Arsenal	L	2-3	C Ford, McInnes	
5	Oct	17	(h)	BRIGHTON UNITED	L	3-5	Durrant, W Ford, Brock	
6	Oct	24	(a)	Rushden	L	2-3	C Ford, Hewitt	
7	Nov	7	(a)	Wellingborough	L	1-7	Dow	
8	Nov	14	(h)	SOUTHAMPTON	W	2-1	W Ford, Kemplay	
9	Nov	21	(a)	Kettering Town	L	0-4		
10	Nov	30	(a)	Bristol City	L	0-6		
11	Dec	27	(h)	WOOLWICH ARSENAL	D	1-1	Kemplay	3000
12	Feb	15	(a)	Brighton United	L	0-5		
13	Feb	27	(h)	BRISTOL CITY	L	1-3	Boutwood	
14	Mar	8	(a)	Southampton	L	0-8		
15	Mar	13	(h)	RUSHDEN	W	3-2	Brock, Dimmock, Kemplay	
16	Mar	20	(h)	READING	D	1-1	McInnes	
17	Mar	27	(h)	MILLWALL ATHLETIC	L	1-2	Dow	
18	Apr	19	(a)	Reading	L	0-6		
19	Apr	24	(a)	Millwall Athletic	L	2-6	Kemplay (2)	
20	Apr	26	(h)	KETTERING TOWN	L	1-2	Kemplay	

	Pld	W	D	L	F	A	Pts
1 Millwall Athletic	20	14	3	3	42	19	31
2 Southampton	20	12	1	7	53	32	25
3 Arsenal	20	10	4	6	40	30	24
4 Tottenham Hotspur	20	11	2	7	36	25	24
5 Bristol City	20	11	0	9	43	31	22
6 Reading	20	8	5	7	36	25	21
7 Brighton U	20	10	1	9	41	42	21
8 Wellingborough Town	20	7	1	12	32	40	15
9 Kettering Town	20	8	1	11	25	38	15
10 Rushden	20	6	1	13	26	45	13
11 LUTON TOWN	20	2	3	15	24	71	7

Kettering two points deducted

1900/01 UNITED LEAGUE

Match No	Month	Day	Venue	Opponents	W,L,D Score	Scorers	Attendance	Allen F	Barker A	Barratt	Blessington J	Boutwood J	Brown WR	Clifford T	Cox AG	Dawson	Dempsey N	Dimmock E	Durrant AF	Ellingham E	Farr H	Garratt A	Hawkes F	Hawkes T	Holdstock HF	Lindsay W	McCurdy W	Molyneux F	Monks J	Ord RG	Plummer MM	Saxton AW	Smart T	Street A	Tierney TT	Turner	White F	Williams H	Match No
1	Sep	3	(a)	Rushden	W 2-1	Blessington, Lindsay				8		7	4										5	2	3	9	1				11		10			6	1
2	Sep	8	(h)	FINEDON	W 2-0	T Hawkes, Plummer		10		7					5			11	4	1	6	8	2							9					3		6	2
3	Oct	8	(h)	RUSHDEN	D 2-2	Barker (2)		10	9		8		7	4				11								5	2	3				1					6	3
4	Nov	24	(a)	Kettering	D 1-1	Brown					8		7	4			10							9		5	2	3				1	11					6	4
5	Dec	15	(h)	ROTHWELL	W 3-1	Barker, Plummer, (og)			9	7								5		11		4	6	8	3						10	1					5	5
6	Dec	22	(a)	Finedon	D 3-3	Dimmock (2), Plummer				7								6		11		4	5	3	8	2					10	1					6	6
7	Dec	26	(h)	NORTHAMPTON	W 2-1	Durrant, Saxton			9				7	8		4				11			5									2	6	7
8	Feb	10	(a)	Wellingborough	W 3-1	Barker, Saxton, Tierney			9	8						5				7			4			2					11		3	10		6	8
9	Mar	4	(h)	WELLINGBOROUGH	W 9-0	Barker (3), Blessington (2), Brown (2), Plummer, Williams			9	8		11								7			4								1	10					5	6	9
10	Mar	16	(h)	KETTERING	W 3-0	Blessington, Brown, Tierney			9	8		11								7			4									2	10			5	6	10
11	Apr	10	(a)	Northampton	D 0-0	-			9	8		11					5			7				6							1	10			2	4	11
12	Apr	13	(a)	Rothwell	L 0-8	-				7		9			4	6			11			5	2			3					10		1		8		12

1 Own Goal

		Apps	2	7	4	1	7	4	3	5	1	3	7	3	4	4	8	4	3	6	4	1	1	7	6	4	3	4	3	3	5	8	
		Goals		7		4		4					2	1				1			1				4	2					2	1	

	Pld	W	D	L	F	A	Pts
1 Rothwell	12	10	0	2	36	11	20
2 LUTON TOWN	12	7	4	1	30	18	18
3 Kettering Town	12	6	3	3	23	18	15
4 Wellingborough Town	12	6	0	6	24	28	12
5 Northampton	12	2	4	6	16	27	8
6 Rushden	12	2	3	7	16	24	7
7 Finedon	12	0	4	8	10	29	4

1905/06 UNITED LEAGUE

Match No	Month	Day	Venue	Opponents	W,L,D Score	Scorers	Attendance	Barnes WE	Blackett J	Brown Alexander	Dobson E	Dow JM	Else A	Farr H	Field A	Gallacher PJ	Gibson	Hawkes F	Hawkes R	Lane H	Latheron R	McCurdy W	McDonald A	Parsons H	Pickering J	Platt P	Wales A	Warner A	Watkins J	White F	Match No
1	Sep	2	(a)	Watford	L 1-2	Pickering		11	2	9				1		7			6		3	4	10		8			5		1
2	Sep	13	(a)	Grays United	W 6-0	Pickering (2), Barnes, Brown, Gallacher, White		11	2	9						7					3	4	10	1	6	8			5	2
3	Sep	18	(h)	GRAYS UNITED	W 9-1	MacDonald (2), Pickering (2), Warner (2), Blackett, White, F Hawkes		11	2									4	6		3	9	10	1		8		7	5	3
4	Sep	27	(a)	Brighton & Hove Albion	L 1-2	Brown			2	9				6							11	3	4	10	1		7		5	4
5	Oct	5	(a)	Southern United	D 1-1	Brown		11	2	9						4					8	3	10	1		7	6	5	5
6	Oct	9	(h)	SWINDON	W 4-2	Brown (2), F Hawkes, Gallacher		11	2	9	2					7		4		8	3	10		1		7	6	5	6
7	Oct	16	(h)	LEYTON	W 5-1	Gibson (3), Blackett, Brown		11	2	9							8	4	6		3		10	1		7		5	7
8	Oct	30	(h)	GILLINGHAM	W 3-0	Brown, Latheron, Warner		11	2	9						6		4		9	3	8	10			7		5	8
9	Nov	20	(h)	SOUTHERN UNITED	W 5-2	R Hawkes (2), Gallacher, Pickering, Warner		11	2	9			2			5		4			3	8	10	1		7		6	9
10	Nov	27	(a)	Gillingham	W 1-0	Brown		11	2	9						6			7		3	8	10	1		7		5	10
11	Dec	30	(a)	Leyton	L 2-3	Pickering, White		11	2	9						6					3	4	10	1		7		5	11
12	Jan	24	(a)	Swindon	L 2-3	Brown, MacDonald		11	2	9						6					3	4	10	1		7		5	12
13	Feb	19	(h)	CRYSTAL PALACE	L 1-2	Warner		11	2	9						6					3	4	10	1	8	7		5	13
14	Feb	26	(h)	CLAPTON ORIENT	D 1-1	Wales		11	2	9			2			4		6	11		3	9	10	1	8	7		5	14
15	Mar	12	(h)	BRIGHTON & HOVE ALBION	D 3-3	Brown, MacDonald, Pickering		11		9			2			5		4		6	3	9	10	1	8	7	3	5	15
16	Mar	17	(a)	Crystal Palace	L 1-2	Pickering		11	2	9	9					5				6	3	9	10	1	8	7		17
17	Mar	19	(a)	Clapton Orient	L 1-2	Barnes		11	2	9						5			6		3	4	10	1	8	7		17
18	Apr	17	(h)	WATFORD	D 0-0	-		11	2	9						6					3	8	4	10	1		7		5	18

		Apps	15	14	14	1	1	3	1	1	15	1	12	4	4	6	17	17	1	16	17	4	16	3	15	
		Goals	2	2	10				1		3	3	2	2		1		9		4		1	5		3	

	Pld	W	D	L	F	A	W	D	L	F	A	Pts
1 Watford	18	7	2	0	28	5	6	2	1	21	10	30
2 Crystal Palace	18	6	2	1	27	13	7	0	2	24	8	27
3 Leyton	18	6	2	1	23	15	2	2	5	10	16	20
4 LUTON TOWN	18	5	3	1	31	12	2	1	6	16	15	18
5 Clapton Orient	18	5	3	1	16	11	0	5	4	8	16	18
6 Swindon Town	18	5	1	3	24	15	2	2	5	9	14	17
7 Brighton & HA	18	5	1	3	19	11	1	3	5	9	17	16
8 New Brompton	18	6	1	2	13	5	1	1	7	13	22	16
9 Grays United	18	2	2	5	9	21	2	0	7	12	43	10
10 Southern United	18	3	1	5	14	21	0	1	8	7	43	8

1906/07 UNITED LEAGUE

Match No	Month	Day	Venue	Opponents	W,L,D Score	Scorers	Attendance	Barnes WE	Brown Alexander	Farr H	Fitzpatrick HJ	Gallacher PJ	Gittins AF	Hawkes F	Hawkes R	Hogg J	Jackson BH	Jones A	Latheron R	McCurdy W	McDonald A	Murphy N	Pickering J	Platt P	Schofield JA	Slater	Starkie	Warner A	Watkins J	White F	Match No
1	Sep	5	(a)	Brighton & Hove Albion	L 2-7	Brown, Warner		11	9					4	2			3		10	1	7			8		6	1
2	Sep	10	(h)	WATFORD	W 2-0	Gittens, MacDonald		11			6	10	4	3	2			3	9		10	1	7		8		2
3	Sep	19	(a)	Watford	W 1-0	Brown		11	9		6		4	2	1			3		10	1	7			8		3
4	Sep	24	(h)	BRIGHTON & HOVE ALBION	D 0-0			11	9		6	10	4	2				3	8		10	1	7			5		4
5	Oct	1	(a)	Gillingham	W 3-1	Barnes, Brown, Gittens		11	9		6	10	4	2				3			10	1	7			5		5
6	Oct	8	(h)	CRYSTAL PALACE	L 0-1								4	6	2			3	8	7	9			5		6
7	Oct	22	(h)	LEYTON	W 3-2	Fitzpatrick (3)		11	9	1	10		4	2		6	3	8	7						7
8	Nov	1	(a)	Norwich	L 0-4			11	1	10		4	2	6		3	8	7	9				5		8
9	Nov	5	(h)	GILLINGHAM	W 3-2	Fitzpatrick, Jones, Murphy		11	1	10		4	2	6	5	7	3	8	9					9
10	Nov	12	(h)	NORWICH	W 5-1	Pickering (3), Barnes, Gittens		11	9		6	10	4			7	3	8	1			2	5		10
11	Dec	10	(h)	HASTINGS	W 2-0	Brown, Pickering		11	9	6		4	2	3		10	8	1			7		5		11
12	Jan	24	(a)	Leyton	W 2-0	Pickering (2)		11	9		4	10	2	6	11	8	7	9	1				3	5		12
13	Feb	13	(a)	Crystal Palace	L 0-7					4	2	6	7	9	1		10	7			5		13
14	Mar	6	(a)	Hastings	L 0-2					4		2	6	11	3	9	1				5		14

		Apps	12	8	3	4	8	4	11	1	10	8	9	5	10	9	5	9	11	6	1	1	7	3	9	
		Goals	2	4		4	3						1		1	6	1					1		

	Pld	W	D	L	F	A	Pts
1 Crystal Palace	14	8	5	1	39	20	21
2 Brighton & HA	14	6	6	2	33	26	18
3 LUTON TOWN	14	8	1	5	23	27	17
4 Norwich City	14	6	4	4	34	22	16
5 Hastings	14	6	2	6	27	24	14
6 Leyton	14	3	4	7	24	27	10
7 New Brompton	14	3	3	8	24	35	9
8 Watford	21	3	1	10	15	38	7

1907/08 WESTERN LEAGUE

The Western League was used to augment Southern League games and was regarded as a "first team" competition.

Match No	Month	Day	Venue	Opponents	W,L,D	Score	Scorers	Attendance	Benham GC	Brown NL	Dimmock WH	Farrant SG	Hall P	Hawkes F	Hawkes R	Hogg J	Jarvis RT	Jones A	Latheron R	McCurdy W	Moody HB	Nicholson B	Pearson F	Platt P	Rankin B	Rigate WJ	Sharpe I	Walders J	Watkins J	White F	Match No
1	Sep	23	(h)	WEST HAM UNITED	W	1-0	Pearson						8	4		2		6	11	3			9	1	7		10		5	1
2	Sep	30	(h)	CRYSTAL PALACE	D	1-1	Walders			3			10	4					6		2	9			1	8	7		11		5	2
3	Oct	9	(a)	Bristol Rovers	W	2-1	Jones, Moody			9	3	11	8					1	4		2	10				5	7				6	3
4	Oct	14	(a)	West Ham United	W	2-1	Moody, Pearson			8	3	11	4						1		2	10	6	9			7				5	4
5	Oct	21	(a)	Millwall Athletic	L	1-4	Jones			9	3		4	8				1	6		2	10					7		11		5	5
6	Oct	28	(h)	BRISTOL ROVERS	D	1-1	F Hawkes				3			4						11	2	10		8	1	9	7			6	5	6
7	Nov	6	(a)	Crystal Palace	D	1-1	Moody						8	4	6	2			4		10			3	9	1	11	7			5	7
8	Nov	11	(h)	MILLWALL ATHLETIC	L	2-3	F Hawkes, (og)			3	10		9	8	6			4			2				1		7		11		5	8
9	Nov	20	(a)	Reading	D	1-1	Walders			3			4	8		2	1	6			10				9		7		11		5	9
10	Nov	25	(h)	READING	W	3-1	F Hawkes (2), Moody		9				4	8		2		6		3	10				1		7	11			5	10
11	Dec	9	(h)	TOTTENHAM HOTSPUR	L	1-5	White			3			4	8		2		6			10				9	1	7		11		5	11
12	Dec	16	(a)	Tottenham Hotspur	L	0-2	-		7		10		4	4		2	1	6			9			8				11	3	5	12

1 Own Goal

| | | | | | | | Apps | | 2 | 3 | 8 | 4 | 9 | 11 | 2 | 6 | 5 | 9 | 2 | 8 | 9 | 2 | 7 | 7 | 6 | 10 | 1 | 7 | 2 | 12 | |
| | | | | | | | Goals | | - | - | - | - | - | 4 | - | - | - | 2 | - | 4 | - | - | 2 | - | - | - | - | 2 | - | 1 | |

		Pld	W	D	L	F	A	Pts
1	Millwall	12	9	2	1	31	13	20
2	Bristol Rovers	12	6	3	3	22	19	15
3	Tottenham Hotspur	12	6	1	5	16	15	13
4	LUTON TOWN	12	4	4	4	16	21	12
5	Reading	12	4	3	5	20	25	11
6	Crystal Palace	12	3	4	5	16	17	10
7	West Ham	12	1	1	10	16	27	3

1908/09 WESTERN LEAGUE

Match No	Month	Day	Venue	Opponents	W,L,D	Score	Scorers	Attendance	Bradley EJ	Brown NL	Chapman R	Dimmock WH	Fleckney T	Folley W	Gregory J	Hawkes F	Hawkes R	Haycock FJ	Holtum FG	Jarvis RT	Johnson J	Jones A	McCurdy W	Menzies AW	Moody HB	Parsons F	Platt P	Rigate WJ	Stansfield H	Tildesley J	White F	Match No
1	Sep	14	(h)	CROYDON COMMON	W	2-1	Johnson, Stansfield		5	7		3				2	4				11	6		9	10		1		8			1
2	Sep	30	(h)	QUEENS PARK RANGERS	W	8-1	Menzies (2), F Hawkes, Brown, Stansfield, Moody, R Hawkes, Haycock			7		2				3	4	6	8				5	9	10		1		8			2
3	Oct	7	(h)	LEYTON	W	2-0	Haycock, Moody			7			6			2	4	8	3					9	10	5	1		11			3
4	Oct	12	(h)	READING	D	2-2	Haycock, Moody			7			6			2	4	8	3				5	9	10		1		11			4
5	Oct	21	(a)	Reading	L	1-3	Menzies		2	7			6			3	4	8						9	10		1		11			5
6	Oct	28	(a)	Brighton & Hove Albion	L	0-2	-		5				6			3	4	8			11			9	10		1	7			2	6
7	Nov	2	(h)	CRYSTAL PALACE	W	5-1	Menzies (3), Moody, Stansfield		8	7			6		2	3	4			1				9	10				11		5	7
8	Nov	9	(a)	Leyton	W	2-1	Johnson, Platt (pen)							2		3	4	8			10	6		9				1	7	11	5	8
9	Nov	18	(h)	BRIGHTON & HOVE ALBION	D	1-1	Moody			7		2				3	4	6	8				5	9	10				11			9
10	Dec	2	(a)	Croydon Common	L	1-2	Haycock		10	7	2		6				4	8			11			9	10		1			3	5	10
11	Feb	21	(a)	Queens Park Rangers	L	0-2	-		6							3	4	8			1	11	2	9	10			7			5	11
12	Mar	8	(a)	Crystal Palace	L	0-8	-		5			2				3	4	8			1	11	6	9	10			7				12

| | | | | | | | Apps | | 7 | 8 | 1 | 4 | 6 | 2 | 11 | 12 | 2 | 10 | 2 | 3 | 6 | 7 | 1 | 12 | 10 | 1 | 9 | 2 | 10 | 1 | 5 | |
| | | | | | | | Goals | | - | 1 | - | - | - | - | - | 1 | 1 | 4 | - | - | 2 | - | - | 6 | 5 | - | 1 | - | 3 | - | - | |

		Pld	W	D	L	F	A	W	D	L	F	A	Pts
1	Brighton & HA	12	5	0	1	16	5	2	2	2	7	8	16
2	QPR	12	5	0	1	18	4	1	1	4	10	20	13
3	Crystal Palace	12	4	1	1	17	6	1	1	4	6	16	12
4	LUTON TOWN	12	4	2	0	20	6	1	0	5	4	18	12
5	Croydon Common	12	3	1	2	9	11	2	1	3	7	13	12
6	Reading	12	2	1	3	8	8	2	1	3	11	13	10
7	Leyton	12	2	1	3	9	12	2	0	4	7	9	9

'STARS OF THE WESTERN LEAGUE'

N. BROWN (Forward).

▶ Norman Brown

W. RIGATE (Forward).

▶ Walter Rigate

(W. McCURDY (Back).

▶ Bill McCurdy

W. DIMMOCK (Back).

▶ Walter Dimmock

1912/13 SOUTHERN ALLIANCE

The Southern Alliance was a mid-week competition aimed at giving opportunity to those who worked Saturdays the chance to see a football match. It was regarded as a a "first team" competition.

Match No	Month	Day	Venue	Opponents	W,L,D Score	Scorers	Attendance	Abbott RH	Bateman H	Chipperfield JJ	Conquest J	Davidson TK	Day JW	Elvey JR	Hawes HG	Hawkes F	Hawkes R	Henderson GG	Holland JJ	Jarvie J	Jelley WG	Johnson J	Murphy N	Ports EJ	Price M	Rogers E	Smith W	Stephenson James	Streeton TA	Thompson S	Toyer W	Webdale	Wileman AH	Wilson TT	Worth A	Match No
1	Sep	2	(h)	SOUTHEND UNITED	W 4-0	Smith (2), Thompson, Worth								1				6	2				10	3			9		7	5			8	4	11	1
2	Sep	4	(a)	Southend United	L 1-5	Stephenson								1				6	2				10	3			9	7		5			8	4	11	2
3	Sep	18	(a)	Southampton	D 2-2	Smith, Wileman								1			6		2				10	3			9	7		5			8	4	11	3
4	Sep	25	(h)	SOUTHAMPTON	W 2-0	Conquest, Davidson					11	9	1				4		2				8	3				7		6			10	5	4	4
5	Oct	2	(h)	BRENTFORD	W 1-0	Thompson		1									4	6	2				10	3				7		9			8	5	11	5
6	Oct	16	(h)	BRIGHTON & HOVE ALBION	W 6-0	Streeton (2), Worth, Wileman, Stephenson, Henderson			1								4		2					3				7	9	10	6		8	5	11	6
7	Oct	30	(a)	Portsmouth	L 0-3			1									4		2				10	3			9	7					8	5	11	7
8	Nov	2	(h)	CROYDON COMMON	D 2-2	Stephenson, Worth		1									4		2		7			3					9	10			8	5	11	8
9	Nov	6	(a)	Brentford	D 2-2	Hawes, Stephenson									1		10	4	8	2				3					9		6		7	5	11	9
10	Nov	13	(a)	MILLWALL	W 2-1	Streeton, Stephenson		1									10	4		2					3					9	8	6		7	5	11	10
11	Nov	20	(a)	Brighton & Hove Albion	D 1-1	Worth									1		10	4		2			9	8	3						6		7	5	11	11
12	Jan	25	(a)	Croydon Common	L 1-3	Wileman				1							4	10	2				11	8	3				9				7	6		12
13	Feb	10	(a)	Millwall	L 0-4					1							4	6					10	8	3				9				7	5		13
14	Mar	25	(h)	PORTSMOUTH	W 2-1	Price, Wileman		1									4								3				9			2	7	5	11	14
15	Apr	19	(h)	CARDIFF CITY	W 2-0	Stephenson, Wileman											4	6		10	2				3				9	7				8	5	11	15
16	Apr	26	(a)	Cardiff City	L 2-5	Chipperfield, Wileman			1	10							4	6		2					3				9	7				8	5	11	16
						Apps		5	5	1	1	1	1	6	1	3	14	9	12	2	3	1	3	9	14	1	2	8	13	3	12	1	1	15	16	14	
						Goals		-	-	1	1	1	-	-	1	-	-	1	-	-	-	-	-	-	-	-	1	-	3	6	3	2	-	-	6	-	4	

	Pld	W	D	L	F	A	W	D	L	F	A	Pts
1 Croydon Common	16	7	1	0	21	5	2	5	1	10	11	24
2 Brighton & HA	16	4	4	0	18	7	4	1	3	10	12	21
3 LUTON TOWN	16	7	1	0	21	4	0	3	5	9	25	18
4 Millwall	16	5	2	1	22	8	2	1	5	14	18	17
5 Portsmouth	16	5	1	2	16	7	2	1	5	13	16	16
6 Southend United	16	5	1	2	16	8	0	3	5	3	23	14
7 Southampton	16	3	2	3	16	16	2	1	5	7	14	13
8 Brentford	16	4	1	3	18	13	1	0	7	12	26	11
9 Cardiff City	16	3	2	3	16	13	1	0	7	8	22	10

1913/14 SOUTHERN ALLIANCE

Match No	Month	Day	Venue	Opponents	W,L,D Score	Scorers	Attendance	Abbott RH	Brandham J	Brewis R	Clark	Dodd EJ	Donaghy Michael	Durrant AF	Elvey JR	Frith RW	Hawkes F	Hawkes R	Hoar SW	Jarvie J	Mitchell JT	Robinson J	Rollinson F	Simms E	Stevens E	Wileman AH	Wilkie J	Wilson TT	Match No
1	Sep	1	(h)	BRENTFORD	W 1-0	Simms									2	5	4	6		1	3	10	9	7	8	11		1
2	Sep	6	(a)	Brentford	W 3-2	Brewis, R Hawkes, Rollinson				8			7		2	5	4	6		3	1	10	9		7	11		2
3	Sep	10	(h)	CROYDON COMMON	L 0-2				4							5	4			3	1	2	10	9	7	8	11		3
4	Sep	24	(a)	Croydon Common	D 1-1	Wileman										5	4			3	1	2	10	9	7	8	11	6	4
5	Oct	8	(h)	BRIGHTON & HOVE ALBION	W 2-0	Brewis, Rollinson				8						5	4		11	3	1	2	10	9	7	6		5
6	Oct	15	(h)	PORTSMOUTH	W 4-3	Brewis, Durrant, R Hawkes, Rollinson				9			7	2	5		4	6		3	1	10		11	8	4	6		6
7	Oct	22	(a)	Brighton & Hove Albion	L 1-2	Simms				10						4	6		3	1	2	10	9	7	8	5	7	7
8	Oct	29	(a)	Portsmouth	W 2-1	Rollinson, Wileman				9						5	6		11	3	1	2	10	9	7	8	4	9	8
9	Nov	5	(a)	Cardiff City	L 1-3	Rollinson				9							6		11	3	1	2	10	9	7	8	4	9	9
10	Nov	12	(a)	Southend United	L 0-1					9					2	5	4	6		3	1	2	10	9	7	8	6	10	10
11	Nov	19	(h)	SOUTHAMPTON	W 3-1	Brewis (3)				9					2	5	4	6		3	1	2	10	9	7	8	5	11	11
12	Dec	3	(a)	Southampton	W 4-2	Stevens (2), Elvey, Wileman								7	2	5	4	6		3	1	2	10	9	8	11	6	12	12
13	Feb	4	(h)	NEWPORT COUNTY	W 3-1	Wileman, Simms, Rollinson										5	4		11	2	1	3	10	9	7	6	6	13	13
14	Feb	26	(h)	Newport County	W 3-1	Brewis, Simms (2)				8	4					5	4			1	3	10	9	7	6	6	14	14
15	Mar	18	(h)	SOUTHEND UNITED	W 7-0	Rollinson (3), Simms (3), F Hawkes				8						5	4		11	2	1	3	10	9	7	6	6	15	15
16	Apr	14	(h)	CARDIFF CITY	W 1-0	Wileman		1				10				5		6		3		1	9	7	8	11	4	16	16
						Apps		1	1	10	1	1	1	2	7	14	11	8	7	11	15	14	14	11	15	11	8	13	
						Goals		-	-	7	-	-	1	-	1	-	2	-	-	-	-	-	9	8	2	5	-	-	

	Pld	W	D	L	F	A	W	D	L	F	A	Pts
1 Brighton & HA	16	7	0	1	27	4	4	2	2	12	11	24
2 LUTON TOWN	16	7	0	1	21	7	4	1	3	15	13	23
3 Croydon Common	16	7	1	0	15	2	3	1	4	9	14	22
4 Cardiff City	16	5	1	2	21	9	3	0	5	5	16	14
5 Newport County	16	4	1	3	15	11	2	1	5	5	12	14
6 Southampton	16	5	1	2	21	12	0	1	7	6	20	12
7 Portsmouth	16	5	0	3	14	8	1	0	7	8	20	12
8 Brentford	16	3	3	2	16	9	1	1	6	7	24	12
9 Southend United	16	4	3	1	12	6	0	0	8	3	27	11

1945/46 FA CUP

Round	Month	Day	Venue	Opponents	W,L,D Score	Scorers	Attendance
3	Jan	5	(h)	DERBY COUNTY	L 0-6	-	16792
3	Jan	9	(a)	Derby County	L 0-3	-	18000

Team on 5th Jan: Duke, Beach, Dunsmore, Goodyear, Vinall, Campbell, Daniel, Brice, Needham, Gardiner, Waugh.
Team on 9th Jan: Duke, Lake, Dunsmore, Goodyear, Gager, Campbell, Isaacs, Daniel, Needham, Vinall, Waugh.

◗ Kenilworth Road in 1913, looking towards the Oak Road goal.

THE INTERNATIONALS

ENGLAND

Ron Baynham - 1956: Denmark, N.Ireland, Spain. (3)
Mick Harford - 1988: Israel 1989: Denmark. (2)
Bob Hawkes - 1907: N.Ireland 1908: Austria (two games), Hungary, Bohemia. (5)
Ricky Hill - 1983: Denmark, W.Germany 1986: Egypt. (3)
Syd Owen - 1954: Yugoslavia, Hungary, Belgium. (3)
Joe Payne - 1937: Finland. (1)
Ernie Simms - 1922: N.Ireland. (1)
Brian Stein - 1984: France. (1)
Bernard Streten - 1950: N.Ireland. (1)
Paul Walsh - 1983: Australia (three games) 1984: France, Wales. (5)

NORTHERN IRELAND

Thomas 'Bud' Aherne - 1950: Wales. (1)
Billy Bingham - 1959: England, Scotland, Wales, Spain 1960: Scotland, England, Wales. (7)
Kingsley Black - 1988: France, Malta 1989: Eire, Hungary, Spain (two games), Chile 1990: Hungary, Norway, Uruguay 1991: Yugoslavia (two games), Denmark, Austria, Poland, Faroe Islands. (16)
Louis Bookman - 1921: Scotland, Wales 1922: England. (3)
Bobby Brennan - 1949: Wales. (1)
Mal Donaghy - 1980: Scotland, England, Wales 1981: Sweden, Portugal, Scotland 1982: Scotland (two games), Israel, England, France, Wales, Yugoslavia, Honduras, Spain, France 1983: Austria, W.Germany, Albania (two games), Turkey, Scotland, England, Wales 1984: Austria, Turkey, W.Germany, Scotland, England, Wales, Finland 1985: Romania, Finland, England, Spain, Turkey 1986: Turkey, Romania, England, France, Denmark, Morocco, Algeria, Spain, Brazil 1987: England (two games), Turkey, Israel, Yugoslavia 1988: Yugoslavia, Turkey, Greece, Poland, France, Malta 1989: Eire, Hungary. (58)
Iain Dowie - 1990: Norway, Uruguay 1991: Yugoslavia, Denmark, Austria. (5)
Warren Feeney - 2005: Poland, Germany 2006: Malta, Azerbaijan, England, Austria, Portugal, Estonia 2007: Finland, Iceland, Spain, Denmark, Latvia, Liechtenstein, Sweden. (15)
Phil Gray - 1993: Denmark, Albania, Eire, Spain 1999: Moldova. (5)
Allan Mathieson - 1921: Wales 1922: England. (2)
Darren Patterson - 1996: Norway, Sweden 1998: Switzerland, Spain. (4)
Steve Robinson - 2006: Azerbaijan 2008: Spain (2)
Danny Wilson - 1988: Yugoslavia, Turkey, Greece, Poland, France, Malta 1989: Eire, Hungary, Spain, Malta, Chile 1990: Hungary, Eire, Norway, Uruguay. (15)

EIRE

Thomas 'Bud' Aherne - 1950: Finland (two games), England, Sweden, Belgium 1951: Norway (two games), Argentina 1952: W.Germany(two games), Austria, Spain 1953: France 1954: France. (14)
George Cummins - 1954: Luxembourg (two games), 1955: Norway (two games), W.Germany 1956: Yugoslavia, Spain 1958: Denmark, Poland, Austria 1959: Poland, Czechoslovakia (two games), 1960: Sweden, Chile, W.Germany, Sweden 1961: Scotland (two games). (19)
Seamus Dunne - 1953: France, Austria 1954: France, Luxembourg 1956: Spain, Holland 1957: Denmark, W.Germany, England 1958: Denmark, Poland, Austria 1959: Poland 1960: W.Germany, Sweden. (15)
Don Givens - 1970: Poland, W.Germany 1971: Sweden, Italy (two games), Austria 1972: Iran, Ecuador, Portugal. (9)
Tony Grealish - 1980: Wales, Czechoslovakia, Bulgaria, USA, N.Ireland, England, Cyprus, Switzerland, Argentina 1981: Holland, Belgium, France, Cyprus, Wales, Belgium, W.Germany, Poland. (17)
Ashley Grimes - 1988: Luxembourg, Romania. (2)
Brendan McNally - 1959: Czechoslovakia 1961: Scotland 1963: Iceland. (3)

▶ Mick Harford wearing the 'Three Lions'.

▶ Ricky Hill was unlucky not to win more than three caps for his country.

▶ Brian Stein and Paul Walsh were both picked for England to play against France in 1984. The press had a field day!

▶ Mal Donaghy was picked 58 times for Northern Ireland during his stay at Kenilworth Road.

SCOTLAND

Mike Cullen - 1956: Austria. (1)

WALES

Andy Dibble - 1986: Canada (two games). (2)

Ceri Hughes - 1992: Holland 1994: Norway, Sweden, Estonia 1996: Albania 1997: Eire. (6)

Iorwerth Hughes - 1951: England, N.Ireland, Portugal, Switzerland. (4)

Peter Nicholas - 1985: Norway, Scotland, Spain, Norway 1986: Scotland, Hungary, Saudi Arabia, Eire, Uruguay, Canada (two games) 1987: Finland (two games), USSR, Czechoslovakia. (15)

Mark Pembridge - 1992: Brazil, Eire, Romania. (3)

Paul Price - 1980: England, Scotland, N.Ireland, Iceland 1981: Turkey (two games), Czechoslovakia, Eire, Scotland, England, USSR. (11)

Jason Rees - 1992: Austria. (1)

BULGARIA

Bontcho Guentchev - 1996: England, Slovenia, Macedonia, UAE, Romania. (5)

CANADA

Geoff Aunger - 1994: Morocco, Brazil, Germany, Spain, Holland. (5)

DENMARK

Lars Elstrup - 1989: Belgium, Holland 1990: Faroe Islands, N.Ireland, Yugoslavia 1991: Bulgaria. (6)

FINLAND

Petri Helin - 2001: England. (1)

Markus Heikkinen - 2006: Macedonia (two games), Romania, Czech Republic 2007: Poland, Portugal, Armenia (two games), Azerbaijan, Serbia, Belgium. (11)

GHANA

Kim Grant - 1996: Egypt, Denmark, S Africa, Angola 1997: Morocco, Zimbabwe. (6)

NIGERIA

Emeka Nwajiobi - 1985: Tunisia. (1)

Enoch Showunmi - 2004: Eire, Jamaica. (2)

TRINIDAD AND TOBAGO

Carlos Edwards - 2005: Bermuda (two games) 2006: Guatemala, Costa Rica, Panama, Mexico, Bahrain (two games), Iceland, Peru, Wales, Slovenia, Czech Republic, Sweden, England, Paraguay 2007: St Vincent, Panama, Austria. (19)

USA

Juergen Sommer - 1994: England, Saudi Arabia 1995: Uruguay. (3)

TOP TEN ALL TIME APPEARANCES

TOTAL	L	NL	FAC	LC	OTH	TOT
Fred Hawkes	2	504	40	0	79	625
Robert "Bob" Morton	495	0	48	7	12	562
Ricky Hill	436	0	33	38	1	508
Brian Stein	427	0	31	35	3	496
Mal Donaghy	415	0	36	34	3	488
Gordon Turner	406	0	25	7	12	450
Marvin Johnson	372	0	21	29	17	439
Ron Baynham	388	0	31	5	10	434
Syd Owen	388	0	27	0	8	423
Robert "Bob" Hawkes	0	349	35	0	26	410

LEAGUE	L	NL	FAC	LC	OTH	TOT
Robert "Bob" Morton	495	0	48	7	12	562
Ricky Hill	436	0	33	38	1	508
Brian Stein	427	0	31	35	3	496
Mal Donaghy	415	0	36	34	3	488
Gordon Turner	406	0	25	7	12	450
Ron Baynham	388	0	31	5	10	434
Syd Owen	388	0	27	0	8	423
Marvin Johnson	372	0	21	29	17	439
David Preece	336	0	27	23	9	395
Matthew Spring	308	0	24	20	5	357

NON-LEAGUE	L	NL	FAC	LC	OTH	TOT
Fred Hawkes	2	504	40	0	79	625
Robert "Bob" Hawkes	0	349	35	0	26	410
Fred White	0	237	21	0	46	304
Herbert Moody	0	232	15	0	19	266
Mark Tyler	0	199	12	0	19	230
Jake Howells	29	191	25	0	31	276
William "Bill" McCurdy	31	162	18	0	40	251
Abe Jones	0	136	5	0	25	166
Harold Stansfield	0	135	9	0	10	154
Peter Platt	0	130	9	0	44	183

▶ Bob Morton, holder of the record for the most appearances in the Football League for the Hatters.

▶ Fred Hawkes, holder of the record for playing in the most competitive games for the Town.

FA CUP	L	NL	FAC	LC	OTH	TOT
Robert "Bob" Morton	495	0	48	7	12	562
Fred Hawkes	2	504	40	0	79	625
Mal Donaghy	415	0	36	34	3	488
Robert "Bob" Hawkes	0	349	35	0	26	410
Ricky Hill	436	0	33	38	1	508
Brian Stein	427	0	31	35	3	496
Ron Baynham	388	0	31	5	10	434
Les Sealey	207	0	28	21	3	259
Syd Owen	388	0	27	0	8	423
David Preece	336	0	27	23	9	395
Mick Harford	168	0	27	17	5	217
Steve Foster	163	0	27	20	2	212

LEAGUE CUP	L	NL	FAC	LC	OTH	TOT
Ricky Hill	436	0	33	38	1	508
Brian Stein	427	0	31	35	3	496
Mal Donaghy	415	0	36	34	3	488
Marvin Johnson	372	0	21	29	17	439
Tim Breacker	210	0	21	24	7	262
David Preece	336	0	27	23	9	395
Les Sealey	207	0	28	21	3	259
Steve Foster	163	0	27	20	2	212
Matthew Spring	308	0	24	20	5	357
Danny Wilson	110	0	8	20	4	142

OTHER	L	NL	FAC	LC	OTH	TOT
Fred Hawkes	2	504	40	0	79	625
Fred White	0	237	21	0	46	304
Peter Platt	0	130	9	0	44	183
Tom McInnes	93	0	16	0	44	153
William "Bill" McCurdy	31	162	18	0	40	251
Jake Howells	29	191	25	0	31	276
Richard Williams	30	11	7	0	30	78
Jimmy 'Punch' McEwen	30	99	17	0	29	175
William Stewart	46	17	12	0	29	104
Thomas Wilson	0	35	3	0	29	67

TOP TEN ALL TIME GOALSCORERS

TOTAL	L	NL	FAC	LC	OTH	TOT
Gordon Turner	243	0	18	4	11	276
Andy Rennie	147	0	15	0	0	162
Brian Stein	130	0	6	15	3	154
Ernie Simms	47	62	13	0	8	130
Herbert Moody	0	86	11	0	9	106
Steven Howard	96	0	5	2	0	103
David Moss	88	0	3	3	0	94
Jimmy Yardley	78	0	16	0	0	94
Mick Harford	69	0	10	10	3	92
Joe Payne	83	0	4	0	0	87

LEAGUE	L	NL	FAC	LC	OTH	TOT
Gordon Turner	243	0	18	4	11	276
Andy Rennie	147	0	15	0	0	162
Brian Stein	130	0	6	15	3	154
Steven Howard	96	0	5	2	0	103
David Moss	88	0	3	3	0	94
Joe Payne	83	0	4	0	0	87
Jimmy Yardley	78	0	16	0	0	94
Anthony "Tony" Thorpe	70	0	3	6	5	84
Syd Reid	70	0	11	0	0	81
Mick Harford	69	0	10	10	3	92

NON-LEAGUE	L	NL	FAC	LC	OTH	TOT
Herbert Moody	0	86	11	0	9	106
Ernie Simms	47	62	13	0	8	130
Andre Gray	0	52	2	0	3	57
Arthur Wileman	0	42	5	0	11	58
Robert "Bob" Hawkes	0	40	3	0	5	48
Alexander "Sandy" Brown	0	32	1	0	14	47
John Smith	0	32	5	0	0	37
Hugh Galbraith	0	28	9	0	6	43
Frank Rollinson	0	28	6	0	9	43
Thomas Quinn	0	26	4	0	0	30

▶ Gordon Turner netted 276 career goals for the Hatters.

▶ Joe Payne scored an amazing 87 goals
in only 77 appearances for the Town.

FA CUP	L	NL	FAC	LC	OTH	TOT
Gordon Turner	243	0	18	4	11	276
Jimmy Yardley	78	0	16	0	0	94
Jimmy Blessington	0	19	15	0	4	38
Andy Rennie	147	0	15	0	0	162
Ernie Simms	47	62	13	0	8	130
Herbert Moody	0	86	11	0	9	106
Syd Reid	70	0	11	0	0	81
Arthur 'Jimmy' Durrant	8	25	10	0	4	47
Mick Harford	69	0	10	10	3	92
Hugh Galbraith	0	28	9	0	6	43
Tom McInnes	20	0	9	0	14	43

LEAGUE CUP	L	NL	FAC	LC	OTH	TOT
Brian Stein	130	0	6	15	3	154
Mick Harford	69	0	10	10	3	92
Roy Wegerle	10	0	0	8	0	18
Phil Gray	43	0	4	6	0	53
Anthony "Tony" Thorpe	70	0	3	6	5	84
Ricky Hill	54	0	6	5	0	65
Lars Elstrup	19	0	2	5	1	27
Laurie Sheffield	12	0	0	5	0	17
Gordon Turner	243	0	18	4	11	276
Malcolm Macdonald	49	0	5	4	0	58
David Oldfield	22	0	0	4	6	32

OTHER	L	NL	FAC	LC	OTH	TOT
William Gallacher	7	14	6	0	18	45
William Stewart	10	6	4	0	18	38
John Pickering	0	13	0	0	15	28
Tom McInnes	20	0	9	0	14	43
Alexander "Sandy" Brown	0	32	1	0	14	47
Frederick Ekins	5	8	1	0	13	27
Gordon Turner	243	0	18	4	11	276
Arthur Wileman	0	42	5	0	11	58
James Coupar	9	12	1	0	10	32
Herbert Moody	0	86	11	0	9	106
Frank Rollinson	0	28	6	0	9	43

THE RECORDS

LONGEST RUN OF WINS - 12 MATCHES

New Division Three	Feb	19	2002	BRISTOL ROVERS	W 3-0
New Division Three	Feb	23	2002	YORK CITY	W 2-1
New Division Three	Feb	26	2002	Lincoln City	W 1-0
New Division Three	Mar	2	2002	Torquay United	W 1-0
New Division Three	Mar	5	2002	LEYTON ORIENT	W 3-0
New Division Three	Mar	9	2002	Rushden & Diamonds	W 2-1
New Division Three	Mar	12	2002	EXETER CITY	W 3-0
New Division Three	Mar	16	2002	KIDDERMINSTER HARRIERS	W 1-0
New Division Three	Mar	23	2002	HALIFAX TOWN	W 5-0
New Division Three	Mar	30	2002	Swansea City	W 3-1
New Division Three	Apr	1	2002	MANSFIELD TOWN	W 5-3
New Division Three	Apr	6	2002	Hull City	W 4-0

LONGEST RUN OF HOME WINS - 15 MATCHES

Southern League 2	Dec	20	1913	ABERDARE	W 7-0
Southern League 2	Dec	26	1913	NEWPORT COUNTY	W 1-0
Southern League 2	Jan	17	1914	CAERPHILLY	W 4-0
Southern Alliance	Feb	4	1914	NEWPORT COUNTY	W 3-1
Southern League 2	Feb	7	1914	BRENTFORD	W 3-1
Southern League 2	Feb	21	1914	BARRY	W 3-1
Southern League 2	Feb	28	1914	LLANELLY	W 5-1
Southern League 2	Mar	7	1914	TON PENTRE	W 2-0
Southern Alliance	Mar	18	1914	SOUTHEND UNITED	W 7-0
Southern League 2	Apr	4	1914	SWANSEA TOWN	W 5-0
Southern League 2	Apr	10	1914	STOKE	W 2-1
Southern Alliance	Apr	14	1914	CARDIFF CITY	W 1-0
Southern League 2	Apr	18	1914	CROYDON COMMON	W 2-1
Southern League	Sep	5	1914	PLYMOUTH ARGYLE	W 2-1
Southern League	Sep	9	1914	SOUTHAMPTON	W 3-2

LONGEST UNBEATEN AWAY RUN - 12 MATCHES

Conference Premier	Nov	12	2013	Braintree Town	W 2-1
Conference Premier	Nov	16	2013	Chester FC	D 1-1
FA Trophy 1st Round	Nov	30	2013	Staines Town	D 0-0
Conference Premier	Dec	7	2013	Alfreton Town	W 5-0
Conference Premier	Dec	26	2013	Barnet	W 2-1
Conference Premier	Jan	4	2014	Lincoln City	D 0-0
FA Trophy 3rd Round	Jan	11	2014	Cambridge United	D 2-2
Conference Premier	Feb	11	2014	Macclesfield Town	W 2-1
Conference Premier	Feb	22	2014	Nuneaton Town	W 5-0
Conference Premier	Mar	8	2014	Salisbury City	D 0-0
Conference Premier	Mar	11	2014	Cambridge United	D 1-1
Conference Premier	Mar	25	2014	Grimsby Town	W 2-1

LONGEST RUN OF AWAY WINS - 6 MATCHES

New Division Three	Feb	26	2002	Lincoln City	W 1-0
New Division Three	Mar	2	2002	Torquay United	W 1-0
New Division Three	Mar	9	2002	Rushden & Diamonds	W 2-1
New Division Three	Mar	30	2002	Swansea City	W 3-1
New Division Three	Apr	6	2002	Hull City	W 4-0
New Division Three	Apr	20	2002	Shrewsbury Town	W 2-0

LONGEST UNBEATEN RUN - 23 MATCHES

Southern League 2	Dec	26	1913	NEWPORT COUNTY	W 1-0
Southern League 2	Dec	27	1913	Croydon Common	D 1-1
Southern League 2	Jan	17	1914	CAERPHILLY	W 4-0
Southern League 2	Jan	24	1914	Caerphilly	W 9-0
Southern Alliance	Feb	4	1914	NEWPORT COUNTY	W 3-1
Southern League 2	Feb	7	1914	BRENTFORD	W 3-1
Southern League 2	Feb	14	1914	Aberdare	W 5-1
Southern League 2	Feb	21	1914	BARRY	W 3-1
Southern Alliance	Feb	26	1914	Newport County	W 3-1
Southern League 2	Feb	28	1914	LLANELLY	W 5-1
Southern League 2	Mar	7	1914	TON PENTRE	W 2-0
Southern League 2	Mar	14	1914	Swansea Town	W 1-0
Southern Alliance	Mar	18	1914	SOUTHEND UNITED	W 7-0
Southern League 2	Mar	28	1914	Mid-Rhondda	D 1-1
Southern League 2	Apr	4	1914	SWANSEA TOWN	W 5-0
Southern League 2	Apr	10	1914	STOKE	W 2-1
Southern League 2	Apr	11	1914	Brentford	D 0-0
Southern League 2	Apr	13	1914	Stoke	W 2-1
Southern Alliance	Apr	14	1914	CARDIFF CITY	W 1-0
Southern League 2	Apr	18	1914	CROYDON COMMON	W 2-1
Southern League	Sep	2	1914	Southampton	D 3-3
Southern League	Sep	5	1914	PLYMOUTH ARGYLE	W 2-1
Southern League	Sep	9	1914	SOUTHAMPTON	W 3-2

LONGEST UNBEATEN HOME RUN - 43 MATCHES

Division Four	May	11	1968	BRENTFORD	W 2-1
Division Three	Aug	10	1968	OLDHAM ATHLETIC	W 4-0
League Cup 1st	Aug	14	1968	WATFORD	W 3-0
Division Three	Aug	24	1968	ROTHERHAM UNITED	W 3-0
Division Three	Aug	28	1968	BARNSLEY	W 5-1
League Cup 2nd, Replay	Sep	11	1968	BRIGHTON & HOVE ALBION	W 4-2
Division Three	Sep	14	1968	TRANMERE ROVERS	W 3-1
Division Three	Sep	18	1968	MANSFIELD TOWN	W 4-2
Division Three	Sep	28	1968	TORQUAY UNITED	W 1-0
Division Three	Oct	12	1968	HARTLEPOOL	W 3-0
Division Three	Oct	26	1968	NORTHAMPTON TOWN	W 2-1
Division Three	Nov	9	1968	SWINDON TOWN	W 2-0
FA Cup 1st	Nov	16	1968	WARE TOWN	W 6-1
Division Three	Nov	23	1968	BOURNEMOUTH	D 1-1
FA Cup 2nd	Dec	7	1968	GILLINGHAM	W 3-1
Division Three	Dec	21	1968	PLYMOUTH ARGYLE	W 2-0
Division Three	Jan	25	1969	WALSALL	W 1-0
Division Three	Feb	1	1969	READING	W 2-1
Division Three	Feb	26	1969	CREWE ALEXANDRA	W 2-0
Division Three	Mar	5	1969	SHREWSBURY TOWN	W 2-1
Division Three	Mar	19	1969	BRISTOL ROVERS	W 3-0
Division Three	Mar	22	1969	GILLINGHAM	D 1-1
Division Three	Mar	26	1969	BARROW	W 5-1
Division Three	Mar	29	1969	ORIENT	W 2-1
Division Three	Apr	8	1969	SOUTHPORT	D 0-0
Division Three	Apr	12	1969	BRIGHTON & HOVE ALBION	W 3-0
Division Three	Apr	25	1969	STOCKPORT COUNTY	W 4-1
Division Three	Apr	30	1969	WATFORD	W 2-1
Division Three	Aug	9	1969	BARROW	W 3-0
League Cup 1st, Replay	Aug	19	1969	PETERBOROUGH UNITED	W 5-2
Division Three	Aug	23	1969	ORIENT	W 3-2
Division Three	Aug	26	1969	HALIFAX TOWN	D 1-1
League Cup 2nd	Sep	2	1969	MILLWALL	D 2-2
Division Three	Sep	6	1969	BRISTOL ROVERS	W 4-0
Division Three	Sep	20	1969	SHREWSBURY TOWN	D 2-2
Division Three	Oct	4	1969	STOCKPORT COUNTY	W 2-0
Division Three	Oct	7	1969	BOURNEMOUTH	D 0-0
Division Three	Oct	25	1969	TORQUAY UNITED	D 1-1
Division Three	Nov	8	1969	BARNSLEY	D 1-1
FA Cup 1st, Replay	Nov	18	1969	BOURNEMOUTH	W 3-1
Division Three	Nov	22	1969	ROCHDALE	W 2-0
Division Three	Nov	25	1969	FULHAM	W 1-0
Division Three	Dec	13	1969	BRADFORD CITY	W 5-0

MATCHES PLAYED IN EACH COMPETITION

		HOME					AWAY				
	Pld	W	D	L	F	A	W	D	L	F	A
Anglo-Italian	12	3	2	1	13	6	0	2	4	5	12
Associate Members Cup	24	4	2	2	11	10	6	1	8	17	22
Conference Premier	228	71	24	19	266	96	48	40	26	153	120
Div 3 South Cup	7	2	0	1	6	5	1	0	3	10	12
FA Cup	365	107	37	47	463	254	56	40	66	224	279
FA Trophy	25	9	3	1	23	4	4	4	4	12	15
Full Members Cup	11	3	0	0	11	3	2	2	3	10	16
League	3624	963	456	393	3514	2051	409	462	941	1977	3199
League Cup	144	28	20	15	112	72	28	16	32	102	128
Play Offs	10	2	1	1	6	4	1	0	3	5	5
Southern Alliance	32	14	1	1	42	11	4	4	8	24	38
Southern League	592	180	53	63	623	316	63	68	165	333	570
Southern Professional Floodlit Cup	14	4	1	1	20	8	4	2	1	13	5
Texaco Cup	3	0	1	0	1	1	1	1	0	4	3
United League	94	30	9	8	143	55	17	6	24	82	115
Watney Cup	1	0	0	0	0	0	0	0	1	0	1
Western League	24	6	4	2	29	17	3	2	7	11	28
TOTAL	5210	1426	614	555	5283	2913	647	650	1296	2982	4568

		NEUTRAL					TOTAL				
	Pld	W	D	L	F	A	W	D	L	F	A
Anglo-Italian	12	0	0	0	0	0	3	4	5	18	18
Associate Members Cup	24	1	0	0	3	2	11	3	10	31	34
Conference Premier	228	0	0	0	0	0	119	64	45	419	216
Div 3 South Cup	7	0	0	0	0	0	3	0	4	16	17
FA Cup	365	3	2	7	14	23	166	79	120	701	556
FA Trophy	25	0	0	0	0	0	13	7	5	35	19
Full Members Cup	11	0	0	1	1	4	5	2	4	22	23
League	3624	0	0	0	0	0	1372	918	1334	5491	5250
League Cup	144	2	0	3	9	10	58	36	50	223	210
Play Offs	10	0	1	1	1	2	3	2	5	12	11
Southern Alliance	32	0	0	0	0	0	18	5	9	66	49
Southern League	592	0	0	0	0	0	243	121	228	956	886
Southern Professional Floodlit Cup	14	0	0	1	0	1	8	3	3	33	14
Texaco Cup	3	0	0	1	2	0	1	2	0	5	4
United League	94	0	0	0	0	0	47	15	32	225	170
Watney Cup	1	0	0	0	0	0	0	0	1	0	1
Western League	24	0	0	0	0	0	9	6	9	40	45
TOTAL	5210	6	3	13	28	42	2079	1267	1864	8293	7523

		HOME					AWAY				
	Pld	W	D	L	F	A	W	D	L	F	A
Division One (Premier League)	658	156	88	85	536	367	57	80	192	327	644
Division Two (Championship)	1425	353	187	173	1331	856	163	176	373	787	1238
Division Three (League One)	1311	379	158	118	1396	710	154	176	326	724	1135
Division Four (League Two)	230	75	23	17	251	118	35	30	50	139	182
TOTAL	3624	963	456	393	3514	2051	409	462	941	1977	3199

		TOTAL				
	Pld	W	D	L	F	A
Division One (Premier League)	658	213	168	277	863	1011
Division Two (Championship)	1425	516	363	546	2118	2094
Division Three (League One)	1311	533	334	444	2120	1845
Division Four (League Two)	230	110	53	67	390	300
TOTAL	3624	1372	918	1334	5491	5250

OLDEST, YOUNGEST, SHORTEST, TALLEST

▶ **Trevor Peake** - The oldest to turn out for the Town in the Football League at 40 years 222 days. Peake (14) is seen here coming on as substitute in his final game against Wrexham in September 1997.

▶ An honourable mention goes to Hatters trainer Arthur Pembleton who was forced to turn out in a Wartime game at Millwall on 9th November 1940 at the grand age of 45 years 289 days!

▶ **Jordan Patrick** - The youngest to appear in the Football League for the Hatters at 16 years 7 days at Grimsby in October 2008.

▶ In recent times Danny Stevens (pictured) is regarded as the shortest player to appear for the Town at 5 feet 4 inches although pre-war wingers Freddie Hogg and Hugh Moffatt were reputed to measure less than this.

▶ Giant goalkeeper Ian Feuer, at 6 feet 7 inches, is the tallest player to figure for the Town.

▶ Ned Liddell

▶ Dally Duncan and George Martin.

▶ Jack Crompton

▶ Bill Harvey

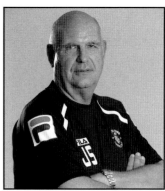
▶ John Still

LUTON TOWN MANAGERS

Name	Appointed	Departed	Former Player
George Thompson	16/02/1925	26/10/1925	
John McCartney	14/09/1927	31/12/1929	Yes
George Kay	01/01/1930	13/05/1931	
Harold Wightman	01/06/1931	09/10/1935	
Edward "Ned" Liddell	13/08/1936	26/02/1938	
Neil McBain	01/06/1938	05/06/1939	
George Martin	04/12/1944	24/05/1947	Yes
Douglas "Dally" Duncan	13/06/1947	16/10/1958	Yes
Syd Owen	27/04/1959	16/04/1960	Yes
Sam Bartram	18/07/1960	14/06/1962	
Jack Crompton	29/06/1962	06/07/1962	
Bill Harvey	24/07/1962	21/11/1964	
George Martin	16/02/1965	03/11/1966	Yes
Allan Brown	04/11/1966	19/12/1968	Yes
Alec Stock	20/12/1968	27/04/1972	
Harry Haslam	04/05/1972	23/01/1978	
David Pleat	24/01/1978	16/05/1986	Yes
John Moore	03/06/1986	16/06/1987	Yes
Ray Harford	16/06/1987	03/01/1990	
Jim Ryan	11/01/1990	13/05/1991	Yes
David Pleat	07/06/1991	11/06/1995	Yes
Terry Westley	03/07/1995	18/12/1995	
Lennie Lawrence	21/12/1995	04/07/2000	
Ricky Hill	10/07/2000	15/11/2000	Yes
Joe Kinnear	07/02/2001	23/05/2003	
Mike Newell	21/06/2003	15/03/2007	Yes
Kevin Blackwell	27/03/2007	16/01/2008	
Mick Harford	16/01/2008	01/10/2009	Yes
Richard Money	30/10/2009	28/03/2011	Yes
Gary Brabin	28/03/2011	31/03/2012	
Paul Buckle	08/04/2012	19/02/2013	
John Still	26/02/2013	to present	

HIGHEST ATTENDANCES AT
KENILWORTH ROAD (OVER 25,000)

Competition	Month	Date	Year	Opponents	Att
FA Cup	Mar	4	1959	BLACKPOOL	30069
FA Cup	Mar	8	1952	ARSENAL	28433
Division One	Nov	5	1955	WOLVERHAMPTON WANDERERS	27911
FA Cup	Feb	23	1952	SWINDON TOWN	27553
Division One	Dec	28	1957	ARSENAL	27493
Division Two	Oct	22	1949	TOTTENHAM HOTSPUR	27319
FA Cup	Jan	28	1959	LEICESTER CITY	27277
Division Two	Apr	9	1955	WEST HAM UNITED	27148
Division One	Dec	28	1959	ARSENAL	27055
Division One	Apr	11	1959	MANCHESTER UNITED	27025
League Cup	Oct	6	1970	ARSENAL	27023
Division One	Aug	22	1956	WOLVERHAMPTON WANDERERS	26715
FA Cup	Jan	27	1951	BRISTOL ROVERS	26586
Division Two	Oct	25	1947	TOTTENHAM HOTSPUR	26496
Division One	Dec	26	1957	MANCHESTER UNITED	26478
FA Cup	Jan	29	1949	WALSALL	26422
Division Two	Nov	16	1946	TOTTENHAM HOTSPUR	26362
FA Cup	Feb	12	1949	LEICESTER CITY	26280
FA Cup	Jan	7	1961	NORTHAMPTON TOWN	26220
Division Two	Feb	28	1953	HUDDERSFIELD TOWN	25841
Division One	Sep	10	1955	NEWCASTLE UNITED	25814
Division One	Nov	19	1955	SUNDERLAND	25802
Division Two	Apr	8	1955	LEEDS UNITED	25775
FA Cup	Jan	22	1938	SWINDON TOWN	25746
Division One	Sep	6	1958	WEST HAM UNITED	25715
FA Cup	Feb	16	1974	LEICESTER CITY	25712
FA Cup	Feb	20	1960	WOLVERHAMPTON WANDERERS	25619
FA Cup	Jan	12	1952	CHARLTON ATHLETIC	25554
Division Two	Nov	30	1946	NEWCASTLE UNITED	25410
Division Two	Sep	1	1937	ASTON VILLA	25349
FA Cup	Feb	2	1952	BRENTFORD	25320
Division Three	Apr	30	1969	WATFORD	25253
Division Two	Apr	3	1971	BIRMINGHAM CITY	25172

HIGHEST ATTENDANCES AT
AWAY GROUNDS (OVER 50,000)

Competition	Month	Date	Year	Opponents	Att
Friendly	May	20	1956	CCA	120000
Friendly	May	23	1956	Dynamo Bucharest	120000
FA Cup	May	2	1959	Nottingham Forest	100000
League Cup	Apr	24	1988	Arsenal	95732
League Cup	Apr	9	1989	Nottingham Forest	76130
FA Cup	Jan	25	1936	Manchester City	65978
FA Cup	Mar	14	1959	Norwich City	65000
Division Two	Jan	3	1948	Newcastle United	64931
Simod Cup	Mar	27	1988	Reading	61740
FA Cup	Apr	9	1994	Chelsea	59989
Division One	Sep	22	1956	Tottenham Hotspur	58960
Division One	Dec	27	1958	Arsenal	56277
FA Cup	Mar	4	1933	Everton	55431
Johnstone's Paint Trophy	Apr	5	2009	Scunthorpe United	55378
FA Cup	Jan	28	1922	Aston Villa	53832
Division Two	Apr	4	1947	Manchester City	53692
Division One	Nov	8	1958	Newcastle United	53488
FA Cup	Feb	3	1937	Sunderland	53235
FA Cup	Mar	17	1973	Sunderland	53151
Division Two	Mar	11	1950	Tottenham Hotspur	53145

▶ Top left: A crowd of 30,069 is shoehorned into Kenilworth Road to see the Town beat Blackpool in the F.A.Cup quarter-final in March 1959.
▶ Top right: The Town play in front of 120,000 in Bucharest in 1956.

LUTON TOWN MEMORIES

▶ **Below** - The Dunstable Road ground which was used by the Town between 1897 and 1905.

▶ **Above** - Luton director Eric Morecambe gets too close to the team bath after the Hatters had won promotion to the top flight in 1974.

▶ **Above** - David Pleat skips across the Maine Road pitch after the Hatters had won 1-0 at Manchester City in 1983 to preserve top flight status.

▶ **Above -** John Aston shocks the St James Park crowd with a goal in an FA Cup 4th round tie in 1973. The Town went on to beat Newcastle 2-0.

▶ **Left -** Manager Harold Wightman addresses his players in 1935.

▶ **Right -** An early post-war crowd at Kenilworth Road take a half-time break during the Town's 6-3 win over Newport in May 1947.

▶ **Above -** The boys of 1929. John Black, Archie Clark, Charlie Fraser and John Fulton pose for the camera. 'Scotch Corner', built over when the Main Stand was extended in 1937, is pictured in the background

▶ **Above Left -** Trainer Billy Lawson stands proudly in front of the old main stand at Kenilworth Road in 1907.

▶ **Left -** In an experiment that did not work, England international goalkeeper Ron Baynham is picked at centre-forward in a home game against Leyton Orient in April 1962.